T0391759

Inclusion in Linguistics

Inclusion in Linguistics

Edited by
Anne H. Charity Hudley
Christine Mallinson
Mary Bucholtz

OXFORD
UNIVERSITY PRESS

OXFORD
UNIVERSITY PRESS

Oxford University Press is a department of the University of Oxford. It furthers
the University's objective of excellence in research, scholarship, and education
by publishing worldwide. Oxford is a registered trade mark of Oxford University
Press in the UK and certain other countries.

Published in the United States of America by Oxford University Press
198 Madison Avenue, New York, NY 10016, United States of America.

Library of Congress Cataloging-in-Publication Data
Names: Charity Hudley, Anne H., editor. | Mallinson, Christine, editor. |
Bucholtz, Mary, 1966– editor.
Title: Inclusion in linguistics / Anne Charity Hudley, Christine Mallinson,
Mary Bucholtz.
Description: New York, NY : Oxford University Press, 2024. |
Includes bibliographical references and index. |
Identifiers: LCCN 2023049338 (print) | LCCN 2023049339 (ebook) |
ISBN 9780197755303 (hardback) | ISBN 9780197755310 (paperback) |
ISBN 9780197755334 (epub)
Subjects: LCSH: Linguistics—Study and teaching–ocial aspects. |
Social justice. | Educational equalization. | LCGFT: Essays.
Classification: LCC P53.8 .I48 2024 (print) | LCC P53.8 (ebook) |
DDC 410.8—dc23/eng/20231220
LC record available at https://lccn.loc.gov/2023049338
LC ebook record available at https://lccn.loc.gov/2023049339

DOI: 10.1093/oso/9780197755303.001.0001

How you language is beautiful. Don't let anyone tell you your language is wrong. Your languaging is the story of your life.
—Jon Henner

We dedicate this volume to the memory of our friend and colleague, Jon Henner.

Jon, it was a joy and pleasure to work with and learn from you. In one of our email exchanges during the final editing of this volume, you wrote, 'What do we do if not argue for inclusion?"

Thank you for teaching us how to crip linguistics brilliantly, inclusively, and authentically. Your memory is a blessing, and your life and work are an inspiration to us all.

Contents

PART 3: CREATING JUST AND INCLUSIVE CLASSROOMS

Preface

Anne H. Charity Hudley (she/her)
Stanford University

Christine Mallinson (she/her)
University of Maryland, Baltimore County

Mary Bucholtz (she/her, they/them)
University of California, Santa Barbara

This volume and its companion, *Decolonizing Linguistics,* were invited by Meredith Keffer, senior acquisitions editor at Oxford University Press. We couldn't have had a more knowledgeable or supportive editor than Meredith, to whom we are deeply grateful. As a scholar in folklore and mythology as well as anthropology herself, Meredith was well aware of the intellectual and practical need for decolonization and inclusion in linguistics in alignment with similar efforts in other disciplines that have been traditionally dominated by Western and Global North white cis male discourse, including anthropology, education, and sociology. Grounded in her efforts to continue to diversify the linguistics catalog at OUP, Meredith reached out to Anne to begin the conversation about proposing these volumes in order to advance efforts to decolonize linguistics and create a more inclusive discipline and profession.

We refer to linguistics as a discipline here intentionally—as opposed to the broader, more inclusive and interdisciplinary vision of linguistics that we advocate throughout both volumes—as a nod to the scholarly communities and power dynamics in the particular scholarly tradition of the study of language that has shaped our careers as researchers and educators. We recognize both the challenges and the benefits of our professional and personal experiences, which have informed our editorial lens and the work that we have done throughout our careers. In line with the contributions throughout each of these volumes, we also discuss in this preface who we are and how our positionalities and subjectivities have shaped our lives and careers.

Anne: I grew up in Varina, Virginia, a rural area zoned for agriculture just east of Richmond, Virginia. I was born there to two Black physicians who were part of two large economically privileged Black families in the Upper South. My local affiliations and my dedication to my community are the driving forces behind my most fundamental interests as an academic. In the Black educational narrative, I represent the prep-school-to-professor experience. I attended St. Catherine's School in Richmond for 13 years, where I had an early interest in studying linguistics and in being a college professor and administrator. I was granted early admission to Harvard and found myself surrounded by supportive faculty and students. My senior/master's thesis explored the idiolect of the African American blues singer Ms. Bessie Smith over time—that is, how her individual language and singing style changed over the years. Through this work, I learned about Southern Black and African American language and culture from a linguistics standpoint, and it was an important start to the work I do today.

After Harvard, I attended graduate school at the University of Pennsylvania, where I began studying in earnest how discrimination based on language and culture leads to educational inequalities. I also became very interested both in the transition from high school to college and in undergraduate research through my work with the Center for Africana Studies Summer Institute for Pre-Freshmen and the Penn McNair Scholars Program. At that time, I thought that my interests in linguistics and in supporting underrepresented students and scholars were somewhat unrelated—but as I began to see how they overlap in crucial ways, it shaped my career path, leading me to where I am today.

For 12 years, I worked in my home community at the College of William and Mary in Williamsburg, Virginia, where I was the first William and Mary Professor of Community Studies and where I co-created the William and Mary Scholars Undergraduate Research Experience (WMSURE) program to support WM Scholars—students who are awarded merit tuition based on their academic excellence. Their experiences are the backbone of all of my work. They are my family, my community, and my home.

For four years after that, I was the North Hall Endowed Chair in the Linguistics of African America at the University of California, Santa Barbara (UCSB), where I was also the Director of Undergraduate Research for the Office of Undergraduate Education for three years. These positions brought together my passions for linguistics and for supporting underrepresented students in their research endeavors. I am also dedicated to the craft of teaching and was a faculty fellow in the Center for Innovative Teaching, Research, and Learning at UCSB, where I worked with other faculty to improve their teaching, particularly with regard to empowering Black students as well as other students who have been underrepresented at Historically White Institutions. In addition, I was a faculty in residence, which means that when I wasn't teaching or doing research, students could often find me hosting parties and barbecues, where we talked about life and what it means to be a college student.

I am now Associate Dean of Educational Affairs and the Bonnie Katz Tenenbaum Professor of Education in the Stanford University Graduate School of Education. In my current role, I oversee degree programs and work with students and faculty to ensure a rich educational experience. I am also affiliated with Stanford's Center for Comparative Studies in Race and Ethnicity, the Program in African and African American Studies, and the Department of Linguistics. I consider myself a humanistic social scientist who describes and documents the linguistic, literary, and cultural experiences of Black learners across their lives. I use a community-based participatory research methodology in all of my work and co-construct information and findings with students, community members, and large teams of researchers. I have a particular focus on sharing those findings with in-service educators who most immediately need them. I have a longstanding relationship with the American Federation of Teachers that I am particularly proud of, as it keeps my work centered on the interests and experiences of large numbers of in-service educators.

My desire to see greater and immediate inclusion of Black students in the academy and in research has led me to design innovative undergraduate and graduate curricula and advising programs as we create liberatory and reparative models for what universities can be both now and in the future. We got this. I'm proud to be at Stanford as we work to establish African and African American Studies as a university department. I am also fortunate to be a faculty member at the same university my nieces attend as undergraduate students. We experience college as a family, and their perspective is invaluable as I do this work. It is, ultimately, for them.

Christine: I am an interdisciplinary scholar of language, culture, and society and have devoted my career to studying linguistic and cultural diversity and inclusion in ways that are shaped by my formative life experiences. I grew up in a small town in North Carolina, in the Southern region of the US where both pride and stigma surrounding Southern language run deep. My parents were first-generation college students, having moved from New York and Pennsylvania to North Carolina to attend college; they both ended up pursuing master's degrees and careers in helping professions related to counseling and social work.

My maternal grandparents, who lived nearby and were the only grandparents I knew, were immigrants from Germany, without a high school education. From them I got my earliest understanding of how complicated language can be. Some of my earliest childhood memories are of my grandmother singing songs in German and reading me books and telling nursery rhymes, and we shared that identity and culture together through language. But I also saw how linguistic insecurity, bias, and discrimination can often surround those who are perceived as speaking differently within a community. As I attended school, I became aware that white Southern English and the local Southern variety of African American English, two important varieties of English used by my peers and teachers, also were subjected to this same complicated mix of social value and stigma. I became intrigued by the social dimension of linguistic differences—the ways that language reflects culture and identity, but also social boundaries and social divisions—which set me on a path of figuring out how to think about and study these dimensions in all their interrelated complexities.

In college and graduate school, my studies were interdisciplinary, centered on sociology, anthropology, gender studies, and linguistics. I completed my master's degree in English linguistics and my PhD in sociology and anthropology at North Carolina State University, working with Walt Wolfram to study how language is used in white and Black communities in the Appalachian region of North Carolina in ways that applied my linguistic, anthropological, and sociological training. In the years I spent studying while working with community members, I added richer scholarly as well as personal understandings of the social dimensions of language use that informed how I understood my own lived experiences with language and the social dynamics that I had seen in the world. I arrived at several key principles that have undergirded and shaped my work ever since: language and society are inseparable, language is a cultural artifact that belongs to those people and communities who use it, and addressing power dynamics and inequalities surrounding language is central to social justice, equity, and inclusion.

After graduate school, I moved to the University of Maryland, Baltimore County (UMBC)—a Minority Serving Institution and a campus known for its innovative teaching, inclusive culture, and dedication to supporting the success of students from historically underserved groups. My interdisciplinary background was a perfect fit for my faculty position in the Language, Literacy, and Culture Program, where I work with faculty and graduate students from numerous fields and disciplines that converge around the study of language and society. When I was on the job market and interviewing for other positions at prominent institutions across the country, I was told by several linguistics departments that my work was not "linguistic enough," and by several sociology departments that my work was not "sociological enough." I rejected those false binaries and the boundary-setting culture of academia, both then and now. Since that time, linguistics has become more open to interdisciplinarity and inclusivity in terms of how we conceptualize language and approach the study of language use—although much more progress needs to be made.

At UMBC, most of the courses I teach focus on language as central to education, equality, social change, and social justice. I am deeply committed to being a mentor and an advocate for graduate students from groups that have been systemically underrepresented in higher education, which includes students of color, women, first-generation students, and members of the LGBTQ+ community. As a white woman, I see my role and responsibility as a professor and mentor as a central part of my dedication to promoting social justice and decolonizing academia through dismantling traditional power structures and established hierarchies and expanding pathways for inclusion. In addition to my faculty positions as professor in the Language, Literacy, and Culture Program and affiliate professor in the Department of Gender, Women's and Sexuality Studies, I hold an appointment as the 2023–2024 Lipitz Distinguished Professor of the Arts, Humanities, and Social Sciences at UMBC. In my administrative roles, I am also the director of the Center for Social Science Scholarship, UMBC's comprehensive social science research center, and Special Assistant for Research and Creative Achievement in UMBC's Office of the Vice President for Research, where I work across our campus to grow social science research, connect it to practice and policy, and foster cross-disciplinary collaborations. The social sciences are critical to tackling pressing social issues, challenging bias and discrimination, addressing social inequalities, and promoting social action.

Across my research leadership, teaching, and mentorship roles, my true academic joys are bringing together great minds and helping faculty, graduate students, and undergraduate students realize their scholarly goals and ambitions. And above all, I do the work that I do for my family—especially for my two children, who already recognize the beauty of language in all its diversity and who, I hope, will always also intentionally work for greater equity and inclusion.

Mary: I became a linguistics professor because I love languages and teaching, but I stayed in linguistics to fight against injustice. My personal and professional commitment to social justice is informed in part from my own first-hand experiences of educational inequity based on my gender and social class. Growing up poor in a very small town in northern Indiana, I was discouraged from going to college by my guidance counselor, who advised secretarial school as a more appropriate aspiration. In college, my (male) professors disparaged my interest in education and in youth language and steered me toward fields and topics they considered more respectable. In graduate school at the University of California, Berkeley, I quickly changed my research specialization from historical linguistics to sociolinguistics after other women students warned me of rampant sexual harassment by male faculty and students in that field (as well as others). This decision, however, did not protect me from being stalked by a faculty member, among many other harassing incidents. Nor did my interest in social issues meet with faculty approval. Several linguistics professors mocked and dismissed my interest in gender in particular, and my piles of assigned linguistics articles languished unread while I devoured books on gender, sexuality, race, and social justice, reading these texts not "for fun" but as a form of self-care in Audre Lorde's (1988) sense, as a lifeline in a hostile environment. In my first semester of graduate school I spoke with the chair of the Department of Ethnic Studies about transferring to that program, but I changed my mind after my conversation with another linguistics professor that semester. I had gone to his office hours in some distress and expressed dissatisfaction with the program's decontextualized, asocial approach to language. His response was to discourage me from continuing in linguistics and to blame his wife and child for frustrations in his own career. At that point, I decided to stay in the department, and the field, simply to prove that I refused to be driven out.

Fortunately, I found supportive colleagues among my fellow graduate students, one of whom, Kira Hall, became my closest collaborator. And I found an advisor, Robin Tolmach Lakoff, who at that time was not only one of the few women among the linguistics faculty but also the only Berkeley linguist writing about issues of power and injustice. (For further discussion of the need for linguistics to become a more just and inclusive discipline, see Bucholtz & miles-hercules 2021; for a discussion of Lakoff's contributions to linguistics and social justice, see Bucholtz 2004.)

Given the reception of my ideas in graduate school, I have not been surprised to face opposition from the linguistics establishment throughout my career—and I have had a far easier time than my friends and colleagues from more minoritized positionalities. As a graduate student and a junior faculty member writing critically both about race and about cherished assumptions in linguistics, I was often the target of harsh comments and sometimes even angry attacks from senior white male faculty. But I also received supportive comments, especially from faculty of color as well as junior scholars and graduate students, which made it easier to keep doing the work I needed to do.

I am deeply indebted to the many linguists and linguistic anthropologists of color who went far out of their way to offer me material support early in my career in the form of recommendation letters, feedback on my work, and professional guidance, among them John Baugh, John Rickford, Marcyliena Morgan, and Ana Celia Zentella. I pledged to pay their generosity forward to the next generation of linguists, and especially linguists of color, an obligation I continue to fulfill to this day.

Linguistics has changed a great deal since I entered the field, and it is encouraging to see the ranks of linguists slowly diversifying, with an accompanying transformation of the discipline's research questions, methods, and professional practices. But this change is far too slow, and now that I am a senior scholar I believe that the greatest impact I can make on linguistics is not through traditional research—after all, the most exciting ideas have always come from those who bring new perspectives to the field rather than those who are firmly established. Instead, I aim to make an impact by using the structural and institutional power I hold as a senior white, cis, relatively able-bodied scholar to make linguistics a welcoming place for students and scholars whose lived experiences and resulting ideas remain marginalized and devalued within the discipline. Although my three-year stint as department chair enabled me to do some of this work, I was frustrated to discover that academic administration is designed to reproduce rather than to undo structural injustice. More important and more rewarding have been my efforts behind the scenes and in collaboration with others—as represented by these two volumes, among many other activities. The lesson I have learned in my career as an academic linguist striving to make our field more inclusive, more equitable, and more humane is that in the never-ending struggle for social justice, the greatest force for change is social connection and collective action, in forms large and small.

Creating *Inclusion in Linguistics* and *Decolonizing Linguistics*

These volumes are directly informed by previous formative collaborations involving the three editors. First was a proceedings paper that we published in 2019 and that led to the first-ever Statement on Race for the Linguistic Society of America, which was adopted by the association. We then drew on this statement to write a subsequent theoretical article, "Toward Racial Justice in Linguistics" (Charity Hudley, Mallinson, & Bucholtz, 2020a), which appeared in the discipline's flagship journal, *Language*, along with a set of responses on racial equity in the field, to which we in turn responded (Charity Hudley, Mallinson, & Bucholtz, 2020b). Brian Joseph, former president of the Linguistic Society of America, referred to this work in his presidential address, published later in *Language* (Joseph, 2020). These efforts and others have pushed the discipline to be more fully inclusive and decolonial and have inspired scholars, departments, universities, and professional organizations to put forward their own initiatives: to host webinars on racial equity for faculty and students, to form workshops and workgroups for white allies, to design new courses on racial justice, and to craft and implement departmental action plans on racial justice.

In our response to the published commentaries that accompanied our *Language* article, we included our call for contributions to these two volumes, and we also spread the word widely online through virtual talks, emails, and social media. In addition, we directly invited scholars from across subfields, regions, and institutions whom we knew had an interest and expertise in these topics. We intentionally invited both well-established senior researchers and emerging scholars to ensure that we were all in conversation with each other. At the same time, we acknowledge that there are persistent challenges in being globally inclusive, given the structural biases of professional networks, and we continue to strive to undo those barriers and hope that future work will continue to do the same.

Interest in the volumes was widespread. We accepted 40 contributions across both volumes, all of which went through an intentionally inclusive process of development, workshopping, and revision, which we adopted in deliberate contrast to the traditional paradigm of scholarly writing, editing, revision, and anonymous critique. That traditional approach is often isolated and isolating, as well as susceptible to processes of injustice, exclusion, and colonization. Through these volumes, we aim to challenge that paradigm and change that process. All contributors met in large and small groups during multiple author sessions, sharing project ideas and feedback, and went through multiple rounds of peer and editors' review. Both *Decolonizing Linguistics* and *Inclusion in Linguistics* were developed simultaneously in order to ensure coverage of and dialogue around core themes across the volumes. To broaden the perspectives we were able to represent, we also invited two linguists whose professional and lived experiences were different from our own, Ignacio Montoya and Jon Henner, to co-author the introduction and conclusion of each volume, respectively. (See the introductions to both volumes for more detail about the process of creating these books.)

We are deeply indebted to our editorial and production team, including Julia Steer, Lacey Harvey, Stuart Allison, Anne Sanow, and Sarah Yamashita. We also sincerely thank our external reviewers, as well as all of the volume contributors for their insights, support, and participation throughout the process of putting together these volumes. We are incredibly grateful to UMBC Language, Literacy and Culture doctoral student Kara Seidel, whose spectacular project management skills allowed the compilation of these volumes to proceed smoothly from start to finish and who was an integral member of our editorial team.

We are immensely grateful for the support of the National Science Foundation's Build and Broaden Program, awards #SMA-2126414 and 2126405, "Linguistic Production, Perception, and Identity in the Career Mobility of Black Faculty in Linguistics and the Language Sciences," which supported both of these volumes, particularly Chapters 5, 14, and 15 in *Decolonizing Linguistics* and Chapters 11 and 12 in *Inclusion in Linguistics*. We thank our Build and Broaden research scholars network, who continue to advance critical work in pursuit of Black linguistic liberation.

We also thank the Bonnie Katz Tenenbaum endowed professorship at Stanford University in support of Anne Charity Hudley's research, and we gratefully acknowledge Stanford University's support of Anne Charity Hudley's Black Academic Lab, https://badlab.stanford.edu/. We additionally wish to express our appreciation of UMBC's support of Christine Mallinson's research, including the 2023–2024 Lipitz Distinguished Professorship in the Arts, Humanities, and Social Sciences and the College of Arts, Humanities, and Social Sciences Student Research Assistance award for Faculty Research and Creative Achievement. We thank UCSB for ongoing support of Mary Bucholtz's research. We further thank the following institutions for supporting open access for these volumes: Stanford University, Swarthmore College, UCSB, UMBC, University of Michigan, University of Pennsylvania, University of Pittsburgh, and University of South Carolina.

The volumes, and the models of decolonized and inclusive research, teaching, advocacy, and action that they present, inform and are informed by each other. We strongly encourage readers to engage with them as a pair. We also encourage using the volumes both as guides for scholarly work and for pedagogical purposes, including as course readers, and we invite readers to consult the supplementary website associated with these volumes for further materials and resources in teaching contexts. We look forward to the ongoing conversations and the decolonizing and inclusive models of linguistics that will result from scholarly engagement with the chapters in these volumes for years to come.

About the Companion Website

www.oup.com/us/inclusioninlinguistics

Oxford has created a website to accompany *Inclusion in Linguistics*. Material that cannot be made available in a book, namely author photos, bios, and additional resources for readers are provided here. The reader is encouraged to consult this resource in conjunction with the chapters.

References

Bucholtz, Mary. (2004). Changing places: *Language and Woman's Place* in context. In Mary Bucholtz (Ed.), *Language and woman's place: Text and commentaries,* original text by Robin Tolmach Lakoff (pp. 121–128). Revised and expanded edition. Oxford University Press.

Bucholtz, Mary, & miles-hercules, deandre. (2021). The displacement of race in language and gender studies. *Gender and Language, 15*(3), 414–422. https://doi.org/10.1558/genl.20882

Charity Hudley, Anne H., Mallinson, Christine, & Bucholtz, Mary. (2020a). Toward racial justice in linguistics: Interdisciplinary insights into theorizing race in the discipline and diversifying the profession. *Language, 96*(4), e200–e235. https://doi.org/10.1353/lan.2020.0074

Charity Hudley, Anne H., Mallinson, Christine, & Bucholtz, Mary. (2020b). From theory to action: Working collectively toward a more antiracist linguistics (Response to commentators). *Language, 96*(4), e307–e319. http://doi.org/10.1353/lan.2020.0081

Joseph, Brian D. (2020). What is time (and why should linguists care about it)? *Language, 96*(4), 908–937. https://doi.org/10.1353/lan.2020.0066

Lorde, Audre. 1988. *A burst of light.* Firebrand Books.

Abstract: This introduction to *Inclusion in Linguistics* begins by explaining the motivation for the volume and its grounding in social justice initiatives within linguistics, the academy, and society more broadly. It then provides an overview of the chapters, organized around the volume's major themes: intersectional inclusion, disciplinary and institutional pathways for inclusion, creating just and inclusive classrooms, and fostering community partnerships and public engagement. Next, reflecting on the insights of the chapters, a key principle of inclusion in academia is discussed, namely, that inclusion and exclusion are both personal and structural. Finally, the inclusive process of developing and creating the volume is described and the reader is called upon to use this volume and its companion, *Decolonizing Linguistics*, to develop their own action plan for advancing social justice in linguistics.

Key Words: accessibility, anti-racism, inclusion, intersectionality, pedagogy, public engagement

Introduction

Inclusion in Linguistics

Christine Mallinson (she/her)
University of Maryland, Baltimore County

Jon Henner† (he/him/☞/🖐)
University of North Carolina, Greensboro

Anne H. Charity Hudley (she/her)
Stanford University

Mary Bucholtz (she/her, they/them)
University of California, Santa Barbara

Inclusion in Linguistics as Intersectional Social Justice

What is inclusion? What is inclusion in linguistics? These are fundamental questions that this volume and its contributors engage with, explicitly and implicitly. The question of inclusion is increasingly recognized as fundamental to academia, higher education, and society writ large, and it should be seen as equally fundamental to the discipline of linguistics.

We started these volumes just before the summer of 2020, when the world saw the #BlackLivesMatter movement intensify in response to the murders of Breonna Taylor, George Floyd, and other Black people in the US and around the globe. At the same time, the world was experiencing intense upheaval, stress, fear, and loss due to the COVID-19 pandemic—which disproportionately affected communities of color and disabled communities, and especially disabled communities of color. The crisis further exacerbated structural and individual racial and ability disparities and inequities related to health and healthcare, education, and the economy. An intense period of activism and

---

Jon Henner died on August 14, 2023. His contributions to this chapter were complete except for the final copyediting and proofreading which was done by the editors.

Christine Mallinson, Jon Henner, Anne H. Charity Hudley, and Mary Bucholtz, *Introduction* In: *Inclusion in Linguistics*.
Edited by: Anne H. Charity Hudley, Christine Mallinson and Mary Bucholtz, Oxford University Press.

media attention spanned the summer and the months that followed, with social movement leaders making direct calls to action for racial equity and racial justice—and, by extension, justice on the basis of disability, gender, sexuality, class, immigration status, Indigeneity, and global geography, as well as the intersection of these and other bases of social oppression.

College and university campuses became and continue to be key sites for this work (Libresco, 2015). Scholar-activists decried the pervasiveness of superficial institutional discourse about diversity, equity, and inclusion, called for explicit awareness of anti-Blackness and white supremacy as issues that directly affect higher education, and demanded specific action-based, solutions-driven, intersectionally informed systemic and institutional-level responses (Charity Hudley et al., 2022; cf. Calhoun, 2021). Such efforts also reached linguistics as a discipline, which over the years had been facing growing demands to address issues of racial inequity, particularly the persistent underrepresentation of faculty and students of color (see, e.g., Linguistic Society of America, 2019a; 2019b; Rickford 1997; 2014). This ongoing period of activism is viewed by many as central both for addressing anti-Blackness and for advancing the broader work of justice, equity, diversity, and inclusion that also needs to happen in linguistics and in higher education. If scholars and activists can work to get it right for Black people, given the history of the world, we can work to get it right for everyone. Work that challenges anti-Blackness and white supremacy encompasses all permutations of inclusive activism.

The time has thus arrived for linguistics departments to take an active stand, and several have risen to the challenge. Numerous departmental statements and action plans for justice, equity, diversity, access, and inclusion have been issued and continue to be put forward around the world. Some examples in the US include the University of California, Berkeley Department of Linguistics (n.d.); the University of Chicago Department of Linguistics (n.d.), the University of Michigan Department of Linguistics (n.d), the University of Washington Department of Linguistics (n.d.), the University of Oregon Department of Linguistics Diversity Committee (2020), the University of California, San Diego Department of Linguistics (2020), and the Western Washington University Department of Linguistics (2022a; 2022b). These statements have ranged from presenting departmental values to thorough attempts at unpacking bias and addressing structural disparities in higher education. As some of these statements acknowledge, writing a statement is easy; following up and implementing direct actions for change is much harder. How many departments that put out statements do not have Black faculty, deaf faculty, or disabled faculty, for example? Paying lip service to supporting linguists from marginalized backgrounds means little when all the faculty making the statements are from hegemonic backgrounds; recognizing the fact that language is not solely spoken is not the same as ensuring that deaf linguists have faculty jobs. Nevertheless, these statements, action plans, and similar efforts by faculty in linguistics and related fields are a critical starting point and are at the heart of the conceptual framework for this book.

The cumulative efforts thus far within the field of linguistics and in higher education more generally lay the groundwork for this volume. Contributors engage with questions of justice, equity, and inclusion and demonstrate how to take this work to the next level in research, teaching, community partnerships, public engagement, and institutional and professional service. They also demonstrate that the term "inclusion," a pivotal legal and activist term for disability communities, has limitations which are often ignored in justice and equity work. Inclusion is less about ensuring that the right kinds of white, cis, abled bodies are in the same room and more about working to create an environment where various types of bodies and minds can fully participate in the room where it happens (Hamraie, 2017). María Cioè-Peña (2022, p. 31) writes that "language is for meaning making, not categorizing people." This must be true of spaces as well, which must be active sites for the process of inclusion, as exemplified through the practices described in the chapters in this volume.

The following chapters present specific models and describe specific practices for how to extend and transcend existing frameworks for inclusion and address their limitations in ways that actively create a meaningfully inclusive linguistics. As the authors establish, it is not sufficient to understand what inclusion is as a theoretical construct; we must also understand how to implement it—and then do so—in relevant, meaningful, and contextualized ways. In this regard, *Inclusion in Linguistics* is a roadmap for inclusion as an active practice in linguistics. The volume places an emphasis on results and impact, with full access, equity, and justice as the goal.

Intersectional Inclusion in Linguistics

Part 1 of this volume widens the frame of inclusion in linguistics beyond academia's traditional focus on race and binary cis gender. The authors present detailed and intersectional inclusion models across disability, sexuality, geography, and gender identity, as well as race.

In Chapter 1, "How to Train Your Abled Linguist: A Crip Linguistics Perspective on Pragmatic Research," Jon Henner argues that true inclusion in linguistics requires linguists to respect disabled people and how they use language. This requires more than simply updating the terms used to refer to disabled people without thinking deeply about their rights or materially benefiting them. Using as an example a special section of the Linguistic Society of America's journal *Language* focused on Autistic languaging, Henner demonstrates that ableism in linguistic analysis prevents the field from being truly inclusive.

In Chapter 2, "Critically Examining Inclusion and Parity for Deaf Global South Researchers of Colour in the Field of Sign Language Linguistics," Lynn Hou and Kristian Ali examine inclusion in signed language linguistics. While the field has considered inclusion as primarily focusing on the needs of deaf communities and secondarily including deaf scholars from these communities, deafness as conceived by the field is still inseparable from whiteness, particularly in the Global North. Hou and Ali argue that true inclusion means making more space for deaf scholars of color, especially those who reside in the Global South, through systematic changes in the infrastructure of Global North PhD programs and signed language research conferences as well as ongoing critical dialogue about racial and geographical disparities in the field.

In Chapter 3, "We Need to Be Telling Our Own Stories: Creating a Home for Filipinx Americans in Linguistics," Julien De Jesus writes about their experiences as a Filipinx American linguist and their complicated relationship with the discipline. They detail the marginalization of Filipinx people within linguistics, not only numerically but also through the exoticization and exploitation of Filipinx and Filipinx American identity and the gatekeeping of research. De Jesus argues that structural change is needed in order for Filipinx American linguists to thrive, including support systems beyond the graduate program as well as emotional, intellectual, and material allyship and support from linguists in societal and institutional positions of power.

In Chapter 4, "(Trans)forming Expertise: Transness, Equity, and the Ethical Imperative of Linguistics," deandre miles-hercules widens the scope of gender inclusion discussions in linguistics, describing the trans-exclusivity of the discipline and detailing specific incidents where cis linguists created a hostile environment for trans people. Asserting that a commitment to scholarship must entail a principled investment in dismantling oppression, miles-hercules describes how the field can progress via trans and nonbinary frameworks and offers recommendations for cis linguists interested in becoming accomplices in creating a truly gender-inclusive field.

In Chapter 5, "Toward a Big Tent Linguistics: Inclusion and the Myth of the Lone Genius," Rikker Dockum and Caitlin M. Green argue that a key element of exclusion in linguistics is the ideology that the discipline is founded on key works by a few white and apparently abled and cisgender men, who are valorized for decades after their core publications appear. The authors call for the discipline to elevate other kinds of linguistic thinkers in order to achieve true inclusion and to reject the reproduction of longstanding disciplinary hierarchies and ideologies.

Linguistics for All: Disciplinary and Institutional Pathways for Inclusion

Part 2 of the volume provides models for working toward inclusion across various disciplinary contexts that have not been addressed in previous discussions, including underexamined student populations, subfields, and geographic regions.

In Chapter 6, "Increasing Access and Equity for First-Generation Scholars in Linguistics," Iara Mantenuto, Tamaya Levy, Stephanie Reyes, and Zhongyin Zhang push for a recognition of the hidden curriculum in higher education and how it hinders first-generation scholars' persistence, retention, publishing, job placement, and overall success. The authors provide in-depth discussion of first-generation scholars as a diverse and intersectional group, who often do not have the kinds of capital available to scholars from families who are experienced in higher education. Mantenuto and colleagues argue that an inclusive linguistics must remove gatekeeping that disproportionately affects first-generation scholars, expand outreach efforts to include these scholars, raise awareness about the experiences and issues that first-generation scholars face in academia, and advocate for more institutional support—academic, social, cultural, financial—to promote and ensure their success.

In Chapter 7, "For the Culture: Pathways in Linguistics for Black and HBCU Scholars," Candice Y. Thornton establishes that an inclusive linguistics must expand programs to Historically Black Colleges and Universities (HBCUs). They explain that linguistics programs rooted in Blackness and Black higher education environments can lead more students to study Black Diaspora-related languaging such as Gullah/Geechee. Thornton also discusses actionable items that can be taken to address and remove barriers that impede Black students, especially from HBCUs, from engaging in linguistics.

Chapter 8, "Towards Greater Inclusion in Practice and Among Practitioners: The Case for an Experience-Based Linguistics in India," by Reenu Punnoose and Muhammed Haneefa, adds important geographic breadth to the discussion of inclusive linguistics. Punnoose and Haneefa argue that in India, where linguistics originated, linguists focus excessively on the discipline as solely theoretical and dismiss experience-based forms of linguistic research as not "real" linguistics. The authors discuss how these ideologies constrain the practice of the discipline as well as the practitioners of linguistics in India. Drawing upon examples from sociology, which they take as a reference point for a relatively more inclusive and reflexive discipline practice, the authors argue for more applied forms of linguistic research and training and offer recommendations for ways that linguistics programs on the subcontinent can become more inclusive.

In Chapter 9, "Power Shift: Toward Inclusive Natural Language Processing," Emily M. Bender and Alvin Grissom II expand the discussion of disciplinary inclusion to the subfield of computational linguistics. They note that big data/ machine learning approaches to linguistic analysis overwhelmingly serve to reproduce hegemonic power. What is good for profits and imperialism is not necessarily good for humanity; as a result, linguists must be more engaged in understanding how linguistic datasets and language technologies are used. For example, Bender and Grissom point out that many researchers and practitioners fail to recognize that biases encoded into datasets can be extraordinarily harmful. The authors call for inclusive, community-engaged language technology work, demand transparent and thorough explorations of negative impacts of new proposed technologies, and claim space for linguists to participate in decision-making about language technology design and deployment.

Creating Just and Inclusive Classrooms

Part 3 of the volume presents examples and resources for teaching linguistics in pre-kindergarten through high school environments as well as in higher education. The chapters in this section represent a range of languages and language varieties in their pedagogical focus.

In Chapter 10, "Disrupting English Class: Linguistics and Social Justice for *All* High School Students," Amy L. Plackowski draws upon her experience as a high school teacher asserts that linguistics should be a part of the public school curriculum as it gives students (and teachers) a framework to engage in social justice-oriented, anti-racist pedagogy and inquiry while centering student voices and teaching media literacy. Plackowski argues that linguistics should be accessible to all students regardless of where they attend school or what classes they take and thus should be part of a core curriculum that promotes inquiry into language study via real-world examples, rather than being organized traditionally by subfield. She provides recommendations for how linguists can help this effort by creating accessible linguistic content for students and teachers.

In Chapter 11, "Bilingual Education in Cabo Verdean: Toward Visibility and Dignity," Abel Djassi Amado, Marlyse Baptista, Lourenço Pina

Garcia, Ambrizeth Helena Lima, and Dawna Marie Thomas discuss how a Massachusetts language-in-education policy allowed a Boston-based research network with explicit linguistic justice goals, the Cabo Verdean Center for Applied Research, to develop a curriculum for Cabo Verdean English language learners attending Boston public schools, using Cabo Verdean Kriolu as a medium of instruction. The authors describe elements of the curriculum and its benefits for the education of a group of students who have been underserved by traditional language instruction that does not acknowledge their linguistic background.

In Chapter 12, "Community College Linguistics for Educational Justice: Content and Assessment Strategies That Support Antiracist and Inclusive Teaching," Jamie A. Thomas argues that if linguistics is serious about being inclusive, it must develop a curriculum that supports students who study in community colleges, who are largely from nontraditional and sociopolitically marginalized backgrounds. Thomas draws upon her pedagogical experience across a range of institutions to show that a curricular emphasis on the significance of language as a tool of exclusion is a productive framework that can draw community college students into the discipline by exploring how tools and approaches of linguistics can be used to advance equity and justice.

In Chapter 13, "Texts, Tweets, Twitch, TikTok: Computer-Mediated Communication as an Inclusive Gateway to Linguistics," Jenny Lederer offers another strategy for inclusive engagement in linguistics teaching, proposing that linguists incorporate media that students themselves use, especially social media platforms such as TikTok and Twitch, as well as data from students' own online interactions. Lederer provides a model for incorporating media examples into an introductory linguistics course in highly accessible and engaging ways. This technique, she explains, facilitates students' view of themselves as scholars and of their language use as worthy of scholarly attention—which increases interest and participation in linguistics, particularly among underrepresented students, who often emerge as linguistic experts in this approach.

In Chapter 14, "Pedagogies of Inclusion Must Start from Within: Landguaging Teacher Reflection and Plurilingualism in the L2 Classroom," Rhonda Chung and John Wayne N. dela Cruz connect ecological and plurilingual learning theories to Indigenous scholarship, in order to support Teaching English as a Second Language (TESL) instructors in designing inclusive land-sensitive plurilingual pedagogies. Accordingly, the authors present a model of an inclusive teacher education curriculum that is rooted in principles of what they call *landguaging*, which confronts systemic inequalities by taking a land-first account of the rich biodiversity of dialects and languages found in a school's local territory. In this way, the authors show that even educators teaching a colonial language can reject monocultural and extractive settler-colonialist teaching practices and transform their classroom into an inclusive translanguaging space through land-sensitive exercises.

In Chapter 15, "Beyond Pronouns 101: Linguistic Advocacy for Trans-Inclusive Language in the College Classroom," Lal Zimman and Cedar Brown take a linguistics-informed approach to gender inclusivity in the classroom, with a focus on the growing but sometimes poorly handled practice of sharing gender pronouns. Drawing on a survey of trans students' experiences with pronoun sharing in classroom contexts, the authors offer specific action items and recommendations to ensure that pronoun usage is respected without assuming that the same approach will work for all students. The authors demonstrate that creating a trans-inclusive classroom requires flexibility and ongoing commitment.

In Chapter 16, "Increasing Inclusion Through Structured Active Learning: Curriculum Changes in an Introduction to Formal Linguistics Class," Florian Schwarz proposes an inclusive model of formal tools used in syntax and semantics that reflects the languaging that students use. He discusses how flipping his introductory linguistics classroom—that is, providing subject-matter content outside of instruction time and using in-class time for hands-on learning—supported diverse groups of linguistics students, resulting in higher attendance rates, performance, and participation in the course as well as positive evaluation responses and feedback. The pedagogical model was also successful in supporting students with different learning styles, which proved helpful in the context of the many challenges to traditional academic learning that arose during the COVID-19 pandemic.

In Chapter 17, "An Action-Based Roadmap for Equity, Diversity, and Inclusion in Teaching Linguistics," Nathan Sanders, Lex Konnelly, and Pocholo Umbal outline a multifaceted model of inclusive linguistics teaching that provides a detailed guide to the process of developing and implementing such an initiative. They focus in particular on the creation of a repository of open-access pedagogical tools specific to linguistics—including lecture notes, datasets, and a cross-linguistic database of names for use in example sentences—that support more inclusive teaching practices in the discipline. The repository also includes a handbook that provides guidance to new instructors and teaching assistants in creating an equitable linguistics classroom. Finally, the authors describe their strategies for sharing their work more widely through workshops, presentations, and collaborations.

Fostering Community Partnerships and Public Engagement

Part 4 of the volume presents examples of collaborations, community partnerships, and other forms of inclusive engagement. The chapters in this section feature linguists' work beyond the academy to advance linguistic justice.

In Chapter 18, "Creating Inclusive Linguistics Communication: Crash Course Linguistics," Lauren Gawne, Gretchen McCulloch, Nicole Sweeney, Rachel Alatalo, Hannah Bodenhausen, Ceri Riley, and Jessi Grieser describe a partnership between academic linguists, specialists in linguistic communication, and media production professionals to create an online linguistics series, Crash Course Linguistics. The authors describe their approach to creating inclusive linguistics content for the public, which involved engaging with a range of languages, varieties, language users, and linguistic practices designed with target audiences and their experiences with language in mind. The authors offer specific guidelines for those interested in communicating about linguistics to the general public, noting that widening our scope to reach audiences who may never enter our classrooms is central to the goals of an inclusive linguistics.

In Chapter 19, "The Justice Language Action Project: Critical Linguistics for Inclusion and Equity in K-12 Classrooms," Jennifer Sclafani, Panayota Gounari, Iuliia Fakhrutdinova, and Vannessa Quintana Sarria describe a professional development workshop, held virtually during the COVID-19 pandemic, in which graduate students and faculty trained public school educators in critical discourse analysis and critical language awareness. Teachers learned via case studies that promoted linguistic and educational equity and inclusion and successfully developed social justice-themed curricular units of their own. At the same time, the project also provided graduate students with the opportunity to connect theory and practice during this turbulent period that affected their own professional, academic, and personal lives.

In Chapter 20, "Linguistic Literacy and Advocacy in Action: Case Studies in Community Engagement from the Language Diversity Ambassadors at North Carolina State University," Marie Bissell, José Álvarez-Retamales, Matthew Champagne, Jessica Hatcher, Shalina Omar, and Walt Wolfram establish the need for inclusive linguistics programs to expand outside of the academy. The authors assert that linguists have a responsibility for clear communication with the public, including students, who benefit from access to knowledge about the relationships between language, identity, and culture and the real-life impacts of linguistic stereotyping and discrimination. The authors discuss their successes with various linguistic outreach programs designed for local students and provide actionable ideas and practical knowledge to facilitate the growth and expansion of inclusive language-science public engagement programs by scholars at other universities and educational institutions.

The volume ends with a conclusion in which the four co-authors reflect on the lessons learned from the chapters in this volume for further advancing inclusion in linguistics.

Inclusion and Exclusion as Both Personal and Structural

In higher education, inclusion must be an active practice and structural goal. Advancing diversity and inclusion in higher education requires active, sustained, and multiscalar efforts by individuals and institutions across all levels (American Association of Colleges and Universities [AAC&U], n.d.; US Department of Education, 2017). At the same time, inclusion is intrinsically personal: To be included, individuals and groups must feel a sense of belonging and community (Center for Postsecondary Research, 2021). Bringing systemically and historically minoritized people into academic spaces without ensuring they feel that they belong or are in community with others is not truly inclusive and can cause harm. Thus, inclusion involves doing, feeling, and being. Inclusion also crucially involves communicating (Rapp & Corral-Granados, 2021).

Too often, academic institutions discuss inclusion without discussing exclusion. But it is impossible to achieve inclusion without also purposefully eliminating exclusion. Doing so requires us to look at the complex relationship between inclusion and exclusion at the structural or systemic level as well as the individual level. Before we decide how to achieve inclusion, we need to understand who isn't currently included as well as why and how they are excluded. We take as an example the range of experiences of those in linguistics who identify as disabled or as living with a disability. (We note that even the language used to refer to this large, heterogeneous, and often marginalized group of people is under debate.) Linguists who focus on the languaging of the mouth and its internal and external movements do not consider themselves obligated to include the languaging of the hands and the body (although they are limited in the generalizations they can make if they choose not to do so). This example may therefore seem to be a simple individual exclusionary practice, a matter of scholarly preference without larger consequences. Yet for marginalized people, such exclusions are frequent and add up to a larger aggregate; in this way, what initially appears to be an individual form of exclusion becomes a systemic exclusion. If there were proportional numbers of publications on the languaging of other modalities, then an individual paper solely focused on the mouth and its internal and external movements would not contribute to systemic exclusion. However, linguistics does not treat languaging in modalities other than the mouth and its internal and external movements as equally central to the discipline (Henner & Robinson, 2023). Linguists who study semiotic, visual, and haptic languaging, among others, must therefore continue to seek the same recognition and validation that linguists who study languaging of the mouth already enjoy. Nor is this simply a matter of individual preference, because deaf linguists overwhelmingly conduct research on signed languages. In other words, limiting our understanding of language, or of linguistics, often creates systemic exclusion within our discipline, regardless of individual intentions.

More generally, being disabled or living with a disability in linguistics, as in the wider world, requires navigating on a daily basis a host of such seemingly small exclusionary practices that together accumulate into systemic exclusion. The disabled person quickly learns that a truly accessible and inclusive world does not exist. Audio recordings may be shared without transcripts, and even when transcripts are available, they are not an equivalent experience (cf. Figueroa, 2022). Video recordings often do not have audio descriptions and are not captioned or subtitled. Images are regularly presented without alt text. Deadlines do not respect crip time (Samuels, 2017). Events like conference talks or classroom lectures that are claimed to be fully accessible and inclusive are not. And many linguists read from dense, complex texts in presentations, or speak rapidly and use extensive jargon, while scholars with intellectual disabilities or neurodivergent people struggle to absorb information presented in those ways. Even if appropriate accommodations are provided, which is more often the exception than the rule, disabled people can experience "access friction" (cf. Hamraie, 2017), where the accommodations that one person requires conflict with those that another person needs. People sensitive to sound may attend an event where a deaf or hard-of-hearing person has requested sound amplification. People sensitive to light may be seated near a deaf-blind person who requires extra light.

The existence of access friction requires a model of inclusion and exclusion as fundamentally complex. There are no one-size-fits-all formulas for inclusion, and exclusion is regularly reproduced even in the most carefully designed inclusion efforts, especially given the nature of academic life. Being disabled is often in conflict with tight tenure or PhD requirements. A sick body and mind cannot often meet the productivity requirements set by an ableist university (Samuels, 2022). Even people who consider themselves abled can run afoul of neoliberal and capitalist production demands due to pregnancy (which can be legally conceptualized as a disability; Cox, 2012) or caretaking obligations. The broader theoretical or conceptual view of inclusion espoused by academic institutions thus does not negate the lived realities of exclusion that are experienced and must be navigated by disabled people every day. Nor does a stated commitment to inclusion negate the structural inequities and financial penalties that can result from being excluded, or diminish the need for the basic supports and accommodations, not to mention the large-scale structural changes, that are critical for full inclusion.

Inclusivity in *Inclusion in Linguistics*

Recognizing the complexities of inclusion and exclusion, we highlight these realities as part of who we are and why we are doing this work. As tenure-line and tenured faculty who work at well-resourced universities in the Global North, we occupy structural and economic positions that allow us to forge models of collaboration and support in order to assist other scholars in navigating around the walls and barriers that still too often exist in the academy. Here we describe how Anne, Christine, and Mary aimed to create a maximally inclusive process for developing and editing this volume, as well as how Jon became part of this collaboration.

From day one, the co-editors actively practiced inclusion along multiple lines in the process of developing the volume. To ensure that the opportunity to submit a chapter proposal was as widely distributed as possible, they conducted multiple open calls for papers and hosted open and accessible webinars to maximally reach contributors across career stages, paths, institutions, and geographic locations. In selecting proposals, they prioritized a range of approaches that advance a more inclusive linguistics, focusing not only on research but also teaching, community partnerships, public engagement, and institutional and professional service, as well as accompanying activism and actions for social change. They also made clear that they consider collaborative work in teams to be just as valuable as solo-authored work in creating rigorous and relevant research (cf. Ledgerwood et al., 2022). With this "big tent" approach to who counts as a linguist and what counts as linguistics, the co-editors resisted exclusionary moves by those who would aim to "police the boundaries of the discipline by declaring certain topics off limits, as 'not linguistics'" (Charity Hudley et al., 2020, e312), which further marginalize scholars who are already often excluded by the discipline on the basis of race, disability, gender identity, geographic region, and/or other parameters of differences. (For additional details on our process, see also the preface to both volumes and the introduction in *Decolonizing Linguistics*.)

The co-editors invited Jon to co-author the introduction and conclusion to this volume in order to broaden the perspectives represented on inclusion in linguistics. At the first stage of the co-authorship process, Christine and Jon workshopped key concepts about inclusion in academia and linguistics framed with a humanizing lens and, in drafting the introduction and conclusion, combined these with ideas generated by the editorial team. As a priority, the main goal was to interrogate what an inclusive linguistics would (and would not) look like. By putting this framework and concept into conversation with the chapters in this volume, they provided ideas and pathways for moving toward that goal. Anne and Mary wove in their own ideas and insights as well, and the final texts represent a collaboration of all four of us, informed by feedback from the contributors.

For all contributions that were selected for the volume, the co-editors followed inclusive publication practices of collective authoring and editing. For the contributed chapters, groups were formed via Zoom for contributors to meet remotely on multiple occasions at different stages in the manuscript preparation process to collectively workshop and discuss ideas with others across this volume and its companion volume, *Decolonizing Linguistics*. Anne, Christine, and Mary ensured that each contributor received multiple rounds of feedback, both written and through Zoom conversations, from peer contributors and from each co-editor. This feedback was designed to constructively shape and refine the work before the volumes proceeded to external review. It also helped build our community of scholars. As Kamran Khan (2022), a contributor to the *Decolonizing Linguistics* volume, noted, "The best thing about this project was in creating communities and space for us."

During their process of writing and editing, the co-editors encouraged all authors to practice inclusion in multiple ways. They also encouraged contributors' discussions of the limitations and failures of their work, as well as its successes, and acknowledgments of the power dynamics that may have shaped and limited their inclusion efforts. They encouraged contributors to engage directly with their own positionality, subjectivity, and intentionality in their work—to write themselves into the text and to explain why they pursued their work and who it is for. (For similar engagement by the co-editors and co-authors, see also the preface and the introductions of both volumes.) In line with our goals of community-based linguistic and cultural inclusion, all contributors were asked to provide their pronouns to accompany their chapters, and many contributors elected to include a second abstract for their chapters in a language or language variety other than standardized English. Contributors were encouraged to use terms for communities they worked with that are guided and informed by the community's preferences (e.g., Brown, 2011), and to use inclusive terminology—such as *language user* or *communicator* instead of *speaker*—in order to avoid treating speech as the default linguistic modality. Throughout the volumes, the co-editors also made deliberate choices to capitalize and decapitalize specific terms. For example, in our introductions and conclusions, we have chosen to use the term "deaf" instead of "Deaf," a term that became a divisive concept in deaf communities often used to gatekeep and marginalize people who did not meet specific constructed criteria to be "true" Deaf, especially BIPOC deaf people. who often have different experiences in deaf communities than white, generationally deaf people. However, we capitalize terms such as "Black," "Native," and "Indigenous" that refer to a shared culture and history, while lowercasing the term "white," which is not a comparably cultural term and has long been capitalized by white-supremacist hate groups (cf. Coleman, 2020). The co-editors similarly use and encouraged contributors to use precise wording that conveys the intended meaning—including such terms as "racism," "white supremacy," "hate," and "anti-Blackness." Conversely, they avoid and encouraged the authors to avoid mitigated language that attempts to sugarcoat inequities (e.g., "less advantaged") or cast them as merely individual-level phenomena (e.g., "prejudice"), or that otherwise is less specific or informative than language that highlights systemic and structural factors (cf. Buchanan et al., 2021).

Moreover, the co-editors asked contributors to practice inclusion and decolonization in their citation practices, making sure to cite scholars of color and other structurally marginalized scholars wherever possible and to avoid routinely citing scholars simply because they are routinely cited. The chapters across these volumes are robustly cross-referenced, as all authors read and extensively commented on others' work, finding linkages and points of commonality. Contributors were also encouraged to seek feedback on their work from those outside their regular spheres and networks, including those from outside academic circles. Each chapter was required to state that IRB approval was received if applicable, acknowledge any funding received, and recognize collaborators and community groups who contributed to their work. Finally, all contributors were asked to write their chapters in an accessible style, with a focus on practical application and clear recommendations, providing citations and resources for readers to use to engage in similar work in their own areas of interest.

Throughout, the co-editors prioritized humanization as central to the scholarly process. For many scholars, academia is neither truly accessible nor truly inclusive. During the course of developing and producing these volumes, this reality was made even more vivid for us. The COVID-19 pandemic was in full swing, along with the pandemic of anti-Blackness—two pandemics of epic proportions that disproportionately harm "academia's essential workers" (Thomas & Bucholtz, 2021, p. 290). This group includes women and faculty of color, pretenure faculty, disabled faculty, trans and nonbinary faculty, and the precariously employed, as well as other groups that are structurally marginalized in academia yet disproportionately carry much of its teaching, service, and community-focused labor. Indeed, some scholars who desired to contribute to this volume were ultimately unable to do so because of the burdens and barriers inflicted by these twin pandemics, and we acknowledge their missing and much-needed contributions here.

The social context surrounding the COVID-19 pandemic also highlighted much of the structural ableism in universities, whereby people who could teach and work in person and forgo masking were valorized over people who needed to continue mitigating risk. During the writing and publication process for these volumes, many of us—co-editors, authors, and contributors across both volumes—experienced personal losses and setbacks, short-term illnesses as well as long-term and chronic health situations and disabilities, and ongoing caregiving responsibilities, all of which were exacerbated by these twin pandemics. We all extended grace as much as possible to ourselves and others with empathy and support, while still advancing the goal of creating volumes that elevate essential perspectives and ideas. In this way, production of the books was an act of Crip Carework (Piepzna-Samarasinha, 2018).

In contrast to the traditional paradigm of solitary scholarly writing, editing, revision, and anonymous critique, which often isolates scholars and prevents true dialogue, we as co-editors and authors therefore have prioritized restorative models of transparency, collaboration, and humanity in the scholarly production of this pair of volumes. These values and practices advance the goals of inclusion and justice that undergird the work presented in and through both *Inclusion in Linguistics* and *Decolonizing Linguistics*.

Going Forward: Creating Your Own Action Plan for Inclusion

As we strive to enact inclusion and decolonization in linguistics and the academy, we reject the colonialist, white-supremacist notion that research discovery and scholarly knowledge must be personally distant or seemingly objective for the author to have authority and expertise. We prioritize multiple ways of knowing, multiple language modalities, and multiple pathways for sharing knowledge that take as a premise the need to dismantle and discard traditional academic hierarchies and power dynamics.

As indicated by the dialogic process of creating these volumes, we also recognize that inclusion and decolonization go hand in hand, but that neither concept is sufficient in and of itself. Models of and strategies for advancing inclusion and decolonization must be accompanied by models of and strategies for eliminating exclusion and colonization, with the goal of full access, equity, and justice.

Sentiment is not enough to challenge longstanding ideologies, to disrupt structural inequities, and to ensure full inclusion and participation: Transformative change requires hard work and skill. The contributions across this volume advance these goals via work that illustrates a range of perspectives, interests, and issues, grounded in the specific perspectives and lived experiences of linguists with different perspectives and experiences that have been shaped by structural inequities. We call upon you, the reader, to envision how you can take the range of models you have before you—from departmental, institutional, and organizational statements, to pedagogical and curricular interventions, community-based research approaches, public engagement endeavors, and more—and create your own action plan for taking this work forward.

References

American Association of Colleges and Universities. (n.d.). Advancing diversity, equity, and inclusion. https://www.aacu.org/priorities/advancing-diversity-equity-and-inclusion

Brown, Lydia X. Z. (2011, August 4). The significance of semantics: Person-first language: Why it matters. Autistic Hoya. https://www.autistichoya.com/2011/08/significance-of-semantics-person-first.html

Buchanan, Nicole T., Perez, Marisol, Prinstein, Mitchell J., & Thurston, Idia B. (2021). Upending racism in psychological science: Strategies to change how science is conducted, reported, reviewed, and disseminated. *The American Psychologist, 76*(7), 1097–1112. https://doi.org/10.1037/amp0000905

Calhoun, Kendra N. (2021). Competing discourses of diversity and inclusion: Institutional rhetoric and graduate student narratives at two Minority Serving Institutions [Doctoral dissertation, University of California, Santa Barbara].

Center for Postsecondary Research. (2021). Building a sense of community for all. Indiana University. https://nsse.indiana.edu/research/annual-results/belonging-story/index.html

Charity Hudley, Anne H., Mallinson, Christine, & Bucholtz, Mary. (2020). Toward racial justice in linguistics: Interdisciplinary insights into theorizing race in the discipline and diversifying the profession. *Language, 96*(4), e200–e235. https://doi.org/10.1353/lan.2020.0074

Charity Hudley, Anne H., Mallinson, Christine, & Bucholtz, Mary. (2022). *Talking college: Making space for Black language practices in higher educaticn*. Teachers College Press.

Cioè-Peña, María. (2022). The master's tools will never dismantle the master's school: Interrogating settler colonial logics in language education. *Annual Review of Applied Linguistics, 42*, 25–33. https://doi.org/10.1017/S0267190521000209

Coleman, Nancy. (2020, July 5). Why we're capitalizing Black. *New York Times*. https://www.nytimes.com/2020/07/05/insider/capitalized-black.html

Cox, Jeannette. (2012). Pregnancy as disability and the amended Americans with Disabilities Act. *Boston College Law Review, 53*(2), 443–488. https://lawdigitalcommons.bc.edu/bclr/vol53/iss2/2/

Figueroa, Megan. (2022). Podcasting past the paywall: How diverse media allows more equitable participation in linguistic science. *Annual Review of Applied Linguistics, 42*, 40–46. https://doi.org/10.1017/S0267190521000118

Hamraie, Aimi. (2017). *Building access: Universal design and the politics of disability*. University of Minnesota Press.

Henner, Jon, & Robinson, Octavian. (2021). Unsettling languages, unruly bodyminds: A Crip Linguistics manifesto. *Journal of Critical Study of Communication and Disability, 1*(1), 7–37. https://doi.org/10.48516/jcscd_2023vol1iss1.4

Khan, Kamran [@SecurityLing]. (2022, August 31). Thinking back on this. The best thing about this project was in creating communities and space for us. Not sure [Tweet]. Twitter. https://twitter.com/securityling/status/1564944757083852801?s=27&t=CaXRdsfXZI0TSiFPXhC5VQ.

Ledgerwood, Alison, Pickett, Cynthia, Navarro, Danielle, Remedios, Jessica D., & Lewis, Neil A. Jr. (2022). The unbearable limitations of solo science: Team science as a path for more rigorous and relevant research. *Behavioral and Brain Sciences, 45*, E81. doi:10.1017/S0140525X21000844

Libresco, Leah. (2015, December 3). Here are the demands from students protesting racism at 51 colleges. FiveThirtyEight. https://fivethirtyeight.com/features/here-are-the-demands-from-students-protesting-racism-at-51-colleges/

Linguistic Society of America. (2019a). LSA statement on race. https://www.linguisticsociety.org/content/lsa-statement-race

Linguistic Society of America. (2019b). The state of linguistics in higher education: Annual report 2018. https://www.linguisticsociety.org/sites/default/files/Annual%20Report%202019%20-%20Final_1.pdf

Piepzna-Samarasinha, Leah L. (2018). *Care work: Dreaming disability justice*. Arsenal Pulp Press.

Rapp, Anna Cecilia, & Corral-Granados, Anabel. (2021). Understanding inclusive education—a theoretical contribution from system theory and the constructionist perspective. *International Journal of Inclusive Education*. https://doi.org/10.1080/13603116.2021.1946725

Rickford, John R. (1997). Unequal partnership: Sociolinguistics and the African American speech community. *Language in Society, 26*(2), 161–198. https://doi.org/10.1017/S0047404500020893

Rickford, John R. (2014, January). Increasing the representation of under-represented ethnic minorities in linguistics: Diversity in linguistics. Paper presentation, Linguistic Society of America Annual Meeting, Minneapolis, MN.

Samuels, Ellen. (2017). Six ways of looking at crip time. *Disability Studies Quarterly, 37*(3). https://doi.org/10.18061/dsq.v37i3.5824

Samuels, Ellen. (2022). Slow time, slow futurity. *Panorama: Journal of the Association of Historians of American Art, 8*(1). https://doi.org/10.24926/24716839.13275

Thomas, Jamie A., & Bucholtz, Mary. (2021). Personal protective equipment against anti-Blackness: Communicability and contagion in the academy. *Journal of Linguistic Anthropology, 31*(2), 287–292. https://doi.org/10.1111/jola.12324

US Department of Education. (2017). Advancing diversity and inclusion in higher education: Key data highlights focusing on race and ethnicity and promising practices. https://www2.ed.gov/rschstat/research/pubs/advancing-diversity-inclusion.pdf

University of California, Berkeley. Department of Linguistics. (n.d.). Climate, inclusion, and community. https://lx.berkeley.edu/about/climate-inclusion-and-community

University of California, San Diego. Linguistics Department. (2020). UC San Diego Linguistics Department commitment to anti-racism. https://linguistics.ucsd.edu/events-info/statements/index.html

University of Chicago. Department of Linguistics. (n.d.). The Department of Linguistics' statement on diversity and inclusion.https://linguistics.uchicago.edu/

University of Michigan, Ann Arbor. Department of Linguistics. (n.d.). Statement of support to community members of minoritized backgrounds. https://lsa.umich.edu/linguistics/about-us/statement-of-support.html

University of Oregon Department of Linguistics Diversity Committee. (2020, June 3). Department of Linguistics racial justice statement.https://linguistics.uoregon.edu/diversity-and-inclusion

University of Washington Department of Linguistics. (n.d.). Diversity. https://linguistics.washington.edu/diversity

Western Washington University Linguistics Department. (2022a). Justice, equity, diversity, and inclusion. https://chss.wwu.edu/linguistics/justice-equity-diversity-and-inclusion-jedi

Western Washington University Linguistics Department. (2022b). Statement on language and social justice.https://chss.wwu.edu/linguistics/wwu-linguistics-department-statement-language-and-social-justice

PART 1
INTERSECTIONAL INCLUSION IN LINGUISTICS

Jonathan (Jon) Henner tragically passed away in August 2023 following a battle with cancer. Jon joined the University of North Carolina Greensboro (UNCG) School of Education faculty in 2016 as assistant professor in the Department of Specialized Education Services and the Interpreting, Deaf Education, and Advocacy Services program. He became the first Deaf tenured professor at UNCG when he was promoted to associate professor in 2022.

Jon was an energetic and accomplished academic who produced rigorous research and groundbreaking scholarship. His impressive work on language deprivation in deaf children advocated for deaf children's proficiency in American Sign Language as the basis for academic success while fostering their fluency in English. In addition, Jon was developing an important theory with colleagues on Crip Linguistics. As a deaf academic, Jon had a unique view of disability in academia. In his own words, he was committed "to help others in the deaf community and allies to deaf academics understand the circumstances faced by the deaf." Jon was a critic of educational policy that often treats deaf and hard-of-hearing people as a homogeneous group, rather than as a diverse group with differing backgrounds. His scholarly contributions have helped break down structural barriers for other deaf scholars and promote equity and social justice for all those in the deaf and disabled communities.

Jon excelled in the classroom, where his passion for teaching was unmistakable. He loved being a mentor and advocate for his students. Students have shared that they felt they could be their true selves in his classes. They mentioned Jon's willingness to help all students academically and to provide support for those who were dealing with personal issues or were members of marginalized groups. Another quote from Jon's work on Crip Linguistics best captures his view on language: "How you language is beautiful. Don't let anyone tell you your languaging is wrong. Your language is the story of your life."

In addition to being an outstanding role model, scholar, and teacher, Jon was a dedicated husband and father to his three children. As a colleague of Jon's wrote, he was a "force, never letting cancer stop him and always standing up for what he believed was right." Jon is deeply missed by the editors and contributors to *Inclusion in Linguistics* and its companion volume *Decolonizing Linguistics*, as well as the greater deaf community, the field, his department and university, his students, and all who knew him professionally and personally.

Abstract: In this chapter, the author talks about how some people think that autistic people are not able to understand that other people have thoughts and feelings. They use their beliefs to make guesses about if language is learned from nothing, or if people are born with language in their brains. The author does not think these people are right. Instead, he believes that their feelings about disabled people affect their understanding of how autistic people live in society. The author tries to explain that these people, who are linguists, need to understand disability and their own feelings about disability before they write about how disabled people use language.

Key Words: autism, crip linguistics, disability justice, linguistics, ableism

1

How to Train Your Abled Linguist

A Crip Linguistics Perspective on Pragmatic Research

Jon Henner† (he/him/☞/✍)
University of North Carolina at Greensboro

Introduction

This chapter centers and uplifts the languaging of autistic people using a Crip Linguistics framework. Crip Linguistics is a recent theoretical framework that combines disability theories with linguistics. It is the extension of several existing linguistic frameworks, such as embodied sociolinguistics (Bucholtz & Hall, 2016) and critical applied linguistics (Pennycook, 2021). The term "Crip" in Crip Linguistics comes from the verb "cripped" or "to crip," which means to make non-normative (see McRuer, 2006). Crip Linguistics was defined in depth in Henner and Robinson (2021). To sum, Crip Linguistics is a way for linguistics to analyze disability as a variationist perspective in languaging. It asks linguists to understand that language cannot be disordered, but bodies can be disordered in a way that affects languaging. And often, how people perceive disordered bodies make them think that the language produced by those bodies is disordered (when it's not).

While different fields recognize variation in languaging especially in terms of modality, or specific identities (e.g., gender), researchers seem hesitant to use disability as a facet of linguistic variation, or any kind of acceptable variation, except when describing things as disordered or deviant (see Mauldin & Brown, 2021 for examples from sociology). Yet as Bucholtz and Hall (2016) explain, language cannot exist without the bodies that produce it. These ideas of embodied language arise in two unpublished essays. First, in "The Ear," Hou (under review) explains that societies have covert scripts regarding expectations of the speaking and listening abilities of its peoples: "The spoken

Jon Henner died on August 14, 2023. His contributions to this chapter were complete except for the final copyediting and proofreading which was done by the editors.

Jon Henner, *How to Train Your Abled Linguist* In: *Inclusion in Linguistics*. Edited by: Anne H. Charity Hudley, Christine Mallinson and Mary Bucholtz, Oxford University Press. © Anne H. Charity Hudley, Christine Mallinson, and Mary Bucholtz 2024. DOI: 10.1093/oso/9780197755303.003.0002 language ability script postulates that to be a speaker is to be an independent agent who can interact with any hearing person spontaneously and freely" (p. 8). What this means is that the average hearing and nonmute person centers their communication expectations on the belief that every single person in their immediate and nonimmediate vicinity uses language in the same way they do. These beliefs are often enforced via physical and emotional violence. I, myself, have been physically assaulted by people who assume that I am ignoring them, when the reality is I cannot hear what they are asking me to do. Second, in "The Lungs," Charity Hudley (under review) points out that even when speaking people share the same language, abled people forget that speakers can still be limited by their bodies, as language is a coordination of several interconnected body parts. Charity Hudley explains that having lost part of a lung, she began to recognize that how much of who she was and how she was perceived was very much reliant on a singular body part that produced, amplified, and propelled speech. Given how much languaging is reliant on bodies, one would think that linguists would be more cognizant of disability studies, which is a broad field that examines bodies and minds. This, however, does not seem to be the case.

My definition of disability comes from Haagaard (2022), who explains that disability is a fluid state wherein people are viewed as harmful to society depending on how many resources, in money, time, or caregiving, are required to help them behave in ways that society considers ideal. The harm is calculated by outlays of resources (e.g., cash or time, among others); disabled people are necessarily more expensive than abled people. This definition includes people whose disabilities have not been marked by the clinical gaze, or formal definition and identification of the disability (e.g., people with invisible and unidentified illnesses). Haagaard's model can be described as a model of parasitic disability—one wherein people who are perceived as non-normative and require state and community intervention to live fruitfully are seen as a drain on social resources. Robinson explains that this kind of debility theory is starkly evident in how government institutions such as the National Institutes of Health specifically recommend implantation and oral therapies for deaf and hard-of-hearing children as a condition for saving society money (e.g., Semenov et al., 2013) (Robinson, personal communication, March 23, 2022).

In Critical Disability Theory or DisCrit (Annamma & Hardy, 2021) the clinical gaze in school systems (identification and intervention) focuses on students who under- or overperform on assessments. Those students are seen as non-normative in that they do not fit into a normative range of expected behaviors. In linguistics and related fields, non-normative languaging is often identified via the use of language assessments. Once the clinical gaze has identified these children, they are given labels such as *disordered language*, *atypical language*, and *specific language impairments*, among others. They are then othered from "typically developing" children. DisCrit parallels parasitic disability theory in that those children who are identified as non-normative are then in need of interventions, which incurs a cost to the school and the communities around the students.

Author Positionality

I move through the world as a cis, white man. I do not quite consider myself cis, but that is how the world perceives me and responds to me. I am large. I take up space. I am heavily tattooed. I am hirsute and bearded. These markers of masculinity combined with my white skin afford me very specific privileges. Although Jewish, I am ashkinormative (Ashkenazi) and matrilineal, which means that my Jewishness and my place in US Jewish discourses have never been questioned. I am deaf, but have speech privileges; I am severely chronically ill, but have systems in place to support me. I acknowledge myself as autistic and neurodivergent, but do not have a formal identification, nor did I receive services for these identifications as a student in the US school system. My US nationality means my perspectives, including what is written in this chapter, are US centered.

I started my academic career working with American Sign Language (ASL) assessments. My experiences developing and norming these assessments helped me realize that how we assess signed languages is unjust, especially in the context of US schools for the deaf. As Cioè-Peña (2022) writes, "Fidelity to linguistic standards will not usher in social justice in schools or anywhere. Language should reflect the capacity of people; as such, we should shift fidelity to people, and we can do this by honoring expansive linguistic practices in research, classrooms, assessments, and applied linguistics" (p. 31). My collaboration with Octavian Robinson on the idea of Crip Linguistics came out of discussions with many different thinkers on how we can ethically assess the language use of deaf people, and disabled people broadly, within the educational institution and outside of it.

I am often asked why I focus my energies on examining ableism in the field of linguistics when other fields (e.g., medicine or special education) target disabled people specifically and arguably with more concrete policy effects. That is a reasonable question. Charity Hudley and Flores (2022) answer this question far better than I can:

It might be tempting to abandon linguistics completely and do critical work in other areas that encourage focusing our language research agendas on issues of power and oppression. But to not contend with linguistics means shutting this line of scholarship and inquiry out of the arts and sciences areas of the academy; in the US, that means keeping this teaching and research away from a great number of undergraduates and from the structurally situated conversations that being in arts and sciences provides researchers at all stages of education. **So, for us, the answer isn't to try to *escape* linguistics but rather to broaden what *counts* as linguistics in an effort to bring more diverse perspectives into linguistics research and practice.** For us, *anybody who studies issues of language is a linguist* and there are multiple intellectual trajectories that scholars from marginalized backgrounds take in becoming linguists. (p. 149; emphasis my own)

I believe that how disabled people language is valid rather than deficient, valuable rather than defective. And I think that this perspective is necessary in the field of linguistics. Gaeta (2019) writes, "Disability justice emphasizes vulnerability, collective access, and interdependence as values necessary in order to survive in an ableist, classist, heteronormative white man's world" (para 4). For me, disability justice in Linguistics requires cripping the field.

Reading the Minds of Abled Linguists

If there is any safe generalization in the field of linguistics, it is probably that linguists love a good theoretical fight. This is famously demonstrated in any squabble between constructionist and generative linguists (e.g., Harris, 2021). These discussions are generally good for the field, provided that living people are not harmed by them. Recently, however, the flagship journal of the Linguistic Society of America (LSA), *Language*, published a series of conversations focused on the constructionist and generative debate that centered autistic people. In the initial article that prompted the conversations, Kissine (2021) argued that the way autistic people learn language means that constructionist theories are likely inaccurate. Specifically, Kissine wrote that learning language through interaction requires Theory of Mind, or an ability to recognize others' intentions, which autistic people have been claimed to lack. While Kissine never outright says that autistic people cannot "read others' minds," section two of the paper is titled "Language Use without Mind Reading" and contains phrases such as "autistic individuals with a deficient theory of mind."

Even researchers like Katsos and Andres-Roquet (2021), who agree with Kissine on a fundamental level, seem uncomfortable with Kissine's description of how autistic people use language. As they write, "it is difficult to base theoretical arguments on the fact that there is a marked 'deficit', 'impairment', or 'difficulty' with pragmatics, especially in autistic people with high structural language skills. This is a challenge for every researcher in autism, of course, and it calls for methodologically different ways of assessing pragmatic competence" (e193). Here Katsos and Andres-Roquet recognize the difficulties any researcher who studies language variation, and any other variation in disabled bodies and minds, must manage—how does one point out variation without pathologizing it? In my own work, I have examined the effects of language deprivation on deaf and hard-of-hearing children. Language deprivation happens when deaf and hard-of-hearing children are not afforded full access to language, either through environmental barriers (e.g., poverty and faulty auditory access equipment) or personal barriers (e.g., parents who refuse to learn a signed language). Language deprivation has a marked effect on both mental health and languaging abilities (Hall et al., 2018; Hall 2017). Language deprivation, as a material downstream effect of not being given an accessible language during critical early years, has led to a marked discussion among linguists, educators, and psychologists on how to handle the debilitating effects of language deprivation without stigmatizing the languagers themselves (Moriarty-Harrelson, 2017; Hou, 2018). Researchers of autistic languagers find themselves in a similar situation—what is difference, what is deviance, what needs intervention, and what is normal? Bottema-Beutel and co-authors (2021) explain that within the field of autism research, autistic researchers, community members, and allies have been pushing for a model of autism research that they call an "integrative model of disability." This is similar to the social model in that it recognizes that society is structured in a way that creates deviance among autistic people, but the model also recognizes impairment. However, as in linguistics, it is not clear that advocacy from disabled researchers and community members has changed how abled researchers perceive autistic people.

The questions of how we examine variation without stigmatizing the languagers, and how we decide that some variation is deviance and not variation, demonstrate the need for Crip Linguistics. It is not enough to state that bodies produce language if it is still acceptable to categorize those bodies as insufficient, lacking, problematic, deviant, or flat-out wrong. More importantly, linguists cannot discuss the languaging of disabled bodies without considering how those bodies are perceived. Katros and Andres Roquet (2021) seem trapped in this quandary. They discuss, for example, that autistic people are terrible with irony and metaphor. But who really is good at those two languaging types? "It's like rain on your wedding day," as Alanis Morrissette sang.

In another response to Kissine (2021), Mazzarella and Noveck (2021) write, "The best one can conclude from the current state of the art is that there is indeed a certain lack of pragmatic stability among autistic individuals regarding each investigated phenomenon, especially when increased mind reading is called for" (e205). What is a lack of pragmatic stability? What is pragmatic stability? Milton (2012) correctly argues that in research concerned with social interaction, there is a tendency "to assume that there is a set of definable social norms and rules that exist for people to follow." This is clearly demonstrated in any expectation that people will adhere to the Gricean maxims regardless of cultural background or neuroexperience (e.g., is the person neurodivergent?). As Surian, Baron-Cohen, and Van der Lely (1996) asked, "Are children with autism deaf to Gricean Maxims?" (Yes, was the answer they provided.) But as Ameka and Terkoufi (2019) point out, even among abled people, Gricean maxims are still culturally specific.

To provide examples of pragmatic instability in autistic people, Mazzarella and Noveck turn to Hochstein and co-authors (2016), who conducted a test in which two boxes are visible and contain strawberries while a third box is hidden. Participants were required to use scalar implicature to determine if the hidden box contains strawberries if the following statement is given: "Some of the boxes have strawberries." According to Hochstein and co-authors, the autistic participants were less likely to give suitably neutral answers about whether the third, hidden box contained strawberries (as Mazzarella and Noveck point out, autistic people tended to say that the thirdbox had no strawberries). However, the whole situation reads like the classic gotcha riddle which requires people to determine if they'd be willing to jump out of an airplane without a parachute. The astute individual responds, "Yes, if the airplane is on the ground." The reality is that there are multiple responses that people provide depending on their understanding of their own bodies and how they understand the airplane. But we do not assume pragmatic instability of the people who do not respond "properly." In a world where people still do not understand that face masks to prevent the spread of covid go above the nose, perhaps not guessing correctly the contents of a hidden box is a bit of a nothingburger. Nothingburger aside, Gernsbacher and Yergeau (2019) extensively documented the challenges of many of the assessments which are used to assess Theory of Mind in autistic (and other kinds of) people. These challenges are not discussed by Mazzarella and Noveck (2021); rather, pragmatic instability is accepted as a fact which does not merit continued thought.

What Is the Obligation for Linguists to Be Anti-Ableist?

In 2014, Humphries and co-authors pointed out that linguists, particularly those who study disabled languaging and signed languages, have an ethical obligation to support the language rights of deaf and hard-of-hearing communities. This was a call that I later echoed in my 2021 paper with Diane Lillo-Martin that focused on the acquisition of signed languages by deaf and hard-of-hearing children. There, we wrote, "As linguists who profit from the study of sign languages, we have an obligation to ensure that the wishes and needs of the communities with whom we work are respected. In this case, our responsibilities include ensuring that the families of deaf and hard of hearing children also have access to signs. Thus, dear reader, we hope that you too will advocate for deaf and hard of hearing children to sign" (p. 413). While the topic of those two papers was language acquisition in deaf and hard-of-hearing children, the point can be generalized across all disabled communities. I would also like to spotlight the phrase "the wishes and needs of the communities with whom we work." If the field of linguistic scholarship is to be truly inclusive, it needs to consider disability and disability communities. And what are the wishes and needs of disability communities? Poulsen, Brownlow, Lawson, and Pellicano (2022) simply state that it is the wish of the autism community not only to be involved in research on autism, but to take a leading role in conducting it. Can an article adequately describe the languaging of autistic people if it is not written by an autistic researcher? Yergeau (2009) weighs in on this topic:

> The typical autism essay is neurotypical: it feels the need to situate a bunch of neurotypical readers who, generally speaking, are incredibly situated in autism and its concomitant rhetorics. It is defensive. It likes numbers so much that you'd think a self-hating spectrumite penned it (if you're into the whole auties-love-numbers-duh thing, that is). I am loath to believe that readers of the typical autism essay doubt the importance of autism: it's the importance of autistics that they largely doubt. But the typical autism essay isn't about autistics—at least, it's not about autistics-as-humans inasmuch as it's about autistics-as-specimens. The typical autism essay s a sealed jar without holes poked in the lid. It's an intellectual vacuum. (section 1, para 2)

From that paragraph, and considering the earlier critiques of Kissine, we can piece out several different important ideas. First, disabled people are first and foremost people. If the initial interpretation of them is rooted in their "impairments" or what they "lack" then the "people" aspect tends to be lost! Rather, it is voided out and only the impairment remains, even if person-first language is used! The impairment of "lack of mind reading" and all its associated costs was discussed earlier in this chapter. Second, these impairments are artificially constructed and often are used to establish borders between people. As Lim, Young, and Brewer (2021) found, sometimes being identified as autistic is enough for nonautistic people to find flaws within the autistic person. This phenomenon is of course not limited to disability. Tripp and Munson (2021), for example, point out, "Judgments regarding the importance of particular features or behaviors for discrimination between bodyminds and person-kinds vary between cultures, which are necessarily practiced locally" (p. 8). Tripp and Munson define *personkind* as an amalgamation of perceived linguistic, physiological, and social features. Basically, if it looks like a duck, talks like a duck, and we've been socially conditioned to think it is a duck, we assume it is a duck. However, these taxonomic categorizations are necessarily artificially derived. And yet assuming that something is a duck would only be problematic in a local culture where being a duck is not just morally wrong but seen as an entity that is in need of intervention. These assumptions about the moral value of existing in a state of perceived wrongness are not necessarily universal across human cultures past and present. What I mean by that is that there is no evidence that disabled people have always been stigmatized by abled people in every human culture in every possible time period.

While Tripp and Munson (2021) were writing about gender categories, their point can be applied to disability broadly. A human taxonomy is only wrong if it is perceived to be wrong within predefined and artificially established criteria. The point of this discussion is to demonstrate two key values. First, linguists need to read extensively outside of the fields of linguistics and psychology. If languages are produced by bodies, then we need to be better educated about the bodies themselves. Second, there needs to be a reckoning about how quickly linguists default to the assumption that there are normative and wrong ways to produce and understand languaging. In a conversation, Tripp (personal communication, January 11, 2022) explained that bounding an entity creates other entities that lie outside the boundary. If linguists believe in good language, then necessarily there is bad language. If good language can only be produced by good body-minds, then bad body-minds necessarily produce bad language. Why are linguists so quick to label any non-normative body as a producer of deviant language? This is partially explained by two different phenomena. First, linguistic research which attempts to explain aspects of languaging as normative imply that those within those language communities who do not conform to expectations are non-normative. Basically, there can be no normal without abnormal. Second, linguists, who are typically abled people integrated into their local cultures, are generally raised to see disability as an abnormal existence that needs to be fixed. Here I respond to each point.

Disabled Bodies Produce Linguistic Variation, Not Incorrect Language!

Some linguists argue that language is necessarily unbounded (e.g., Otheguy, Garcia, & Reid, 2015). What this means is that languages such as English or ASL exist only as political actors to represent communities or state decisions about national ideologies (e.g., language education and requirements). It may seem a bit odd that even languages in different modalities such as ASL and English can in fact exist simultaneously and unbound by modality differences. Yet as demonstrated by how signers actually use these languages, there is clear contact, crossover, and influence between languages among deaf signers of American Sign Language that shows an unbounding across modalities (e.g., Scott & Henner, 2020). Even among signers who speak, evidence for modality crossover exists. For example, Pyers and Emmorey (2008) demonstrated that ASL signers speaking English will often incorporate ASL nonmanual markers (e.g., raised and furrowed eyebrows for yes/no questions) into their languaging regardless of the language orientation of their audience.

Otheguy, Garcia, and Reid (2015) point out that bounded languages are contrived as political ontologies. The actual use of language varies from person to person in ways that are not necessarily sanctioned by the state. The core belief behind this thought process is that language that exists outside of political boundaries can never be incorrect. Every single idiolect, or individual way of languaging, regardless of modality, is appropriate and is representative of linguistic variation. Yet it seems in many societies, language produced by disabled body-minds is naturally bounded by abled people's negative perception of disability. In our 2021 Crip Linguistics paper, Robinson and I argued that language produced by disabled body-minds is an accepted form of variation and that attempts to thoughtlessly remediate that linguistic variation should be treated in the same class as speech therapies for accent reduction or forced eradication of community-based dialectal variation (e.g., Ramjattan, 2018; Flowers, 2019). However, many abled people seem to disagree with this notion. Disabled languaging is a reminder, to them, of lost potential, what could be if not for this wretched brokenness.

Abled Linguists Are Conditioned to See Disability as Bad

Many years ago, I visited pre-flood New Orleans and found myself chatting with a group of women in the French Quarter. At that time, I had more patience for engaging in oral conversation with hearing people and was at least willing to try to engage with them in less-than-optimal conditions. One of the women pointed out that I talked funny and asked me where I was from. I responded that I was from Chicago. The women disbelieved me and became angry because they thought I was intentionally lying to them. In their minds, people from Chicago could only sound a certain way, and someone who talked funny like me had to be foreign. And no amount of telling them that I was from Chicago, I was just deaf, would make them believe me.

The purpose of this story is to illuminate a point about abled people's expectations of what disability looks like, sounds like, and acts like. In disability studies and culture, the "freakery" or "freak show" is an archetype of a historical and current phenomenon: a metaphor for how disabled bodies and minds are perceived by abled people and put on display as a spectacle (Thompson, 1997; Bodgan, 1990). These spectacles were not necessarily limited to the Global North, as described by Nair (in press), but also extended to colonial institutions in the Global South such as colonial India. The freak shows were a contrast to "Ugly Laws," laws that existed in the twentieth-century United States that prevented visibly disabled people from existing in public view (Schweik, 2009). When disabled people were not displayed as entertainment for abled people, they were locked away either in their homes or in institutions. While for deaf people, institutions became a cultural mythos where they would finally have access to people like them and languages that were compatible with their body-minds, many other disabled people found themselves in unimaginably abusive environments.

In our Crip Linguistics work, Robinson and I proposed a parallel to the freakery, which typically focuses on disabled body-minds, by centering the languaging created by disabled people. These are "freakish languages." And much like with freak shows, the goal of abled people is both to use disabled languaging as spectacle and to hide it away so that no one can see the broken communication. When an abled person beholds disabled languaging, which Nair (in press) terms "enfreakening," they often assume that it exists only because of intervention and therapy. Kissine (2021) uses the spectacle of language acquisition among autistic children to make a point about linguistic frameworks (generative versus socially based acquisition). The humanity and joy of language acquisition among autistic people is washed out to score points in a linguistic war where the battles do not have qualitative effects on their daily lives.

The enfreakening of disabled languaging is not limited to autistic communities. Dumas (2016) detailed how comedians who stutter use their languaging disability to perform a freak show for abled audiences. In these comedy acts, stuttering is the point of the joke, but also a commentary on existing as someone who has a perceived linguistic deficiency in a world where this kind of existence is either mocked or eliminated via intervention.

Similarly, Freeman (2018) notes that hearing kids are often right assholes to deaf kids who are identified as speaking but not hearing. That is certainly true. And rather than recognizing the structural issues that surround why speaking in a way that is perceived as less than ideal is cause for condemnation, Freeman and co-authors (2017) describe how therapists should take care of the "speech intelligibility deficit," as they call it. Imagine an entire life of support, therapy, and effort only to be labeled as having a speech intelligibility deficit by a linguist with only marginal and minimal interaction in the affected community. As the participants in Freeman's study were implanted with cochlear implants, a device that a Med-El advertisement called "The Greatest Gift" [to deaf people], there is an underlying assumption that to develop speech that hearing people assume is not intelligible is evidence of individual failure. Similarly, for autistic people, there are therapies that attempt to train Theory of Mind; however, as Fletcher-Watson, McConnel, Manola, and McConachie (2014) point out, these therapies have limited longterm effectiveness. Quite frankly, disabled people rightly resist attempts to normalize us, because our normal state is what we already are.

To take another example, Figueroa (2024) critiques the "word gap," the belief that low-income children of color do not have access to the same number of words as middle-class white children raised with very specific parenting philosophies. The idea that this gap is a lifelong harm is also related to enfreakening. The children affected by the "word gap" are disabled, or cripped, by the fact of being racialized, or by the experience of poverty.

Cripping Linguistics

Here is some guidance on how linguists can consider improving how they perceive the language produced by disabled people.

1. Research on the languaging of disabled people needs to center not only the communities affected by the research, but researchers who

are themselves members of those communities. As Hochgesang (2022) mentioned in her plenary presentation for the 2022 LSA conference, linguists need to consider their positionalities when doing research with minoritized communities. Autistic researchers like Yergeau have already dismissed concepts like Theory of Mind and mind-reading as rather minimal in the autistic experience. Why then was there an entire special issue by presumably nonautistic linguists debating if autistic people could read minds well enough to learn language via social interaction?

2. Linguists need to avoid doing "parachute science" (Stefanoudis et al., 2021). Stefanoudis and co-authors define this phenomenon as "the practice whereby international scientists, typically from higher-income countries, conduct field studies in another country, typically of lower income, and then complete the research in their home country without any further effective communication and engagement with others from that nation" (p. R184). In some contexts, this practice has also been called FIFO, or "fly in, fly out." While some linguists engage in parachute science in the original definition of the term, in the context of this chapter, communities are centered rather than countries. Basically, linguists should not exploit disabled communities for the purpose of publication. Extractive research must not exist in a people-based field. Languages are used by people; disabled people are people, and disabled ways of languaging are valid.

3. There needs to be increased recognition of disabled ways of languaging as valid. If one only perceives disabled languaging as relative to abled languaging then the point of variety in languaging and humanity is missed. This is not a thing requiring an anti-thing, as Alayo Tripp would say. While bad languaging implies good languaging, as I discussed above, good languaging does not necessitate bad languaging. It is not necessary to establish that bad languaging exists in order to prove that good languaging is possible. I have made this mistake in my own work on language deprivation in deaf and hard-of-hearing children. At the time, I viewed these kinds of analyses as necessary for the sake of showing the harms of language deprivation. Currently, I am working on ways of doing data analysis that can show that language deprivation is bad without shaming the language of language-deprived deaf and hard-of-hearing people. I do not entirely know how to do that, but the effort is worth enduring, which is to say: physician, heal thyself.

Robinson and I summed up our Crip Linguistics paper by proclaiming that the languaging of disabled people is pretty cool if attended to properly. I would like to do the same here: there is absolutely nothing wrong with how autistic people, and other disabled people, use language. As Mary Bucholtz wrote in a comment on previous drafts of the chapter, "Autistic language is not wrong, but it has the potential to revolutionize linguistics if understood on its own terms."

References

Annamma, S. A., & Handy, T. (2021). Sharpening justice through DisCrit: A contrapuntal analysis of education. *Educational Researcher, 50*(1), 41–50. https://doi.org/10.3102/0013189X20953838\

Ameka, F. K., & Terkourafi, M. (2019). What if . . . ? Imagining non-Western perspectives on pragmatic theory and practice. *Journal of Pragmatics, 145*, 72–82. https://doi.org/10.1016/j.pragma.2019.04.001

Bogdan, R. (1990). *Freak show: Presenting human oddities for amusement and profit.* University of Chicago Press.

Bottema-Beutel, K., Kapp, S. K., Lester, J. N., Sasson, N. J., & Hand, B. N. (2021). Avoiding ableist language: Suggestions for autism researchers. *Autism in Adulthood, 3*(1), 18–29. https://doi.org/10.1089/aut.2020.0014

Bucholtz, M., & Hall, K. (2016). Embodied sociolinguistics. In N. Coupland (Ed.), *Sociolinguistics: Theoretical debates*, 173–197. Cambridge University Press. https://www.cambridge.org/core/books/abs/sociolinguistics/embodied-sociolinguistics/5F49298B4597ECAE7741964E47D50AF5

Cioè-Peña, M. (2022). The master's tools will never dismantle the master's school: Interrogating settler colonial logics in language education. *Annual Review of Applied Linguistics, 42*, 25–33. https://doi.org/10.1017/S0267190521000209

Charity Hudley, A. (under review). The lung. In Mary Bucholtz and Kira Hall (Eds.), *Parsing the body: Language and the social life of embodiment.*

Charity Hudley, A. H.., & Flores, N. (2022). Social justice in applied linguistics: Not a conclusion, but a way forward. *Annual Review of Applied Linguistics, 42*, 144–154. doi:10.1017/S0267190522000083

Dumas, N. W. (2016). "This guy says I should talk like that all the time": Challenging intersecting ideologies of language and gender in an American stuttering English comedienne's stand-up routine. *Language in Society, 45*(3), 353–374. https://doi.org/10.1017/S0047404516000233

Figueroa, Megan. (2024). Decolonizing (psycho)linguistics means dropping the language gap rhetoric. In Anne H. Charity Hudley, Christine Mallinson, & Mary Bucholtz (Eds.), *Decolonizing linguistics.* Oxford University Press.

Fletcher-Watson, S., McConnell, F., Manola, E., & McConachie, H. (2014). Interventions based on the Theory of Mind cognitive model for Autism Spectrum Disorder (ASD). *Cochrane Database of Systematic Reviews, 3*. https://doi.org/10.1002/14651858.CD008785.pub2 https://www.ncbi.nlm.nih.gov/pmc/articles/PMC6923148/

Flowers, K. (2019). Resisting and rewriting English-only policies: Navigating multilingual, raciolinguistic, and translingual approaches to language advocacy. *Literacy in Composition Studies, 7*(1): 67–89.

Freeman, V. (2018). Speech intelligibility and personality peer-ratings of young adults with cochlear implants. *The Journal of Deaf Studies and Deaf Education*, 23(1), 41–49. https://doi.org/10.1093/deafed/enx033

Freeman, V., Pisoni, D. B., Kronenberger, W. G., & Castellanos, I. (2017). Speech intelligibility and psychosocial functioning in deaf children and teens with cochlear implants. *The Journal of Deaf Studies and Deaf Education*, 22(3), 278–289. https://doi.org/10.1093/deafed/enx001

Gaeta, A. (2019). Cripping emotional labor: A field guide. https://disabilityvisibilityproject.com/2019/06/03/cripping-emotional-labor-a-field-guide/

Gernsbacher, M. A., & Yergeau, M. (2019). Empirical failures of the claim that autistic people lack a Theory of Mind. *Archives of Scientific Psychology*, 7, 102–118. http://dx.doi.org/10.17605/OSF.IO/3R2QY

Haagaard, A. (2022). Complicating disability: On the invisiblilization of chronic illness throughout history. https://blog.castac.org/2022/02/complicating-disability-on-the-invisibilization-of-chronic-illness-throughout-history/

Hall, M. L., Eigsti, I. M., Bortfeld, H., & Lillo-Martin, D. (2018) Executive function in deaf children: Auditory access and language access. *Journal of Speech, Language, and Hearing Research*, 61(8), 1970–1988. doi: 10.1044/2018_JSLHR-L-17-0281. PMID: 30073268; PMCID: PMC6198917.

Hall, W. C. (2017). What you don't know can hurt you: The risk of impairing visual language development in deaf children. *Journal of Maternal and Child Health*, 21(5), 961–965. https://doi.org/10.1007/s10995-017-2287-y

Harris, R. (2021). *The linguistics wars: Chomsky, Lakoff, and the battle over deep structure*. Oxford University Press.

Henner, J., & Robinson, O. (2021, July 8). Unsettling languages, unruly bodyminds: Imaging a Crip Linguistics.https://doi.org/10.31234/osf.io/7bzaw

Hochgesang, J. A. (2022, January 6). Documenting signed language use while considering our spaces as a Deaf* linguist. Invited Plenary Presentation. The 96th Annual Meeting of the Linguistic Society of America, Virtual/Washington, DC.

Hochstein, L., Bale, A., Fox, D., & Barner, D. (2016). Ignorance and inference: Do problems with Gricean epistemic reasoning explain children's difficulty with scalar implicature?. *Journal of Semantics*, 33(1), 107–135.

Hou, L. (under review). The ear. In Mary Bucholtz and Kira Hall (Eds.), *Parsing the body: Language and the social life of embodiment*.

Hou, L. (2018). Iconic patterns in San Juan Quiahije Chatino sign language. *Sign Language Studies*, 18(4), 570–611. https://doi.org/10.1353/sls.2018.0017

Humphries, T., Kushalnagar, P., Mathur, G., Napoli, D. J., Padden, C. A., & Rathmann, C. (2014). Ensuring language acquisition for deaf children: What linguists can do. *Language*, 90(2), e31–e52. https://doi.org/10.1353/lan.2014.0036

Katsos, N., & Andrés-Roqueta, C. (n.d.). Where next for pragmatics and mind reading? A situation-based view (Response to Kissine). *Language*, 97(3), e198–e197.

Kissine, M. (2021). Autism, constructionism, and nativism. *Language*, 97(3), e139–e160. https://doi.org/10.1353/lan.2021.0055

Lillo-Martin, D., & Henner, J. (2021). Acquisition of sign languages. *Annual Review of Linguistics*, 7(1), 395–419. https://doi.org/10.1146/annurev-linguistics-043020-092357

Lim, A., Young, R. L., & Brewer, N. (2021). Autistic adults may be erroneously perceived as deceptive and lacking credibility. *Journal of Autism and Developmental Disorders, 52*: 490–507. https://doi.org/10.1007/s10803-021-04963-4

Mauldin, L., & Brown, R. L. (n.d.). Missing pieces: Engaging sociology of disability in medical sociology. *Journal of Health and Social Behavior*, 62(4): 477–492.

Moriarty Harrelson, E. (2017). Deaf people with "no language": Mobility and flexible accumulation in languaging practices of deaf people in Cambodia. *Applied Linguistics Review*, 10(1): 55–72. https://doi.org/10.1515/applirev-2017-0081

Mazzarella, D., & Noveck, I. (2021). Pragmatics and mind reading: The puzzle of autism (Response to Kissine). *Language*, 97(3), e198–e210. https://doi.org/10.1353/lan.2021.0037

McRuer, R. (2006). *Crip theory: Cultural signs of queerness and disability*. NYU Press.

Milton, D. E. M. (2012). On the ontological status of autism: The "double empathy problem." *Disability & Society*, 27(6), 883–887. https://doi.org/10.1080/09687599.2012.710008

Nair, A.(In press). *Fungible bodies: Disability histories of British India, 1850-1950*. University of Illinois Press.

Otheguy, R., García, O., & Reid, W. (2015). Clarifying translanguaging and deconstructing named languages: A perspective from linguistics. *Applied Linguistics Review*, 6(3), 281–307. https://doi.org/10.1515/applirev-2015-0014

Pennycook, A. (2021). *Critical applied linguistics: A critical re-introduction*. 2nd ed. Routledge.

Poulsen, R., Brownlow, C., Lawson, W., & Pellicano, E. (2022). *Meaningful research for autistic people? Ask autistics!* 26(1), 3–5. https://doi.org/10.1177/13623513211064421

Pyers, J. E., & Emmorey, K (2008). The face of bimodal bilingualism: Grammatical markers in American Sign Language are produced when bilinguals speak to English monolinguals. *Psychological Science*, 19(6), 531–535. https://doi.org/10.1111/j.1467-9280.2008.02119.x

Ramjattan, V. A. (2018). Raciolinguistics and the aesthetic labourer. *Journal of Industrial Relations*, 002218561879299. https://doi.org/10.1177/0022185518792990

Schweik, S. M. (2009). *The ugly laws*. NYU Press.

Scott, J. A., & Henner, J. (2020). Second verse, same as the first: On the use of signing systems in modern interventions for deaf and hard of hearing children in the USA. *Deafness & Education International*, 1–19. https://doi.org/10.1080/14643154.2020.1792071

Semenov, Y. R., Yeh, S. T., Seshamani, M., Wang, N.-Y., Tobey, E. A., Eisenberg, L. S., Quittner, A. L., Frick, K. D., & Niparko, J. K. (2013). Age-dependent cost-utility of pediatric cochlear implantation. *Ear & Hearing*, 34(4), 402–412. https://doi.org/10.1097/AUD.0b013e3182772c66

Stefanoudis, P. V., Licuanan, W. Y., Morrison, T. H., Talma, S., Veitayaki, J., & Woodall, L. C. (2021). Turning the tide of parachute science. *Current Biology*. 31(4), R184–R185.

Surian, L., Baron-Cohen, S., & van der Lely, H. K. J. (1996). Are children with autism deaf to Gricean maxims? *Cognitive Neuropsychiatry*, 1(1), 55–72. https://doi.org/10.1080/135468096396703

Thomson, R. G. (2017). *Extraordinary bodies: Figuring physical disability in American culture and literature*. Columbia University Press.

Tripp, A., & Munson, B. (2021). Perceiving gender while perceiving language: Integrating psycholinguistics and gender theory. *WIREs Cognitive Science*. https://doi.org/10.1002/wcs.1583

Yergeau, M. (2009). Circle wars: Reshaping the typical autism essay. *Disability Studies Quarterly*, 30(1). https://doi.org/10.18061/dsq.v30i1.1063

Lina Hou is assistant professor in the Linguistics Department at University of California, Santa Barbara. She received her PhD in linguistics from the University of Texas at Austin in 2016. Her dissertation was a linguistic ethnographic description of family sign languages known as "making hands" in a Mesoamerican (Chatino) community in Oaxaca, Mexico. She completed a postdoctoral fellowship in Communications at University of California, San Diego from 2016 to 2018, before moving to her current job. Her research interests encompass usage-based linguistics, language documentation and description of sign languages, linguistic ethnography, first language acquisition and language socialisation, and inclusion of deaf people of colour and social justice in linguistics.

Kristy (Kristian) Ali is Chancellor's Fellow and PhD student at the University of California, Santa Barbara. She is hearing and was born and raised in Trinidad and Tobago, where she completed her undergraduate degree in Linguistics at the University of the West Indies, St Augustine Campus, and wrote an MPhil thesis on the history and structure of Bay Islands Sign Language. She has published on Caribbean signed languages, and Caribbean research methodologies, and worked on documenting signed languages in Trinidad and Tobago, Guyana, and the Bay Islands of Honduras. Her research interests broadly include social and linguistic justice for Caribbean people.

Abstract: There is a problem with the inclusion of deaf researchers particularly when it comes to racial parity in sign language research. This chapter foregrounds the discussion to examine the particular case of some deaf researchers from the majority People of Colour Global South. The chapter uses a multipronged methodology, starting with auto-ethnographic data to describe how the authors arrived at the point of carrying out this research. Secondly, an analysis of the recent meetings of a major sign language conference was conducted. Finally, the authors conducted individual interviews of and group discussions among deaf researchers of colour in the Global South and examined certain emerging themes. The chapter ends with concrete suggestions and actions for improving equity and parity for these researchers, which the authors argue is critical for improving the field of sign language linguistics.

Key Words: sign language linguistics, deaf people, intersectionality, racism, Global South

2

Critically Examining Inclusion and Parity for Deaf Global South Researchers of Colour in the Field of Sign Language Linguistics

Lynn Hou (she/they)
University of California, Santa Barbara

Kristian Ali (she/her)
University of California, Santa Barbara

Introduction

There is a problem with the inclusion of deaf linguists when it comes to racial parity in sign language research (Hill et al., 2020; Hou et al., 2022). This chapter addresses the general lack of attention to the intersectionality of race and deafness in linguistics by looking at the disparity in the representation of deaf linguists from the white-majority Global North and the People of Colour-majority Global South. For some purposes, it may be logical to categorise "deaf linguists" as an underrepresented minority within sign language research (Hochgesang, 2019; Kusters, 2021a). While this category can be empowering at times, it also conflates the experiences of People of Colour with those of white people (Hill et al., 2020), obscuring the complexity of racial disparities among these groups, especially in the twenty-first-century context of global hegemony.

The hearing, white, Global North scholars Bernard Tervoort and William Stokoe are credited with laying the foundation for sign language linguistics with their publications in the 1950s and 1960s respectively (McBurney, 2006). Stokoe's work was made possible with the vital support of two deaf research assistants, Carl Croneberg and Dorothy Casterline (née Sueoka). More

Lynn Hou and Kristian Ali, *Critically Examining Inclusion and Parity for Deaf Global South Researchers of Colour in the Field of Sign Language Linguistics* in: *Inclusion in Linguistics*. Edited by: Anne H. Charity Hudley, Christine Mallinson and Mary Bucholtz, Oxford University Press. © Anne H. Charity Hudley, Christine Mallinson, and Mary Bucholtz 2024.
DOI: 10.1093/oso/9780197755303.003.0003

scholars of similar backgrounds continued to dominate the academic field in the 1970s, 1980s, and 1990s. From the 2000s onwards, there was a blossoming of research on the diversity of sign languages of the world, though this did not necessarily equate to a diversity of scholars. The absence of deaf researchers of colour from the Global South reduces not only intellectual diversity in the field but also epistemic diversity (de Sousa Santos, 2015) as well as cultural diversity that would benefit scholarship. Sign languages used by deaf communities in the Global South are of increasing theoretical interest, and so the inclusion of researchers from these backgrounds is essential to minimise the exoticisication of these languages and communities (Braithwaite, 2020). Moreover, the inclusion of deaf researchers of colour of the Global South is not to be taken superficially but must come with the same labour rights and privileges as their hearing, White, Global North counterparts who dominate sign language linguistics research.

The necessary changes to the field therefore depend not only on time but also on space. The effects of time on knowledge in sign linguistics are evident. The assumptions held about deaf and deafblind people, signing communities, and sign languages have all shifted to more complex and accurate representations in the 60 years since the field emerged and discipline-wide ideas about what constitutes a language, or even what constitutes linguistics, have also radically changed as a result of these findings (Hou & de Vos, 2021). Though equally important, critical examination of the effects of space or the geography of knowledge-making have been missing in sign linguistics.

With this context in mind, the following questions guided this research: Where is sign language linguistics being done? Who is doing the work there and where are they originally from? It also served us well to look at the inverse in conceptualising this research—that is, who is excluded from doing research, or from setting in the major scientific trends and agendas of sign linguistics? The rest of this chapter presents our findings in exploring these questions. Our research design combines auto-ethnographic reflection data, an analysis of the diversity of sign linguistics conference presenters, and interviews and focus groups with deaf researchers of colour in the Global South. We then provide recommendations based on our findings.

In this chapter, we use the term "Global South" as not an exclusively geographical term. It is a dynamic and complex concept that refers to lower-income countries with shared experiences of subjugation under contemporary global capitalism (Mahler, 2017). These experiences are essential for the ways in which research is carried out, particularly research done in the Global South on Global South communities. This chapter follows the framework of Boaventura de Sousa Santos's epistemologies of the South that he proposes "epistemologies of the South, a set of inquiries into the construction and validation of knowledge born in struggle, of ways of knowing developed by social groups as part of their resistance against the systematic injustices and oppressions caused by capitalism, colonialism, and patriarchy" (2015, p. x). In this framework, Global North academia is not deferred to. Rather, Global South knowledges are privileged, and not seen to be less than hegemonic traditional Global North academia. This is the first time this framework will be applied to the field of sign language linguistics. Though other scholars have written about these relations in linguistics (see for example, Punnoose & Haneefa, this volume) and other fields, sign language linguistics is still burgeoning and discussions of equity and parity are still extremely new. The term "Global North" refers here to those settler colonies which have benefited from the exploitation of the Global South. The research carried out there is broadly what we know as traditional Western academia. One must look broadly at these distinctions without getting lost in the divisions, for example, how research is done in Australia versus Italy. We must zoom out to see that "there is no global social justice without global cognitive justice" (de Sousa Santos 2015, p. viii), meaning we must liberate the Global South from the shackles of Global North epistemic hegemony.

Before turning to our data, we would like to briefly address why we focus on Global South researchers and not Global North deaf researchers of colour too. It is not our intention to imply that structural barriers are not stacked against deaf researchers in the Global North. The fact is that Global South scholars face particular challenges that are not well represented in discourse on inclusion of deaf researchers in sign language research, because most of the discussion on inclusion of deaf researchers has been centred on the Global North. Some of the particular issues surrounding doing research in the Global South are the global direction in which research happens, the continued underdevelopment of Global South research, and the marginalisation and devaluation of Global South knowledges. Migration to the North for schooling and training is seen as natural, whereas migration to the South is not. Brain drain is a result of the expected migration to the North. Additionally, universities and research institutions recruit prospective students and researchers from the Global South, which causes the displacement of talent from Global South societies to work and live in Global North countries, thereby encouraging the underdevelopment of those societies. Collaborations also tend to go one way—from North to South, not vice versa as Global North scholars tend to have the resources to initiate collaborations with Global South scholars. Helicopter or parachute research is common in Global South communities, which involves the quick extraction of academic resources in a Global South community for use in the Global North with little to no real connections to the local community. The "trickle-down science" approach is the view that improving resources and funding in the Global North will trickle down to the Global South (Reidpath & Allotey, 2019). The move towards open source data practices does not have the same consequences for Global South scholarship as it does for Global North researchers (Serwadda et al., 2018 Villarreal & Collister, 2024). Additionally, Global North researchers are able to use data gathered by Global South people to advance their careers. As a result, there is anxiety and distrust of Global North researchers. There are several parallels between Global South researchers' and deaf researchers' experiences in academia. There is the marginalisation and devaluation of their knowledge and ways of knowing—they have been historically the subjects of research. So-called *mesearch* (Ray, 2016) is a denigrating term used to describe the study of People of Colour by themselves which is seen as navel-gazing, insignificant and indulgent and is sometimes extended to other communities researching themselves. Finally, they are both disconnected from the core spaces of academia, physically and financially. All of these are rationales for our primary focus on Global South deaf researchers of colour in this chapter.

We also would like to state the intended audience of this chapter. This contribution is targeted towards hearing, white Global North senior scholars in the field. They are the ones who have the most opportunities to include junior scholars from different backgrounds, fund or apply for funding for equitable research in deaf communities in the Global South and hold administrative positions in which they can lobby for structural changes. This contribution may also serve as a guide to governing bodies and institutions in the field such as the Sign Language Linguistics Society (SLLS). The data presented here has significance to future conference hosts and organisers wanting to make their meetings more inclusive. Finally, this contribution is also intended for the deaf scholars of colour in the Global South doing sign language research. It is our hope that this chapter affirms your needs and organises your concerns.

Researcher Positionalities and Auto-Ethnographies

We begin with brief auto-ethnographic reflections and our positionalities. Kristian (Kristy) Ali is a PhD student in the Department of Linguistics at the University of California, Santa Barbara. She is a hearing Trinidadian researcher who works with signing communities in the Caribbean. She was born, grew up, worked, and studied in Trinidad and Tobago. Lynn (Lina) Hou is a deaf Assistant Professor of Linguistics at the University of California, Santa Barbara. She was born to a Chinese-Taiwanese immigrant family and was raised in the US and received her PhD in Linguistics from the University of Texas at Austin. She has conducted research within the US and rural southern Mexico (Oaxaca). In the following sections, we recount our experiences and motivations for carrying out this research.

Lina

My journey to linguistics was motivated by a lifelong curiosity about multiply minoritised and marginalised deaf people, their signing practices, and signing communities in diverse language ecologies. This curiosity is a product of my lived experiences. I belong to the millennial generation, born between 1981 and 1996; this generation witnessed numerous social, institutional, and political changes in the US. One corollary of these changes was that more deaf people could pursue higher education and academic careers (Chua et al., 2022).

I entered graduate school with very little background in linguistics and no research experience, which translated to a lot of naivety about the field of sign language linguistics. Very quickly, I learned that much of this field had yet to engage meaningfully with theories of race, racism, and racialisation and therefore lacked the appropriate language to theorise the role of race in sign language linguistics. I struggled to understand how race and racism shaped theoretical and methodological approaches to researching sign languages and signing communities in various global contexts. This struggle coincided with the rapid expansion and diversification of academic research on sign languages that are largely concentrated in the Global South—but that line of research is dominated by white hearing people from the Global North. At that time, I had the general impression that sign languages occupied the periphery of the broad purview of linguistics, so the ethical implications of who was doing most of the research and producing the scholarship did not fully sink in. Eventually I saw that there were few deaf linguists and even fewer deaf linguists of colour on the PhD level, so I felt compelled to carve out my own research trajectory (Hou, 2016; 2017; Chua et al., 2022). The trajectory led me to the world of academic training, presentations, and publications, where I experienced various aspects of structural exclusion first-hand and saw how deaf people of colour, especially from the Global South, were overrepresented as research subjects but underrepresented as researchers.

Kristy

I received my first two degrees in linguistics at the University of the West Indies in Trinidad and Tobago. Being a hearing Global South researcher working in the Global South shapes the research that I produce. Because I'm hearing and I speak and write English, I had access to secondary and tertiary education, as well as academia when I decided to pursue academic research. Now, I'm in an international PhD program. This experience of moving into a research institution in the Global North provides a contrast to the way academia is carried out in the Caribbean. It means that I receive the privileges associated with being in a prestigious US academic institution but also the losses that come with moving from the Global South as a researcher who works in the Global South. The complicated issue of losses and gains of Global South students in the Global North is one of the many repercussions caused by the colonial geography of linguistics which is explored in my contribution with Ben Braithwaite (Braithwaite & Ali, 2024). My first time at a major international sign language linguistics conference, Theoretical Issues in Sign Language Research (TISLR), I was surprised to see so very few presenters of colour. There were almost no deaf presenters of colour and none from the Global South. It surprised me because I work with deaf researchers of colour and know for a fact that many communities being researched are in the Global South. It is important to note here that we use the term "researcher" broadly—researchers aren't limited to academic researchers with advanced degrees and formal training. The SLLS statement of ethics on working with deaf individuals and communities does not offer any concrete actions for researchers to train deaf people to become sign language linguists, nor does it offer any ethical considerations when working with deaf people in the Global South (Sign Language Linguistics Society, 2016). The most disappointing part of it all is that there were no explicit references to this imbalance of lack of equity in the field. It seemed that those who were there were there because it was naturalised, and there was no need to discuss who was not there.

Our respective experiences prompted us to reach out to several deaf researchers of colour from the Global South to talk to them about their experiences getting involved with sign language research. We also connected with a few deaf tenured professors from the Global North who wanted to share some of their insights into these racial disparities based on their experiences of interacting with deaf people of colour from the Global South.

Having taken these auto-ethnographic reflections as a starting point to flag parity and inclusion issues in the contemporary sociopolitical context of sign language linguistics, in the next two sections, we discuss our analysis of conference presenters and then discuss our interview data.

Diversity of Conference Presenters

We assessed the diversity of stage presenters at the last four meetings of Theoretical Issues in Sign Language Research (TISLR). These meetings corresponded to TISLR 10 through TISLR 13, held in the US, UK, Australia, and Germany, respectively. TISLR is perceived as the leading international conference for the linguistic study of signed languages and attracts a critical mass of scholars who research different signed languages. TISLR is a triennial conference supported by the Sign Language Linguistics Society (SLLS). Since 1986, there have been 13 conference meetings hosted at various academic institutions, mostly in Europe and the United States; two exceptions to the pattern are Brazil and Australia. Our assessments focused on three types of diversity that distinguished presenters: hearing status, institutional affiliation, and geographic region. We present the findings to further highlight the disparities as represented by the diversity of talks presented at these meetings. We do not report the race and ethnicity of the presenters, since that information was not readily obtained through conference programs, personal knowledge, or social connections. Moreover, the understanding of race and ethnicity vary enormously across the presenters, something that we also experienced in the interviews with our participants.

Each TISLR meeting varied in the number of presenters and presentations. We counted a total of 207 stage presentations, including invited keynotes, and a total of 495 presenters from all four TISLR meetings. Many stage presentations were multiauthored; the collaborators were not always affiliated with the same institution and the same region of the institution. Figure 2.1 represents the summary of the hearing status and the general location of the institutional affiliations of the presenters. The hearing status refers to whether the presenter identifies as or is identified by others as deaf, hearing, or CODA (hearing child of deaf adults). We were able to identify the hearing status of all presenters except for four; these four presenters are excluded from the data. We counted 374 hearing presenters, 88 deaf presenters, and 29 CODA presenters. These counts are slightly redundant, as some of the presenters appeared on the stage more than once within a meeting and/or across the meetings. The location refers to the institutional affiliation that the presenter was employed at the time of their presentation. There are six locations: Africa,

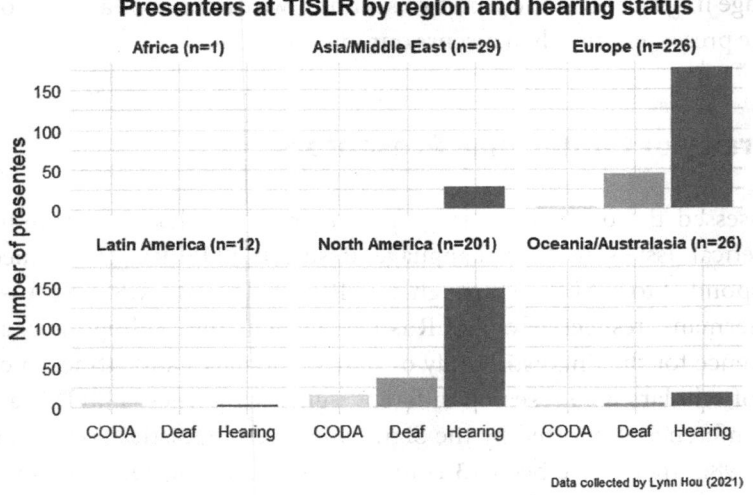

Presenters at TISLR by region and hearing status

Data collected by Lynn Hou (2021)

Figure 2.1 Results of the hearing status and location of institutional affiliation of presenters at TISLR 10-13 meetings
Alt text: there are six sets of bar graphs. On the y axis is "Number of presenters." On the x axis is "CODA," "Deaf" and "Hearing." The titles of the bar graphs from top left to bottom right are as follows: "Africa (n=1)," "Asia/Middle East" (n = 29), "Europe (n=226)," "Latin America (n=12)," "North America (n=201)," "Oceania/Australasia (n=26)".

Asia/Middle East, Europe, Latin America, North America, and Oceania/Australasia.

Out of all the four TISLR meetings, hearing presenters from Europe and North America clearly dominated the stage. By stark contrast, presenters from other regions were severely underrepresented. We took a closer look at the data and tracked unique presenters from the other regions. There was only one hearing presenter affiliated with a university in Africa (South Africa); this presenter does not appear to be African. There were nine unique presenters, including one deaf presenter, affiliated with universities in Asia (7 Hong Kong and two in Japan). There were four unique presenters, of which one is identified as CODA and another as hearing; they were affiliated with universities in Latin America (mostly Brazil and one in Mexico). There were 20 unique presenters, including 17 hearing, two deaf, and one CODA presenters, affiliated with universities in Oceania/Australasia (mostly Australia and two in New Zealand).

Now that we have provided demographic information on who is presenting and who is invited to present at a major and prestigious conference in the field, we move to in-depth discussions of personal experiences and collective solution-building through personal interviews and focus group discussions.

Interviews and Focus Groups

We conducted semistructured one-on-one interviews and focus groups with the approval of University of California, Santa Barbara's Institutional Review Board (IRB Protocol #4-21-0562). To recruit potential interviewees, we made a recruitment flyer in the form of a video in International Sign (IS) supplemented by a mix of mainstream British and US English. In the video, we introduced ourselves and explained our project in IS, as many deaf people find signing more accessible than writing. IS operates as a global lingua franca that has been used among deaf signers of different language backgrounds in international contexts, including large international deaf organisations including the World Federation of the Deaf. Our choice to use IS was intentional—we believed it would convey a more inclusive and neutral stance of communication compared to using ASL, another global lingua franca that carries a certain global prestige as English does (Kusters, 2021b). We tapped into our social media networks to advertise the flyer and used personal contacts and snowball sampling. Most participants who consented to the interviews were already part of our social networks. We knew them for their own published research, their research assistance and collaboration with white hearing researchers on academic publications and/or their language advocacy in their local deaf signing communities. The interviews took place over Zoom in November and December 2021.

The first round of interviews focused on individuals' experiences of inclusion and exclusion in sign language research. In the first round, we interviewed 13 participants individually. Table 2.1 details the participants' region background and the focus groups. All but four participants were born and raised in countries in the Global South; they represented the Caribbean, East Africa, Middle East, and Southeast Asia. The other regions represented were the US, Western Europe, and Western Asia. For most interviews, we took a co-interviewing approach, but we each individually interviewed a few participants. The second round aimed to initiate collaborative theorising about how sign language research conferences and academic programs could be more inclusive. We organised four focus groups based on the participants' background, experiences, and availability. One focus group consisted of two educators from the Caribbean and another educator from East Africa who were not previously acquainted with each

Table 2.1 Number of participants in individual interviews and focus groups

	No. of participants	East Africa	Southeast Asia	Middle East	Western Europe	Caribbean	USA
Individual interviews	14	5	3	1	2	2	1
		Caribbean and African researchers		API PhD students		Global North tenured professors	
Focus groups		9		3		3	

other. Another focus group consisted of three PhD students from Southeast Asia who were already acquainted with each other. The other two focus groups consisted of three deaf tenured professors employed at predominantly hearing research or teaching institutions in the US and Europe. Lina met with one pair of two professors and another pair of two professors separately since scheduling conflicts did not allow all professors to meet at once, so Lina and one of the three professors participated in the focus group interviews twice. One pair was already acquainted with one another; the other pair was not. All participants were deaf. Kristian facilitated the focus group of Caribbean and African researchers. Lina facilitated the rest of the focus groups.

All participants were receptive to our questions and willingly shared many stories about their experiences. They also shared their insight about what would make their experiences more inclusive or what would allow them to advance their training in sign language research. The interviews were conducted ASL and/or IS, and everyone was skilled at translanguaging (de Meulder et al., 2019). Our understanding and interpretation of the stories depended on our relationship to the participants in the individual interviews as well as the relationship between the participants in the group interviews. If the participant is a friend of Lina, then the shared contextual background rendered the contents of the responses more familiar. Our varied relationships to the participants make it difficult to reduce the rich diversity and heterogeneity of their stories. Therefore, we present our own impressions of selected elements of the participants' stories with respect to identity politics and research and conference experiences.

All participants identified as deaf and are multilingual in different signed, written, and spoken languages. Some were born deaf while others became deaf in childhood. Some came from hearing nonsigning families and reported learning to sign when they entered a deaf school. Others were mainstreamed and learned to sign when they met other deaf children and adults in social contexts. Two participants came from deaf signing families and were mainstreamed.

Most participants identified as a member of at least one racial or ethnic group that would classify them as people of colour (POC). Two participants identified as white of European descent. The racial and/or ethnic construction of one's identity must be understood in the sociohistorical context of where one generally lives and works, and this can change across nation-states. POC is a distinctly US category that distinguishes race from ethnicity and includes any group that is racialised in the US context. This perspective does not translate cleanly to many other nation-states, as confirmed by some of our participants' responses about how they self-identify and how they are seen in local and nonlocal contexts. For example, one participant identifies as a member of the dominant ethnic group in their home country but is perceived as an ethnic minority in their current country of residence, and might be variously perceived as white, Middle Eastern, Asian or "other race" in US and European contexts. As another example, the participants from East Africa identified as members of various ethnic groups in their local contexts, but they are aware of how they are perceived as African and/or Black in the US and Europe. Our classification of the participants as POC is not intended to erase their diverse ethnic identities, but rather to highlight the skewed disparities of representation of deaf people of colour from the Global South as researchers in conference and institutional spaces.

Most interviews were filmed on Zoom. One was not due to a technical error and had to be summarised from the interviewers' memory and double-checked by the interviewee. We independently watched them to identify any broad arising themes that could be generalised to some or most of the interviewees' experiences. When we selected quotes from the interview and focus group data for this chapter, we translated the participants' signing to English. Otherwise, the data was not translated. From our analysis of the interviews and the focus groups, two sites of exclusion repeatedly emerged in the data for Global South deaf researchers of colour: research conferences and academic institutions.

Conferences as Spaces of Knowledge Production

In contrast to other conferences, more participants from the Global South had attended conference meetings via SIGN (formerly known as Cross-Linguistic Sign Language Research, CLSLR), the World Congress of African Linguistics (WOCAL), and/or the World Congress of the World Federation for the Deaf

(WFD). SIGN is a more community-oriented conference that represents three areas of research: linguistics, Deaf studies, and Deaf education. The SIGN conference series is coordinated by the International Institute for Sign Languages and Deaf Studies (iSLanDS) at the University of Central Lancashire; there have been nine meetings held in various Global South and Global North countries including the UK, India, Turkey, China, Brazil, and Poland, since the 2000s (Nick Palfreyman, p.c.).[1] Unlike TISLR and most other academic conferences, SIGN is entirely conducted in the host country's national sign language and IS without the presence of sign language interpreters. The participants who attended SIGN reported basking in the ease and pleasure of direct communication, meeting new people and reuniting with old friends, and learning about research.

WOCAL, established in the 1990s, is the only international conference that specialises in the linguistic study of African languages with an emphasis on the participation of African scholars. Since 2008, WOCAL has had a separate workshop dedicated to African sign languages that has been held in various African countries and elsewhere.[2] Our participants from East Africa had attended WOCAL before since they were key members of a research collaboration on sign languages in Africa and had some financial support to travel, though not without difficulty. The World Congress of WFD, another international conference, draws multiple national deaf organisations and large crowds of deaf people to engage in the exchange of information about a wide range of deaf-related topics not limited to linguistics, such as advocacy for sign language rights. Since 1951, various Global North countries have hosted the Congress, but in recent decades, a few Global South nations have hosted it. Some of our participants who were able to attend the Congress received financial support from research collaborators affiliated with academic universities or governmental or nonprofit organisations. These participants reported positive experiences of attending the Congress for meeting and networking with other deaf people from different countries and absorbing useful information from presentations that appealed to their research and personal interests.

Our participants' stories—like our analysis of the conference data—confirmed our observations about the low representation of deaf people of colour, especially those from the Global South, at TISLR. Very few interviewees from the Global South have attended the conference or even knew what it was. Though TISLR is a large and prestigious international sign language linguistics conference, this is not surprising as our demographic analysis in the third section reveals that Global South scholars are not well represented at all at TISLR. Those who were unaware of TISLR were those who were not enrolled in a master's or doctoral program and did not have the financial and institutional support to attend, since the budget would involve paying for international visas, air and ground transportation, lodgings, per diem expenses, and conference registration fees, which are fixed in euros and therefore are very high after currency conversion. Two PhD students from Southeast Asia were able to attend TISLR 13 because they were affiliated with US universities and received support from a National Science Foundation conference grant available through TISLR. Another PhD student from the same region, who was not affiliated with a US university, was able to attend through support from their previous employer, a nonprofit organisation dedicated to sign language research. One PhD student from the Middle East could not attend the conference due to strict visa requirements and the politics of travelling to certain nation-states, including the US; this student had not been able to travel to any international conference during their graduate career.

Out of all the conferences mentioned in the interviews, TISLR was the least familiar and most inaccessible to the participants. TISLR is strictly an academic conference that university professors and their graduate students are more likely to attend and present at. Often it is a professor's research funding that supports their own and their students' travel. Moreover, most attendees are predominantly hearing, white Global North researchers who vary enormously in their proficiency in different sign languages and in their experience of translanguaging. The current practice at TISLR is that many stage presentations are delivered in spoken English and interpreted into ASL, IS, and a few other sign languages. Many hallway conversations and social gatherings, which are key to professional networking, are mixed with respect to the modality and language used. Conferences like TISLR are of known importance to acquiring research jobs and PhD positions. For prospective deaf candidates who are able to attend the conference, the inaccessibility to hallway conversations represents an additional barrier. For these reasons, many interview participants who had attended TISLR found the experience ambivalent because their access to presentations and conversations was variable.

One interview participant recalled attending TISLR in Amsterdam in 2000 and attending many spoken talks without sign language interpreters. They relied on presentation slides and/or handouts for accessing information and watching hearing sign language researchers debating during the question-and-answer session. Their experience was shared by other deaf Global North academics, who created the Amsterdam Manifesto.[3] Since then, the Sign Language Linguistics Society has implemented recommendations from the Amsterdam Manifesto for more inclusive practices and accessibility.[4]

The same participant also recalled asking a very prominent hearing sign language researcher, one who is well-known in the larger field of linguistics and other related fields, about how they managed to collaborate with so many other researchers on various projects. The hearing researcher replied that people just ask them, often approaching them at conferences and proposing collaborations. These interactions naturally happened through direct communication—speaking English—an implicit but significant privilege that the participant did not have. Most potential collaborators would not approach the participant the same way, because they either did not have the level of signing proficiency to converse about research or they likely harboured some bias about the participant not being able to collaborate with them due to the participant's research interests and knowledge, which did not align with the goals of other researchers' projects.

The deaf POC participants reported various forms of discrimination and bias from hearing and deaf white Global North people, especially senior researchers. They suspected the discrimination and bias were related to their status, background, and research, which was perceived as "niche." We interpreted these incidents as motivated by implicit global racism. Regrettably but unsurprisingly such racism was not specific to TISLR but also occurred in the general space of academia in the Global North.

All but one of the participants reported never attending or knowing about Formal and Experimental Advances in Sign Language Theory (FEAST). The one participant who attended FEAST said that the small size of the conference made in-depth feedback possible. However, they reported a very low presence of deaf researchers and a very high attendance of hearing European researchers.

By comparison, SIGN and WFD are more familiar and accessible conferences, especially WFD, given its mission to promote the human rights of deaf people all over the world. These conferences draw more diverse groups and do not strictly require institutional affiliation, or financial, intellectual, and moral support. The greater diversity of the attendees gave our interview participants more networking opportunities without the hidden cultural expectations of academia. Although professors and graduate students may have the resources to travel to SIGN and WFD, these conferences do not carry the same prestige as TISLR does and may not appear as impressive on one's curriculum vitae in the general academia especially universities with very high research activities. A consequence is that there is little overlap among the conferences, which minimises the visibility of deaf people of colour from the Global South for the more privileged Global North researchers and excludes Global South researchers. Graduate students and faculty in the Global North can more easily attend TISLR and present their research, learn about other people's research, and network with other researchers for future collaboration, a privilege that Global South researchers do not have.

Universities as Privileged Institutions of Higher Learning

Out of the 13 participants we interviewed, three participants were not affiliated with any advanced linguistics or linguistics-related programs at an accredited university. These participants were from Global South nation-states that already have some history of sign language linguistics research in academic, missionary, and nongovernmental contexts. They have been involved in extensive sign language research, teaching, and advocacy, and at least two participants played a fundamental role in advancing the projects of their collaborators at research universities. Yet they were unable to enrol in a linguistics program due to various institutional, economic, and social barriers, of which many were used as gatekeeping factors.

First, participants were not successful in applying for or getting admitted for an advanced degree in a local or international linguistics program, because the requirements for admissions often call for a completed undergraduate degree, high level of standardised US or UK English in application materials, writing samples, standardised exam scores, and letters of recommendation from faculty. Second, they lacked the financial means, including scholarships and fellowships, to support themselves as students without giving up their full-time jobs. Third, local programs did not offer professional sign language interpreters that would facilitate communication with hearing nonsigning faculty and peers; more critically, these programs also lacked signing faculty for direct communication. International programs would most likely require the participants to immerse themselves in a mainstream sign language variety used by the interpreters in order to quickly gain a high level of fluency to follow complex academic lectures and conversations. Interview participants acknowledged inaccessibility to linguistics as a major keep back. They reported having to read up for themselves on the subject due to a lack of accessible textbooks, classes, or training.

The following is a quote from a participant who does linguistic research in Puerto Rico. She describes the specific colonial situation in Puerto Rico and the way it affects them being a deaf Puerto Rican: "Puerto Rico is under the USA. We are colonised by them. Deaf Puerto Ricans are doubly colonised." We are reminded that colonisation is not just a metaphor for deaf people—they are in many states part of larger colonised communities. The participant describes the push back she receives when using her own sign language variety and the consequences of moving to the mainland for education.

When I use the signs we use in Puerto Rico, I'm told, "Why are you using your signs? You must use ASL in Puerto Rico!" But we don't use full ASL in PR. We use our own sign language.

When Hispanic families from Mexico, Cuba, etc. move to the USA, they have to change their signing to match the signing in the USA. Schools and universities force them to use ASL. I want to see how the US can work with a diversity of deaf cultures. There is no one deaf culture. It is not just white deaf culture. There are indigenous ways of signing, Mexican ways of signing, Puerto Rican ways of signing. How will interpreters learn these different ways of signing to be able to interpret well for us?

I want more inclusivity. I know my signing is not ASL.

For the participants who are already studying, they reported encountering numerous barriers to advancing their studies. Five participants were currently enrolled in a linguistics or linguistics-related master's and/or doctoral program. Two students were studying in their home countries, of which one was a Global South nation-state; they reported spending inordinate amounts of labour in advocating for themselves for linguistic access and catching up on their coursework or putting in extra time to educate themselves in order to distinguish themselves from their hearing peers. Three students from Global South nation-states were studying at universities in the US and Europe and had scholarships and accommodations to support their studies. These experiences nod to the bigger problem of sign language linguistics as an exclusively privileged Global North endeavour due to the high costs of academic mobility as well as an extremely inaccessible space for deaf people, limiting their ability to directly engage in formal and informal conversations.

As further evidence of this point, mobility occurred within Global North spaces for all three professors in our interviews. Two professors had to leave their home countries to obtain their doctorates and to secure permanent employment, requiring them to teach, write, and publish in other languages. One professor obtained their doctorate in their home country but worked in another country for a decade before they moved back home. All professors, including Lina, expressed a strong desire to train future generations of deaf (and nondeaf) doctoral scholars but either were not in a PhD-granting program or were not in an ideal position for capacity building by recruiting and training critical masses of potential candidates. These participants acknowledged their own privileges and recognized some of the institutional, economic, and social barriers that deaf people of colour from the Global South faced but could not individually address the barriers or change the standards of meritocracy, due to gatekeeping practices and pushback from faculty colleagues and university administrators. For example, in one interview, by way of reflecting on their privileges, one deaf white Global North professor shared a memorable story with Lina. This professor recalled being a baby linguist (that is, a graduate student in linguistics) when they met many deaf researchers of colour from the Global South at the SIGN conference in 2004. Eighteen years later, the baby linguist was now a tenured professor of linguistics, but most people they had met at that conference had not advanced as much in their academic linguistics training by comparison. One person in this professor's story is another of our interview participants. This story highlights the magnitude of the differences of some structural disparities between Global North and Global South researchers.

Calling for Social Justice Action: Recommendations

Our findings drawn from analysing our auto-ethnographic reflections, conference presenter data and the interviews and focus groups all underscore the marginalisation and exclusion of deaf researchers of colour of Global South in sign language linguistics. The corollary is the clear lack of cultural, linguistic, and intellectual diversity among academic sign language linguistics researchers, particularly at the doctoral level and in senior faculty ranks. This problem also occurs for other marginalised populations in linguistics including Native and Indigenous scholars (Leonard, 2020) and Black scholars (Charity Hudley et al., 2020). To make more space for deaf researchers of colour from the Global South, we call for social justice in action through the following institutional, structural, and attitudinal changes. These changes are not entirely our invention but rather have been collaboratively brainstormed by our interview participants. These proposed changes are very specific to our participants' needs. More work is needed to understand how to support deaf researchers of colour in the Global South in other situations. We present the changes as follows.

First, PhD-granting linguistics programs must revise their admissions requirements to minimise bias. Extensive research experience, community relationships, and letters of recommendation from mentors and collaborators can be prioritised over a completed undergraduate or master's degree, demonstration of "standardised" English literacy skills, writing samples, and exam scores. The programs also need to invest in student cluster recruiting so potential deaf students will have access to peers that they can relate to and incorporate community capacity building in which the students and local deaf signing communities, including deaf community stakeholders, may have opportunities to collaborate on community-based research projects. Such collaborations could lead to the production of more accessible scholarship that would include community forums and sign language vlogs.

Second, conference organisers can hold more space for Global South deaf researchers of colour. As WFD is symbolic in the Global South, it can offer more financial support for people to attend conferences. Sign language linguistics conferences should have panels and/or workshops that would allow for more opportunities for researchers to engage in collaboration. Third, researchers can aim to hold workshops and summer schools in more accessible spaces outside of the US and Europe. These workshops and summer schools would be targeted at people who are not US and EU citizens and who are not enrolled in graduate linguistics programs. There would not be any academic prerequisites in place, which would emerge as major gatekeeping practices.

These above spaces should aim for direct communication to encourage everyone to engage with translanguaging. Ideally, these spaces could be in person. High-speed internet access is not a feasible option in many Global South nation-states and many deaf people value face-to-face interaction over videoconferencing, print-based communication, and even sign language interpreters. Although interpreters can facilitate access between deaf signers and nondeaf signers, the interpreters would be most likely accustomed to prestigious and standardised signing varieties from the US and Europe, which could lead to the devaluation of signing varieties from the Global South. Direct communication also would reduce the cost of hiring interpreters, which often are a significant barrier for conferences, workshops, and summer schools and tend to feed the widespread implicit bias of deaf people as "an economic burden."

Finally, we need to have more open and explicit dialogue, beyond informal and private conversations, about the disparities of our field. We need to acknowledge that these parities cannot be reduced to "deaf education problems" and/or "audism." We need to take a more radical approach to redefining and revaluing "literacy." One starting point would be to revisit and re-evaluate the SLLS statement of ethics (SLLS, 2016) for sign language research and dedicate a section to the discussion of ethical responsibilities and considerations when researchers get involved with deaf and signing communities in the Global South.

The field of sign language linguistics will thrive from the greater inclusion and valuation of deaf researchers of colour from and in the Global South. While there is a clear trend of increased attention towards the diversity of sign language varieties and signing communities in the Global South, the attention is largely motivated by intellectual purposes for a more comprehensive understanding of the human capacity for language. But languages are more than bounded and disembodied objects; they exist in the bodies of people with lived experiences and knowledges that have been all too often exoticized and extracted to reproduce and reinforce global, racial, and ableist hierarchies entrenched in white hegemony. This chapter calls for a radical shift in the power dynamics between the researchers and the researched, especially between the predominantly hearing, white Global North senior scholars and the deaf Global South people of colour. The shift must prioritise establishing, sustaining, and nurturing meaningful relationships in which the people are valued as equal partners who participate in all stages of research rather than participating in research as exemplary and tokenised signing models.

Notes

1. Although there does not appear to be much print or digital documentation of SIGN, a collage of photos of various meetings is available at https://www.youtube.com/watch?v=I5yk i5ZegCM.
2. A collage of photos of a few past WOCAL workshops is available at http://sign.wocal.net/. Accessed Nov. 9, 2023.
3. The Amsterdam Manifesto, revised August 21, 2000, http://www.deafacademics.org/conf erences/amsterdam_manifesto.pdf.
4. See Sign Language Linguistics Society, "Inclusive Practices and Accessibility," June 11, 2018, https://slls.eu/inclusive-practices/.

References

Braithwaite, Ben. (2020). Ideologies of linguistic research on small sign languages in the global South: A Caribbean perspective. *Language & Communication, 74*, 182–194.

Braithwaite, Ben, & Ali, Kristian. (2024). The colonial geography of linguistics: A view from the Caribbean. In Anne H. Charity Hudley, Christine Mallinson, & Mary Bucholtz (Eds.), *Decolonizing linguistics.* Oxford University Press.

Chua, Mel, de Meulder, Maartje, Geer, Leah, Henner, Jon, Hou, Lynn, Kubus, Okan, O'Brien, Dai, & Robinson, Octavian. (2022). 1001 small victories: Deaf academics and imposter syndrome. In M. Addison. M. Breeze, & Y. Taylor (Eds.), *The Palgrave Handbook of Imposter Syndrome in Higher Education* (pp. 481–496). Springer.

De Meulder, Maartje, Kusters, Annelies, Moriarty, Erin, & Murray, Joseph J. (2019). Describe, don't prescribe. The practice and politics of translanguaging in the context of deaf signers. *Journal of Multilingual and Multicultural Development, 40*(10): 892–906. doi: 10.1080/ 01434632.2019.1592181

de Sousa Santos, Boaventura. (2015). *Epistemologies of the South: Justice against epistemicide.* Routledge.

Hill, Joseph, Hou, Lynn, Lim, Anna, Harrison, Dominic, & Player, David. (2020). Race, racism, and racialization in sign language research and deaf studies. Introduction for the panel. High Desert Society Linguistics 14, Albuquerque, NM.

Hochgesang, Julie A. (2019). Inclusion of deaf linguists and signed language linguistics [Invited Panel Presentation]. Georgetown University Roundtable (GURT) 2019: Linguistics and the Public Good, Georgetown University, Washington, DC.

Hou, Lynn, Hochgesang, Julie, Occhino, Corrine, & Lepic, Ryan. (2022). Where do we go from here? Faculty placement of deaf linguists in US PhD programs. Poster presentation for Linguistics Society of America. January 6, 2022. Washington, DC. https://doi.org/10.6084/m9.figshare.17912228.v1

Hou, Lynn, & de Vos, Connie. (2021). Classifications and typologies: Labeling sign languages and signing communities. *Journal of Sociolinguistics* 26(1): 118–125.

Hou, Lynn. Y-S. (2017). Negotiating language practices and language ideologies in field-work: A reflexive meta-documentation. In Annelies Kusters, Maartje de Meulder, & Dai O'Brien (Eds.), *Innovations in deaf studies: The role of deaf scholars* (pp. 339–359). Oxford University Press.

Hou, Lynn Y.- S. (2016). "Making hands": Family sign languages in the San Juan Quiahije community [Doctoral dissertation, University of Texas at Austin].

Hudley, Anne Charity, Mallinson, Christine, & Bucholtz, Mary. (2020). Toward racial justice in linguistics: Interdisciplinary insights into theorizing race in the discipline and diversifying the profession. *Language*, 96(4), e200–e235. https://doi.org/10.1353/lan.2020.0074

Kusters, Annelies. (2021a, December 14). [Twitter]. https://twitter.com/AnneliesKusters/status/1470675630903681027

Kusters, Annelies. (2021b). International Sign and American Sign Language as different types of global deaf lingua francas. *Sign Language Studies, 21*(4): 391–426. doi:10.1353/sls.2021.0005

Leonard, Wesley Y. (2020). Insights from Native American studies for theorizing race and racism in linguistics: Response to Charity Hudley, Mallinson, and Bucholtz. *Language*, 96(4), e281–e291. https://doi.org/10.1353/lan.2020.0079

Mahler, Anne. G. (2017). Global South. In Eugent O'Brien (Ed.), *Oxford Bibliographies in Literary and Critical Theory* (pp. 1–2). Oxford University Press.

McBurney, Susan L. (2006). *Sign Language: History of Research*. In Keith Brown (Ed.), Encyclopedia of Language & Linguistics (pp. 310–318). Oxford: Elsevier Science.

Ray, Victor. (2016, October 21). The unbearable whiteness of Mesearch. *Inside Higher Ed*. https://www.insidehighered.com/advice/2016/10/21/me-studies-are-not-just-conducted-people-color-essay

Reidpath, Daniel D., & Allotey, Pascale. (2019). The problem of "trickle-down science" from the Global North to the Global South. *BMJ Global Health*, 4(4), e001719.

Serwadda, David, Ndebele, Paul, Grabowski, M. Kate, Bajunirwe, Francis, & Wanyenze, Rhoda K. (2018). Open data sharing and the Global South—Who benefits? *Science*, 359(6376), 642–643.

SLLS Ethics Statement for Sign Language Research. (2016, August). Sign Language Linguistics Society. https://slls.eu/slls-ethics-statement.

Villareal, Dan, & Collister, Lauren. (2024). Open Methods: Decolonizing (or not) research methods in linguistics. In Anne H. Charity Hudley, Christine Mallinson, & Mary Bucholtz (Eds.), *Decolonizing linguistics*. Oxford University Press.

Julien De Jesus is a graduate student and Doctoral Scholars Fellow at the University of California, Santa Barbara, located on Chumash territory. Born in Manila, Philippines, they are a trans Filipinx American settler on Tongva land (Los Angeles). Their work is in liberatory linguistics, spanning language reclamation and decolonization; Asian American transness broadly (specifically relationships between language, racioethnicity, gender, nationality, and sexuality); and Filipinx American experiences and language use. Their undergraduate honors thesis was a speaker-based approach to morphosyntactic phenomena in Numu (Northern Paiute), while their master's thesis focused on the experiences of Filipinx Americans in US academia.

Abstract: The guiding question for this chapter is: How can Linguistics be made to feel like a home, intellectually and otherwise, for Filipinx American students and scholars? The author takes a simultaneously ethnographic and autoethnographic approach to answering this question, utilizing a combination of reflections on their own experiences as a Filipinx American linguist in the US and qualitative IRB-approved interviews with seven other Filipinx American scholars in Linguistics and adjacent fields. The author describes how they ended up writing this project in the first place, then delves into several themes from the interviews that reveal ways in which colonial structures and thinking impact Filipinx Americans in academia. Finally, the chapter ends with recommendations and actionable steps for faculty who work with and/or hope to work with Filipinx American students.

Key Words: autoethnography, Filipinx diaspora, decolonization, Philippines, interdisciplinary

3

We Need to Be Telling Our Own Stories

Creating a Home for Filipinx Americans in Linguistics

Julien De Jesus (they/them/siya)
University of California, Santa Barbara

Introduction

It has been my experience that Linguistics is hostile to Filipinx Americans—a fact that is perhaps unsurprising given the history of the field's exclusion of Asians of all kinds (see Yoo et al., 2023). My guiding question for this chapter is therefore the following: How do we make Linguistics feel like a home, intellectually and otherwise, for Filipinx American students and scholars? At its core, this project is for myself and my Filipinx American peers in Linguistics, as well as future Filipinx American linguists. It serves as a starting point for my upcoming work in increasing and supporting Filipinx Americans in Linguistics and academia broadly, increasing interdisciplinary work and international collaboration within the field of Linguistics, and contributing to theories of racialization, decolonization, and inclusivity. This project is also a call to action for departments, programs, and the discipline—and especially white tenured faculty as well as other faculty who currently work or hope to work with Filipinx American scholars—to support Filipinx American students in creating a home in Linguistics.

I first provide an autoethnographic account of my journey in the writing of this chapter. I then discuss my interviews with Filipinx American scholars in Linguistics and related fields, drawing out key themes that arose across my discussions with the participants. Those themes are (1) the exoticization and exploitation of Filipinx American identity; (2) the gatekeeping of research; and (3) the importance of support systems beyond the program. These themes, and my discussion of them, reveal ways in which colonial structures and thinking impact Filipinx Americans in academia. Finally, I end with a set of recommendations for faculty.

Julien De Jesus, *We Need to Be Telling Our Own Stories* In: *Inclusion in Linguistics*. Edited by: Anne H. Charity Hudley, Christine Mallinson and Mary Bucholtz, Oxford University Press. © Anne H. Charity Hudley, Christine Mallinson, and Mary Bucholtz 2024. DOI: 10.1093/oso/9780197755303.003.0004

Before I begin, I want to warn my Filipinx American and Asian American readers broadly that this chapter uses some explicit and potentially triggering language; still, I hope that they can come away from this work feeling affirmed in their experiences and hopeful about their academic futures.

Some final introductory notes on terminology: firstly, in this chapter, I follow Wesley Leonard (2017) in "capitalising the names of academic disciplines but using lower-case to refer to what professionals in the discipline study (e.g., scholars in Linguistics do research in linguistics)" (p. 18). Secondly, I find that when referring to people of the Philippines, "Filipinx" is unsatisfactory, for it is a name derived from a false nation; the Philippines is named after Philip II of Spain, and as a country would not exist if it had not been "unified" (i.e., forced together under colonization) by Spain. Moreover, the Philippines is extremely diverse in its people, communities, and languages, and "Filipinx" (as well as any of its variants, i.e., "Filipino," "Filipina," "Filipin@," "Filipine") erases that diversity and obscures ethnoracial politics, privileges, and oppressions within the archipelago. Further, precolonial Indigenous groups may not identify themselves with the Philippines at all, and people who have ancestral ties to the Philippines but do not reside there likewise have complex identities. For all these reasons, it is important to be very deliberate, intentional, and explicit in deciding how to refer to specific groups. My own label of choice when referring to the postcolonial Philippine diaspora in the United States context is "Filipinx American." My decision to use "Filipinx" as opposed to the more conventional "Filipino" is rooted in my own understanding of colonialism in the Philippines as well as my desire to signify the gender variance of my existence; it is also my way of indicating to other queer/trans people of the Philippine diaspora that I am part of their community. See Kay Ulanday Barrett, Karen Buenavista Hanna, and Anang Palomar (2021) for a more sustained and historically rich discussion of the term "Filipinx."

Doing research as a Filipinx American linguist

For this project I took a simultaneously ethnographic and autoethnographic approach, utilizing a combination of reflections of my own experiences as a Filipinx American linguist in the US and qualitative interviews with seven other Filipinx American scholars in Linguistics and adjacent fields. Christopher Poulos, a professor of communication studies, states, "Qualitative researchers are human actors—inexorably impacted and influenced by their responses to unfolding events and their cultural and historical premises, rules, and backgrounds" (Poulos, 2021, p. 7). Thus, it follows that my positionality informed my methods in this project, and my methods greatly impacted me due to my positionality. I am the light-skinned, queer/trans child (they/them/their pronouns in English) of a Tagalog Filipina mother and a white American military father, raised middle-class. I was born in the Philippines and raised in Guam, the Kingdom of Hawai'i, and various parts of the "country" colonially known as "the United States." The United States, much like the Philippines, is a false country, a nation of various lands, cultures, peoples, and languages, forcibly brought together by the domineering hands of colonialism and imperialism. Further, the Philippines was for years a literal colony of the United States (see, for example, Renato Constantino, 1969 on the colonial history of the Philippines.) I am currently a graduate student in the Department of Linguistics at the University of California, Santa Barbara (UCSB) and I am a settler on Tongva land in Los Angeles. Much of my work has been in language documentation, revitalization, and reclamation work and sociolinguistic research in the American West, and therefore has had to engage with the colonialism of linguistic research (for the colonial legacy of Documentary Linguistics, see Errington, 2008; Leonard, 2018; Montoya, 2024). The process of self-analyzing my place in this colonial legacy has been an ongoing one; because of this, I strive to be more thoughtful and think more critically about how that place informs my analysis. At the same time, I am constantly learning and changing my perspective, so this analysis has never been completely satisfactory. Additionally, as a non-Indigenous person in the United States, I have had to and continue to reckon with and reflect on my own role in settler-colonialism; for a more sustained discussion on Asian settler-colonialism, see Eve Tuck and Wayne Yang (2012), Dean Itsuji Saranillio (2013), Iyko Day (2018), and Candace Fujikane and Jonathan Okamura (2008).

As scholars in the accompanying volume have noted (see, e.g., Braithwaite & Ali, 2024; Fuller Medina, 2024), in order to decolonize Linguistics, linguists must acknowledge the divide between the Global South and the Global North. Although I was born in the Global South and still have strong ties to the Philippines, I am a Global North researcher and thus must acknowledge the privileges that come with this position, such as the financial, institutional, and educational resources that accompany my affiliation with a highly resourced institution in the Global North. Additionally, it is important to note that I am a diasporic Filipinx, having spent most of my life outside of the Philippines, and therefore I cannot and will not claim to speak for my Philippine-residing kababayan. While my own positionalities and relative places in power dynamics are constantly shifting depending on context, I am conscious of the fact that my own experiences and background impact my analysis, and that there are a multitude of actual, potential, and possible different perspectives on this journey and on my role of being a Filipinx scholar in academia.

How I Got Here (Literally): An Autoethnographic Account

I began this project out of sheer necessity: I needed both an outlet to share my experiences and frankly, a way to keep myself in graduate school. In the early spring of 2021, the latter half of my first year of graduate school at UCSB, I almost dropped out—out of my program, out of my school, and out of academia altogether. From the first month in my graduate program I lived in Goleta, the small city adjacent to Santa Barbara, both situated on Chumash land, wherein most UCSB graduate students reside, and I kept wondering if I'd made a mistake. Despite its official designations as both a Hispanic-Serving Institution (HSI) and an Asian American Native American Pacific Islander-Serving Institution (AANAPISI), UCSB is still a Predominantly White Institution (PWI) (UCSB Diversity, Equity, and Inclusion, 2022). A PWI is a very specific type of institution: one with whiteness and white supremacy imbued in nearly every facet of its history and its existence. The seemingly paradoxical distinction of UCSB's dual statuses as both PWI and Minority-Serving institution may lead to contradictory experiences, and is jarringly clear when comparing the undergraduate and graduate populations: 36% of UCSB's undergraduates and 57% of its graduate students are white (Institutional Research, Planning & Assessment, 2022). I had already spent four years at a PWI as an undergraduate and was hesitant to commit the better part of a decade to another one. However, in the end, I chose UCSB for its mentorship possibilities, its reputation, and the broad expertise of its faculty (and, admittedly, the benefits of the fellowship they offered me) over other schools where the student body and local population were both much more diverse and ethnically similar to me.

During my first year at UCSB, I was one of 32 self-identified Filipinx graduate students, out of a total of 2,097 students at the university (Institutional Research, Planning & Assessment, 2021); Filipinx graduate students made up only 2% of the school's graduate students (Institutional Research, Planning & Assessment, 2021). "Filipino" is a substantial enough ethnic group in California—the only larger Asian group is Chinese—to warrant its own subcategory in UCSB's yearly "Campus Profile." The "Filipino" category is an improvement upon the reductive racial categorization of the city of Goleta, "Asian alone" (demographics), and of the largest organization of American linguistics, the Linguistic Society of America, "Asian or American," (Linguistic

Society of America, 2021). The "Asian alone" and "Asian or Asian American" categories are especially problematic in that they disregard differences between Asian regions, such as South Asia versus Southeast Asia, and Global South versus Global North; ignores ethnic, linguistic, and cultural differences; and overlooks Asian people in the diaspora (see also Yoo et al., 2023). Nor does this flattened Pan-Asianism account for factors such as socioeconomic disparity, Western imperialism, and regional colonialism as enacted, for example, by the Empire of Japan. This approach ignores key details about the Philippines: that it is a poor country, that it is part of the Global South, and that it was occupied by Spain, Japan, and the United States.

Regardless of the labels used, numbers and statistics cannot fully portray the months of cultural and racioethnic isolation I experienced as a Filipinx graduate student, which were exacerbated by the COVID-19 pandemic. I could spend the entirety of this chapter detailing the micro and macro aggressions and loneliness that slowly eroded the hope I held as a nervous but excited first-year graduate student, with self-doubt quickly filling its place.

But allow me to fast-forward to the fifth month of my graduate program. I finally hit my breaking point in February 2021, when I was once more subjected to racism by my academic community. Even now, this incident is still painful for me to talk about, and what I write is as much as I am able to share here. That year, Lunar New Year, a major holiday for much of Asia and the Asian diaspora, fell on Friday, February 12. The only other Asian people I saw that day, period, were the Chinese American employees working at the restaurant where I picked up my takeout dinner. What should have been a moment of celebration was instead one of intense loneliness. This feeling was compounded by fear: during that time, across the United States, anti-Asian hate crimes were markedly higher than usual due to racist rhetoric around the COVID-19 pandemic, fanned by Trump and his supporters. My feelings were only confirmed by what happened two weeks later.

I was at a virtual social gathering in a supposedly "safe" graduate student space hosted by a graduate student organization that I belonged to, wherein I was the only person racialized as Asian. Someone typed on the screen the word "chink," an anti-Asian slur rooted in xenophobia against Chinese immigrants to the United States (Wu, 1972). A second unknown person followed with an anti-Latinx slur. It was and still is striking to me how easily people's minds turn to racism, and how comfortable they are using negative racialized terms. In this case, I wonder how much these people were emboldened by their anonymity.

As the only racialized-as-Asian person present, and in the absence of any Latinx people saying anything (I was not familiar with everyone in the group, and thus cannot say for certain whether or not anyone identified as Latinx), I was the only one to call out these racist acts. The fact that nobody else said anything is significant because it shows how white supremacy and racist sentiments are so normalized—even in academia, a space that is often attacked by conservatives as "overly liberal." Further, this situation shows how white people are resistant to call each other out for racist acts, and how "doing nothing" is actually doing something: it is supporting those who are doing wrong. I received a perfunctory apology from the person who typed "chink," who was an organizer of the event and a leader of the organization, but nobody admitted to the anti-Latinx slur. Maybe because a Latinx person did not call them out? The event otherwise continued as if nothing had happened. The silence from the other attendees resulted in me self-gaslighting. As many racialized people know, being "the only one" in a space is made all the more difficult when you attempt to call something out, while everyone else pretends that it did not happen in the first place. I did not receive an apology from the other organizers until I sent an email formally withdrawing my labor from the group—I had, only a few days prior, accepted a position on this organization's executive board—an indication that racialized people in such spaces are only valued for their labor (see Fuller Medina, 2024).

I still clearly remember seeing "chink" flash across the screen, but what I remember even more vividly is feeling my face burn with shame and embarrassment, wondering if my emotions were readable over Zoom. At the time, I could not figure out why I felt this way. I found the answer a few months later, when reading Cathy Park Hong's (2020) timely book *Minor Feelings: An Asian American Reckoning*. The following line, about Hong's aversion to reading about anti-Asian hate crimes ranging from rape and assault to murder, resonated deeply with me: "I don't want to care that no one cares, because I don't want to be stranded in my rage" (Hong 2020, p. 173). Yet even while writing this chapter, I fear that I am overreacting; I wonder if I am being ridiculous by comparing the hate speech that I endured to the physical violence Hong discusses. But then I remember that Ronald Ebens, a white man, used anti-Asian slurs when he cracked open Chinese American Vincent Chin's head with a baseball bat in 1982, in one of the most notorious anti-Asian hate crimes in US history. Language does not only uphold racism; it is part of racism. In reading the reporting on the aftermath of this crime I was struck by one detail: Ebens eventually "sought refuge in Nevada" (Guillermo, 2012). Knowing that fact, it feels strange to say that after my own encounter with anti-Asian hate, I also "sought refuge in Nevada," where my mother was living at the time. The day after the event, I texted my mom, asking if I could come home to Las Vegas, a city situated on Nuwu land, but refusing to tell her why. The next day,

I retreated, driving five-and-a-half hours and 390 miles/628 km inland. In the days, weeks, and months that followed, I found myself emotionally paralleling that motion, mentally curling inward as if around a wound, away from my department, from UCSB, and from academia.

Several weeks later, I moved to Los Angeles, situated on Tongva land—the metropolitan area with the largest Filipinx population of any city in the United States, and where I have had family since the 1970s. Los Angeles is barely 100 miles from Santa Barbara; I realized that all along, I had been so close to a community that could have supported me, yet due to the pandemic and my time and financial restrictions as a graduate student, I did not have access to it. While settling into my new home in Los Angeles, I began working on my proposal for this chapter. I was fueled by my need for catharsis in the wake of everything that had happened to me in Santa Barbara, but I was also motivated by my ever-present desire to build community. This project became a way to achieve both of those goals.

Filipinx Americans in Academia

Racist incidents like the one I described above are only part of the picture. The structural racism of Linguistics as a whole creates a hostile climate for Filipinx students and scholars. Filipinxs are the third-largest Asian ethnic group in the United States (AAPI Data, 2021), yet from the time I began my BA (August, 2015) until the writing of this chapter, I know of only one other Filipinx American who studied linguistics at my undergraduate institution, a large state school that was a PWI. This is not to say that there are no Filipinx Americans in Linguistics and adjacent fields. At the time this chapter was written, Filipinx American scholars at the faculty level included but are not limited to Catherine Ceniza Choy (Asian American and Asian Diaspora Studies, and Comparative Ethnic Studies, UC Berkeley), Denise Cruz (English and Comparative Literature, Columbia University), E. J. R. David (Psychology, University of Alaska Anchorage), Martin Manalansan IV (American Studies, University of Minnesota, Twin Cities), Robyn Magalit Rodriguez (Asian American Studies, UC Davis), Angela Reyes (English and Anthropology, Hunter College, City University of New York), and Dan Villareal (Department of Linguistics, University of Pittsburgh). However, we are certainly not a critical mass, in terms of numbers; Filipinx Americans are sorely underrepresented in US academia, especially among tenured faculty (Maramba & Nadal, 2013). Within Linguistics, this lack of visibility is evident at the Linguistic Society of America annual meeting, one of the largest linguistics conferences in the world. The work of Filipinx American linguists is not widely discussed or engaged with generally. What could potentially be a visible and cohesive contingent of Filipinx American linguists is often folded into the broader—and flatter—group of "Asian American linguists" or even "Asian linguists."

Conversations with Filipinx American Scholars

In the fall of 2021, I put out a call for participants for this study. I was seeking to interview Filipinx/a/o Americans residing in the US above the age of 18, who had at least a bachelor's degree in Linguistics and/or an adjacent field (e.g., Anthropology, Education, Ethnic Studies, Sociology). Prior to putting out my call for participants, I told several friends that I would be surprised to find multiple Filipinx Americans in Linguistics to interview, since there are so few; this is why I kept my eligibility criteria relatively flexible in regard to discipline. In retrospect, I believe that this flexibility allowed for more fruitful and interesting conversations, as well as an expansion of my own academic circle beyond the realm of Linguistics. I recruited seven participants in total. One was my junior at my undergraduate institution; the other six were recruited through Twitter, an important space for Filipinx American scholars to find each other, given our sparse distribution in the academy. Participants were in their twenties and older, with educational levels ranging from bachelor's degree to doctorate; all had attended and/or were attending institutions in the United States. The interviews were about an hour long, conducted over Zoom video and/or chat, and participants were financially compensated for their time through a mini-grant I received from my department. I received IRB approval from UCSB to conduct these interviews. In all but two cases, Krisna Balolong and Joseph Bernardo, participants' names are pseudonyms, per each interviewee's individual preference. See Table 3.1 for participant information.

However, because of the small number of Filipinx Americans not only in Linguistics but also in adjacent fields and academia more generally (Maramba & Nadal, 2013), I was concerned about preserving the privacy of my interviewees who chose to remain anonymous. JR, a PhD student in a social science program in the Midwest, was only half-joking when he said that even specifying that much detail ("Filipino in [his field] in the Midwest") would be enough information to reveal his identity. This self-awareness reflects an issue that Long T. Bui (2021) touches upon in his discussion of Southeast Asian American scholars, a term which for Bui (and me) includes Filipinx

Table 3.1 Participant information

Participant (*indicates pseudonym)	Pronouns	Field	Educational Level at Time of Interview	Area of Current or Most Recent Institution
Krisna Balolong	she/her	Linguistics	BA	Nevada
Joseph Bernardo	he/him	History	PhD	Washington
*Maricel	she/her	Social science and natural science interdisciplinary program	BS	South
*JR	he/him	Social science	PhD candidate	Midwest
*Angel	they/them	Social science and natural science interdisciplinary program	BS	South
*Gabriela	she/her	Linguistics	PhD candidate	Northeast
*Tita Baby	they/them	Interdisciplinary social science	PhD student	Northeast

Americans: "There are so few [Southeast Asian American] scholars that they can be identified even with the smallest of demographic information" (p. 4).

My primary research goals with these interviews were, first, to learn more about what other Filipinx Americans of different positionalities experience in Linguistics; second, to determine some of the most common issues that Filipinx Americans in academia face and to collaborate with my interviewees to come to solutions for those issues; and third, to build community with other Filipinx American scholars. The interviews were semistructured but casual in tone and more like conversations: after all, tsismis (a Tagalog term that often translates to "gossip") is an inherently dialogic cultural practice. Learning about other Filipinx Americans' experiences in academia allowed me to reflect on and share my own, resulting in an autoethnographic component in the interviews that, quite honestly, I didn't expect. I began with basic demographic questions before delving into questions about each participant's academic journey, their experiences as a Filipinx American in US academia, and whether they thought a community of Filipinx American scholars exists. For example, I asked, "How many other Filipinx Americans were in your program?" and followed up by asking how they felt about that number. I also asked each participant how they felt about their own discipline and about academia broadly. For those who were not in Linguistics, I asked how they perceived the field, and how they thought it could be in better conversation with their own.

julien de jesus
@julien_de_jesus

...

just finished conducting my first interview for my
master's thesis and my cheeks hurt from smiling &
laughing so much.

a physical reminder that this work, while emotionally
difficult, can be immensely joyful, too ✦

Figure 3.1 Screenshot of my tweet after my first interview
Alt text: screenshot of Tweet from author's Twitter account, @julien_de_jesus, reading,
"just finished conducting my first interview for my master's thesis and my cheeks hurt
from smiling & laughing so much. a physical reminder that this work, while emotionally
difficult, can be immensely joyful, too [sparkle emoji]." Profile picture is of the author,
a light-skinned Filipinx American with short green hair, smiling in front of a large
green bush.

I wrote a tweet in October 2021 that offers a neat summation of what the
interviews were like (Figure 3.1).

However, my emotions while working on this project, and especially immediately after the interviews, were anything but neat. To be able to mutually share experiences (and tsismis) in academia with other Filipinx American
scholars was extremely rewarding, and I am so grateful to have made those
connections. From this project, I have gained so many things, among them
community, knowledge, support, new friends, even a Los Angeles independent bookstore recommendation. At the same time, though, I was wholly
unprepared for the physical weight that I felt as a result of conducting the research. The very reason that the interviews were rewarding—I was able to
commiserate with people who really, truly *got it*—was also the reason that
they were so difficult. While I am relieved to be affirmed that yes, what I am
experiencing and feeling is real, that I was not overreacting in response to
what I now call "the slur incident," it pains me to know that other people have
undergone and continue to undergo experiences similar to the ones I did.

Interview Findings

I identified three key themes in the interviews regarding Filipinx American
scholars in the academy that arose across seven interviews: (1) the
exoticization and exploitation of Filipinx American identity; (2) the gatekeeping of research; and (3) the importance of support systems beyond departmental graduate programs. I discuss each theme in more detail below.

The Exoticization and Exploitation of Filipinx (American) Identity

The Philippines and Southeast Asia broadly have long been exoticized, fetishized, and exploited by the Global North. Western linguists have been instrumental and foundational in perpetuating this colonial viewpoint by positing the Philippines as a fascinating treasure trove of languages to be studied with no regard to the actual humanity of the country's inhabitants. This theme was well-illustrated in my interview with Gabriela, a PhD candidate in Linguistics, who had completed her MA at another institution before starting her PhD program. When I asked Gabriela about other Filipinx Americans in either of her graduate programs, she responded that there were none, adding, "The very few Fil Ams I encounter in both institutions tend to occupy different roles/be in other depts [like . . .] wives to fellow researchers." Gabriela expressed surprise at how common it is for her non-Filipinx fellow researchers, upon finding out that she is Filipino (Gabriela's own term to identify herself), to want to introduce her to their Filipina wives (I use the -*a* ending here to specifically denote the gendered dynamics at play). Later in the interview, Gabriela explicitly stated, "I feel exoticized sometimes." Gabriela's experience reflects how non-Filipinx researchers exoticize and even fetishize Filipinx identity, often in a specifically gendered way, and/or try to force awkward connections between people with very little in common. Despite having met several linguists who have done the same as Gabriela's colleagues, it never fails to surprise me how unabashed—even excited—white male linguists are to tell me about their Filipina, or other Asian wife, or in-law. This Filipinx person they are so proud to have a connection to is, of course, always a woman, and never a man. This fact is a direct consequence of the historically and contemporarily racialized and gendered view of the Filipinx body in the white and non-Filipinx gaze (for more on this topic, see, for example, Choy, 2003; Cruz, 2012; Manalansan, 2003; Suzuki, 2007; Winkelmann, 2023).

Related to these exoticizing microaggressions are faculty's assumptions about Filipinx American scholars' access to "the Philippine community" and subsequent attempts to exploit them for access to "data." Making assumptions about who has which access to communities is problematic, and exploitation of this kind can manifest in ways such as expecting Filipinx American students to perform certain work they are uncomfortable with. Similarly, Joyhanna Yoo and colleagues (2023) write about how "non-Asian mentors and colleagues frequently advise their Asian and Asian American graduate students to study a particular language or speech community based solely on their ethnic background." I have experienced this pressure myself. When

I was an undergraduate student, I conducted a mini-experiment for a course paper inspired by my work as a research assistant and involving Filipinx people from my own social circles. This paper meant a lot to me on a personal level. The next school term the professor that I wrote the paper for excitedly shared my work with their colleague, who suggested that I conduct similar research on ("on" being the key word here, as opposed to "with," a distinction also brought up by Khan, 2024) a specific population of Filipinx Americans in a particular region *for their own project*, even though I had little to no connection to that community. In essence, this professor tried to leverage their institutional and societal power to appropriate my research and take advantage of my assumed access to "the Filipinx community." I felt uncomfortable participating in the project, especially as I became more (self-)critical of the ways in which Linguistics upholds settler-colonialism and realized that the project as a whole was exploitative. My refusal to participate cost me the favor of this professor, demonstrating the high price of standing by one's ethics in academia.

My experience is parallel to that of many of my interviewees. Tita Baby, a PhD student in Cognitive Science at a university on the East Coast, mentioned that when they were interviewing for their graduate program, a Linguistics professor assumed that they knew Tagalog. This professor made comments like "You'll be so helpful with [my] projects," and Tita Baby felt that the professor was disappointed to learn that they actually were not fluent in Tagalog. I have had similar experiences with faculty, who have expressed thinly veiled disappointment at my lack of fluency in Tagalog, with seemingly no thought about why that might be; in my case, the reasons include growing up in a mixed-race household, the general hegemony of English in the United States public school system, and the cultural currency of English—topics that I am not eager to explain to faculty, especially those in Linguistics, who should know better.

The Gatekeeping of Research: Who Deserves the Title of Researcher?

A second theme that emerged in the interviews was the gatekeeping of Filipinx American scholars' own research. The gatekeeping of Linguistics is such a powerful force that some of my interviewees expressed resistance to the label of "linguist" for themselves due to ideologies upheld in parts of the field. Near the beginning of our conversation, Gabriela confided, "I still have hang-ups about being called 'linguist,'" despite working toward a PhD in

Linguistics. When asked about these hang-ups, she told me, "There are expectations people have about what a linguist should do. Go out in the field, do research on a linguistic minority group, publish in journals. And to be able to do all those is to finally get the privilege of being called a 'linguist.' My professors at [institution] kind of implied those 'requirements' to be a linguist too." Likewise, Krisna, who had studied Linguistics as an undergraduate, struggled with the discipline and with academia broadly, citing her "decolonial agenda" and the marginalized status of her community-centered research on Philippine linguistics and history as the reasons for her hesitancy to apply to graduate school in Linguistics.

These "requirements" for "linguists" lead to false ideas about the type of work linguists should do: in my own and my interviewees' experience, acceptable research is largely documentary and almost certainly exploitative. These ideas in turn lead to accusations that Filipinx American scholars' research is "too personal" and "not *real* scholarly work." Filipinx Americans, like other minoritized groups in academia, are often told that the work that we are interested in is not "real linguistics," particularly if our work is less traditionally "theoretical" and "more applied." More generally, qualitative research is often taken less seriously by researchers who use quantitative methods. Due to "science envy," linguists say things like "the more data, the better" when what they really mean is "the more participants, the better," as if we can reduce the human experience to numbers and statistics. Of course, numbers and statistics are useful too (I use them in this very piece), but they don't mean anything without context, without stories. Anne Charity Hudley, Christine Mallinson, and Mary Bucholtz (2020) critique this divide, and contrast the work of fields like Linguistics with "interdisciplinary fields that are concerned with critically theorizing race," noting that the latter "understand that what traditional disciplines often consider 'data' produced by people of color is better conceptualized as grounded theoretical knowledge in its own right" (e211).

Moreover, Filipinx Americans are oftentimes interested in doing ethnographic research with *our own* communities, which is very different from the racist assumption that Filipinx researchers have access to *every* Filipinx community, since as stated earlier, the Philippines and its peoples are richly diverse. Linda Tuhiwai Smith (2012) wrote of how non-Indigenous people are framed as experts on the validity and authenticity of "Indigeneity" and even Indigenous people's existence. Similarly, non-Filipinx (and typically white) researchers are framed as the experts on "Filipinx-ness." Thus, if Filipinx Americans engage in in-group ethnographic research, and pursue research interests in their own communities, ideas of Western authenticity can be disrupted. However, these interests may be discouraged by faculty.

This discouragement can translate to a lack of Filipinx American graduate students and therefore Filipinx American faculty, because potential Filipinx American scholars are gatekept from doing the work they actually want to do, so they leave their field or academia altogether. JR, the Midwest social science PhD candidate, recalled the response he received when he told a white faculty member about a project idea he was particularly passionate about: "You can't do that, it's too personal." This sort of work is threatening to white linguists because the idea of "objectivity" is still pervasive in many academic circles (see Clemons, 2024); a more insidious assumption held by many scholars is that only the unmarked (white) researcher can be objective. I suppose this makes sense, given that Linguistics as a field was made by and for white people (see, for example, Flores & Rosa, 2015). Racialized scholars are not allowed to do the work we want to do; we have to fight for it in ways that white scholars do not. Because "white" is the unmarked racioethnic identity in academia, white researchers are allowed, in fact, *expected and even entitled,* to study other communities or even the world as a whole without interrogating their own positionality.

But not even the unmarked can escape from subjectivity. Angel, who completed an interdisciplinary social science and natural science BA, said of their program, "We talked so much about how, like queer and trans youth of color are at like, extremely high at a high risk for like suicide, increased suicidality, and like anxiety, and all these different things, and it's like, okay, so you have people that are these identities, like in your space, like, you do this research and have these like groundbreaking findings, but what are you doing, like interpersonally to, like, actually support the population that you're like doing research on?" Although Angel is not a linguist, their critique of research that doesn't directly benefit participants or consider researchers themselves resonated deeply with me. As linguists, we cannot just look at a decontextualized aspect of someone's language—like the disembodied syntax of a minoritized Philippine language, or the sociophonetics of West Coast Filipinx Americans—and ignore the whole person, their life, and their community (also see Fuller Medina, 2024).

One remedy for these issues that Krisna and I collaboratively came up with during our conversation was that "we need to be telling our own stories"— hence the title of this chapter. Filipinx American students must be allowed and encouraged to pursue the topics that we are most passionate about, which are necessarily often highly personal. In many ways, the topics that are most personal to us are those that we are the greatest experts on, and Linguistics as a field will benefit from these different types of knowledge and expertise.

The Importance of Support Systems Beyond the Departmental Graduate Program

A third theme that arose in the interviews was the extreme importance of support systems beyond the departmental graduate program. For Filipinx Americans in academia, the stakes are high. As JR said, "Academia is a tool of white supremacy so it's never really made for other folks. For folks of color and other minoritized groups to put themselves through this process, you need to understand that it's going to kill us." JR said that this was why he tells people that if they don't have specific types of support, then they should definitely not consider academia. But what are these "specific types of support"? How are we supposed to know what we need if we don't know anything about academia, or don't know any Filipinx Americans in academia?

Every single interviewee mentioned, at least in passing, how their support systems were largely outside of their programs. Maricel and Joseph talked at length about the importance of having kababayan to commiserate, celebrate, and engage in tsismis with. Joseph, who earned a PhD in History, stated, "It wasn't necessarily the cohort that was supporting me, it was the friends that I made, both in my department and outside my department." Maricel, who was in the same interdisciplinary social science and natural science under-graduate program as Angel, expressed the same sentiment, saying, "As an Asian American person on campus, the resources and the support that I felt in that community were things outside of academics, like organizations and friend groups and things like that. It wasn't necessarily built into the pro-gram, or the classes that I took." This has been my experience as well: I had to look beyond my "batch" (as my mother would call the group I started grad-uate school with), my department, and Linguistics as a discipline. In order to be able to do this work of telling our own stories—in order to survive in academia—it is crucial for Filipinx American scholars to have strong support systems and thriving communities.

Recommendations

Building on the insights from my conversations I had with interviewees as well as my reflections on my own experiences, in this section I present a set of recommendations, for faculty instructors, advisors, and mentors, particularly those who hold societal and institutional power (e.g., those who are white, tenured, and so on). These recommendations should be implemented both in smaller advisor–advisee relationships as well as on broader departmental and institutional levels. A number of these recommendations are discussed more generally in Beronda Montgomery et al. 2014 and Sarah Fletcher and Carol Mullen 2012. Similarly, many of the resources cited below focus on graduate students of color who are not Filipinx American, given the dearth of research specifically on this group.

1. Faculty with Filipinx American students and those considering taking on Filipinx American students: Do your homework so you don't burden your students with educating you about their history and lived experience. At the same time, remember that you are not the expert, your student is. Understand that the advisor-advisee relationship involves mutual teaching and learning (cf. Ross-Sheriff et al., 2017).
   • Educate yourself on Philippine and especially Filipinx American history. Read Renato Constantino, Jose Rizal, Carlos Bulosan, and the work of the scholars in the Filipinx Americans in Academia section. Also engage with more contemporary work, especially by Filipinx women and gender-variant people, such as Elaine Castillo's *America Is Not the Heart* (2018) and Kay Ulanday Barrett's *More Than Organs* (2020). If a student is particularly excited about a certain work, read it, even if it is not "linguistics" or even "academic." For example, Castillo and Barrett are contemporary literature and poetry, respectively, but both works center Filipinx American experiences.
   • Attend presentations by Filipinx American scholars, both within and ideally beyond Linguistics (e.g., on your home campus). If your student is comfortable and interested, attend presentations together or meet afterward to discuss.
2. Support Filipinx American students in pursuit of work they are passionate about, even if you personally do not fully understand it. Provide students with financial and intellectual support to do fieldwork, research, and present their research at conferences and other venues. Interdisciplinary work in particular may be necessary for students' survival in academia, especially since Linguistics as a field currently cannot provide what marginalized scholars need (Liu, 2006 discusses a similar issue in the field of Geography). As Krisna explained, "I was able to do my own research on Philippine history, because I had a professor who was like, 'Do what you want. You need this. We need this.' So yeah, so even if I don't have professors that even know much of Philippine history, as long as they'll accommodate my research and my studies, that's fine. And I really want that freedom to say, 'I don't want to work on your project, you can do that. I want to work on mine. Trust me.'"

- Prioritize Filipinx American students who study Philippine languages and Filipinx American language over non-Filipinx students who study those languages.
- Foster and maintain strong, positive relationships with faculty and programs in other disciplines that may be able to help support and mentor your Filipinx American students. More specifically, foster more substantive relationships with departments and programs in Asian American Studies and Southeast Asian Studies.
- Encourage your graduate students to meet students, faculty, and mentors in other departments, programs, and institutions. Further, be humble and recognize when your students may need an outside member on their committee; encourage your students to reach out to outside members, or even do so on their behalf through a virtual introduction (email has a CC function for a reason).
- Invite Filipinx American graduate students and faculty from other departments, institutions, and disciplines to give paid talks and presentations at institutional and departmental events. Advertise these presentations within the department, and potentially outside of the department, too; your students may be able to make connections this way.
- Several interviewees explicitly mentioned the importance of and need for more Philippine Studies and Philippine American Studies programs—there are some programs in the United States, but many are limited to the undergraduate level and most are in California and especially the San Francisco Bay Area (e.g., City College of San Francisco and University of San Francisco). Outside of California, the University of Hawai'i Mānoa, the University of Wisconsin-Madison, the University of Michigan, and the University of Washington offer interdisciplinary graduate programs wherein students may specialize in the Philippines; however, this is not enough. Support your colleagues who are fighting to create and maintain Philippine, Southeast Asian, and Asian American Studies programs. Lobby administration, sign and forward petitions, and make sure that these are agenda items.
- Give Filipinx American students money to attend conferences so that they can network and meet with other Filipinx Americans, even if those conferences are "not strictly linguistics." I don't believe I'll ever be able to have a strong Filipinx American academic community at UCSB, but with increased travel and conference funding, I could have been better connected to Filipinx people in Los Angeles and elsewhere.

- Help students submit abstracts and present at those conferences where Filipinx American scholars are likely to congregate, such as the Association for Asian American Studies Annual Conference. Even if it is not your specific area of expertise, you know how to write a good abstract. At the very least, copy-edit abstracts and do practice run-throughs with your students.

3. Acknowledge that minoritized scholars experience an increased workload and set of expectations. For example, students who are similarly minoritized may (justifiably) seek out these scholars as mentors; Maricel, for instance, noted that she is "more drawn to" Asian American mentors. Being mindful of this increased workload and set of expectations is not enough. Hiring and tenure committees need to acknowledge and reward this type of "service" work *much* better than they currently do. This type of service work includes unofficial mentoring and advising, organizing events for minoritized scholars, and the creation of new courses that may attract new students to the department. Potential rewards for such work could include lowering other service requirements, lowered teaching loads, and increased pay or research funds. Richard Reddick, an associate dean for equity, community engagement, and outreach, suggests "time out from teaching a course, an extra office or a graduate assistant" as possible forms of compensation (Gewin, 2020).

- Students who engage in service work (e.g., leadership in campus organizations, peer mentorship, recruitment and retention of other Filipinx American students) should be rewarded and compensated as well, especially financially. My own department has recently committed to recognizing graduate students' work of this kind as a kind of scholarly activity.

4. Provide students with financial and intellectual support to do fieldwork, research, and present their research at conferences and other venues.

5. Provide students with emotional support and backup on micro (and macro) aggressions both in real time and in the aftermath of such incidents. If you do not know where to start—and even if you think you do—see Derald Wing Sue et al. (2019) for intervention strategies and Michelle Haynes-Baratz et al. (2021) for analysis of bystander training.

- Call shit out.
- Believe your students when they tell you what they are going through. Never minimize their experiences; this can be harmful to your adviser-advisee relationships, but more importantly, it can be damaging to the overall wellbeing of your students (Johnson et al., 2021).

6. As Joseph said: "Tenure-line faculty are needed! The students will follow." Hire more Filipinx Americans into tenure-track positions.

- Engage in cluster hiring of Filipinx and Filipinx American scholars with specialties in a variety of fields (Susana Muñoz et al. (2017) reflect on a diversity-focused cluster hire at their own university, with recommendations for others interested in cluster hiring). That is, hire *actual* Filipinxs (as opposed to non-Filipinxs) to study, research, and teach about Philippine languages. Additionally, provide secure, well-paid positions for Filipinx Americans scholars who study Filipinx American language practices and communities. However, be cautious of falling into the trap of assumptions about access; you should also hire Filipinx Americans who don't study Philippine or Filipinx American language(s). And remember to recognize the other types of work that minoritized scholars perform, and to adjust your expectations accordingly when hiring.
- Even at the individual faculty level, there is work to be done: lobby the university administration in order to create more tenure-track positions for Filipinx and Filipinx American scholars.

Conclusion

In this chapter, I have offered a piece of myself in the form of autoethnography alongside the experiences of the Filipinx American scholars that I interviewed. I have described and discussed three major themes of the interviews: the exoticization and exploitation of Filipinx American identity; the gatekeeping of research; and the importance of support systems. My interviewees were all Filipinx, but the themes that arose have commonalities with the experiences of other racialized academics. Admittedly, I am left wondering which kinds of experiences are unique to Filipinx Americans and which are not, but in order to answer that question, more work needs to be done. We don't yet know where all the common ground lies, and so further work on minoritized and specifically racialized communities in Linguistics must be done.

Since moving away from Santa Barbara, every time I visit, I fantasize about what life would have been like with a better support system. If, in my first year of graduate school, I had had the community that I have cultivated since moving to Los Angeles—and since beginning this project—I think I would have fared better. I think about what sort of pushback I would have been able to create against the racist hate speech I encountered, what it would have been like to feel like I was not alone. I wonder if, rather than curling inward as I did,

I could have branched outward. While I still wonder if Linguistics can ever truly feel like home to me, and to other Filipinx Americans, to people who were directly subjugated by the discipline and in its name, I hope that this work may help create some semblance of belonging for Filipinx Americans who are so far from the homes of our families and ancestors. I also hope that it will create a sense of urgency among linguists in societal and institutional positions of power, and to the field of Linguistics overall, to do better by us.

References

AAPI Data. (2021). Detailed origin for Asian Americans (national) version B: AAPI data quick stats.http://aapidata.com/stats/national/detailed-origin-for-asian-americans-national-version-b/

Barrett, Kay Ulanday. (2020). *More than organs*. Sibling Rivalry Press.

Barrett, Kay Ulanday, Hanna, Karen Buenavista, & Palomar, Anang. (2021). In defense of the X: Centering queer, trans, and non-binary Pilipina/x/os, queer vernacular, and the politics of naming. *Alon: Journal for Filipinx American and Diasporic Studies, 1*(2), 125–147. https://doi.org/10.5070/LN41253177

Braithwaite, Ben, & Ali, Kristian. (2024). The colonial geography of linguistics: A view from the Caribbean. In Anne H. Charity Hudley, Christine Mallinson, & Mary Bucholtz (Eds.), *Decolonizing linguistics*. Oxford University Press.

Bui, Long T. (2021). On the struggles and experiences of Southeast Asian American academics. *Journal of Southeast Asian American Education and Advancement, 16*(1). https://doi.org/10.7771/2153-8999.1218

Castillo, Elaine. (2018). *America is not the heart*. Viking.

Charity Hudley, Anne H., Mallinson, Christine, & Bucholtz, Mary. (2020). Toward racial justice in linguistics: Interdisciplinary insights into theorizing race in the discipline and diversifying the profession. *Language, 96*(4), e200–e235. https://doi.org/10.1353/lan.2020.0074

Choy, Catherine Ceniza. (2003). *Empire of care: Nursing and migration in Filipino American history*. Duke University Press.

Clemons, Aris Moreno. (2024). Apolitical linguistics doesn't exist, and it shouldn't: Developing a Black feminist praxis toward political transparency. In Anne H. Charity Hudley, Christine Mallinson, & Mary Bucholtz (Eds.), *Decolonizing linguistics*. Oxford University Press.

Constantino, Renato. (1969). *The making of a Filipino: A story of Philippine colonial politics*. Malaya Books.

Cruz, Denise. (2012). *Transpacific femininities: The making of the modern Filipina*. Duke University Press.

Day, Iyko. (2018). Settler colonialism in Asian North American representation. In J. Lee (Ed.), *Oxford Research encyclopedia of literature*. Oxford University Press.

Demographics. (n.d.). City of Goleta. https://www.cityofgoleta.org/community/about-goleta/demographics

Errington, J. Joseph. (2008). *Linguistics in a colonial world: A story of language, meaning, and power*. Blackwell.

Fletcher, Sarah, & Mullen, Carol A. (Eds.). (2012). *SAGE Handbook of Mentoring and Coaching in Education*. SAGE Publishing.

Flores, Nelson, & Rosa, Jonathan. (2015). Undoing appropriateness: Raciolinguistic ideologies and language diversity in education. *Harvard Educational Review*, 85(2), 149–171. https://doi.org/10.17763/0017-8055.85.2.149

Fujikane, Candace, & Okamura, Jonathan. Y. (Eds.). (2008). *Asian settler colonialism: From local governance to the habits of everyday life in Hawai`i*. University of Hawai'i Press.

Fuller Medina, Nicté. (2024). We like the idea of you but not the reality of you: The whole scholar as disruptor default colonial practices in linguistics. In Anne H. Charity Hudley, Christine Mallinson, & Mary Bucholtz (Eds.), *Decolonizing linguistics*. Oxford University Press.

Gewin, Virginia. (2020). The time tax put on scientists of colour. *Nature*, 583(7816), 479–481. https://doi.org/10.1038/d41586-020-01920-6

Guillermo, Emil. (2012, June 22). *Ronald Ebens, the man who killed Vincent Chin, apologizes 30 years later*. Asian American Legal Defense and Education Fund. https://www.aaldef.org/blog/ronald-ebens-the-man-who-killed-vincent-chin-apologizes-30-years-later/

Haynes-Baratz, Michelle C., Metinyurt, Tugba, Li, Yun Ling, Gonzales, Joseph, & Bond, Meg A. (2021). Bystander training for faculty: A promising approach to tackling microaggressions in the academy. *New Ideas in Psychology*, 63, 100882. https://doi.org/10.1016/j.newideapsych.2021.100882

Hong, Cathy Park. (2020). *Minor feelings: An Asian American reckoning*. One World.

Institutional Research, Planning & Assessment. (2021). *2020–2021 Campus Profile*. University of California Santa Barbara. https://drive.google.com/file/d/1iUG5djO8FB-0X9mBmc-3OKGMf8YSseHU/view?usp=sharing&usp=embed_facebook

Institutional Research, Planning & Assessment. (2022). *2021–2022 Campus Profile*. University of California Santa Barbara. https://drive.google.com/file/d/1Rs1Pn0iVDEbzxhLV2Y3DUY6k8HsI_qq7/view?usp=embed_facebook

Johnson, Veronica E., Nadal, Kevin. L., Sissoko, D. R. Gina, & King, Rukiya. (2021). "It's not in your head": Gaslighting, 'splaining, victim blaming, and other harmful reactions to microaggressions. *Perspectives on Psychological Science*, 16(5), 1024–1036. https://doi.org/10.1177/17456916211011963

Khan, Kamran. (2024). Unpacking experiences of racism in European applied linguistics. In Anne H. Charity Hudley, Christine Mallinson, & Mary Bucholtz (Eds.), *Decolonizing linguistics*. Oxford University Press.

Leonard, Wesley Y. (2017). Producing language reclamation by decolonising language. *Language Documentation and Description*, 14, 15–36.

Leonard, Wesley Y. (2018). Reflections on (de)colonialism in language documentation. In B. McDonnell, A. L. Berez-Kroeker, & G. Holton (Eds.), *Reflections on language documentation 20 Years after Himmelmann 1998* (pp. 55–65). Language Documentation & Conservation.

Linguistic Society of America. (2021). *The state of linguistics in higher education annual report 2020* (No. 8). https://www.linguisticsociety.org/sites/default/files/Annual%20Report%202020%20Jan2021%20-%20final.pdf

Liu, Laura Y. (2006). On being "hen's teeth": Interdisciplinary practices for women of color in Geography. *Gender, Place & Culture*, 13(1), 39–48. https://doi.org/10.1080/09663690500530966

Manalansan, Martin F. (2003). *Global divas: Filipino gay men in the diaspora*. Duke University Press.

Maramba, Dina C., & Nadal, Kevin L. (2013). Exploring the Filipino American faculty pipeline: Implications for higher education and Filipino American students. In R. Bonus & D. C. Maramba (Eds.), *The "other" students: Filipino Americans, education and power* (pp. 297–307). Information Age Publishing.

Montgomery, Beronda L., Dodson, Jualynne E., & Johnson, Sonya M. (2014). Guiding the way: Mentoring graduate students and junior faculty for sustainable academic careers. *SAGE Open*, 4(4), 1–11. https://doi.org/10.1177/2158244014558043

Montoya, Ignacio L. (2024). Manifestations of colonialism in linguistics and opportunities for decolonization through refusal. In Anne H. Charity Hudley, Christine Mallinson, & Mary Bucholtz (Eds.), *Decolonizing linguistics*. Oxford University Press.

Muñoz, Susana, Basile, Vincent, Gonzalez, Jessica, Birmingham, Daniel, Aragon, Antonette, Jennings, Louise, & Gloeckner, Gene. (2017). (Counter)narratives and complexities: Critical perspectives from a university cluster hire focused on diversity, equity, and inclusion. *Journal of Critical Thought and Praxis*, 6. https://doi.org/10.31274/jctp-180810-71

Poulos, Christopher N. (2021). Conceptual foundations of autoethnography. In *Essentials of autoethnography* (pp. 3–17). American Psychological Association.

Ross-Sheriff, Fariyal, Berry Edwards, Janice, & Orme, Julie. (2017). Relational mentoring of doctoral social work students at historically Black colleges and universities. *Journal of Teaching in Social Work*, 37(1), 55–70. https://doi.org/10.1080/08841233.2016.1270250

Saranillio, Dean Itsuji. (2013). Why Asian settler colonialism matters: A thought piece on critiques, debates, and Indigenous difference. *Settler Colonial Studies*, 3(3–4), 280–294. https://doi.org/10.1080/2201473X.2013.810697

Smith, Linda Tuhiwai. (2012). *Decolonizing methodologies: Research and Indigenous peoples* 2nd ed. Zed Books.

Sue, Derald Wing, Alsaidi, Sarah, Awad, Michael N., Glaeser, Elizabeth, Calle, Cassandra Z., & Mendez, Narolyn. (2019). Disarming racial microaggressions: Microintervention strategies for targets, White allies, and bystanders. *American Psychologist*, 74(1), 128–142. https://doi.org/10.1037/amp0000296

Suzuki, Nobue. (2007). Marrying a Marilyn of the tropics: Manhood and nationhood in Filipina-Japanese marriages. *Anthropological Quarterly*, 80(2), 427–454.

Tuck, Eve, & Yang, K. Wayne. (2012). Decolonization is not a metaphor. *Decolonization: Indigeneity, Education & Society*, 1(1), 1–40. https://jps.library.utoronto.ca/index.php/des/article/view/18630

UCSB Diversity, Equity, and Inclusion. (2022). *Minority Serving Institution*. https://diversity.ucsb.edu/about/minority-serving-institution

Winkelmann, Tessa (2023). Dangerous Intercourse: Gender and Interracial Relations in the American Colonial Philippines, 1898–1946. Cornell University Press.

Wu, Cheng-Tsu. (1972). *"Chink!" A documentary history of anti-Chinese prejudice in America*. World Pub.

Yoo, Joyhanna, Lee, Cheryl, Cheng, Andrew, & Ànand, Anusha. (2023). Asian American racialization and model minority logics in linguistics. *Daedalus*, 152(3), 130–146. https://www.jstor.org/stable/48739986

deandre miles-hercules is a PhD Candidate in linguistics at the University of California, Santa Barbara. They study how discourse organizes culture, power, and identification across intersecting axes of social differentiation, especially as regards race, gender, and sexuality. miles-hercules' research has explored such topics as the semantic bleaching of intersectionality in academic and popular discourse, virtue signaling within the linguistic repertoire of anti-Blackness, and methodological issues in phonetic analysis of nonbinary voices. Supported by a National Science Foundation Graduate Research Fellowship, their work has appeared in the *Journal of Linguistic Anthropology*, *The Oxford Handbook of Language and Sexuality*, *Pedagogy*, and *Gender and Language*. miles-hercules holds a BA in linguistics, anthropology, and African American studies from Emory University, as well as an MA in linguistics from UC Santa Barbara.

Abstract: This chapter explores the state of linguistics' engagement with (trans) gender inclusion. The author's discussion is framed by a call to insist upon increased competence around issues of inequality as necessarily entailed by the notion of scholarly expertise. Setting the discipline's consideration of trans and nonbinary scholars and issues within the context of regressive sociopolitical undercurrents in higher education, the author highlights instances of linguists' interactions, or lack thereof, with the concerns of trans and nonbinary scholars in the field in terms of the methodological, structural, and interpersonal aspects of scholarly activity. These occurrences are drawn from both public discourse and personal experience, detailing circumstances that range in character from general disregard around gender inclusion to outright antagonism of trans and nonbinary linguists. The author offers concrete actions and strategies for combating cisnormativity and transphobia in linguistics, ultimately advocating for a sea change in linguists' orientation to questions of equity and justice.

Key Words: translinguistics, transgender, inclusion, nonbinary, language and gender

4

(Trans)forming Expertise

Transness, Equity, and the Ethical Imperative of Linguistics

deandre miles-hercules (they/them)
University of California, Santa Barbara

Introduction

Historically, linguists' modus operandi regarding prominent issues of language tied to transphobia has been silence. On December 4, 2017, however, linguist Geoffrey Pullum published a controversial post to Language Log on gender-neutral singular *they*.[1] Pullum, Professor Emeritus of General Linguistics at the University of Edinburgh and Fellow of both the American Academy of Arts and Sciences and the British Academy, wrote, "for me singular *they* is **ungrammatical** with a personal name as antecedent" (boldface in original). His post was spurred by a news article detailing Philadelphia resident Phillip Garcia's write-in victory for a local area electoral judge position; the article referred to Garcia with the gender-neutral third-person singular pronoun (Bowden, 2017). Noticing the author's usage, Pullum (2017a) observed of Garcia that, "he is—sorry, that they are—one of the opponents of gender binarity whose own choice is that they would prefer to be referred to with the pronoun *they* all the time." Despite intentionally misgendering Garcia and including an impudent self-correction to accentuate the act, Pullum (2017a) claimed that he "[didn't] want to offend anyone," but rather sought readers' understanding of the apparently Herculean effort involved in referring to others appropriately.

Pullum's desire for sympathy engendered polarized commentary from members of the Language Log community, most of whom are linguistics faculty and graduate students. The comments section on the original post was closed, and so responses to his metalinguistic tantrum appeared elsewhere, most notably in the comments on a December 5, 2017 guest post by Kirby

deandre miles-hercules, *(Trans)forming Expertise* In: *Inclusion in Linguistics*. Edited by: Anne H. Charity Hudley, Christine Mallinson and Mary Bucholtz, Oxford University Press. © Anne H. Charity Hudley, Christine Mallinson, and Mary Bucholtz 2024. DOI: 10.1093/oso/9780197755303.003.0005

Conrod, a sociosyntactician who expressed "disappointment" in Pullum's message, pointing to research demonstrating the harm trans people experience from misgendering.[2] Less than 16 hours later, he posted a rebuttal and, in keeping with the grand tradition of individuals invoking bigoted rhetoric, Pullum doubled down. He argued that "the use of *they* under consideration here has (normally) nothing to do with being trans," and clarified his misgendering by noting, "It was not snarky; it was an honest admission that [he] had found it hard to make an instant change to [his] syntactic habits" (Pullum, 2017b). "If I could roll my eyes any harder, they would fall out of my skull," Conrod wrote. Pullum also revealed, erasing any lingering concerns of transphobia, that he has a "young friend" who was "born about 18 years ago as the daughter of a good friend . . . but [is] now militantly trans-identified and male" (Pullum, 2017b). The implication is that Pullum respects that man's pronouns, which indisputably evidences his ardent support of trans people— he is a consummate ally. And yet in the final point of his rebuttal, Pullum declares the following: "Telling me I am required for political reasons to use a construction that strikes me as ungrammatical, and judging me morally and politically for not instantly obeying, is the most extreme manifestation of prescriptivist Stalinism I have ever encountered" (Pullum, 2017b). Prescriptivist. Stalinism.

Does it matter that one senior linguistics professor encounters personal difficulty using nonbinary pronouns appropriately? Hardly. However, Pullum likening interpretations of his comments as transphobic to the policies of a totalitarian regime that operated concentration camps and carried out mass executions is a different story. It is part and parcel of an attitude that has been and remains pervasive in linguistics, as well as academia in general. Pullum's suggestion that labeling the sentiments of fellow linguists as transphobic, racist, ableist, or otherwise bigoted is unproductive and overblown, even bordering on censorship, is not an idiosyncratic anomaly in the field. It is reflective of a perception that efforts to minimize language conveying intolerance, particularly in higher education, have increasingly encroached upon individuals' free-speech rights. Oklahoma, for instance, passed HB 3543 to establish the Free Speech Committee, tasked with "oversee[ing] the state of campus discourse at public institutions of higher education." (Moody, 2022) The academic professionals supporting this political activity, rabid defenders of free speech, would sooner resign from their positions altogether than relinquish the ability to misgender a trans student or quote racist slurs from a James Baldwin novel while lecturing.

This free speech panic was also on display on April 26, 2022, when the Linguistic Society of America (LSA) posted to its website—and removed just days later—a draft resolution proposing that the organization adopt a modified version of the University of Chicago's controversial "Report of the Committee on Freedom of Expression" (Jaschik, 2016). The draft, authored by Noam Chomsky, Sabine Iatridou, Pauline Jacobson, Jason Merchant, Pritty Patel-Grosz, Yael Sharvit, Philippe Schlenker, Tim Stowell, Harold Torrence, and Charles Yang, asserted, "it is not the proper role of the Society to attempt to shield individuals from ideas and opinions they find unwelcome, disagreeable, or even deeply offensive." This type of language constitutes a high-register dog whistle (Saul, 2018), as might be ascertained from consideration of a couple questions. Why is it necessary now to affirm the rightful place in our discipline of ideas and opinions that many people find reprehensible? Who precisely stands to benefit from such an affirmation in the current political climate? No, the answer is not "everyone." In fact, during the brief window the draft resolution was hosted online for comment from LSA members, scores of linguists expressed grave misgivings over its implications regarding equity and inclusion in the field. An associate editor of the LSA's flagship journal, *Language*, wrote that if the resolution passed, she would consider resigning from the position and revoking her lifetime membership with the organization. Six days after the resolution was released, the Executive Committee of the LSA withdrew the resolution, citing parliamentary error but acknowledging the "highly disruptive episode" it had caused.

Taken together, the Geoffrey Pullum singular *they* affair and the LSA free-speech resolution debacle underscore the need for scrutinizing metadiscourse around equity in linguistics. Though I focus in this chapter specifically on disrupting transphobia and cisnormativity, much of my framing applies as well to anti-Blackness and misogyny, as it emerges from my experience as a scholar who is at once Black, femme, and gender-creative. To march toward progress on these and other issues of oppression, I argue, we must recast the notion of individualized moral responsibility regarding such matters into a sweeping professional imperative. In other words, if one finds themself averse to sustained discussion of and initiatives around issues of inequality in higher education, they should steer far clear of academic occupations. (I'm told that veterinary acupuncture can be a lucrative profession.)

Regardless of one's research interest, no matter how esoteric or socially detached, a commitment to scholarship must entail a principled investment in dismantling oppression. This is less a question of conscience than competence. Should one truly be considered an expert in the scientific study of language with no scholarly understanding of the role that language plays in social organization and the maintenance of inequality? Ultimately, I suggest that articulating a notion of scholarly proficiency from this posture represents a promising path forward toward advancing equity in linguistics and beyond. I first discuss a number of contexts in which I have witnessed the exclusion of trans and nonbinary identities in the discipline. I then offer recommendations for cisgender linguists interested in becoming accomplices in creating a truly gender-inclusive field.

(Trans)forming Linguistic Scholarship

There is copious room for improvement in the ways linguists engage trans and nonbinary issues as a scholarly community. By *engagement* I am referring especially to the methodological, structural, and interpersonal aspects of scholarly activity. An illustrative example of the inadequate consideration of trans people in linguistic research occurred during my first year as a linguistics PhD student. For a term paper in a sociophonetics course, I decided to study the acoustic properties of "nonbinary voices." I was interested in the vocal production of individuals who identify within the constellation of gender-nonconforming identities, and consequently interviewed Alex (pseudonym), a nonbinary graduate student at my institution, as a pilot study. I extracted a roughly seven-minute segment of the interview and manually segmented and annotated each intonation unit of the excerpt in PRAAT, the primary software used by linguists for acoustic analysis. The next step of my methodology was to extract Alex's vowel formants using the Dartmouth Linguistic Automation tool (DARLA). When attempting to upload the necessary files, however, I ran into an issue: DARLA required that users identify their speakers as *female*, *male*, or *child*, none of which accurately described Alex.

The programmers' logic was consistent with the theretofore prevailing view in phonetics that physiological factors produce different average fundamental frequency and pitch ranges and ceilings across binary genders; children's less developed larynxes produce a separate phonetic profile within that model. An ever-supportive ally, my fellow then-PhD student Jazmine Exford emailed one of DARLA's designers, cc-ing me, and alerting them to this issue of exclusion. They responded sympathetically, but wrote: "What DARLA needs is a way to know which voices are higher versus lower in pitch, so that the system can properly extract the formant values. This is necessary for the acoustic analysis. It's not a gender issue within DARLA, simply a matter of pitches" (J. Stanford, personal communication, February 11, 2019). I still needed to submit a final paper but was not willing to misgender my interviewee to do so. I consequently became interested in the accuracy of the claim that programs like DARLA are designed to account for acoustic patterns that incidentally coalesce along binary, gendered lines.

My research question became whether such programs produced the gendered difference they were purported merely to represent. I twice-duplicated my files of the interview excerpt and processed them through DARLA, labeling two *female* and the others *male*. Eschewing the finer technical, methodological, and analytical details, my results showed significant differences between the two gender designations in the formant values produced by the program for several vocal segments. In other words, DARLA, which employs a suite of other standard programs used for phonetic analysis, had inserted gender difference into my data.

Beyond the initial problem of the program excluding nonbinary speakers, my results also suggested that the voices of individuals whose phonetic profiles are not within the historically established parameters for their gender may be inaccurately analyzed, which has adverse ramifications for both trans and cisgender individuals. This work developed into a collaboration with Lal Zimman, who taught the sociophonetics course (and is a far more skilled statistician than I). We presented our results at the 2019 New Ways of Analyzing Variation conference; incidentally, one of DARLA's designers, James Stanford, was in the audience. He approached us afterward to praise our talk, acknowledge the problem we had presented, and affirm his commitment to resolve it. As it now stands, DARLA's setting options are *low voice* and *high voice*; *child* has been removed altogether. While users may still interpret those settings as corresponding to binary genders, the change represents a good-faith, if imperfect, effort to be more inclusive of trans people in linguistic research.

As this example indicates, linguistic research has tended to operate based upon implicit cisnormative ideas about gender. To take another example, reporting gender as metadata within quantitative linguistic studies is common practice, especially in experimental research; the effort put into collecting that information is laudable and shows that researchers recognize that participant gender may affect their results. However, these studies near-universally approach gender on a binary basis, excluding nonbinary individuals in the process. A rather obvious solution is to standardize the practice of offering participants more than two categorical gender options, or providing open-ended questions about gender identity. A less intuitive situation arises when gender is not within the focus of the study at the outset but has a statistical effect on the results. Explanations as to why gender matters for the phenomena under study are often relegated to the dark abyss of "future directions," leaving readers to draw their own interpretive conclusions and reinforcing entrenched, cisnormative and often misogynistic ideas about gender in the process. To avoid this problem, quantitative researchers should more carefully operationalize gender as a variable, specifically considering why it might demonstrate an effect in the first place. To that end, researchers should draw on the vast amount of scholarship available on language, gender, and sexuality (Angouri & Baxter, 2021; Hall & Barrett, 2018; Zimman et al., 2014) and include it as background in their publications.

Like phonetic analysis, publication is a sphere in which subtle but important structural issues around transness arise. I am concerned here with one in particular: pronouns. Historically and currently, if a writer is not well acquainted with an author to whom they would like to refer in writing using a pronoun, they are likely to simply guess the author's gender based upon their first name. What may seem an innocuous mistake arising from an incorrect guess results in misgendering a scholar in a medium that may be accessed by generations of readers to come. Again, the remedy is simple: publication venues should include authors' pronouns alongside other basic identifying information such as institutional affiliation. For instance, thanks to editors Rodrigo Borba, Kira Hall, and Mie Hiramoto, articles published in *Gender and Language* now appear with pronouns following authors' names—as do those in this book and its accompanying volume. Unfortunately, few other publication venues follow these examples. In fact, I once wrote pronouns for myself (they/them) in a manuscript draft for a well-known journal and emailed the production editor to tell them explicitly why I had done so. The pronouns remained on the manuscript through completion of the proofs stage but had disappeared without explanation by the time the publication was released. If writers insist to editors who, in turn, insist to presses that authors are always given the option to include their pronouns, that will be a victory for trans inclusion in the field.

I would be remiss if I did not note that some researchers do actively oppose trans inclusion in academia. As my exchange with the production editor indicates, just as important as the methodological and structural issues I have described are interpersonal negotiations around inequity and exclusion. In addressing this point, it must be said in no uncertain terms that some academics are transphobes; some are racists; some are misogynists; some are anti-Semites. In short, some academics are bigots, and we must reckon with that fact directly. I had just such an opportunity in April 2022 when I received an email from Ráhel Katalin Turai. Turai's email was sent as a reply on a thread containing nearly 80 language and gender scholars that was initiated over the news that Oxford University Press UK planned to publish a book on gender-critical feminism, which has been widely castigated for inciting transphobia. Her email asserted—with no supporting evidence—that pro-trans advocacy generates negative consequences for (cisgender) women, girls, and lesbians. She went on to paraphrase a proposed petition in support of the book, arguing that so-called transgenderism endeavors to invalidate women as a class, which is a routine talking point for gender-critical feminists, also known widely as Trans Exclusive Radical Feminists (TERFs) or Feminist Appropriating Radical Transphobes (FARTs). I responded in detail to this hateful and outrageous message, as did several others, many voicing support for me specifically. More than anything, though, that interchange illustrates the need for the support of cisgender scholars in combatting transphobia.

How to Be an Accomplice

A few years ago, I heard someone say, "We don't need allies. We need accomplices. We need folks who will put skin in the game." Toward eradicating transphobia and increasing equity in linguistics broadly, a few guiding principles of academic accomplicehood may prove useful.

Rule 1: Hold your colleagues accountable by making explicit that microaggression (e.g., misgendering) of any kind is unacceptable. While those conversations can be uncomfortable and are rarely well-received, they are nonetheless crucial for disrupting the air of resignation to deleterious behavior which relies heavily upon bystander passivity.

Rule 2: Stand behind those who are targeted academically or professionally for being vocal on issues of inequality, both publicly and behind closed doors (e.g., when decisions are made about admissions, hiring, tenure and promotion). Naturally, direct confrontation is not every person's strong suit, but openly supporting professionally vulnerable individuals in some form is an important role, else they are likely to become the victim of any retribution to which their antagonists have institutional recourse.

Rule 3: Do not remain silent about who those antagonists are. At every level of academic organization, there are politics around discussing the misconduct of others in the same field, department, and so on, and this situation is complicated by the differential access to structural power of those involved. Those circumstances notwithstanding, disrupting the silence is significant for both advocacy in the moment and for maintaining integrity of the historical record. The people deserve to know.[3]

Rule 4, if applicable: Teach your graduate students to follow Rules 1, 2, and 3.

As indicated by Rule 4, engaging with students in the classroom is another important area for inclusion. Classrooms are spaces of stress and discomfort for many trans students, and instructors can play a role in mitigating that negative experience; one way to do so can be to use pronoun rounds, that is, including individuals' preferred pronouns during the course of introduction. While recommending the practice, Lal Zimman and Cedar Brown (this volume) illustrate how trans students' responses to them are neither monolithic nor unilateral. The latter author has conducted ethnographic research examining the complex ways in which pronoun rounds are a semiotic resource enabling the construction of trans selfhood, but can also be a virtue signaling instrument for voicing superficial support of trans communities (Brown, forthcoming). I suggest that at the start of a course, before students introduce themselves, one should instruct them on what information they may wish to share when doing so, such as name, major, hometown, and so on, being certain to include pronouns. As Catherine Anderson (2022) demonstrates, it is also possible to integrate extended discussion of gender and pronouns into introductory linguistics courses. Regarding initial pronoun rounds, you should model the preferred format when introducing yourself as an instructor. Some students may not disclose theirs for a variety of reasons, and it is inappropriate to ask for an explanation, but overall, pronoun rounds can help facilitate a trans-inclusive classroom space. As many classes take place virtually (e.g., on Zoom) in the wake of COVID-19, an additionally helpful practice is including pronouns in one's screen name. When I taught a college-level dual-enrollment introduction to sociocultural linguistics course to high school students as part of the University of California, Santa Barbara's School Kids Investigating Language in Life and Society (SKILLS) program, I conducted a pronoun round early on. The students had never done one before, and when I conducted post-course feedback interviews with them, the pronoun round was one element of my teaching for which the students voiced strong appreciation. Related to sharing pronouns for the comfort of trans students and to model inclusive practices for all students, it is also important to avoid assuming students' pronouns based on the extent to which they appear cisgender to you. Destabilizing cisnormativity requires reorienting to gender such that you refrain from assuming the gender of students who you don't read as trans in the absence of self-identification.

Lastly, cis linguists should actively look for opportunities to use their academic knowledge for political participation outside of the ivory tower. Making linguistics a discipline where trans and otherwise-marginalized students, faculty, and staff can thrive requires challenging inequality in the broader world from which we enter the educational landscape in the first place. One way to do so is by submitting op-ed pieces to local or national news outlets when prominent social issues could benefit from a linguistic analysis. For example, conservative politicians and activists in the United States have recently taken the tack of advancing transphobia by demanding that individuals define what a *woman* is. At the judicial committee hearing for Supreme Court nominee Judge Ketanji Brown Jackson, Republican Senator Marsha Blackburn asked her to do just that. That strategy certainly warrants a semantic analysis, for example. Scholars of language should use their/our professional expertise to disrupt linguistic levers of inequality wherever they/we see them.

Conclusion

In this chapter, I have issued a call to reevaluate how to conceive of and demonstrate expertise as a linguist and as a scholar, through a lens that centers the rights and dignity of trans and nonbinary people. It must become beyond the bounds of possibility to thrive as an academic professional with no principled investment in challenging inequality. We all must insist that destabilizing entrenched power structures in academia is a professional imperative in our discipline. In the final instance, linguists must strive to shift our professional modus operandi from silently standing by to steadily speaking out.

Notes

1. Language Log is a collaborative blog launched in 2003 by Mark Liberman and none other than Geoffrey Pullum. Posts tend to focus on language use in media and popular culture.
2. Granted, most of Geoff Pullum's posts on Language Log are submitted with closed comments sections.
3. Regarding the sharing of potentially private information, it is worth noting that under United States copyright law, emails are protected as intellectual property and reproducing or publishing their contents without the authors' express permission can be grounds for suit. Hence, I paraphrase Turin's email above, refraining from quoting it directly.

References

Angouri, Jo, & Baxter, Judith. (Eds.). (2021). *The Routledge handbook of language, gender, and sexuality*. Routledge.

Anderson, Catherine. (2022). Pronouns and social justice in the linguistics classroom. *Journal of Language and Sexuality*, *11*(2), 251–263. https://doi.org/10.1075/jls.20024.and

Bowden, John. (2017). Philadelphia write-in candidate: I won with one vote. *The Hill*. https://thehill.com/homenews/campaign/362934-philadelphia-write-in-candidate-shocked-by-surprise-victory/

Brown, Cedar. (forthcoming). Misgender or out yourself: vulnerability in pronoun sharing practices. *Gender and Language*.

Hall, Kira, & Barrett, Rusty (Eds.). (2018). *The Oxford handbook of language and sexuality*. Oxford University Press.

Jaschik, Scott. (2016). The Chicago letter and its aftermath. *Inside Higher Ed*. https://www.ins idehighered.com/news/2016/08/29/u-chicago-letter-new-students-safe-spaces-sets-inte nse-debate.

Moody, Josh. (2022). Monitoring free speech on Oklahoma's campuses. *Inside Higher Ed*. https://www.insidehighered.com/news/2022/05/05/oklahoma-creates-committee-oversee-college-free-speech.

Pullum, Geoffrey. (2017, December 4). *A letter saying they won*. Language Log. https://language log.ldc.upenn.edu/nll/?p=35641.

Pullum, Geoffrey. (2017, December 6). *Courtesy and personal pronoun choice*. Language Log. https://languagelog.ldc.upenn.edu/nll/?p=35688.

Saul, Jennifer. (2018). Dogwhistles, political manipulation, and philosophy of language. In D. Fogal, M. Cross, D. Harris (Eds.), *New work on speech acts* (pp. 360–383). Oxford University Press.

Zimman, Lal, Davis, Jenny, & Raclaw, Joshua (Eds.). (2014). *Queer excursions: Retheorizing binaries in language, gender, and sexuality*. Oxford University Press.

Rikker Dockum is visiting assistant professor of linguistics at Swarthmore College. He earned his doctoral degree in linguistics at Yale University. His research focuses on phonology and sound change in tonal languages, with a combination of quantitative and qualitative methods, as well as fieldwork and language documentation. His research focuses especially on Tai languages of the past and present, and the Mainland Southeast Asia linguistic convergence area.

Caitlin M. Green is an independent researcher with a PhD in linguistics from the University of California, Davis. She teaches about language in Silicon Valley and writes articles for a public audience. Her research is on discourses online, focusing on academic freedom, civility, and bigotry in public discourses around higher education.

Abstract: Linguistics has a documented history of divisiveness and remains poorly understood by the general public. Nevertheless, linguistics also has great unrealized potential for positive impact on global society, hand in hand with scholarship. This chapter argues for an inclusive big tent linguistics that will help the discipline achieve its potential, and the authors outline three sources of current exclusion: socialization into gatekeeping what counts as linguistics, with legitimacy tied to outdated opinions of what is more scientific, rigorous, rational, or prestigious; epistemic injustice, including a tendency for hero-worship of lone geniuses of the field; and a pattern of ignoring power imbalances in interactions, such as the demand for civility, often from the discipline's least powerful members. The authors discuss the origins of these problems, some recent events that exemplify them, and suggest ways that all linguists, inclusively defined, can contribute to helping our scholarly community achieve a more uplifting culture.

Key Words: sociology of linguistics, history of linguistics, teaching linguistics, pedagogy, discourse studies, composite case study, big tent linguistics, inclusion

5

Toward a Big Tent Linguistics

Inclusion and the Myth of the Lone Genius

Rikker Dockum (he/him)
Swarthmore College

Caitlin M. Green (she/they)
independent scholar

Introduction

In the preface to his book on the "linguistics wars," Randy Allen Harris (1993, p. vii; 2021, p. xiii) laments that "widespread ignorance and trepidation about linguistics" hamper the study of language, something "unutterably fundamental to our humanhood." While progress has been made, the field of linguistics remains poorly understood by the general public and often still lives up to its reputation for the fractiousness, dysfunction, and exclusion that Harris documented. Until we can fearlessly identify root causes for this reputation, we cannot expect the full participation of those who are excluded by a culture that communicates that it will reproduce and reinforce hierarchies of race, gender, class, and professional renown, undermining and endangering marginalized scholars at every turn.[1]

Our field is rife with binary divisions like "formal" versus "functional" (Mackenzie, 2015; Newmeyer, 2016), "theoretical" versus "applied" (Newmeyer, 1990), "p-side" versus "s-side" (Sarvasy, 2016), or "academic" versus "industry" (Trester, 2022). At every stage of professional advancement, linguists may feel pressured to identify with one side or another or find ourselves involuntarily lumped into one side of a binary. Whole linguistics departments often consider themselves aligned with one side or the other of some of these binaries, and students are socialized into choosing alignments, whether implicitly through selecting departments and programs or explicitly as part of their training (e.g., Sarvasy, 2016). Constructing a field mainly in terms of mutually exclusive teams encourages the thinking of a single approach, or subset of approaches, as superior, as more rigorous or

Rikker Dockum and Caitlin M. Green, *Toward a Big Tent Linguistics* In: *Inclusion in Linguistics.*
Edited by: Anne H. Charity Hudley, Christine Mallinson and Mary Bucholtz, Oxford University Press.
© Anne H. Charity Hudley, Christine Mallinson, and Mary Bucholtz 2024. DOI: 10.1093/oso/9780197755303.003.0006

more explanatory, and to elevate those who do our preferred kind of research above others. This situation has led to territorial gatekeeping, which is often felt on both sides of a given dichotomy. This gatekeeping is fueled and exacerbated by the academy's more general problem of competition for limited grant funding and the increasing reliance of higher education on precarious faculty (AAUP, 2020).

Further, gatekeeping in linguistics intersects with white supremacy (Charity Hudley et al., 2020), hegemonic gender ideologies (Ayres-Bennett & Sanson, 2020b), classism, and other structural harms by devaluing approaches that focus on social or applied approaches to language, disproportionately impacting work by minoritized and marginalized scholars (Charity Hudley, 2020). To give one example, gatekeeping is deeply felt by linguists outside of theoretical paradigms like generative linguistics, and research that takes language as inextricable from the social bodies that produce it is often considered too interdisciplinary to be accepted by journals that focus on certain methods or subfields (Charity Hudley & Flores, 2022). At the same time, lack of critical attention on the nature of power in the academy and how it shapes scholarly interaction, whether in publication, in person, or on social media; perpetuates exclusion and marginalization within our field; and has resulted in conflicts where participants and onlookers alike are in disagreement on how linguists at different career stages should engage with one another. One thing is clear: the intersection of disciplinary rivalry with power hierarchies is detrimental to the field. This problem is not unique to linguistics, of course, as shown by recently documented issues in anthropology (Jobson, 2020), sociology (Meghji, 2020; 2021), and others. Regardless of the general nature of many of these issues, we as linguists must reckon with those issues. It is doubly important because how we address them impacts the way the field is perceived by the public.

In this chapter, we identify and reject disciplinary and social divisions as false dichotomies and a hindrance to the great potential of linguistics to have a positive impact on global society. We respond to the call in Anne Charity Hudley et al. (2020) to move from theory to action, informed by both past events and recent ones, such as those documented in Itamar Kastner et al. (2021; 2022). We identify and discuss three major sources of these problems within linguistics: exclusionary socialization, epistemic injustice, and unexamined power imbalances. These practices uphold an exclusionary version of our field, what we term "small tent linguistics," which is often better known to the public for its disputes than for its successes and core principles. The metaphor of a tent originates in political discourse to describe the restrictive or expansive nature of the backgrounds, viewpoints, and interests represented by a political party's members. We reject small tent linguistics and outline action-able ways to better achieve an inclusive big tent linguistics that welcomes and makes space for all. The goals of this chapter are, first, to make the discipline's hierarchies more visible and show linguists where they have influence to en-sure constructive professional interactions, and second, to invigorate linguists at all levels of training and professional development to feel empowered to make a positive impact on the field within their sphere of influence.

Part of doing thorough research is making our positionality explicit. This chapter has two authors: Rikker and Caitlin. Many of our experiences are sim-ilar: we are both white linguists of millennial age who grew up in predom-inantly English-monolingual households that valued learning a European second language. We are both the first in our families to earn a PhD degree, but we both come from households where our parents attended college or higher. We have benefitted from both whiteness and the class advantages entailed by having access to guidance by those who have navigated higher-education institutions before us. We have both been positioned as profes-sional, knowledgeable, and easy to work with because of language ideologies held by professional gatekeepers. We have also both experienced the jarring realization that our whiteness and class advantages have shielded us from scrutiny by a discursive environment that treats us as the default, and as a re-sult we have been energized by the examples of many colleagues to help seek out and foreground the expertise both of people who have worked toward a more equitable and inclusive linguistics and of those who would most benefit from achieving that goal.

Rikker

I earned my PhD in Linguistics at Yale University in 2019. I grew up in rural communities in the Pacific Northwest of the United States, which were predominantly white, politically conservative, and extremely Christian. I attended an Ivy League college in the Northeast United States, and spent about 10 of the past 20 years living in Thailand, with Thai as the primary lan-guage of my home life. Since completing my PhD I have taught in the linguis-tics department of an elite liberal arts college in the Northeast United States as a non–tenure-track (visiting) faculty member on time-limited contracts. As an undergraduate, I was in Anne Charity Hudley's first ever solo-taught course, so I had some excellent training in sociolinguistics early in my linguis-tics career, but it did not become my research focus, and my graduate program offered no formal training in sociolinguistics. I began to work on inclusion in linguistics toward the end of graduate school, and have co-authored papers on, e.g., gender representation in linguistic example sentences (Kotek et al., 2021) and on decolonizing the historical linguistics curriculum (Bowern & Dockum, 2024).

Caitlin

I earned my PhD in linguistics at University of California, Davis in 2018. I have always lived in middle-class, liberal, mostly white areas in or near large cities in the western half of the United States. My father funded his college education with military service, attending a combination of junior college and a small local college and graduating just before my birth. My mother attended various colleges off and on while working for an hourly wage, earning a bachelor's degree when I was four. Despite their early life experiences, my parents raised me with the expectation that I would be able to attend a high-ranking public university straight after high school without having to work full-time, which I did thanks to upward class mobility afforded them by their positionalities as educated white Americans. After graduate school, I chose not to pursue a career in higher education due to concerns about relocating and starting a family. Instead, I have been working as a teacher, an independent researcher and a public linguist specializing in discourse studies, pragmatics, and foreign language pedagogy. Having found some moderate success on social media, I try to use that platform as well as contributions to online publications to do public linguistics. I also use social media to connect with justice-oriented scholars and call attention to issues of equity.

We began collaborating in the aftermath of the 2020 Open Letter to the Linguistic Society of America, at first informally and then as part of a group of linguists exploring methods of correcting the public record and providing support to signatories impacted by public and private harassment. Deeply upset by the ways public scholars and media worked together to reproduce harmful discourses around fraught political concepts like "cancel culture" and to silence the fact-checking efforts of less prominent scholars, we began to consult on projects to address these (Kastner et al., 2021; 2022; Green, 2021; 2022). This led us to form theoretical explanations for what we were witnessing. We know that as signatories (but not authors) of the LSA open letter, and recipients of resulting abuse, we cannot see all angles of the events in question, but in the interest of political transparency (Clemons, 2024), we choose to take that closeness as motivation for finding ways to address the culture of exclusion, fractiousness and abuse of power that we have witnessed. We are limited in our search for avenues for justice by our own imaginations: we can only conceptualize the kinds of social changes that are allowed by our own epistemologies. Similarly, while we might be able to imagine sweeping systemic changes, we are focusing on the kinds of decisions that people can make in their own individual practice.

Exclusionary Socialization: The Myth of the Lone Genius in Linguistics

Like many other academic disciplines, linguistics has suffered from ill effects of the myth of the lone genius, which is a variation of Great Man theory. The Great Man approach to history, popularized by Thomas Carlyle in the nineteenth century, considers progress to be the result of actions by a sequence of individual heroes (Sorensen & Kinser, 2013). This paradigm privileges wealthy white men who have been the primary recipients of formal education and professional opportunities and accepts as valid the values of the white supremacist heteropatriarchy in which it is situated (Lerner, 1975). The great man is to historical leaders as the "lone genius" is to scholars: it is the idea that great academic discoveries are each attributable to one incredibly brilliant person, someone like Albert Einstein or Aristotle. Laura C. Ball (2012) notes that narrativizing the development of the discipline in the form of a chronological list of scholars is a common pedagogical tool. For some students, learning about the lives of the field's geniuses allows them to see themselves, their interests, and their struggles in the story of the people described. But for so many others who pass through our classrooms, departments, and degree programs, the parade of lone (predominantly white, male, abled, American/European, cisgender, straight) geniuses held up as representatives of the field is as alienating a picture of linguistics as it is incomplete. Most importantly, for all of our students, from those who will pursue careers in linguistics to those taking only a single course and everyone in between, the myth of the lone genius socializes them to buy into and perpetuate the false notion that scholarly progress is led by individual geniuses rather than by and with communities. It also discourages them from seeking help when they need it, as they may become convinced that their worthiness to be a scholar depends on their ability to do it alone (Nobel Prize Outreach, 2022). A tentpole of the big tent approach, in contrast, is that linguistics, just like language itself, is a team effort.

The myth of the lone genius means treating linguistics as a ladder with a genius on each rung leading from the dark ages of early linguistic writing into an enlightened "modern linguistics." This thinking is mired in Western chauvinism, Eurocentrism, scientific racism, and prejudiced language ideologies masquerading as objective facts. Treating our discipline this way reinforces colonialist perceptions that the history of an academic discipline is a series of forward leaps bringing us from an irrational past into a rational, empirical, and enlightened present. Discourses that assume rationality and science as the domain of Western whiteness have been critically investigated in many fields, including cultural studies (e.g., Quijano, 2007) and education (e.g., Ideland, 2018). This issue is rarely addressed in linguistics (but see Clemons, 2024). Continuing to promote the myth of the lone genius imbues each genius of our discipline with a halo of rationality, casting the marginalized voices that might disagree with him as irrational by contrast. It also exposes us to the danger of considering our field to be finished with making social progress, since identifying weaknesses or shortcomings in linguistics or its theories threatens the mythological progress already brought about by recent geniuses. One way that this danger exhibits itself is in declarations that the removal of bias and discrimination from our work has already been sufficiently accomplished. Another frequent variation is when well-meaning linguists, upon hearing calls for greater inclusion and justice in the field, defensively cite more inclusive subfields as if to suggest that we can stop there.

Tying ideas in our field so tightly to individuals can also make critiquing or rejecting their work or their behavior feel equivalent to rejecting that figure personally, and because many prominent figures in linguistics are still alive, and because we live in the age of television, online media, and social media, they can continue to "manage their brand" and respond to criticism using multiple wide-reaching platforms that their critics may simply not have access to. In some cases, the lone geniuses of linguistics may even have attained celebrity status, often both within and outside of academia, which brings with it fans who can be summoned to defend them or who volunteer to do so on their own. Prominent linguists who claim the mantle of public scholar especially present such a problem, as their reach extends far beyond the linguistics community in which they ground their epistemic authority. They cross a strange threshold from lone genius academic into a public brand, whose reputation must be actively and constantly defended (Kastner et al., 2021). This situation further reinforces the ideology that the best ideas are those with the best publicity, while limiting the privilege of publicity to only those ideas that resemble those already voiced by the most famous "geniuses."

A significant factor in the exclusionary nature of linguistics research and teaching is linguists' tendency to place ourselves on tracks modeled after and credited to famous lone genius figures. The greater the figures associated with your particular research interest, and the closer your academic lineage is to them, the more prestige your work (and by extension, you) will garner. The past—and present—of linguistics is filled with such figures (see Thomas, 2024), yet when scholars in other disciplines were questioning this tendency at the end of the twentieth century, linguists were not doing the same regarding our best-known lone genius characters (Ayres-Bennett & Sanson, 2020a). These men are often granted monikers like "Father of (Modern) Linguistics." Men referred to this way include Noam Chomsky (e.g., Shenker, 1971; Fox, 1998; O'Regan, 2013), Edward Sapir (Britton, 1972), Roman Jakobson (Harvard Crimson Staff, 1982; Boudraa et al., 2008), Ferdinand de Saussure (e.g., Lepschy, 1975; Pilcher & Richards, 2022), William Jones (e.g., Cannon, 1990; Singh, 2017), and Pāṇini (e.g., Bod, 2013; Karsten, 2011). No linguist has ever been referred to as the "Mother of (Modern) Linguistics" with any frequency that permits detection. Rather, the phrase "Mother of Linguistics" has been used exclusively for abstractions, including academic disciplines, such as semiotics (Barnstone, 1993) or psychology (Chomsky, 2004), a language, especially Sanskrit (Kidwai, 2015), or a country, such as India (Bhuvaneswar, 2020).

It is no accident that some of the most prominent recent "lone geniuses," especially starting in the mid-twentieth century, focused their work in formal linguistic theory: "As linguistics becomes institutionalized, notably in the mid-twentieth century with the work of the American structuralists, the crystallization of the definition of linguistics as the 'scientific study of language' means that the focus narrows to particular approaches to language study which favour a canon of male figures holding academic posts" (Ayres-Bennet & Sanson, 2020a, p. 5). This epistemological narrowing coincided with an influx of funds from the US military, which added to the prestige and power of formal theoretical lines of inquiry (Martin-Nielsen, 2012; Hutton, 2019). This injection of funding and attention created a center of gravity of funding and plaudits that drew linguists to work on the questions of the most interest to well-funded and prestigious academics and universities and to the US government, contributing to a sense that other approaches to linguistics were less valuable and, by extension, less rigorous.

One manifestation of this narrowing of the field is in what the unmodified term "linguistics" includes and excludes. As more linguistics departments started to appear in the twentieth century, domains that were once integral to linguistics stayed in other departments. The notion of the "core" areas of linguistics that emerged in this era represented a clear shrinking of the tent. Much human-focused and culturally focused work, rebranded as "linguistic anthropology," "anthropological linguistics," or "ethnography of communication," remained in longstanding anthropology departments. The field of applied linguistics established itself as a reaction to this narrowing definition (Davies & Elder, 2004), becoming home to the study of discourse and conversation analysis, language pedagogy, second language acquisition, language planning, speech-language pathology, and more. Linguistics and sociology diverged in the same period, with sociology of language mainly being pushed into the latter field—a divide that still persists (Mallinson, 2009). Evidence of this narrowing is also found in which types of linguistics are represented by the tenure lines of linguistics PhD programs, by which types they continue to hire, and by their required courses. For far too many linguists, "linguistics" became mutually exclusive with social and "applied" research so that other linguists often spent their whole careers hearing their work dismissed as "not (real) linguistics" (Charity Hudley & Flores, 2022; Lanehart, 2021). That narrow view, now increasingly seen as counterproductive, has proved difficult to undo (Ayres-Bennett & Sanson, 2020a; Charity Hudley, 2020; Eckert & Inkelas, 2018). It is quite the irony that linguists struggle to reject linguistic and scholarly prescriptivism around the term "linguistics" itself.

Feminist history has a long history of discussing how to treat marginalized figures in the field's metadiscourse. Gerda Lerner (1975) shows that thinking about marginalized figures in history tends to follow a similar progression: first, exceptional individuals from marginalized backgrounds are celebrated. However, as Wendy Ayres-Bennett and Helena Sanson (2020a) note, "the danger associated with this approach is that it may result in overshadowing the experience of those who could not escape exceptionality because of a number of limitations, including not least social class" (p. 1). For example, seventeenth-century intellectual Anna Maria van Schurman is known for her writings on language (McLelland, 2020). She was the first woman to attend a Dutch university, a groundbreaking achievement that she was able to negotiate thanks in part to her elevated class and social connections. Spotlighting her life and work brings important attention to the existence of women as analysts of language throughout history, but it is just as important to remember and highlight the stories of women who are marginalized not only by gender but also by race, class, and other social forces. In the next step in Lerner's progression, "contribution history" focuses on the contributions that the less-celebrated have made to the work of others, an approach which continues to reinforce the hegemonic perspective as the measure of value. Nicola McLelland describes the treatment of women translators in seventeenth-century Germany, whose work involved considerable linguistic analysis but which textbooks and historians treat as simplistic, and even dismiss it as a hobby rather than the scholarly pursuit it was. Lerner argues that women—and, we would add, by extension all marginalized groups—should be recognized as operating within an unequal hierarchical frame but on their own terms, so that their work is not devalued when it differs from hegemonic scholarly views. If we hope to reverse this course, we must own up to the fact that since its inception, "modern linguistics" has been exclusionary, quite literally by definition.

Epistemic Injustice: The Outsized Influence of Small Tent Linguistics

The potential for linguistics to contribute to social good in the mid-twentieth century was more limited than it is today. The field was too young, too white, too narrowly focused too paternalistic, too deeply rooted in unexamined colonialism and racism. The fights were too fierce, the borders too strong. Linguistics had certainly not matured enough then, and some may argue it still has not. We argue that today the potential for linguistics to be a force for good in the world is vastly increased, yet still largely unrealized. A key factor preventing this realization is epistemic injustice (Dotson, 2012; Fricker, 2007). The concept of epistemic injustice highlights that someone can be wronged or undermined in their capacity as a knower, and in their way of arriving at knowledge. Epistemic injustice is an attack on marginalized people's status as linguists and shuts off avenues for them to be full participants in the study of language.

Epistemic injustice can come in the form of overvaluing the work done at one institution at the expense of others, and by extension, only giving resources and respect to the academic lineages of a limited set of scholars. In a study of hiring practices of linguistics departments that offer PhD programs, Jason D. Haugen et al. (forthcoming) show that "market share" of job placements is distributed very unevenly across departments. Of 733 full-time permanent positions in the United States and Canada, Massachusetts Institute of Technology placed 87, or 11.9%. The next highest program is University of Massachusetts, Amherst with 49 (6.7%). The third highest, University of California, Berkeley, placed 47 (6.4%), meaning that fully 25% of all permanent linguistics faculty positions in the United States and Canada were trained in these three departments. It bears repeating that linguistics is not unique in this regard, as the Haugen et al. study was itself inspired by studies on hiring trends in archaeology (Speakman et al., 2018) and anthropology (Kawa et al., 2019; Speakman et al., 2018). The field has not yet had a widespread reckoning with how this imbalance has been impacting hiring pipelines for decades and contributing to the outsized influence of a small number of departments and researchers.

Departments obviously change their membership over time, but given that a faculty member can spend three decades or more in a department, and considering the diminishing supply of tenure-track positions in favor of precarious employment and casualization (Brenn & Magness, 2018; AAUP, 2020; Los Angeles Times Editorial Board, 2021), we argue that there is no way that a field so small and so lopsided in theoretical and methodological approaches can currently be considered inclusive or representative of much beyond the interests of a small contingent of disproportionately white, male, Anglophone linguists and their academic progeny, who graduated from a small number of departments and study a relatively narrow range of topics.

At the same time, the unfounded and harmful belief among some linguists that to produce a "rigorous" account of a community's language, one should be an "objective" community outsider, has created conditions where the people most qualified to describe the community—its members—have regularly been deprived of the opportunity to do so. Scholars who refuse to divorce language from the bodies and communities that produce it have been devalued and discouraged from their work (Charity Hudley & Flores, 2022). Many communities have a history of negative encounters with outside linguists and view us with well-earned suspicion, meaning much reclamation and documentation work simply never gets done, or what does get done is exploitative (see Gregory, 2021 for one such cautionary tale). The work of Indigenous linguists and others with training in anthropology and ethnography can show us how to produce high-quality research while advancing and prioritizing community perspectives (e.g., Leonard, 2018; Tsikewa, 2021). Furthermore, the casual erasure of signed languages continues to plague our field (Henner & Robinson, 2021a; see also Hou & Ali, this volume); if we cannot adequately represent signing in our analyses, we will continue to see troubling public misconceptions, such as that signed languages are not full languages, that they are simply pantomime or iconic representations of spoken languages, or that all signed languages are mutually intelligible. Instead, the practical linguistic needs of minoritized and endangered language communities have almost always come second to perceived scientific and pedagogical value or the career value to linguists (Henner & Robinson, 2021a, 2021b; Hochgesang, 2019; Flores, 2020; Keicho, 2021; see also Henner, this volume).

To be maximally clear: whether or not you personally value or agree with the work of any given cult figure in our field is beside the point of this chapter. We do not argue for dismissing their work. Rather, we ask you to recognize that the linguists who disproportionately represent our field have always carried out their research within their own political frames, and thus a linguistics that perpetuates the propping up of a small number of voices is inherently flawed (see also Clemons, 2024). We need to abandon pretensions to being above or outside of politics and think about our impact as researchers, as members of an academic community, as workers, as mentors, as ambassadors for our field. Linguistics can take as a model Ryan Cecil Jobson (2020), who makes the case for "letting anthropology burn," identifying academic discourses of "moral perfectibility" and liberal humanism as insufficient in creating work that combats existential threats of climate change and authoritarianism. We must let small tent linguistics—the idealized, unrealizable concept of linguistics as a disembodied pursuit by naturally superior minds—burn, or risk continuing to ice out scholars we should be welcoming with respect and joy. Research and the communication thereof, as human activities, cannot be divorced from the structural inequities that humans create, and these inequities must be acknowledged for us to be able to see beyond them to lift up the contributions of people who are not traditionally seen as candidates for lone genius cult figure status.

As the present volumes illustrate, a growing body of linguists are working toward making these visions for our field into a reality. Another recent example of positive improvement is the renewed interest in how our teaching and publishing perpetuate gender stereotypes and bias (Cépeda et al., 2021; Kotek et al., 2021, both building on Macaulay & Brice, 1997). Linguists have also frequently raised the issue of citational injustice, a pattern in which minoritized scholars are not cited in an equitable share (Charity Hudley & Flores, 2022; Charity Hudley et al., 2024). We should document and discuss how citational injustice affects various groups as has been done for gender in sociology (King et al , 2017), physics (Teich et al., 2022), astronomy (Caplar et al., 2017), neuroscience (Dworkin et al., 2020), psychology (Hill, 2019), and other fields. In a recent statement, the American Psychological Association acknowledged and apologized for how scholars and gatekeepers in psychology appraise, train, and reward only limited knowledge production, and how psychologists have harmed the research participants on whom their work relies (APA, 2021). Linguistics would benefit from similar investigations and apologies, as well as reparations and restorative justice.

Linguists who fight for a more just and equitable linguistics, who are not a homogeneous group but skew younger and more junior in rank, have faced an evolving range of criticisms for their efforts, everything from "political correctness" to "wokism" to "illiberalism" to "cultural Marxism" and "cancel culture" (see discussion in Kastner et al., 2021). Those who engage in liberatory linguistics are told that their work is not "real" linguistics because it does not resemble the work of the lone geniuses (Charity Hudley & Flores, 2022; Lanehart, 2021). It is interesting to note, then, how the history of modern linguistics has ties to the 1960s US counterculture. Even as formal theoretical approaches were reshaping the field, US military and intelligence agencies were finding ways to use formal linguistics to strengthen the power of the state (Hutton, 2019). Noam Chomsky became and remains a household name for his reputation as a left-wing political dissident, ultimately authoring many dozens more books on politics than he has on linguistics. Many of today's elder US linguists were youths of this counterculture of the 1960s and 1970s who came of age during a period of historic turmoil and social progress. They may feel as though they are under uncomfortable scrutiny within linguistics, are not given the benefit of the doubt by younger scholars, and are at risk of being publicly criticized for any gaffe. Nevertheless, it is the nature of social progress that unless a person's views evolve, they may very well go from being progressive to conservative in the course of their adult life. Without necessarily having changed, their opinions may come to be viewed by society as regressive, even bigoted, and even debunked by the very academic disciplines that formerly supported those views. Add to that new methods for accountability in the form of democratized publishing and social media, and the perception of amplified risk for senior scholars is understandable. However, this trepidation is also constantly exaggerated and used to whip up outrage (e.g., Clark, 2020; Green, 2022; Kastner et al., 2021). Both participants and onlookers in any conflict around making linguistics more inclusive should be conscious of the current debate regarding "cancel culture" and "free speech." These are volatile issues that are often weaponized by those with the most power (Clark, 2020) and that extend well beyond the boundaries of our profession (Norris, 2021), taking on aspects of a moral panic (Ng, 2020; Sailofsky, 2022). We should resist reinforcing those toxic discourses, which only serve to exacerbate the damage done to the careers and well-being of less powerful scholars, keeping the tent small.

It is important to bear in mind that youth-centric movements pushing for change against the status quo by their very nature will always be alienating or offensive to some in older generations. It takes real work to continue to learn and grow with a changing society. For that reason, rather than being criticized, dismissed, or simply ignored, the activist energy of linguists who make the time to do that work and share it with the field is an invaluable resource that needs to be supported and amplified by senior linguists.

For some of our most prominent linguists, who perhaps even grew up supporting their own youthful ideals in the 1960s and 1970s counterculture, a different kind of political activism now holds the greater allure (see also miles-hercules, this volume). These champions of the status quo, branding themselves as brave truth-tellers in the face of an "intolerant orthodoxy," are still de facto representatives of the field and regularly appear in some of the largest media outlets on the planet.

How can we improve this state of affairs? One way is to democratize access to linguistics research methods and findings, especially those with practical applicability beyond academia. This could mean creating or identifying outlets that allow for the dissemination of work to communities that most need it (cf. Villarreal & Collister, 2024). This includes anyone heavily involved in language work who is less likely to identify as a linguist: teachers, podcasters, journalists, public relations and marketing professionals, and more (cf. Gawne et al., this volume; Plackowski, this volume; Figueroa, 2022). Linguists would benefit from a linguistics-specific outlet similar to *Nature*, *Science*, and *Smithsonian Magazine* to communicate with the public so that when harmful language ideologies are promoted in high-profile places, we have a public-facing venue to tell people that the popular line is not right, while also diffusing the influence of the top two or three prominent names, who tend to be the first invited to comment or give interviews on language-related topics. Even without such an outlet, as linguists we need to be more strategic in how we share our expertise in news and other media contexts. There are already good examples to look toward. When in the midst of a global pandemic involving an airborne virus, a significant part of the United States was arguing for children to forgo wearing masks due to misplaced concerns about their language development, Megan Figueroa spoke with an Arizona radio journalist to correct this misinformation (Gilger, 2022). When public discourse about "cancel culture" was weaponized against the left, Nicole Holliday spoke about it to the NPR show *Consider This* (National Public Radio, 2021). When the most famous linguists in the US were spreading misconceptions about slurs, denying the very concept that words might have a material effect on their recipients, mainstream outlets were not receptive to counternarratives. Instead, Caitlin appeared on the politics podcast *Polite Conversations* (Mohammed-Smith, 2021) to explain the most commonly adopted semantic and pragmatic theories regarding the effects of slurs, and distributed the same arguments in text form as a blog post (Green, 2021). Linguists should reach out to media outlets as much as possible and work together to raise the profile of those doing liberatory linguistics, despite the structures that work to prevent liberatory messages from reaching mainstream outlets.

Power Imbalances in Linguistics: Making the Hierarchy Visible

To illustrate the ways in which power, civility norms, and disciplinary fractiousness have caused dysfunction in our discipline, in this section we present a composite case study (Willis, 2019). A composite case study is a narrative in which elements of multiple separate events are woven together to create a coherent story, with general applicability beyond the specific incidents, without drawing further undesirable attention to those involved. Readers may recognize elements of this case study from recent public conflicts involving Steven Pinker, John McWhorter, Noam Chomsky, Daniel Everett, and other publicly prominent linguists, but the details are a compilation of several events. Quotes are invented or paraphrased but convey the general message and tone of real statements made by participants in the original interactions.

One goal of presenting this case study is precisely to draw attention to the fact that there will be future incidents of this kind, and it is important both to recognize how they reflect on the field and to be prepared to handle them appropriately in the future. We were both involved in some of these events, and therefore complete partiality is not a reasonable expectation. The details are represented as accurately as possible in honor of the larger goal of justice.

We present here the case of a famous academic, whom we call Big Linguist, who is well known for his scholarly work as well as his popular science writing. Big Linguist is a tenured professor at one of the most influential institutions in the world. He recently made disparaging remarks about what he called "gendered language," taking shots at singular *they* and other nonbinary language, sometimes in ways which struck audiences as racially insensitive or dead on racist. He made these comments to his nearly one million followers, most of whom were not linguists, as well as in his radio programs, and he even wrote up a blog post complaining about nonbinary language in the guise of linguistic analysis, critiquing its proponents for their "bustling wokeness" (see also miles-hercules, this volume; Zimman & Brown, this volume).

When an anonymous group of presumably junior linguists arrived at the conclusion that Big Linguist should no longer be treated as a spokesperson for the field, they solicited support for this view in the form of signatures to an open letter calling for some small professional consequences for his history of misrepresenting current issues in linguistics. Graduate student Lilly tweeted that she "can't stand" Big Linguist, referring to his work, which she considered culturally chauvinistic and lacking in anthropological rigor. This remark prompted a securely employed linguist to comment on her tweet from an account associated with his research lab, asserting that it was inappropriate to speak this way about a serious scholar such as Big Linguist. A close associate of the disapproving linguist took this comment and quote-tweeted it, recirculating it to her own followers, while using the opportunity to further chastise Lilly. In this new stream, Lilly no longer received notifications when linguists said something about her. Linguists began threads on Facebook discussing Lilly's behavior on social media. When some linguists suggested that the tweets about Lilly amounted to harassment, one tenured professor asked, "How was it harassment to inform her that she'd been uncivil? If you tweet something mean, it's you who are in the wrong, not people who inform you of such." Because the primary political frame by which we interpret academic conflict is "free speech" (Green, 2022; Scott, 2017f), the conversation inevitably centered itself around this frame: "Do students have the freedom to say anything they want just because they are supposedly less powerful? Do securely employed scholars have no intellectual freedom because their insights might hurt the feelings of someone below them on the ladder?" Emotions ran high, and those who had defended Lilly were called childish and entitled. Her statement was exaggerated in the retelling, and several participants minimized the senior scholars' admonitions as mere disagreements.

When Big Linguist became aware of the open letter, he wrote a social media post that the letter seemed like a satire on "woke" irrationality and that such incidents of "cancel culture" were a threat to academic freedom, even to science itself. He shared the letter, along with the list of signatories, with his followers. Other household names and prominent academics outside of linguistics became involved, using inflammatory language describing the signatories as "illiberal" "monsters," "barbaric hordes" who "would seem at home in Maoist struggle sessions." Big Linguist himself insisted that the signatories were "a bunch of jealous nobodies" who seemed like they had "a screw loose," though the signatory list in reality included many of his peers at all levels of seniority. Others questioned the legitimacy of the signatory list, and some trolls signed the list with fake names or falsely signed the list with someone else's name. Big Linguist was interviewed by major news outlets about the "traumatic" experience. "I'm Being Attacked By Woke Big Brother," read one headline. Opinion writers and journalists weighed in with comments like, "His academic achievements insulate him from the dangers of cancel culture, but you won't be so lucky when the mob comes for you." When readers who knew the stories were factually incorrect attempted to alert the journalists, they were met with mockery; one responded to factual corrections by a signatory by saying, "You'd better hope none of your colleagues dig through your old tweets and find something they can use to get you in trouble based on skewed interpretations of what you said." No signatories were able to get their side of the story told in major media outlets—when Big Linguist has something to say, the media can make room, but the same is not true for some random "nobody"—so they resorted to self-publishing their counterarguments.

The letter's signatories, including Lilly, were criticized for their lack of civility, while the incivility of the securely employed and celebrity linguists was not questioned despite its much larger impact. Big Linguist was cast as the victim of baseless ad hominem attacks no matter how many factual arguments the signatories made, while he and his allies used as many hateful names as they wished without significant pushback and with no negative consequences.

What can we learn from the experiences of Lilly and the signatories? We reflect on this composite case study in the context of the recommendations we have made in previous sections. Assumptions about the types of discourses that can take place on social media should be re-examined. For some, social media is a place to share and discuss professional linguistic work only. For others, it is a place to be a social individual without having to be professional. For others still, it is both (Chugh et al., 2021). When expectations are misaligned on this dimension, misunderstandings and even damaged relationships can result. For too many, it is assumed that social media is necessarily and naturally a place where bullying and insults take place, and where attempts to engage in deeper conversation will be fruitless, and that this reality should therefore be expected and accepted. We should refuse to accept this view, both by avoiding participation in discourses that reinforce animosity within the field, and by actively trying to shape the norms of acceptable online discourse in just the same way we would in the halls of our campus buildings or in our classrooms.

We should also be conscious that the power to set the frame for discussing conflicts belongs to those with the most to protect and be mindful that academic work involves not only arguing for the relevance and correctness of our research, but also fostering a culture in which those we work with are able to engage constructively and healthily. One of the troubling aspects of Lilly's treatment was that the more powerful figures who expressed disapproval of her conduct were not conscious of the ways in which an individual's vulnerability is magnified when the audience is shifted from that individual to all members of a social media platform. More consideration and explicit discussion of the mechanics and pragmatics of social media use are needed to reduce such incidents, and to provide onlookers with the tools to identify and critically discuss them when they do.

Moreover, those who objected to the language used by Lilly and the signatories were interested in directing them toward "playing the game" the way they expect it to be played, rather than interrogating (working to change) the ways in which "the game" is unfair. The content of Lilly's critiques of Big Linguist were ignored for several reasons: the reverence some feel for Big Linguist, Lilly's informal language in formulating the critique, and the fact that her arguments came from one side of the formal/functional false binary, while Big Linguist's work was more focused on the other side. When we see someone critiquing the lone geniuses or so-called fathers of our subfields, even in a way that seems impolite, we have to resist the urge to police them on grounds of civility. And when we see someone with institutional or cultural power bringing negative attention to a junior, we have to stand in solidarity with that junior scholar and defend their right to belong. A big tent linguistics should recognize that a well-rounded and well-argued linguistic analysis should involve considerations from multiple perspectives in order to avoid the pitfalls and assumptions that can hamper each.

Senior scholars often object to the communication styles of their juniors, but they are not always consistent in how they justify their objections. In an interview for *the Chronicle of Higher Education*, David Bromwich joined a chorus of respected senior academics who fundamentally misunderstand the challenge facing young scholars. He recalled, "A student said, 'I want to piggyback on what Raymond just said, and add . . .' But what he was adding was *the exact opposite* of what Raymond just said. So, if you're saying the opposite, you still have to say it in the grammar of agreement" (Gutkin, 2022). In a conversation about students being afraid to disagree with each other, Bromwich provides an example in which a student easily disagrees with another, but objects to the way he framed his disagreement. At the same time, his interview does not consider the ways that early career researchers and minoritized scholars are policed by people like himself, those with institutional power. Lilly stated her criticism boldly, just the way Bromwich wishes his students would, and she was harshly criticized in public by her seniors. How can students' politeness strategies possibly compare to the effects of knowing that your professors might unite against you should you choose to report a serial sexual harasser for his crimes, as a group of Harvard professors did (Anthropologists, 2022)? Or that they might suddenly choose to rescind your honors and degree after being contacted by your abuser (Aviv, 2022)? Or the fear that your name and contact information could be listed by a conservative watchdog group, resulting in harassment and even threats (Green, 2022; Tiede et al., 2021), and that that group's materials might even be shared by respected academics even as they argue that it is progressive students who create a chilling effect on free speech in academia (e.g., John McWhorter as cited in Friedersdorf, 2020)? Is it really more important that we encourage our students to use fewer face-threat mitigation strategies, or that we take opportunities to proactively affirm our dedication to promoting psychologically and physically healthy environments in which to engage in knowledge production?

Creating opportunities to reduce the salience of professional hierarchies in students' day-to-day life would do more to reduce student discomfort than chiding them for their politeness strategies (Green, 2018). We should consider the ways in which a standard of civility, unevenly applied, is often a tool to reinforce power imbalances rather than one which encourages collegiality (hooks, 1991; Itagaki, 2021; Zamalin, 2022). Simply questioning the reasons behind norms or hegemonic discourses can be seen as disruptive, a threat to the status quo which requires correction, regardless of the style or politeness strategies involved in that questioning. Conventionalized politeness practices should not be confused with true civility, which we understand as actions undertaken to improve the ethical and professional practices of linguistics and thus may be achieved through language not typically considered "civil" by established members at the top of the professional hierarchy. The Linguistic Society of America (LSA) has a policy on civility in its annual meetings and sponsored events (LSA, 2017), which notably focuses on discrimination and harassment rather than any particular concept of politeness. We ought to continue to develop our position on civility in more detail, as power disparities are exacerbated by unexamined ideologies around civility due to the hypervisibility and therefore overpolicing of minoritized scholars (Settles et al., 2019). Emotions such as anger and indignation in the face of systems of oppression or individual cruelty are important and valid, yet are often dismissed (Lorde, 1981; Srinivasan, 2018). As such, minoritized scholars advocating for their own rights and dignity are often denied, in what Koritha Mitchell calls an act of "know-your-place aggression" (Mitchell, 2018). The repression of this questioning and advocacy on the basis of tone will not bring us closer to either a just field or a just world.

The insistence on suppressing critique in order to preserve the existing hierarchy, often expressed as "civility," presented itself in public discussion on the LSA website regarding a proposal by a group of 10 scholars to adopt a lightly modified version of the controversial Chicago Principles of Freedom of Expression (Stone et al., 2015). The Chicago Principles have been criticized as overly vague, as protecting the "rights" of nonminoritized, securely employed scholars to promote unfounded and potentially anti-justice views at the expense of less powerful researchers, and as playing into a moral panic that supports political efforts to weaken higher education as a public good (Ben-Porath, 2018). The majority of comments posted on the website in response to the proposal were critical, and virtually all comments focused on the content of the arguments presented and their relevant context. Outside of the LSA website, critical comments were similarly focused on these issues (e.g., Fruehwald, 2022; Stickles, 2022). Despite a clear lack of ad hominem or defamatory comments toward those who had proposed the resolution, they nonetheless began their own response by saying they would reply "in the interest of constructive debate, to what we take to be the main substantive objections and questions raised, at a length that the resolution format itself did not permit (while disregarding comments that we take to be ad hominem and/or defamatory)" (Patel-Grosz et al., 2022). By claiming that there had been personal attacks, the group used "civility" as a cover for shifting the discourse away from critiques that are difficult to answer on the merits. Civility is also a way to sneak in uncivil ideas under the cloak of politeness: the signatories to the proposal state that they "support the LSA's work on making the field more inclusive, and do not see such inclusivity work to be in conflict with the expression of controversial ideas where such ideas are expressed in a civil and professional manner." As several LSA members had pointed out in their comments on the proposal, the academic terrain is littered with long-debunked ideas that rest on bigoted logics, whose defenders insist on relitigating them despite their lack of evidentiary support. Very often they do so under the auspices of precisely this argument: that the expression of so-called controversial ideas is a cornerstone of any organization that values freedom, and that any idea is acceptable if it is delivered with all the trappings of professionalism. The LSA Executive Committee opened the proposal up for public comment and found that there was strong opposition. The Executive Committee eventually withdrew the matter and it was not put to a vote by the membership, indicating that speaking out against policies that perpetuate injustice can be effective.

Conclusion: A Way Forward

In this chapter we have identified and examined three major sources of inclusion problems in linguistics: exclusionary socialization, epistemic injustice, and unexamined power imbalances. In order to move forward, we urge all who consider ourselves part of the linguistics community to rethink and update our socialized norms at all career stages, as a way to help reshape the field into one where we achieve "ambient belonging" for scholars of all backgrounds (Cheryan et al., 2009). The focus must be twofold: first, on reversing the narrowing of the field by adopting an inclusive definition for "linguist" and "linguistics" and by consciously creating a culture that recognizes the collaborative nature of research; and second, promoting discussion of ways for all linguists to evaluate our power and influence in order to act to increase inclusion towards the big tent linguistics we hope to build. Because this effort requires us to make systemic cultural changes within our field, every person has a role regardless of their level of experience or seniority. We all have different positions regarding our ability to effect change, but we all have the potential to contribute. As such, we briefly consider the variety of professional stages and positions within linguistics and examine how each stage offers you, the reader, opportunities for proactive inclusion. And since many of these ideas and resources apply to more than one career stage, we also encourage you to read through suggestions for all stages.

1) **Undergraduate students**, who study a linguistics curriculum. You may additionally occupy a role such as teaching assistant, writing tutor, or other peer mentor positions. You can offer feedback to your instructors, whether directly or in the form of course evaluations, on topics like equitable citation in course syllabi, or inclusion of signed languages in basic course materials. You can advocate for inclusive major requirements, such as requiring training in sociolinguistics, or for a selection of different major tracks, allowing greater flexibility for courses outside conventionally "core" subfields, to better serve the needs and interests of all students. You also have the opportunity to spread the message against everyday linguistic prejudice with your full networks of acquaintances, especially those who have never studied linguistics. The LingComm project, which includes events, advice, and grants about communicating linguistics to a wider audience, is one place to get started (McCulloch & Gawne, 2021). Similarly, you can follow podcasts like The Vocal Fries, social media accounts like @sunnmcheaux or @LaymansLinguist on TikTok, or YouTube channels like MikeMena or Crash Course Linguistics (Gawne et al., this volume).

2) **Graduate students**, who are taking steps toward professionalization in the field. In your role as students you can advocate to your instructors for topics such as citational justice and inclusive degree program design. You may also teach undergraduates or fellow graduate students and have the ability to build solidarity and provide positive mentorship in that sphere. You may start to participate in peer scholar interactions such as reviewing, publishing, and editing. You may run reading groups, organize speaker series, or plan conferences. These all present opportunities for inclusion advocacy. You can reach out to other students who have done these things, like the chairs of the Cluster on Language Research at University of California, Davis (Cluster on Language

Research, 2022). You can also seek and contribute to professionalization training from your department and help ensure that it covers inclusive topics, including career opportunities beyond academia. In departments where student representatives formally participate in faculty meetings, you have another avenue for advocacy and influence. Some resources to use as a starting point include books about navigating linguistics career paths like *Surviving Linguistics* (Macaulay, 2011) and *Employing Linguistics: Thinking and Talking About Careers for Linguists* (Trester, 2022).

3) **Non–tenure-track faculty** or **early career academics** who are in the (increasingly long) phase of nonpermanent employment, including postdoctoral researchers, adjunct and visiting professors, lecturers, and other temporary or part-time teaching positions. Although employment precarity is a serious obstacle to the large number of linguists at this stage, you may have significant teaching duties and influence within your sphere. Opportunities for influence arise as you design and teach courses, plan and run events, advise students, and more. You may also be active in research, bringing the opportunity to practice inclusion in your own writing, especially by lifting up junior and minoritized scholars by reading, citing, as well as teaching, their work. Teach students how to be critical of the hero status afforded those society treats as "lone geniuses." As a reviewer for conferences and journals, you can adopt a constructive view of the peer review process as one of peer support rather than gatekeeping. Be conscientious about building the field, while avoiding fractious pitfalls. It is also important for more senior and more stably employed academics to acknowledge that many early career linguists are in a state of constant employment precarity and therefore lack power in the field; they are in special need of mentorship and other support in this stage.

4) **Tenure-track faculty**, who though still professionally vulnerable, are entering a stage of increasing autonomy, stability, responsibility, and influence. Many of the opportunities in this stage mirror those of early career academics. In addition to opportunities for influence through teaching, course design, and other professional activities, you may increasingly oversee student research, apply for grant funding, run research labs, plan larger conferences, and take journal editorial roles. All of these provide opportunities to exert positive influence on the field. You may influence more inclusive representation among invited speakers at events. Your service responsibilities may also give you a voice in academic job searches and curriculum planning, which bring their own opportunities to strengthen the field. Make sure you are aware of the ethics of journal

editing (e.g., Committee on Public Ethics, 2022) and course design (e.g., Culver et al., 2021) to maximize your effectiveness. Look into ways to challenge dominant ideologies about pedagogy that might hamper a just teaching environment in your classroom by reading works like *Antisocial Language Teaching* (Gerald, 2022) from the field of English Language Teaching and finding ways to incorporate its lessons in other kinds of linguistics teaching.

5) **Tenured faculty,** who enjoy significant stability and increasing responsibility. You have opportunities for influence that mirror all those of your junior faculty colleagues. You are also likely in a position of greater influence within your department and may have substantial reputation and influence within your research areas or the field at large. You may be holding journal editorial positions, serving on grant review panels, leading job searches, or filling an administrative role in your department. You may have more freedom to steer your research towards issues that contribute to the greater good for both society and our field. At this career stage, you are also especially well situated to amplify the work and voices of junior and minoritized scholars, to implement better practices in your department, and to work with other linguists to make the field more inclusive. For inspiration in the classroom, look to projects like *Talking College* (Charity Hudley et al., 2022), and for inspiration in creating inclusive student research experiences, see guides like Charity Hudley et al. (2017).

6) **Full professors,** who are in a position of maximal stability and influence, which you may occupy for decades. You may serve as a department chair, lead influential committees, or occupy other executive roles within your university and the discipline. This stage presents perhaps the greatest opportunity to influence trends of socialization in the field, both structurally through administrative roles, but also often by acting as a role model to students and more junior scholars, as your work and name are often what draw in new students. For some, this might be a frustrating stage as you rise high enough in the decision-making ranks to see many of the limits on the influence that academics have within contemporary higher-education institutions, but you have all of the opportunities for influence that those at more junior stages have, and you can use the substantial power and influence you have for positive impact and listen to and amplify the voices of junior colleagues. It is important to become familiar with the various ways that academics can abuse their power, including undermining their victims' ability to seek justice (Keashly & Neuman, 2010; Mahmoudi, 2019; van Scherpenberg

et al., 2021). If you are contacted by another senior linguist asking you to defend them against a complaint of harassment or bullying, it is crucial that you not take their claims at face value and speak on their behalf in public—or private—without knowing the details of the case from all sides.

7) **Public linguists,** who are a very small group that wield a disproportionate influence on the public perception of linguistics. This group also includes linguists who engage with the general public on a large platform, whether in traditional media or social media. You are uniquely situated to influence public perception of our field for better or worse, because people in this group are often the only linguists known to the wider public, to leaders in industry, or to politicians in a position to influence public policy and control public grant programs. Maintain—or exercise, if atrophied—the humility to acknowledge that being a famous linguist does not qualify you as an expert in all aspects of linguistics, let alone on all public issues of the day. Be intentional about sharing opportunities to access large platforms with like-minded colleagues who do not typically have this access, such as suggesting other names when invited for media comment or appearances. Actively combat the myth of the lone genius by refusing to become a brand that defines you as synonymous with academic advancement. Name and credit linguists who are more junior and/or members of marginalized groups in your work, and advocate for the funding and public recognition of underappreciated kinds of linguistics.

8) **Linguists beyond academia,** who are employed (or hobbyists, or unemployed) in areas that involve discussing and working with language. This group includes the many linguists in tech or other industry roles, as well as speech-language pathologists, teachers, public relations and marketing professionals, journalists, and more. Take steps available to you to improve diversity in your workplace. Resist harmful language ideologies and participate in the implementation of liberatory linguistics in your sphere of influence. You can also become a member of organizations like the LSA, if you currently aren't, and exercise your voting rights to support officers who share these goals. Participating in social media with your linguist colleagues in academia may be another way for you to maintain your connections to the field, and help be a voice in support of justice.

Furthermore, it is important for our field to recognize that there are many who have chosen to leave academia at any stage, or who have received minimal or no formal training in linguistics, but who nonetheless identify as linguists and seek to be part of the linguistics community. We strongly assert that our field must be inclusive of those who do not follow the traditional academic path. We must consider how socialization in linguistics is relevant to adjacent academic disciplines, careers in industry, P-12 teaching, government, and beyond. We must also confront how the academic/nonacademic divide is yet another false dichotomy that has frequently been a source of exclusion. In part this false dichotomy can be addressed by committing ourselves to live by an inclusive definition of "linguist," like the one given by the LSA demographic data workgroup: "By 'linguist,' we mean people who have a graduate degree in Linguistics, as well as people who knowingly recruit knowledge of linguistics or teach linguistics as part of their profession, avocation, or advocacy work" (Brosselow et al., 2021).

All linguists have some power to challenge harmful discourses, and this responsibility must be undertaken by everyone to some degree. However, power differentials mean that different strategies are available to each person, and there are different consequences for challenging dominant discourses. To readers at all career stages, we invite you to consider your present positionality, your potential future career stages, and the influence—realized or unrealized—that you have on those in other stages, both earlier and later. We urge you to take action wherever you see exclusion and injustice to the extent that you safely can, given your structural and institutional positionality.

As we stated at the start of this chapter: linguistics has incredible potential for doing transformative good in society, and a big tent vision will enable us to better realize this potential. We hope that the preceding discussion will help to energize all linguists, in the inclusive definition, to identify ways that we can each contribute to achieving that potential, hand-in-hand with scientific and professional advancement. By rethinking our disciplinary norms, we will move beyond the small tent approach that linguistics has inhabited and which has prevented it from achieving the widespread understanding and appreciation by the general public that many other disciplines of study enjoy. Our field is changing, and it must continue to change. We each have a role in rehabilitating and resocializing it, to create an inclusive and just linguistics.

Note

1. Thank you to our co-authors on The Open Letter: Responses and Recommendations (Kastner et al., 2022): Itamar Kastner, Hadas Kotek, Michael Dow, Maria Esipova, Todd Snider, Elise Stickles, and anonymous author(s), for feedback on this chapter, and helping us

analyze these issues during a challenging moment. Thank you also to Aris Clemons, Anne Charity Hudley, Christine Mallinson, Mary Bucholtz, Colin Reilly, and Adina Williams for indispensable support and comments on drafts. Thank you to students in Advanced Research Methods Spring 2022 at Swarthmore College for thoughtful discussion on a draft. And thank you to the audience at NWAV50 at Stanford University, October 2022, both in-person and virtual, for valuable feedback on a talk based on this chapter.

References

American Association of University Professors. (2020). *The annual report on the economic status of the profession, 2019–20.* https://www.aaup.org/sites/default/files/2019-20_ARES.pdf

American Psychological Association. (2021). *Apology to people of color for APA's role in promoting, perpetuating, and failing to challenge racism, racial discrimination, and human hierarchy in U.S.* https://www.apa.org/about/policy/racism-apology

Anthropologists. (2022). Anthropologists' response to Harvard sexual harassment stories. https://docs.google.com/document/d/1GN0JAfqQ42rxmLOdZFA75sYJA0HleJBEv7E_olTcn-o/edit

Aviv, Rachel. (2022, March 28). How an Ivy League school turned against a student. *The New Yorker.* https://www.newyorker.com/magazine/2022/04/04/mackenzie-fierceton-rhodes-scholarship-university-of-pennsylvania

Ayres-Bennett, Wendy, & Sanson, Helena. (2020a). Women in the history of linguistics: Distant and neglected voices. In Wendy Ayres-Bennett & Helena Sanson (Eds.), *Women in the history of linguistics* (pp. 1–29). Oxford University Press.

Ayres-Bennett, Wendy, & Sanson, Helena. (Eds.). (2020b). *Women in the history of linguistics.* Oxford University Press.

Ball, Laura C. (2012). Genius without the "great man": New possibilities for the historian of psychology. *History of Psychology, 15*(1), 72–83. https://doi.org/10.1037/a0023247

Barnstone, Willis. (1993). *The poetics of translation: History, theory, practice.* Yale University Press.

Ben-Porath, Sigal. (2018, December 11). Against endorsing the Chicago principles. *Inside Higher Ed.* https://www.insidehighered.com/views/2018/12/11/what-chicago-principles-miss-when-it-comes-free-speech-and-academic-freedom-opinion

Bhuvaneswar, Chilukuri (2020). Towards de-colonization of ELT theory: A critique. *International Journal of Innovations in Liberal Arts, 1*(1). http://www.ijila.org/wp-content/uploads/2020/12/6-Towards-De-colonization-of-ELT-Theory-A-Critique.pdf

Bod, Rens. (2013). *A new history of the humanities: The search for principles and patterns from antiquity to the present* Oxford University Press.

Boudraa, Bachir, Boudraa, Malika, & Guerin, Bernard. (2008). Arabic diagnostic rhyme test using minimal pairs. *Journal of the Acoustical Society of America, 123*(5), 3324–3324. https://doi.org/10.1121/1.2933808

Bowern, Claire, & Dockum, Rikker. (2024). Decolonizing historical linguistics in the classroom and beyond. In Anne H. Charity Hudley, Christine Mallinson, & Mary Bucholtz (Eds.), *Decolonizing linguistics.* Oxford University Press.

Brennan, Jason, & Magness, Phillip. (2018). Estimating the cost of justice for adjuncts: A case study in university business ethics. *Journal of Business Ethics, 148*(1), 155–168. https://doi.org/10.1007/s10551-016-3013-1

Britton, James N. (1972). Writing to learn and learning to write. [Spoken lecture]. National Council of Teachers of English. Troy State University, Alabama.

Brosselow, Ellen, Orozco, Rafael, Narayan, Chandan, Grieser, Jessi, Syrett, Kristen, Mallinson, Christine, Salehi-Nejad, Alireza, Baese-Berk, Melissa, Salmons, Joe, Hanson, Aroline, Collister, Lauren, Ginsberg, Daniel, Reed, Alyson, Ananthanarayan, Sunny, & Pace, Emily. (2021). *Framework for LSA ad-Hoc Workgroup on demographic data in linguistics*. Linguistics Society of America. https://www.linguisticsociety.org/content/framework-lsa-ad-hoc-workgroup-demographic-data-linguistics

Cannon, Garland. (1990). *The life and mind of Oriental Jones: Sir William Jones, the father of modern linguistics*. Cambridge University Press.

Caplar, Neven, Tacchella, Sandro, & Birrer, Simon. (2017). Quantitative evaluation of gender bias in astronomical publications from citation counts. *Nature Astronomy, 1*(6) 1–5. https://doi.org/10.1038/s41550-017-0141"https://doi.org/10.1038/s41550-017-0141

Cépeda, Paola, Kotek, Hadas, Pabst, Katharina, & Syrett, Kristen. (2021). Gender bias in linguistics textbooks: Has anything changed since Macaulay & Brice 1997? *Language, 97*(4), 678–702. https://doi.org/10.1353/lan.2021.0061

Charity Hudley, Anne H. (2020). *Fostering a culture of racial inclusion in linguistics: For the children of the 9th ward circa 2005*. [Conference presentation]. 94th Annual Meeting of the Linguistics Society of America, New Orleans.

Charity Hudley, Anne H., Dickter, Cheryl L., & Franz, Hannah A. (2017). *The indispensable guide to undergraduate research: Success in and beyond college*. Teachers College Press.

Charity Hudley, Anne H., & Flores, Nelson. (2022). Social justice in applied linguistics: Not a conclusion, but a way forward. *Annual Review of Applied Linguistics, 42*, 144–154. https://doi.org/10.1017/S0267190522000083

Charity Hudley, Anne H., Mallinson, Christine, & Bucholtz, Mary. (2020). Toward racial justice in linguistics: Interdisciplinary insights into theorizing race in the discipline and diversifying the profession. *Language, 96*(4), 200–235. https://doi.org/10.1353/lan.2020.0074

Charity Hudley, Anne H., Mallinson, Christine, & Bucholtz, Mary. (2022). *Talking college: Making space for Black language practices in higher education*. Teachers College Press.

Charity Hudley, Anne H., Mallinson, Christine, Monét, Kahdeidra, Clemons, Aris Moreno, Randolph, L. J. Jr., Bucholtz, Mary, Calhoun, Kendra, Hankerson, Shenika, Peltier, Joy P. G., Thomas, Jamie A., McQuitty, Deana Lacy, & Seidel, Kara. (2024). Solidarity and collectivity in decolonizing linguistics: A Black Diasporic perspective. In Anne H. Charity Hudley, Christine Mallinson, & Mary Bucholtz (Eds.), *Decolonizing linguistics*. Oxford University Press.

Cheryan, Sapna, Plaut, Victoria C., Davies, Paul G., & Steele, Claude M. (2009). Ambient belonging: How stereotypical cues impact gender participation in computer science. *Journal of Personality and Social Psychology, 97*(6), 1045–1060. https://doi.org/10.1037/a0016239

Chomsky, Noam (2004). *The generative enterprise revisited*. Mouton de Gruyter.

Chugh, Ritesh, Grose, Robert, & Macht, Stephanie A. (2021). Social media usage by higher education academics: A scoping review of the literature. *Education and Information Technologies, 26*, 983–999. https://doi.org/10.1007/s10639-020-10288-z

Clark, Meredith D. (2020). DRAG THEM: A brief etymology of so-called "cancel culture." *Communication and the Public, 5*(3–4), 88–92. https://doi.org/10.1177/2057047320961562

Clemons, Aris Moreno. (2024). Apolitical linguistics doesn't exist, and it shouldn't: Developing a Black feminist praxis toward political transparency. In Anne H. Charity Hudley, Christine Mallinson, & Mary Bucholtz (Eds.), *Decolonizing linguistics*. Oxford University Press.

Cluster on Language Research. (2022). Cluster on language research at UC Davis. https://www.languagecluster.com/home

Committee on Publication Ethics. (2022). COPE: Committee on Publication Ethics. https://publicationethics.org/

Culver, K. C., Harper, Jordan, & Kezar, Adrianna. (2021). *Design for equity in higher education*. Pullias Center for Higher Education.

Davies, Alan, & Elder, Catherine. (2004). Applied linguistics: Subject to discipline? In Alan Davies & Catherine Elder (Eds.), *The Handbook of Applied Linguistics* (pp. 1–15). Wiley.

Dotson, Kristie. (2012). A cautionary tale: On limiting epistemic oppression. *Frontiers: A Journal of Women Studies*, *33*(1), 24–47. https://doi.org/10.5250/fronjwomestud.33.1.0024

Dworkin, Jordan D., Linn, Kristin A., Teich, Erin G., Zurn, Perry, Shinohara, Russell T., & Bassett, Danielle S. (2020) The extent and drivers of gender imbalance in neuroscience reference lists. *Nature Neuroscience*, *23*(8), 918–926. https://doi.org/10.1038/s41593-020-0658-y

Eckert, Penny & Inkelas, Sharon (2018). Our linguistics community: addressing bias, power dynamics, harassment. [Conference presentation]. 92nd Annual Meeting of the Linguistics Society of America, Salt Lake City. https://www.linguisticsociety.org/news/2018/01/11/our-linguistics-community-addressing-bias-power-dynamics-harassment

Figueroa, Megan. (2022). Podcasting past the paywall: How diverse media allows more equitable participation in linguistic science. *Annual Review of Applied Linguistics*, *42*, 40–46. https://doi.org/10.1017/S0267190521000118

Flores, Nelson. (2020). From academic language to language architecture: Challenging raciolinguistic ideologies in research and practice. *Theory Into Practice*, *59*(1), 22–31. https://doi.org/10.1080/00405841.2019.1665411

Fox, Margalit. (1998, December 5). A changed Noam Chomsky simplifies. *New York Times*.

Fricker, Miranda. (2007). *Epistemic injustice: Power and the ethics of knowing*. Oxford University Press.

Friedersdorf, Conor. (2020, September 21). The fight against words that sound like, but are not, slurs. *The Atlantic*. https://www.theatlantic.com/ideas/archive/2020/09/fight-against-words-sound-like-are-not-slurs/616404/

Fruehwald, Josef. (2022). What does "freedom" mean? *Medium*. https://medium.com/@JoFrhwld/what-does-freedom-mean-a4624e89dcf5

Gerald, J. P. B. (2022). *Antisocial language teaching: English and the pervasive pathology of whiteness*. Multilingual Matters.

Gilger, Lauren. (2022). Do masks delay language in little kids? This Arizona psycholinguist says no. *KJZZ 91.5 FM*. https://kjzz.org/content/1765870/do-masks-delay-language-little-kids-arizona-psycholinguist-says-no

Green, Caitlin M. (2018). *Toward increased retention in university computer science programs: A language socialization approach* [Doctoral Dissertation, University of California, Davis].

Green, Caitlin M. (2021). Beyond "mention vs. use": The linguistics of slurs. *Medium*. https://c-moriah-green.medium.com/beyond-mention-vs-use-the-linguistics-of-slurs-3e0bfff11c5d

Green, Caitlin M. (2022). Framing, stance, and discourses in reporting of political bias on college campuses [Conference presentation]. Annual Meeting of the Linguistics Society of America, January 6–9, 2022. Washington, DC.

Gregory, Alice. (2021, April 12). How did a self-taught linguist come to own an Indigenous language? *The New Yorker*. https://www.newyorker.com/magazine/2021/04/19/how-did-a-self-taught-linguist-come-to-own-an-indigenous-language

Gutkin, Len. (2022, March 15). "An elaborate new decorum has crept in": David Bromwich on politics, manners, and therapeutics. *Chronicle of Higher Education*. https://www.chronicle.com/article/an-elaborate-new-decorum-has-crept-in

Harris, Randy Allen. (1993). *The linguistics wars*. Oxford University Press.

Harris, Randy Allen. (2021). *The linguistics wars: Chomsky, Lakoff, and the battle over deep structure*. Oxford University Press.

Harvard Crimson Staff. (1982). Roman Jakobson to be honored as father of modern linguistics. https://www.thecrimson.com/article/1982/11/10/roman-jakobson-to-be-honored-as/

Haugen, Jason D., Margaris, Amy V., & Calvo, Sarah. (forthcoming). A snapshot of academic job placements in linguistics in the US and Canada. *Canadian Journal of Linguistics*.

Henner, Jon, & Robinson, Octavian. (2021a). Signs of oppression in the academy: The case of signed languages. In Gailynn Clements & Marnie jo Portray (Eds.), *Linguistic Discrimination in U.S. Higher Education* (pp. 92–109). Routledge.

Henner, Jon, & Robinson, Octavian. (2021b). Unsettling languages, unruly bodyminds: Imaging a crip linguistics.https://doi.org/10.31234/osf.io/7bzaw

Hill, Darryl B (2019). Androcentrism and the Great Man Narrative in Psychology Textbooks: The Case of Ivan Pavlov. *Journal of Research in Gender Studies, 9*(1), 9–37.

Hochgesang, Julie A. (2019). *Inclusion of Deaf linguists and signed language linguistics* [Invited Panel Presentation]. Georgetown University Roundtable (GURT) 2019: Linguistics and the Public Good, Georgetown University, Washington, DC. https://linguistics.georgetown.edu/research/round-table/

hooks, bell. (1991). Theory as liberatory practice. *Yale Journal of Law and Feminism, 4*(1), 1–12. https://doi.org/10.4324/9780203700280-11

Hutton, Christopher. (2019). Linguistics and the state: How funding and politics shape a field. *Items.* https://items.ssrc.org/sociolinguistic-frontiers/linguistics-and-the-state-how-funding-and-politics-shape-a-field/

Ideland, Malin. (2018). Science, coloniality, and "the great rationality divide." *Science & Education, 27*(7), 783–803. https://doi.org/10.1007/s11191-018-0006-8

Itagaki, Lynn Mie. (2021). The long con of civility. *Connecticut Law Review, 52*(3),1169–1186.

Jobson, Ryan Cecil. (2020). The case for letting anthropology burn: Sociocultural anthropology in 2019. *American Anthropologist, 122*(2), 259–271. https://doi.org/10.1111/aman.13398"https://doi.org/10.1111/aman.13398

Karstens, Bert. (2011). Recursion, rhythm and rhizome: Searching for patterns in the history of the humanities. *Beiträge Zur Geschichte Der Sprachwissenschaft, 21*, 153–162.

Kastner, Itamar, Kotek, Hadas, Anonymous, Dockum, Rikker, Dow, Michael, Esipova, Maria, Green, Caitlin M., & Snider, Todd. (2021). Who speaks for us? Lessons from the Pinker letter [Manuscript]. https://ling.auf.net/lingbuzz/005381

Kastner, Itamar, Kotek, Hadas, Anonymous, Dockum, Rikker, Dow, Michael, Esipova, Maria, Green, Caitlin M., & Snider, Todd. (2022). The open letter: Responses and recommendations. *Proceedings of the 96th Annual Meeting of the Linguistic Society of America.*https://doi.org/10.3765/plsa.v7i1.5257

Kawa, Nicholas C., Clavijo Michelangeli, José A., Clark, Jessica L., Ginsberg, Daniel, & McCarty, Christopher. (2019). The social network of US academic anthropology and its inequalities. *American Anthropologist, 121*(1), 14–29. https://doi.org/10.1111/aman.13158

Keashly, Loraleigh, & Neuman, Joel H. (2010). Faculty experiences with bullying in higher education. *Administrative Theory & Praxis, 32*(1), 48–70. https://doi.org/10.2753/ATP1084-1806320103

Keicho, Momoka. (2021). Raciolinguistic socialization and subversion at a predominantly white institution [BA thesis, Swarthmore College].

Kidwai, Shafey. (2015, August 6). Making sense of Sanskrit. *The Hindu.* https://www.thehindu.com/features/friday-review/making-sense-of-sanskrit/article7508389.ece

King, Molly M., Bergstrom, Carl T., Correll, Shelley J., Jacquet, Jennifer, & West, Jevin D. (2017). Men set their own cites high: Gender and self-citation across fields and over time. *Socius, 3.* https://doi.org/10.1177/2378023117738903

Kotek, Hadas, Dockum, Rikker, Babinski, Sarah, & Geissler, Christopher. (2021). Gender bias and stereotypes in linguistic example sentences. *Language, 97*(4), 653–677. https://doi.org/10.1353/lan.2021.0060

Lanehart, Sonja L. (2021). Say my name: African American women's language. *Gender and Language, 15*(4), 559–568. https://doi.org/10.1558/genl.21523

Leonard, Wesley Y. (2018). *Reflections on (de)colonialism in language documentation.* University of Hawai'i Press.

Lepschy, Giulio C. (1975). Some problems in linguistic theory. In Eric H. Lenneberg & Elizabeth Lenneberg (Eds.), *Foundations of Language Development* (pp. 35–42). Academic Press.

Lerner, Gerda. (1975). Placing women in history: Definitions and challenges. *Feminist Studies*, 3(1/2), 5–14. https://doi.org/10.2307/3518951

Linguistic Society of America. (2017). LSA meeting conduct policy. https://www.linguisticsociety.org/content/lsa-conduct-policy

Lorde, Audre. (1981). The uses of anger. *Women's Studies Quarterly*, 9(3), 7–10.

Los Angeles Times Editorial Board. (2021, November 28). Editorial: Colleges' overreliance on adjunct faculty is bad for students, instructors and academic freedom. *Los Angeles Times*.

Macaulay, Monica. (2011). *Surviving linguistics: A guide for graduate students.* 2nd ed. Cascadilla Press.

Macaulay, Monica, & Brice, Colleen. (1997). Don't touch my projectile: Gender bias and stereotyping in syntactic examples. *Language*, 73(4), 798–825. https://doi.org/10.1353/lan.1997.0031

Mackenzie, J. Lachlan. (2015). Functional linguistics. In Keith Allan (Ed.), *The Routledge Handbook of Linguistics* (pp. 470–484). Routledge.

Mahmoudi, Morteza. (2019). Academic bullies leave no trace. *BioImpacts*, 9(3), 129–130. https://doi.org/10.15171/bi.2019.17

Mallinson, Christine. (2009). Sociolinguistics and sociology: Current directions, future partnerships. *Language and Linguistics Compass*, 3(4), 1034–1051. https://doi.org/10.1111/j.1749-818X.2009.00144 x

Martin-Nielsen, Janet. (2012). "It was all connected": Computers and linguistics in early cold war America. In M. Solovey and H. Cravens (Eds.), *Cold war social science* (pp. 63–78). Palgrave Macmillan.

McCulloch, Gretchen, & Gawne, Lauren. (2021). LingComm: Communicating linguistics to broader audiences. *Lingthusiasm*. https://lingcomm.org/about/

McLelland, Nicola. (2020). Women in the history of German language studies: "That subtle influence for which women are best suited"? In Wendy Ayres-Bennett & Helena Sanson (Eds.), *Women in the History of Linguistics* (pp. 193–217). Oxford University Press.

Meghji, Ali. (2020). *Decolonizing sociology: An introduction.* Wiley.

Meghji, Ali. (2021). Just what is critical race theory, and what is it doing in British sociology? From "BritCrit" to the racialized social system approach. *British Journal of Sociology*, 72(2), 347–359. https://doi.org/10.1111/1468-4446.12801

Mitchell, Koritha. (2018). Identifying white mediocrity and know-your-place aggression: A form of self-care. *African American Review*, 51(4), 253–262. https://doi.org/10.1353/afa.2018.0045

Mohammed-Smith, Eiynah (host). (2021, May 29). The linguistics of slurs [Audio podcast episode]. Polite Conversations. https://soundcloud.com/politeconversations/episode-63-the-linguistics-of-slurs

National Public Radio. (2021, July 9). Co-opted and weaponized, "cancel culture" is just today's "politically correct." *Consider This*.

Newmeyer, Frederick J. (1990). Competence vs. performance; theoretical vs. applied: The development and interplay of two dichotomies in modern linguistics. *Historiographia Linguistica*, 17(1–2), 167–181. https://doi.org/10.1075/hl.17.1-2.13new

Newmeyer, Frederick J. (2016). Formal and functional explanation. In Ian Roberts (Ed.), *The Oxford handbook of universal grammar* (pp. 129–152). Oxford University Press.

Ng, Eve. (2020). No grand pronouncements here . . . : Reflections on cancel culture and digital media participation. *Television & New Media*, 21(6), 621–627. https://doi.org/10.1177/1527476420918828

Nobel Prize Outreach. (2022, February). Nobel prize inspiration initiative. https://www.nobelprize.org/events/nobel-prize-inspiration-initiative/kenya-2022/

Norris, Pippa. (2021). Cancel culture: Myth or reality? *Political Studies*. https://doi.org/10.1177/00323217211037023

O'Regan, Gerard. (2013). Noam Chomsky. In Gerard O'Regan (Ed.), *Giants of computing: A compendium of select, pivotal pioneers* (pp. 71–74). Springer.

Patel-Grosz, Pritty, Chomsky, Noam, Iatridou, Sabine, Jacobson, Pauline, Merchant, Jason, Sharvit, Yael, Schlenker, Philippe, Stowell, Tim, Torrence, Harold, & Yang, Charles. (2022). Executive Committee update on the resolution to adopt the Chicago principles. https://www.linguisticsociety.org/comment/5009#comment-5009

Pilcher, Nick, & Richards, Kendall. (2022). *Enhancing student support in higher education: A subject-focused approach*. Palgrave Macmillan.

Quijano, Aníbal. (2007). Coloniality and modernity/rationality. *Cultural Studies*, *21*(2–3), 168–178. https://doi.org/10.1080/09502380601164353

Sailofsky, Daniel. (2022). Masculinity, cancel culture and woke capitalism: Exploring Twitter response to Brendan Leipsic's leaked conversation. *Palliative Medicine*, *57*(5), 444–453. https://doi.org/10.1177/0269216319896955

Sarvasy, Hannah. (2016). Monolingual fieldwork in and beyond the classroom: The Logooli experience at UCLA. In *Proceedings from the annual meeting of the Chicago Linguistic Society 51*, 471–484.

Scherpenberg, Cornelia van, Bultema, Lindsey, Jahn, .Anja, Löffler, Michaela, Minneker, Vera, & Lasser, Jana. (2021). Manifestations of power abuse in academia and how to prevent them. *Elephant in the Lab*. https://doi.org/10.5281/zenodo.4580544

Scott, Joan W. (2017). On free speech and academic freedom. *Journal of Academic Freedom*, *8*, 1–10.

Settles, Isis H., Buchanan, NiCole T., & Dotson, Kristie. (2019). Scrutinized but not recognized: (in)visibility and hypervisibility experiences of faculty of color. *Journal of Vocational Behavior*, *113*, 62–74. https://doi.org/10.1016/j.jvb.2018.06.003

Shenker, Israel. (1971, October 11). Jakobson: Great in any language. *New York Times*.

Singh, Varun (2017). Origin of Hindu religion and Sanskrit in Central Asia: a recent claim and its rebuttal. *Indian Historical Review* 44(1), 1–20. https://doi.org/10.1177/0376983617694720

Sorensen, David R., & Kinser, Brent E. (Eds.) (2013). *On heroes, hero-worship, and the heroic in history*. Yale University Press.

Speakman, Robert J., Hadden, Carla S., Colvin, Matthew H., Cramb, Justin, Jones, K. C., Jones, Travis W., Kling, Corbin L., Lulewicz, Isabelle, Napora, Katharine G., Reinberger, Katherine L., Ritchison, Brandon T., Jose Rivera-Araya, Maria, Smith, April K., & Thompson, Victor D. (2018). Choosing a path to the ancient world in a modern market: The reality of faculty jobs in archaeology. *American Antiquity*, *83*(1), 1–12. https://doi.org/10.1017/aaq.2017.36

Speakman, Robert J., Hadden, Carla S., Colvin, Matthew H., Cramb, Justin, Jones, K. C., Jones, Travis W., Lulewicz, Isabelle, Napora, Katharine G., Reinberger, Katherine L., Ritchison, Brandon T., Edwards, Alexandra R., & Thompson, Victor D. (2018). Market share and recent hiring trends in anthropology faculty positions. *PLOS ONE 13*(9), e0202528. https://doi.org/10.1371/journal.pone.0202528

Srinivasan, Amia. (2018). The aptness of anger. *Journal of Political Philosophy*, *26*(2), 123–144. https://doi.org/10.1111/jopp.12130

Stickles, Elise (2022). Thoughts on the LSA resolution to adopt the Chicago principles on freedom of expression. *Ms.* https://drive.google.com/file/d/1bwphXfTVK3Jni-gOEj9fIo7YN0pGcV4B/view

Stone, Geoffrey R., Bertrand, Marianne, Olinto, Angela, Siegler, Mark, Strauss, David A., Warren, Kenneth W., & Woodward, Amanda. (2015). *Report of the Committee on Freedom of Expression*. University of Chicago.

Teich, Erin G., Kim, Jason Z., Lynn, Christopher W., Simon, Samantha C., Klishin, Andrei A., Szymula, Karol P., Srivastava, Pragya, Bassett, Lee C., Zurn, Perry, Dworkin, Jordan D., & Bassett, Dani S. (2022). Citation inequity and gendered citation practices in contemporary physics. Nature Physics, 18(10), 1161–1170. https://doi.org/10.48550/arXiv.2112.09047

Thomas, Margaret. (2024). Racialization, language science, and nineteenth-century anthropometrics. In Anne H. Charity Hudley, Christine Mallinson, & Mary Bucholtz (Eds.), Decolonizing linguistics. Oxford University Press.

Tiede, Hans-Joerg, McCarthy, Samantha Kamola, Isaac, & Spurgas, Alyson K. (2021). Data snapshot: Whom does campus reform target and what are the effects? American Association of University Professors.

Trester, Anna Marie. (2022). Employing linguistics: Thinking and talking about careers for linguists. Bloomsbury Academic.

Tsikewa, Adrienne. (2021). Reimagining the current praxis of field linguistics training: Decolonial considerations. Language, 97(4), e293–e319. https://doi.org/10.1353/lan.2021.0072

Villarreal, Dan, & Collister, Lauren. (2024). Open Methods: Decolonizing (or not) research methods in linguistics. In Anne H. Charity Hudley, Christine Mallinson, & Mary Bucholtz (Eds.), Decolonizing linguistics. Oxford University Press.

Willis, Rebecca. (2019). The use of composite narratives to present interview findings. Qualitative Research, 19(4), 471–480. https://doi.org/10.1177/1468794118787711

Zamalin, Alex. (2022). Against civility: The hidden racism in our obsession with civility. Penguin Random House.

PART 2

LINGUISTICS FOR ALL: DISCIPLINARY AND INSTITUTIONAL PATHWAYS FOR INCLUSION

Iara Mantenuto is assistant professor of linguistics and program coordinator for the Masters in Teaching of English as a Second Language at California State University Dominguez Hills (CSUDH) in Carson, California. She is from Italy, and she earned a PhD in linguistics from the University of California Los Angeles (UCLA). Mantenuto's research focuses on revitalization, reclamation, documentation, and morphosyntactic analysis of understudied languages, in particular Teramano (her heritage language) and San Sebastián del Monte Mixtec. She also conducts research on how we can improve the teaching of linguistics.

Stephanie Reyes is a recent graduate with a MA in linguistics from the University of Chicago. Her research interests are in psycholinguistics, semantics, pragmatics, bilingualism, and language variation and change. She worked on Tagalog, with general interests in Austronesian languages. Prior to linguistics, she completed a master's degree in philosophy from the University of Calgary.

Tamaya Levy is a PhD student of linguistics at the University of Oregon. As an aspiring junior scholar, her research interests include sociophonetics, African American Language (AAL), and raciolinguistics. Her sociophonetics work analyses speech perceptions and stereotypes toward speakers of African American language. Likewise, she investigates and describes the prosodic processes associated with emotion and how phonological and phonetic variables are realized in AAL.

Zhongyin Zhang is an undergraduate student in psychology at Haverford College. She is interested in the interface of neurobiology and linguistics, in particular neurodevelopmental disorders related to speech and language, as well as other cognitive impairments. Additionally, she is also enthusiastic about the clinical applications of neurolinguistic findings, including but not limited to the integration of speech language therapy and other therapy services.

Abstract: This chapter provides information about who first-generation scholars are in the field of linguistics, and the work that the authors have done with their First Gen Access and Equity (FGAE) committee. The authors argue that the field of linguistics needs to do better to recruit and retain first-generation scholars, and to do so linguists need to educate themselves, by reflecting on some of the hurdles that institutions create. The chapter focuses in particular on two main issues the authors have faced in their experiences as first-generation scholars: financial barriers to success and the culture of exclusion. This chapter and the FGAE committee offer tools to start improving and advocating for the first-generation scholar experience, while also creating a supportive community.

Key Words: first-generation students, first-generation scholars, linguistics, financial barriers, academic culture, intersectional inclusion, academic success, higher education, underrepresentation in linguistics

6

Increasing Access and Equity for First-Generation Scholars in Linguistics

Iara Mantenuto (she/her)
California State University Dominguez Hills

Tamaya Levy (she/her)
University of Oregon

Stephanie Reyes (she/her)
Independent scholar

Zhongyin Zhang (she/her)
Haverford College

Introduction

The aim of this chapter is to educate graduate students, faculty members at any career stage, and anyone interested in linguistics about first-generation scholars: who we are and how we can engage the field to foster a sense of belonging for first-generation scholars in academia.[1] Although more data is increasingly being collected and made available on demographic diversity in linguistics (LSA, 2020), we lack information on the number of first-generation scholars within our field. In order to meet the urgent need for greater disciplinary resources and recognition, we created the First Gen Access and Equity Committee (FGAE) with the support of the Committee on Gender Equity in Linguistics (COGEL), which is part of the Linguistic Society of America (LSA). This chapter is primarily intended for scholars in the United States. Although some content may be relatable for scholars in other countries (especially those with strong North European-centric academic approaches), we mostly investigate our experiences as people who are either attending or teaching in undergraduate and/or graduate institutions in the US.

Iara Mantenuto, Tamaya Levy, Stephanie Reyes, and Zhongyin Zhang, *Increasing Access and Equity for First-Generation Scholars in Linguistics* In: *Inclusion in Linguistics*. Edited by: Anne H. Charity Hudley, Christine Mallinson and Mary Bucholtz, Oxford University Press. © Anne H. Charity Hudley, Christine Mallinson, and Mary Bucholtz 2024. DOI: 10.1093/oso/9780197755303.003.0007

We begin this chapter by introducing what researchers know about first-generation students, drawing from literature in the field of education, which is far more robust than what currently exists in linguistics. We then describe who we are and what has brought us together as a group of scholars from diverse backgrounds who are asking for and working towards more support for first-generation scholars in linguistics. We use the word "scholars" to include both current first-generation students and previous first-generation students who are now faculty members or professionals. We describe our roles in the formation of our committee and its goals, which we tie to our experiences and needs as first-generation scholars in linguistics and to our ideas for recommendations and action plans.

First-Generation Scholars in Linguistics

A first-generation student is defined by Anne Charity Hudley, Cheryl Dickter, and Hannah Franz (2017) as follows: "A student who will be the first person in their immediate family to graduate from a 4-year college. More specific descriptors are students whose parents have attended a 4-year college but did not graduate and students whose parents attended and graduated from a 2-year college" (p. 19).

We want to emphasize that these students are not a minority in US colleges. In fact, according to the US Department of Education (RTI International, 2019), as of the academic year 2015–2016, 24% of US students from a variety of institutions had parents who did not earn any postsecondary credential, 56% of students had parents who did not have a bachelor's degree, and 59% of students whose parents did not have a bachelor's degree were also the first sibling in their family to go to college. It seems obvious from this data that when we are talking about first-generation scholars, we are not talking about a small group, but rather about a large but underrepresented group of individuals, many of whom are racially minoritized and/or low-income (Sarcedo et al., 2015).

Moreover, there are multiple levels to first-generation student identities. Studies are still progressing on how to represent the continuum of the first-generation experience, from families with some experience of higher education to those with none (Darrah et al., 2022; Toutkoushian et al., 2015). In this chapter we do not cover this point in depth, but we emphasize the importance of viewing this group from an intersectional perspective (Crenshaw, 1989) and not defining it as monolithic, since the first-generation experience differs among people from different racial, national, and socioeconomic backgrounds, as well as based on the schooling experience of the parents. Students whose parents completed college in the US have a different experience than students whose parents completed college outside of the US. Students of the Global Majority have a different experience than white students, and their experiences differ among different racial/ethnic groups as well.[2] Students from a low-income background have a different experience than students coming from a higher income background. From an intersectional perspective, the diversity within first-generation scholars is part of the strength of this group. Understanding the needs and strengths of first-generation students can help bring positive change, for example by increasing the number of underrepresented students in higher education (Dowd & Bensimon, 2015; Ives & Castillo-Montoya, 2020) and thus in linguistics (Mantenuto, 2021).

Underrepresentation within the field of linguistics heightens the need to develop a more inclusive and diverse scholarly community (Charity Hudley & Mallinson, 2018; Friedman & Reed, 2014; Rickford, 1997; 2014). As we discuss later in this chapter, some problems that are present in academia for first-generation students are often related to the cultural capital that academia, including linguistics as a discipline, is centred on. By cultural capital we mean "the set of cultural knowledge that provides an advantage within a particular setting" (Haeger et al., 2018, p. 2). With regard to higher education specifically, Christa Winkler and Rishi Sriram (2015) refer to "academic capital," defined by St John and colleagues (2010) as "the social processes that build family knowledge of educational and career options and support navigation through educational systems and professional organizations" (p. 1). At the end of this chapter, we address some of the issues related to cultural capital and how faculty members in linguistics can make them more explicit.

First-generation students are usually described as different from the (tacitly) "normative" student (Ilett, 2019; Pascarella et al., 2004), namely students who by virtue of their family academic background and experiences possess and reproduce academic capital. As Alicia Chávez and Susan Longerbeam (2016) and Tara Yosso (2005) point out, it is not that students who do not have academic capital are lacking cultural capital completely, but that they just have a different form of cultural capital that is not valued in academia. First-generation students are expected to be aware of academic capital to which they have not been exposed, which includes hidden norms and expectations that define their success and their career; this set of hidden norms and expectations is often referred to as the "hidden curriculum" (Conley, 2005; Freire, 1972, among others).

As Heather Haeger and colleagues (2018) indicate, the hidden curriculum is formed by the set of norms, expectations, and rules that are learned when a student is being socialized into an academic discipline and into higher education more generally. The hidden curriculum has consequences for how easily a scholar can navigate their surroundings, relate to professors and mentors, succeed in a major, and understand the path to a career, among many other things (p. 15). Often professors assume that this set of norms, expectations, and rules is familiar to every student, without introducing them or making them explicit to the students.

In linguistics, even more than in other fields, we need to be aware of the challenges that the hidden curriculum creates for first-generation scholars and other underrepresented scholars in academia. Students in general, and first-generation students in particular, are often unaware of linguistics until they get to college, especially since linguistics is still rarely presented to high school students (Plackowski, this volume). Therefore, as we have experienced in our own lives, first-generation students in linguistics may take longer to start their bachelor's degree, potentially truncating time for research experiences, internships, and professional development, and thus potentially slowing the pursuit of graduate education in linguistics and/or the development of a career in the field. Graduate programs in linguistics are quite competitive, yet the criteria necessary to gain admission are often opaque; we are aware of only two books that clarify the hidden curriculum written for and by linguists (Charity Hudley et al., 2017; Macaulay, 2011), while some books outside of linguistics are for graduate students and early faculty members of colour (Mack et al., 2014), for first-generation students in legacy universities (Gable, 2021) and for professionalization and preparation for the job market (Kelsky, 2015). Likewise, there are still very limited conversations on jobs outside of academia for linguists and how to get them, although the LSA's Linguistics Beyond Academia Special Interest Group, which works to promote nonacademic career paths for linguists and has made great progress in this area.

Given these factors, the field of linguistics needs to offer academic resources and strategies that are realistic and transparent, in ways that will benefit first-generation students. Research suggests that academic programming explicitly designed to uncover the hidden curriculum increases the impact of undergraduate research (Haeger et al., 2018, p. 20). Strategies such as recruiting and mentoring first-generation undergraduate students, providing accessible group networking opportunities, and advertising the diversity of career pathways in the field are all crucial for the success of first-generation scholars in linguistics. We also recommend the inclusion of first-generation students in conversations about this group. Undergraduate and graduate students who are first-generation may not know that they are, or if they do, they may feel isolated, unrepresented, and unaware of how to obtain mentorship, because of the lack of overt discourse within the field about who is and who is not first-generation and why these students are important to linguistics as a discipline. Increasing high-quality teaching and mentorship for first-generation students within the field is therefore key (Charity Hudley et al., 2017; Childs, 2018; LSA, 2018; Mantenuto, 2021; Truong, 2021; Welch, 2021). More initiatives are needed, both in number and reach, not only for students, but also for linguists in later stages of their career, whether in academia or not.

Who We Are

We take a moment to share our personal trajectories as scholars relevant to the topic of this chapter. We share our positionality statements because we want to offer some examples of first-generation students and former students within linguistics. We also include them because the inclusion of positionality statements can support an antiracist ethos by demonstrating "research subjectivities affect the kinds of questions that get asked as well as the interpretation of findings" (Clemons & Lawrence, 2020, e259; see also Clemons, 2024). This acknowledgement is particularly important because it highlights our individual endeavours to find our positions in linguistics with few established resources available to us to do so. Our experiences exemplify what is necessary to support first-generation students and how doing so can be beneficial as linguistics tries to be a more inclusive field.

We all came together when we decided to create the LSA's First Gen Access and Equity Committee, which originally was a subcommittee of COGEL. Stephanie and Iara met at the COGEL meeting during the LSA annual conference in January 2021. We then started connecting with others interested in the creation of a committee for first-generation students. Tamaya was introduced to Iara and to the committee when she reached out to the LSA mentorship program. Similarly, Zhongyin was introduced to the committee after reaching out to the chair of COGEL at the time, who is also a first-generation scholar and part of the founding group of the committee. The way we met exemplifies how important mentorship and networking has been for us as first-generation scholars, and how these practices allowed us to create a community and start working to find and disseminate resources.

The following positionality statements illustrates the common thread of the first-generation experience, reported as a continuum from scholars with parents who have not attended a postsecondary institution (Tamaya and Iara), to those whose parents have attended postsecondary institutions but do not have graduate degrees (Stephanie and Zhongyin). We also represent different academic levels in linguistics (an assistant professor, a BS student, an MA student and a former PhD student/current independent scholar), from both private and public institutions in the US. Finally, we offer examples of first-generation experiences that are intersectional across class, race and immigration status. Although our experiences are far from being comprehensive of all the realities of first-generation scholars, they provide some insight into why first-generation scholars should not be considered a monolithic group.

Tamaya Levy, MA Student in Linguistics

It was not until I was accepted into a university that I learned I was first-generation, but by then the transition from high school to college had already been abrupt and rough. I did not learn how to handle the adjustment or what I should expect as a newly admitted student. I felt overwhelmed by the thought of being an undergraduate because I lacked a support system in academia, and I did not believe I had the knowledge to survive the next four years by myself. At the University of Illinois at Chicago, a huge public university, professors seemed not to have the capacity to offer their undergraduate students research positions, and I was not familiar with learning environments where there were more than a hundred students in a classroom. I thought of myself as a burden on professors when I needed to ask for help or resources, and I did not take advantage of office hours as I should have. I thought I should not be asking for help—I just needed to do better and be better on my own. I carried the expectations of my parents, who did not graduate high school, because as a first-generation student I felt responsible to uplift my community at the same time I was trying to uplift myself.

I subsequently felt unprepared to apply for graduate school because I had not had the chance to enrich my classroom learning and development of new skills through undergraduate research opportunities. Having such research experiences are expected in higher education in graduate programs, and yet my undergraduate program had very limited resources to provide them. Academics and administrators need to critically assess the university programs that are supposed to serve undergraduates and advocate for more college-based initiatives geared towards retention of first-generation students. Today, my positionality as a first-generation Black woman in academia has shown me that I have to adapt to the challenges that I and others like me encounter, just as I had to navigate my undergraduate experience. By examining my own beliefs and practices, and through moments of self-awareness, I learned how to use discomfort as a source of empowerment. I joined the LSA

FGAE committee to have a space to openly engage and discuss with other first-generation scholars, to know I am not in this struggle alone. Through cultivating awareness, being resilient to challenges, and encouraging inclusion, I am confident that our experiences can serve as a resource for diversity in thought and perspective in the field of linguistics.

Iara Mantenuto, Assistant Professor of Linguistics

I am white, I am from Italy, I come from a low-income family of immigrants, I am the first person in my family to go to college, and I am currently an assistant professor of linguistics at California State University Dominguez Hills (CSUDH), a Minority-Serving and Hispanic-Serving Institution, with a majority first-generation student population. I learned that I was a first-generation student in my third year of my PhD program at the University of California, Los Angeles. La'Tonya Rease Miles, the director of the First Year Experience at UCLA at the time, gave a presentation on first-generation students, and on their perspectives and experiences. I remember looking through the list of characteristics of first-generation students and finally feeling validated: her words resonated with me, and it suddenly became clear that I was not the only one who thought for the longest time that something was wrong with herself; other first-generation students shared many of my experiences. From this moment onward I started to understand myself and my surroundings better. I was blessed in having had incredible mentors throughout my graduate career, as I still do today—people who taught me how to collect data, build relationships with communities, apply to graduate school, present at conferences, write papers, network, and apply for jobs. However, I often wonder what would have happened to me if I did not have these wonderful mentors, and thus what happens to first-generation students who are not as lucky as myself. As an undergraduate, I did not have mentors, and as a consequence I tried multiple majors before finding linguistics, and I started my MA in the field at the age of 29. I always felt I was missing a lot of experiences: I did not have research experience until my master's program; I did not know that different conferences have different levels of importance and that to move forward you are expected to attend them; it was not clear to me that proceedings are not peer-reviewed but that they are still very important on a graduate student curriculum vitae; and I did not know of the importance of networking with senior faculty members outside of my institution, who could provide recommendation letters. These are just some examples of what I needed to know. Moreover, as a low-income student I had to hold multiple jobs in undergraduate and graduate school, which was an obligation outside of my studies, and as an international student I was also trying to navigate a culture different from my own.

Once I became a faculty member, I decided to start a bigger conversation about first-generation students and the ways that we can support them in our field, both financially and through mentorship. In order to do so, I started writing and presenting about what I had been learning and practicing, and I led in the creation of the FGAE committee.

Stephanie Reyes, Independent Scholar

Before graduating with an MA in linguistics, I was a first-generation PhD student in linguistics at the University of Chicago, which means that I would have been the first in my family to attend a PhD program and earn a doctorate. Both of my parents earned undergraduate degrees in the Philippines. During my undergraduate studies, it was difficult to imagine a career path in academia because I did not encounter any faculty mentors who looked like me or shared the same immigrant upbringing. My family immigrated to Canada when I was five years old. Before we moved, my mother was a professor at a university in the Philippines and was ready to start the thesis writing portion of her master's of journalism program. She quit the program after we immigrated to focus on getting settled in Canada.

I learned that I was a first-generation graduate student during a conversation with peers. We were talking about our families, and I learned that a majority of my peers' parents had graduate degrees and helped them navigate academia, from the process of applying to graduate school to networking strategies. My mother's graduate experience has been helpful to me, but some of it does not apply to the North American context and I still need other resources and support. I joined the FGAE committee to learn from and meet other first-generation students, to share the academic resources I have gathered over the years with other first-generation students, and to learn about other resources from them.

Zhongyin Zhang, BS Student in Psychology

It was not until my first year at Haverford College that I realized I was an aspiring first-generation academic researcher. Both of my parents had careers in finance after attending college in China, so their work and academic experience was not transferable to me. During my first semester at college, I had a long conversation with a history professor who mentioned that both of his parents were college professors and talked about professional advice he got from his parents early in his education and career. This conversation lingered and made me start to reflect on my own identity: Am I alone just because I am the first person in my family who wants to become an academic?

As an international undergraduate student, I often found shut doors when I sought additional research opportunities outside of my home institution: for example, many summer research programs for undergraduates only accept US citizens primarily due to visa issues, and as a result, sometimes I had to pause my research plan and head back to my home country in order to solve visa problems.

I joined the FGAE committee hoping to find peers that share similar concerns, and I felt for the first time that I was not alone. After talking to other first-generation scholars and hearing their personal stories, I started to see myself in academia more. Those conversations motivated me to participate in gatherings, conferences, and mentorship programs, and I familiarized myself with the social circle in linguistics outside of my classroom experiences.

The First Gen Access and Equity Committee

Our goal is to become a permanent committee that provides support and resources for first-generation students and faculty, as well as a source of information for other scholars interested in learning how to support first-generation scholars. We created the LSA FGAE subcommittee together with Caitlin Moriah Green, Inî G. Mendoza, Jessica Rett, and Tran Truong. The committee's purpose and agenda were generated from the needs that some of us expressed at the organized session on Scholarly Teaching in the Age of COVID and Beyond at the 2021 LSA annual meeting (Hiramatsu & Temkin Martinez, 2021). We organically formed as a group at that point and have subsequently met every month. During the subcommittee's first year of existence, we decided upon our priorities and created our mission statement: "The FGAE committee is on a mission: to empower first-generation linguists by providing resources, advice, and opportunities often not extended to those whose families do not have experience navigating academia or linguistic careers; to highlight the work and careers of first-generation linguists; to educate others about the strengths and resourcefulness of first-generation linguists" (FGAE Committee, 2023).

We use the word "linguists" similarly to how we use "scholars," in order to be inclusive of current and former students in linguistics, including those in academia and those in industry or in other areas, as well as to be inclusive of the different definitions of first-generation students. To the best of our knowledge, our committee is unique in that it is associated with a national professional organization and not with a single institution of higher education. Although resources for first-generation students exist, they seem to be fragmented at the institutional level, and rarely is there clear communication between different institutions, let alone a whole field. The FGAE committee allows people belonging to different institutions and different disciplines related to linguistics to communicate, share ideas, inspire, and collaborate with each other.

The goal of our first meeting was the creation of a list of resources that members need, such as a list of conferences and fellowships, and information about networking, mentorships, and career opportunities. The major focus so far has been to highlight and address the needs of undergraduate and graduate students in particular. We created a website (https://tinyurl.com/firstgen lsa) that we are still building, where we have begun collecting these resources (FGAE Committee, 2023).

Our next goal was to find others like us. Currently, in the field of linguistics, very few professors have any information on their website indicating that they were first-generation students, and very few introduce themselves as such on the first day of class or in professional settings like conferences. We decided to start a competition to create a logo to represent the subcommittee; the logo would not only easily identify the group, but it would also be an easy means for first-generation scholars to identify ourselves (Figure 6.1). To us this little logo means a lot: it means representation, it means that others have shared some of our experiences and it identifies people to whom we can reach out with questions or in solidarity. The logo is downloadable from our website

Figure 6.1 First Gen Access and Equity Subcommittee logo
Alt text: Digital illustration of First Gen Access and Equity Subcommittee logo. The illustration is credited by member, Iyad Ghanim. Multicolored speech bubbles surround the space to create the number one. Underneath the image is the words First Gen Access & Equity.

(FGAE Committee, 2023) for scholars to identify themselves in their signature files, websites, virtual meetings, and so forth.

The logo was launched at our virtual mixer during the 2022 LSA conference, First Gen Access and Equity Mixer 2022, the first event dedicated to first-generation scholars in linguistics, was a great success. Fourteen scholars attended: five professors, eight graduate students, and one undergraduate student. Two faculty members, Iyad Ghanim (the creator of the FGAE logo) and Jennifer Nycz, spoke at the mixer and shared their experiences as first-generation scholars.

We are working towards three additional future-facing goals that were further defined by the conversation at our mixer. The first goal is to collect quantitative data as to the numbers of first-generation scholars in linguistics, with demographic information regarding income, dependents, race, ethnicity, and gender. Along with demographic information, we also want to learn more about their immigration experiences (if applicable) and family backgrounds to better inform our understanding of this group of scholars and find ways we can best support them. The second goal is to collect resources and organize events in linguistics for first-generation scholars, instructors, and allies—people who might not have the same shared experience as first-generation scholars, but who are interested in learning about our experiences and supporting us. The final goal is to facilitate additional networking opportunities with other first-generation scholars in linguistics, to feel validated, to learn from each other, to find mentors, and to form a supportive community. For example, we are pushing for institutional changes, starting from the LSA. We asked for first-generation to be included in the demographic information with two purposes: allow people to connect with each other and be able to track us statistically as per other fields (e.g., ethnicity and gender). The LSA included the checkbox, but without a definition next to the entry and it is not possible to find people who self-identify (cf. ethnicity and gender). Many first-generation students do not know they are first-generation because of the discourse, or lack thereof, around their identities; moreover, the directory should be able to connect scholars in our field through the visibility of the first-generation category. We hope that in the future our presence and work will continue advocating for what first-generation scholars need in our field.

In the past two years, we achieved many successes directly linked to starting conversations about first-generation students in linguistics. For example, Iyad Ghanim was interviewed for the LSA spotlight article in December 2021 (LSA, 2021); Tamaya Levy won a Committee of Ethnic Diversity in Linguistics travel grant; Iara Mantenuto was invited to talk about mentorship at a special session at the LSA annual meeting (Baese-Berk & Cepeda, 2022); Monica

Macaulay will include a discussion of first-generation students in the new edition of her book *Surviving Linguistics* (Macaulay, in progress); we became a full fledge LSA committee in February 2023; and we are writing this chapter, which we hope to be followed by a trilogy of articles expanding in more detail on the ethnographically studying first-generation students, mentoring, and the teaching of first-generation.

Understanding and Advocating for First-Generation Scholars in Linguistics and in Academia

First-generation representation is integral to advancing inclusivity and diversity in the field of linguistics. First-generation students like us may find it difficult to consider postgraduate career paths because they do not see themselves represented in the field. In this section we highlight two main issues we have faced in our experiences as first-generation scholars: financial barriers to success and the culture of exclusion that too often exists in academia. Throughout, we provide recommendations for ways to advocate for first-generation scholars in building a culture of inclusion and ways that the FGAE committee is starting to address these issues.

Addressing Financial Barriers to Success

Academic success cannot be detached from social status and economic resources. First-generation students in the US primarily come from low-income families: the medial parental income among dependent first-generation students is $40,000, compared to the $90,000 medial parental income of their non–first-generation counterparts (RTI International, 2019). For this reason, faculty members need to be aware of the burden of university costs on students' experiences, the consequences that those economic limitations have on their scholarly trajectories, and how to mentor students on these topics.

For example, many first-generation students have to work multiple jobs to support themselves and their families: 66% of first-generation students are employed (RTI International, 2019) students, and their jobs have an impact on the way professors perceive them, including circumstances when they may have to miss class due to work or limitations on when they can attend office hours. A student who does not have a job has more time available, a disparity faculty members need to keep in mind in evaluations, in mentorships, and in understanding student experiences in undergraduate and graduate programs. Just advising a student to focus exclusively on their studies, without considering their full experiences and commitments as low-income first-generation scholar who must work outside of school, is problematic. Faculty members should make sure to not judge a student's level of commitment to their research and studies based on whether or not they can dedicate themselves completely to it, as opposed to taking on additional employment. For example, faculty can share with students what resources are available for funding, explain that funding is available for graduate school, and that there are alternative ways to make income; faculty should also ask their offices on campus what resources are available and have a list accessible to their students. Moreover, one of the first skills faculty should teach their students (even at the BA level) is grant writing, which is a skill also transferable outside of academia. Faculty should also make clear what is expected from a student when doing research and work together with the student to come up with a clear plan on how to schedule their research while also working and/or caring for others, for example by creating to do lists and planning together a realistic timeline for a project. Faculty should also promote widely through a BA/MA listserv and the department listserv jobs available for students that relate to their studies and help them to apply for these jobs. Programs should recommend the creation of a professionalization course which would help students learn the necessary skills for graduate school and later for the job market. Although some programs have these opportunities, not all of them do. We suggest that some of the resources needed for this course could be implemented by offices already doing professionalization on campus and others which are able to create safe spaces for students to ask what they need (e.g., career center, Diversity Equity and Inclusion office, various alliances, First-Generation office).

Universities should also make it a priority to financially support students in order to give everyone the opportunity to move forward. As recent graduate student protests across the US have shown (Zahneis & Patel, 2020), universities need to offer higher stipends to graduate students. If a first-generation student enters graduate school, they face an even higher level of economic burden. For example, in linguistics, only 22% of graduate programs are funded (LSA, 2020). Moreover, if admission to graduate school requires undergraduate research-based experiences, which are increasingly necessary for competitive applications, then those opportunities need to be made available to everyone. An excellent example of this type of model is the UC-HBCU Initiative Pathways Grants at the University of California (Franz et al., 2022) and the Developing Research Experiences for Native American Undergraduates Through a Transdisciplinary Approach, created by Gabriela Pérez Báez and Melissa Baese-Berk at the University of Oregon in 2022.

It would be also helpful to create bridge programs between schools that serve mostly first-generation students and graduate programs, and to inform students early in their career of fellowships such as the McNamara Fellowship, the Mellon Mays Undergraduate Fellowship, and the NSF Graduate Research Fellowship. We need to be mindful, however, that often students discover linguistics later in their undergraduate studies; thus, it is not always possible for them to apply on time for these opportunities. Further, some PhD programs favour students with a master's degree, or students may need to complete a master's degree because they were not able to build a competitive curriculum vitae based on the external restrictions we discussed above. However, many master's programs in the US are unfunded. Student loans are not available for most international students, in either the US nor in their home country. Furthermore, loans may also be unattainable for students coming from low-income families, as the mean need that remains after applying for financial aid (unmet financial need) before the loan represents half of the student's median annual income, while funding for the Federal Pell Grant and Work-Study programs has not kept up with tuition and fees increases (Engle & Tinto, 2008). Creation of nonloan financial aid resources, such as grants, scholarships, and work-study, have been shown to improve the retention of first-generation students (Engle & Tinto, 2008; Lohfink et al., 2005; Somers et al., 2004). We want to emphasize, however, that those resources need to reflect the cost of living and the possibility of having dependents.

Finally, there should be mandatory allocations for professionalization to be used at the student's discretion. This specifically refers to departments including in all student's aid packages funding for conferences, and/or summer schools for linguistics that is not reliant on reimbursement, or students paying out of pocket. Departments should be invested in our success and that includes opportunities such as these through specific allocation of funding. Related to this point, a particularly burdensome financial limitation that surfaces during graduate study (and sometimes also during undergraduate study) is the way that the academic financial system is structured to require students to pay up front for conference registration or other research-related activities and wait a month or more to receive reimbursement. This situation is financially untenable for many students, including first-generation students from low-income backgrounds, who may face accruing credit card debt and paying interest on it—or they may be unable to pay in advance at all because they are unable to obtain a credit card. Students thus face a bind, as conferences and other such activities are important networking events. When institutions limit the possibility of students going to these events, or when institutions demand that they pay up front, we limit their opportunity to succeed. We are unfortunately unaware of any university which has implemented such a system, and we hope that a change will be possible, it is unsatisfactory to accept bureaucratic limitations as an answer. A way to solve this kind of problems would be to work with the department in paying for some of the expenses for the event in question, for example by paying for the event registration and the ticket via a purchasing card or to assign purchasing cards to graduate students for a conference.

First-generation international scholars, who are rarely discussed in the literature on first-generation scholars, may face challenges that are often related to financial concerns and constraints. For first-generation international scholars in the US, visa status remains a central issue (Khanal & Gaulee, 2019). Some scholars are only permitted visas with limited campus and off-campus work options, which restricts their financial, academic, and research opportunities. First-generation international students also often face the additional pressures of higher tuition and fees, limited scholarship and bursary opportunities (since most of these opportunities are reserved for US citizens), limited summer research opportunities, and financial obligations to their families whether they live in the US or abroad. These additional pressures make first-generation international students' advancement in academia more difficult. Academic institutions and organizations can mitigate immigration and financial barriers by not restricting funding and research opportunities based on citizenship status, by increasing the number of scholarships earmarked for first-generation international students, and by ensuring that international students have a support system with strong networks of mentors who can assist them with navigating academia in the US.

The FGAE committee aims to increase the transparency of discussions about the financial toll faced by many first-generation and low-income scholars in linguistics is by collecting quantitative data on first-generation scholars, including their incomes and dependents, as noted earlier. One of the committee's goals is to educate other linguists about the first-generation experience, about mentorship best practices, and about financial considerations, including how they affect specific student populations such as first-generation international students. Our plan to continue to expand and publicize the list of financial and other resources for first-generation scholars will also help address this area of concern.

Building an Academic Culture
of Intersectional Inclusion

In addition to financial support, fostering a sense of belonging is essential for first-generation student success. As Allison Morgan and colleagues (2022) reported in their study looking at 7,204 US-based tenure-track faculty across disciplines and institutions between 2017 and 2020, faculty members are 25 times more likely to have a parent with a doctorate, and this number almost doubles in prestigious institutions. The lack of diversity among linguistics faculty (Rickford, 2014) as well as in many linguistics curricula does not facilitate a sense of belonging and makes the acquisition of academic capital harder. First-generation students often see and experience lack of social-emotional understanding of their situation "dysconscious" educators. Dysconsciousness is a psychological state in which individuals' perceptions, attitudes, assumptions, and beliefs justify inequity by accepting "the existing order of things as given" (King, 1991, p. 135). Educators that embody this trait fail to support academic and cultural diversity in the classrooms. Such educators may compare first-generation students to students with greater academic capital, who have had easier circumstances and often more favourable experiences, disregarding how different the two students compared are, their different resources and most importantly disregarding the first-generation student's strengths. First-generation scholars are often the recipient of educators' unwarranted expectations in the form of implicit or explicit questions like "Why can't you be more like them?" These harmful comparisons ostracize and belittle first-generation scholars who do not have the same access to academic capital as their more structurally advantaged counterparts. Instructors need to take an asset-based approach, which is concerned with recognizing students' strengths both inside and out of the classroom. Many scholars have argued for students' strengths, experiences, and identities to be reflected in educational institutions (Freire, 1972; hooks, 1994; Ladson-Billings, 1995; Thomas, this volume), and we urge scholars in linguistics to follow up on this work to address the culture of educational exclusion that we as first-generation scholars have experienced. Scholars like us bring more to the table than what has been traditionally valued in academia, grounded in our life experiences and positionalities that inform our approaches to research and our contributions to academia.

Some of our strengths are compassion, curiosity, persistence, and resourcefulness, all characteristics that allow us to strive once we understand how the system works and we are given the right institutional support. We are excellent multitaskers because of how many tasks we have to balance while studying, we are good at relating to a nonacademic audience what we do because that is what we are used to doing with our families. Many of us want to support future generations of scholars and make their learning experience better than ours, we recognize the importance and the need for mentorship. One goal of the FGAE committee, to educate others about our varied strengths and resourcefulness while also making very clear that we are not a homogenous group of people, needs to be taken into account. Similarly to Joyhanna Yoo, Cheryl Lee, Andrew Cheng, and Anusha Ánand (2023), we urge linguists to "embrace a deeply relational politics rooted in historical and comparative understanding of race." We want to emphasize that our experience as first-generation students are similar in some ways, but they differ based on aspects such as race, class, gender, and status, and we highly recommend to other linguists to not group us together under one label but to look at us as intersections of first-generation in addition to our other identities. We do not want people to police our identity and we also do not want people to take out of context what it means to be a first-generation scholar and use it for "diversifying" their institutions in a manner that is colour blind and perpetuates white supremacy; thus, we want linguists to understand who we are and how to support us.

First-generation scholars often feel familial and self-imposed pressure to be "the best," since they are the first in their family to go to college (Ramos, 2019). This can also be the case for scholars who are the first person in their family to receive a postsecondary degree. For this reason, part of creating inclusion for first-generation scholars requires addressing the academic culture that for too long has perpetuated the idea that constant productivity is an indicator of a scholar's self-worth and dedication. For many scholars, especially first-generation scholars, this expectation leads to burnout, as they are also more likely to be scholars of the Global Majority and from low-income backgrounds and thus to face many circumstances that place additional burdens and take an added toll as they navigate their educational journeys. For example, Maya Smith (2024) discusses experiences of "classroom anxiety as the lone Black student," who is worried that their mistakes would reflect on their communities. In our experience, these same concerns and expectations, which are mentally exhausting, also affect first-generation scholars, who may begin overcompensating and whose achievements may feel diminished because, in academia, the question is always "What is next?" We also point out that some first-generation scholars of the Global Majority interact with community or family members who believe that academia correlates with whiteness. For example, being called "boujie," "saddity," or "uppity" is often familiar to first-generation students who identify as Black. These labels are handed out as if a scholar is acting beyond their expected societal role when they decide to pursue postsecondary education. Similarly, international first-generation scholars may face cultural differences, lack a sense of community, and experience alienation when they study in the United States. The limited literature on this topic suggests that to improve the academic experience of first-generation international scholars requires academic-focused interactions with professors outside of the classroom and classrooms that create a supportive environment for cross-cultural engagement enhancement (Glass et al., 2017).

To address these issues in our own lives, we have found it helpful to have a network of mentors to help us navigate the academic system. Research shows that academic programs that offer mentorship to first-generation scholars are more likely to retain them (Plaskett et al., 2018; Ramos, 2019). Part of building an academic culture of inclusion for first-generation scholars is addressing how academia and traditional academic narratives are experienced by and affect first-generation scholars from a variety of social backgrounds and positionalities. Our committee aims to help build a culture of inclusion that will validate and support first-generation scholars through creating a community with wide networks, including mentors, and with as many resources to assist scholars as possible.

Conclusions

In this chapter we have highlighted the importance of understanding first-generation scholars as a diverse and intersectional group. We suggested that reflecting on first-generation scholars and their experiences lends insight into some fundamental changes needed in the field of linguistics in particular to recruit and retain them, in the discipline as well as in academia. Outreach and education are important tools to improve the first-generation scholar experience. Through the FGAE committee, we will continue to compile and offer resources to first-generation scholars and to create a strong community within linguistics. We will also continue to raise awareness, educate, and offer tools for faculty and others to use to support first-generation scholars. The greater goal is to know that we can send our friends, students, and colleagues to these programs where faculty members are directly working for inclusion, confronting issues of institutional and structural discrimination, and informing themselves in order to take action and be inclusive of first-generation scholars. We urge first-generation scholars and allies to contact our committee and be involved with our community-building efforts how little or how much they can, which also includes sharing our contact and resources with their students and contacting the FGAE committee for any consulting they might need.

Notes

1. We would like to thank all the members of the First Gen Access and Equity (FGAE) Committee and the Committee on Gender Equity in Linguistics of the Linguistic Society of America. In particular, we are grateful to Iní G. Mendoza, Jessica Rett, Caitlin Moriah Green, Tran Truong, Melissa Baese-Berk, Ander Beristain Murillo, Ivano Caponigro, Jennifer Cox, Iyad Ghanim, Claudia Holguin Mendoza, and Jennifer Nycz for working with us in building the foundation of the FGAE committee. We thank the other authors in this volume for the enriching exchange of ideas. We would also like to thank Mary Bucholtz, Anne Charity Hudley, Christine Mallinson, Maya Smith, and Jamie Thomas for their feedback. Christine Mallinson saw multiple versions of this draft and we are thankful for her patience and helpful suggestions. We are grateful to Anne Charity Hudley, Mary Bucholtz and Christine Mallinson for all their support, guidance, encouragement and for creating a writing experience that generated a supportive community of scholars. Finally, we want to thank those who identify as first-gen; we hope you feel appreciated and validated. Any errors are ours.
2. Following Rosemary Campbell-Stephens (2021) we use the term "Global Majority" to indicate "those people who identify as Black, African, Asian, Brown, Arab and mixed heritage, are indigenous to the Global South, and/or have been racialized as 'ethnic minorities.' Globally, these groups currently represent approximately eighty-five per cent of the world's population, making them the Global Majority" (p. 7).

References

Baese-Berk, Melissa, & Cepeda, Paola (organizers). (2022). Challenges and opportunities for mentoring in linguistics session, Linguistics Society of America annual meeting, Washington, DC.

Campbell-Stephens, Rosemary M. (2021). *Educational leadership and the global majority: Decolonising narratives*. Springer Nature.

Charity Hudley, Anne H., Dickter, Cheryl L., & Franz, Hannah A. (2017). *The indispensable guide to undergraduate research: Success in and beyond college*. Teachers College Press.

Charity Hudley, Anne H., & Mallinson, Christine. (2018). Introduction: Language and social justice in higher education. *Journal of English Linguistics*, 46(3), 175–185. https://doi.org/10.1177/0075424218783247

Chávez, Alicia F., & Longerbeam, Susan D. (2016). *Teaching across cultural strengths: A guide to balancing integrated and individuated cultural frameworks in college teaching*. Stylus Publishing.

Childs, Becky. (2018). Student voice and linguistic identity: Digital badging as a tool for retention of first year and first generation undergraduates. *Journal of English Linguistics*, 46(3), 186–198. https://doi.org/10.1177/0075424218783444

Clemons, Aris Moreno. (2024). Apolitical linguistics doesn't exist, and it shouldn't: Developing a Black feminist praxis toward political transparency. In Anne H. Charity Hudley, Christine Mallinson, & Mary Bucholtz (Eds.), *Decolonizing linguistics*. Oxford University Press.

Clemons Moreno, Aris, & Lawrence, Anna. (2020). Beyond position statements on race: Fostering an ethos of antiracist scholarship in linguistic research (Response to Charity Hudley et al.). *Language 96*(4), e254–e267. https://muse.jhu.edu/article/775380

Conley, David. (2005). *College knowledge: What it really takes for students to succeed and what we can do to get them ready*. Jossey-Bass.

Crenshaw, Kimberlé. (1989). Demarginalizing the intersection of race and sex: A Black feminist critique of antidiscrimination doctrine, feminist theory and antiracist politics. *University of Chicago Legal Forum, (1)*8: 139–167.

Darrah, Marjorie, Stewart, Gay, & Humbert, Roxann. (2022, March 2). Understanding levels of first-generationness. *Chronicle of Higher Education*. https://www.insidehighered.com/views/2022/03/02/first-gen-category-encompasses-varied-group-opinion

Dowd, Alicia C., & Bensimon, Estela M. (2015). *Engaging the "race question": Accountability and equity in U.S. higher education*. Teachers College Press.

Engle, Jennifer, & Tinto, Vincent. (2008). Moving beyond access: College success for low-income, first-generation students. Washington, DC: Pell Institute for the Study of Opportunity in Higher Education. https://files.eric.ed.gov/fulltext/ED504448.pdf

First Gen Access and Equity Committee. (2023). https://tinyurl.com/firstgenlsa

Franz, Hannah, Charity Hudley, Anne H., Scarborough King, Rachael, Calhoun, Kendra, miles-hercules, deandre, Muwwakkil, Jamaal, Edwards, Jeremy , Duffie, Cecily A., Knox, Danielle, Lawton, Bishop, & Merritt, John Henry. (2022). The role of the graduate student in inclusive undergraduate research experiences. *Pedagogy 22*(1), 121-141. https://doi.org/10.1215/15314200-9385522

Freire, Paulo. (1972). *Pedagogy of the oppressed*. Penguin Books.

Friedman, Lauren, & Reed, Alyson. (2014). The state of linguistics in higher education: Annual report 2013. Linguistic Society of America. http://www.linguisticsociety.org/files/Annual_Report_2013.pdf

Gable, Rachel. (2021). *The hidden curriculum: First generation students at legacy universities*. Princeton University Press.

Glass, Chris R., Gesing, Peggy, Hales, Angela, & Cong, Cong. (2017). Faculty as bridges to co-curricular engagement and community for first-generation international students. *Studies in Higher Education, 42*(5), 895–910. https://doi.org/10.1080/03075079.2017.1293877

Haeger, Heather, Fresquez, Carla, Banks, John E., & Smith, Camille. (2018). Navigating the academic landscape: How mentored research experiences can shed light on the hidden curriculum. *Scholarship and Practice of Undergraduate Research, 2*(1), 15–23. https://doi.org/10.18833/spur/2/1/7

Hiramatsu, Kazuko, & Temkin Martinez, Michal (organizers). (2021). Scholarly teaching in the age of Covid-19 and beyond session, Linguistics Society of America annual meeting, San Francisco, CA.

hooks, bell. (1994). *Teaching to transgress: Education as the practice of freedom*. Routledge.

Ilett, Darren. (2019). A critical review of LIS literature on first generation students. *Portal: Libraries and the Academy, 19*(1), 177–196. https://doi.org/10.1353/pla.2019.0009

Ives, Jillian, & Castillo-Montoya, Milagros. (2020). First-generation college students as academic learners: A systematic review. *Review of Educational Research, 90*(2), 139–178. https://doi.org/10.3102%2F0034654319899707

Kelsky, Karen. (2015). *The professor is in: The essential guide to turning your Ph.D. into a job*. Crown.

Khanal, Jeevan, & Gaulee, Uttam. (2019). Challenges of international students from pre-departure to post-study: A literature review. *Journal of International Students, 9*(2), 560–581.

King, Joyce E. (1991). Dysconscious racism: Ideology, identity, and the miseducation of teachers. *The Journal of Negro Education*, 60(2), 133–146. https://doi.org/10.2307/2295605

Ladson-Billings, Gloria. (1995). Toward a theory of culturally relevant pedagogy. *American Educational Research Journal*, 32(3), 465–491. https://doi.org/10.2307/1163320

Linguistic Society of America. (2021). December 2021 members spotlight: Iyad Ghanim. https://www.linguisticsociety.org/content/december-2021-members-spotlight-iyad-ghanim

Linguistic Society of America. (2020). Annual report: The state of linguistics in higher education. https://www.linguisticsociety.org/sites/default/files/Annual%20Report%202020%20Jan2021%20-%20final.pdf

Linguistic Society of America. (2018, October 5). LSA webinar: How to be a successful grad school applicant. https://www.youtube.com/watch?v=JDCNZjp7nRM&t=4228s

Lohfink, Mandy Martin, & Paulsen, Michael B. (2005). Comparing the determinants of persistence for first-generation and continuing-generation students. *Journal of College Student Development* 46(4), 409–428.

Macaulay, Monica A. (2011). *Surviving linguistics: A guide for graduate students.* Cascadilla Press.

Macaulay, Monica A. (in progress). *Surviving linguistics: A guide for graduate students.* Cascadilla Press.

Mantenuto, Iara. (2021). Diversifying the field: Activities to make linguistics more relevant. *Proceedings of the Linguistics Society of America*, 6(2), 5094–5100. https://doi.org/10.3765/plsa.v6i2.5094

Mack, Dwayne A., Watson, Elwood, & Madsen Camacho, Michelle. (2014). *Beginning a career in academia: A guide for graduate students of color.* Routledge.

Morgan, Allison C., LaBerge, Nicholas, Larremore, Daniel B., Galesic, Mirta, Brand, Jennie E. & Clauset, Aaron. (2022). Socioeconomic roots of academic faculty. *Nature Human Behaviour*, (6)12: 1625–1633. https://doi.org/10.1038/s41562-022-01425-4

Pascarella, Ernest T., Pierson, Christopher T., Wolniak, Gregory C., & Terenzini, Patrick T. (2004). First generation college students: Additional evidence on college experiences and outcomes. *The Journal of Higher Education*, 75(3), 249–284. https://doi.org/10.1080/00221546.2004.11772256

Plaskett, Sean, Bali, Diksha, Nakkula, Michael J., & Harris, John. (2018). Peer mentoring to support first-generation low-income college students. *Phi Delta Kappan*, (99)7, 47–51. https://doi.org/10.1177%2F0031721718767861

Ramos, Bianca Natalie. (2019). Moving from access to success: How first-generation students of color can build resilience in higher education through mentorship. *The Vermont Connection*, (40)1, 55–61.

Rickford, John R. (1997). Unequal partnerships: Sociolinguistics and the African American speech community. *Language in Society*, 26(2), 161–197. https://doi.org/10.1017/S0047404500020893

Rickford, John R. (2014). Increasing the representation of under-represented ethnic minorities in linguistics. Paper presented as part of the Symposium Diversity in linguistics, at the Linguistic Society of America annual meeting. Minneapolis, MN.

RTI International. (2019). First-generation college students: Demographic characteristics and postsecondary enrollment. NASPA. https://firstgen.naspa.org/files/dmfile/FactSheet-01.pdf

Sarcedo, Geneva L., Matias, Cheryl E., Montoya, Roberto, & Nishi, Naomi. (2015). Dirty dancing with race and class: Microaggressions toward first-generation and low income college students of color. *Journal of Critical Scholarship on Higher Education and Student Affairs*, 2(1), 1–17. https://ecommons.luc.edu/jcshesa/vol2/iss1/1

Smith, Maya Angela. (2024). Centering race and multilingualism in French linguistics. In Anne H. Charity Hudley, Christine Mallinson, & Mary Bucholtz (Eds.), *Decolonizing linguistics*. Oxford University Press.

Somers, Patricia, Woodhouse, Shawn R., & Cofer Sr., James E. (2004). Pushing the boulder uphill: The persistence of first-generation college students. *NASPA Journal, 41*(3), 418–435.

St John, Edward P., Hu, Shouping, & Fisher, Amy S. (2010). *Breaking through the access barrier: How academic capital formation can improve policy in higher education.* Routledge.

Toutkoushian, Robert K., Hossler, Don, DesJardins, Stephen, McCall, Brian, & Gonzalez Canche, Manueal. (2015). The effect of participating in Indiana's twenty-first century scholars program on college enrollments. *The Review of Higher Education 39*(1), 59–95. doi:10.1353/rhe.2015.0042

Truong, Tran. (2021, January 9). Course design principles for a more diverse professoriate. Paper presented at the Scholarly Teaching in the Age of Covid-19 and Beyond session, Linguistics Society of America annual meeting, San Francisco, CA.

Welch, Katie. (2021). Rethinking extra credit: How gamification can reduce grade inflation and strengthen soft skills. *Proceedings of the Linguistics Society of America, 6*(2), 5094–5100. https://doi.org/10.3765/plsa.v6i2.5070

Winkler, Christa, & Sriram, Rishi. (2015). Development of a scale to measure academic capital in high-risk college students. *Review of Higher Education, 38*, 565–587. https://doi.org/10.1353/rhe.2015.0032

Yosso, Tara J. (2005). Whose culture has capital? A critical race theory discussion of community cultural wealth. *Race Ethnicity and Education, 8*(1), 69–91. https://doi.org/10.1080/1361332052000341006

Yoo, Joyhanna, Lee, Cheryl, Cheng, Andrew, & Ànand, Anusha. (2023). Asian American racialization and model minority logics in linguistics. *Daedalus, 152*(3), 130–146. https://www.jstor.org/stable/48739986

Zahneis, Megan, & Patel, Viaml. (2020, April 30). Covid-19 changes the calculus of grad-student activism. *Chronicle of Higher Education.* https://www.chronicle.com/article/covid-19-changes-the-calculus-of-grad-student-activism/

Candice Thornton earned their BA in art history from the illustrious Spelman College in 2019, and their MA in English from Texas Southern University in 2021. Shortly after, they enrolled in the humanities doctoral program at Clark Atlanta University and began teaching College Composition as an adjunct professor. Thornton's research centers the literary traditions of women and gender expansive people of the African Diaspora. They are specifically interested in highlighting how authors contextualize intergenerational and transcontinental trauma and healing through signifying Diasporic cosmologies/epistemologies in autobiography and fictional narratives.

Abstract: Based on their experiences as a Black, disabled, queer, gender-expansive, neurodivergent doctoral student and adjunct faculty member who deeply loves language, the author sought to identify and document the pathways of Black and HBCU linguists in part to contextualize the opportunities for Historically Black Colleges and Universities (HBCUs) to create or further develop their existing linguistic coursework and programs. By providing a short review of the state of Black linguists, HBCUs, and the linguistics field at large, this chapter intends to document and legitimize the rich legacy of Black scholars in linguistics and language-related disciplines, name institutional and systemic barriers that contribute to the inaccessibility and lack of inclusion for Black scholars, and offer actionable solutions for academic institutions to recruit, engage, and support Black linguists to increase linguistics course offerings, departments, research, and the overall population of Black linguists.

Key Words: linguistics, HBCUs, HBCU linguistics programs, inclusive education, sociolinguistics

7

For the Culture

Pathways in Linguistics for Black and HBCU Scholars

Candice Y. Thornton (they/them/theirs)
Clark Atlanta University

Introduction

Several months after the world initially shut down from the onset of COVID-19, I found myself doom scrolling on Instagram, looking for yet another dopamine-inducing distraction. I was nearly an hour into social media surfing when I clicked on a post that led me to the Instagram page of Anne Charity Hudley. Within minutes, I clicked the link to her website and was thrilled to learn about her research and pedagogical contributions. Because her Instagram posts were so warm, extremely candid, and revolutionary, she felt familiar, akin to the mentors from each of my historically Black institutions. Charity Hudley's unapologetic Blackness, critical thinking, and ability to shake tables and make things happen was evident with every hyperlink that I clicked. As I explored her website and read her curriculum vitae, I squealed with excitement, thinking to myself that she is 100% bout dat life!!! She not only critiques inequity in academia, but also found fifty-leven ways to address systemic barriers through pedagogical workshops, mentorship initiatives, publications, and a whooooole partnership with Historically Black Colleges and Universities (HBCUs). Her social media presence and professional contributions lessened the impact of inaccessibility by providing resources to learn more about and engage with linguistics in culturally affirming and relevant ways. Charity Hudley is an exceptional example of how Black educators bridge proverbial and actual gaps while simultaneously navigating them *and* doing the seemingly impossible. For a Black American HBCU scholar like myself, reading the titles of her research, professional contributions, and personal biography inspired me to attend the second annual Advancing African American Linguistics (#2AAAL) Symposium.

Candice Y. Thornton, *For the Culture* In: *Inclusion in Linguistics.* Edited by: Anne H. Charity Hudley, Christine Mallinson and Mary Bucholtz, Oxford University Press. © Anne H. Charity Hudley, Christine Mallinson, and Mary Bucholtz 2024.
DOI: 10.1093/oso/9780197755303.003.0008

Charity Hudley's Instagram, website, and the #2AAAL Symposium were my earliest introductions into linguistics. I highlight these three entry points- because they mark the beginning of my own pathway. The symposium marks the day that I learned that my interdisciplinary research interests, although deeply rooted in humanities, were also closely aligned with sociolinguistics. During my lunch break on that first day, with my mind racing and brain flooded with all the dopamine, I leaned into my neurodivergent impulsivity and simultaneously ran several Google queries. I had no fewer than nine tabs open, trying to identify what I needed to know and do to swiftly switch gears and pursue a linguistics program. In the midst of this chaotic search, I also realized that I needed more information about the history of the discipline, so in another tab, I opened a link from the Linguistic Society of America's website. While my short time at the virtual #2AAAL Symposium was pleasantly diverse, accessible, and engaging, in contrast, LSA's website seemed to communicate otherwise. If the #2AAAL Symposium and Charity Hudley's website were the sparks that set my linguistic candle ablaze, the LSA website was a candle snuffer.

Although the #2AAAL symposium featured countless African American scholars and research that engaged decolonial epistemologies, the Linguistic Society of America's website did not. With one click from the homepage, I arrived at a page entitled "What Is Linguistics?" that defined linguistics as the "scientific study of language" in which linguists "apply the scientific method to conduct formal studies of speech sounds and gestures, grammatical structures, and meaning across the world's 6000+ languages" (LSA, 2022). As an HBCU scholar, my observations regarding the dichotomy of scientific versus humanistic studies of language illustrates the history of education and science-based disciplines being inaccessible to Black people. HBCUs have a rich legacy of developing preachers, teachers, and social justice warriors, and were created because white institutions did not permit Black students to enroll. Because of the inaccessibility of institutions of higher learning and scientific disciplines, students like me have struggled to navigate institutions and disciplines that are deeply entrenched in ableist, classist, racist, sexist, and xenophobic practices and policies.

A bit further down the page, a small section "The Science of Linguistics" explained that "Linguists are . . . researchers dedicated to the systematic study of language who apply the scientific method by making observations, testing hypotheses, and developing theories" (LSA, 2022). As a person who studies ideological hegemony, as perpetuated by and through language and "science," LSA's descriptions communicate a very colonial sentiment; their definitions and summaries riddled with language that signifies an intellectual taxonomy, with implied distinctions of value and validity that contributes to the marginalization and misrepresentation of colonized peoples and their history, knowledge, and language. Eduardo Bonilla-Silva and Tukufu Zuberi's *White Logic, White Methods: Racism and Methodology* explains that "a careful reading of the history of social statistics reveals that it was born when mathematical statistics an evolutionary theory met in the racially bent eugenic mind of Francis Galton [who was] obsessed with explaining the racial hierarchy in social status and achievement" (2008, p. 11). They further explain that "data do not tell us a story. We use data to craft a story that comports with our understanding of the world. If we begin with a racially biased view . . . then we will end with a racially biased view . . . Data may indeed speak to some users of statistics; however, it only speaks to the rest of us in the voice of research" (Bonilla-Silva et al., 2008, p. 12). In relation to linguistics, methodologies and resulting data often perpetuate colonial hegemony.

Just above "The Science of Linguistics," a link to "Studying Linguistics" offered additional information about the discipline along with a series of resources. One of these resources, "The Domain of Linguistics," is "a series first published by the Linguistic Society of America in 1982 . . . [and] was written to explain the discipline to the general public" (LSA, 2022). "The Domain of Linguistics" series features seven articles, with topics ranging from grammar, language variation, and linguistics and literature. I clicked the final article, entitled "The History of Modern Language," by Frederick Newmeyer, and learned that the modern field of linguistics was established in the nineteenth century, and that "while ancient India and Greece had a remarkable grammatical tradition, throughout most of history, linguistics had been the province of philosophy, rhetoric, and literary analysis" (Newmeyer, n.d.). While reading Newmeyer's summation, I could not help but think "so he just gon' act like Greek scholars ain' learn from KmT?! Like people of the African diaspora (pre and postcolonial contact) weren't exemplifying linguistics, philosophy, and rhetoric through diverse oral traditions?! Like languages of the African diaspora ain' been explicitly articulatin' and signifyin' all the cosmologies, epistemologies, and ontologies?!" I tried to quiet my thoughts so that I could get through the remainder of the summary and resumed with Newmeyer's assertion that at the beginning of the twentieth century, "the attention of the world's linguists turned more and more to the study of grammar—in the technical sense of the term the organization of the sound system of a language and the internal structure of its words and sentences" (Newmeyer, n.d.). Although I wanted to get through the information, I murmured something along the lines of "and who pray tell were the world's linguists, sir?!" as he briefly described the contributions of Swiss linguist Ferdinand de Saussure, American linguist Noam Chomsky, German mathematician and philosopher

Gottlob Frege, and British philosopher Bertrand Russell to the development of linguistics. While these individuals' contributions are significant, Newmeyer's brief survey reveals Eurocentric perspectives that perpetuate the erasure of nonwhite, nonmale history and scholarly contributions. Newmeyer concludes by acknowledging:

> In the past 50 years, there has been increasing attention to the social side of language as well as the mental . . . In addition, the movements for minority rights in the United States and other Western countries has led to a close examination of social variation that complements earlier work in geographical variation. Scholars have turned the analytical tools of linguistics to the study of nonstandard varieties like African American Vernacular English and Chicano Spanish. And the women's movement has led many linguists to investigate gender differences in speech and whether our language has to perpetuate sexual inequality. (n.d.)

For me, this article amplifies all-too-familiar sentiments of Eurocentric male consciousness that perpetuates the erasure and marginalization of non-white people with marginalized genders. I was disheartened by the lackluster documentation of linguistic scholarship, but frankly, not at all surprised. Whereas the #2AAAL Symposium inspired me to pursue linguistics because of the diversity and innovative research, LSA's website was a jarring reminder that the #2AAAL was more like the exception than the standard. This observation was further exacerbated in April 2022, when a resolution sponsored by Noam Chomsky, Sabine Iatridou, Pauline Jacobson, Jason Merchant, Pritty Patel-Grosz, Yael Sharvit, Philippe Schlenker, Tim Stowell, Harold Torrence, and Charles Yang called for the adoption of the Chicago Statement on free speech.

On her social media, Charity Hudley explained the nuances of how this proposal was harmful. On the day it was announced, she noted, "The Linguistic Society of America actively chose to put this proposal through [without] comment or debate. We spent years in open forums & faced direct questions & comments from EC members to get our race statement shared in a restoratively just manner. None of that here. They wanted us to do the labor here and once again put our bodies and reputations on the line . . . These authors know what they are doing. They waited until my term on the LSA executive committee was over to launch this. And no current leader wrote a dissent or rejoinder" (Charity Hudley, 2022). Additional commentary was provided by various individuals both affiliated and not affiliated with the LSA, and in the "Linguistic Society of America Considers Free Speech Resolution," Weinberg provides additional context surrounding the aforementioned resolution.

Numerous other members also dissented, and days later, the LSA removed the statement from their website (for additional discussion, see miles-hercules, this volume; Dockum & Green, this volume).

The (2019) LSA Statement on Race acknowledges "the essential intellectual contributions of people with various racial identities to the study of language." In the statement's preamble, the LSA asserts that "a consideration of race, racialization, and racial implications of linguistic scholarship is important for linguists who study the relationship of social factors to language as well as those from whom social factors are not the primary focus of linguistic research, as all linguistic research has the potential to reproduce or challenge racial notions" (2019). The LSA's statement also articulates the linguistic consequences of racial classification in the United States, highlighting the eradication of Indigenous languages and systemic penalization of racially minoritized people who speak varieties of standardized languages. The LSA offers strategies to address the perpetuation of erasure, inequity, and violence in the discipline and profession of linguistics. The statement asserts:

> Linguists must be active participants in creating an intellectually inclusive community. For linguists seeking to mentor and support [racially marginalized students], listening to and respecting their experiences is crucial, as is acknowledging and addressing rather than overlooking or denying the role of the discipline of linguistics in the reproduction of racism. To ensure equity and inclusion in the theory, practice, and teaching of linguistics, framing efforts with a linguistic empowerment approach can help ensure that the institutional racism that leads to linguistic injustice is disrupted.

The statement also calls for linguists to "reject the marginalization of the intellectual interest of those who are traditionally underrepresented in the discipline and the profession." This call requires that linguists actively "scrutinize and dismantle privilege within linguistics," in part by embracing an inclusive cross-disciplinary approach and assessing exclusionary boundaries and engaging systematically marginalized scholars and their respective communities. It also advocates for more research that explores "how race intersects with other social categories and forms of social identification and grouping," and for linguists to "explicitly examine the connection between racism and capitalism as well as racism and colorism, both within and outside communities of color" (LSA, 2019). These salient points could all be addressed by cultivating new and developing existing linguistics programs at HBCUs.

I am writing this chapter because I want to be abundantly clear that linguistics is for everybody, to contextualize the barriers and subsequent pathways that Black and HBCU scholars have forged into the field and provide additional information for new pathways. It documents the rich contributions of Black and HBCU scholars, while examining data that contextualizes the disparities of higher education and the current/developing landscape of linguistics. Most importantly, it provides specific strategies to develop sustainable, equitable, and inclusive pathways for Black and other marginalized scholars, including those at HBCUs.

HBCUs and Linguistics

According to the United Negro College Fund, HBCUs are only 3% of the United States' colleges and universities, however, are responsible for 10% of enrolled African American students. The National Center for Education Statistics (2019c) explains that "HBCUs are institutions that were established prior to 1964 with the principal mission of educating Black Americans ... These institutions were founded and developed in an environment of legal segregation and, by providing access to higher education, they contributed substantially to the progress Black Americans made in improving their status." While HBCUs were established for "Black Americans," since their inception, Black scholars from across the Diaspora have and continue to matriculate through these institutions. As a descendent of enslaved West Africans who is American-born, but who also was educated through Pan-Africanism, my research centers the pathways of Black and HBCU scholars, acknowledging our racial identity cannot be reduced to an anti-Black policy such as the one-drop rule—nor will I deny the ways in which our Diasporic identities, though intrinsically connected, may differ based on the respective ethnicities and nationalities of folks racially categorized as Black. Nevertheless, my intention is to highlight the barriers, contributions and pathways of Black scholars who received their degrees from both HBCUs and predominantly white institutions (PWIs).

Although HBCUs were developed to provide Black American scholars an equitable opportunity to pursue higher learning, unfortunately, due to sentiments resulting from assimilation, some curricula and policies within HBCUs perpetuate systemic racism. For example, at each of the three HBCUs that I've attended, standardized English was required for all core curriculum coursework. Although Black English and other varietal dialects were and are commonly used throughout public and private spaces at each of these institutions, student learning outcomes required that written assignments and oral presentations adhere to standardized English. Let me be clear in stating that requiring standardized English, particularly at an HBCU, is one example of how anti-Black racism is perpetuated—even in spaces intended to affirm people whose ethnicity, race, and nationality are marginalized by anglo/euro/white hegemony.

Another challenge that HBCUs must address is the limited language and linguistics course offerings. While many offer Romance languages like French or Spanish as majors or core language requirement courses, there is a great need for Black diasporic language courses. In "Critical Race Pedagogy for More Effective and Inclusive World Language Teaching," Uju Anya (2021) asserts that "to address racial inequity and the exclusion of African Americans in applied linguistics, second-language acquisition, and world language education, our field must reckon with social justice problems of racism and anti-Blackness" (p. 1055). They propose a series of steps that include:

(1) to conduct inquiry and self-assessment of language programme policies, stakeholders, practices, and materials through the lens of CRT to determine if and to what extent they promote Black students' meaningful, equitable participation and success in WL.
(2) careful examination of power and inequity in language teaching. This requires educators' awareness of their racial identities and positionality in racial hierarchies, which influence their perception of materials, how they teach, and their attitude toward and treatment of their students.
(3) translating understanding from inquiry and self-reflexivity into a liberatory practice for antiracism and social justice.

In my own search for African Language programs in which to potentially cross-register, I encountered yet another barrier. According to the National African Language Resource Center (2021), there are nearly 30 US postsecondary institutions that have programs that offer at least one African language course. In the NALRC's list of African language programs in the US, however, the only HBCUs listed include Howard University and Georgia Southern University. I continued searching and discovered that over the last decade many HBCUs have expanded their language course offerings; however, few of the new offerings center languages of the African Diaspora.

In my survey of language course offerings at HBCUs, I found that Spelman College currently offers Chinese, French, Japanese, Portuguese, and Spanish, the University of Maryland Eastern Shore (n.d.) offers Fundamentals of Arabic, and Texas Southern University offers Chinese, French, and Spanish. As noted in the Clark Atlanta University (2018) graduate catalog, the university offers three graduate level linguistics courses, including African American Dialects, but their modern languages include Spanish and French. Bowie State University (n.d.) offers Amharic for beginners, the African American Vernacular Tradition, and Introduction to General Linguistics I and II (which are classified as English courses rather than social sciences). Howard University offers Somali, Swahili, Wolof, Yoruba, and Zulu language courses; additionally, they offer the Howard African Language Summer Institute, which "is an annual program dedicated to increasing students' proficiency in the seven African languages that Howard offers" (Howard University, n.d.). They also have a forthcoming African Language Lab, which is a collaborative development of "the Center for African Studies, the Founders Library, and the Department of World Languages" Howard University, n.d.). While these additions are encouraging, they also illustrate layers of inaccessibility that affect Black and HBCU scholars to enroll in African language and linguistics courses.

According to the National Center for Education Statistics (2019c; 2019a; 2019b), 207,858 Black students enrolled at HBCUs in 2018; however, only 12.6% of Black students enrolled at an HBCU received bachelor's degrees. Even more astounding is that 2.6% of Black students enrolled at an HBCU received their master's, and only .74% received doctoral degrees. These disparaging figures amplify how systemic racism impacts the accessibility of academia. While HBCU scholars arrive from across the nation and globe, there are several barriers for HBCU scholars to secure adequate funding to enroll and matriculate through postsecondary institutions. In an article entitled "How HBCUs Are Addressing the Cost of College," Sarah Wood (2021) cites data from the NCES and explains that "Black graduates . . . owe $25,000 more in student loans on average compared to their white counterparts. Wood also cites Lodriguez Murray, the United Negro College Fund's senior vice president of public policy and government affairs, who asserts that "the colleges are underinvested in, like many African Americans and their communities." The article thus broadly contextualizes how systemic racism negatively impacts Black students as well as HBCUs and their financial resources.

Despite the multidisciplinary nature of linguistic studies, the data about Black scholars with linguistic degrees remains minimal. Indeed, the "population of ethnic minorities with advanced degrees in linguistics is so low in the U.S. that few federal agencies report data for these groups" (Linguistic Society of America 2018, p. 28). Because existing data fails to quantify how and how many Black and HBCU scholars are actively engaged in the discipline, it is imperative for researchers to actively engage race by clearly defining racial categorizations used in their data collection. Furthermore, there are several HBCUs that offer linguistic courses by way of speech-pathology, classical and comparative literature, communications, and foreign and modern languages. Unfortunately, however, out of the 100 accredited HBCUs, there are currently no HBCUs that confer linguistics degrees.

Included on the publication website are the most recent figures about conferred linguistics and language related degrees from the National Center for Education Statistics (2019c; 2019a; 2019b). Although these figures are not exhaustive and do not distinguish the race of degree recipients, or whether the awarding institutions are predominantly white or historically Black, it is clear that few linguistics degrees are awarded. In a report on fall enrollment and degrees conferred at HBCUs, the National Center for Education Statistics (2019c) notes that its data "excludes historically Black colleges and universities that are not participating in Title IV programs" and that "totals include persons of other racial/ethnic groups not separately identified."

In 2020, Charity Hudley, Christine Mallinson, and Mary Bucholtz published "Toward Racial Justice in Linguistics: Interdisciplinary Insights Into Theorizing Race in the Discipline and Diversifying the Profession." This article offers a nuanced perspective about many of the barriers that prevent racially marginalized scholars from navigating the discipline. They provide a survey of the sociohistorical landscape of the linguistics discipline, along with countless strategies for addressing inequitable circumstances. According to their article, "many scholars with a deep interest in language and race center their own scholarship and professional activity not in linguistics departments, but rather in departments of communication, English, modern languages, or education, where they often receive a warmer reception, more support to pursue research on race, and more opportunities to take part in professional initiatives that advance racial justice. These disciplines, though often devalued within linguistics (Mallinson & Charity Hudley, 2018), collectively provide a model for linking theoretical racial knowledge to the real-world contexts in which language users go about their day talking, writing, learning, and expressing themselves" (Charity Hudley et al., 2020).

This assertion resonates immensely with my experience navigating three different HBCUs. I earned my bachelor's in art history and master's in English Literature at one HBCU, and I am currently enrolled in a humanities doctoral program at another HBCU. Although the underlying theme of my research has been and remains rooted in studying the relationships between language, identity, power, and value, I recognize that my research would benefit immensely from a comprehensive foundation in linguistics. My desire to disrupt ideological and linguistic hegemonies perpetuated in curriculum development, literary criticism, media representation, and social justice movements exists because my HBCUs have encouraged me to synthesize my knowledge and experiences through my scholarship. Although I have had very limited access to linguistic programs or even Black linguistics faculty members, I am privileged to be able to leverage resources like the internet to find opportunities that allow me to collaborate across disciplines and institutions.

My Linguistics Pathway

As previously mentioned, my pathway into linguistics began with Charity Hudley's social media and website. I am privileged enough to have internet access and devices that connect me to individuals and institutions beyond my physical location. Because of Charity Hudley's internet presence, I was able to learn about the #2AAAL Symposium, which was hosted by the University of California Santa Barbara Department of Linguistics. Although at the time I had no affiliation with the institution or discipline, the website for the symposium clarified that nonaffiliated and multidisciplinary scholars were welcome. Additionally, the symposium was virtual and free to attend, thus permitting me access that I otherwise would not have. Attending the symposium allowed me to familiarize myself with Black linguistics scholars, but most importantly, attending allowed me to identify viable opportunities to transition from English literature to linguistics.

Although initially after learning about linguistics, I sought linguistics programs to apply to, but learned very quickly that it would be counterproductive and financially impossible to pursue. At that time I was more than halfway through my master's program and in the process of selecting doctoral programs to apply to. I briefly considered finding a master's program in linguistics, but upon reviewing the different requirements for each program it was clear that I would still have to enroll in more than a semester's worth of foundational coursework. I therefore decided to pursue my doctorate degree in a humanities program. Nevertheless, I did not lose sight of linguistics. Within weeks of attending the #2AAAL Symposium and contacting Charity Hudley, I received an email to collaborate with other scholars who were developing their publications for Students' Rights to Their Own Language. I also continued to develop my teaching in ways that incorporated linguistics. After attending the #2AAAL Symposium and witnessing Charity Hudley and Calhoun discuss pedagogical approaches for introductory linguistics, their conversations revealed several opportunities for me to examine how I could better serve my institution and peers as a graduate student, supplemental English instructor, and humanities tutor.

The information and connections that #2AAAL provided me have been invaluable resources to my development of affirming coursework and research. During #2AAAL Symposium, Charity Hudley and Calhoun discussed pedagogical approaches for introductory linguistics, their conversations revealed several opportunities for me to examine how I could better serve my institution and peers. Because of my experiences during and the resulting connections from the #2AAAL, I have been able to develop my pedagogical praxis in culturally affirming ways. Nearly two years after attending #2AAAL, I am serving in my second year as a full-time doctoral student and adjunct English professor at my third HBCU. As the spring semester of my first year ended, my students wrote short semester recaps in which one shared that they "never had a professor . . . allow [them] to free write with AAVE included. You've helped me realize how complex AAVE can be and it's not only a dialect but something we should be proud of." Another shared that "the thing that I like about the course is the discussions we had, specifically the one about AAVE. I felt like this class allowed me to talk and write about subjects that I was genuinely interested in." The assignment they were referring to was developed in part because of what I learned during Calhoun's presentation at #2AAAL and the co-authored publications I read from Calhoun and Charity Hudley. The #2AAAL Symposium was a pivotal moment in my academic and professional journey, and I am privileged and thankful for Charity Hudley, her colleagues, and mentees—all of whom work tirelessly to address systemic barriers through their scholar-activism.

As a Black student with multiple marginalized identities, academia has often been challenging to navigate. Because I was a military dependent, I attended nearly 10 different schools before enrolling in college. In most of my schools, diversity was limited to three or four non-white students, and very seldom did I have teachers who shared any similar marginalized identities. Over the course of my K-12 education, I experienced significant racialized violence that occurred during school hours, on school property, by educators and students alike. At one institution, my family withdrew my brother and me after I was penalized for appropriately responding to a racial epithet. After the administration failed to hold the teacher and student who used the epithet accountable, my parents enrolled us in an entirely different district. This experience was one of many, and due to these unfortunate and common experiences, I committed to attend HBCUs for the entirety of my postsecondary education.

One of the greatest barriers to my academic progress throughout my journey has been the lack of support from non-Black educators. I often felt isolated or othered by my teachers and struggled immensely with navigating what I now understand was the adultification of Black students. This barrier was further exacerbated by the fact that my HBCU alum parents, who worked (in varying degrees) in education, were very transparent about the misrepresentation of Black and American history. The education that I received at home differed immensely from my classroom learning and the discrepancies that I observed and experienced often made me feel unsafe to engage at school. Despite these issues in my formative years, in my first semester at my undergraduate HBCU, it was apparent that I was receiving an entirely different education, one that centered culturally affirming curricula.

During my first few semesters, I struggled immensely to adapt to my new environment, in part because much of what I'd previously learned was being debunked. Additionally, my professors engaged my peers and I differently. I was encouraged to articulate my thoughts and pursue research topics that in predominantly white spaces, were rejected. I recognized that much of my foundational education centered romanticized misrepresentations of white supremacist delusion. My HBCU undergraduate experience marked a new period of developing language to articulate how class, gender, nationality, race, and other intersections of identity inform experiences, perspectives, and values. With each course, I learned from and with scholars who shared their diverse knowledge about Black culture, US history, and global citizenship, and because the majority of my peers and professors were Black, I felt safe to intimately engage and synthesize my coursework in affirming ways.

My undergraduate research examined the Yoruba philosophical concept of àse as an aesthetic criterion to legitimize extrinsic and intrinsic metaphysical attributes of artists and their creations. Although it is categorized as art history criticism, it is inherently sociolinguistic. My master's thesis briefly discusses the role of standardized and vernacular language in the characterizations, mythic constructions, and archetypal figures and patterns that are specific to Black English and African oral tradition. Because of my academic pathway, I have often approached my research interests as an interdisciplinary scholar, drawing from art history, comparative literature, philosophy, psychology, and sociology. My interdisciplinary pathway is one that is not unusual for many Black scholars, as can be seen in the diverse pathways that other Black linguists and Black linguistic scholarship have taken.

Diverse Pathways of Black Linguists

One of the earliest Black linguists to publish research in the field is Lorenzo Dow Turner. Turner received his bachelor's and master's degree from

Howard University and was of the "first generation of African Americans to be able to earn a living wage from the pursuits of their mind" (Wade-Lewis, 2001, p. 238). Turner served as an English professor at Fisk University, and in 1930, he attended the Linguistics Institute in New York City. Turner became the first African American member of the Linguistics Society of America and in 1932, and he was awarded a grant from the American Council of Learned Societies, which, along with other funding, permitted him to begin his comprehensive study of Gullah speakers. According to Wade-Lewis, "Turner interviewed twenty-one Gullah speakers, filling a notebook on each with the details of [their] ideolect—phonology, morphology, syntax, and semantics" (2001, p. 236). Turner ensured that his data reflected generational variations by selecting "two speakers over the age of sixty and one speaker between forty and sixty years . . . from each island" (2001, p. 236). Turner subsequently returned during the summers of 1933, 1934, and 1935 to continue his research. Turner shared his research interests with the president of the International Phonetic Association, explaining that "I should like to study the phonetic structure of certain West African languages with a view to determine, if possible, the nature and content of African survivals in Gullah" (2001, p. 240). After having attended the School of Oriental and African Languages at the University of London during 1936 and 1937, Turner returned to the Sea Islands to collect additional data. Turner's *Africanisms in the Gullah Dialect* (1949) was the first linguistic study of Gullah, and the first body of research to illustrate the survival of Niger Kordofanian languages in the United States. Turner's research is arguably a catalyzing force for academia's legitimization of Gullah and other creolized languages. More importantly, Turner's research restores severed transcontinental ties for descendants of enslaved African people.

Nearly a century after Turner's publications, there are many Black scholars who continue to do the work that must be done, reconnecting Black people to the languages, epistemologies, and ontologies that are indigenous to the people and lands from which we were violently removed. It is by no coincidence that one of the first things enslaved people were stripped of was their mother tongue. As Morrison once said, "There is no time for despair, no place for self-pity, no need for silence, no room for fear. We speak, we write, we do language. That is how civilizations heal" (2015). While there are many ways to do language beyond the confines of academia, it is important to disrupt anti-Blackness that manifests as misinformation and cultural appropriation, especially within linguistics. In order for this to happen, equity and inclusion must be prioritized on all levels. One of the barriers for Black students in academia and linguistics is the lack of representation and inclusion of marginalized people. This barrier is in part the consequence of inaccessibility, and requires several strategies to overcome. While I do not believe the onus of addressing inequity is on Black students or HBCUs alone, I believe that by intentionally centering marginalized scholars and their work, academia and the linguistics discipline can reduce the harm of erasure and white supremacist delusion.

Although there is a small population of scholars in general—and Black scholars in particular—who are obtaining linguistics degrees, this section highlights several of the many contemporary scholars whose research demonstrates the diverse pathways that they have forged in doing research related to linguistics and language-based disciplines. In this section I highlight several Black scholars, such as Sunn m'Cheaux, Lisa Green, Temptaous Mckoy, Daryl Dance, and David F. Green, because their research provides culturally relevant information to incorporate in introductory linguistics, literature, and language-related courses that provides opportunities to expand how Black and HBCU students engage within and across linguistics and language-based disciplines. Because much of these scholars' work is rooted in diverse linguistic variations of Black people, instructors at HBCUs and PWIs should integrate their work to disrupt racially hegemonic misrepresentations of language variation. By doing so, institutions develop culturally competent curriculum that equips Black students with methodological frameworks to develop their own innovative research. HBCU and PWIs can and should assess existing programs, course offerings, and syllabi to identify opportunities to equitably include diverse scholarship. Additionally, supplemental courses, institutional partnerships, and recruitment initiatives need to be established to develop sustainable pathways for Black and HBCU students.

In 2017, Sunn m'Cheaux became the first native-speaking Gullah person to teach Gullah/Geechee in the African Languages Program at Harvard University through the Project Teach program (Harvard University, n.d.a). Project Teach is a community initiative that uses a research-based approach to encourage "a college-going culture among students"; according to post-program surveys, there was a 6% increase "in students' belief that people who look like them go to college" (Harvard University n.d.a). Harvard's development of Project Teach and partnership with m'Cheaux demonstrates how institutions can create opportunities for marginalized people and develop curriculum and partnerships that are diverse and inclusive. m'Cheaux's involvement with the program, and subsequent affiliation with Harvard University, demonstrates the importance of legitimizing culturally acquired knowledge beyond the confines of academia. In an interview with National Public Radio, m'Cheaux explains that people "have no idea that there's a whole community, a whole culture, a whole language system that's indigenous to this country"

(McCammon, 2019; see also m'Cheaux, n.d.). He asserts that while Gullah is indigenous to the United States, it is uniquely African because of its preservation of diasporic linguistic components. Because academia is inaccessible in many ways, partnering with individuals like m'Cheaux expands pathways for Black students to identify the significance of linguistic variations and to preserve the legacy of diasporic traditions.

Lisa Green is an associate professor in the Department of Linguistics and founding director of the Center for the Study of African American Language at the University of Massachusetts, Amherst (n.d.). Green earned a BS from Grambling State University in English education, MA from University of Kentucky in English, and a PhD in linguistics from the University of Massachusetts. Green holds membership with the Linguistic Society of America and the National Alliance of Black School Educators. Her research "[investigates] variation within and across varieties of English, with a focus on African American English (AAE)" (umass.edu). Some of Green's publications include Language and the African American Child (2011), African American English: A Linguistic Introduction (2002), and a paper entitled "Syntax and Semantics," which was included in the 2019 publication of the Oxford Handbook of African American Language.

Temptaous Mckoy is an assistant professor of English with a focus in technical and professional communication at Bowie State University. She teaches courses such as "Developmental Writing, First-Year Writing, Research Writing, and Technical and Report Writing" (Mckoy, 2019). Mckoy also serves as the coordinator of graduate studies in the Department of Language, Literature, and Cultural Studies. Mckoy received a BA in English from Elizabeth City State University, an MA in professional communications and leadership, and a PhD in rhetoric, writing, and professional communication from East Carolina University.

Mckoy's research explores "the use of amplification rhetorics in Black communities and their implications for technical and professional communication studies" (2019). Additionally, Mckoy has presented on eliminating privileged socialization practices for minority students in graduate TPC programs, diversifying graduate programs through recruitment, and HBCU faculty's role in diversifying technical communication. Mckoy's research brilliantly articulates that "amplification rhetorics are discursive and communicative practices, both written/textual and embodied/performative" and that amplification rhetorics "are characterized by three tenets: (a) the reclamation of agency, (b) the accentuation and acknowledgment of narratives, and (c) the inclusion of marginalized epistemologies" (2019). In her dissertation, Mckoy asserts that "this project identifies rhetorical practices located in Black spaces and communities" and that "it illustrates just what it means to pass the mic and remind fold that we not 'bout to act like there aren't people of color at the TPC table" (2019). Mckoy's theoretical contributions are deeply sociolinguistic and would be useful to integrate in linguistic introductory courses.

Daryl Lynn Dance earned a BA in English from Hampton University, an MA in English from Virginia Commonwealth University, and a PhD in English from the University of Kansas. As noted in her university profile (Hampton University, n.d.), her research interests include African American rhetoric and literature, writing theory and pedagogy, and service learning. In 2015, Dance published an article entitled "Can Rachel Jeantel Speak?" which poignantly highlights sociolinguistics as it relates to the dismissal of Rachel Jeantel's testimony in the George Zimmerman trial. Dance analyzes several accounts about Rachel Jeantel to demonstrate how writers "re-present Jeantel by showing how she is like other African Americans [making it] clear that African American English is normal and legitimate" (Dance, 2015, p. 142). Articles like "Can Rachel Jeantel Speak" should be incorporated in introductory linguistics, communications, composition and rhetoric, and sociology courses to help Black students identify the implications of language variation in the media and as an aspect of social justice reform.

David F. Green Jr. is the director of first-year writing and an associate professor at Howard University. He earned his BA in English from Hampton University and a PhD in English from Penn State University. According to his official profile (Howard University, n.d.), Green is "deeply invested in culture, language, and the performance of self in writing" and "African American expressive cultures." Green explains that his research is grounded in "a distinctive understanding of African American Rhetoric," which specifically examines the "artistic and political forms of communication that African descendants within the New World developed to both form and critique community" (2019). In a publication entitled "Flow as Metaphor for Changing Composition Practices," Green (2017) asserts that "English studies can benefit from increased attention to hip-hop language practices" and that "the concept of flow within hip-hop nation language studies has been largely overlooked for its value to the rhetorical development of students in English studies." Green (2017) further explains that "agency can be found in academic writing through the fluid and confident manner with which one defines and links an idea, phrase, or expression to a larger issue." Green continues by asserting that "sensitivity to linguistic differences does not alone invest students with agency," and that educators must incorporate texts that contextualize rhetorical devices in standardized and dialectic English. Green offers in-depth analysis of several songs, highlighting the linguistic relevance and literary strategies that hip-hop artists employ. His examples illustrate culturally competent pedagogical approaches for engaging first-year writers that are integral for engaging Black and HBCU students in existing and developing linguistic programs.

Solutions for Inclusivity

In "Toward Racial Justice in Linguistics," Charity Hudley, Mallinson, and Bucholtz (2020) explain that "race has been integral to how the study of language has developed as a research area and to how languages have been academically, socially, and politically defined over time" (e200). They also assert that "linguistic research concerning language variation and linguistic diversity within and across racial and cultural categories has traditionally centered on who speaks (or does not speak) a particular language or variety" (2020, e201). Because academic institutions have historically marginalized Black people, HBCUs are particularly significant because their populations include people who possess multilingual capabilities that transcend standardized language and white-centering traditions.

In order to improve diversity and inclusion, the University of California developed the UC-HBCU Scholars in Linguistics program. The initiative cultivates diversity and inclusion in the linguistic sciences through collaborative partnerships with "HBCUs and other Minority Serving institutions that do not offer linguistics as a major" (UC-HBCU Scholars in Linguistics, n.d.). This initiative offers promising opportunities for existing institutions to leverage their resources to provide equitable learning and research for racially marginalized scholars. One of the impactful developments from the UC-HBCU/NSF REU Talking College Project and UC Santa Barbara is their presentation of the #2AAAL Symposium, which invited was free and open to all scholars.

In 2021, Kendra Calhoun, Charity Hudley, Mary Bucholtz, Jazmine Exford, and Brittney Johnson published "Attracting Black Students to Linguistics Through a Black-Centered Introduction to Linguistics Course." They developed an online introductory course as part of "a specially funded research program that serves Black undergraduates" from HBCUs and PWIs (2021, e12). Their course was asynchronously offered and centered Black content to address "the lack of culturally sustaining pedagogies for Black students in linguistics" (20201, e12). While there are many barriers that prevent Black students from studying linguistics, they explain in great detail that "if a conventional introductory linguistics course is a Black student's first encounter with the field, then it is very possible that their first impression is that linguistics is a field in which their experiences are not relevant and one that would not provide them with valuable skills and knowledge for everyday life or for a career in their area of interest" (2021, e13). While many Black scholars do engage in linguistic-related disciplines and careers, as previously demonstrated, there are inadequate courses and programs for Black scholars to sustainably navigate linguistic programs and receive degrees in linguistics specifically. As Calhoun et al. explain:

> Introductory linguistics courses are also an opportunity to meet students where they are academically, intellectually, and socially. For Black students, these courses offer opportunities to learn that their language has been studied (i.e. recognized by linguists as being worthy of study), that analytic skills in linguistics can shed light on phenomena studied in other disciplines, and that users of diverse languages and varieties . . . are integral to linguistic advancement because they bring new perspectives and insights to the predominantly white field. (2021, e15)

For this reason, HBCUs are invaluable to the diversification of the linguistics discipline, in that their populations, although predominantly Black, are composed of scholars who are often multilingual and dialectic. In the 2017–2018 academic year, 223,163 Black students were enrolled at an HBCU, and 43,000 HBCU degrees were conferred (approximately 1.4% of total conferred degrees). While these figures seem miniscule, even a small portion of this population would increase the diversity of linguistics.

In "Toward Racial Justice in Linguistics," Charity Hudley, Mallinson, and Bucholtz assert that "in order to adequately address issues of racism . . . the discipline of linguistics must take at least the following steps:

- Fully acknowledge the ongoing legacy of the field's history of racism and colonialism (Bolton & Hutton, 2000; Errington, 2001; Leonard, 2018);
- End scholarly practices of racial erasure and racial displacement through reliance on untheorized conceptual and methodological substitutes for race such as "culture" (Ladson-Billings, 2008);
- Eliminate research that considers racially minoritized groups and their language only as marked and "exotic" and the treatment of whiteness as the unmarked norm rather than as a phenomenon requiring critical analysis (Lanehart, 2009; Trechter & Bucholtz, 2001);

- Understand racialization as a system for reproducing white supremacy (Murji & Solomos, 2005) as well as the centrality of raciolinguistic ideologies in supporting that system (Rosa & Flores, 2017);
- Critique research that reproduces inequality through (what may even be benevolently intended) claims of racially minoritized groups' linguistic deficits; and
- Restructure the discipline to be fully inclusive of the ideas, work, and presence of scholars of color and the experiences, practices, contributions of racially minoritized language users (Lanehart, 2019), even—and especially—when these differ from disciplinary norms and traditions" (Charity Hudley, Mallinson, & Bucholtz, 2020, e212–213)."

These steps are paramount for linguistic scholars who are racially and institutionally privileged, however, HBCUs and PWIs serving racially minoritized students should also implement these recommendations. HBCU and PWI faculty members, especially those with tenure and other privileged positionality, must assess the institutional, departmental, and personal barriers that affect students' ability to engage and contribute to the discipline. PWIs should evaluate the accessibility of their institutions and programming. As mentioned earlier, the University of California Santa Barbara offered the #2AAAL in a virtual capacity with no cost. This one event shifted my entire trajectory because if it were not offered virtually and without cost, I would not have been able to attend because I was still working two jobs and recuperating from COVID-19.

On an institutional level, empowered constituents, particularly those who are protected by their full-time fully vested employment status, must leverage their positions of power to cultivate collaborative initiatives with individuals, institutions, and organizations who lack access to opportunities and resources. Institutions can establish expectations for hiring culturally competent faculty and staff, while ensuring that adequate funding is available for existing linguistics, literature, and language-related studies programs to develop more diverse and comprehensive courses. Financial aid and scholarship offices can ensure that students receive the necessary funding to successfully complete their programs. Deans of arts and sciences, education, and graduate education can partner with department chairs to foster interdisciplinary learning that introduces marginalized students to the linguistics discipline. Academic advisors and career development staff can familiarize themselves with linguistics courses, programs, and professional opportunities within and outside of their institutions, so that they can offer diverse pathways for students with linguistics, literature, and language-related concentrations.

Undergraduate and graduate resource centers should offer consistent grant-writing and publication workshops so that students are equipped to generate funding and partnerships for their research. Alumni affairs offices and department chairs can be diligent in cultivating comprehensive mentoring and research opportunities for students in linguistics and language-related studies. Department chairs can incorporate Black-centered Introduction to Linguistics courses. Educators in communications, communicative disorders sciences, English, education, and foreign and modern languages can incorporate Black linguistic scholarship into their syllabi to demonstrate the relevance and necessity for innovative research.

Students can be diligent in advocating for expansive course offerings, enrolling in said courses, cultivating relationships within and beyond their discipline(s) and institution(s), and leveraging their use of language through their research. By addressing the barriers within and across disciplines and institutions, HBCUs and PWIs can ensure that racially marginalized students are provided equitable and sustainable institutions that prepare them for their respective pathways.

References

Anya, Uju. (2021). Critical race pedagogy for more effective and inclusive world language teaching. *Applied Linguistics, 42*(6), 1055–1069. https://doi.org/10.1093/applin/amab068.

Bonilla-Silva, Eduardo & Zuberi, Tukufu (Eds.). (2008). *White logic, white methods*. Rowman & Littlefield.

Bolton, Kingsley, & Hutton, Christopher (Eds.) (2000). Orientalism and linguistics. Special issue of *Interventions: International Journal of Postcolonial Studies, 2*(1). https://doi.org/10.1080/136980100360751.

Bowie State University (n.d.). Course descriptions. www.bowiestate.edu/academics/colleges/college-of-arts-and-sciences/departments/language-literature-and-cultural-studies/undergraduate-program/course-descriptions.php.

Calhoun, Kendra, Charity Hudley, Anne H., Bucholtz, Mary, Exford, Jazmine, & Johnson, Brittney. (2021). Attracting Black students to linguistics through a Black-centered Introduction to Linguistics course. *Language, 97*(1), e12–e38. doi:10.1353/lan.2021.0007

Charity Hudley, Anne H., Mallinson, Christine, & Bucholtz, Mary. (2020). Toward racial justice in linguistics: Interdisciplinary insights into theorizing race in the discipline and diversifying the profession. *Language, 96*(4), e200–e235. doi:10.1353/lan.2020.0074

Clark Atlanta University. (2018). Graduate catalog. www.cau.edu/registrar/files/Graduate-Catalog-2018-2020--11-14-2019.pdf

Dance, Daryl Lynn. (2015). Can Rachel Jeantel speak? *CLA Journal, 58*(3/4), 139–146. http://www.jstor.org/stable/44324389

Errington, Joseph. (2001). Colonial linguistics. *Annual Review of Anthropology, 30*, 19–39. doi:10.1146/annurev.anthro.30.1.19

Green Jr., David F. (2017). Flow as a metaphor for changing composition practices. *Changing English, 24*(2), 175–185. doi:10.1080/1358684X.2017.1310460

Hampton University. (n.d.). Directory: Daryl Dance. https://directory.hamptonu.edu/index.cfm?bio=daryl.dance.

Harvard University. (n.d.a). *Froject Teach*. https://www.projectteach.community.harvard.edu/.

Harvard University. (n.d.b) Sunn M'Cheaux. https://www.alp.fas.harvard.edu/people/sunn-mcheaux.

Howard University. (n.d.a). Department of African Studies. https://africanstudies.howard.edu/undergraduate.

Howard University. (n.d.b). People profiles: David F. Green Jr. https://profiles.howard.edu/david-green-0.

Hudley, Anne Charity. (2022) (acharityhudley). "The Linguistic Society of America actively chose . . .", https://www.instagram.com/p/Cc270CMr42F/.

Ladson-Billings, Gloria. (2008). It's not the culture of poverty, it's the poverty of culture: The problem with teacher education. *Anthropology & Education Quarterly, 37*(2), 104–109. doi:10.1525/aeq.2006.37.2.104

Lanehart, Sonja L. 2009. Diversity and intersectionality. *Texas Linguistics Forum (SALSA XVII Proceedings),* 53.1–53.8. http://salsa.ling.utexas.edu/proceedings/2009/01 _TLS53_ Lanehart.pdf.

Lanehart, Sonja L. (2019). Can you hear (and see) me now?: Race-ing American language variationist/change and sociolinguistic research methodologies. In Jessica T. DeCuir-Gunby, Tandeka K. Chapman, and Paul A. Schutz (Eds.), *Understanding critical race research methods and methodologies: Lessons from the field* (pp. 34–47). Routledge.

Leonard, Wesley Y. (2018). Reflections on (de)colonialism in language documentation. Reflections on language documentation 20 years after Himmelmann 1998. In Bradley McDonnell, Andrea L. Berez-Kroeker, and Gary Holton (Eds.), *Language Documentation & Conservation special publication 15)* (55–65). University of Hawai'i Press.

Linguistic Society of America. (2018). Annual report: The state of linguistics in higher education. https://www.linguisticsociety.org/resource/state-linguistics-higher-education-annual-report Accessed July 1, 2022.

Linguistic Society of America. (2019). Statement on race. https://www.linguisticsociety.org/content/lsa-statement-race

Linguistic Society of America. (2022). What is linguistics. https://www.linguisticsociety.org/ Accessed July 1, 2022.

McCammon, Sarah. (2019, December 29). A dying language of enslaved Africans lives on at Harvard. National Public Radio. https://www.npr.org/2019/12/29/792221923/a-dying-language-of-enslaved-africans-lives-on-at-harvard.

m'Cheaux, S. (n.d.). Official site for academic, artist, & advocate, Sunn M'Cheaux aka Gullah teacha.https://www.sunnmcheaux.com/.

Mckoy, Temptaous. (2019). *Implications for technical and professional communication*. East Carolina University, www.thescholarship.ecu.edu/bitstream/handle/10342/7421/MCKOY-DOCTORALDISSERTATION-2019.pdf?sequence=1.

Morrison, T. (2019, December 23). No place for self-pity, no room for fear. No Place for Self-Pity, No Room for Fear | The Nation. https://www.thenation.com/article/archive/no-place-self-pity-no-room-fear/

Murji, Karim, & Solomos, John (Eds.). (2005). *Racialization: Studies in theory and practice*. Oxford University Press.

National African Language Resource Center. (2021). African language programs in the US. www.nalrc.indiana.edu/doc/newsletters/ULIMI-2021-Vol-21.pdf

National Center for Education Statistics. (2019a). Digest of education statistics. Bachelor's degrees conferred by postsecondary institutions, by race/ethnicity and sex of student: Selected years 1976–2017–18. www.nces.ed.gov/programs/digest/d19/tables/dt19_322.20.asp

National Center for Education Statistics. (2019b). Digest of education statistics. Doctor's degrees conferred by postsecondary institutions, by race/ethnicity and sex of student: Selected years 1976–2017–18. www.nces.ed.gov/programs/digest/d19/tables/dt19_322.20.asp

National Center for Education Statistics. (2019c). Digest of education statistics. Fall enrollment, degrees conferred, and expenditures in degree-granting historically Black colleges and universities, by institution: 2017, 2018, and 2017–18. www.nces.ed.gov/programs/digest/d19/tables/dt19_313.10.asp

National Center for Education Statistics. (2019d). Digest of education statistics. Master's degrees conferred by postsecondary institutions, by race/ethnicity and sex of student: Selected years 1976–2017–18. www.nces.ed.gov/programs/digest/d19/tables/dt19_322.20.asp

Newmeyer, Frederick J. (n.d.). The history of modern linguistics. Linguistic Society of America. https://www.linguisticsociety.org/resource/history-modern-linguistics.

Rosa, Jonathan, & Flores, Nelson. (2017). Unsettling race and language: Toward a raciolinguistic perspective. *Language in Society, 46*(5), 621–647. doi:10.1017/S00474045 17000562

Trechter, Sara, & Bucholtz, Mary. (2001). White noise: Bringing language into whiteness studies. *Journal of Linguistic Anthropology, 11*(1), 3–21. doi:10.1525/jlin.2001 .11.1.3

UC-HBCU Scholars in Linguistics. (n.d.). https://ucsbhbculing.com/research-experience/

University of Maryland Eastern Shore. (n.d.) Course descriptions. https://wwwcp.umes.edu/english/course-descriptions/.

University of Massachusetts, Amherst. (n.d.). Lisa Green associate professor. www.people.umass.edu/lisag/CV.pdf.

Wade-Lewis, Margaret. (2001). Lorenzo Dow Turner: Beyond Gullah studies. *Dialectical Anthropology, 26*(3–4), 235–266.

Weinberg, Justin. (2022, April 28). Linguistic Society of America considers free speech resolution. Daily Nous. www.dailynous.com/2022/04/28/linguistic-society-of-america-considers-free-speech-resolution/?fr=operanews

Wood, Sarah. (2021, September 29). How HBCUs are addressing the cost of college. U.S. News.https://www.usnews.com/education/best-colleges/paying-for-college/articles/how-hbcus-are-addressing-the-cost-of-college

Reenu Punnoose is an early career linguist whose areas of interest include phonetics, sociolinguistics, and language acquisition. She is currently assistant professor at the Indian Institute of Technology Palakkad (Kerala, India). Earlier, she was awarded a postdoctoral fellowship by the University Grants Commission, India, which she completed at the Centre for Linguistics, Jawaharlal Nehru University, New Delhi. She has a PhD from the University of Newcastle (United Kingdom) and degrees from the University of York (United Kingdom) and the University of Madras (India). Her publications have featured in *Phonetica*, *R-atics*, and the *Economic and Political Weekly*.

Muhammed Haneefa is a postdoctoral fellow at the Department of Humanities and Social Sciences at the Indian Institute of Technology Delhi (New Delhi, India), where he looks at how constructed identities such as caste decide the master status and distribution of social capital among the Muslims of Malabar. He has completed his MA, MPhil, and PhD from the Centre for the Study of Social Systems, Jawaharlal Nehru University, New Delhi. His publications have featured in the *Economic and Political Weekly*, *Journal of Muslim Minority Affairs*, and *Anthropology Today*.

Abstract: This chapter initiates a call for reflexivity in the practice of linguistics in India by demonstrating that the secondary status assigned to experience (as constitutive of empiricism and inextricable to the knowledge of a language) in the discipline's practice is related to a lack of inclusion among its practitioners which in turn continues to narrow the scope of knowledge produced in the field. The authors examine the case of a neighbouring discipline, sociology, in the light of positive shifts over the last 30 years that reflect the early outcomes of a discipline attempting to be reflexive and its consequences for the practitioner-practice relationship in knowledge production. Preliminary recommendations are made on ways to strengthen the undergraduate programme in linguistics, reimagine the MA curriculum, popularise the discipline, and collaborate with the Global North to decentre their position of privilege in the knowledge economy while participating as allies in centring the practice and practitioners of linguistics in the Global South.

Key Words: reflexivity, linguistics in India, inclusion, experience, empiricism, Global South

8

Towards Greater Inclusion in Practice and Among Practitioners

The Case for an Experience-Based Linguistics in India

Reenu Punnoose (she/her)
Indian Institute of Technology Palakkad

Muhammed Haneefa (he/his)
Indian Institute of Technology Delhi

Introduction

The ancient, rich pedigree of linguistic scholarship in India and its undeniable influence on modern linguistics as a discipline (Allen, 1953; Emeneau, 1955) makes the Indian context a significant site at which to begin any discussion surrounding decolonisation and inclusion in this field. However, as currently practised, linguistics in India is not inclusive both in terms of subject matter purview as well as representation of marginalised communities. The present chapter aims to draw attention to the need for more inclusion of experience in the practice of linguistics in India, which we argue is related to the need for inclusion of a wider socioeconomic demographic as the practitioners of linguistics in the country. We use the term "experience" both as constitutive of empiricism, which has conventionally been treated in opposition to theory in Western philosophical thought, and as inextricable to the knowledge of a language. Therefore, the users and use of a language merit as much attention as the structural properties of a language. It is also worth pointing out here that the understanding of what constitutes empiricism in linguistics is open to question because there is no consensus among practitioners regarding what constitutes the study of language (Chapman, 2008). By advocating the significance of experience in linguistics, we strive to go beyond a conventional view of linguistics wherein language is treated as an *object* of inquiry independent of its use and thus its users. Equally importantly and by extension, such a view

Reenu Punnoose and Muhammed Haneefa, *Towards Greater Inclusion in Practice and Among Practitioners* In: *Inclusion in Linguistics*. Edited by: Anne H. Charity Hudley, Christine Mallinson and Mary Bucholtz, Oxford University Press. © Anne H. Charity Hudley, Christine Mallinson, and Mary Bucholtz 2024. DOI: 10.1093/oso/9780197755303.003.0009 also calls attention to the *practitioners* of linguistics, who we argue have a significant impact on the *practice* of linguistics.[1]

In light of this argument, we begin with our own positionality. The authors are, in very different ways, both insiders and outsiders to the world we describe in the chapter. A second-generation learner, Reenu completed all her linguistics training in the Global North and has been a practitioner of linguistics in India for over five years. Haneefa is a first-generation learner and a Mappila Muslim from South Malabar, a region and a religious community that was historically excluded from higher education in India. He is also a beneficiary of India's constitutional safeguards for members of marginalised communities in the education sector, enacted in 1992, which enabled him to complete all his training in sociology in some of the premier educational institutions in the country. We met at different stages of our research training years at Jawaharlal Nehru University, New Delhi, an institution that has significantly shaped the ways we think about the world and higher education in particular.

As a linguist who is interested in phonetics, sociolinguistics, and its intersectional areas, Reenu struggled to find a peer community with similar interests when she returned to India after her PhD in the UK. There were no specific forums dedicated to work in these areas. The few people she did get acquainted with worked individually for the most part. Even though a hierarchy of subdisciplines is not unique to linguistics in India or even linguistics as a discipline, the wide chasm between the status of theoretical linguistics and that of empirical linguistics in India is quite unlike anything she had encountered before. Conversations with Haneefa on the matter led to being quizzed about who the practitioners of linguistics in India are. Unlike Reenu, for Haneefa, questions surrounding who is producing knowledge and why, and the habitus of a scholar, are his primary concerns as a sociologist. On the other hand, it was the first time Reenu had thought about who does linguistics in India, who is missing in the discipline, and how that has a significant relationship with how the discipline is practised. In short, it was an examination of the areas neglected in the practice of linguistics in the country and debates on reflexivity in neighbouring disciplines that led to an understanding of the significant relationship between the practice of a discipline and its practitioners.

In this chapter, we initiate a call for reflexivity in the practice of linguistics in India. The chapter is divided broadly into three parts: the first part discusses the prevalent features that characterise the practice of linguistics in India. The second part attempts to understand who the practitioners of linguistics in India are and to situate the discipline's practice and practitioners against significant shifts in the development of its neighbouring discipline, sociology.

This is because sociology has been described as the most reflexive discipline in India about its practitioners (Jodhka, 2009). The third part suggests ways forward for linguistics in India, which includes, among other things, the role that institutions in the Global North must play in actively decentring their position of privilege in the knowledge economy and participating as allies in the processes that help centre the practice and practitioners of linguistics in the Global South (see also Gibson et al., 2024).

The Practice of Linguistics in India

The first department of modern linguistics in India was established in 1939 at Deccan College, Pune. Eight decades later, while the number of linguistics departments have grown, the discipline's presence in Indian higher education is overwhelmingly restricted to the postgraduate level, with only a negligible presence as an undergraduate field of study. Although there is no official data on the total number of linguistics departments in the country and on the number of linguistics departments offering undergraduate programmes, it is some indication of the discipline's lack of undergraduate engagement that there is no mention of linguistics in the list of 97 undergraduate course syllabi on the website of the University Grants Commission (a statutory body set up by the Ministry of Education, Government of India, that is responsible for the determination, coordination and maintenance of the standards of university education in the country) (UGC, 2015). Moreover, with regard to the UGC's quality improvement programme to develop a Learner-based Outcome Framework (LOCF) at the undergraduate and postgraduate level, initiated in August 2018, linguistics does not figure in the list of 33 courses for which updated undergraduate curricula have been uploaded.

The major curriculum revision initiated by the UGC prior to the LOCF was the development of the model curriculum for various disciplines including linguistics, which were published in 2001 (UGC, 2001). The preamble of the model curriculum in linguistics, prepared by some of the leading linguists in India, reflects the long-standing dominant views among Indian linguists about what constitutes the discipline. The first point states that although "popular opinion might relegate the study of language to Language Arts programmes (with their associated emphasis on literary and cultural values)," India has a long tradition of studying language dating back to Panini, wherein language is an "object of enquiry in its own right" (UGC, 2001, p. 1). This clearly makes a distinction between the study of language in relation to literature and culture and the study of language in linguistics. The reasons for the superiority of linguistics as an academic discipline in relation to the language arts programmes (as implied by "relegated") can be attributed to the central notion that linguistics is the scientific study of language. Phrases such as "scientific study" and "language sciences," which turn up in points 2 and 3 of the preamble, appear in tandem with declarations about linguistics providing "the most promising window on how the mind works" and feeding "into the discipline of cognitive science." Not surprisingly, these statements echo the dominance of the Chomskyan, mentalist view in linguistics in India, as is the case for linguistics in many other parts of the world (Lukin, 2011).

The preamble characterizes the subject matter of linguistics as comprising "the orthodox and central domains of syntax, semantics, morphology and phonology," "applied domains such as the sociology of language, the psychology of language and language processing (human and machine)," and "applications such as Psycholinguistics . . . psycho-linguistic approaches to language disorders . . . the psychological approaches to the teaching and learning of languages, mass media, lexicography, machine translation etc." According to the preamble, all of these domains are "theoretical and applied manifestations" of the inherent relationship between language and cognition (UGC, 2001). While the wording suggests the constitutive role of language in cognition and, therefore, the influence of linguistics on cognitive science, linguistics is only seen as "interfac[ing] with societal concerns" rather than focusing on the social world as inherent and integral to language. The social and the cognitive aspects of language are seen, therefore, as distinct from each other: the latter is inherent and central to the goal of linguistics, while the former is merely an application (see also Gibson et al., 2024).

The conventional dichotomy between the fundamental ("central") cognitive enterprise of language and its social ("applied") "interface" is an extension of the larger opposition between theory and experience in Western philosophical tradition (see also De Jesus, this volume). In the practice of linguistics in India, as is likely the case in other parts of the world, this dichotomy manifests itself in the dominance of theory over experience, evident in the hierarchy of subdisciplines seen in the model curriculum above. Our broader point also finds an indirect mention in the latest masters-level linguistics syllabus of a top university in the capital of India, in which the major highlight of their linguistics programme is stated to be the representation in equal measure of both "theoretical" and "empirical" orientations in the variety of diverse teaching and research areas it offers, which they note is unlike most other linguistics departments in the country. Documentary linguist Shobhana Chelliah succinctly underscores the underlying philosophy of language science in India and its consequences thus (Chelliah, 2018, p. 248):

A common viewpoint in linguistics departments in India is that extended and varied data collection, such as that needed for the creation of a documentary corpus, is time consuming and not useful for scientific publications. As a result, much of the language data collected is at the level of the word or clause and is collected through responses to questionnaires. Language science, produced and sanctioned in this way, is reflected in the very successful society and related summer school, known as the Formal Studies in the Syntax and Semantics of Indian Languages (FOSSSIL).

Chelliah further adds, "Many of the leading linguists in India are on the governing body of FOSSSIL, and likewise, many of the programs around the country have this same focus. A consequence of this focus is the lack of encouragement towards resource creation, especially the lack of language data in the form of annotated corpora" (2018, p. 249). In fact, FOSSSIL is the only scholarly society in India based on specific linguistics subdisciplines. Given that for any subdiscipline to have and sustain an academic association and its activities would be a challenging feat in a country where linguistics is not a well-known or sought-after discipline, the continued active presence of FOSSSIL is a testament to the clout of formal syntax and semantics and the significant numerical strength of practitioners of these subfields within Indian linguistics.

The hegemony of theory/ideas/mind over empiricism/experience is not unique to linguistics as a discipline in the academic landscape of India and other nations. The prioritisation of ideas over experience as characterised in Western constructs and the dominance of this view in the theorization of social sciences in India has been previously pointed out by noted political scientist Gopal Guru (2002). In his landmark essay "How Egalitarian Are the Social Sciences in India?," he places the social reality of caste, untouchability, and Dalit life at the centre of his analysis and argues that "social science practice in India has harboured a cultural hierarchy, dividing it into the vast, inferior mass of academics who pursue empirical social science, and the privileged few who are considered the theoretical pundits, with reflective capacity that makes them intellectually superior to the former," that is, a distinction between "empirical Shudras" and "theoretical Brahmins" (Guru, 2002, p. 5003). While Guru points to the hegemony of knowledge produced by "theoretical Brahmins" over the 'empirical Shudras" in the Indian context, several postcolonial thinkers have situated the dominance of universalism, classification and comparison—which are some of the major constituents of theory building—in colonialism (Bhabha, 2012; Dabashi, 2019). Ugandan political scientist Mahmood Mamdani points out the link between theory and the colonial cause (2019, p. 16):

> Theory is born of comparison. Comparison is older than colonialism . . . But the most comprehensive comparative work was carried out during the European colonial project. It is this work that is of concern to us today as we seek to define the problem of decolonization. With the European colonial project, classification became global . . . Comparison requires a standard, the familiar, through which the not-so-familiar is understood, sometimes as not-quite-yet, at other times as an outright deviation. All ordering has a reference point. For those who did the classifying and ordering of everything around the world, the reference point was the West, the reality they knew and considered natural.

Mamdani also draws attention to the grounding of modern humanities and social sciences in the European Enlightenment experience characterised by a focus on the oneness of humanity, where oneness is defined as sameness from a European perspective.

The practice of linguistics in India is characterised by a singular focus on a kind of universality which sanctions the peripheralization of real-world experience and observation and by extension, diversity and variation. Interestingly, this characteristic reveals both colonial as well as casteist overtones: it echoes the Eurocentric universalism for which postcolonial thinkers like Said attacks the West's positioning of itself as the representative of universal values and reason while distancing others as primitive, chaotic, and irrational (Said, 1979). Universalism of this kind, in other words, "is abused as part of a culturalistic strategy of exclusion" (Scherer, 2014). A similar strategy of exclusion is reflected in Guru's metaphor for the pernicious divide in the practice of social science disciplines in India between "theoretical Brahmins" and "empirical Shudras" (Guru, 2002). He further elaborates this point thus:

> Social science discourse in India is being closely disciplined by self-appointed juries who sit in the apex court and decide what is the correct practice according to the canons. These juries decide what is theory and what is trash. It is a different matter that these canons lack authenticity as they are borrowed from the west unreservedly. The apex court in social sciences with its full bench in Delhi keeps ruling out subaltern objections as absurd and idiosyncratic at worst and emotional, descriptive-empirical and polemical at best. (Guru, 2002, p. 5004)

These strategies of epistemic exclusion in the practice of linguistics in the country cast under the guise of a reductive interpretation of universalism has significantly contributed to the discipline's disinterest in considering who practises linguistics in India, who is excluded from the field, who produces knowledge in linguistics and who decides what is real linguistics.

Practitioners of Linguistics: Reflexivity in Sociology and Implications for Linguists

There is hardly any data in the public domain on the practitioners of linguistics in India, whether students, teachers, or researchers. We therefore present first a general overview of the representation of members of marginalised groups both as students and faculty in the field. Subsequently, we discuss the link between who is missing in linguistics as practitioners and what is missing in the curriculum, compared to significant developments in sociology that reflect the practitioner-practice relationship in knowledge production.

Religion and caste-based marginalised communities in India are placed within one of three constitutional classifications: The Scheduled Castes are groups traditionally regarded as "untouchables," and the Scheduled Tribes are Indigenous, also sometimes referred to as Adivasis. The third group, called Other Backward Classes (OBC), are castes or communities that are socially and educationally backward, and which include groups from various religious communities. The Other Backward Classes are subdivided into many groups and subgroups, and the Central List of OBCs contains more than a thousand castes and communities from various states. According to the 2011 census, the Scheduled Castes and Scheduled Tribes constitute 16.6% and 8.6% of India's population respectively. Though India's Census does not provide data on Other Backward Classes, various reports have shown that they constitute nearly half of the Indian population. In 1990, the National Front government led by V. P. Singh implemented the report of the Mandal Commission, named for its chairman, B. P. Mandal, which had noticed that due to poor access to land and education, the situation of the OBCs was desperately urgent and in dire need of assistance. The commission further concluded that a program of positive discrimination was needed to improve the condition of the OBCs, and it recommended 27% reservation for them in public sector employment and education in addition to the 15% and the 7% in favour of the Scheduled Castes (SCs) and the Scheduled Tribes (STs) that were mandated by the Indian Constitution (Jaffrelot, 2006).

The unofficial term for the first two groups, "Dalit,"[2] is a Marathi term which means "the oppressed, the resourceless" (Thorat, 2009). Over the years, Dalit came to refer to those who were oppressed economically, culturally, and politically on the basis of their caste. In order to ameliorate their position, the Indian Constitution gives the Scheduled Castes, Scheduled Tribes, and the Other Backward Classes certain constitutional safeguards as mentioned above. These include reserved posts in government jobs, reservations in public education, and special welfare provisions. But studies have shown that even after decades of constitutional safeguards, these groups remain the most educationally, economically, and socially marginalised and exploited communities in India.

These patterns are evident in higher education: according to the 2011 census, the total percentage of graduates in India is 9.51% (males 11.54%, and females 7.41%). However, the total percentage of graduates among the Scheduled Castes is only 4.84% (6.45% males and 3.18% females), and among Scheduled Tribes, it is only 3.10% (4.21% males and 2% females). The higher the educational level, the lesser the representation of students from marginalised backgrounds. Because linguistics is mainly a postgraduate discipline in India, the number of scholars from Scheduled Castes, Scheduled Tribes, and Other Backward Classes is very low in number.

Unsurprisingly, the situation is even worse for faculty members: the results of the most recent All India Survey of Higher Education (AISHE) published by the Ministry of Education in 2018 revealed that 57% of faculty in Indian universities belong to the socially privileged general category. Though the Scheduled Castes and Scheduled Tribes populations represent 16.6% and 8.6% of the total Indian population, they only constitute 8.6% and 2.27% of teaching staff in India. In fact, 38% of faculty posts reserved for the Scheduled Castes, 43% of posts reserved for the Scheduled Tribes, and 52% of those reserved for Other Backward Classes remain vacant in central institutions of higher education (Jebaraj, 2021). While the abysmal representation of these candidates in academia is a much larger problem in India and not specific to linguistics, our point is that this lack of representation is not discussed as having consequences for the discipline: given what is evident from the overall representation of marginalized communities in higher education in India, it should come as no surprise that the committee members involved in developing the UGC Model Curriculum of 2001 were overwhelmingly from privileged backgrounds. Furthermore, neither in the 2001 model curriculum nor in the most recent MA syllabi available online are stand-alone courses offered, for instance, on topics such as caste and language or ethnolinguistics, and there are only a handful of departments that list language policy and planning even as an elective course on offer. These topics typically find mention in most cases as one topic in one unit of a course on sociolinguistics, in a country where it has been reported that the difference between home language and school language among students from marginalised communities plays a significant role in their educational outcomes (Mohanty, 2018), and where the primarily linguistic reorganisation of regions into states postindependence was a transformative event in India's history (Guha, 2017). In short, the lack of inclusion among the practitioners of linguistics has consequences for the practice of linguistics and its real-world impact.

While there are numerous historical reviews and genealogies of linguistics in India, the only critical reflection on the practice of linguistics in India is Chelliah (2018). By contrast, sociology[3] is the social science discipline in India that is the most reflexive with regard to its practitioners (Jodhka, 2009), who have traditionally belonged to upper-caste backgrounds but whose dominance has been challenged by the presence of marginalised scholars in the discipline over the last three decades. Although a relatively more reflexive discipline with a stronger undergraduate presence than linguistics, sociology is not widely taught compared to other social science disciplines in India.

Since the 1990s, sociologists in India have been producing literature that critically analyses the history of the discipline, its practitioners, and how the habitus of a sociologist shapes their knowledge production. The development of sociology as a discipline in India can be understood in three phases: the preindependence period, the postindependence period, and the post-Mandal period. The preindependence period was characterised by male Brahmin practitioners who later came to be called the "pioneers" of the discipline in India and their "book view"; that is, their emphasis on the role of Sanskrit texts in understanding social phenomena. In contrast, the postindependence period was characterised by the "field view" (Jodhka, 1998), "which placed the sociologist under obligation to observe and record life as it was actually lived, without embellishment" (Béteille, 2009, p. 199). The post-Mandal period, from the 1990s onwards, witnessed significant changes in Indian sociology, reflecting the major events and changes that characterised India during that time, namely the belated implementation of the Mandal Commission recommendations, communal tensions that arose between Hindus and Muslims due to the demolition of the Babri Masjid by Hindu nationalists, and the liberalisation of the Indian economy. Consequently, discussions on minoritised groups' rights and a stronger presence of members of marginalised communities in the public sphere, including the education sector, contributed significantly to questioning existing practices in sociology.

As noted by various sociologists, the entry of marginalised scholars into academia raises questions of how scholars from upper-caste backgrounds can genuinely represent the experiences, lives, and ambitions of socially marginalised communities (Guru, 2002; Kumar, 2016). This questioning of the status quo has resulted in a revival of the works of the social thinker, Dr Bhimrao Ramji Ambedkar, much like the revival of the works of W. E. B. Du Bois in American sociology (Morris, 2015). Born in a Dalit, Mahar community, Ambedkar and his works have had a hallowed place and an emancipatory role in the political and intellectual lives of Dalits and other marginalised people who continue to be forced to live under the socially and religiously sanctioned caste system. During this period, some scholars from the Global North have played a crucial role in mainstreaming Ambedkar's works and framing him as a "pioneer" of Indian sociology (Jaffrelot, 2005; Omvedt, 2004).

A decade back, when Haneefa was pursuing his MA in sociology from one of the premier sociology centres in India, the Centre for the Study of Social Systems (CSSS), at Jawaharlal Nehru University, Ambedkar's writings were not included in the core readings of even social stratification courses. Now, however, the syllabus of Sociology of Social Stratification in India at CSSS lists his works as major readings and the same is true for courses on sociological theory. Though change has been slow to occur, Ambedkar's works are no longer limited to the domain of social stratification and his theories form an integral part of sociological courses at Indian universities.

However, Ambedkar's writings on the language question in India—that is, the reorganisation of states postindependence on a linguistic basis—have not received much scholarly attention. Political scientist Asha Sarangi argues that Ambedkar's notion of linguistic states is an attempt to "reconcile the tension between cultural pluralism and political democracy, as well as between social heterogeneity (multilingualism) and political authority (federalism)." She notes that he was especially concerned about the caste composition of such linguistic states asking if smaller communities would find states organised on the basis of language socially and politically advantageous and whether the notion would eventually lead to a communal majoritarianism under the guise of shared linguistic identity. While some linguists have examined Ambedkar's views even if not as the main focus of their work on the linguistic reorganisation of states (e.g., Abbi, 2009; Agnihotri, 2015; Babu, 2017; Gupta, 1955), a more comprehensive engagement with his writings on the language question comes from political scientists like Sarangi.

To be fair to practitioners of linguistics in India, the role of the state as an external factor contributing to the prevalent state of affairs also needs mention for a better understanding of the different ways that the discipline's practice is affected. In this regard, a brief discussion on the hierarchy of languages in India is useful to understand that beyond the core-applied, cognitive-social dichotomy, the issue of which languages in a plurilingual India find constitutional favour and state support also has significant implications for the discipline's practice. Scholars from various academic backgrounds have dealt with the topic of the hierarchy of languages directly or indirectly and have taken different positions on the matter. Hany Babu's (2017) position, in particular, raises significant questions for the practice of linguistics in India: he broadly classifies the language hegemony in India as operating on two levels, the centre (the Union government) and the states. He further invokes the basic four-tier caste hierarchy in India—the notion of Chaturvarna—to analyse how both the Constitution and the official language policy of the Indian state have created a similar system of linguistic hierarchy. The first and top tier is occupied by Sanskrit, the chief source of many Indian languages including Hindi, which is in second place and is the official language of the Union. The third tier includes the 22 languages recognised by the Eighth Schedule of the Constitution as official languages of the Republic of India (2011 Census). Such provisions necessitate that the Government is obligated to take measures for the development of these languages (among other benefits). The fourth and bottom tier of the language hierarchy is occupied by the 99 languages that the Census identifies but are not listed in the Eighth Schedule of the Constitution (2011 Census). These are referred to as nonscheduled languages and do not receive any state support for their development and/or use. Sanskrit, Hindi, the 22 scheduled languages, and the 99 nonscheduled languages occupy the different rungs of the ladder "with an ascending order of privilege and a descending order of prestige" (Babu, 2017, p. 113)—and with English as a rank outsider with emancipatory potential. English is only mentioned as an ancillary language of the Union and is neither classified as scheduled nor nonscheduled. It is the "untouchable" language (p. 117) because it is outside of the legitimised hierarchy of languages and no group would request its promotion or inclusion as a scheduled language due to its existing aspirational value. It is a source of cultural capital that aids access to resources and upward mobility. Furthermore, many Dalit/Bahujan thinkers and anti-caste activists like Kancha Ilaiah (2006) and Chandrabhan Prasad (2013), and young intellectuals like Suraj Yengde (2019) and Yashica Dutt (2019), advocate for the emancipatory power of English for Dalits and other marginalised groups as it does not carry the memory of caste, unlike Indian languages (Babu, 2017; Kothari, 2013). However, the ambivalent policy on English further widens the gap between the English-knowing elite and the vast majority of those who are denied opportunities and social mobility on account of not knowing the language, thus creating an English-based hierarchy.

Among the 121 languages enumerated by the most recent Indian census in 2011, the majority are nonscheduled. This raises important questions about the threat to survival for these languages with little or no state support and by extension to the identities and cultural heritage of communities who speak these languages. Worse still, what about varieties not classified as languages that are reported by citizens as mother tongues? How many of these varieties (classified, unclassified, nonscheduled) are subjects of linguistics research? How might the lack of such research limit the questions we ask and the solutions we seek about various linguistic phenomena? Without a reliable language census methodology, identifying hitherto unclassified varieties is difficult, and equally, the language census exercise calls for massive involvement from the linguistics community both in number and range of expertise. All the more reason why topics like these must become a central focus of linguistics practice in India and find a deserving place in classroom teaching and learning and in active research.

Even in the case of those languages which are studied, it is pertinent to ask, who studies whose languages as an object? After all, "For the colonized subject, objectivity is always directed against him" (Fanon, 1961, p. 37). In the case of sociology, it was only after scholars from marginalised communities became practitioners that upper-caste male members who single handedly dominated the field were challenged on their production of harmful, condescending knowledge (for instance, G. S. Ghurye's discussion of tribal assimilation in Oommen, 2011) about minorities, Dalits and Adivasis. The lack of reflexivity in the practice of linguistics in India, therefore, serves to further enable the Chaturvarna linguistic hierarchy sanctioned by the Constitution and the official language policy.

In short, in the prevalent practice of linguistics in India, language is viewed as an object of enquiry independent of its users and their circumstances and so questions about the social dimension of language, let alone about who produces linguistics knowledge, are seen as being outside the central purview of the discipline. Such views also presumably affect hiring patterns, such that poorly funded humanities and social science departments that face hiring freezes focus on recruiting more of those who can teach the core courses than the elective/applied domains. Mirroring global trends in academia, this, in turn, results in a vicious cycle of lack of inclusivity and diversity both among practitioners and in the practice of such disciplines. Given the absence of relevant data for all disciplines in India, the case of sociology is particularly worth mentioning due to the undeniable impact of the presence of marginalised scholars on knowledge production in the field. The shift in knowledge production in sociology from the objective knowledge about the "Indian" social experience produced mainly by the upper-caste male perspective to the subjective, life experience-based writing of the marginalised scholars discussed earlier can be viewed as an early outcome of some degree of reflexivity in the discipline's practice.

Recommendations for Ways Forward

Based on our analysis of the current state of linguistics in India, we offer the following suggestions for creating an inclusive, experience-based discipline.

Strengthen the Undergraduate Programme

Although the preamble to the UGC model curriculum (2001) includes no direct description of the current status of undergraduate education in linguistics in India, its necessity is emphasized. The preamble highlights the central role that an undergraduate linguistics programme can play in providing a more solid foundation for higher-level programmes in the discipline as well as career options. Some attempts have been made over the years to persuade concerned authorities about the need to ramp up undergraduate programmes in linguistics. The limited success of these previous attempts is likely due to factors both internal and external to the practice of the discipline. The close association of linguistics with language arts programmes in public perception, as noted in the preamble, and particularly with English is also worth mentioning. Reenu's own educational background includes a BA in English before she pursued an MA in linguistics. This appears to be the predominant trend and may explain the prevalent public perception that linguistics is a specialization within English rather than a discipline in its own right. Additionally, the conservative view of what counts as linguistics, as evident in the model curriculum discussed above, does not realize the inherently interdisciplinary potential and the wide scope of linguistics (see also Thornton, this volume), thereby weakening the case for more undergraduate programmes in linguistics among policymakers.

How do we attract more students to opt for an undergraduate programme in linguistics? Moving beyond an ivory tower approach to a more outward-looking, participatory model of teaching and learning linguistics is the way forward (see also Lederer, this volume). This could include but is not limited to:

- Designing a cafeteria-style programme where students, based on their interests, can choose to specialize in linguistics with focused minors, both within linguistics and interdisciplinary areas (e.g., computer science/ data science, sociology, anthropology, history, cognitive science, statistics) to increase employment opportunities. For example, the University of Leiden[4] offers seven areas of specialisation in their linguistics MA programme which includes Language and Communication, Language Description, and Documentation apart from the more conventional theoretical linguistics and applied linguistics options.

- Incorporating mini projects into courses in several subdisciplines that help students appreciate empirical aspects of linguistics. For example, a course on sociolinguistics or bilingualism could involve group projects that collect small-scale community data to examine a relevant topic.
- Creating and facilitating opportunities for internships that provide experience of working in a wide range of areas based on interest (see for example information related to external internship opportunities available to students of the Department of Linguistics at California State University[5]). For instance, students might:
  o Hold entry-level roles in one or more processes involved in the language census in the form of data collection, preparation, and analysis.
  o Assist in creating and curating linguistically sound language teaching materials for schools together with teachers and community members.
  o Collaborate with community members of lesser-known and minoritized languages and dialects to document the varieties.
  o Intern with firms in the information technology sector in areas at the intersection of computer science and linguistics.
  o Participate in newly developed semester-long exchange programmes between linguistics departments and institutions offering undergraduate programmes in Audiology and Speech Language Pathology at the All-India Institute of Speech and Hearing, the National Institute of Speech and Hearing, and similar institutions.

Reimagine the MA Curriculum

The theory-experience imbalance in linguistics is reflected in the fact that the majority of compulsory core courses are theoretical in orientation while those that are empirical in orientation are largely electives, in keeping with the central/applied domain distinction in the UGC model curriculum. Individual departments, depending on their history and the type of subdiscipline expertise available, vary considerably in the number and diversity of electives offered. To offer students a balance of theoretical and empirical courses, international faculty may be invited to teach in areas where there is a dearth of expertise in India. One avenue for such collaboration is the Global Initiative of Academic Networks, a scheme launched in 2015 and funded by the Indian Ministry of Education, which is aimed at facilitating engagement of international academics and entrepreneurs with higher education institutions in India in an attempt to strengthen the country's existing academic resources and enhance India's global influence in science and technology. Since the initiative was launched, seven courses which fall under the purview of linguistics have been offered, including courses on Indo-Aryan syntax, biolinguistics and evolutionary linguistics, language endangerment, language policy and human rights, and more. Such courses are free for students of the host institutions and available to other students for a nominal fee. Four of these seven courses involved international faculty based in the US, one in the UK, one in Denmark, and one in Japan. As is obvious, there is scope for more courses to be offered under this scheme in a wider range of subdisciplinary and interdisciplinary areas.

Once there is a regular arrangement in the form of sustained collaboration among groups of Indian and international faculty, they could also consider signing a Memorandum of Understanding to offer joint degrees and/or to develop local expertise in those linguistics subdisciplines where there is currently a dearth in India. MA programmes with the option for specialization in one or more subdisciplines could also be planned in order to offer more flexibility to learners and nurture future linguists with expertise in different areas. For example, MA and/or PhD programmes can be designed in areas like Indigenous language revitalisation which actively aims at recruiting members of Indigenous communities as students via attractive scholarships and bursaries. Similar programmes are being offered via the MIT Indigenous Languages Initiative (MITILI) in the US; the MA programme in Indigenous Language Revitalisation at the University of Victoria, Canada; and the PhD programme in Linguistics, Language Documentation, and Revitalisation at Carleton University, Canada.

Popularise Linguistics

Even though linguistics is not a new discipline in India, sustained and conscious efforts could be made to popularise linguistics among the larger public. This could include but need not be limited to:

o Writing grant proposals to implement more projects which involve small-scale and large-scale community participation and engagement. A Citizen Sociolinguistics approach (Rymes & Leone, 2014; Svendsen, 2018), although not originally intended to popularise linguistics, has the potential to communicate awareness about the discipline while academics and nonprofessionals co-construct knowledge about language (see also Chetty et al., 2024 for more on research funding).

o Workshops and seminars could be organised by departments individually or jointly for high school students in their region.

o A proposal to introduce linguistics at the high school level may also be considered (see also Plackowski, this volume). In line with the Indian Constitution's encouragement of scientific temper, analysis of one's own language at the school level could add value to the beginning of a scientific training for students. Language can then be appreciated as a natural phenomenon to be analysed in terms of the abstract units of its structures, the systematicity that underlies its social patterning and the various real-life implications of its social associations.

o Open days for the public can be co-organized by existing linguistics societies and associations and linguistics departments in different parts of the country every year. Several similar initiatives are being used to increase awareness of and promote STEM in India (Varghese, 2021). Although STEM institutions/organisations have access to far greater funding than the social sciences, it would still be feasible to organise similar events on a smaller scale.

Foster Global North–Global South Collaboration

Given that the Global North continues to dominate the knowledge economy as a consequence of its colonial past, it is imperative that measures for inclusivity be adopted at the global level too. It is pertinent to highlight at the outset that the Global North–South power divide is not the central issue faced by practitioners in India who are from marginalised backgrounds. The effects of the long-standing systemic privilege enjoyed by the upper-caste scholars combined with their academic gatekeeping is prevalent within the Global North too. This is evident in the recent case of the addition of caste as a protected category in university policy at the California State University. The move, hailed by Dalit activists as a watershed moment, was immediately followed by more than 80 Indian-origin professors in the US demanding that the policy, which would make discrimination on the basis of caste an offence, be removed (Naik, 2022). Scholars from privileged caste backgrounds position themselves as victims in the global discourse on decolonisation while concealing their caste privilege in the Indian context to negotiate better opportunities for themselves in the Global North. In this regard, anthropologist Gajendran Ayyathurai, argues that many postcolonial theorists, who have not experienced caste humiliation, fail to understand the problem of caste/casteism. He further argues that "for Indian post-colonialists in the Western academy, caste, unlike race, is largely not a crisis in their own life experiences. Their subjectivities and their theoretical proclivities are consequently geared towards seeing colonial racism and racial capitalism but not the collusion of brahminical casteism and capitalism with it" (Ayyathurai, 2021). Caste, therefore, is not only an Indian problem; it has been imported to the Global North through the upper-caste Indian immigrants. The creation and implementation of affirmative actions in this regard lies at the heart of fostering inclusion across the Global North–South divide.

This can take the form of greater geographical and social diversification of memberships in journal editorial boards and publishing houses, international professional organisations, and funding agencies that offer international and collaborative grants with special calls for underrepresented areas and scholars in linguistics (see also Braithwaite & Ali, 2024; Chetty et al., 2024, Gibson et al., 2024) The option for virtual attendance at conferences, seminars, and workshops must be made mandatorily available and at low cost, especially for students and faculty from socioeconomically oppressed backgrounds. Virtual academic events have proven to be feasible in recent years when the world has been affected by the COVID-19 pandemic (see also Sclafani et al., this volume). Finally, faculty based in the Global North, particularly those who have benefitted from Indian languages and Indian students for their research (for instance, those who work on Indian languages or on Indian varieties of English, and those who are members of centres or departments of South Asian Languages), must consider contributing to designing and teaching courses and joint doctoral supervision to promote underrepresented areas and underrepresented scholars. Collaborative networks, not transactional ones, are the way forward as these enable the creation of more democratic and reflexive research communities wherein all involved are participant-observers, co-construct knowledge and share voice, power, and privilege (Cooper, 2006; see also Plumb et al., 2024).

In contrast to the prevalent intellectual traditions in elite academic institutions in the Global North that reflect their colonial heritage, Braithwaite and Ali (2024) draw our attention to Caribbean traditions of linguistic study, which are "broad in their scope and explicitly liberatory in their ambitions" and provide a powerful situated model to those interested in liberatory linguistics. In this tradition, the methodological emphasis is on "direct observation and field research," and "theoretical concerns without immediate social consequences are explicitly treated as secondary." The Caribbean tradition is very much in sync with our own stance in this chapter in favour of a greater inclusion of experience in the practice of linguistics. The opposite has been the dominant trend in linguistics in India thus far, which has contributed significantly to the stunted growth of the discipline in the country. Both historically and in modern times, linguistics in India has produced pioneering work. That notwithstanding, if linguistics is to be a thriving academic discipline in India, there is an urgent need to be continually reflexive about its practice and its practitioners while also demanding that the Global North become allies and actively participate in centring the practices and practitioners of linguistics in the Global South.

Notes

1. We wish to thank several professional acquaintances, students and faculty, in educational institutions around India, who wish to remain anonymous, for the many discussions that provided valuable insights into the topic. Special thanks are due to Basil Philip Kunnath, Jobin M. Kanjirakkat, Kamran Khan, and Julien De Jesus for their valuable comments on earlier versions of the chapter.
2. The term "Dalit" contains multitudes (For more, see (Yengde, 2019). While some scholars interpret the term to include only the Scheduled Castes and use the term "Adivasis" to refer to the Scheduled Tribes, others interpret it to include both Scheduled Castes and Scheduled Tribes.
3. Much like the US, sociology and social anthropology are merged into one department in Indian universities.
4. See the University of Leiden's MA in linguistics programme information at https://www.uni versiteitleiden.nl/en/education/study-programmes/master/linguistics/linguistics-special isation/about-the-programme.
5. See California State University Long Beach, linguistics internships, https://cla.csulb.edu/ departments/linguistics/internships/.

References

Abbi, Anvita. (2009). Vanishing diversities and submerging identities: An Indian case. *Language and Politics in India*, 67, 299–311. http://www.linguapax.org/wp-content/uploads/2015/03/2_abbi.pdf

Agnihotri, Rama Kant. (2015). Constituent assembly debates on language. *Economic and Political Weekly*, 50(8), 47–56. https://www.jstor.org/stable/24481425

Allen, W. Sidney. (1953). Phonetics in Ancient India. *Journal of the American Oriental Society*, 74(4). https://doi.org/10.2307/595521

Ayyathurai, Gajendran. (2021, July 5). It is time for a new subfield: "Critical caste studies." https://blogs.lse.ac.uk/southasia/2021/07/05/it-is-time-for-a-new-subfield-critical-caste-studies/

Babu, Hany M. T. (2017). Breaking the chaturvarna system of languages the need to overhaul the language policy. *Economic and Political Weekly*, 52(23), 112–119.

Béteille, André. (2009). Sociology and ideology. *Sociological Bulletin, 58*(2), 196–211. https://doi.org/10.1177/0038022920090203

Bhabha, Homi K. (2012). The location of culture. Routledge.

Braithwaite, Ben, & Ali, Kristian. (2024). The colonial geography of linguistics: A view from the Caribbean. In Anne H Charity Hudley, Christine Mallinson, & Mary Bucholtz (Eds.), *Decolonizing linguistics*. Oxford University Press.

Chapman, Siobhan. (2008). *Language and empiricism: After the Vienna circle.* Palgrave Macmillan.

Chelliah, Shobhana. (2018). Reflections on language documentation in India. In Bradley McDonnell, Andrea L. Berez-Kroeker, & Gary Holton (Eds.), *Reflections on Language Documentation 20 Years after Himmelmann 1998* (pp. 248–255). University of Hawai'i Press.

Chetty, Rajendra, Gibson, Hannah, & Reilly, Colin. (2024). Decolonising methodologies through collaboration: Reflections on partnerships and funding flows from working between the South and the North. In Anne H. Charity Hudley, Christine Mallinson, & Mary Bucholtz (Eds.), *Decolonizing linguistics*. Oxford University Press.

Cooper, Camille Wilson. (2006). Refining Social Justice Commitments through Collaborative Inquiry: Key Rewards and Challenges for Teacher Educators. *Teacher Education Quarterly, 33*(3), 115-132.

Dabashi, Hamid. (2019). *Europe and its shadows: Coloniality after empire.* Pluto Press.

Dutt, Yashica. (2019). *Coming out as Dalit: A memoir.* Aleph Book Company.

Emeneau, Murray Barnson. (1955). India and linguistics. *Journal of the American Oriental Society, 75*(3), 145. https://doi.org/10.2307/595166

Fanon, Frantz. (1961), *The Wretched of the Earth.* Grove Press, New York.

Gibson, Hannah, Jerro, Kyle, Namboodiripad, Savithry, & Riedel, Kristina. (2024). Towards a decolonial syntax: Research, teaching, publishing. In Anne H. Charity Hudley, Christine Mallinson, & Mary Bucholtz (Eds.), *Decolonizing linguistics*. Oxford University Press.

Guha, Ramachandra. (2017). *India after Gandhi: The history of the world's largest democracy.* Picador.

Gupta, R. S., & Abbi, Anvita. (1955). The eighth schedule: A critical introduction. In A. A. and K. S. A. R S Gupta (Eds.), *Language and the state: Perspectives on the eighth schedule* (pp. 1–7). Creative Books.

Guru, Gopal. (2002). How egalitarian are the social sciences in India? *Economic and Political Weekly, 37*(50), 5003–5009. https://www.jstor.org/stable/4412959?seq=1

Ilaiah, Kancha. (2006). Merit of reservations. *Economic and Political Weekly, 41*(24), 2447–2449.

Jaffrelot, Christophe. (2005). Dr Ambedkar and untouchability: Analysing and fighting caste. Orient Blackswan Private Limited.

Jaffrelot, Christophe. (2006). The impact of affirmative action in India: More political than socioeconomic. *India Review, 5*(2), 173–189. https://doi.org/10.1080/14736480600824516

Jebaraj, Priscilla. (2021, March 16). Over 60% OBC, SC positions vacant in IIMs. *The Hindu.* https://www.thehindu.com/education/93-of-st-professor-positions-at-central-universities-80-of-st-posts-at-iims-unfilled/article34076556.ece

Jodhka, Surinder. (1998). From "book view" to "field view": Social anthropological constructions of the Indian village. *Oxford Development Studies, 26*(3), 311–331. https://doi.org/10.1080/13600819808424159

Jodhka, Surinder. (2009). Review: Plural histories of sociology and social anthropology. *Economic and Political Weekly, 44*(17), 35–38.

Kothari, Rita. (2013). Caste in a casteless language?: English as a language of "Dalit" expression. *Economic and Political Weekly, 48*(39), 60–68.

Kumar, Vivek. (2016). How egalitarian is Indian sociology? *Economic and Political Weekly, 51*(25), 33–39. https://www.academia.edu/download/47260451/How_Egalitarian_Is_Indian_Sociology__0.pdf

Lukin, Annabelle. (2011, November 14). *The paradox of Noam Chomsky on language and power*. The Conversation. https://theconversation.com/the-paradox-of-noam-chomsky-on-language-and-power-4174

Mamdani, Mahmood. (2019). Decolonising universities. In J. Jansen (Ed.), *Decolonisation in Universities: The Politics of Knowledge* (pp. 15–28). Pluto Press.

Mohanty, Ajit. K. (2018). Multilingualism of the unequals and predicaments of education in India: Mother tongue or other tongue? In Ofelia García, Tove Skutnabb-Kangas, & María E. Torres-Guzmán (Eds.), *Imagining Multilingual Schools* (pp. 262–283). De Gruyter.

Morris, Aldon. (2015). *The scholar denied W. E. B. Du Bois and the birth of modern sociology*. University of California Press.

Naik, Raqib Hameed. (2022, February 1). "Watershed": Dalits hail US university's caste discrimination ban on news. Al Jazeera. https://www.aljazeera.com/news/2022/2/1/us-csu-dalits-hail-university-caste-discrimination-ban

Omvedt, Gail. (2004). *Ambedkar: Towards an enlightened India*. Penguin.

Oommen, T. K. (2011). Scheduled castes, scheduled tribes, and the nation: Situating G. S. Ghurye. *Sociological Bulletin, 60*(2), 228–244. https://doi.org/10.1177/0038022920110202

Plumb, May Helena, Dubcovsky, Alejandra, Guzmán, Moisés García, Lillehaugen, Brook Danielle, & Lopez, Felipe H. (2024). Growing a bigger linguistics through a Zapotec agenda: The Ticha Project. In Anne H. Charity Hudley, Christine Mallinson, & Mary Bucholtz (Eds.), *Decolonizing linguistics*. Oxford University Press.

Prasad, Chandra Bhan. (2013, September 19). Hail English, the Dalit goddess. *DNA*. https://www.dnaindia.com/analysis/comment-hail-english-the-dalit-goddess-1060755

Rymes, B., & Leone, A. R. (2014). Citizen sociolinguistics: A new media methodology for understanding language and social life. In *Working Papers in Educational Linguistics, 29*(2), https://repository.upenn.edu/wpel/vol29/iss2/4/

Said, Edward W. (1979) *Orientalism*. Penguin Books.

Scherer, Bernd M. (2014). *Edward Said's universalism: The perspective of the margins*. https://journeyofideasacross.hkw.de/out-of-academia-in-places/bernd-m-scherer.html

Svendsen, Bente Ailin. (2018). The dynamics of citizen sociolinguistics. *Journal of Sociolinguistics, 22*(2), 137–160. https://doi.org/10.1111/josl.12276

Thorat, Sukhadeo. (2009). Dalits in India: Search for a common destiny. SAGE Publishing.

UGC. (2001). UGC model curriculum: Linguistics. https://www.ugc.gov.in/oldpdf/modelcurriculum/linguistics.pdf

UGC. (2015). Syllabi for the following under graduate courses under choice based credit system (CBCS). https://www.ugc.ac.in/ugc_notices.aspx?id=MTA3Nw==

Varghese, Manoj. (2021). Interventions to promote, propagate and popularise science in schools. *Journal of Scientific Temper, 9*(1–2), 97–109. http://nopr.niscair.res.in/handle/123456789/57573

Yengde, Suraj. (2019). *Caste matters*. Penguin India.

Emily M. Bender is professor of linguistics and adjunct professor in the School of Computer Science and Engineering and the Information School at the University of Washington and the faculty director of the Master of Science program in Computational Linguistics at the University of Washington. Her research areas include the intersection of syntax and sociolinguistics, computational methods in linguistic analysis, the role of linguistic knowledge in natural language processing, and ways of bringing considerations of societal impact into the design of language technology.

Alvin Grissom II is assistant professor of computer science at Haverford College. He has done research in computational approaches to incremental language processing, including simultaneous interpretation between distant language pairs and sentence-final verb prediction; the analysis of racially biased language in large corpora using machine learning techniques; and examining the susceptibility of neural networks to undesirable behaviors when given unexpected inputs.

Abstract: This chapter explores the ways in which lack of inclusion in natural language processing encourages the development of inequitable and harmful technology, both through the exclusion of the language and perspectives of marginalized populations and through overexposure and surveillance, especially of these same populations. The authors review the ways in which research funding and corporate interests influence the field and the growing awareness within the research community of the deleterious potential of current language technologies, from the level of individuals to the level of societies and beyond. Finally, the authors look to some paths forward, with particular emphases on shifting power to affected communities and the role that linguists can play in shaping the development of more inclusive and less harmful language technology.

Key Words: NLP, language technology, bias, dual use, surveillance, community governance

9

Power Shift

Toward Inclusive Natural Language Processing

Emily M. Bender (she/her)
University of Washington

Alvin Grissom II (he/him)
Haverford College

Introduction

The field of natural language processing (NLP) seeks to build software that processes language—speech, text, or, far more rarely, sign—for various practical applications. These applications include consumer-facing technology such as spell checkers and autocorrect, machine translation services, automatic transcription, computer-assisted language learning apps, customer service chatbots, and digital voice assistants (Apple's Siri, Google Assistant, Amazon Alexa, Samsung's Bixby, etc.). Other applications impact what users see without being directly visible to us: NLP is potentially involved in both web search results and the selection of ads to display alongside them, in recommender systems that shape our feeds on social media sites, as well as in such applications as matching patients to clinical trials. Still other applications of NLP involve surveillance in various respects, so that the technology remains invisible to those subjected to it. These applications might be relatively benign (e.g., companies running sentiment analysis systems over social media data to gauge consumer opinions about their brands) but many are not: these include systems which purport to gauge job applicants' agreeableness or conscientiousness through automated interviews[1] and software that aids police and intelligence organizations in sifting through large quantities of captured audio or text data. Consumer-facing applications such as automatic transcription or machine translation can also be used in such surveillance contexts; this scenario, where a single technology can have positive or neutral as well as negative applications, is called dual use.

Emily M. Bender and Alvin Grissom II *Power Shift* In: *Inclusion in Linguistics*. Edited by: Anne H. Charity Hudley, Christine Mallinson and Mary Bucholtz, Oxford University Press. © Anne H. Charity Hudley, Christine Mallinson, and Mary Bucholtz 2024. DOI: 10.1093/oso/9780197755303.003.0010

In this chapter, we explore the ways in which NLP fails at inclusion, the impacts of such failures, and the issues that arise with dual use of language technology. Because language technology can also be used for surveillance, and thus used to surveil already overpoliced populations, broadening the training and testing data to include minoritized languages and varieties is not enough and can even be harmful. What's needed is a path to opt-in inclusion, where data contribution comes with individual privacy rights as well as community-level, democratic governance of both data collection and the resulting tech. We do not claim to offer easy solutions to these complex and evolving problems, but given that language technologies have been integrated into nearly every aspect of modern life, language scientists and professionals must wrestle with these issues.

Background: Author Positionality

In order to situate the discussion that follows, and give the reader context for our analysis, we briefly describe our own positionality.

Emily M. Bender

I am a professor of linguistics, working in the area of computational linguistics/natural language processing. I also run the Computational Linguistics Master of Science program at the University of Washington. In 2016, a member of our advisory board urged me to look into including content on ethics and NLP in our curriculum. After searching in vain for someone to come teach or even give a short presentation on the topic, I decided I would have to gear up to teach it myself and began collecting all the references I could find about the societal impacts of language technology to prepare for a graduate seminar on the topic in early 2017. I have been working in this space ever since and have taught the class twice more so far (in 2019 and 2021). Through this work, I have learned from the research and activism of Black scholars and in particular have been impressed with the importance of understanding technology in its social context.

As a white American, my direct experience with the racial construct could have made it very simple to believe that the opposite of racism was colorblindness. Some of my experiences helped mitigate that, however: first, I was fortunate to attend a racially diverse public high school in Seattle while our city still provided bussing for integration (though it was no longer mandated). I believe that the experience of being in my high school community, forming friendships with Black and Asian peers, gave me a starting point from which to understand racism and racialization that I might not have had otherwise. Second, I lived in Japan for a year in college and experienced being constantly and immediately perceived as "other" by those around me, even as I established a community to belong to. Importantly, this is not parallel to the experience of racialized people in the US, not least because the stereotypes I was subject to were largely positive.

I see racial inequality as a key problem facing society today, one bound up with just about every other problem we face: inequities in healthcare, increasing economic inequality, and climate change and environmental racism, to name a few. I am motivated to research and teach about the ways in which language technology can reinscribe and amplify racism (together with other systems of oppression) because I see those dangers and because it is a way to use the skills I have to work to contribute to addressing these problems.

Alvin Grissom II

I am an assistant professor of computer science, working primarily in computational linguistics and machine learning at Haverford College, a small undergraduate liberal arts college. As a liberal arts college professor, I spend the majority of my time teaching students whose first introduction to computational linguistics, machine learning, or other topics is likely what I teach them, and I have been fortunate to be able to explore many of the topics raised here in my courses. As a Black American computer scientist, I am unfortunately still quite rare. My experiences inform my views, but not reductively or exclusively. I have lived and worked in Japan several times since I first studied abroad there in 2004, which provided me with many invaluable experiences and relationships, further developing my passion for cross-cultural connections and enabling me to see my country from the outside, while also having the privilege to temporarily shed the racial baggage that follows me around it. I have worked in both the United States and Japan, in both academia and industry.

My life has taught me to be resistant to tokenism and to being placed in a box, including the box of working on issues of diversity, race, and the like, however essential. When I write about these issues, it is because I believe they are important and my perspective has something to offer.

Research in NLP

NLP research takes place in academia, industry, and government labs, and many researchers are active participants in the research community, publishing papers at conferences, serving as reviewers, and so on, though there is some industrial and government research not made public through academic publications.

Most research in NLP, whether in industry or academia, is organized around "tasks," conceptualized as particular competencies that system developers can create in a computer (Belz & Kilgarriff, 2006; Schlangen, 2019). Such tasks usually have inputs and outputs: for the task of automatic transcription (otherwise known as speech recognition or speech to text), the input is an audio recording and the output is text in an appropriate orthography; for machine translation, the input is text in one language and the output the translated text in another language; and for a search engine, the input is a query and the output a ranked list of results. Most modern approaches to NLP use machine learning, and most of these use supervised machine learning. (For a brief, accessible overview of machine learning, see Heath, 2020.) In machine learning, rather than crafting the logic to solve a task, programmers create a system that can construct (or "learn") a model from data. In supervised learning, these data consist of labeled examples, where the sample inputs are each paired with expected outputs (for example, spam or not spam for a spam filter). The labels are typically, though not always, created by human annotators. The annotations provided by the annotators are usually treated as "ground truth," that is, a true and objective reflection of what outputs the system should provide for each input. In some cases, such as spam detection, the assumption that one can ignore the positionality (language competencies, lived experience) of human annotators may be mostly innocuous. In contexts like automatic hate speech detection, on the other hand, it can be problematic. For example, Maarten Sap and colleagues (2019) found that tweets with features of African American Language were more likely to be labeled as hate speech than other varieties of English in existing datasets. This outcome is likely related to the language competencies of the crowd workers—people employed by researchers on online platforms to perform research tasks for a small fee per task—who were not specifically recruited based on competence in African American Language. For a survey and critical analysis of data collection and handling practices in machine learning, see Paullada et al. (2021).

Who Sets the Research Agenda?

With the increased prevalence and profitability of NLP has come the requisite corporate and governmental investment and influence, and this influence exerted by investors on the research agendas of scientists must be interrogated. Funding influences research priorities as well as research results.[2] For example, those in power have sought in NLP the tools to exert control not only at the level of societies but also at the granularity of momentary psychological states (Kosinski et al., 2013; Kramer et al., 2014; Tufekci, 2015). Out of all possible research directions, why is this focus on controlling others the road that NLP has taken? We can follow the money: the funding for this research (and thus the agenda setting) comes in large part from government agencies and large corporations. (While we know of no systematic study quantifying this for NLP in particular, we refer the reader to Whittaker, 2021 and Abdalla & Abdalla, 2021 for discussions of corporate influence on research in machine learning and artificial intelligence.)

In the US, the government agencies involved in NLP research include the National Science Foundation (NSF), the National Institute of Standards and Technology (NIST) and especially the Department of Defense and related agencies, including the Defense Advanced Research Projects Agency (DARPA) and the Intelligence Advanced Research Projects Agency (IARPA). Not all government funding schemes are driven by military or corporate agendas. For example, the NSF Dynamic Language Infrastructure–National Endowment for the Humanities Documenting Endangered Languages program[3] includes funding for computational linguistics work on language documentation, though this focus is motivated by anticipated benefits for science and society rather than the communities whose languages are studied. However, NSF is also involved in stewardship of the corporate agenda, administering, for example, the Program on Fairness in Artificial Intelligence in Collaboration with Amazon.[4]

In the last decade, large tech companies have become increasingly important funders of research, both in their own research labs and through sponsoring academic research. Meredith Whittaker (2021) documents this "corporate capture" of the machine learning research space (which includes NLP and is now usually branded as artificial intelligence or AI). Whittaker further shows the resulting impact on work taking a critical view of the creation and application of machine learning technology: researchers in industry risk losing their jobs if they publish critical work (Metz, 2021; Schwab, 2021), and even researchers in academia are strongly incentivized to make nice with corporations, lest they and their students lose access to the large datasets and computing power required for what are currently considered leading-edge approaches to building language technology. As Whittaker (2021) points out, even proposals for dedicating public resources toward "democratizing" (p. 53) AI by creating publicly available computing resources still play into corporations' goals, because those computing resources are rented by the government from those same corporations as cloud infrastructure providers. Meanwhile, more indirectly, the imperatives of these corporations both incentivize educational institutions to prioritize the skill sets that propel their bottom lines and stifle criticism from those who may be on the job market.

NLP is Data-Driven, But Who Drives the Data?

The effect of the financial incentives behind NLP research can be observed in the type and range of datasets created and used, both for training systems and testing them, and, consequently, in the resulting technology. On the one hand, there is an enormous focus on (standardized varieties of) English (Bender, 2011; Blasi et al., 2022; Joshi et al., 2020), which can likely be traced to a few sources, all amplified by the global dominance of the United States: (1) the culture of computer science departments in the United States, where the typical practice has been to focus on a contrast between "natural languages" and programming languages, and to use English as the primary example of a natural language (usually without naming it); (2) the prevalence of funding by the US government, especially the military, with an eye toward creating software for such tasks as voice control of robots by English speakers;[5] and (3) the attention of corporate research on the English language market. There is also a vicious cycle at work in the research community, where reviewing standards demand comparison of new systems to previous systems. A research group working outside the Anglosphere on their own language faces higher hurdles to publication (Church, 2020; Rogers & Augenstein, 2020), as reviewers will ask why they didn't try their ideas on English for better comparison. (Two important recent exceptions to this tendency are the Universal Dependencies project (Nivre et al., 2020), which has fostered the creation of dependency treebanks in 122 languages as of version 2.9[6] and the UniMorph project (Kirov et al., 2018), which has provided annotated data for 142 languages.[7])

On the other hand, NLP research on "low-resource" languages frequently stems from US military support. A low-resource language is one for which the kinds of resources on which NLP work usually relies (for example, corpora, treebanks, pronunciation dictionaries, bitexts) are in short supply.[8] US military-funded work on such languages is motivated by the military's desire to have language processing tools available on short notice for languages they haven't previously been concerned with. For example, in 2014–2019, the DARPA LORELEI (Low Resource Languages for Emergent Incidents) program funded the development of technology to be used in the context of "emergent missions such as humanitarian assistance, disaster relief, peacekeeping or infectious disease response" where "a sudden need emerges for assimilation of information by U.S. Government entities about a region of the world where low-resource languages are frequently used in formal and/or informal media."[9] By comparison, there is vanishingly little funding available for communities working to develop language technology for their own languages and for their own purposes, including language reclamation. In fact, NSF's Dynamic Language Infrastructure program, mentioned above, specifically excludes such work, stating, "DLI does not support projects to revive or expand the actual use of endangered languages" and referring such projects to a program within the US Department of Health and Human Services.[10]

Another key trend in dataset development is the current focus on ever larger datasets, driven in turn by the trend since about 2016 toward the application of neural networks across most NLP tasks. The performance of neural networks is highly dependent on the availability of sufficient computing power and large datasets, the larger the better. Since the publication of two influential papers (Brown et al., 2020; Devlin et al., 2019), significant effort has been directed to a research paradigm based on language models—that is, systems trained to predict words given their surface context. These systems are "pretrained" on the task of predicting words and sentences given their context, using enormous amounts of text (typically scraped from the internet), and then "fine-tuned" with a small amount of task-specific data. Performance on various tasks, as measured by standard benchmarks, has gone up with the size of the pretraining dataset, now measured in hundreds of billions of gigabytes (see Bender, Gebru et al., 2021 for a summary through early 2021). As Emily, Timnit Gebru, and their colleagues discuss, when the research field is organized to prioritize methods that are extremely data-hungry and computing resource-intensive, this excludes work on languages for which such large datasets can't be amassed and work by researchers who don't have access to sufficient computing resources (Bender, Gebru et al., 2021). Further, they argue, datasets at such a large scale cannot be appropriately curated or documented, and thus, given the forces shaping who has access to the internet and can freely express themselves there, end up overrepresenting hegemonic views. Technology trained on such data sets stands to perpetuate systems of oppression, including racism, misogyny, ableism, transphobia, Islamophobia, and more. This isn't a mere academic observation, because the technology is used both to classify texts (for example, in selecting resumes to show to a recruiter (Weissmann, 2018)) and to generate or synthesize text. In the latter case, there may be errors in speech recognition or machine translation output where the text is skewed toward hegemonic views, for example, translating the Turkish gender-neutral pronoun *o* in *O bir kadın doktor* as English *he* in *He is a doctor*, but as *she* if the sentence is about a nurse (Caliskan & Lewis, 2022). In sum, the resulting systems "hold the power biases of those who are able to propagate such systems" (Noble, 2018, p. 137). This is not to say that such research is not valuable, but that the disproportionate resources allocated for it, at the expense of others, and the effect of deploying it in consequential applications, leads to unjust and exclusionary outcomes.

Growing Awareness of the Issues

Recently, both researchers and the general public have grown more aware of the potential negative effects, unintentional or otherwise, of the deployment of NLP and other algorithmic technologies. For example, the documentary *Coded Bias* (Kantayya, 2020) scrutinizes not only the ways in which algorithms disadvantage vulnerable populations through algorithmic and data bias, but also how such systems are being used for surveillance and control. A key example is risk-assessment algorithms which purport to predict recidivism among individuals caught in the US incarceration system, with no recourse against the determinations of the algorithms. Likewise, internet studies scholar Safiya Noble (2018) demonstrated that Google's algorithms serially returned results from text searches that stereotyped people of color of all genders and women of all races. A key example is the search phrase "Black girls," which at the time of Noble's work returned links to pornography. Noble shows how this outcome is due to the economic incentives for both Google and the websites that it indexes, which were set up in such a way that terms describing identities were effectively for sale. African American studies scholar Ruha Benjamin (2019) uses a Black feminist framework to analyze how biases are actualized in the real world, catalyzing much-needed conversations about the price of this rapid technological deployment. Benjamin (2019) notes:

> The key is that all this takes time and intention, which runs against the rush to innovate that pervades the ethos of tech marketing campaigns. But, if we are not simply "users" but people committed to building a more just society, it is vital that we demand a slower and more socially conscious innovation. (p. 183)

Within the NLP research community, there has been increasing awareness of the issues of fairness, transparency, and harm mitigation, through research papers, talks, and other initiatives, such as tracks at major NLP venues dedicated to ethics and sustainability. (Some examples are Ethics in NLP and Green NLP in Association for Computational Linguistics (ACL)-affiliated conferences, and the ACL 2021 theme track NLP for Social Good.) Several major NLP conferences now have ethics reviews for flagged papers as part of the peer review process, and venues such as the Association for Computing Machinery Conference on Fairness, Accountability, and Transparency[11] explicitly specialize in research on ethics in NLP and other fields where machine learning is applied. This is necessary work. Because of its importance and potential influence, however, it is a tantalizing target for corporate interests to co-opt, to the extent that some researchers have argued that the whole notion of "ethical AI" originates as a corporate contrivance to avoid legal limitations on their projects (Ochigame, 2019), providing openings for corporate influence into the ethics agendas of academic and public-sector interests, including the military (Bandler et al., 2019). Under these circumstances, then, the question in focus at these venues becomes not whether but how such technologies are to be researched, developed, and deployed, as it is taken for granted that the technology can and should be developed.

An example of this reframing from *whether* to *how* in NLP is the work on documenting and then attempting to remove bias in word embeddings (Bolukbasi, et al. 2016; Caliskan et al., 2017; Gonen & Goldberg, 2019). Word embeddings—an application of distributional semantics—are representations of words in terms of their co-occurrence with other words: the word embedding training algorithms learn to predict a word's surrounding words, leading to a model which projects these words into a high-dimensional mathematical space, with more "similar" words (according to the corpus on which the model is trained) being closer to each other, sometimes along dimensions that intuitively align with human-understandable concepts. The word's semantics, then, is defined by its mathematical relationship to other words as gleaned from the corpus. Word embeddings are frequently used as a stand-in for what words mean in a broad range of NLP tasks. This "meaning," however, reflects not just what a linguist might consider the dictionary definition, but also information better considered as stereotypes, neither true of the world nor part of the inherent meaning of words, such as associations between immigration and criminality (Speer, 2017). Thus word embeddings recapitulate, and even enhance, the biases both blatant and subtle, of the datasets on which they are trained. Documenting this fact is extremely important work, and word embeddings and similar models of distributional semantics can in fact be illuminating when used to examine the kinds of biases that arise within data (e.g., Garg et al., 2018; Herbelot et al., 2012).

Attempts to address these biases, however, appear only to do so at the surface level (Gonen & Goldberg, 2019). The biases are multidimensional and run deep; they cannot be excised with a scalpel. Even if they could, whose notions of race and gender, for instance, should be used? These are complex concepts with many uses and interpretations. Who decides which biases are worth "debiasing" and how? Most, if not all, debiasing work involves identifying a single dimension in the mathematical representation space that corresponds to a legally protected identity category such as gender or race and then working to remove that dimension from the embeddings for other words. This work is rarely, if ever, grounded in an explicit theory of race. However, viewing race as a dimension in a mathematical space, as in this approach, aligns with essentialist theories of race, and is far from the constructivist theories which political scientists Maya Sen and Omar Wasow (2016) argue provide a more effective foundation for social-scientific work on the functioning of race in society. It remains an open question how Maya Sen and Omar Wasow's "bundle of sticks" model, which represents race as constituted by a variety of elements—including such things as wealth, power relations, and diet, alongside region of ancestry and skin color—could inform a system designed to "debias" word embeddings, or if the result of such a study would ultimately quantify the ways in which such "debiasing" is futile.[12]

If attempts to "debias" word embeddings in many cases only effect cosmetic improvements, what would give us a better understanding of how biases expressed through language come to permeate language technology? Following Benjamin's (2019) view of "race as technology," we can understand racist language use, both subtle and overt, as a constitutive technology of race. The ability of word embeddings to model this constitutive technology means they are ripe for dual use: on the one hand, they can be used as a tool to study the linguistic technology of race at a population scale (Garg et al., 2018). On the other hand, when word embeddings are used in applications, they quietly and not so quietly include the technology of race: the biases propagate to downstream tasks. Moreover, neural network-based text models in general are susceptible to insidious errors across tasks, including question answering (Feng et al., 2018) and machine translation (Raunak et al., 2021, Shi et al., 2022), sometimes with serious consequences, such as when a Facebook post by a Palestinian man was mistranslated—mistaking *yusbihuhum* (Arabic for "good morning") for "attack them" (Hern, 2017).[13] It is also possible to coax large language models, and products that use them, to output offensive text with simple triggers (Noor, 2021; Wallace et al., 2019; de Zwart, 2021). It is of critical importance to measure and understand the ways in which language technology absorbs biases and reproduces systems of oppression. As Ruha Benjamin (2019, p. 7) notes, "the road to inequity is paved with technical fixes," and that road won't lead to solutions to what are really societal problems.

Beyond Data Bias

Data are a source of bias, but bias in language technology and other applications of machine learning is not reducible to data alone. System outputs are also shaped by engineering and research decisions, particularly how systems are designed and evaluated (Raji et al., 2020). These decisions, in turn, are often shaped by the economic pressures and incentives surrounding the technology. Such economic pressures and incentives can be both formidable and inconspicuous: formidable because language technology is presently a very lucrative market, attracting large amounts of investment, and inconspicuous because the pressures themselves are, like the air we breathe, ubiquitous and often banal.[14] While individual examples of bias or prejudice in system outputs can evoke visceral reactions, the fact that they come from automated systems means that the harm can be perpetuated at scale (Buolamwini, 2022; O'Neil, 2016; Zuboff, 2019). Google can influence the information accessed by millions of people with a small tweak, while Facebook can profile users based on posts, mining our innermost selves and sharing our private selves with others without our awareness or control (Dance et al., 2018). Never before in history has technology existed which targets users based on their internal psychological states as externalized by their language and behavior. And never before in history has anyone, let alone an elite "priesthood" (Zuboff, 2019) of software developers, had the power to instantaneously alter the information access, emotions, and behavior of billions of people. (One proof of concept, often criticized, involved a study showing "emotional contagion" on Facebook, which involved manipulating users' feeds to examine the effect on the emotional content of their posts (Kramer et al., 2014).)

Corporate power's objective is profit maximization. As Noble (2018) notes, "Google's monopoly status, coupled with its algorithmic practices of biasing information toward the interests of the neoliberal capital and social elites in the United States, has resulted in a provision of information that purports to be credible but is actually a reflection of advertising interests" (p. 36). These interests are not all benign. Both Google and Facebook, for instance, have been implicated in enabling discriminatory ad targeting, allowing ads for housing and employment to discriminate against protected groups. But even absent these egregious cases, why is it that so much human expertise is directed toward targeted ads—that is, customized manipulation? This is in service to what social psychologist Shoshana Zuboff terms "instrumentarianism," an objectifying form of power, which manipulates through intentionally surreptitious Skinnerian behavior modification and data collection, primarily for profit, but also to other ends, including political manipulation and social control (Zuboff, 2019, p. 352). Of the numerous popular digital assistants, she exhorts that we "do not mistake these soothing sounds for anything other than the exploitation of [our] needs." (2019, p. 377) Where totalitarianism's project was one of an all-encompassing state, instrumentarianism signals "the transformation of the market into a project of total certainty, an undertaking that is unimaginable outside the digital milieu" (2019, p. 382). As with totalitarianism, Zuboff argues, it is sold as a solution to real problems.

This is a new frontier of colonization: the colonization not only of our digital footprints, but of our innermost selves and self-determination. First, the technologies themselves, through surveillance and calculated "nudging" (Eyal, 2014), are designed for explicit behavior modification; and second, the fact that we are aware that we are being spied on changes our behavior (Penney, 2016). We may self-censor (Oulasvirta et al., 2012) because we know we are being mined—watched—and studied, the technologies at once using language to manipulate us and manipulating our language.

Much of modern NLP is driven by machine learning and data-hungry deep neural networks in particular. Research avenues that eschew this paradigm have largely been pushed to the margins. Is this because such research is less interesting or less important? What motivates emphasizing data hungry approaches over others? The common argument is that it's more effective, which may be true—but more effective for whom and for what? The controlling narrative is that this direction is inevitable; it is progress. But it is not inevitable that a major thrust of NLP be one of control and extraction. It is not inevitable that NLP be used in ways that hurt our mental health (Kramer et al., 2014) and distort our societies rather than enhancing our lives. Nor is it inevitable that universities play to the tune of corporate and military interests.

What can be done? Universities have the opportunity to educate conscientious, thoughtful researchers and practitioners through ethically aware curricula (Bender et al., 2020), examination of the social impacts of NLP (Fort et al., 2016; Hovy & Spruit, 2016), and increased prioritization of research outside of that which is potentially profitable. The value of a scientific question is not solely determined by its applicability to business interests. Just how much NLP research—and scientific research generally—is driven by potential business and military applications is worth interrogating not only once, but constantly. The very structures of academia encourage and even necessitate bringing in money, individually and collectively, for funding research and, often, for obtaining tenure. Alvin connects this to the propaganda model of Herman and Chomsky (2010) in Grissom 2019. Furthermore, students trained by university NLP programs often, not unreasonably, expect to have desirable, marketable skills, providing another incentive to structure curricula around the priorities of corporate interests. We need not assume that corporate objectives are always undesirable to understand that corporate power over academic priorities is undesirable. The fact of the profit motive is reason for extreme skepticism, a priori, of such influence and its effects. Corporations will do what corporations do: maximize profit. If researchers in academia follow corporate directives, they too pursue this imperative by proxy; they are merely worse at it and paid less.[15]

Shifting Power to Communities

Inclusive NLP requires shifting power to communities. We want to draw a clear distinction here between tokenism—placing a few visible members of marginalized communities into existing hegemonic power structures—and inclusive approaches to technology design and application which intentionally, meaningfully, and permanently shift power. Technology by and for those in power in a society with vast power asymmetries will primarily benefit those in power, but NLP practitioners can take steps in the right direction. Including stakeholders—the communities affected, not just tokens from these communities—in the process of designing and testing the technology gives them a voice in how and even whether they want a given technology, potentially bringing transparency regarding whom that technology actually serves. Indeed, some technologies should not be developed at all, and the communities affected are often aware of this fact. Media, communications and cultural studies scholar Mirca Madianou (2021) conducts an extensive examination of ways in which even data science technologies developed and deployed for humanitarian purposes can actually be a form of what Mirca calls "technocolonialism," driven by market forces and reifying colonial legacies and power asymmetries. (See also Zaugg, 2020 for a discussion of surveillance technologies of linguistically marginalized groups.)

We see the process of peer review as one place where pressure can be exerted to improve this situation: transparent discussion of dual use should be a standard part of research papers in NLP. Since 2020, conferences run by

ACL, as well as machine learning conferences like the Conference on Neural Information Processing Systems (NeurIPS), have instituted ethics review of publications. In this practice, reviewers tend to look for discussions of dual use, though it remains to be seen how this review will affect the culture of the research field. Providing such discussion in research papers would not only be a step toward making dual use issues apparent to community advocates, but would potentially also motivate researchers to direct their research effort in ways aligned with the values and goals of the communities whose languages are being studied.

The field of NLP as a whole also needs to let go of its colonizer's mentality. Damián Blasi et al. (2022) present important work in quantifying the disparities in language technology outside English plus a handful of other languages associated with politically, militarily, and economically powerful nation-states. However, they do so from an unacknowledged Western perspective: they quantify the "utility" of language technology to users of a given language via a proxy for their own ideal measurement of such things as "how successfully the user can obtain information from an automatically translated web page, or how satisfied the user is by a speech-based virtual assistant's execution of a series of verbal commands" (Blasi et al., 2022, p. 5487). But they don't show that such technology is in fact desired by all or even most of the communities in question.

Scholarship on Indigenous data sovereignty presents an alternative model, wherein data governance is in the hands of communities and thus so is control of the resulting technology. Tahu Kukutai and John Taylor (2016) bring together a collection of studies, featuring primarily Indigenous authors, theorizing Indigenous data sovereignty and exploring implementations with respect to social-science research, governmental policy and planning, and questions of data governance. These studies are grounded in specific Indigenous perspectives and interpret and draw on the United Nations Declaration on the Rights of Indigenous Peoples.[16] Similarly, the Indigenous Protocol and Artificial Intelligence Working Group (2020) reports on a series of international workshops devoted to exploring what Indigenous protocols for AI could look like, articulating goals including making sure that AI technologies are designed for, rather than against, Indigenous people and making sure that global conversations around AI ethics aren't mired in a philosophical monoculture. The position paper includes essays by Caroline Running Wolf, Dr. Noelani Arista, Michael Running Wolf, Caleb Moses, and Joel Davison describing Hua Kiʻi, an app that performs image recognition with Hawaiʻian vocabulary as a language learning tool and serves as an initial prototype for a much larger envisioned app, Kuanoʻo, providing immersive language education to Native Hawai'ians and visitors to the Queendom of Hawai'i alike. Donavyn Coffey (2021) describes how Te Hiku Media, a radio station in Aotearoa/New Zealand, collected data required to create a te reo Māori speech to text system and have since worked to fend off outside interests seeking to gain access to theirs or similar training data for their own commercial purposes.

In a world that respects Indigenous data sovereignty, the questions that an NLP researcher asks shift from "How do I use this technique to make better tech for that language?" to "How do I use what I know about technology to help my community/this community who has asked for my help to achieve their goals?" and "How do I use what I know about the precise capabilities of this kind of technology and the risks it opens up to help my community/this community which has asked for my help to decide what technology they would like built?" Asking these questions helps us to move away from an extractive notion of inclusion, which is limited to including "their" data in "our" dataset, toward one that shifts power and stands a chance of developing language technology that serves communities.

Conclusion: What Linguists in NLP Can Do

NLP, like any other technology, is the product of human effort and decisions, which means that nothing about it is inevitable. Linguists from all subfields who choose to work in NLP should be aware of current issues within the field, in order to be best positioned to bring about a future in which language technology is built to serve the needs of language communities, especially racialized and overpoliced communities.

The first issue is technosolutionism, or the culture of optimism around technology where every idea is sold as solving problems and the solutions are rarely critically examined. One approach to combating this is the idea of value scenarios (Nathan et al., 2007) from value sensitive design (Friedman & Hendry, 2019), where technologists explore the possible impacts of their proposed technology beyond the typical practice of imagining just rosy scenes of happy customers. Instead, they also consider what might happen to other people impacted by the technology, usually not those actually using the technology and especially those in marginalized or otherwise vulnerable positions; what might happen if the technology is deliberately used for negative purposes, as in dual use, described above; or what might happen if it's used as intended, at scale, and there are side effects of that pervasive use. For example, who might be cut off from government services if automated voice-based assistants become ubiquitous as the first point of contact? Relatedly, developers typically focus on users similar to themselves and thus easy for them to imagine, with little or no consideration for other users and especially those who the technology might be used on rather than by. Here, too, value sensitive design provides useful methodologies for identifying people potentially impacted by technology so that their values and well-being can be considered (Friedman & Hendry, 2019; Yoo, 2021).

The second issue is the problem of dual use. Language technology products, like other forms of technology, are often described, even to developers, in terms of beneficial and pro-social uses, while simultaneously being developed for surveillance or other harmful purposes. One striking example is the DARPA LORELEI program cited above, which was motivated in terms of "humanitarian assistance/disaster relief, peacekeeping or infectious disease response," where "peacekeeping" (which must surely mean military action) is sandwiched between two humanitarian use cases. Dirk Hovy and Shannon L. Spruitt (2016) identify several possible cases of dual use: educational technology, including grammar checkers, reinforcing stigmatization of nonprestige linguistic varieties, stylometric analysis developed to identify authorship of historical texts being used for outing political dissenters, and systems designed to detect maliciously produced text, such as fake reviews, fake news, or hate speech, instead being used to generate such text.

So how can linguists help address these problems? How can knowledge of linguistics be used to build a more inclusive NLP and resist the trends toward using NLP for surveillance, policing, and concentration of power? Linguists bring several strengths to this effort, starting with a deep understanding of how language works. This can be key in handling discourses where language technology is asserted to have magical powers (e.g., detecting whether someone is lying or trustworthy based on their facial movements and voice; see Feathers, 2021). In addition, knowledge about the nature and function of sociolinguistic variation positions us to reason about harms that arise from inequitable access to language-mediated technology. This includes both general reasoning about how those harms fall disproportionately on users of stigmatized varieties, who are already marginalized in other ways, and specific reasoning about what harms would need to be addressed for which communities. At the same time, linguists' understanding of how language variation is particularly relevant to decisions of how and when to extend language technology to stigmatized varieties. For example, research on how marginalized communities use language variation to prevent surveillance by powerful outgroup individuals or to establish solidarity with in-group members—both of which, it is worth noting, were accomplished by songs of the Underground

Railroad (Hudson, 2006)—can potentially help communities decide what language technology they want and how to govern its use.

In short, linguists have skills and knowledge that are highly relevant to the development of just and inclusive language technology. This doesn't mean, however, that linguists are necessarily included in the conversations where decisions about the design, deployment and governance of technology happen. One hurdle is what Timnit Gebru (2021) calls the "hierarchy of knowledge," where those in control of funding (academic and otherwise), hiring, and other decision making value computer science above fields like linguistics as more general, profitable, or even objective. A key step, then, is to not cede that ideological ground: linguists can and should enter into interdisciplinary conversations with confidence in the value of linguistic expertise to the development of language technology. One strategy for showing confidence is to ask proactive questions based on linguistic considerations, such as "How can we ensure that our product will work for language users who . . . ?," "How can we fulfill our responsibility to protect user privacy in light of . . . ?," and, when the technology is not being developed by the relevant language community, "How do we connect with the community for this language to find out if they even want this technology?" Some of Emily's recent collaborative work (Bender, Gebru et al., 2021; Shah & Bender, 2022) is written in this spirit, seeking to use linguistics to inform discussions of language technology.

It is also valuable to think ahead to the eventuality of witnessing wrongdoing and thus needing to decide whether or not to become a whistleblower. We recommend preparing in advance, both to be able to recognize when it would be worthwhile to take action but also to know how to balance and mitigate the risks of doing so. Such preparation could involve writing down personal answers to questions such as "What are the bright lines that I will not cross?" and "What are examples of things that I would feel compelled to become a whistleblower over?," networking with like-minded people, so as to have someone to talk things over with, and importantly, being knowledgeable about legal issues, about how to effectively talk with the media, and about how find legal representation. On these points, the *Tech Worker Handbook*[17] provides extremely valuable information.

We have argued that language technology development exists in an environment heavily influenced by corporate and military priorities, a fact which will likely not change any time soon. But a linguist who is aware of this reality can more shrewdly navigate this environment with knowledge and awareness rather than naiveté, empowering them to make decisions about research, employment, or projects in line with their values. Linguists, in particular, have expertise which is highly relevant to these issues and desperately lacking in many of the key conversations where decisions about language technology are being made. We hope that this chapter will inspire people to work within natural language processing to reorient the field in ways that shift power to communities in the development, deployment, and governance of language technology.

Notes

1. Sheridan Wall & Hilke Schellman (2021), "We Tested AI Interview Tools. Here's What We Found," MIT Technology Review, July 7, 2021, https://www.technologyreview.com/2021/07/07/1027916/we-tested-ai-interview-tools/.
2. See Farrell (2016) for a discussion of this in the context of climate change research.
3. National Science Foundation, "NSF Dynamic Language Infrastructure–National Endowment for the Humanities Documenting Endangered Languages," https://www.nsf.gov/pubs/2020/nsf20603/nsf20603.htm.
4. National Science Foundation, "Program on Fairness in Artificial Intelligence in Collaboration with Amazon," https://www.nsf.gov/pubs/2021/nsf21585/nsf21585.htm.
5. There is now also a good deal of work on Mandarin, likely the result of high levels of funding from the Chinese government and large corporations. See, for example, the Wu Dao 2.0 model, for which there is little information available: Oliver Freeman, "Chinese AI Model Wu Dao 2.0 Unnerves Europe," AI Magazine, June 11, 2021, https://aimagazine.com/technology/chinese-ai-model-wu-dao-20-unnerves-europe.
6. Universal Dependencies project, https://universaldependencies.org/.
7. UniMorph project, https://unimorph.github.io/.
8. For an alternative conception that honors the resources that communities working on language reclamation have, see Bird (2022).
9. Defense Advanced Research Projects Agency, "Low Resource Languages for Emergent Incidents (LORELEI)," https://www.darpa.mil/program/low-resource-languages-for-emergent-incidents.
10. National Science Foundation (2020), "NSF Dynamic Language Infrastructure–NEH Documenting Endangered Language (DLI-DEL)," https://www.nsf.gov/pubs/2020/nsf20603/nsf20603.htm.
11. Association for Computing Machinery, "ACM Conference on Fairness, Accountability, and Transparency," https://facctconference.org/.
12. A study such as Dhamala et al. (2021), which uses actual individuals' names as proxies for race in probing word embeddings for racial bias, resembles social scientific exposure studies as described by Sen and Wasow (2016), which use single racial cues representing one "stick" as a proxy for the full bundle. However, no studies we are aware of are on solid theoretical footing when trying to move on from demonstrating racial bias in word embeddings to removing it.
13. For other examples of harmful incidents at the hands of algorithms, see the AI Incident Database at https: //incidentdatabase.ai.
14. Various market analysts estimated the natural language processing market size in 2029 to be over USD 160 billion; see Q.ai, "What Companies Are Fueling The Progress In Natural

Language Processing? Moving This Branch Of AI Past Translators And Speech-To-Text ," Forbes. 6 Feb 2023. https://www.forbes.com/sites/qai/2023/02/06/what-companies-are-fueling-the-progress-in-natural-language-processing-moving-this-branch-of-ai-past-translators-and-speech-to-text/?sh=3db88eab4a8f.

15. We are not advocating that graduate students turn down funding; we are, however, making the observation that money influences priorities and behavior.

16. United Nations, "Declaration on the Rights of Indigenous Peoples," March 2008, https://www.un.org/esa/socdev/unpfii/documents/DRIPS_en.pdf.

17. *Tech Worker Handbook*, https://techworkerhandbook.org/.

References

Abdalla, Mohamed, & Abdalla, Moustafa. (2021). The grey hoodie project: Big tobacco, big tech, and the threat on academic integrity. *Proceedings of the 2021 AAAI/ACM Conference on AI, Ethics, and Society*, 287–297. https://doi.org/10.1145/3461702.3462563

Bandler, James, Tsui, Anjali, & Burke, Doris. (2019, August 22). How Amazon and Silicon Valley seduced the Pentagon. *ProPublica*. https://www.propublica.org/article/howamazon-and-silicon-valley-seduced-the-pentagon]

Belz, Anja, & Kilgarriff, Adam. (2006). Shared-task evaluations in HLT: Lessons for NLG. *Proceedings of the Fourth International Natural Language Generation Conference*, 133–135.

Bender, Emily M. (2011). On achieving and evaluating language independence in NLP. *Linguistic Issues in Language Technology*, 6, 1–26.

Bender, Emily M., Gebru, Timnit, McMillan-Major, Angelina, & Shmitchell, Shmargaret. (2021). On the dangers of stochastic parrots: Can language models be too big? *Proceedings of FAccT 2021*: 610–623. https://doi.org/10.1145/3442188.3445922

Bender, Emily M., Hovy, Dirk, & Schofield, Alexandra. (2020). Integrating ethics into the NLP curriculum. *Proceedings of the Association for Computational Linguistics: Tutorial Abstracts*, 6–9. https://doi.org/10.1145/3545945.3569792

Benjamin, Ruha. (2019). *Race after technology: Abolitionist tools for the New Jim Code*. Polity Press.

Bird, Steven. (2022). Local languages, third spaces, and other high-resource scenarios. *Proceedings of the 60th Annual Meeting of the Association for Computational Linguistics*. https://doi.org/10.48448/511d-wr51

Blasi, Dami´an, Anastasopoulos, Antonios, & Neubig, Graham. (2022). Systematic inequalities in language technology performance across the world's languages. *Proceedings of the 60th Annual Meeting of the Association for Computational Linguistics (Volume 1: Long Papers)*, 5486–5505. https://doi.org/10.18653/v1/2022.acl-long.376

Bolukbasi, Tolga, Chang, Kai-Wei, Zou, James Y., Saligrama, Venkatesh, & Kalai, Adam T. (2016). Man is to computer programmer as woman is to homemaker? Debiasing word embeddings. In D. D. Lee, M. Sugiyama, U. V. Luxburg, I. Guyon, & R. Garnett (Eds.), *Advances in neural information processing systems 29* (pp. 4349–4357). Curran Associates.https://doi.org/10.48550/arXiv.1607.06520a

Brown, Tom B., Mann, Benjamin, Ryder, Nick, Subbiah, Melanie, Kaplan, Jared, Dhariwal, Prafulla, Neelakantan, Arvind, Shyam, Pranav, Sastry, Girish, Askell, Amanda, Agarwal, Sandhini, Herbert-Voss, Ariel, Krueger, Gretchen, Henighan, Tom, Child, Rewon, Ramesh, Aditya, Ziegler, Daniel M., Wu, Jeffrey, Winter, Clemens, . . . Amodei, Dario. (2020). Language models are few-shot learners. In Hugo Larochelle, Marc'Aurelio Ranzato, Raia Hadsell, Maria-Florina Balcan, & Hsuan-Tien Lin (Eds.), *Advances in neural information processing systems 33: Annual conference on Neural Information Processing Systems 2020, NeurIPS 2020, December 6–12, 2020, virtual.* https://proceedings.neurips.cc/paper/2020/hash/1457c0d6bfcb4967418bfb8ac142f64a-Abstract.html

Buolamwini, Joy. (2022). *Facing the coded gaze with evocative audits and algorithmic audits* [Doctoral dissertation, Massachusetts Institute of Technology].

Caliskan, Aylin, Bryson, Joanna J., & Narayanan, Arvind. (2017). Semantics derived automatically from language corpora contain human-like biases. *Science, 356*(6334), 183–186. https://doi.org/10.1126/science.aal4230

Caliskan, Aylin, & Lewis, Molly. (2022). Social biases in word embeddings and their relation to human cognition. In Morteza Dehghani & Ryan Boyd (Eds.), *The handbook of language analysis in psychology* (pp. 478–493). Guilford Press.

Church, Kenneth Ward. (2020). Emerging trends: Reviewing the reviewers (again). *Natural Language Engineering, 26*(2), 245–257.https://doi.org/10.1017/S1351324920000030

Coffey, Donavyn. (2021, April 28). Māori are trying to save their language from big tech. *WIRED.* https://www.wired.co.uk/article/maori-language-tech

Dance, Gabriel J. X., LaForgia, Michael, & Confessore, Nicholas. (2018, December 18). As Facebook raised a privacy wall, it carved an opening for tech giants. *New York Times.* https://www.nytimes.com/2018/12/18/technology/facebook-privacy.html

Devlin, Jacob, Chang, Ming-Wei, Lee, Kenton, & Toutanova, Kristina. (2019). BERT: Pre-training of deep bidirectional transformers for language understanding. *Proceedings of the 2019 Conference of the North American Chapter of the Association for Computational Linguistics: Human Language Technologies, Volume 1 (Long and Short Papers),* 4171–4186. https://doi.org/10.18653/v1/N19-1423

de Zwart, Hans. (2021). Racist technology in action: An AI for ethical advice turns out to be super racist. Racism and Technology Center. https://racismandtechnology.center/2021/11/26/racist-technologyin-action-an-ai-for-ethical-advice-turns-out-to-be-super-racist

Dhamala, Jwala, Sun, Tony, Kumar, Varun, Krishna, Satyapriya, Pruksachatkun, Yada, Chang, Kai-Wei, & Gupta, Rahul. (2021). Bold: Dataset and metrics for measuring biases in open-ended language generation. *Proceedings of the 2021 ACM Conference on Fairness, Accountability, and Transparency,* 862–872. https://doi.org/10.1145/3442188.3445924

Eyal, Nir. (2014). *Hooked: How to build habit-forming products.* Penguin.

Farrell, Justin. (2016). Corporate funding and ideological polarization about climate change. *Proceedings of the National Academy of Sciences, 113*(1), 92–97.

Feathers, Todd. (2021, January 19). This app claims it can detect "trustworthiness." It can't. *Motherboard, Tech by VICE.* https://www.vice.com/en/article/akd4bg/this-app-claims-it-can-detecttrustworthiness-it-cant

Feng, Shi, Wallace, Eric, Grissom II, Alvin, Iyyer, Mohit, Rodriguez, Pedro, & Boyd-Graber, Jordan. (2018). Pathologies of neural models make interpretations difficult. *Proceedings of the 2018 Conference on Empirical Methods in Natural Language Processing,* 3719–3728.

Fort, Karën, Adda, Gilles, & Cohen, K. Bretonnel (Eds.). (2016). Tal et éthique. *Traitement automatique des langues, 57*(2), 7–110.

Friedman, Batya, & Hendry, David G. (2019). *Value sensitive design: Shaping technology with moral imagination.* MIT Press.

Garg, Nikhil, Schiebinger, Londa, Jurafsky, Dan, & Zou, James. (2018). Word embeddings quantify 100 years of gender and ethnic stereotypes. *Proceedings of the National Academy of Sciences, 115*(16), E3635–E3644. https://doi.org/10.1073/pnas.1720347115

Gebru, Timnit. (2021). The hierarchy of knowledge in machine learning and related fields and its consequences [Talk presented at the Spelman College Center of Excellence for Minority Women in STEM, April 14]. https://www.youtube.com/watch?v=OL3DowBM9uc

Gonen, Hila, & Goldberg, Yoav. (2019). Lipstick on a pig: Debiasing methods cover up systematic gender biases in word embeddings but do not remove them. *Proceedings of the*

2019 Conference of the North American Chapter of the Association for Computational Linguistics: Human Language Technologies, Volume 1 (Long and Short Papers), 609–614. https://doi.org/10.18653/v1/N19-1061

Grissom II, Alvin. (2019). Thinking about how NLP is used to serve power: Current and future trends [Keynote Talk, The Third Workshop on Widening NLP@ACL]. https://www.youtube.com/watch?v=xpq4FLyLsyE

Heath, Nick. (2020, December 16). What is machine learning? Everything you need to know. ZDNet. https://www.zdnet.com/article/what-is-machine-learning-everything-you-need-to-know/

Herbelot, Aurelie, von Redecker, Eva, & Mu¨ller, Johanna. (2012). Distributional techniques for philosophical enquiry. Proceedings of the 6th Workshop on Language Technology for Cultural Heritage, Social Sciences, and Humanities, 45–54. https://www.aclweb.org/anthology/W12-1008

Herman, Edward S, & Chomsky, Noam. (2010). Manufacturing consent: The political economy of the mass media. Random House.

Hern, Alex. (2017, October 24). Facebook translates "good morning" into "attack them," leading to arrest. The Guardian. https://www.theguardian.com/technology/2017/oct/24/facebook-palestine-israel-translates-good-morning-attack-them-arrest

Hovy, Dirk, & Spruit, Shannon L. (2016). The social impact of natural language processing. Proceedings of the 54th Annual Meeting of the Association for Computational Linguistics (Volume 2: Short Papers), 591–598. https://doi.org/10.18653/v1/P16-2096

Hudson, J. Blaine. (2006). Encyclopedia of the underground railroad. McFarland.

Indigenous Protocol and Artificial Intelligence Working Group. (2020). Position paper: Indigenous protocol and artificial intelligence.

Joshi, Pratik, Santy, Sebastin, Budhiraja, Amar, Bali, Kalika, & Choudhury, Monojit. (2020). The state and fate of linguistic diversity and inclusion in the NLP world. Proceedings of the 58th Annual Meeting of the Association for Computational Linguistics, 6282–6293. https://doi.org/10.18653/v1/2020.acl-main.560

Kantayya, Shalini. (2020). Coded bias. 7th Empire Media.

Kirov, Christo, Cotterell, Ryan, Sylak-Glassman, John, Walther, Geraldine, Vylomova, Ekaterina, Xia, Patrick, Faruqui, Manaal, Mielke, Sabrina J., McCarthy, Arya, Kübler, Sandra, Yarowsky, David, Eisner, Jason, & Hulden, Mans. (2018). UniMorph 2.0: Universal morphology. Proceedings of the Eleventh International Conference on Language Resources and Evaluation (LREC 2018). https://aclanthology.org/L18-1293

Kosinski, Michal, Stillwell, David, & Graepel, Thore. (2013). Private traits and attributes are predictable from digital records of human behavior. Proceedings of the national academy of sciences, 110(15), 5802–5805. https://doi.org/10.1073/pnas.1218772110

Kramer, Adam, D. I., Guillory, Jamie E, & Hancock, Jeffrey T. (2014). Experimental evidence of massive-scale emotional contagion through social networks. Proceedings of the National Academy of Sciences, 111(24), 8788–8790. https://doi.org/10.1073/pnas.1320040111

Kukutai, Tahu, & Taylor, John (Eds.). (2016). Indigenous data sovereignty: Toward an agenda. Australian National University Press.

Madianou, Mirca. (2021). Technocolonialism: Digital innovation and data practices in the humanitarian response to refugee crises. In Lilie Chouliaraki and Anne Vestergaard (Eds.), Routledge handbook of humanitarian communication (pp. 185–202). Routledge.

Metz, Rachel. (2021, March 11). How one employee's exit shook Google and the AI industry. CNN Business. https://www.cnn.com/2021/03/11/tech/google-ai-ethics-future/index.html

Nathan, Lisa P., Klasnja Predrag V., & Friedman, Batya. (2007). Value scenarios: A technique for envisioning systemic effects of new technologies. CHI '07 Extended Abstracts on Human Factors in Computing Systems, 2585–2590. https://doi.org/10.1145/1240866.1241046

Nivre, Joakim, de Marneffe, Marie-Catherine, Ginter, Filip, Haji˘c, Jan, Manning, Christopher D., Pyysalo, Sampo, Schuster, Sebastian, Tyers, Francis, & Zeman, Daniel. (2020). Universal Dependencies v2: An ever-growing multilingual treebank collection. *Proceedings of the 12th Language Resources and Evaluation Conference*, 4034–4043. https://aclanthology.org/2020.lrec-1.497

Noble, Safiya Umoja. (2018). *Algorithms of oppression: How search engines reinforce racism.* NYU Press.

Noor, Poppy. (2021). "Is it OK to . . .": The bot that gives you an instant moral judgment. *The Guardian.* https://www.theguardian.com/technology/2021/nov/02/delphi-online-ai-botphilosophy

Ochigame, Rodrigo. (2019). The invention of "ethical AI": How big tech manipulates academia to avoid regulation. *The Intercept, 20.* https://theintercept.com/2019/12/20/mit-ethical-aiartificial-intelligence/

O'Neil, Cathy. (2016). *Weapons of math destruction: How big data increases inequality and threatens democracy.* Broadway Books.

Oulasvirta, Antti, Pihlajamaa, Aurora, Perki¨o, Jukka, Ray, Debarshi, Vähäkangas, Taneli, Hasu, Tero, Vainio, Niklas, & Myllymäki, Petri. (2012). Long-term effects of ubiquitous surveillance in the home. *Proceedings of the 2012 ACM Conference on Ubiquitous Computing*, 41–50.

Paullada, Amandalynne, Raji, Inioluwa Deborah, Bender, Emily M., Denton, Emily, & Hanna, Alex. (2021). Data and its (dis)contents: A survey of dataset development and use in machine learning research. *Patterns, 2.* https://doi.org/10.1016/j.patter.2021.100336

Penney, Jonathon W. (2016). Chilling effects: Online surveillance and Wikipedia use. *Berkeley Technology Law Journal, 31*(1), 117.

Raji, Inioluwa, Deborah, Smart, Andrew, White, Rebecca N., Mitchell, Margaret, Gebru, Timnit, Hutchinson, Ben, Smith-Loud, Jamila, Theron, Daniel, & Barnes, Parker. (2020). Closing the AI accountability gap: Defining an end-to-end framework for internal algorithmic auditing. *Proceedings of the 2020 Conference on Fairness, Accountability, and Transparency*, 33–44. https://doi.org/10.1145/3351095.3372873

Raunak, Vikas, Menezes, Arul, & Junczys-Dowmunt, Marcin. (2021). The curious case of hallucinations in neural machine translation. *Proceedings of the 2021 Conference of the North American Chapter of the Association for Computational Linguistics: Human Language Technologies*, 1172–1183. http://dx.doi.org/10.18653/v1/2021.naacl-main.92

Rogers, Anna, & Augenstein, Isabelle. (2020). What can we do to improve peer review in NLP? *Proceedings of the 2020 Conference on Empirical Methods in Natural Language Processing: Findings*, 1256–1262. http://dx.doi.org/10.18653/v1/2020.findings-emnlp.112

Sap, Maarten, Card, Dallas, Gabriel, Saadia, Choi, Yejin, & Smith, Noah A. (2019). The risk of racial bias in hate speech detection. *Proceedings of the 57th Annual Meeting of the Association for Computational Linguistics*, 1668–1678. https://doi.org/10.18653/v1/P19-1163

Schlangen, D. (2019). Language tasks and language games: On methodology in current natural language processing research. *ArXiv, abs/1908.10747.* https://doi.org/10.48550/arXiv.1908.10747

Schwab, Katharine. (2021, February 26). "This is bigger than just Timni" ': How Google tried to silence a critic and ignited a movement. *Fast Company.* https://www.fastcompany.com/90608471/timnit-gebru-google-ai-ethics-equitable-tech-movement

Sen, Maya, & Wasow, Omar. (2016). Race as a bundle of sticks: Designs that estimate effects of seemingly immutable characteristics. *Annual Review of Political Science, 19*, 499–522.

Shah, Chirag, & Bender, Emily M. (2022). Situating search. *ACM SIGIR Conference on Human Information Interaction and Retrieval*, 221–232. https://doi.org/10.1145/3498366.3505816

Shi, Ruikang, Grissom II, Alvin, & Trinh, Duc Minh. (2022). Rare but severe neural machine translation errors induced by minimal deletion: An empirical study on Chinese and English. *Proceedings of the 29th International Conference on Computational Linguistics*, 5175–5180.

Speer, Robyn. (2017). Conceptnet numberbatch 17.04: Better, less-stereotyped word vectors [blog post]. https://blog.conceptnet.io/2017/04/24/conceptnet-numberbatch-17-04-better-lessstereotyped-word-vectors/

Tufekci, Zeynep. (2015). Algorithmic harms beyond Facebook and Google: Emergent challenges of computational agency. Colorado Technology Law Journal *13*, 203–215.

Wallace, Eric, Feng, Shi, Kandpal, Nikhil, Gardner, Matt, & Singh. Sameer. (2019). Universal adversarial triggers for attacking and analyzing NLP. *Proceedings of the 2019 Conference on Empirical Methods in Natural Language Processing and the 9th International Joint Conference on Natural Language Processing (EMNLP-IJCNLP)*, 2153–2162. https://doi.org/10. 18653/v1/D19-1221

Weissmann, Jordan. (2018, October 10). Amazon created a hiring tool using A.I. It immediately started discriminating against women. *Slate*. https://slate.com/business/2018/10/amazon-artificial-intelligence-hiring-discrimination-women.html

Whittaker, Meredith. (2021). The steep cost of capture. *Interactions, 28*(6), 50–55. https://doi.org/10.1145/3488666

Yoo, Daisy. (2021). Stakeholder tokens: A constructive method for value sensitive design stakeholder analysis. *Ethics and Information Technology, 23*(1), 63–67. https://doi.org/10.1007/s10676-018-9474-4

Zaugg, Isabelle A. (2020). Digital surveillance and digitally-disadvantaged language communities. *International Conference Language Technologies for All (LT4All)*. https://data-ethics.jonreeve.com/static/papers/zaugg2019.pdf

Zuboff, Shoshana. (2019). *The age of surveillance capitalism: The fight for a human future at the new frontier of power*. Profile Books.

PART 3
CREATING JUST AND INCLUSIVE CLASSROOMS

Amy Plackowski is a high school English teacher with the Hudson Public Schools in Hudson, Massachusetts, where she has taught since 2005. Inside and outside the classroom, she is interested in making linguistics accessible to high school students, integrating linguistics into existing high school curricula, and using linguistics to teach social justice and antiracism. She has served as chair of the Linguistics in the School Curriculum Committee of the Linguistic Society of America. She holds degrees from Alma College and Georgetown University. Her publications have appeared in the journal *American Speech,* the volumes *Teaching Language Variation in the Classroom: Strategies and Models from Teachers and Linguists* and *Theoretical Linguistics in the Pre-University Classroom*, and the website Scary Mommy. Her resources for teachers and students interested in learning more about linguistics can be found on her website at www.hslinguistics.com.

Abstract: This chapter describes a high school linguistics course developed by the author in the 2020–2021 school year for the public school where she teaches English Language Arts. Unlike most high school linguistics courses, this course is not an elective, but can be taken for core English credit. The course is organized around thematic units rather than traditional linguistic subfields. These units use linguistics to provide students with a framework for investigating social issues, problems, and questions related to social justice and media literacy. The course is aimed at exposing all students to linguistics, including students who have not typically been offered opportunities to take linguistics (e.g., students on education plans, students designated English language learners, and non–college-bound students). This chapter discusses the necessity of including linguistics in social justice teaching, as well as challenges and limitations.

Key Words: high school, teaching, education, social justice, curriculum, English Language Arts, accessibility, prescriptivism, standardized language ideology, language variation

10

Disrupting English Class

Linguistics and Social Justice for *All* High School Students

Amy L. Plackowski (she/her)
Hudson Public Schools

Introduction

In May of 2021, at the end of what had been the hardest year of teaching for most educators up to that point, a card was slipped under my classroom door. It read, in part,

> I wanted to thank you for teaching Linguistics this year. I have truly never taken a class before where I could relate the content to my everyday life until this one. My friends and I will always say, "linguistic moment!" whenever we say or hear something that relates to content from class (usually multiple times a day ha!). This is knowledge that I will carry with me forever, as I use and apply it everyday. . . . I became so much more aware of the importance of language, and the value how all languages matter. . . . I wish everyone was fortunate enough to take a course in linguistics, because all society can become better with this knowledge.

That was the first year I had taught this linguistics class as a core course, and it was also the first time I had ever taught the class using a thematic approach to curriculum design. Prior to the 2020–2021 school year, I had offered a semester-length linguistics elective through the English Language Arts (ELA) department in our small public high school in Massachusetts. In 2020, with electives on the chopping block due to budget cuts, our department revised our program of study so that two electives, Linguistics and Media Literacy, were combined to make a single course, renamed Linguistics and Media Studies. It became one of six options students could take to meet their 11th or 12th grade ELA graduation requirement. In 2020–2021, I taught three sections of the course. In 2021–2022, we offered four sections of the course, two of them taught by the former Media Literacy teacher, Elizabeth Albota. In this chapter, when I use the pronoun "we" regarding curricular decisions and

Amy L. Plackowski, *Disrupting English Class* In: *Inclusion in Linguistics*. Edited by: Anne H. Charity Hudley, Christine Mallinson and Mary Bucholtz, Oxford University Press. © Anne H. Charity Hudley, Christine Mallinson, and Mary Bucholtz 2024.
DOI: 10.1093/oso/9780197755303.003.0011

instructional reflections, I am referring to the work that she and I have done together as the course continues to evolve. I am grateful for her contributions.

As I reimagined the course content and engaged with big questions of what linguistics in high school can and should be, four major questions presented themselves:

- How can this course integrate the two separate but related disciplines of linguistics and media studies while fulfilling ELA content area standards?
- How can this course empower any ELA teacher to teach linguistics, including those without a linguistics background?
- How can this course be relevant and accessible to all students?
- How can this course be built on an anti-racist, culturally responsive foundation?

I am a white, cishet, female teacher, and I have always spoken and written something close to a mainstream variety of American English. As a district, our students are 83% white, 10% Hispanic, and 2% Black (Massachusetts Department of Elementary and Secondary Education 2021).[1] A significant number are Brazilian or Portuguese. These students often identify as white or multiracial but are linguistically and culturally minoritized. Twenty-five percent of the student body uses a language other than English at home. Our community is working-class, and 38% of students qualify as low-income. That said, most of my students look and talk like me. As a white teacher who teaches many students whose language variety is privileged, I believe it is especially important for me to design instruction from an antiracist foundation while taking care not to "other" users of minoritized language varieties. It is also important to note that I work for a district that has historically been intentionally committed to academic freedom, antiracist teaching, and social justice. This affords me a freedom that a growing number of teachers are losing due to the increased constraints on curriculum by right-wing school boards and state governments. The curricular decisions described in this chapter may not be available to all PK-12 teachers without significant risk to their livelihoods.

Guiding Principles

As an ELA teacher, my practice has been guided by children's literature professor Rudine Sims Bishop's metaphor of "mirrors, windows, and sliding glass doors" (1990). Bishop writes that literature should provide a reflection in which "we can see our own lives and experiences as part of the larger human experience" (p. ix). However, too often students of color do not see their image reflected back to them in the ELA curriculum, or the image they see is "distorted, negative, or laughable" (p. ix). Further, Bishop writes, "Children from dominant social groups . . . need [multicultural books] as windows onto reality. . . If they see only reflections of themselves, they will grow up with an exaggerated sense of their own importance and value in the world" (p. xi). Bishop's metaphor was originally conceived to offer guidance for educators diversifying their literature curriculum. However, I believe that the study of language should also provide mirrors and windows for all students. In our course, students study their own language(s) in a way that intends to be validating and affirming, but it also provides, especially for white students, a window into often ignored or misrepresented lived experiences.

In addition to this guiding metaphor, the development of the Linguistics and Media Studies course was also grounded in a few of my fundamental beliefs about what high school linguistics should be:

1. *Linguistics should be available to all high school students, not just privileged or college-bound students.* Existing opportunities for students to engage with linguistics in high school—clubs, competitions, and elective linguistics courses—are important points of access to the field, but are not widely accessible. Students who work or are responsible for childcare after school often can't be involved in extra-curricular activities, and most schools are limited in the electives they offer due to staffing and scheduling. I believe that high school linguistics should be accessible to and inclusive of all students, including those who require individualized education plans, whose heritage language is not English, and/or who do not intend to pursue postsecondary education (see Thomas, this volume). If PK-12 schools are to do the work of anti-racism, as we must, providing a background in linguistics is as essential for future first responders, childcare providers, and retail managers as it is for those who might pursue a postsecondary degree in education, law, or technology.

2. *Linguistics in high school should center student voices, language varieties, and lived experiences.* As Kendra Calhoun et al. (2021) have noted, the traditional sequencing of topics in introductory undergraduate linguistics courses appeals to students who already have an interest in linguistics, but showing the relevance of linguistics to all students requires an overhaul in the way instructors approach introductory linguistics. If the study of linguistics is to gain more of a foothold in PK-12 schools, this rethinking must extend to those levels as well. In my class, students

use their own language variety as data to analyze some of the rules and patterns that govern it. This inquiry-based approach allows students who use an institutionally devalued language variety to appreciate its complexity and beauty. It also demonstrates to privileged language users—most of them white students—that their language use often does not conform to notions of "correct" or "standardized" language. ELA teachers cannot center student voices without teaching students to value all language varieties.

3. *Standardized language ideology is a pillar of systemic racism (Lippi-Green, 1997), and linguistics provides a framework for helping dismantle it.* In teaching students to examine the attitudes and beliefs about language expressed by people around them, including in the media, they begin to notice and question standardized language ideology. Students explore how standardized language ideologies are intertwined with power structures by targeting people of color, women (especially young women and women of color), LGBTQ+ people, immigrants, and disabled people, among others.

4. *Linguistics provides a framework for critical examination of media and its relationship to politics, science, marketing, education, technology, race, gender, and geography.* Linguistics can help students notice and deconstruct linguistic bias and how it is perpetuated. In a class brainstorming session, students readily identified school as a major perpetuator of standardized language ideology, but also named parents and families, peers, social media, and popular culture (Figure 10.1).

5. *High school linguistics can do the liberatory work of knocking down disciplinary silos and showing students the connections among academic disciplines and the world at large.* Linguistics is a fundamentally human inquiry, with connections to literature and writing, technology, psychology, music, mathematics, science, and the social sciences. Traditional education does students a tremendous disservice in segmenting and separating fields of study—and consequently students' own experiences of the world—into STEM, the humanities, the arts, and so on. Writing about the benefits of interdisciplinary learning, Rebecca Hill (2016) argues that in taking an interdisciplinary approach, "we are allowed not just to ask *more* questions but to *question* the questions we are used to asking, to mix insights from multiple types of scholarship." With its inherent multidisciplinary connections, linguistics can help students understand the ways in which traditionally segmented fields of study and insights about the human experience are in fact connected.

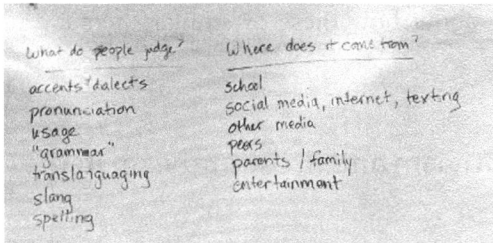

Figure 10.1 The brainstorming my students and I did as a class about standardized language ideology
Alt text: Two columns written on a whiteboard. The first column is labeled, "What do people judge?," and lists accents/dialects, pronunciation, usage, "grammar," translanguaging, slang, and spelling. The second column is labeled "Where does it come from?" and lists school, social media, internet, texting, other media, peers, parents/family, and entertainment.

Thematic Units

When the linguistics course was an elective, the content was organized in a more traditional format, beginning with phonology, morphology, and syntax, moving on to language acquisition and psycholinguistics, and ending with sociolinguistics (Plackowski, 2020). The recategorization of the course from elective to core meant that some students would not enter the class with an established interest in linguistics. I therefore wanted to pursue a more inquiry-based approach to organizing linguistics content (see also Lederer, this volume; Thomas, this volume). I thought about the ways I, a high school teacher without a linguistics degree, have accessed linguistics content outside the academy, and the ways some linguists have made the field accessible to nonacademic audiences via books, podcasts, and web content (see also Gawne et al., this volume). These resources often engage linguistics as a framework to answer questions or examine a larger problem or issue.

To plan my course, I built thematic units around a social issue, problem, or question, and used linguistics as a framework for examining that topic in more depth. I developed 10 units that drew on various linguistic subfields (morphology, syntax, pragmatics, sociolinguistics, and so on) and gave students the tools to analyze these issues through a linguistic lens. The thematic units helped students apply linguistic concepts to their immediate, lived experiences. Teachers of any content area, especially those without a deep background in linguistics, can integrate linguistic study into their content areas by thinking about how these or similar thematic units support pre-existing curricula.

Unit 1: Descriptivism and Prescriptivism in the Public Sphere

In the first unit, students consider where our attitudes and beliefs about language come from, how they shape our worldview, and how our attitudes about language reflect our attitudes about users of different language varieties and vice versa. We study examples of language ideologies and how they are perpetuated by popular culture, social media, and education. One accessible resource for instructors interested in learning about and teaching this unit is Gretchen McCullough's *Because Internet* (2019).

Unit 2: True Biz: Language Development and Linguistic Identity

Our second unit originally used the case study of Genie, the abused child who grew up without human interaction, to cover linguistic content like morphosyntax and psycholinguistics, while also asking students to consider the ethical implications of linguistic research and science in general. However, as my co-teacher and I reflected on the course, we decided that the emphasis on Genie felt, at times, guilty of the exploitation we have sought to question. At the same time we were struggling to revamp the unit, author Sara Nović published her novel *True Biz* (2022), set in a school for Deaf children and featuring nuanced discussions of themes related to language and deafness. It fortuitously offered us an opportunity to cover the same topics we had covered in the Genie unit while grounding them in a high-interest whole-class novel, as the novel weaves in discussions of ASL morphosyntax and grammar along with information about Deaf culture, identity, and history. It also allows us to guide students through the reading of a fictional text through the lens of linguistic identity, which they will practice independently later in book clubs.

Unit 3: The (Myth of the) 30-Million Word Gap

We begin this unit by examining the shortcomings of the highly sensationalized hypothesis of the purported 30-million-word gap between lower- and higher-income children, and how the resultant ideologies have contributed to harmful public policy (see Figueroa, 2024). We then move on to learning about multilingualism and second language acquisition, providing students with an opportunity to reflect on their own second language learning. This also specifically centers the linguistic experiences of multilingual students, which are often de-centered in traditional ELA courses. The documentary *Do You Speak American?* (Cran & Buchanan, 2005) and Gloria Anzaldua's essay "How to Tame a Wild Tongue" (1987) both introduce bilingualism, culture, and linguistics in a way that's accessible to both teachers and students.

Unit 4: Speaking "American": The Invention of an American Language

This unit examines the history of language in the United States and how it reflects and perpetuates systems of power, colonization, and racism. Students learn about Indigenous languages, endangered/dormant languages, and language revitalization/reclamation. Students also learn about regional language varieties in the United States and how they arose, especially in the context of settlement and colonization. The documentary *We Still Live Here—Âs Nutayuneân* (Makepeace, 2011) can provide teachers with some background regarding Indigenous languages in the United States. The books *We Do Language* (Charity Hudley & Mallinson, 2014) and *Teaching Language Variation in the Classroom* (Devereaux & Palmer, 2019) provide many real-world pedagogical strategies for teachers teaching language variation.

Unit 5: Black Language on Trial

This unit examines Black Language through the lens of the courts—real-life examples of how perceptions of Black Language have influenced trial outcomes, as well as examples of when Black Language itself was on trial in what became known as the Oakland Ebonics controversy (Rickford & King, 2016). This unit exposes my students, who are mostly not users of Black Language, to its grammatical, lexical, and phonological features, as well as to its history. Students examine and confront how standardized language ideology has shaped their beliefs about Black Language. We also analyze Black Language in popular culture, and how whiteness appropriates Black Language even as it is used as a site for discrimination (Baker-Bell, 2020). Just a few of the many accessible resources related to this topic are the book *Articulate*

While Black (Alim & Smitherman, 2012) and the documentary *Talking Black in America* (Hutcheson & Cullinan, 2017) and its follow-up, *Signing Black in America* (Hutcheson & Cullinan, 2020).

Unit 6: Policing Voices, Policing Bodies: Gender, Gender Identity, and Sexuality

This unit begins by looking at perceptions of women's voices, especially concerning purportedly feminine features of language such as so-called vocal fry and uptalk. We also examine how greater understandings of gender and sexuality have led to important discussions about language. My co-teacher and I have added lessons about trans and nonbinary identities and their relationship to language use and language change, and students have studied the discourse around pronouns and other lexical items used by or for nonbinary people. This unit provides a useful site for discussion of intersectionality and how linguistic innovation is often driven by people in minoritized groups. A helpful resource on this topic for teachers is *Language, Gender, and Sexuality* (Kiesling, 2019), while students may be interested in Amanda Montell's *Wordslut: A Feminist Guide to Taking Back the English Language* (2019).

Unit 7: Marketing and Manipulation

This unit leans heavily on pragmatics, semantics, and phonology to examine how marketers manipulate language to brand and sell products. For example, students learn about the use of presupposition and implicature in advertising (Sedivy & Carlson, 2011). Students use the same analytic lens to study images in advertising and explore how language and visuals work together to manipulate consumers. We examine how marketers target specific types of consumers according to race, region, gender, class, and so on by using language and images. This unit helps students become more critical consumers by analyzing the semiotics of marketing. Julie Sedivy and Greg Carlson's *Sold on Language* (2011) is a good resource for teachers interested in this topic.

Unit 8: Politics, Fanaticism, and Language

This unit segues from the previous unit to examine how politicians and leaders of political groups use language and marketing tools to perpetuate their message. As a white teacher of mostly white students, countering messages of fanaticism and radicalization with media literacy is an especially important tool in combating white supremacy. Montell's *Cultish: The Language of Fanaticism* (2021) and George Lakoff's *Don't Think of an Elephant* (2004) are both useful resources for this unit.

Ongoing Unit: Vocabulary

Students examine how the history of language connects to patterns of colonization and oppression. For example, students learn about the transition from Old English to Middle English, and how power differences between English and French speakers contributed to modern ideologies about academic language, which is often uses lexical items derived from French and Latin. Later, we study how English has borrowed words from people who were colonized by English speakers. This unit also involves morphological study, examining word formation and empowering students to interpret unfamiliar words or create their own, emphasizing to students that language constantly changes. The unit consists of mini-lessons on vocabulary every week or two throughout the year (Plackowski, 2023). Thomas Carnicelli's *Words Work* (2001) and Deb Glaser's *Morpheme Magic* (2020) provide useful overviews of both history and morphology related to vocabulary study.

Ongoing Unit: Linguistics Book Clubs

Inspired by April Baker-Bell's (2020) sample unit of study on Angie Thomas's *The Hate U Give*, students form groups and choose a Young Adult novel where characters' linguistic identity is an important site of plot or character development. They lead small-group discussions on how the author portrays language and linguistic identity. To prompt discussion, my co-teacher and I ask students to consider questions like, "Where do you see that characters in this book have internalized ideas about their language being 'incorrect' or problematic? Alternatively, where do you see characters taking pride in using a nonstandard or nondominant language variety?" (These questions were adapted from Ian Cushing and Anthony Carter's 2021 article in the journal *Literacy*.) We also ask students to consider how race, gender, class, and setting impact characters' language. Students read a new book every few months and meet periodically with their group during class time.

Successes and Challenges

In end-of-year reflections, students generally reported that they understood standardized language to be an oppressive construct and that they had become more adept at identifying standardized language ideology, developed the habit of checking themselves when judging others' language use, and noticed linguistic framing in the news media. One white nonbinary student contacted me almost a year after their graduation to tell me that "[linguistic] discrimination is something I barely thought of before and now I use the lessons you told mould the way I interact w/ others on a daily basis. . . The lessons abt learning to treat others who may not have your linguistic privilege have been incredibly helpful." While one course is not enough to dismantle systemic racism and harmful language ideology, such comments indicate that the course was successful at some level in providing students with windows into other lived experiences that they had not encountered before.

Students also reported enjoying the opportunity to reflect on their own language use in an affirming way. Minoritized students in particular found mirrors in the course content that were meaningful to them. One heritage speaker of Portuguese wrote:

> [This course] touched a place deep in my heart. My dad always pushed us to learn english and to speak it in the house as well as outside the house. I believe my father wanted to let his kids have the best "American experience" possible, [but] apparently that meant pushing away so much of our culture.

Another student reported, "My favorite topic was definitely learning Black language because I already speak Black language and have my whole life so I found it very interesting seeing my classmates try to learn the way I talk and understand it."

The work of mirroring students' own linguistic lives and helping students to see fully and consistently through windows to others' lived experiences is ongoing and never fully realized. As in traditional ELA courses, students tend to respond more readily to mirrors than windows. Harmful language ideologies often manifest in ways that students do not critically reflect upon without prompting. This is especially true for students who use the prestige varieties of our community. One white student, who reported feeling disengaged from school, wrote that he enjoyed the class because "Linguistics [class] helps me be myself and talk the way that I wanna talk. It lets you use slang in any way that you want, because it is a new language that everyone is speaking and every kid uses." However, when this same student reflected on the documentary *We Still Live Here—Âs Nutayuneân* (Makepeace, 2011), about the Wampanoag Language Reclamation Project, he wrote, "there is not really a point to learning a language that nobody uses. . . . What is the point of learning [Wampanoag] when they all speak English." Another white student, when asked what variety of English should hypothetically be sent into space to represent English to aliens, said, "Definitely not Southern because we wouldn't want aliens to think we're dumb." In a discussion of the possibility of using "y'all" as a gender-neutral second-person plural pronoun, one Black student said, "My 'y'all' is fine, but not the redneck 'y'all.'" In each case, the ideologies behind these statements were addressed in class or individually, but their expression reveals that harmful language ideologies are so ingrained that students who have been exposed to a critical linguistics perspective nevertheless may easily revert to them without questioning. Furthermore, as a teacher, these attitudes can only be addressed when expressed overtly, limiting my opportunities for intervention.

What Can Linguists Do?

Much has been written about the inclusion of linguistics in PK-12 education and the thematic approach I've described is one of many that has provided a way to integrate linguistics into a public school curriculum (see Mallinson, 2024). But the challenge of making linguistics accessible to teachers without a linguistics background remains. Because there is no certification to teach linguistics for public school teachers, very few teachers have a linguistics degree. I was fortunate to be able to take some linguistics courses to complete my degrees in English, but it has taken me years of independent study to be able to teach high school linguistics with confidence. I've used institutional resources like textbooks and conferences to teach myself, but I've also used many linguistics-related books written for a popular audience, podcasts, YouTube videos, and even Twitter to fill in the gaps in my knowledge. PK-12 teachers face many constraints on their ability to do this work, both financial (including the inability to access scholarly journals) and what Megan Figueroa (2022) calls the "psychological paywall," or the impenetrable nature of discipline-specific academic language for outsiders. Other blockades to teachers engaging fully with linguistics include a lack of funds to pursue postgraduate study, lack of time to engage in study, and limitations on teacher autonomy to make curricular decisions. As noted in the beginning of this chapter, many teachers are also facing increased pressure from right-wing attacks on curriculum, limiting their ability to teach antiracism and social justice.

For the field of linguistics to continue contributing to PK-12 education, linguists need to produce content that is accessible to people outside of the field, including teachers. Many linguists have contributed significant resources to linguistic communication, such the Crash Course series (Gawne et al., this volume) and podcasts like *Lingthusiasm* and *The Vocal Fries*, and these provide excellent models for free and accessible resources for teachers and students. Such materials should provide the depth of knowledge that teachers need to pursue our own avenues of inquiry without assuming prior knowledge. Even more importantly, linguists need to produce material accessible to students that teachers can use in our classrooms. It takes a great deal of teacher resourcefulness to find and adapt high-interest resources for use in the classroom. On a broader scale, postsecondary institutions and the organizations they're affiliated with (such as the College Board) must use their leverage to denounce racist, misogynistic, anti-Semitic, and homophobic/transphobic attacks on teachers and schools doing the work of social justice.

Linguists who hope to make linguistics more widely available in PK-12 schools can help by partnering with teachers who are interested in teaching the subject, making contacts with professional teacher organizations, and showing teachers how linguistics can enhance our already-existing curricula. As the 2022 chair of the Linguistics in the School Curriculum Committee (LiSC) for the Linguistic Society of America, I helped facilitate networking between university linguists and PK-12 educators; this committee can help linguists who are interested in getting involved in PK-12 linguistics connect with PK-12 educators in-person and virtually.

Although all ELA courses can and should center student voices, build on a foundation of antiracism, and teach media literacy, high school linguistics is an ideal site for the immediate integration of those pedagogies. The thematic approach to curriculum design centers problems, issues, and questions from the real world and shows students how linguistics provides a framework for understanding them. This approach can be helpful in facilitating the incorporation of linguistics into the PK-12 curriculum, especially for teachers without a strong background in linguistics, and it can provide another avenue for students to access the mirrors and windows that promote an inclusive curriculum across subjects. An inclusive approach to high school linguistics—making it accessible to all students regardless of their background, their future plans, or the school they attend—cannot single-handedly dismantle white supremacy. But it can offer students the mirrors that allow for self-reflection and affirmation, and the windows into others' lived experiences that help create empathy and change.

Note

1. "Hispanic" is the term the Massachusetts Department of Elementary and Secondary Education uses in its demographic data. Many Brazilian students might identify as Latinx if given the option, but do not identify as Hispanic, and therefore choose "white" instead. This creates a situation where the official data do not necessarily reflect the linguistic/cultural demographics of our school.

References

Alim, H. Samy, & Smitherman, Geneva. (2012). *Articulate while Black: Barack Obama, language, and race in the U.S.* Oxford University Press.

Anzaldua, Gloria. (1987). "How to tame a wild tongue." In *Borderlands: The new mestiza—la frontera* (pp. 53–64). Aunt Lute Book Company.

Baker-Bell, April. (2020). *Linguistic justice: Black language, literacy, identity, and pedagogy.* Routledge.

Bishop, Rudine Sims. (1990). Mirrors, windows, and sliding glass doors. *Perspectives: Choosing and Using Books for the Classroom, 6*(3), ix–xi.

Calhoun, Kendra, Charity Hudley, Anne H., Bucholtz, Mary, Exford, Jazmine, & Johnson, Brittney. (2021). Attracting Black students to linguistics through a Black-centered introduction to linguistics course. *Language, 97*(1), e12–e38. https://doi.org/10.1353/lan.2021.0007

Carnicelli, Thomas A. (2001). *Words work: Activities for developing vocabulary, style, and critical thinking.* Heinemann.

Charity Hudley, Anne H., & Mallinson, Christine. (2014). *We do language: English language variation in the secondary classroom.* Teachers College Press.

Cran, William, & Buchanan Christopher. (producers). (2005). *Do you speak American?* [film]. Films for the Humanities & Sciences.

Cushing, Ian, & Carter, Anthony. (2021). Using young adult fiction to interrogate raciolinguistic ideologies in schools. *Literacy, 56*(2), 106–119. http://doi.org/10.1111/lit.12277

Devereaux, Michelle D., & Palmer, Chris. (Eds.). (2019). *Teaching language variation in the classroom: Strategies and models from teachers and linguists.* Routledge.

Figueroa, Megan. (2024). Decolonizing (psycho)linguistics means dropping the language gap rhetoric. In Anne H. Charity Hudley, Christine Mallinson, & Mary Bucholtz (Eds.), *Decolonizing linguistics.* Oxford University Press.

Figueroa, Megan. (2022). Podcasting past the paywall: How diverse media allows more equitable participation in linguistic science. *Annual Review of Applied Linguistics, 42*, 40–46. http://doi.org/10.1017/S0267190521000118

Glaser, Deb. (2020). *Morpheme magic: Lessons to build morphological awareness for grades 4–12.* Deborah Glaser Publishing.

Hill, Rebecca. (2016). What is this thing called interdisciplinarity? *American Quarterly, 68*(2), 361–364. http://doi.org/10.1353/aq.2016.0016

Hutcheson, Neal, & Cullinan, Danica. (Eds.). (2020). *Signing Black in America* [film]. The Language and Life Project.

Hutcheson, Neal, & Cullinan, Danica. (Eds.). (2017). *Talking Black in America* [film]. The Language and Life Project.

Kiesling, Scott F. (2019). *Language, gender, and sexuality: An introduction.* Routledge.

Lakoff, George. (2004). *Don't think of an elephant! Know your values and frame the debate.* Chelsea Green Publishing.

Lippi-Green, Rosina. (1997). *English with an accent: Language, ideology, and discrimination in the United States.* Routledge.

Makepeace, Anne (director). (2011). *We still live here—Âs nutayuneân* [film]. Makepeace Productions.

Mallinson, Christine. (2024). Linguistic variation and linguistic inclusion in the US educational context. *Annual Review of Linguistics, 10.* https://doi.org/10.1146/annurev-linguistics-031120-121546

Massachusetts Department of Elementary and Secondary Education. (2021). Enrollment data (2021–2022)—Hudson. https://profiles.doe.mass.edu/profiles/student.aspx?orgcode=01410000&orgtypecode=5&

McCullough, Gretchen. (2019). *Because internet: Understanding the new rules of language.* Riverhead Books.

Montell, Amanda. (2021). *Cultish: The language of fanaticism.* Harper Collins.

Montell, Amanda. (2019). *Wordslut: A feminist guide to taking back the English language.* HarperCollins.

Nović, Sara. (2022). *True biz.* Penguin Random House.

Plackowski, Amy L. (2023). A linguistic approach to vocabulary instruction: Using etymology and morphology to learn vocabulary, improve writing, and read the world. In Alice Corr and Anna Pineda (Eds.), *Theoretical linguistics in the pre-university classroom.* Oxford University Press.

Plackowski, Amy L. (2020). Using understanding by design to build a high school linguistics course. *American speech, 95*(2), 235–242. http://doi.org/10.1215/00031283-8501379

Rickford, John R., & King, Sharese. (2016). Language and linguistics on trial: Hearing Rachel Jeantel (and other vernacular speakers) in the courtroom and beyond. *Language, 92*(4), 948–988. http://doi.org/10.1353/lan.2016.0078

Sedivy, Julie, & Carlson, Greg. (2011). *Sold on language: How advertisers talk to you and what it says about you.* Wiley-Blackwell.

Abel Djassi Amado is assistant professor of political science and international relations at Simmons University. He holds a PhD in political science/African studies from Boston University. He researches and has published on the politics of language in West Africa/Cabo Verde and the political history of national liberation in Cabo Verde and Guinea-Bissau. Amado is the current chair of the Lusophone African Studies Organization (LASO) and the president of the Cabo Verdean Center for Appl ed Research (CVCAR).

Marlyse Baptista is the President's Distinguished Professor of linguistics at the University of Pennsylvania. She specializes in the morpho-syntax of Creole languages and in theories of creole genesis. In addition to conducting generative and descriptive analyses of a variety of Creoles, she is involved in several collaborations using experimental methods and agent-based modeling to examine cognitive processes involved in language emergence. She is deeply committed to the study of Creoles in education and has been collaborating with members of the Cabo Verdean Center for Applied Research in designing K-12 heritage language and culture curricula.

Ambrizeth Lima is an educator in Massachusetts. Her research areas of interest include urban education; race, class, gender, and culture in education; first and second language acquisition; and immigrant studies. She has presented at numerous workshops that focus on the integration of immigrant communities in the US and teaching immigrant families the role that their schools and communities play. She received her doctorate in education and her master's in education at the Harvard Graduate School of Education. She is also the author of the book *The Socialization of Cabo Verdean Immigrant Youth in Urban America*.

Lourenço Pina Garcia is assistant superintendent of Equity and Inclusion and chair of the Equity Advisory Board of Revere Public Schools. He provides leadership on critical issues in diversity, inclusion, and equity throughout the district to ensure anti-racism education, programs, policies, practices, and systems are thoughtfully constructed and consistently implemented to create a fairer, equitable, and uniform school system for all students and families, particularly those deemed historically underserved and marginalized. His areas of expertise include equity and inclusion, civil rights, public policy, educational leadership, curriculum, instruction and assessment, special education, sociolinguistics, second-language acquisition, intercultural and cross-communication, family engagement, and systems change. He has been featured in two educational books, *Five Practices for Improving the Success of Latino Students* and *The Human Side of Changing Education*, as well as numerous other articles and case studies on urban education, leadership, and school reform.

Dawna Marie Thomas is professor and chair of the Critical Race, Gender and Cultural Studies Department, chair of the Department of Public Health, and director of the

Law and Justice Minor at Simmons University. She teaches a cross-section of courses that relate to women, culture, gender, race, family violence, and health and disability. Thomas's research is grounded in her Cabo Verdean and African American cultural roots and in Boston's Roxbury neighborhood where she grew up and continues to live. Her research includes health and disability policy, racial/ethnic and gender disparities in health, family violence, and identity development. Her latest study, the Cape Verdean Women's Project, includes four generations of Cabo Verdean women throughout New England and explores their experiences with domestic violence, healthcare and disability, and concepts of womanhood. Thomas's research has been published in journals and books. Her book *Women's Health: Readings on Social, Economic, and Political Issues* includes a collection of articles on the history of women's health, access to health and disability services, health disparities, and culturally relevant approaches to more effective service delivery.

Abstract: The focus of this chapter is the use of Cabo Verdean Creole as a language of instruction in Baystate Public Schools. The authors discuss the development of the Cabo Verdean Heritage Language and Culture curriculum that took place during Summer and Fall 2020, designed specifically to meet the needs of Cabo Verdean learners of English currently attending Baystate Public Schools. The curriculum was implemented in 2021. This chapter provides a brief historical overview of the use of Cabo Verdean Creole in Massachusetts Bilingual Education programs and then describes the overall vision for a new policy regarding the use of mother tongues in educational systems, which is driving the Cabo Verdean Center for Applied Research (CVCAR) to conceptualize and implement this new curriculum for Cabo Verdean learners of English. The authors introduce the various components of the curriculum while demonstrating that linguistic frameworks can be used successfully when they are applied in the instruction of Cabo Verdean learners of English. Es artigu ta sentra na uzu di kriolu kabuverdianu komu un instrumentu di ensinu na Skolas Públiku di Baystate. El ta relata dezenvolvimentu di un kurríkulu na kriolu kabuverdianu na verãu y outonu di 2020, konsebidu spesifikamenti pa Aprendizis Kabuverdianu di Inglês, ki ta frekuenta Skolas Públiku di Baystate. Es kurríkulu foi inplementadu na 2021. Es artigu ta fornese un brevi kontextu stóriku di uzu di língua kabuverdianu na idukasãu bilíngi na Massachusetts y dipos el ta oferese uma vizãu jeral di un novu pulítika di uzu di línguas na sistemas idukasiunal, ki permiti Cabo Verdean Center for Applied Research (CVCAR) lidera konsepsãu y inplementasãu di es kurríkulu pa Aprendizis Kabuverdianu di Inglês. Nu ta prezenta konponentis di kurríkulu y nu ta mostra ma nu pode uza struturas linguístiku ku susesu na idukasãu di Aprendizis Kabuverdianu di Inglês.

Key Words: culturally responsive teaching, decolonizing the curriculum, language and identity, bilingual/transitional bilingual education, Creole language, high school curriculums, dual language program

11

Bilingual Education in Cabo Verdean

Toward Visibility and Dignity

Abel Djassi Amado (he/his/him)
Simmons University

Marlyse Baptista (she/her)
University of Pennsylvania

Lourenço Pina Garcia (he/him/his)
Revere Public Schools

Ambrizeth Helena Lima (she/her)
Boston Public Schools

Dawna Marie Thomas (she/her)
Simmons University

Introduction

More than 140 languages are spoken in Boston, Massachusetts (Lima & Melnik, 2012). The most spoken languages include Spanish, Cabo Verdean *Kriolu* (Cabo Verdean Creole or simply Cabo Verdean language), Haitian Creole, Chinese, Vietnamese, and French. In the past, the school district, Baystate Public Schools (BPS, a pseudonym) had utilized native languages in its transitional bilingual education (TBE) programs to support the academic achievement of English language learners. However, proponents of English-only education heavily criticized TBE as a program that promoted native language to the detriment of English language learning. The English-only movement gained traction in the early 2000s, and in 2002 a new law (*An Act Relative to the Teaching of English in Public Schools*) dismantled transitional bilingual programs. Consequently, there has been a dramatic increase in what Massachusetts Department of Elementary and Secondary Education

Abel Djassi Amado, Marlyse Baptista, Lourenço Pina Garcia, Ambrizeth Helena Lima, and Dawna Marie Thomas, *Bilingual Education in Cabo Verdean* In : *Inclusion in Linguistics*. Edited by: Anne H. Charity Hudley, Christine Mallinson and Mary Bucholtz, Oxford University Press. © Anne H. Charity Hudley, Christine Mallinson, and Mary Bucholtz 2024. DOI: 10.1093/oso/9780197755303.003.0012

(DESE) calls the achievement gap for English language learners. To address the achievement gap, another law, *An Act Relative to Language Opportunity for Our Kids*, or the LOOK Act, was enacted to create a favorable environment for reforming school curricula and reinstating programs to support minoritized languages in the state.

Centering on the use of the Cabo Verdean language as a medium of instruction in BPS, this chapter reports on the lead role played by the Cabo Verdean Center for Applied Research located in Massachusetts in the development and implementation of a Cabo Verdean *Kriolu* curriculum, designed specifically for Cabo Verdean English language learners attending BPS.

This chapter is organized as follows. In the first section, we provide a brief historical background of the use of Cabo Verdean in bilingual education in Massachusetts. The second section provides an overview of the new language-in-education policy. In the third section, we introduce the components of the curriculum and show that linguistic frameworks can be effectively utilized in the education of Cabo Verdean English language learners. This chapter contributes to the literature on the Cabo Verdean language in education policy and, by so doing, helps deconstruct old myths about Creole languages not being suitable in the context of formal education. The discussion of the Cabo Verdean bilingual education centers on demonstrating that far from being a problem, the language can indeed be a powerful resource at the disposal of their speakers (Macedo, 1980; Ruiz, 1984).

It is important to note that the authors of the chapter are themselves of Cabo Verdean descent and speakers of the language. In addition, some of the authors are former students and/or educators in Cabo Verdean transitional bilingual education in the United States. Moreover, the authors, through their studies, have found that the Cabo Verdean language plays a fundamental role in the socialization, adaption, and political incorporation of Cabo Verdean immigrants in the United States (Amado, 2020; Baptista, 2002; Lima, 2022).

Cabo Verdean as a Language of Education in Massachusetts

Cabo Verde is a small archipelagic nation off the coast of Senegal, with a population of about 500,000. The islands were part of the Portuguese colonial empire since the mid-1400s and in the following three centuries, Cabo Verde functioned as a depot of enslaved Africans to be forcibly shipped to the Americas (Duncan, 1972). The confluence of Portuguese and West Africans in the territory led to the formation of a creole society with a distinct Creole language. Disastrous colonial policies had since the mid-1800s led hundreds of thousands to migrate throughout the Atlantic world, making Cabo Verde a "transnational archipelago" (Batalha & Carling, 2008; Carreira, 1983).

The settlement of Cabo Verdeans in Massachusetts dates back to the mid-1800s, during the height of the whaling industry in New England, especially in the city of New Bedford. Many Cabo Verdean men were recruited as crew members in the US whaling ships (Halter, 2008, 1993; Meintel, 2002). The decline of the whaling industry compelled many Cabo Verdeans to find alternative jobs on land, which allowed them to bring their families. In the 1960s and 1970s, the civil rights movement impacted the Cabo Verdean community in the United States, initiating an ethnic revival among its members (Halter, 2008). The politically conscious community began to influence education policy and practice. Following the approval of the Massachusetts Transitional Bilingual Education Act in 1971, the Cape Verdean Educators Collaborative lobbied the state authorities for the recognition of the Cabo Verdean *Kriolu* as a "living foreign language," a required status for its use as a medium of instruction in bilingual education.

Enacting Cabo Verdean *Kriolu* as a medium of instruction involved many challenges. Many people, including its speakers, believed it was inadequate as a medium of instruction and argued that the Portuguese language could better serve the needs of Cabo Verdean children (Macedo, 1980). Despite much opposition, Cabo Verdean transitional bilingual education became a reality in many Massachusetts school districts in the mid-1970s and early 1980s. To build community support and awareness, in 1996, the Capeverdean Creole Institute (CCI) was founded by a group of Cabo Verdean scholars and community leaders. (Capeverdean Creole Institute, n.d.). The organization's motto and mission were "Advocating for the Capeverdean Language Around the World." The CCI devised strategies to increase recognition and legitimacy of the Cabo Verdean language by creating opportunities to discuss the representation of Cabo Verdean in the classroom. It also promoted the passage of the Cabo Verdean language from orality to the written word by organizing workshops to train community members to read and write in the Unified Alphabet for the Writing of Cabo Verdean (better known by its Portuguese acronym, ALUPEC). This orthography was approved by the Cabo Verdean government in 1998. The workshop proceedings were published in the 1999 volume of *Cimboa*, a journal edited by the General Consulate of Cabo Verde in Boston. A related objective was to promote the officialization of the Cabo Verdean language, taking advantage of the newly officialized ALUPEC script.

As the Cabo Verdean bilingual program took root in the 1980s and early 1990s, opposition to bilingual education across the US became more vigorous (May, 2017). Anti-bilingualism grew bolder with the passing of legislation in

California (1998) and Arizona (2000) that resulted in the supremacy of the Sheltered English Immersion approach, in which books and academic instruction are solely in English, with minimal support in the native language of the student. Businessman Ron Unz, who spearheaded the shattering of bilingual education in those two states, persuaded Massachusetts voters to approve Question 2 in 2002. Following the vote, the Massachusetts legislature passed new legislation that entailed ending transitional bilingual education and adopting English as the exclusive medium of instruction for bilingual students (Uriarte et al., 2009).

The 2002 law was approved on the assumption that the English-only policy would accelerate the English acquisition by multilingual students—thus, improving their academic success. However, a post–Question 2 study showed that Cabo Verdean multilingual students did not thrive in Sheltered English Immersion or general education classes. Instead, these students' enrollment in special education increased exponentially. In the same vein, they did not make sufficient progress to be promoted to the next grade. Consequently, Cabo Verdean multilingual students dropped out of school in significant numbers (Uriarte et al., 2009).

By the first half of the 2010s, it had become clear that the Sheltered English Immersion model was failing multilingual students, thus creating wider educational inequalities between them and native English speakers. Social and political actors, ranging from immigrant community activists and professional organizations, such as the Language Opportunity Coalition founded in 2014, to state lawmakers and media rallied to reintroduce bilingual education. The arguments against the 2002 law were based on two key points: first, that educational inequalities had been caused by the elimination of native language supports, and second, that bilingualism was perceived as an asset in the global community (DiDomenico & Chang-Diaz, 2016; Boston Globe Editorial Board, 2015; Uriarte et al., 2009).

The 2017 LOOK Act proposed four main policy innovations (Aguiar, 2017). First, it granted school districts more flexibility in choosing the language acquisition program that best fit their multilingual community. The LOOK Act effectively removed the rigidity that the 2002 law had imposed. Second, it ensured that the Massachusetts DESE would provide leadership and guidance to districts. Third, the DESE was tasked with licensure endorsements for the language acquisition programs. Finally, the new law established an English language parent advisory council, thus bringing the parents of multilingual students into the conversation about their children's language acquisition programs. The LOOK Act also established the State Seal of Biliteracy, an award given to students who meet the state criteria of proficiency in

English and another language (often the students' mother tongue). In fact, in California, it is easier for white students from monolingual English homes to get the seal of biliteracy than for truly bilingual students of color (e.g., Chang-Bacon and Colomer, 2022). In line with the LOOK Act, selected community members developed a heritage language curriculum to help ensure equity for Cabo Verdean multilingual students.

The Cabo Verdean Heritage Language and Culture Curriculum

The Cabo Verdean Center for Applied Research (CVCAR) consists of scholars of Cabo Verdean descent representing the community, based on the Gramscian concept of organic intellectual, that is, intellectual laborers who represent the interests of the community (Gramsci et al., 2014). Working closely with BPS, CVCAR developed the Cabo Verdean Heritage Language and Culture Curriculum in 2020, which was implemented in 2021 at a high school that houses the Sheltered English Instruction for Cabo Verdean students. The curriculum was designed specifically for ninth and tenth graders, whose heritage language is Cabo Verdean. The class, designed to be year-long, was taught by a Cabo Verdean native speaker as a social studies course. The curriculum used Cabo Verdean *Kriolu* as the medium of instruction to teach students content from different areas of study. It was deeply influenced by efforts to augment language prestige and promote positive attitudes toward it (Ager, 2001; Haarmann, 1990; Kamwangamalu, 2016).

CVCAR followed the innovations in the written Cabo Verdean, as sanctioned by the Cabo Verdean government since the late 1990s. Therefore, writing the curriculum was based on strict adherence to the ALUPEC rules.

To ensure that Cabo Verdean *Kriolu* could fulfill the functions of a medium of instruction for high schoolers, the curriculum development entailed two fundamental dimensions of corpus planning: lexical modernization and stylistic development (Liddicoat, 2005). CVCAR made conscious choices to introduce a new scientific lexicon to the Cabo Verdean language. For instance, many social-scientific lexica from linguistics were added to the curriculum.

The source languages for the borrowing were English and Portuguese, and the pattern of word formation in Cabo Verdean guided the construction of these neologisms. Stylistic development entailed using the Cabo Verdean to produce academic text styles that were previously seldom used.

The new curriculum is composed of three modules: "The Cabo Verdean Language," "Negotiating Identity: Then and Now," and "Immigration: Past and Present." Module 1 focuses on the Cabo Verdean language and has several objectives: (1) to introduce students to the history of the Cabo Verdean language; (2) to provide them with grammatical tools to analyze their language as a rule-governed system, like any other natural language; (3) to present the new alphabet to help students read and write in the Cabo Verdean language; (4) to explore language variation; (5) to examine linguistic models that help students understand the colonial sociohistorical reasons responsible for the negative perception of Creoles compared to their lexifiers; and finally (6) to introduce students to code-switching as a marker of identity.

For reasons of space, we focus on objective (5). Students examine Rosina Lippi-Green's (2012) Language Subordination Model, which, combined with her discussion of the Standard Language Ideology, explains how hierarchies between languages get established and the social motivations behind them. This model was initially intended to show how "Standard English" is situated compared to "nonmainstream varieties" such as Appalachian English or African American English. When transposing the model's tenets to the hierarchical relationship between Creoles and their colonial European lexifiers, the guiding questions we prepared help students critically assess how the model's tenets—mystification, claiming authority, misinformation, trivialization, reward, and penalization—operate in such contexts. Students examine how creolophone speakers are born into a system that mystifies them into believing that their own language is impoverished and inadequate compared to the European language, which is portrayed as complex and as having a long-written history. Promoters of the European languages claim authority by maintaining that their language's long literary tradition makes it more suitable for education than the Creole language. That claim generates misinformation, as it conveys that the European language is historically, aesthetically, and logically superior. The system trivializes the Creole, casting it in a deprecating light. It rewards speakers who use the European language by holding them up as positive examples of how one should speak and promoting their socioeconomic advancement. In contrast, it penalizes those who only speak the Creole language by keeping them in the lower rungs of society. Given its subordinate position, the Creole language is denied official status and representation as a language of instruction in the classroom. As a result, the European language remains the only official language in the country, the only language of instruction in the classroom, and the only language of prestige in society, thus perpetuating its power while delegitimizing the Creole language. In brief, the Language Subordination Model and the Standard Language Ideology provide high schoolers with valuable tools to critically examine and demystify the hierarchies that Creole languages inherited from their colonial past (see Braithwaite & Ali, 2024; Bancu, Peltier et al., 2024).

Module two, "Negotiating Identity: Then and Now," argues that language cannot be taught without the context of Cabo Verdean history, culture, heritage, and identity. Students' lessons are centered on the concept of identity, specifically using the prompt "Who am I?" through which students explore their roles and relationships within their family, school, and friendship networks. Students are asked to define race, culture, ethnicity, and gender—how they see themselves and how others see them. Understanding identity is valuable for students' social, moral, and intellectual development and serves as a foundation for examining choices regarding language and identity—this goal is specifically crucial for Cabo Verdean students. It is important to recognize that Cabo Verdeans, as colonized people, bring with them a history of linguistic and cultural oppression. When they arrive in the social context of the United States, Cabo Verdeans are then confronted with the US society's exclusionary practices and ideologies, resulting in their identity being consistently undervalued and scrutinized. Therefore, the goal of this module is to connect students to their history and language not only in the classroom but also within the community context.

In the last module, "Immigration: Past and Present," the course unpacks the history of immigration to the United States, focusing on the Cabo Verdean experience in the past two centuries. To begin, students delve into the history of US immigration by analyzing the immigration experiences of different ethnic and racial groups. They next conduct short research projects on "famous immigrants." Through a combination of different academic activities, ranging from mock interviews with peers and analysis of important political documents such as the US Constitution and the Universal Declaration of Human Rights, students develop a hands-on knowledge of the push-pull factors of immigration In the following unit, students critically analyze Cabo Verdean songs and poems connected to immigration to the United States. From poetry and Cabo Verdean traditional musical genre of *mornas*, students glean the main themes that characterized Cabo Verdean immigration to the US. Students also engage in comparative analysis of major American cultural artifacts and historical immigration sites like Ellis Island. They study "the road to citizenship" while being mindful of factors leading to deportation. In sum, the module allows students to make personal connections as they research Cabo Verdean immigrants and learn about their contributions to US society.

The development and implementation of the Heritage Curriculum took place within a short time span due to a deadline set by the Department of

Education, which in turn was following the LOOK ACT guidelines. Therefore, the curriculum developers, using a rigorous curriculum map, not only explicitly laid out the lesson planning but also ascertained that the assessments could correctly assess content, rigor, and learning. students were actively engaged in activities and were continuously assessed throughout the module. In Module 1, which focused on the Cabo Verdean language, the final assessment entailed students documenting the profiles of Cabo Verdean individuals in their community who code-switched, whether these individuals code-switched with mainstream English or African American English. Their research culminated in a class presentation using sound files illustrating the code-switching samples they collected in their research. In Module 2, which encompassed ethnic, racial, and gender identities, the engaging activities were also utilized as formative assessments. As the final assessment, students wrote an analytical essay on the intersection of gender, race, and ethnicity. They had the opportunity to share their essays as class presentations. Finally, module three, which discussed Cabo Verdean immigration to the United States, also was very rich in interactive activities that were also used as ongoing assessments within each lesson. As a final assessment, students drew from their analyses of texts and research done through units one, two, and three and wrote an informative/explanatory text on topics from the three units: (1) why people immigrate, migrate, or emigrate; (2) push and pull factors and their connection to Universal Declaration of human rights and US Constitution Amendments; and (3) US immigration policies and their impact on world immigration, including Cabo Verde.

Conclusion

After three consecutive decades of transitional bilingual education (1975–2002), the passing of the 2002 law severely curtailed bilingual education in the state. Nonetheless, many social and political actors joined forces to pressure the state government to restore bilingual education, which eventually led to the enactment of the LOOK Act in 2017. The new language-in-education policy created a favorable environment for reinstating Cabo Verdean bilingual education. Against this backdrop, the CVCAR was formed as an organization to advocate for the cultural and linguistic interests of the Cabo Verdean community. CVCAR has partnered with Baystate Public Schools to develop a comprehensive high school curriculum showcasing the Cabo Verdean language. Furthermore, as part of the curriculum development, CVCAR also organized many workshops on the Cabo Verdean language and culture for different departments of the school district—with particular emphasis on teachers. These workshops have contributed enormously toward the visibility and new perception of the Cabo Verdean language by the school district and its speakers alike.

The development of the new Cabo Verdean bilingual curriculum, which has stood on the four-decade-long tradition of advocacy, inclusion, and dual language education, has made a significant impact in the United States and Cabo Verde. With a growing trend of city and state governments in Rhode Island and Massachusetts using Cabo Verdean as a medium of communication, understanding the rules of grammar and writing has become a powerful resource that can assist in career development. In Cabo Verde, CVCAR was invited to present on the ongoing experience in the President of the Republic-sponsored international conference on the Cabo Verdean language, held in February 2022. Despite obstacles and linguistic myths regarding Cabo Verdean, it has become evident that the language continues to impact the Cabo Verdean communities worldwide.

References

Ager, Dennis E. (2001). *Motivation in language planning and language policy*. Multilingual Matters.

Aguiar, Paul. (2017). *Board of Elementary and Secondary Education* [PowerPoint slides]. Massachusetts Department of Elementary and Secondary Education. https://www.doe. mass.edu/ele/2017-1219presentation.pdf

Amado, Abel Djassi. (2020). Whose independence? Cabo Verdean-Americans and the politics of national independence of Cabo Verde (1972–1976). *Journal of Cape Verdean Studies 5*, 36–53. https://vc.bridgew.edu/jcvs/vol5/iss1/5

Bancu, Ariana, Peltier, Joy P. G., Bisnath, Felicia, Burgess, Danielle, Eakins, Sophia, Gonzales, Wilkinson, Saltzman, Moira, Sedarous, Yourdanis, Stevers, Alicia, & Baptista, Marlyse. (2024). Revitalizing attitudes toward Creole languages. In Anne H. Charity Hudley, Christine Mallinson, & Mary Bucholtz (Eds.), *Decolonizing linguistics*. Oxford University Press.

Baptista, Marlyse (2002). *The syntax of Cape Verdean Creole: The Sotavento varieties*. John Benjamins Publishing.

Batalha, Luís, & Carling, Jørgen (Eds.) (2008). *Transnational archipelago: Perspectives on Cape Verdean migration and diaspora*. Amsterdam University Press.

Boston Globe Editorial Board (2015, July 13). Bring back bilingual education for Boston schools. *Boston Globe*. https://www.bostonglobe.com/opinion/editorials/2015/07/13/eells/xM7jtgtwgcs1wZ80MewCvL/story.html

Braithwaite, Ben, & Ali, Kristian. (2024). The colonial geography of linguistics: A view from the Caribbean. In Anne H. Charity Hudley, Christine Mallinson, & Mary Bucholtz (Eds.), *Decolonizing linguistics*. Oxford University Press.

Capeverdean Creole Institute (n.d). Capeverdean Creole Institute. http://www.capeverdean creoleinstitute.org

Carreira, A. (1983). *The People of the Cape Verde Islands: Exploitation and emigration*. C. Hurst.

Chang-Bacon, Chris K & Colomer, Soria. (2022) Critical Biliteracies: The Mutually Reinforcing Endeavors of Freirean Criticality and Bilingualism. In Sandro R Barros & Luciana C de Oliveira (Eds.), *Paulo Freire and Multilingual Education*. (pp.26–41). Routledge. DOI:10.4324/9781003175728-3

DiDomenico, Sal, & Chang-Diaz, Sonia. (2016, July 29). Flexibility needed in educating English language learners. CommonWealth. https://commonwealthmagazine.org/education/flexibility-needed-in-educating-english-language-learners/

Duncan, Thomas Bentley. (1972) *Atlantic Islands: Madeira, the Azores, and the Cape Verdes in seventeenth-century commerce and navigation*. University of Chicago Press.

Gramsci, Antonio. (2014). *Selections from the prison notebooks of Antonio Gramsci*. International Publishers.

Haarmann, Harald. (1990) Language planning in the light of a general theory of language: A methodological framework. *International Journal of the Sociology of Language, 86*, 103–126. https://doi.org/10.1515/ijsl.1990.86.103

Halter, Marilyn. (2008). Cape Verdeans in the U.S. In Luís Batalha & Jørgen Carling (Eds.), *Transnational archipelago: Perspectives on Cape Verdean migration and diaspora* (pp. 35–46). Amsterdam University Press.

Halter, Marilyn (1993). *Between race and ethnicity: Cape Verdean American immigrants, 1880–1965*. University of Illinois Press.

Kamwangamalu, Nkonko M. (2016). *Language policy and economics: The language question in Africa*. Palgrave Macmillan.

Liddicoat, Anthony J. (2005). Corpus planning: Syllabus and materials development. In Eli Hinkel (Ed.), *Handbook of research in second language teaching and learning* (pp. 993–1011). Routledge.

Lima, Alvaro & Melnik, Mark. (2012). *Boston by the Numbers. Foreign-Born*. Boston Planning & Development Agency. http://www.bostonplans.org/documents/research/population-and-demographics/2013/boston-by-the-numbers/boston-by-the-numbers-foreign-born-2012

Lima, Ambrizeth Helena. (2022). *The socialization of Cabo Verdean immigrant youth in urban America: Family, school and neighborhood contexts*. Brill.

Lippi-Green, Rosina. (2012). *English with an accent: Language, ideology, and discrimination in the United States*. Routledge.

Macedo, Donaldo. (1980). A Língua Caboverdiana na Educação Bilingue. In Donaldo Macedo (Ed.), *Issues in Portuguese bilingual education* (pp. 183–200). National Assessment and Dissemination Center for Bilingual/Bicultural Education.

May, Stephen. (2017). Language education, pluralism, and citizenship. In Teresa L. McCarty and Stephen May (Eds.), *Language Policy and Political Issues in Education* (pp. 31–45). Springer.

Meintel, Deirdre. (2002). Cape Verdean transnationalism, old and new. *Anthropologica 44* (1), 25–42.

Ruíz, Richard. (1984) Orientations in language planning, *NABE Journal, 8*(2), 15–34. DOI: 10.1080/08855072.1984.10668464

Uriarte, Miren, Lavan, Nicole, Agusti, Nicole, Kala, Mandira, Karp, Faye, Kiang, Peter Nien-chu, Lo, Lusa, Tung, Rosann, and Villari, Cassandra. (2009). English learners in Boston public schools: Enrollment, engagement and academic outcomes of native speakers of Cape Verdean Creole, Chinese dialects, Haitian Creole, Spanish, and Vietnamese. *Gastón Institute Publications 130*. https://scholarworks.umb.edu/gaston_pubs/130

Jamie A. Thomas is Dean of Social Sciences at Cypress College, and equity facilitator for the California Virtual Campus/ Online Education Initiative (CVC/OEI) and the Online Network of Educators (@ONE). She is also adjunct lecturer in linguistics at California State University, Dominguez Hills. During 2021–2022, she was a Mellon/ ACLS Community College Faculty Fellow and principal investigator for the project Closing Racial Equity Gaps Through Online Teaching of Introductory Linguistics. In her other research, Thomas explores discourses and semiotics of antiracism, Blackness, cityscapes, and African languages in relation to language learning, embodiment, the workplace, and popular culture. She is author of the forthcoming ethnography *Zombies Speak Swahili: Race, Horror, and Sci-fi from Mexico and Tanzania to Hollywood,* and co-editor of the multidisciplinary volume *Embodied Difference: Divergent Bodies in Public Discourse.*

Abstract: This chapter provides a practical roadmap to transforming introductory linguistics with lesson plans and assessment strategies that facilitate the success of Black, Latinx, Indigenous, and/or disabled college students. These strategies are particularly useful in community college online teaching, and include intentionally welcoming students with an encouraging message before the semester begins; incorporating content that centers perspectives on linguistic racism and exclusion early in the semester, particularly through the voices of Black d/Deaf and DeafBlind people and other people of color, multilingual people, and Indigenous communities; and enacting student-centered, interactive assessments through video/audio discussions that facilitate personalized engagement and peer learning. The author describes the effectiveness and value of these strategies with help from student reflections on their experiences. These course design recommendations make use of free and emerging educational resources and technologies in ways that enable college students to see and hear themselves, and their concerns, in the introductory linguistics curriculum.

Key Words: humanizing linguistics, growth mindset, multimodal assessment, linguistic discrimination, disabilities

12

Community College Linguistics for Educational Justice

Content and Assessment Strategies That Support Antiracist and Inclusive Teaching

Jamie A. Thomas (she/they)
Cypress College and California State University, Dominguez Hills

Introduction: Language Is Unavoidably Personal

> In a Little Rock [Arkansas] high school, I tested in the low average range, with an IQ of 82. I barely missed being placed in the special education classes by 3 IQ points. My counselor placed me in a vocational trade curriculum, because he said I did not have college ability. He told me that I did not talk right, that I did not have college ability. He told me that my grammar was poor. I spoke Ebonics.

This statement appears on one of the online pages of my introductory linguistics course at a Los Angeles area community college. The page includes a video clip and transcription of US Congressional testimony given by a scholar whose research is formative to studies of language, identity, and educational assessment. Students in my course are able to view and listen to the seven-minute video clip, the length of which I customized through the C-SPAN archival website, and they can read the quoted text that I have typed and transcribed into standardized English, with annotation in the form of captioned images (e.g., an Arkansas state map and a photo of the researcher), as well as hyperlinks to related websites. Students can additionally choose to experience the quoted text with the aid of the embedded screen-reader (immersive reader) function of the online course software (also known as a learning management system).[1]

So, can you guess who authored this quoted testimony? (I reveal the answer in the next section of this chapter.)

Incorporating course material such as this scholar's Congressional testimony facilitates access to sociopolitically subordinated varieties of English, in

Jamie A. Thomas, *Community College Linguistics for Educational Justice* In: *Inclusion in Linguistics.*
Edited by: Anne H. Charity Hudley, Christine Mallinson and Mary Bucholtz, Oxford University Press.
© Anne H. Charity Hudley, Christine Mallinson, and Mary Bucholtz 2024. DOI: 10.1093/oso/9780197755303.003.0013

ways that validate and valorize users and creators of these varieties. You will notice below that I intentionally transcribe the scholar's use of "Lawdy," and spell it in a way that telegraphs its cultural significance and is also consistent with orthographies of African American Language (AAL) and literature. At the same time, I include the term's near equivalent in standardized English, "Lord," to allow access for students of other backgrounds. Providing multiple modalities of engagement with these texts is also particularly helpful to users of other varieties of English and students who are multilingual learners, as well as students with disabilities such as deafness, blindness, auditory and visual processing disorders, dyslexia, and attention deficit disorder.

> Through a fluke, however, I went to a junior college [community college], and then on to Philander Smith College, a small, Historically Black College in Little Rock, Arkansas. It was there that I learned the rules of Standard English from an English teacher and a French instructor. I graduated with honors in 1953, cum laude, laude laude, and thank you, Lawdy [Lord]!

I feature this scholar's narrative because many of my students can relate to it: their account exhibits a growth mindset (Hammond, 2015; see also, Sims in his recorded keynote address, 2020), and discloses both a personal experience with linguistic racism and an educational path that is highly relevant to my students. My students are enthusiastic, ambitious, and creative. They live in different time zones, and take classes remotely, a course modality which has been helpful to many due to the COVID-19 pandemic, among other reasons. They are Black, Latinx, and Indigenous; single parents changing careers, multilingual learners, working adults, unhoused and/or undocumented students, first-generation college students (see Mantenuto et al., this volume), and people with disabilities and/or mental health concerns. Many of them will use what they learn in linguistics in their chosen careers in nursing, education, speech-language pathology, counseling, academia, or in data science, marketing, public relations, and journalism. By the time these students find their way into introductory linguistics, many of them have already encountered evidence of linguistic discrimination and oppression and have many such experiences of their own to reflect upon (see also, for example, Plackowski, this volume).

Often, pedagogical strategies for inclusion on the basis of disability are addressed separately from racialization with educators of color excluded from considerations of how to enact and sustain transformative learning that uplifts students of color (see Lisa Delpit's (1995) description of "The Silenced Dialogue.") In fact, discussions of inclusion in education began gaining traction in the early 1990s within the K-12 arena, based in concerns about "mainstreaming" disabled students (previously "handicapped children") as a direct result of a newly enacted US federal law, now known as Individuals with Disabilities Education Act or IDEA (Villa & Thousand, 1995). Here, I advocate for an approach that considers the intersectionality of exclusion on the basis of race and disability at the college level, and facilitates personalized academic engagement and critical thinking for all students. As part of this effort, I acknowledge the insights and recommendations of disabled scholars, particularly the importance of *cripping* the college and university setting through investing in amplifying the authentic voices, concerns, and presence of d/Deaf and disabled students, faculty, and community members (Robinson & Henner, 2018); and shifting from narrow, ableist, and racist framings of "literacy" to openly value and appreciate signed languages and the embodied nature of communication (see Hou & Ali, this volume). I also learn from *DisCrit,* or disability critical race theory, and its foci on the connected oppressions at work within education—an intervention which builds upon Black feminist scholarship (Annamma et al., 2018).

With all of this in mind, and as important as it is to provide students with access to scholarly publications, and guidance in how to meaningfully engage with their contents, I also find it equally—if not more—effective to contextualize research insights within explanations of researchers' personal journeys (on the personal nature of linguistics research, see Clemons, 2024). These explanations assist in both humanizing and problematizing higher education, by showing how a researcher's real-world experiences and observations, particularly of exclusion and injustice, contribute to their critical thinking and worldview, and hence, the forward development of language-related studies. It is important that students see linguistics as a field they can participate in, and also transform, with their cultural patterns of talk and life experiences as critical assets. We can consider this imperative in linguistics with respect to similarly motivated shifts in mathematics pedagogy, as advocated by proponents of *ethnomathematics,* who guide the learning of mathematics principles through affirming explanations, descriptions, and exercises grounded in students' cultural lifeways, language, and understanding (see, for example, Trinick & Meaney (2020) on Māori contexts with reference to Māori maritime navigation; Stavrou & Miller (2017) on Indigenous Canada; and Gurza (1999) on the community college setting in Southern California).

Indeed, the field of linguistics is in urgent need of the talent, critical insights, and creativity of both community college students and community college educators. Community colleges are the postsecondary, two-year public institutions that enroll 44% of US undergraduates in adult and continuing education, with skills preparation for transfer to four-year colleges and universities for degree completion (CCRC, 2021). Community college educators are leaders in online education, and in innovation that facilitates the success of all students (Kim, 2021). At the same time, students of color intending to transfer to four-year colleges and universities often begin—and too often, end—their higher education journey at community colleges. In California, where 70% of Black and Latinx undergraduates begin in community colleges, only 9% of Black students and 10% of Latinx students transfer within four years (Gallegos, 2022). Additionally, Blind students are unable to succeed in courses that utilize textbooks unaccompanied by a Braille or audio supplement. Such situations effectively amount to *de facto* discrimination, even in community college districts where Blind students may number in the hundreds, amid a total student population of more than 200,000 (Jones, 2021).

As a community college professor of linguistics, I have taught as many as 350 undergraduates each year. More than 30% of my students self-identify as Latinx or Hispanic, while 6% identify as Black or African American, 22% as Asian or Pacific Islander, and less than 1% as Native American or Alaska Native, and 24% as white. Linguistics is a gateway to many degree paths of great interest to students of color because of its connections to the social sciences, humanities, natural sciences, and computer science. And yet white students are awarded 58.1% of linguistics bachelor's degrees in the US (LSA, 2021). Meanwhile, national membership in the Linguistic Society of America, a major professional association of some 3,618 student, nonstudent, and international members, is only 3% Latinx or Hispanic, 2% Black or African American, 10.5% Asian or Asian American, 0.85% Indigenous or Native American, and 35% white (LSA, 2021). These demographic contrasts help us to hazard a guess at the profound potential that our discipline overlooks. Such contrasts are particularly stark with regard to the prolific study of Black language, and the steady exclusion of Black scholars of language. Disparities in educational outcomes also manifest the "unequal partnership" that John Rickford (1997) has observed, whereby linguistics benefits from the study of AAL, without extending reciprocal support in the form of "the induction of African Americans into linguistics, the representation of African Americans in our writings, and [advocacy by linguists] in courts, workplaces, and schools" (p. 161).

As an African American woman scholar who grew up in the Los Angeles area and now teaches in this region, it is also my goal to continually facilitate opportunities for students to see themselves in the people, voices, and communities—inclusive of Indigenous California—we encounter throughout the semester. I take up a mantle of courageous care and educational justice in this heart-work. Language is unavoidably personal, not only in the study of how language works, but also in pedagogy, especially when educators lead with inclusion in mind for our students and their communities. When students feel that their identities and concerns are respectfully and meaningfully included in the curriculum, and that their abilities are supported with ample opportunities for growth, they are more likely to stay with the course, succeed, and exceed their own expectations. The strategies I describe herein have enabled me to deliver the highest success and retention rates for Black, Latinx, and Native (Indigenous) students in my department during the years of the pandemic.

In this chapter, I present specific strategies and lesson plans for providing students with opportunities to personalize the linguistics curriculum, with a view toward the highly diverse populations I serve in my role as a community college instructor. These lesson plans explore two topics. The first topic is language in education policy, and the second is the on-campus college experiences of d/Deaf women of color. Each of these topics and lesson plans presents ways to critically engage with race and linguistic racism early in the course and throughout the semester, rather than addressing these issues only in the final weeks of a curriculum, if at all, as is more typical in linguistics courses. I explain these individual lessons in the context of broader, weeklong content units, and as part of an intentional effort to signal to students through regular communiques and supportive course policies that I value them (e.g., through assignment instructions in plain and encouraging language, "no-zero" grading scores on unsatisfactory assignment attempts, select opportunities to revise and resubmit assignments, and student-centered approaches in *ungrading* (for more on ungrading, see Blum, 2020)), and aim to facilitate their imminent success in introductory linguistics.

Additionally, I share my strategy for transforming tests into fun, interactive assessments that build peer learning, particularly in asynchronous online learning. Traditional classroom assessments are biased and exclusionary, as acknowledged by the trend of major universities in California shifting away from using national standardized tests as evaluation measures in student admissions (Chavez, 2021). I argue that both educators and students in linguistics win when we transition our orientation away from timed tests as an expression of "what you should have learned according to me, your instructor," and toward a more open-ended opportunity to "demonstrate what was most salient to you."

An important note: while this semester-long pedagogy is largely enacted through inclusive content lessons and student-centered course policies, a key component of the strategy begins prior to the start of the semester, when

I send a friendly and encouraging welcome email to all students. This message establishes an inclusive tone that helps to build supportive community, by implicitly setting expectations for respectful online communication, and indicating to students that I have designed the course with their success in mind. In this welcome email, which I send one to two weeks prior to the start of the course, I include a hyperlink to the course syllabus. This syllabus resource is not simply an online, searchable PDF version of the typical paper document, but instead is presented in the form of an engaging website or "Liquid Syllabus" that can be easily viewed on mobile devices (Pacansky-Brock, 2014).

I find that the syllabus website, which is not yet a common syllabus format, is greatly effective in communicating the key goals and expectations of a course in ways that facilitate the success of Black, Latinx, and Indigenous, and/or disabled students. This is especially the case when the syllabus website is intentionally tailored with separate webpages featuring student-centered course policies, a teaching philosophy addressed to students in the form of a letter, linguistics-related resources, explicit guidance on online communication etiquette, and a range of related and diverse images that do not center whiteness and ableism.

The Liquid Syllabus also improves the accessibility of key information for my courses that have scheduled meetings on campus, as well as those taught asynchronously with no class meetings. When I introduced the syllabus website to students during in-person courses prepandemic, many were surprised to learn that there would be no paper or PDF syllabus document, but quickly came to appreciate the ease with which they could access the web version. (A list of all of the teaching resources I discuss in this chapter, including my course syllabus, sample lesson plans, and hyperlinks to relevant websites and video clips, is available on the supplementary website associated with these volumes.) In my online teaching, the welcoming and inclusive tone of the course is further expanded through an activity in which students can "meet" each other by posting brief, friendly video/audio entries and replies within a low-stakes discussion.

Contextualizing Language-in-Education Policy: Example Lesson 1

The first-person statements that open this chapter come from testimony given to the US Senate in January 1997 by Dr. Robert L. Williams (1930–2020), emeritus professor of psychology and African American studies at Washington University in St. Louis. His well-circulated research on the biased language and culture of standardized assessments such as IQ tests, his theorizing on AAL, and his coining of the term "Ebonics" (Kifano & Smith, 2000) have greatly contributed to the development of linguistics as well as other fields of study. Williams concluded his live remarks thus: "I close, Senator, with these two thoughts: One, you cannot appreciate or value what you do not understand, and you cannot understand what you do not know. Two, how do you know where I'm at if you ain't been where I've been?" (Senate Hearing 105–120; for video, see also Thomas, 2020).

On the day of his testimony, Professor Williams was accompanied in the Senate Appropriations Committee by other expert witnesses, including Ms. Jean Quan, Oakland School Board President (later Mayor of Oakland, California 2011–2015), as well as linguists Dr. William Labov, Dr. John Rickford, and Dr. John Baugh. At the time, educators in Oakland, California had recently chosen to designate academic language and literacy resources for African American children, in a decision based on linguistics and education research. This 1996 policy decision was also designed to remedy a set of troubling, disproportionate statistics: while 53% of Oakland Unified School District (OUSD) identified as African American, these students comprised 71% of those enrolled in Special Education, and only 37% of enrollments in gifted and talented education enrichment programming (OUSD, 1996/2000). However, the OUSD Board of Education's move to value and legitimate the home language of all students—including a growing Cambodian immigrant population who shared language patterns with their African American counterparts—was fiercely mocked and criticized by politicians, pundits, comedians, and others (for further discussion, see Baugh, 2018; Thomas, 2019). The Senate hearing was convened as part of this political firestorm.

Today, revisiting the Ebonics debate in introductory linguistics illustrates for students how our field can contribute to changes in educational policy that bring visibility to marginalized languages and communities (Smitherman, 1998). I position this content within Week 9 of my 12-week course, under the banner "Affirming Language and Education as Human Rights" (for the lesson plan, see the supplementary website associated with these volumes). This lesson on AAL is part of a larger weeklong content unit on "Zapotec and AAL in Arts and Education," which contextualizes the structure of these languages (e.g., phonology, morphology, syntax) within a discussion of their cultural significance. This broader unit, which reflects the demographics of both my course enrollments and of Los Angeles, includes a lesson on transnational Zapotec communities in Yalálag (Oaxaca), Mexico and Los Angeles, California, as well as an encounter with the free, online galleries of the

National Museum of African American History and Culture (NMAAHC) and the Museum of Latin American Art (MOLAA).

By focusing this lesson on Black children, with examples of how the issue of linguistic racism impacts multiple communities, I draw attention to the way prescriptivist, racist language ideologies are anchored in the systemic anti-Blackness that underpins American schooling (Wiley & Lukes, 1996). This content also historicizes for students of all racialized backgrounds how their own experiences of marginalization are connected to systemic practices, as well as policy developments, that respond to previous decades and centuries of Black struggle.

The presentation of this information is carefully timed in my course design, because by this point in the course, we have already begun to explore racialization, white supremacy, intersectionality, language ideology, semiotics, and colonialism as related to popular orientations toward different communicative modalities. We have also studied phonetics, phonology, morphology, and neurolinguistics. Put together, this background helps students appreciate the distinct structure of AAL. I arrived at this timing through experimentation with previous iterations of the course. Previously, I waited until Week 10 to present a focus on AAL and the Ebonics debate, which allowed me to introduce syntax more fully in Week 9. However, after three semesters with that sequence, I sought to disrupt the disciplinary perception that a unit on "Zapotec and AAL in Arts and Education" could be postponed until the final three weeks of the semester. Now, I use my AAL lesson to preintroduce some of the concepts of syntax before we focus on these in Week 10. I encourage you to similarly experiment with the sequencing of topics in your own courses to make them more engaging and relevant to students from marginalized backgrounds.

This lesson on the Ebonics debate is designed to humanize and illuminate the concerns of speakers of AAL. Students are presented with the official testimony of three expert witnesses who appeared at the 1997 congressional hearing, including Professor Williams. After reviewing these brief videos and their annotated transcripts, students are then introduced to key features of AAL, and assessed online in two ways: (1) participation in discussion, and (2) annotation of linguistic features of AAL dialogue within Zora Neale Hurston's (1937) novel *Their Eyes Were Watching God*.

In my teaching I use Canvas, the online learning management software (LMS) to which my institution has subscribed. However, this lesson can be adapted to other LMS systems such as Moodle or Blackboard, which likewise allow for the creation of sequenced content pages and assignment types such as discussions and quizzes, as well as the incorporation of PDF readings and embedded external content like videos and exercises made with alternative online educator tools (e.g., VoiceThread, Perusall, Flip (previously Flipgrid)).

When teaching on-ground (in campus classrooms), I use an abridged version of this lesson plan, tailored for two or three class periods. In addition to in-class discussion, I have students take five to 10 minutes at the end of class to respond individually and privately in writing to a related prompt. These paper "Exit Tickets" mirror the online "Reality Checks" I create through Canvas "text" assignment-types (or, alternatively through Canvas discussions), to guide personalized engagement and solicit student questions. *Reality Check* is a term I adapted from the Online Network of Educators (@ONE), a training division funded by the California Community Colleges for faculty and staff professional development. Apart from more comprehensive assessments, like tests, I use Reality Checks as low-stakes check-ins in the form of brief quizzes, short-answer questions, and discussions. I explain to students that these provide an "opportunity to pause with our course materials, so that you can check your understanding of our important concepts." I share my Reality Check prompt for the AAL lesson and select student responses below.

Sample Student Responses to Assessment: Reality Check on AAL and Oakland School Board Resolution

For the Reality Check that accompanies the content on the Ebonics debate, I use the following prompt:

So, let's take another breather.

Choose at least one of the following questions to respond to:
1. Which key concepts from our course can you connect to what you have learned about African American Language (AAL) so far?
2. Why does it matter how we linguistically describe a language?
3. How do the concerns of linguistics connect with the fields of psychology, education, law, and special education, in particular?

In addition, feel free to go beyond these questions. You are encouraged to reply to your peers with supportive feedback.

Below are a few of my students' responses to this prompt, and the instructional content it accompanies:

I found Dr. Williams's testimony regarding AAL (or Ebonics, as he called it) very compelling and closely related to the material we've covered in class. Dr. Williams draws a distinction between AAL as a language with a lexicon and morphology and how AAL's detractors (his high school guidance counselor, for example) see it: English spoken with poor grammar. Dr. Williams and Dr. Labov are both careful to point out that AAL isn't slang and grammatical errors but a systematic language spoken by a speech community.

—Student 1

[in response to another student]
Hi XX!
I appreciate that you bring up diglossia. I had a similar thought. I think it is also important to note the elements of white supremacy and how it relates to what is stereotypically viewed as 'proper' or 'improper.' I think much of the reactions to AAL are of an inherently privileged and racist nature (whether consciously or systemically ingrained). I'm really happy we've started to talk about this in this class. Thanks for a great post!

—Student 2

The concept of communicative burden relates to that of AAL considering these speech communities are required to effortfully communicate and alter their language in order to succeed in education, occupational, and other settings. The idea that AAL speech communities should conform to Standard English is not acceptable and needs to be more actively fought against by speech communities who are not as disproportionally affected.

—Student 3

I can definitely relate communicative competence to our learning about Ebonics or AAL. As a Black woman, the way I speak with my friends is different than how I speak at work or school, and the way I speak with my Black friends can vary also. I haven't really thought of Ebonics as a real language or dialect, but seeing these three talented scholars talk about the importance of it is an eye-opener.

—Student 4

These responses, which are anonymized but otherwise unchanged, illustrate that students are ready for more inclusive approaches to linguistics, and eager to engage with instructional content that brings insight to their own experiences of racialized linguistic difference.

Addressing Disability, Intersectionality, and Educational Access: Example Lesson #2

Several years of curricular experimentation across a range of institutions, from a large state university to small liberal arts colleges and community colleges, have taught me that the significance of language as a tool of exclusion becomes even more comprehensible to students, particular those in denial about racism (i.e., mostly white students), when put in conversation with discrimination on the basis of gender and disability. This is why I introduce the concerns of d/Deaf, DeafBlind, and Hard of Hearing women of color in Week 2 of my course, as part of a larger content unit on "Accents, Dialects, and Language Ideologies," which also addresses modality and intersectionality (a more complete lesson plan is available on the supplementary website associated with these volumes). These topics are not typically included, and certainly not together, within linguistics textbooks. Therefore, by presenting these issues early in the semester, I signal a welcoming of social difference within my teaching, and guide students in exploring how tools and approaches of linguistics can be used to further equity and justice efforts.

In addition to captioned videos, I also include two assigned readings within this content unit, in the form of research articles that accessibly utilize key concepts explored in the course to focus on peer populations—namely, other college/university students. Each of these readings examines how hegemonic lenses on difference impose a communicative burden on college students of color who are bilingual and multilingual, creating linguistic barriers to their success in educational settings. These readings include Stephanie Lindemann's (2002) experimental sociolinguistic study "Listening with an Attitude," which challenges bias against "nonnative speakers" by demonstrating the successful comprehension of groups of US American and Korean-speaking multilinguals (international students) when paired in English-language mapping tasks. I liken the study to asking a stranger for directions, and the various biases implicated in our choices of who to approach for help, as well as our concerns about whether we are *heard* (i.e., comprehended) when we talk with others.

Because for many of my students, Lindemann's study is their first encounter with a research article, I scaffold our exploration by explicitly detailing key aspects of its literature review and experimental design. Then, based on these details, I ask students to make a prediction about the study's outcome, with regard to which pairings of students will be most successful in completing the experimental task (students enter their predictions into Canvas, using a prompt I create as a text-type assignment in which their responses remain viewable only to the instructor). Building upon this scaffolding experience, which demonstrates how to engage meaningfully with a research study, and encourages students to take risks with their learning, I then provide less direct scaffolding for their reading of Lissa Stapleton's (2015) "When Being Deaf is Centered." This qualitative study examines d/Deaf women of color's student identities and explores these students' challenges with obtaining necessary and appropriate disability accommodations, including ASL interpreters, in the college/university setting. Students respond to this reading by participating in an all-class prose discussion.

Structuring this content unit in this way, with two accessible journal articles as assigned readings, also means that I postpone use of a textbook until the third or fourth week of the semester. This delay in our textbook use also allows more time for students to obtain their copy, and ask me for help with getting the textbook, if needed. I find this practice particularly useful within the community college setting because many students face financial constraints that present challenges to textbook rental or purchase, as well as consistent access to computing resources and the internet. Students with limited funding may, for example, be unable to commit to a textbook purchase until they are certain they will stay in a course. Such challenges are also part of the reason I continue to explore open educational resources (OER) options that minimize and eliminate the need for a textbook or personal student subscriptions to paid online tools and services. I also intentionally structure and prepare my course materials and assignments so that a student unable to obtain the textbook can still succeed in the course. For example, if I reference specific textbook pages in course content, I also provide a summary of the information covered within those pages. If you are unable to adapt your course into a zero-textbook or fully OER model, this can be an effective alternative.

Assigned readings and other materials provide opportunities to center contributions of Black women scholars and activists, and engage students beyond textbooks. Visual images and discursive imagery are also central in creating an inclusive and welcoming learning environment in which students see themselves in the curriculum. Consider, for example, whether the faces, silhouettes, hands, voices, and other stock images you use in your course center white embodiments—how can you more effectively visibilize inclusion? Do you consistently include alt-text descriptions for each image in your course, so that blind students and others using screen-reader options can participate in all of your course content? Figures 12.1 and 12.2 provide sequential views of my content page "Modalities," in which I present students with introductory explanations and examples of a range of visual-gestural means of human expression.

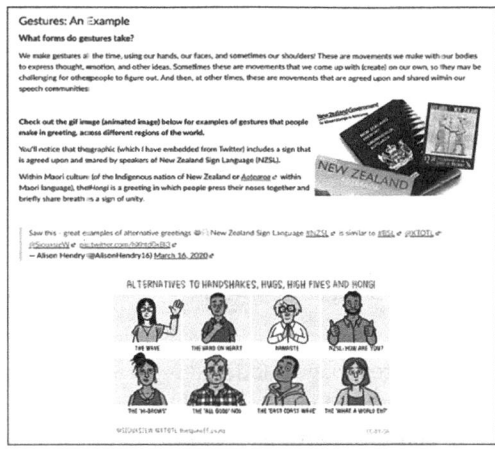

Figure 12.1 Excerpt of the content page "Modalities" with a GIF image inclusive of New Zealand Sign Language

Alt text: This image is a screenshot of an online course page on the topic of gestures. The page begins with the question "What form do gestures take?" and explains these as movements we make with our bodies to express thought, emotion, and other ideas. The Māori cultural practice of Hongi is also described as a greeting in which people press their noses together and briefly share breath as a sign of unity. This page further explains different kinds of gestures with an illustrated image of eight people with various body movements and expressions, including hand-waving, hand on heart, hands together in expression of namaste or peace, how are you? as expressed in New Zealand Sign Language, raised eyebrows, a head nod, a head raise, and a shoulder shrug.

In Figure 12.1, I present a view of "Gestures: An Example," which refers to signs from New Zealand Sign Language, as well as the *Hongi*, a greeting of particular social currency within New Zealand or Aotearoa (the current Māori endonym for the region). The course page includes links to further information, and an image that features Aotearoa, as well as an animated GIF image that centers and validates a range of Black, Brown, and women embodiments.

Figure 12.2 offers a view of a different, later portion of the "Modalities" course page, which centers upon "Digital Braille: The Story of Haben Girma," as an example of the use of tactile, graphic, and aural/oral communicative modalities. This section of the page also introduces the BrailleNote, a digital tool producing the organized, raised dots of English Braille orthography that can be read in real time, in response to typed prose input from an interpreter. I center the experiences of Haben Girma in this portion of the lesson because she is a Black DeafBlind woman, and also because she began her path as a disability advocate while a student at a university in California, the same state where I teach. All of this provides multiple points of connection for my students and

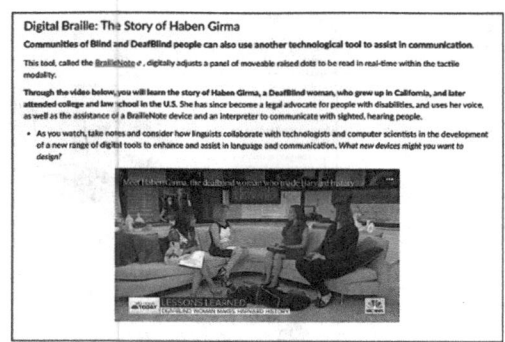

Figure 12.2 Excerpt of the content page "Modalities and Signed Languages" featuring Haben Girma's use of BrailleNote technology
Alt text: This image is a screenshot of an online course page on the topic of digital Braille and the story of Haben Girm, a legal advocate for people with disabilities and a DeafBlind woman who grew up in California, and later attended college and law school in the US. The page explains that communities of Blind and DeafBlind people may use a technological tool called the BrailleNote to communicate, particularly with hearing people. The BrailleNote digitally adjusts a panel of moveable raised dots to be read in real-time within the tactile modality. This course page also includes a clickable video of a news interview with Haben Girma, which shows her using the services of a BrailleNote device and a woman hearing interpreter, who types into a device connected to the BrailleNote so that Haben Girma can read the spoken conversation and reply verbally during the interview. An accompanying discussion question for students to consider while watching the interview video is what new devices might you want to design?

encourages them not only to see themselves in her story, but also to seek points of convergence with their own career goals in education, technology, healthcare, and other fields. The course page also includes a brief, six-minute video from Girma's 2019 appearance on the *Today* show, and invites students to watch the video with the following open-ended prompt: "As you watch, take notes and consider how linguists collaborate with technologists and computer scientists in the development of a new range of digital tools to enhance and assist in language and communication. *What new devices might you want to design?*"

Sample Student Responses to Assessment: Reality Check on d/Deaf Women of Color

For the second Reality Check that accompanies the content on the modalities and "Digital Braille: The Story of Haben Girma," I use the open-ended prompt below as a graded survey question. With this Canvas assignment type, students receive automatic credit for participating, meaning that the instructional focus is not on passing judgment on students' responses, but rather on celebrating their meaningful engagement with course materials.

> In Unit 2, what have you most enjoyed learning about so far? (Share your thoughts in 2–3 sentences here.)

Below are a few of my students' responses to this prompt, and the instructional content it accompanies:

> This unit really changed my perception on "communication." For so long I would associate the word to oral exchange but now I understand that communication isn't just a language skill
>
> —Student 5

> Getting to know that a couple of things that I thought was true turned out to be myths was the part I enjoyed the most so far. For instance, I also thought that signed languages derive from spoken languages, but that it was a myth changed my perspective. Furthermore, learning about a new term 'language modality' helped me to expand my knowledge.
>
> —Student 6

> I have enjoyed gaining insight on the many forms of language that exist in within the Deaf community. I am guilty of having little knowledge on how sign language works or the many varieties that exist around the world. I am fascinated to learn that even in this form of communication, accents exist! In addition to this, I also enjoyed learning about the different modalities in which we communicate, I never really reflected enough to realize that we are always communicating and being real time examples of language and the study of linguistics.
>
> —Student 7

These anonymized student responses demonstrate the importance of including perspectives on disability and difference in introductory study of linguistics, as well as the value of open-ended, nonevaluative assessments and check-ins in online learning. After this content unit, students are excited to learn more about Deaf communities and communicative modalities.

> I have really enjoyed learning about the different modalities of language, especially the tactile and visual-gestural modalities, and how they relate to each other in sign languages. Another thing I really enjoyed was reading about Professor Lindemann's study

on communicative burdens and racial biases in accents. My prediction [about the outcome of the study] was partly correct but it only scratched the surface of the many factors that contribute to the way we perceive people through their use of language.

—Student 8

Learning about alternative communication has been very enlightening. Seeing the rich lives of Deaf and Blind people, like Haben, who expect inclusivity is inspiring. Additionally, shedding light on the biases that nonnative English speakers face through Rubin's (2002) experiment [described in the literature review of Lindemann (2002)] was equally fascinating.

There is a lot I do not understand about how linguistics is organized. I have realized that I take my abilities to communicate for granted. Having learned about how disabled people cope has leveled any expectation I had coming in, so thank you.

—Student 9

As these responses show, students become energized by learning information that challenges their prior beliefs about language and how it works, and by opportunities to reflect on their learning.

Rethinking Tests as Pedagogy: Inclusion Through Interactive, Multimodal Online Assessment

What if tests were enjoyable learning experiences? What if these assessments were authentic to the ways that students will use course content in practical career settings? As the preceding example illustrates, yet another way we can support students is by facilitating flexible assessments that connect instructional content to their everyday lives, and provide space for ample demonstrations of understanding (e.g., Kurbanoğlu & Nefes, 2015). In my teaching of linguistics I see myself in each of my students, and I believe in their success. I want to know what students are gathering from our course materials, and how they are connecting what they learn to their personal experiences. Therefore, in rethinking the role of tests and quizzes in my teaching, I am guided by my previous experiences as a student, and particularly, the range of uninspiring multiple-choice tests I encountered. For these reasons, I have experimented with different testing strategies—something I encourage other educators, such as yourself, to try, as well. The resulting incremental and transformational success of my students has led me to develop an alternative approach in which I primarily consider tests as opportunities to learn from my students (see also Thomas, 2022a).

I conceive of tests, not as opportunities to trick students and point out what they *don't* know, but as occasions for exploration and peer learning that amplify what students *do* know. Shifting from timed, individual response formats to untimed, asynchronous discussions within a community configuration transforms testing from taking a deficit perspective on intellectual ability and linguistic inferiority (e.g., Hammond, 2015), to an appreciative outlook on learning as a process. This shift results in a supportive environment that encourages students to learn from one another.

In my on-ground teaching, students complete open-book (use of notes and textbook allowed) tests and quizzes in community—in groups of two to three students—and write up their responses individually. In the online version of my course, open-ended questions that similarly guide students in applying key concepts to the exploration of data sets become discussion prompts for individual video/audio replies of up to two minutes each. I design these open-book tests as weeklong asynchronous discussions using the video/audio functions of Flip (previously Flipgrid), an online educational discussion platform that can integrate with Canvas for ease of access and grading (this can also be achieved using Canvas's own video/audio discussion functions). Students create their own recordings and respond to one another through additional recordings, all of which remain viewable only to the class (with use of the privacy settings available through Flip). This test design is suitable for a variety of class sizes and accommodates students who do not feel comfortable on video, or who prefer visual-gestural modalities, subtitles, and automatic captioning.

In online course discussions, responding to each student's individual posts can quickly become cumbersome for instructors, and this is where increased opportunities for peer learning and interactivity are particularly helpful. For these reasons, I typically divide my assessment into two parts, each with its own Flip discussion (sample test prompts are available on the supplementary website associated with these volumes, and see Thomas (2022b) for my recorded video presentation for @ONE on their website). Part 1 of my test design provides practice with defining concepts, and Part 2 guides students in applying these concepts to an audiovisual data set that centers the dignity of marginalized languages and communities. This creates a test that facilitates an encounter with Black and Indigenous epistemologies (i.e., through the content of the chosen data set), which, in turn, can be adapted into in-class activities and take-home assignments. My instructions include tips for troubleshooting the technology, as well as a rationale for students: "Why a video discussion for our test? Participating together allows us to learn from one another, and check what we know and understand." By this point, students are already familiar with Flip, because we have used the platform for our opening week of friendly video/audio introductions (another strategy I learned through @ONE).

With this form of student-centered, interactive assessment, my students report lowered testing anxiety and increased confidence:

> I actually really enjoyed our first test together! I completely feel like the test formatting allowed me to convey what I learned about the subject matter.
>
> —Student 10

> The testing format was an entirely new experience for me. I had never had to give video responses for a test before, however by the end of it, I had enjoyed the experience. I feel like it tested me on understanding what I was talking about.
>
> —Student 11

> I found the test to be doable and cool that it was interactive. I think it was a cool way to share my knowledge from what we learned so far and got me to think further. I wish more courses utilized that type of exam.
>
> —Student 12

> This supports my learning because most of us have accents. We used Flipgrid [Flip] to challenge ourselves to be confident in the way we talk and sound, not shyness. Also, the video reply is a good way to support each other and share hints/tips about this class.
>
> —Student 13

> My experience with the test format was interesting because usually when it comes to test I think of multiple-choice questions. But having to talk on video about what I learned and what I found interesting was a new experience because I can explain it in my own words. When my classmates watch my video about this, maybe it could answer their questions if they had any, or I gave them a better understanding of that one topic. So, this gave me a chance to review and understand the material better.
>
> —Student 14

Conclusion: Teaching a More Humanizing Linguistics

Transforming linguistics begins with signaling to students, particularly Black, Latinx, Indigenous, and disabled students who have been systemically marginalized in our field, that we value and welcome their participation and their ways of speaking and ways of knowing. We must present linguistics as a force for social change and useful in seeking justice. For these reasons, I choose a culturally responsive pedagogy (Gay, 2000) that humanizes the theoretical approaches underpinning modern linguistics, embeds diverse forms of accessibility for all students, and embraces antiracist Universal Design for Learning (UDL) principles. Educator and author Andratesha Fritzgerald (2020, p. 48) explains that antiracist UDL is centered upon the premise "that all students are capable of learning and really want to learn," and that it is "our instructional design that prevents them from doing so." This approach eliminates practices that "hold the genius of Black and Brown children hostage to white rhetoric" (p. 5) by "providing multiple means of engagement, multiple means of representation, and multiple means of action and expression" (p. 49). Accessibility and equity-mindedness are a matter of both course content and pedagogical strategies; these are dynamic processes that will continue to shift and grow with what we learn about our students, the insights we develop as instructors, and the capabilities of educational tools, including technology, to support our differences. In other words, and as another community college educator advises: "Community colleges pride themselves on being *open access* institutions, with no admissions requirements . . . By design, we provide access to the top 100%" (Glapa-Grossklag, 2018).

With this in mind, an antiracist linguistics is one that does not shy away from addressing in the (online) classroom the mutually constitutive roles of language and racialization in supporting racism (see also Arnold, 2024; Lederer, this volume; Plackowski, this volume). It requires instructors of linguistics to replace and reenvision course policies and assignments that harm and sabotage the success and creativity of Black, Latinx, Indigenous, and disabled students. Within the community college setting, an antiracist linguistics demands that we actively and intentionally facilitate access to linguistics and frame its study as achievable by all of our students. For these reasons, I have focused in this chapter on providing a practical roadmap to inclusive teaching that makes use of free and emerging educational resources and technologies in ways that enable students to see and hear themselves, and their concerns, in the introductory linguistics curriculum. As we continue to expand inclusion in linguistics, I encourage you to seek further opportunities to learn from others invested in pedagogical transformation.

Note

1. This research was funded through generous support from a 2021–2022 Mellon/ACLS Community College Faculty Fellowship from the American Council of Learned Societies. I also wish to express appreciation to the volume editors and my fellow contributors for their helpful feedback and dialogue.

References

Annamma, Subini Ancy, Ferri, Beth A., & Connor, David J. (2018). Disability critical race theory: Exploring the intersectional lineage, emergence, and potential futures of DisCrit in education. *Review of Research in Education, 42*, 46–71.

Arnold, Lynette. (2024). From gatekeeping to inclusion in the introductory linguistics curriculum: Decolonizing our teaching, our psyches, our institutions, and our field. In Anne H. Charity Hudley, Christine Mallinson, & Mary Bucholtz (Eds.), *Decolonizing linguistics*. Oxford University Press.

Baugh, John. (2018). *Linguistics in pursuit of justice*. Cambridge University Press.

Blum, Susan D. (Ed.) 2020. *Ungrading: Why rating students undermines learning (and what to do instead)*. West Virginia University Press.

Chavez, Jose. (2021, May 23). UC agrees to no longer consider ACT/SAT scores in admissions. *The UCSD Guardian*. https://ucsdguardian.org/2021/05/23/uc-agrees-to-no-longer-consider-act-sat-scores-in-admissions/

Clemons, Aris Moreno. (2024). Apolitical linguistics doesn't exist, and it shouldn't: Developing a Black feminist praxis toward political transparency. In Anne H. Charity Hudley, Christine Mallinson, & Mary Bucholtz (Eds.), *Decolonizing linguistics*. Oxford University Press.

Community College Research Center, Columbia University Teachers College. (2021). Community college FAQs: Community college enrollment and completion. https://ccrc.tc.columbia.edu/

Delpit, Lisa. (1995). *Other people's children: Cultural conflict in the classroom*. New Press.

Fritzgerald, Andratesha. (2020). *Antiracism and universal design for learning: Building expressways to success*. CAST Professional Publishing.

Gallegos, Emma. (2022, February 24). The transfer maze: How to streamline transferring into CSU and UC. *EdSource*. https://edsource.org/2022/how-to-streamline-entry-into-csu-and-uc-panelists-discuss-the-transfer-maze/667984

Gay, Geneva. (2000). *Culturally responsive teaching: Theory, research, and practice*. Teachers College Press.

Glapa-Grossklag, James. (2018). When we talk about accessibility. California Virtual Campus/Online Network of Educators (CVC/@ONE). https://onlinenetworkofeducators.org/2018/05/29/when-we-talk-about-accessibility/

Gurza, Agustin. (1999, August 21). A classroom where math includes history, ethnicity. *Los Angeles Times*. https://www.latimes.com/archives/la-xpm-1999-aug-21-me-2295-story.html

Hammond, Zaretta. (2015). *Culturally responsive teaching and the brain: Promoting authentic engagement and rigor among culturally and linguistically diverse students*. Thousand Corwin (SAGE).

Jones, Carolyn. (2021, December 30). "Unintentional discrimination" at the heart of disability lawsuit against California Community College District. *EdSource*. https://edsource.org/2021/unintentional-discrimination-at-the-heart-of-disability-lawsuit-against-california-community-college-district/665076#

Kifano, Subira, & Smith, Ernie A. 2000. Ebonics and education in the context of culture: Meeting the language and cultural needs of limited English proficient (LEP) African American students. In David J. Ramirez, Terrence G. Wiley, Gerda de Klerk, Enid Lee, & Wayne E. Wright (Eds.), *Ebonics in the urban education debate* (pp. 63–85). Center for Language Minority Education and Research, California State University Long Beach.

Kim, Joshua. (2021, June 23). 11 takeaways from the 2021 CHLOE [Changing Landscape of Online Education] report. *Inside Higher Ed*. https://www.insidehighered.com/blogs/learning-innovation/11-takeaways-2021-chloe-report

Kurbanoğlu, Namudar İsset, & Nefes, Fatma Koç. (2015). Effect of context-based questions on secondary school students' test anxiety and science attitude. *Journal of Baltic Science Education, 14*(2), 216–226.

Lindemann, Stephanie. (2002). Listening with an attitude: A model of native-speaker comprehension of non-native speakers in the United States. *Language in Society, 31*(3), 419–441.

Linguistic Society of America (LSA). (2021). The state of linguistics in higher education: Annual report 2020, eighth edition, 1–32. https://www.linguisticsociety.org/sites/default/files/Ann ual%20Report%202019%20-%20Final_1.pdf

Oakland Unified School District (OUSD). (1996/2000). Clarification and synopsis of the adopted policy on standard American English language development. In David J. Ramirez, Terrence G. Wiley, Gerda de Klerk, Enid Lee, & Wayne E. Wright (Eds.), *Ebonics in the urban education debate* (pp. 114–125). Center for Language Minority Education and Research, California State University Long Beach.

Pacansky-Brock, Michelle. (2014). The liquid syllabus: Are you ready? *Michelle Pacansky-Brock Blog.* https://brocansky.com/2014/08/the-liquid-syllabus-are-you-ready.html

Robinson, Octavian, & Henner, Jonathan. (2018). Authentic voices, authentic encounters: Cripping the university through American Sign Language. *Disabled Studies Quarterly, 38*(4), 1–23.

Rickford, John Russell. (1997). Unequal partnership: Sociolinguistics and the African American speech community. *Language in Society, 26*(2), 161–197.

Sims, Jeremiah. (2020). Intersections in times of crisis: Coming together and taking action. Recorded video of keynote address for Green River College "Opening Day" event for faculty and staff professional development. https://youtu.be/8EM8wWxS4io

Smitherman, Geneva. (1998). Ebonics, *King*, and Oakland: Some folk don't believe fat meat is greasy. *Journal of English Linguistics, 26*(2), 97–107.

Stapleton, Lissa. (2015). When being Deaf is centered: d/Deaf women of color's experiences with racial/ethnic and d/Deaf identities in college. *Journal of College Student Development, 56*, 570–586.

Stavrou, Georgios Stavrou, & Miller, Dianne. (2017). Miscalculations: Decolonizing and anti-oppressive discourses in Indigenous mathematics education. *Canadian Journal of Education/ Revue canadienne de l'éducation, 40*(3), 92–122.

Thomas, Jamie A. (2019). Between Zora Neale, *Hamlet*, and a "dope Black woman": Revisiting language ideology through Alysia Harris' performance poetry. *Altré Modernita/Other Modernities, 22*, 167–181.

Thomas, Jamie A. (2020). "User Clip: Dr. Robert Williams." Remarks at 1997 United States Senate Ebonics hearing. C-SPAN video clip of "Ebonics in Education" (7:12 minutes): https:// www.c-span.org/video/?c4876400/user-clip-dr-robert-williams.

Thomas, Jamie A. (2022a). "Don't stress this test!: Inclusive assessment strategies that may reduce test anxiety and expand success. California Virtual Campus/ Online Network of Educators (CVC/@ONE). https://onlinenetworkofeducators.org/2022/04/01/dont-str ess-this-test/

Thomas, Jamie A. (2022b). From gotcha to "you got this!": Online teaching strategies that uplift students, build interactivity, and increase retention. Presentation for @ONE Equitable Online Teaching workshop series, April 27, 2022. https://onlinenetworkofeducators.org/ equitable-online-teaching-archives/

Trinick, Tony, & Meaney, Tamsin. (2020). Ethnomathematics and Indigenous teacher education: Waka migrations / Ngā Hekenga: Te Tātai me Nga Kura Akoranga-Taketake. *Revemop, 2.* 10.33532/revemop.e202008

Villa, Richard A., & Thousand, Jacqueline S. (Eds). (1995). *Creating an inclusive school.* Association for Supervision and Curriculum Development, Alexandria, VA.

Wiley, Terrence G., & Lukes, Marguerite. (1996). English-only and standard English ideologies in the U.S. *TESOL Quarterly, 30*(3), 511–535.

Jenny Lederer is associate professor of linguistics and Linguistics Program coordinator in the Department of English Language and Literature at San Francisco State University. As a cognitive linguist with special interest in marginalized communities, her corpus-based research focuses on how conceptual metaphor is instantiated in language use, grammar, and co-speech gesture. Her publications in journals such as *Cognitive Linguistics*, *Metaphor and Symbol*, *Metaphor and the Social World*, the *International Journal of Corpus Linguistics*, and the *Journal of Pragmatics* show how metaphorical reasoning reinforces negative stereotypes of marginalized people, from Latinx immigrants to individuals with gender queer identities. Her current book project examines how computer-mediated communication can be used to teach introductory concepts in linguistics and inspire passion for language analysis.

Abstract: Increasing racial diversity in linguistics rests on capturing BIPOC student interest, ideally upon first exposure. This chapter introduces a replicable introductory course design, which focuses on computer-mediated communication (CMC) as a means to inspire passion for language analysis. The case study is a general education course at San Francisco State University, titled Language Evolution in the Digital Age. In the course, students investigate patterns in language use from a variety of online and smartphone platforms including text messaging, social media interaction, online gaming, vlogging, and other every-day mediated interaction. By elevating students' own linguistic competencies and expertise, the traditional asymmetry between instructor and student inverts: the CMC student is a data source, a data analyst, and a teacher, leading to student empowerment and comfort in the linguistics classroom. Meanwhile, the CMC data itself becomes the entree to lessons on grammatical analysis, semantics, pragmatics, and sociolinguistic theory.

Key Words: computer-mediated communication, inclusive pedagogy, course design, introductory linguistics, experiential learning, linguistics recruitment

13

Texts, Tweets, Twitch, TikTok

Computer-Mediated Communication as an Inclusive Gateway to Linguistics

Jenny Lederer (she/her)
San Francisco State University

Introduction

Decolonizing linguistics, in part, centers on recruiting and training students of color. By teaching linguistics to first-year college students and making the study of language patterns accessible, interesting, and personally meaningful, instructors wield immense power in liberating the field from constraints of the past (Calhoun et al., 2021). Racially minoritized groups, for a variety of reasons, have been discouraged from joining the discipline of modern linguistics.[1] The pipeline into the field is crucial: first experiences are highly consequential in determining which areas of study a student pursues (Malgwi et al., 2005). With the right course placement and inclusive pedagogical practice, instructors can open students' eyes toward the richness of a hidden discipline.

An important approach to attract a more diverse student demographic is to focus linguistic instruction on engaging and familiar data, drawing on the everyday linguistic behavior of students themselves, who are increasingly communicating through computers and smartphones. Computer-mediated communication (CMC) encompasses a vast array of media and discourse genres and a variety of modalities from orthographic to pictorial to video, and scholarship on CMC ranges from early study in discourse analysis (cf. Herring, 1996, 1997) to recent attention from a wide-ranging audience in linguistics (cf. McCulloch, 2019) and communication studies (cf. Carr, 2021). In general, any non–face-to-face language interaction that occurs on smartphones, tablets, or personal computers is ripe for documentation and analysis in CMC.

Drawing on the broad appeal of computer-mediated communication, I present a replicable case-study course design centered on CMC as a vehicle to introduce a variety of elementary linguistic concepts. The case study course

Jenny Lederer, *Texts, Tweets, Twitch, TikTok* In: *Inclusion in Linguistics*. Edited by: Anne H. Charity Hudley, Christine Mallinson and Mary Bucholtz, Oxford University Press. © Anne H. Charity Hudley, Christine Mallinson, and Mary Bucholtz 2024.
DOI: 10.1093/oso/9780197755303.003.0014

is a lower-division social science general education elective at San Francisco State University (SFSU) titled Language Evolution in the Digital Age. Based on a discovery-learning model (Josephson, 1969), the curriculum reimagines the roles of instructor and students in order to expand linguistics recruitment by centering students' empowerment, interest, comfort, and confidence.

Several chapters of this volume address pedagogical approaches to increase diverse representation in linguistics, including the application of anti-racist, critical pedagogy in the white-dominant classroom (Arnold, 2024; Plackowski, this volume) and considerations and implications of teaching linguistics to a diverse first-generation audience (Mantenuto et al., this volume; Thomas, this volume). To expand this conversation, my contribution focuses on two related themes. First, I explore how to use CMC as a means to achieve what I call "positionality flip" in the classroom. That is, student becomes teacher and teacher becomes student. (See Schwarz, this volume, for discussion on the efficacy of a related approach, the "flipped classroom" model.) Second, I outline concrete strategies to translate student-generated computer-mediated communication data into broader lessons on grammatical analysis, pattern recognition, hypothesis formulation, and sociolinguistic observation.

When linguistic inquiry is expanded to encompass self-produced language data, the student is both data source and analyst (Bucholtz et al., 2014). This approach avoids the colonizing and exoticizing tendencies of many introductory linguistics courses in which lesser-known languages function as objects to be examined. Instead, student-collected computer-mediated communication serves simultaneously as both a data reserve for investigating linguistic patterns and a knowledge leveler, where young people of color, especially, are experts, and the instructor enters the student's world, rather than vice versa.

Context and Course Genesis

At San Francisco State University, linguistics is one of four undergraduate concentrations within the English major, and, historically, the program includes about 40 majors and minors. Most students elect the English major in order to pursue a concentration either in Literature or in English Education. They are first exposed to linguistics in their third year when required to take the department's Introduction to Language Studies course. By that point, many have already settled on a concentration other than linguistics. As linguistics program coordinator, I have strategized ways both to recruit students earlier in their undergraduate studies and to racially diversify the field by drawing on the demographically diverse and multilingual student population of the university. SFSU comprises a highly diverse student population. In 2020, 86% of first-time SFSU students were students of color (including 24% Asian, 7% Black, 43% Latinx, 5% multiracial, <1% Native American), 45% Pell-eligible low-income, and 38% the first generation of their family to attend college (Office of Institutional Research, SFSU, 2020). On the other hand, SFSU academic faculty and staff are predominantly white and Asian (50% white, 24% Asian, 19% Latinx, 6% Black, 1% multiracial, <1% Native American) (Department of Human Resources, 2020). The racial mismatch between a mostly nonwhite student population and a majority white faculty presents opportunities for the unintentional perpetuation of a racist status quo, where whiteness is embedded in everyday teaching practices (Hyland, 2005).

Nationally, white women make up the preponderance of the teaching workforce, which increasingly serves BIPOC K-12 student constituencies (Brockenbrough, 2014), a gender and racial asymmetry common in higher education as well. As part of this group—a white, middle-aged professor (and mother) of Black and Latinx students—I have noticed potentially problematic patterns in my teaching. Two specific tendencies, in particular, stand out. First, I catch myself falling into the familial pedagogical pattern of what has been characterized as "other mothering" or "further mothering," in which the teacher takes on a mother persona with her students (Brockenbrough, 2014). While there are certainly positives to this sociocultural model of education— one often adopted whether or not the instructor is a parent—I increasingly question the efficacy of this authority hierarchy and parental dynamic within the classroom. Does this model disempower BIPOC students? Second, I notice myself enacting a "helper" persona with racially minoritized students, in particular, who, in my experience, are often working long hours outside of the university to financially support themselves and their families. As Nora Hyland (2005) frames the issue, how much does the "helper model" of white teachers "perpetuate patronizing forms of whiteness and racism grounded in historic, hierarchical race relationships" (p. 456)?

This introspection has fueled both the pedagogical design of Language Evolution in the Digital Age and the core content of the course. I cannot change who I am, but I can change how I teach. In order to minimize my tendency toward "other mothering" and reframe my position from helper to guide, I designed a class which purposely incorporates thematic units on media platforms with which I have little familiarity (e.g., Twitch TV; TikTok, Snapchat). Due to my genuine naiveté, the students are positioned as the source of knowledge, mitigating, to some degree at least, a potentially problematic practice of understanding education as disseminated expertise or worse, a patronizing parent-child enactment. By inverting knowledge transfer, the classroom is more leveled, and instructor authority is decentered: as the trained linguist, I model and guide analysis while my students, as social media experts, provide cultural fluency and explanation. My hope is that this classroom model, featuring cultural and linguistic exchange, results in mutual learning and empowers BIPOC students to share their online linguistic practices with me and with their peers.

Computer-Mediated Communication as a Tool to Disrupt Linguistics

Just as online communication has enriched and accelerated language change, linguists should consider CMC a mechanism to accelerate interest in the field. There are two main reasons to learn linguistics through CMC: it is ubiquitous, and it is changing language.

New mediums—synchronous and asynchronous video, text, and pictorial—allow for the documentation and preservation of linguistic patterns to a greater degree than in any other era in modern history. As is the common refrain in the CMC literature, the medium shapes the message, a concept first introduced by Marshall McLuhan (1964). With an endless stream of new apps and platforms, language use online is shaped, constrained, and expanded in unanticipated ways, evidenced by the changing communication habits of the last two decades, changes in which young people of color and those with non-normative sexual identities have been particularly influential (Huffaker & Calvert, 2005; Murthy et al., 2016).

Linguists typically discourage a focus on textual data in introductory linguistics since orthography is at best an incomplete representation of oral languages. This point is important, certainly, as students need to understand that language exists independently of writing systems. In the modern era, however, students' communicative social practice is increasingly text-based, and the visual representation of language is changing quickly: many aspects of smartphone texting and social-media posting mirror patterns of face-to-face language use. Language users around the globe tend to text like they talk, unlike the formal registers characteristic of academic essays, letters, and emails (Tan et al., 2007). Thus, new media has resulted in a semicollapse of a type of English diglossic system: with the prolific increase in text-based communication, written language, formerly considered formal, becomes more like spoken language. These changing patterns in the written representation of language allow student and teacher to examine every-day, informal language through not just the audio signal of recorded speech, but also through the newest orthographic representations of word pronunciation, formation, and invention, yielding patterns linguists may not have noticed by solely examining in-person spoken or signed interaction.

While written and spoken varieties of English are collapsing in specific ways, paradoxically, diversification is proliferating due to the ongoing invention of new visual symbols like emojis, gifs, and memes. Written forms of language in CMC now encompass an abundant set of symbols that do not exist in spoken discourse. Entirely new sets of research questions arise as to how these symbols interact with standard text-based orthography, and new inquiry focuses on a myriad of projects dedicated to understanding the meaning and use of these emergent symbols of communication. Just when texters think they understand the meaning and usage of one new sign, another comes into practice.

So, unlike past eras of human language, in which daily communication was either exclusively or almost entirely through oral or signed face-to-face interaction, this new century has brought about an inversion: mediated communication is drastically increasing within many communities and especially among the young. In fact, the COVID-19 pandemic era has only accelerated the movement away from face-to-face, in-person communication. In 2019, the average American teenager (13- to 18-year-olds) spent almost seven and a half hours (7:22) on a screen device daily. This average increased to almost nine hours (8:39) in 2021, and screen use is highest among Black and Latinx adolescents, with daily averages of 7:49, 9:50, and 10:02 for white, Black, and Latinx students respectively (Rideout et al., 2022). Entering the world of language study through what users do on a daily basis makes sense in a time when the tools for linguistic expression are expanding and changing with each new software application and technological invention.

Just as the smart phone and personal computer have altered linguistic behavior, employing CMC as the centerpiece of linguistic data disrupts traditional approaches to introductory linguistics. Although the study of CMC is treated by many as peripheral to the field of linguistics, the driving forces behind CMC patterns are the same as those that underlie spoken and signed language grammar and usage. Regardless of medium, language is a social behavior and linguistic style is based on the unconscious drive for social acceptance (Giles, 2016). Investigating these novel media and what seems to outsiders to be unintelligible new language reveals a great deal about traditional notions of language and how it is structured at a conceptual and social level. This innovation reflects the same cognitive and social mechanisms that have historically shaped language grammar and language change, while being far more accessible and engaging to students than traditional discussions of these topics.

Translating CMC Patterns into Introductory Linguistic Content

Through a syllabus organized by communicative modality (e.g., synchronous and asynchronous texting, social media, online gaming, video blogging), the instructor of a CMC course can incorporate lessons on phonetic, morphological, syntactic, semantic, discourse-analytic, and pragmatic touchstones. For example, innovative CMC spelling practices include phonetic spellings that may or may not reflect dialectal variation (*u*, *nite*, *fo sho*), adjacent character repetition (*yessss*), abbreviations (*pls = please*), acronyms (*lmao = laughing my ass off*), and keyboard smash to express strong emotion (*sdfghjkl*). In a unit on phonetic spelling, students discover relationships between the phonemic inventory of English and its quite archaic orthographic system, as represented in dictionaries. (Why is *nite* replacing *night*?) In CMC, adjacent character repetition is used pragmatically for emphasis, but follows predictable and nonobvious patterns about which character can repeat. (Why does *yesssss* look familiar but *yyyyyyyes* doesn't?) The patterns of abbreviation in CMC reveal the phonetic and cognitive load differentials between consonants and vowels. (How is it that we recognize *pls* for the word *please*, but *eae* doesn't work as an acronym for the same word?) An investigation into acronym formation not only touches on new word formation processes in morphology, but also suggests the formulaic and idiomatic nature of phrasal storage in the mind. (Why is there an acronym for *fuck my life* (FML) but not *thank you for helping me* (TYFHM)?) There are even good (*sdfghjkl*) and bad (*nmnmbnm*) examples of keyboard smash, which support exemplar-based models of language representation.

Emoji (☺) and emoticon (:-/) use can be introduced as an entry into discussion of pragmatics, embodied linguistics cues such as facial expression and co-speech gesture, and syntax (emoji placement is restricted in the linear relationship to text). Asynchronous and synchronous texting and messaging yield lessons on conversation analysis and phenomena such as turn-taking, overlaps, and politeness. Data from YouTuber vlogging underlies units on narrative structure and on language and identity. Orthographic creativity such as small caps aesthetic (*i love u*) and Tumblr-style camel case (*aMaZiNg*) yield sociolinguistic modules on language and identity as well as language and gender since affinity spaces in the online environment are equivalent to in-person language communities. And, just as in face-to-face communication, linguistic patterns of translanguaging, borrowing, and second language acquisition all show up in CMC data.

A brief classroom interaction from Fall 2021 illustrates the richly diverse nature of CMC data. In a unit on innovative spelling practices, "Michelle," a student whose parents emigrated from Mexico, introduced the class to a remarkable and fascinating example of phonetic spelling they found in a group text on their phone. The CMC phrase *mailob* ("my love"), used within the California Latinx community, is a phonetic spelling of the English phrase "my love," in which Spanish orthographic rules are imposed on the English phrase (a quasi-reverse example of a common Latinx CMC pattern in which English orthography is used to phonetically spell Spanish words (e.g., *k* = *qué* "what")). During Michelle's presentation, another student, "Adam," who also identifies as Latinx, nodded his head in recognition. Many of the non-Latinx students in the class were unfamiliar with the word, but clearly intrigued by its etymology and its use within the community. As this example illustrates, discovery, revelation, and analysis symbiotically spark interest, and more importantly, pride in forms of language too often devalued or ignored. The more students see the astonishing linguistic, social, and cognitive complexity of their daily communication, the deeper is their involvement in research and analysis.

Safe Classroom Spaces Lead to Better Learning

Freely sharing personal language practice comes about only when students feel secure and safe with the instructor and their peers, which can be especially difficult to achieve when the instructor is white and the students are of diverse backgrounds (Cooper, 2012). There are multiple ways a curricular focus on CMC results in a more comfortable classroom setting. Although these practices are not part of traditional university pedagogy, I have found them to increase participation and attendance. Most of the in-class data gathering assignments involve students' direct data collection from their own phones, laptops, and tablets, and data analysis often focuses on slang, profanity, and other taboo aspects of the typical uncensored language use of a young demographic. Having multiple screens active within the class period can be distracting for some students, and instructors should consider inclusive ways to accommodate students with learning differences that might be exacerbated such as Attention Deficit Disorder. However, in most cases, the setup mirrors students' home environments and seems to disarm the apprehension and nerves that often accompany first-year college students.

Unlike most linguistics classrooms, the data in the course is not precurated, and therefore the instructor must model real-time analysis, somewhat akin to the instruction that takes place in a field methods course with language consultants. As Hannah Sarvasy (2015) notes, a fieldwork approach has the potential to "give students a taste of serendipity . . . give them glimpses of intriguing facets of language they could not have anticipated finding" (p. 477). Rather than serving as expert, the instructor's role is that of facilitator, helping students form testable hypotheses, work on linguistic methodology, and analyze their collected data through the theories presented in course readings. Lesson plans can be structured around the instructor's own research interests, a strategy I have adopted in my course. Example units include in-class group mini-projects focused not only on emerging text-based patterns in creative spelling and new word formation but also units in which students investigate social media participation to explore how language use functions as an index of sociocultural identity.

In one activity, student research groups are asked to analyze differences between the words and emotes (similar to emojis) of two Twitch gamer livestream channels, one Fortnite and one Call of Duty streamer. Through prompting questions, students are instructed to formulate hypotheses about how the game's objectives, environments, and player communities (younger vs. older; multigender vs. male-dominated) will both affect and reveal participant identity as indexed by language use in the chat. Students work together to specify a testable hypothesis and debate investigative methodology; they discuss what to document, what to count, how results corroborate or refute proposed hypotheses, and which variables confound conclusions. In a separate unit on narratives of gender transition, students work collaboratively to find and research trans vloggers on YouTube to not only probe questions about common, socially constructed stories of gender discovery and affirmation but also to consider the malleability of idiolectal features as gender identity shifts over time.

By building units based on a variety of online practices, media, and platforms, I aim for inclusivity. Every student will connect with at least one online community, whether they be a gamer, an athlete, an amateur chef, a makeup aficionado, a car enthusiast, an artist, or a musician, and each student commands expertise in their own language community. In this way, student-directed, discovery-based pedagogical practice aligns with frameworks such as Black Feminist Thought, which questions and inverts traditional assumptions about epistemology itself: what counts as legitimate knowledge, whose knowledge counts, and who has access to such knowledge (Collins, 2009). In my experience, this epistemological inversion empowers learners, especially those from racially minoritized backgrounds. In fact, students with access to the most minoritized dialects—students whose idiolects include African American Language and Chicanx English—become stars of the classroom, as they have knowledge of interesting CMC patterns born out of both English varieties. It is important to note, however, that the sharing of expertise of racialized dialects is emergent, not expected: students in the classroom should not feel on the spot, singled out, nor exoticized for their linguistic practice. By allowing students to control topic investigation and data collection, the sharing of personal language practice is not coerced but rather invited and welcomed.

Successes and Challenges

After five semesters of teaching Language Evolution in the Digital Age, I have witnessed an amazingly creative collection of research projects. These include papers investigating gender differences in emoji use on Twitter, schematic patterns in genre-specific video blogging on YouTube (e.g., day-in-the-life videos, slime videos, unboxing videos), how toxic masculinity is expressed in Twitch video game chat participation through acronyms and emotes, the narrative differences between Asian American and white makeup tutorialists on YouTube, the spread of African American Language features through Black Twitter, and the innovative online spelling practices of Crips and Bloods gang members, to name a few. I have also received plentiful anonymous student evaluation feedback that the focus on CMC data in the course and homework assignments results in a comfortable and dynamic learning environment, as summarized in several student evaluation comments:

> Fun and analytical course. I am able to learn things about my language use that I wouldn't know otherwise. Interesting way to get teenagers interested in research.
>
> This course was extremely enjoyable and I connected to it quite well in terms of our modern era and how we communicate with one another. Personally this course challenged me to not only think critically and deeper but look at a variety of perspectives and analysis. Therefore I found many of the assignments to be focused and engaging with only three main assignments and lots of group work and discussion.
>
> A nurturing welcoming environment in which students could express themselves and explore new ideas. . . . not only did I have fun but I considered ideas and explored areas of linguistics that I otherwise would not have.
>
> Amazing class content and a very safe environment.
>
> This was one of the most interesting classes I signed up for at SFSU.

While student testimonials overall have been encouraging and suggest that first-year and second-year students of color are stimulated, interested, and comfortable, I have limited evidence that students who take the course are choosing to pursue further linguistic study. Though five out of roughly 40 current and recently graduated linguistics students (three white, two Latinx) have taken Language Evolution in the Digital Age, it is not clear that the course alone has done much to increase BIPOC enrollment in the major.

There are several confounding factors that have stymied recruitment from the course into the major: the course cap is small (20–25 students) in order to foster student connection and group work, the course was introduced just a year before the COVID-19 pandemic in which SFSU pivoted to four semesters of distance learning (exacerbating already high attrition rates of first-year students and hindering student advising practices), and SFSU humanities majors overall have disproportionately decreased over the last five years. These specific obstacles, nonetheless, should not be taken as evidence against the potential for BIPOC recruitment through a CMC gateway.

At the same time, a CMC recruitment course needs to be aligned with broader and more explicit departmental and disciplinary inclusion initiatives. My experience teaching the course and my program's accelerated focus on issues of racial justice raise several considerations for faculty at other institutions. A first consideration is the link between the gateway course and enrollment in the major. How can a department capture BIPOC students' interest through first-year general education curriculum and subsequently draw them into a linguistics major or concentration? Departments should consider what institutional support exists to identify and follow nonmajors and continue recruitment into the major as they move through their lower-division general education coursework; in addition, specific recruitment strategies should be developed and shared across courses. A second consideration centers on the continuity of inclusionary practice: Do upper-division courses in the linguistics major support BIPOC students? Capturing student interest in linguistics and language study through CMC does not necessarily translate to sustained interest and comfort within the subdisciplinary suite of courses like syntax, phonetics, phonology, morphology, and semantics, the courses that comprise the core of the major within most universities. Thus, a wholesale rethinking of curricular content and delivery is warranted (Charity Hudley & Mallinson, 2018). A final takeaway is to consider the benefits of a CMC approach even without the addition of a stand-alone course. How can a focus on CMC data and analysis be incorporated into existing linguistics curriculum? Should institutional barriers make new course proposal and development cumbersome or impossible, linguistics faculty may consider an integrational approach in which CMC-based discovery learning is woven into curriculum already taught within the major (cf. Van Herk, 2008; Kemp et al., 2016; Welch, 2021). Together with larger scale efforts, CMC-focused linguistics can be a valuable tool for recruiting and retaining students of color.

Conclusion

Computer-mediated data is inherently diverse as users of oral and signed languages now communicate online in a variety of dialects and registers. In order to increase inclusivity and BIPOC student participation in the field of linguistics, programs should consider ways to make the study of introductory linguistics welcoming, interesting, and relevant to the lives of underrepresented students. One vehicle to achieve these goals is to seed first exposure with data from students' own online interaction. The study of computer-mediated communication facilitates students' ability to see their own language practice as worthy of academic study while simultaneously positioning them as analysts themselves within academia.

Computer-mediated communication is a unique vehicle to introduce students to elementary linguistics. The unrestricted and diverse nature of CMC itself aligns with multiple institutional student learning outcomes and enables a (CMC-focused) linguistics course to meet a variety of categorical general education requirements (Welch & Shappeck, 2020). Placing this type of course in the first or second-year lower-division experience extends the department's reach to an attentive audience of potential future linguists, including students who may have never considered a linguistics or language studies major. By teaching the course to a broad range of lower-division students, mostly those outside of the linguistics concentration or major, departments can use it to attract students of color into the discipline.

Moreover, computer-mediated communication is fun and familiar. And not only is the study of CMC enjoyable for both instructor and student, but it is also a tool for student empowerment. As Kristin Denham (2020) notes, grammatical knowledge is useful as a instrument for equality because students come to see language use not through a lens of right or wrong, nor through a lens of standardization in which minoritized dialects are considered inferior; rather, they learn to understand language as variable, ever-evolving systematic data ripe for investigation. In this egalitarian view of language, the innovative and creative language practices of youth-driven online communities are recast as central to understanding communication, not peripheral or secondary to some type of illusory standard.

Almost every linguist would agree that language is the single most interesting, compelling, important, and consequential of all human behaviors. Our enthusiasm for the subject is unquestionable and, often, evangelical. Yet we frequently fail to translate this message to our students by getting bogged down in fossilized approaches to teaching grammatical analysis through pedagogy based on unfamiliar language samples, which can feel like disembodied linguistic puzzles. The inaccessibility of precurated, unfamiliar problem sets may unintentionally exclude students of color when they are unable to connect language analysis to their own lived experience and life goals (Calhoun et al., 2021, e15). Student-generated CMC avoids these potential turn-offs. Meanwhile, core grammatical theory and analysis can be saved for additional courses in a curricular sequence once the value of language analysis is already established. I liken CMC to a bridge, a pathway that ties BIPOC student linguistic competence and interest with the renewed social justice goals of the field. CMC is one tool in the quest to recruit and support a racially diverse and representative next generation of linguists.

Note

1. Although certainly an underreported sample, statistics from National Science Foundation surveys published in the 2020 Linguistic Society of America annual report suggest that white students comprise about 60% of linguistics majors while Latinx and Black students make up less than 20% (Linguistic Society of America, 2021). The numbers at the postbaccalaureate level are much starker, with white students comprising at least 76% of MA and PhD linguistics students (LSA 20).

References

Arnold, Lynette. (2024). From gatekeeping to inclusion in the introductory linguistics curriculum: Decolonizing our teaching, our psyches, our institutions, and our field. In Anne H. Charity Hudley, Christine Mallinson, & Mary Bucholtz (Eds.), *Decolonizing linguistics*. Oxford University Press.

Bucholtz, Mary, Lopez, Audrey, Mojarro, Allina, Skapoulli, Elena, VanderStouwe, Chris, & Warner-Garcia, Shawn. (2014). Sociolinguistic justice in the schools: Student researchers as linguistic experts. *Language and Linguistics Compass*, 8(4), 144–157. https://doi.org/10.1111/lnc3.12070

Brockenbrough, Ed. (2014). Further mothering: Reconceptualizing white women educators' work with Black youth. *Equity & Excellence in Education*, 47(3), 253–272. https://doi.org/10.1080/10665684.2014.933758

Carr, Caleb T. (2021). *Computer-mediated communication: A theoretical and practical introduction to online human communication*. Rowman & Littlefield.

Calhoun, Kendra, Charity Hudley, Anne H., Bucholtz, Mary, Exford, Jazmine, & Johnson, Brittney. (2021). Attracting Black students to linguistics through a Black-centered Introduction to Linguistics course. *Language 97*(1), e12–e38. doi:10.1353/lan.2021.0007

Charity Hudley, Anne H., & Mallinson, Christine. (2018). Introduction: Language and social justice in higher education. *Journal of English Linguistics, 46*(3), 175–185. https://doi.org/10.1177/0075424218783247

Collins, Patricia H. (2009). *Black feminist thought: Knowledge, consciousness, and the politics of empowerment.* 2nd ed. Routledge.

Cooper, Kristy S. (2012). Safe, affirming, and productive spaces: Classroom engagement among Latina high school students. *Urban Education, 48*(4), 490–528. https://doi.org/10.1177/0042085912457164

Department of Human Resources, San Francisco State University. (2020). *Affirmative action plan workforce analysis for Academic Affairs Division.*

Denham, Kristin. (2020). Positioning students as linguistic and social experts: Teaching grammar and linguistics in the United States. *L1-Educational Studies in Language and Literature, 20*(3), 1–16.

Giles, Howard. (2016). Communication accommodation theory. In K. B. Jensen, E. W. Rothenbuhler, J. D. Pooley, & R. T. Craig (Eds.), *The International Encyclopedia of Communication Theory and Philosophy.* Wiley Online Library. https://www.wiley.com/en-us/9781118290736

Herring, Susan C. (1996). *Computer-mediated communication: Linguistic, social, and cross-cultural perspectives.* John Benjamins Publishing.

Herring, Susan C. (1997). Computer-mediated discourse analysis: Introduction. *Electronic Journal of Communication, 6*(3). http://www.cios.org/www/ejc/v6n396.htm"http://www.cios.org/www/ejc/v6n396.htm

Huffaker, David A., & Calvert, Sandra L. (2005). Gender, identity, and language use in teenage blogs. *Journal of Computer-Mediated Communication, 10*(2), JCMC10211. https://doi.org/10.1111/j.1083-6101.2005.tb00238.x

Hyland, Nora E. (2005) Being a good teacher of Black students? White teachers and unintentional racism. *Curriculum Inquiry, 35*(4), 429–459. doi:10.1111/j.1467-873X.2005.00336.x

Josephson, Irving. (1969). Linguistics and discovery teaching. *College English, 30*(5), 376–380.

Kemp, René, Moline, Emily, Escalante, Chelsea, Mendes, Alexander, & Bayley, Robert. (2016). Where have all the participles went? Using Twitter data to teach about language. *American Speech 91*(2), 226–235. https://doi.org/10.1215/00031283-3633129

Linguistic Society of America. (2021). *The state of linguistics in higher education annual report 2020, eighth edition.* https://www.linguisticsociety.org/sites/default/files/Annual%20Report%202020%20Jan2021%20-%20final.pdf

Malgwi, Charles A., Howe, Martha A., & Burnaby, Priscilla A. (2005). Influences on students' choice of college major. *Journal of Education for Business, 80*(5), 275–282. https://doi.org/10.3200/joeb.80.5.275-282

McCulloch, Gretchen. (2019). *Because internet: Understanding the new rules of language.* Riverhead Books.

McLuhan, Marshal. (1964). *Understanding media: The extensions of man.* Routledge & Kegan Paul.

Murthy, Dhiraj, Gross, Alexander, & Pensavalle, Alexander. (2016) Urban social media demographics: An exploration of Twitter use in major American cities. *Journal of Computer-Mediated Communication 21*(1), 33–49. https://doi.org/10.1111/jcc4.12144

Office of Institutional Research, San Francisco State University. (2021). *Five year trend report: First time freshmen.* https://rpubs.com/ir-sfsu/ftf-fiveyear-f21

Rideout, Victoria, Peebles, Alanna, Mann, Supreet, & Robb, Michael B. (2022). *Common sense Census: Media use by tweens and teens, 2021.* Common Sense. https://www.commonsenseme dia.org/sites/default/files/research/report/8-18-census-integrated-report-final-web_0.pdf

Sarvasy, Hannah. (2015). Monolingual fieldwork in and beyond the classroom: The Logooli experience at UCLA. *Proceedings of the Chicago Linguistics Society 51,* 471–484.

Tan, Kenny W.P, Swee, Debbie, Lim, Corrine., Detenber, Benjamine H., & Alsagoff, Lubna. (2007). The impact of language variety and expertise on perceptions of online political discussions. *Journal of Computer-Mediated Communication, 13*(1), 76–99. https://doi.org/10.1111/j.1083-6101.2007.00387.x

Van Herk, Gerard. (2008). The very big class project: Collaborative language research in large undergraduate classes. *American Speech 83*(2), 222–230. https://doi.org/10.1215/00031 283-2008-014

Welch, Katie. (2021). Discovery learning in the sociolinguistics classroom: Using boojie to teach American English history. *American Speech 96* (2), 253–265. https://doi.org/10.1215/00031283-9089626

Welch, Katie, & Shappeck, Marco. (2020). Linguistics in general education: Expanding linguistics course offerings through core competency alignment. *Language 96*(2), e59–e76. doi:10.1353/lan.2020.0033

Rhonda Chung is a PhD candidate in education (applied linguistics) whose research focuses on acts of listening, specifically dialectal perception. Because dialect is tightly bound to place, her interest in critical sociophonology focuses on the affordances of land sensitivity for language learning and the role it plays in embodied cognition, which she views through a critical ecological lens. For over 10 years, she has taught both English and French as a second language to a wide range of students and lectures in Concordia and McGill University's Bachelor of Education TESL programs.

John Wayne N. dela Cruz is a PhD candidate in educational studies-language acquisition at McGill University. Drawing from plurilingualism and critical applied linguistics, his research explores the intersection of language, culture, and identity in Filipino immigrant lived experiences within the context of Canadian second language education and language policies. He has taught ESL in primary, secondary and postsecondary levels, and he has been teaching courses for BEd and MEd programs at various Canadian universities.

Abstract: Before contact, the Americas were a multilingual pastiche of Indigenous communities. The arrival of colonial linguistic policies disrupted this biodiversity with monolingual (i.e., English-only) pedagogies. To reverse this noninclusive trend, Indigenous scholarship asks settler teacher programs to self-locate their teaching practices on the land and confront TESL's role in maintaining settler-only linguistic futures. To explore a land-based resistance to monolingual pedagogies, the authors piloted and then conducted a two-hour online workshop with ESL instructors in a Canadian university in Québec. The first half of the workshop combined individual self-reflection and self-location activities, followed by small group discussions that located attendees' language teaching practices and learning experiences on the land (Landguaging). The second half explored maintaining multilingual landscapes via three plurilingual teaching strategies, which attendees evaluated in small groups. Participants positively perceived the Landguaging exercises and plurilingual strategies, viewing them as helpful combinations to foster inclusion in the ESL classroom.

Key Words: teacher reflection, teacher education, translanguaging, plurilingualism, land-sensitive pedagogy

14

Pedagogies of Inclusion Must Start from Within

Landguaging Teacher Reflection and Plurilingualism in the L2 Classroom

Rhonda Chung
Concordia University

John Wayne N. dela Cruz
McGill University

Land operates in a time of its own—beyond human experience (Deloria & Wildcat, 2001), communicating itself through billion-year-old cycles, which are uniquely interpreted by each Indigenous nation across the globe (Armstrong, 2017). Colonizing policies interrupt these land-based knowledges, aiming to replace linguistic biodiversity across the landscape with settler monoculture (Wolfe, 2006). Educational institutions in North America are engineered and funded by settler governments, leading Donaldo Macedo (2019) to argue that colonial (English, French, Spanish, etc.) second language (L2) programs can never be decolonized because they are the colonizers. Fracturing the Eurocentric hold that colonial languages have over L2 teacher education programs will require L2 teachers to be actively reflective and ecologically sensitive to the territory upon which they teach and use their languages (Pennycook, 2022), critical of their profession's insistence on using monolingual (e.g., English-only), often monodialectal curriculum (Chung & Cardoso, 2022b), and strategically inclusive of voices traditionally excluded from L2 pedagogies.

Although Canada calls itself a multicultural society, it officially functions in English and French alone, marginalizing other migrant languages, and continuously endangering the more than 70 Indigenous languages that pre-date them (Statistics Canada, 2016). Each Canadian province and territory employs Eurocentric monolingual policies, which often prohibit students

Rhonda Chung and John Wayne N. dela Cruz, *Pedagogies of Inclusion Must Start from Within* In: *Inclusion in Linguistics*. Edited by: Anne H. Charity Hudley, Christine Mallinson and Mary Bucholtz, Oxford University Press.
© Anne H. Charity Hudley, Christine Mallinson, and Mary Bucholtz 2024. DOI: 10.1093/oso/9780197755303.003.0015

from using nonstandardized dialects and other languages in the L2 classroom (Lau, 2022), making L2 teacher education programs sites of ongoing colonization. Rather than operating on a principle of "linguistic gratuity" and creating a more linguistically inclusive space toward non-native users (Wolfram, 1993), whose perceptions and productions have informed the discipline's knowledge (see also Figueroa, 2024), settler-colonial custom has always been to force L2 learners to participate in hierarchical systems designed to oppress and assimilate them (Pennycook, 2022). So long as settler-language classrooms uphold monolingual models, they preserve a linguistic barrier. Our case study focuses on eliminating language-related barriers in English L2 teaching (TESL) programs by using "Landguaging" teacher reflection exercises and plurilingual teaching techniques.

Our interactive workshop, Conversations That Include, was piloted and then conducted with English L2 (ESL) instructors in Tiohtià:ke (Montréal, Canada). Attendees were guided in a self-reflective dialogic process, which focused on the relationship between language teaching and learning experiences and the lands those events occurred on. Because teacher self-reflection exercises are criticized for lacking in-class application (Beauchamp, 2015), participants were supported with plurilingual strategies that encourage students to make connections between English and their pre-existing communicative repertoires (dela Cruz, 2022). In conceptualizing land as a multilingual space, TESL instructors can remove the linguistic barrier of English-only policies that inhibit multilingual classrooms by using plurilingual strategies rooted in Landguaging. This subverts the settler-colonial concept of a "second" language classroom, which ignores students' other dialects and languages, and cultivates a "de/colonial" (Bhattacharya, 2021) translanguaging space that restores linguistic biodiversity by being inclusive of students' entire communicative repertoire (Kubota, 2020).

Landguaging: Self-Locating Language on the Land

Indigenous scholars have long urged settler education programs in Canada to self-reflect and trace their relationship to the colonial process (Battiste, 2013; Tuck & Yang, 2012). Teacher reflection "in, on, for and as action" is described as an internal process driven by cognitive and emotional mechanisms (Beauchamp, 2015, p. 124), and necessitates conscious temporal shifting from past language teaching and learning experiences to present-day pedagogical practices with a focus on future professional development (Farrell, 2022). Reflection is also an external "grounded" process, connected to specific locations and events (Collin et al., 2013, p. 106). It involves externalizing one's teaching and learning experiences with peers, being open to uncertainty regarding these experiences, and being curious about other practices (Jay & Johnson, 2002). Teacher reflection, therefore, is a subjective and critical act of self-location that entails land-based awareness, which has the capacity to unsettle instructors' worldviews (Henhawk, 2013; Tuck & Yang, 2012), and their curriculum design (Kouri, 2020).

When critical self-location is applied to language teaching and learning experiences, it transforms into Landguaging—a land-based awareness involving consciously thinking about the land(s) where one's past language experiences and teaching practices occurred, being both curious and uncertain about these practices, and externalizing one's reflections with colleagues to receive professional feedback (Chung & Cardoso, 2022a). Viewing "land as pedagogy" means understanding the land as both the context and a process of learning (Simpson, 2014). Whereas linguistic landscape research focuses on teacher's sensitivity to semiotic processes of language use visible and audible on the landscape (Sterzuk, 2020), Landguaging views language as flowing *from* and in relationship *with* the land, producing autochthonous or allochthonous relationships. When instructors provide personal examples of how land influences particular language practices, it enables practitioners to cultivate a more engaged citizenship toward the territory they teach on (Tanchuk et al., 2018), a professional competency with which TESL instructors often struggle (Borg & Edmett, 2019).

A main source inhibiting the use of reflexive practices is the practitioner's own institution, which may be uninterested in shifts away from its established hierarchies (Beauchamp, 2015). To mitigate the power differentials inherent to settler systems of domination and subordination, TESL instructors must clarify their positionality toward the languages they have learned, their teaching practices, and the lands these events occurred on, a subjective process that entails seeking commonalities but resists generalizations or universalities (Kovach, 2021; Henhawk, 2013; see also Clemons, 2024). Anti-oppressive and anti-racist language pedagogies specifically state that self-reflection is necessary for instructors seeking to reverse the historically oppressive nature of English-language teaching so as to repair relationships with the communities it continues to marginalize (Charity Hudley, et al. 2020; Flores & Rosa, 2015), actualizing a more inclusive language-learning classroom environment (Anya, 2021). Landguaging is part of a larger movement in critical education scholarship that is land-centered, and focused on repairing the socioecological damage of imperialism through localized community efforts (Calderon, 2014).

Plurilingual Futures

In the settler-colonial state of Canada, Landguaging for TESL practitioners entails confronting native speakerism and English-only approaches to instruction and materials (Cook, 1999; 2016; Cummins, 2007). Plurilingualism is a theoretical-pedagogical framework that offers an alternative to these exclusionary practices (Marshall & Moore, 2018), where all of a learner's languages, varieties, and associated sociocultural experiences are interconnected within a composite repertoire (Coste et al., 1997/2009). Language learners have the agency and plurilingual competence to fluidly draw from their entire semiotic repertoire when acquiring new languages, and to combine them when mediating with peers and making meaning of course content (Council of Europe, 2020). Plurilingualism taps into students' plurilingual repertoires and transforms the classroom into a translanguaging space (Kleyn & García, 2019; Li, 2011), which empowers students to embrace their subjectivities and learn the target language via creative language use. Plurilingual instruction thus scaffolds students' global language learning (Piccardo, 2019) by developing both the target language and their entire communicative repertoire simultaneously. Plurilingual instruction equally empowers teachers to affirm, draw from, and further develop their students' emerging plurilingual awareness, competence, and identities (for sample tasks and assessments, see dela Cruz, in press; Galante et al., 2022).

Plurilingual pedagogies rooted in Landguaging and enacted on settler-colonial lands foster critical awareness regarding which languages, cultures, and identities are traditionally featured in TESL practices and materials. This awareness urges both teachers and students to challenge hierarchical views toward language learning (Lau, 2022), and to resist colonial and raciolinguistic logics that view learners as passive receivers of knowledge (Flores, 2016). Plurilingual pedagogies hence lead to a more democratized language education whereby learners are treated as active knowledge users (dela Cruz, 2022).

Design and Application of Inclusive Language Pedagogies: An Ecological Model

Removing barriers is a cornerstone of inclusive pedagogies (UNESCO, 2017). Within Canada, inclusivity in curriculum design focused on disability issues (Whitley & Hollweck, 2020) and raising cultural awareness of minoritized groups (Ghosh & Galczynski, 2014). Within settler-colonial institutions, minoritized people are the most vulnerable because settler policies are designed to assimilate them and their languages into the majority culture (Bhattacharya, 2021; Pennycook, 2022). Designing inclusive language pedagogies, therefore, first requires language teachers to confront the systemic inequalities that their students will be subjected to and expected to participate in, as well as replicate (Battiste, 2013; Charity Hudley et al., 2020; Otsuji & Pennycook, 2011). Secondly, before adding variation to the classroom, instructors need to reflect on why it is missing from the language learning classroom to begin with. Applying inclusive pedagogies rooted in Landguaging assists instructors in identifying which dialects and languages have been neglected from the L2 classroom, and enables them to strategically eliminate these "language-related barriers" by purposely shifting from monolingual pedagogies toward plurilingual instruction (Motschenbacher, 2016, p. 166; see also dela Cruz, in press).

Removing barriers also entails decolonizing TESL's cognitive imperialism (Battiste, 2013), by expanding our understanding of language learning beyond an anthropocentric computer-based model of cognition (i.e., speech is "input" or "output"; Ellis & Wulff, 2020). This means asking not "what's inside your head, but what your head's inside of" (Mace, 1977, p. 43). Such ecological perspectives involve noticing, for example, how elements in the "macrosystems" of the land(s) and institutions spiral out and influence elements within the "microsystem" of the classroom and home in bi-directional and nonlinear ways, uniquely affecting each member of the classroom population (van Lier, 2004). Ecologists refer to these influential moments as sociocultural relationships, affording the learner opportunities to attune to the animate (animal, human) and inanimate (land, signs, technology) elements found in their linguistic landscape (van Lier, 2011). These moments of relationship either draw the learner closer to engagement with communities within their socioecosystem or drive them away.

Removing language barriers in the language-learning classroom means maintaining a translanguaging space that enables learners' multiple dialect and language resources to interact, thereby validating learners' sociocultural knowledge. If what is more frequently occurring is better noticed and remembered (i.e., usage-based theory; Ellis & Wulff, 2020), then pervasive raciolinguistic ideologies in settler-colonial L2 classrooms undermine the possibility of a translanguaging space because these ideologies deem minoritized/racialized students' home language practices as deficient in order to maintain a monolingual, Eurocentric, and white supremacist structure (Flores & Rosa, 2015; see also Plackowski, this volume). To address the ongoing exclusion of minoritized languages and nonstandardized varieties, our plurilingual-multidialectal model (Figure 14.1) demonstrates that when high frequencies of monolingual/raciolinguistic issues are confronted with the grounded self-locating notions of Landguaging, the L2 classroom is afforded opportunities to

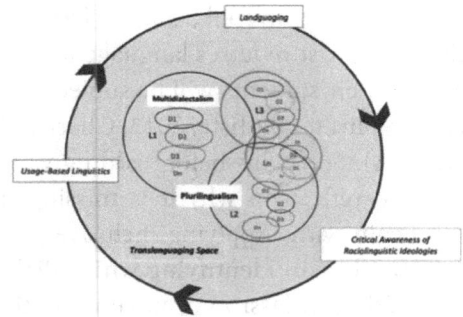

Figure 14.1 Plurilingual-multidialectal model for inclusive language pedagogies
Alt text: Circular chart of the plurilingual-multidialectal model for inclusive language
pedagogies containing multiple nested circles. The large outer circle is labeled
with "critical awareness of raciolinguistic ideologies," "Landguaging," and "usage-
based linguistics" along its circumference. The space inside that circle is labeled
"translanguaging space," within which there are multiple overlapping and intersecting
smaller circles labeled "plurilingualism," representing an individual's multiple
languages (L1, L2, Ln). Inside those smaller circles are even smaller circles labeled
"multidialectalism," representing the dialects and varieties of each language (D1, D2, Dn).

transform into a translanguaging space. Landguaging guides TESL instructors
and their students to notice that the land has always been multidialectal and
plurilingual, and that the curriculum should reflect this reality and foster
these competencies. By focusing on the "system of nested, interdependent,
dynamic" socioecological landscapes that learners navigate (Bronfenbrenner,
1993, p. 4), our model emphasizes that learning about and from variation
within (multidialectalism) and across languages (plurilingualism) should be
the learning goal. This model, which was developed prior to the workshop and
informed its organization, is connected to the context and experiences of the
authors' own teaching and learning experiences.

Workshop Design

This section details the workshop design, including a description of the institutional context, an overview of the three facilitators, and our positionalities.

Institutional Context

Ecolinguists theorize that the land decides how multilingual it will be; for
example, the presence of rainfall and large water reserves is a key factor in

fostering multilingual populations in coastal and island regions compared to arid zones with markedly less linguistic diversity (Nettle, 1999). This land-first perspective posits that it is precisely because the Kahrhionhwa'kó:wa (great-sized river) flows around the island of Tiohtià:ke that a multilingual space emerged and continues to thrive. This study takes place on the ancestral territories of the Kanien'kehá:ka nation, who state that this island served as a natural stopping point for diverse Indigenous nations, making it rich with linguistic biodiversity. Yet present-day settler-colonial linguistic policies continue their attempts to convert the multilingual Tiohtià:kea into a French-only Montréal.

The province of Québec is home to Canada's largest francophone community and operates on a sociocultural policy of "integration" into *québécois* values (Québec, 1977; 2021). The equality of non-Francophone cultures is rejected in this policy because it threatens francophones' minority status in an overwhelmingly anglophone continent, undermining Québec's nation-building aspirations (James, 2008). However, Tiohtià:ke/Montréal, the province's largest city, retains its multilingual characteristic and is Canada's most trilingual city, with Montrealers identifying as plurilinguals, using languages other than the two official ones: English and French (Galante & dela Cruz, 2021). This complex linguistic reality poses distinct challenges: one for ESL learners to attune to the multiple language varieties spoken in this metrolingual environment (Otsuji & Pennycook, 2011), and another for TESL instructors to update their monolingual teaching model to include and reflect this multidialectal and plurilingual reality (Cummins, 2021).

To respond to these challenges, in Fall 2021 we created a two-hour interactive online workshop: Conversations That Include (Ethics certification # 30015467), which involved participants completing a series of Landguaging exercises and plurilingual strategies (described below). The workshop was designed both for preservice ESL teachers enrolled in the undergraduate TESL program leading to Ministry certification to teach at the elementary and secondary levels, and for in-service ESL teachers enrolled in graduate programs. Of the 19 universities located in Québec (Government of Canada, 2021), our workshop was conducted in one of the three anglophone universities.

Facilitators and Our Positionality

The authors are active members in the Belonging, Identity, Language, and Diversity (BILD) group, a critical applied sociolinguistics research group founded at McGill University in Tiohtià:ke/Montréal. BILD provides us a space where we can explore topics not typically discussed in mainstream education, like producing pedagogies which purposely decenter colonial languages. Our shared interests in variation from within (multidialectalism) and across (plurilingualism) languages came from our own understanding of our plural identities, which we describe below.

Rhonda

Landguaging was co-created with my son, whom I homeschooled from March 2020 until August 2022 due to the COVID-19 pandemic, and was developed to satisfy Cycle 1 competencies of Quebec's Education Plan (Chung & Chung Arsenault, 2023). The land-based project was designed to sensitize my then six-year-old to the plurality of his citizenships while living on Tiohti:àke, colonially called Montréal by francophone settlers to whom he is ancestrally related. From my side, I was born in Canada and am connected to ethnic groups indigenous to Madeira, China, West Africa, India, and Guyana; my mixed identity is directly related to the relocating/colonizing actions of British imperialists on Abya Yala (South America/West Indies). In ecological terms, I am mostly allochthonous to the Americas, but have history with five of the seven continents for my livelihood, yet speak none of my ancestral languages because of colonization. I research and teach languages (English and French) connected to the enslavement, indenture, and relocation of my ancestors.

Following Leanne Simpson's (2014) approach to nonlinear intergenerational learning (i.e., child-led) and Kakali Bhattacharya's (2013) arts-based inquiry, I employed several arts-based dialogic reflections with my son, like photo collage (Chung, 2020) and infographics (Chung, 2022), to increase our sensitivity to the land and explore our shared intercontinental identity. For example, we employed the iterative aspects of grounded self-location and followed the timeline of British invasion of our ancestral homelands, excising the countries from a paper map, thereby visually representing the intercontinental and extractive methods of imperialism in the British West Indies (Chung, 2021). We then responded to the Sḵwx̱wú7mesh saying "Rocks are our oldest teachers" (Todd, 2008), asking what the land could teach us about our ancestors' displacement. If understood by its movements, rocks communicate three major orientations: convergence, which create mountains (foundational communities of practice); divergence, which stretches the tectonic of plates (creating social valleys), and; transformation, where the plates shimmy together (transactional or occasional communication); but for our family, the continents collided in ways that rocks don't (Figure 14.2). By employing the Landguaging process, we attempted to re-enact our ancestral relationships with the five continents, articulating why and how we only have present-day knowledge of English and French. This arts-based process clarified and

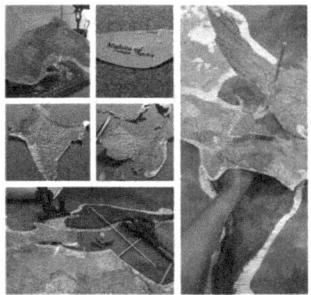

Figure 14.2 "Ho(i)sting the Land": hoisting our ancestral homelands upon Guyana
Alt text: Collage of pictures. To the left, multiple cut-outs of countries from a world map. To the right, these cut-outs are skewered with China on top, followed by Madeira, India, and the African continent at the bottom, all hoisted/hosted atop a map of Guyana.

reaffirmed my commitment to eliminating language-related barriers in my English and French teaching practices.

John

Parts of the workshop's content and its overarching themes reflect and draw from my own lived experiences as an L2 learner and teacher of English, and as a plurilingual and immigrant from the Philippines. European colonialism forms a long part of the Philippines' history—my name alone readily signals both Spanish and American colonial regimes. As a settler to Canada, I bear this history and it informs my approach to language education both as a teacher and a researcher: I see language teaching and learning as implicated in issues of social injustices, inequities, and discrimination rooted in (neo)colonialism and white supremacy (Pennycook, 2022). Further, though Filipino society is highly plurilingual, ESL education there was fairly monolingual. I grew up in a household where Tagalog, Ilocano, Kapampangan, English and even bits of Cantonese were spoken (my parents once worked blue-collar jobs in Hong Kong), but I learned English after a native speakerist ideology: inside the classroom, English-only policies were enforced during English classes, and outside, English was treated as more socially, academically, and economically valuable than the local languages. I saw a similar scenario when I started teaching and researching second languages in Canada: Indigenous and immigrant languages are often neglected to prioritize a native-like command of English and French, which are colonial, and official, languages. My linguistic experiences, and my choice to use linguistics theory to address existing linguistic inequities (Charity Hudley & Flores, 2022), inform the plurilingual orientation in my research and teaching praxis, which is also what our workshop and model articulate.

Although we come from differing backgrounds, we share similar histories as diaspora speaking colonial languages because of an extractive imperial process that resulted in our families' migration from our homelands. We therefore view a multidialectal and plurilingual stance, rooted in Landguaging principles, as pedagogies of resistance to the settler-colonial norms of monolingual-learning classrooms, and consider our approach as an avenue toward repairing TESL's history of epistemic injustice (Fricker, 2017).

The following research questions were intended to document aspects of TESL practitioners' ideological shifting that may have occurred as a result of the workshop:

1) How do Landguaging exercises support participants in identifying:
   a) educational experiences that were inclusive and noninclusive of certain cultures and languages?
   b) how they might begin revising their teaching practices to become more inclusive?
2) How does the plurilingual model for language teaching address the need for more inclusion and diversity in the classroom?

Methodology

Participants were recruited via emails to the university's Department of Education and by postings to social media, inviting attendees to engage in teacher self-reflection activities and learn plurilingual strategies for their language-learning classroom. Eligibility for participation required enrollment in a current education program and experience with teaching ESL. All participants claimed native or advanced proficiency in English with a minimum knowledge of three languages of varying proficiencies (either basic, intermediate or advanced/native), among them: Arabic ($n = 3$), Berber ($n = 1$), Bulgarian ($n = 1$); Cantonese ($n = 1$), French ($n = 12$); German ($n = 4$), Hebrew ($n = 1$), Italian ($n = 3$), Korean ($n = 1$), Mandarin ($n = 2$), Norwegian ($n = 1$), Portuguese ($n = 1$), Russian ($n = 3$), Spanish ($n = 8$), and Vietnamese ($n = 2$). Most considered themselves plurilingual ($n = 12$); however, none reported receiving training on plurilingual or inclusive strategies in their ESL training. Table 14.1 summarizes the biographical, educational, professional, and citizenship backgrounds of the 13 workshop participants.

In order to ensure that attendees understood our terminology, the workshop provided a brief overview of the literature on teacher self-reflection,

Table 14.1 Participants' demographics

Variables		Participants ($N = 13$)
Gender	Female	11
	Male	2
Age	18–35 years old	9
	56–60 years old	4
Education	TESL undergraduates	2
	Education graduate students	11
ESL levels taught*	K-12	10
	Postsecondary/Adult education	11
	Teaching internship	1
Teaching experience	> 6 years	5
	1–5 years	5
	< 1 year	3
Student status	International	5
	Canadian	8

*Note: Numbers reported here reflect overlaps, e.g., most participants had taught in both K-12 and post-secondary/adult contexts.

self-location, and plurilingualism (15 minutes). The first portion focused on Landguaging exercises that connected participants' language learning and teaching experiences with the lands where these events occurred (50 minutes). After a brief break (5 minutes), three plurilingual strategies were then explained to and evaluated by attendees (50 minutes). These strategies were chosen because they occur most regularly during ESL peer-to-peer interactions (dela Cruz, 2022). Note that the workshop was first piloted with four language teachers and three professors from two Canadian TESL programs. Based on their interactions and feedback: individual reflection time was decreased, plurilingual activities were reduced, and group discussion time was increased. Wording in the Landguaging exercises was modified to remove specific mention of colonialism and avoid potentially triggering what Eve Tuck and K. Wayne Yang (2012) describe as "settler moves to innocence" (p. 4), a reactionary defense tactic that may inhibit settlers from confronting their complicity in the ongoing colonial project.

Part 1: Landguaging Exercises

The Landguaging exercises were drawn from Indigenous self-location methodologies, which emphasize the role of land in language use (Armstrong, 2017; Deloria & Wildcat, 2001; Kovach, 2021). The Landguaging acts included self-reflection and group discussion exercises, which asked attendees to reflect on their language learning and teaching experiences. Facilitated by the first author, each individual reflection (duration three minutes) asked participants to identify specific cultural and linguistic experiences, and was followed by a longer (20 minutes) group discussion of two to three people (see the appendix for the list of individual and group questions). These questions were intended to orient attendees to the concept of land as pedagogy, unsettling the Eurocentric discourse of their Canadian education programs, and expanding participant's epistemological repertoire to include land-based reflections of linguistic citizenship (Battiste, 2013). Participants were then given a brief break.

Part 2: Plurilingual Strategies

Participants were then introduced to three plurilingual strategies by the second author, including how to apply them in language classroom tasks:

(1) translation for mediation (Galante, 2021; Muñoz-Basols, 2019): translating from one or more languages to carry out tasks in the target language;

(2) translanguaging for meaning-making (Cenoz, 2017; Hornberger & Link, 2012): mixing and switching across languages when discussing or making meaning of course content;

(3) cross-linguistic analysis (Auger, 2005): drawing from linguistic forms and meanings in the first or additional languages to systematically compare and contrast with novel forms and meanings in the target language.

In groups of two to three, participants had 15 minutes to adapt an existing ESL task and incorporate a plurilingual dimension. Afterward, participants returned to the main group to discuss their adaptations, including how they would implement the tasks, and the benefits/challenges of using plurilingual strategies in their teaching contexts.

Data were collected using video recordings and online surveys that included both scalar judgments and open-ended questions before and after the workshop. Quantitative data from the survey scales (from 1 = *strongly disagree* to 4 = *strongly agree*; negatively worded statements were reverse scored) were analyzed using descriptive statistics to look for patterns pertaining to data distribution and frequency (e.g., means). Qualitative data from the video recordings, open-ended survey questions, and workshop discussions were coded using in vivo coding (Saldaña, 2021) to keep the codes rooted in the participants' own words, which were then analyzed using content analysis (Patton, 2015) to seek emergent thematic patterns.

Results and Discussion

In response to the first research question: How did the Landguaging exercises support participants in identifying educational experiences that were inclusive and noninclusive of certain cultures and languages? Participants strongly agreed ($M = 3.38$; $SD = 0.51$; 3;4) that the Landguaging exercises helped them identify language learning experiences that were inclusive and noninclusive of certain sociocultural knowledges. During group dialogues, those most adept at discussing their reflections were those with teaching experiences outside of Canada. The experience of being unable to use the majority language had sensitized those instructors to the power dynamics of language and place. One United States-born participant stated that the culture shock of teaching English as a foreign language (EFL) in Asia had inspired her to share aspects of her Mayan-Mexican culture in subsequent ESL classes, and she encouraged her learners to also share their own cultural backgrounds. Contrastively, two international students stated that English should be the only language and culture discussed in EFL contexts precisely because it was nonindigenous to the region. EFL learners, they explained, wanted to learn about anglophone cultures, so discussing other cultures seemed pedagogically inappropriate. In the Canadian context, however, both agreed that teaching content related to Indigenous issues was important but were unsure how best to proceed. This reflexive weaving in and out of different territorial macro/microsystems, ecological theory explains, appears to have enabled practitioners to develop ethical relationships to the sociocultural settings they navigated.

In response to the second research questions: How did the Landguaging exercises support participants in identifying how they might begin revising their teaching practices to become more inclusive? Responses toward creating a more inclusive ESL curriculum fell into two categories: linguistic activities and sociocultural content. Most participants ($n = 11$) identified specific plurilingual activities they would use in their future ESL teaching (i.e., translanguaging, translation tables, including more dialectal variation and linguistic diversity). Five mentioned sociocultural tasks focused on: identifying students' cultural/linguistic backgrounds (i.e., through questionnaires), developing students' personal sociocultural knowledge (traditions, customs, and holidays) over those from anglophone countries, and including Indigenous content, particularly related to land acknowledgments.

Participants interested in using Landguaging exercises still felt they needed more guidance and training, and one feared institutional backlash: "I never asked students not to speak other languages. I did do a few plurilingual activities with them but didn't want to push it and get in trouble with the school." In the context of teaching ESL in Québec, this is a valid concern, as TESL programs specifically prohibit the use of languages other than English in the ESL classroom (Québec Education Program, 2011; n.d.); however, to what extent nontarget language is policed in ESL classrooms is an avenue for future research.

With regards to the final research question: How did the plurilingual model for language teaching address the need for more inclusion and diversity in the classroom? Participants gave the highest rating ($M = 3.46$; $SD = 0.50$; 3;4) to plurilingual strategies (translation, translanguaging, cross-linguistic analysis) as one way of creating more linguistically inclusive classrooms that go beyond mainstream English-only orientations and policies, which one participant described as "the main thing that keeps me from making my classroom as inclusive as I actually want it to be." Participants also strongly agreed ($M = 3.43$; $SD = 0.63$ 2;4) that plurilingual instruction should include topics and lessons that help learners self-locate on the land, and that Landguaging exercises made them more comfortable with using plurilingual instruction in their language classroom ($M = 3.14$; $SD = 0.66$; 2;4). This relationship between Landguaging and plurilingualism, as one participant expressed, "was a useful starting point" as a preservice teacher who had no experience with inclusive and plurilingual approaches. Another participant who had received little plurilingual training but had comparatively more professional experience with it "strongly believe[d] that the self-locating reflection is (and should be) necessary" when implementing inclusive/plurilingual pedagogies. Overall, participants agreed that the workshop helped them understand the importance of Landguaging for creating inclusive pedagogies ($M = 3.38$; $SD = 0.49$; 3;4) and made them more comfortable using plurilingual instruction in the future ($M = 3.23$; $SD = 0.80$; 2;4).

These findings support our plurilingual-multidialectal model for land-based inclusive pedagogies. First, Landguaging exercises that consciously explore how land is linked to language teaching and learning experiences is a necessary prerequisite for TESL instructors to shift toward more inclusive plurilingual teaching practices. Because current monolingual pedagogies produce high frequencies of raciolinguistic input, Landguaging encourages acts of professional unsettlement, subverting settler-colonial discourses via inclusive multidialectal and plurilingual translanguaging practices in the classroom. Second, participants' view that plurilingual strategies foster linguistically inclusive instruction affirms our model's perspective that learners' languages and dialects are interconnected and equally valuable. This notion refutes persistent native speakerist English-only approaches in TESL, which privilege a white, monolingual standard, and view linguistic diversity as an instructional barrier. In sum, Landguaging exercises may enable TESL instructors to articulate their English-language learning and teaching experiences, and lead to conversations that acknowledge how land plays a pivotal role in developing their responsibilities to teaching English in settler-colonial and international contexts. Plurilingual strategies rooted in Landguaging exercises may guide attendees to reflect on and develop linguistically and culturally inclusive activities in their curriculum.

Implications and Limitations

Despite participants' positive view, our results should be viewed critically. Since 12 of the 13 participants identified themselves as plurilingual, it is possible that ESL instructors who do not identify as plurilingual may not view Landguaging exercises favourably and exhibit defensiveness or "settler moves to innocence," resisting such conversations. However, since Tiohtià:ke (Montréal) is an increasingly plurilingual landscape (Galante & dela Cruz, 2021), our results may reflect how an increasingly pluricultural and plurilingual ESL teaching population understand their role as instructors of a colonial language in a multilingual settler context.

Moving forward, those wishing to use Landguaging exercises with pre-service and in-service teachers should ensure that each group has members with experiences from abroad to scaffold students who have never lived outside of settler-colonial territories. To further explore land-based relationships to language, instructors can use tools, like portraiture (which supports discussions of user's competing linguistic citizenships; Busch, 2012) or autobiographies (which facilitate connections between language practices and speech communities; Charity Hudley & Mallinson, 2014), as they both enable users to externalize metalinguistic critiques about their linguistic knowledges and ground them to place (see Chung & Chung Arsenault, 2023, for an example). To encourage students' pedagogical engagement with Landguaging, teachers must assess which plurilingual strategy best suits the discussion of the linguistic variety, cultural knowledge, and sociolinguistic practice of that target community. In doing so, students become better informed in making personal (i.e., subjective) decisions about how they want to connect to English, its colonial history, and its ongoing imperialism.

Conclusion

All language users live in relationship with their landscape, which is teeming with linguistic biodiversity and incongruent with the plantation-style monolingualism of colonial language policies. When ESL teachers develop curriculum that is land-sensitive and plurilingual, they confront the allochthonous relationship of English to the territory colonially known as Canada, and help dismantle settler-colonial pedagogies, which are socioculturally unethical and unsustainable in a linguistically biodiverse world. Inclusive language teaching curriculum is a strategic pedagogy of confronting systemic inequalities, identifying which voices are being excluded, and eliminating those language-related barriers by normalizing multidialectal and plurilingual language use on the land, which resists the assimilatory goals of settler-colonialism. As our inclusion model details, engaging the ecological perspectives of Landguaging via plurilingual instruction de-centres colonial languages and transforms the supposed L2 classroom into a translanguaging space, restoring the multilingual biodiversity of the landscape. Inclusivity means honouring the diverse voices of the land, and inclusive pedagogies are reflective actions that first must begin from within.

References

Anya, Uju. (2021). Critical race pedagogy for more effective and inclusive world language teaching. *Applied Linguistics, 42*(6), 1055–1069. https://doi.org/10.1093/applin/amab068

Armstrong, Jeannette. (2017). Land speaking. In S. McCall, D., Gaertner, D. Reder, & G. Hill (Eds.), *Read, listen, tell: Indigenous stories from Turtle Island* (pp. 141–155). Wilfrid Laurier University Press.

Auger, Nicole. (2005). *Comparons nos langues: une démarche d'apprentissage du français auprès des enfants nouvellement arrivés.* Centre régional de documentation pédagogique.

Battiste, Marie. (2013). *Decolonizing education: Nourishing the learning spirit.* Purich Publishing Limited.

Beauchamp, Catherine. (2015). Reflection in teacher education: Issues emerging from a review of current literature. *Reflective Practice, 16*(1), 123–141. https://doi.org/10.1080/14623943.2014.982525

Bhattacharya, Kakali. (2013). Voices, silences, and telling secrets: The role of qualitative methods in arts-based research. *International Review of Qualitative Research, 6*(4), 604–627.

Bhattacharya, Kakali. (2021). De/colonizing educational research. In *Oxford research encyclopedia of education* (pp. 1–19). https://doi.org/10.1093/acrefore/9780190264093.013.1386

Borg, Simon, & Edmett, Adam. (2019). Developing a self-assessment tool for English language teachers. *Language Teaching Research, 23*(5), 75–91.

Bronfenbrenner, Urie. (1993). The ecology of cognitive development: Research models and fugitive findings. In R. Wozniak & K. Fischer (Eds.), *Development in context: Acting and thinking in specific environments* (pp. 3–44). Lawrence Erlbaum.

Busch, Brigitta. (2012). The linguistic repertoire revisited. *Applied Linguistics*, *33*(5), 503–523.

Calderon, Dolores. (2014). Speaking back to manifest destinies: A land education-based approach to critical curriculum inquiry. *Environmental Education Research, 20*(1), 24–36.

Cenoz, Jason. (2017). Translanguaging in school contexts: International perspectives. *Journal of Language, Identity & Education, 16*(4), 193–198. https://doi.org/10.1080/15348458.2017.1327816

Charity Hudley, Anne, Bucholtz, Mary, & Mallinson, Christine. (2020). Toward racial justice in linguistics: Interdisciplinary insights into theorizing race in the discipline and diversifying the profession. *Language, 96*(4), e200–e235. https://doi.org/10.1353/lan.2020.0074

Charity Hudley, Anne, & Flores, Nelson. (2022). Social justice in applied linguistics: Not a conclusion, but a way forward. *Annual Review of Applied Linguistics, 44*, 144–154. https://doi.org/10.1017/S0267190522000083

Charity Hudley, Anne, & Mallinson, Christine. (2014). *We do language: English language variation in the secondary English classroom*. Teachers College Press.

Chung, Rhonda. (2020, May 4). A love letter to the land. *Belonging, Identity, Language, and Diversity*. http://bild-lida.ca/blog/uncategorized/a-love-letter-to-the-land-by-rhonda - chung/#more-3510

Chung, Rhonda. (2021, October 18). Part 1: Rocks are our oldest teachers. *Belonging, Identity, Language, and Diversity*.http://bild-lida.ca/blog/uncategorized/rocks-are-our-oldest-teach ers-by-rhonda-chung/#more-4508

Chung, Rhonda. (2022, February 28). Welcome to the Chungle: Reconnection as colonial defiance. *Belonging, Identity, Language, and Diversity*. http://bild-lida.ca/blog/uncategorized/welcome-to-the-chungle-reconnection-as-colonial-defiance-by-rhonda-chung/

Chung, Rhonda, & Cardoso, Walcir. (2022a). The art of "landguaging" in the city: Teacher reflection for inclusive linguistic futures. In T. Bastiaens (Ed.), *Proceedings of EdMedia + Innovate learning* (671–676). Association for the Advancement of Computing in Education. https://www.learntechlib.org/p/221355

Chung, Rhonda, & Cardoso, Walcir. (2022b). Variation in the L2 French audiovisual input: Ya basic! In J. Levis & A. Guskaroska (Eds.), *Proceedings of the 12th pronunciation in second language learning and teaching conference*. https://doi.org/10.31274/psllt.13264

Chung, Rhonda, & Chung Arsenault, Willem-Loup. (2023). Landguaging the L2 classroom: Inclusive pedagogies and land-sensitive curriculum through teacher reflection art. *Concordia Working Papers in Applied Linguistics, 7*, 29-54.

Clemons, Aris Moreno. (2024). Apolitical linguistics doesn't exist, and it shouldn't: Developing a Black feminist praxis toward political transparency. In Anne H. Charity Hudley, Christine Mallinson, & Mary Bucholtz (Eds.), *Decolonizing linguistics*. Oxford University Press.

Collin, Simon, Karsenti, Thierry, & Komis, Vassilis. (2013). Reflective practice in initial teacher training: Critiques and perspectives. *Reflective Practice, 14*(1), 104–117.

Cook, Vivian. (1999). Going beyond the native speaker in language teaching. *TESOL Quarterly*, *33*(2), 185–209.

Cook, Vivian. (2016). Where is the native speaker now? *TESOL Quarterly 50*(1), 186–189.

Coste, Daniel, Moore, Danièle, & Zarate, Geneviève. (1997/2009). Plurilingual and pluricultural competence. Council of Europe. https://rm.coe.int/168069d295

Council of Europe. (2020). Common European framework of reference for languages: Learning, teaching, assessment: Companion volume with new descriptors. Council of Europe. https://rm.coe.int/common-european-framework-of-reference-for-languages-learning-teaching/16809ea0d4

Cummins, Jim. (2007). Rethinking monolingual instructional strategies in multilingual classrooms. *Canadian Journal of Applied Linguistics/Revue canadienne de linguistique appliquée, 10*(2), 221–240. https://journals.lib.unb.ca/index.php/CJAL/article/view/19743

Cummins, Jim. (2021). The role of teachers as knowledge-generators and agents of language policy. In E. Piccardo, A. Germain-Rutherford, & G. Lawrence (Eds.), *The Routledge handbook of plurilingual language education* (pp. 112–129). Routledge.

dela Cruz, John Wayne N. (2022). "I subtitle myself": Affordances and challenges of Canadian EAL students' plurilingual learning strategies in a francophone college. *TESL Canada Journal, 38*(2), 36–62. https://doi.org/10.18806/tesl.v38i2.1356

dela Cruz, John Wayne N. (2023). Teaching and assessing plurilingually using the CEFR: Towards linguistically inclusive additional language instruction. *Concordia Working Papers in Applied Linguistics, 7,* 59-74.

Deloria Jr., Vines, & Wildcat, Daniel R. (2001). *Power and place: Indian education in America.* Fulcrum.

Ellis, Nick, & Wulff, Stefanie. (2020). Usage-based approaches to L2 acquisition. In B. VanPatten, G. D. Keating, & S. Wulff (Eds.), *Theories in second language acquisition: An introduction.* 3rd ed. (pp. 63–82). Routledge.

Farrell, Thomas. (2022). *Reflective practice in language teaching.* Cambridge University Press.

Figueroa, Megan. (2024). Decolonizing (psycho)linguistics means dropping the language gap rhetoric. In Anne H. Charity Hudley, Christine Mallinson, & Mary Bucholtz (Eds.), *Decolonizing linguistics.* Oxford University Press.

Flores, Nelson. (2016). A tale of two visions: Hegemonic whiteness and bilingual education. *Educational Policy, 30*(1), 13–38. https://doi.org/10.1177/0895904815616482

Flores, Nelson, & Rosa, Jonathan. (2015). Undoing appropriateness: Raciolinguistic ideologies and language diversity in education. *Harvard Educational Review, 85,* 149–171.

Fricker, Miranda. (2017). Evolving concepts of epistemic injustice. In I. Kidd, J. Medina, & G. Pohlhaus Jr. (Eds.), *Routledge handbook of epistemic injustice: Routledge handbooks in philosophy* (pp. 53–60). Routledge.

Galante, Angelica. (2021). Translation as a pedagogical tool in multilingual classes: Engaging the learners' plurilingual repertoire. *Journal of Translation and Translanguaging in Multilingual Contexts, 7*(1), 106–123. https://doi.org/10.1075/ttmc.00064.gal

Galante, Angelica, & dela Cruz, John Wayne. N. (2021). Plurilingual and pluricultural as the new normal: An examination of language ese and identity in the multilingual city of Montreal. *Journal of Multilingual and Multicultural Development.* https://doi.org/10.1080/01434632.2021.1931244

Galante, Angelica, Chiras, Maria, dela Cruz, John Wayne N., & Zeaiter, Lana F. (2022). *Plurilingual guide: Implementing critical plurilingual pedagogy in language education.* Plurilingual Lab Publishing.

Ghosh, Ratna, & Galczynski, Mariusz. (2014). *Redefining multicultural education: Inclusion and the right to be different.* 3rd ed. Canadian Scholars' Press.

Government of Canada. (2021). List of designated educational institutions. https://www.canada.ca/en/employment-social-development/programs/designated-schools.html

Henhawk, Daniel. (2013). My critical awakening: A process of struggles and decolonizing hope. *International Review of Qualitative Research, 6*(4), 510–525. https://doi.org/10.1525/irqr.2013.6.4.510

Hornberger, Nancy, & Link, Holly. (2012). Translanguaging and transnational literacies in multilingual classrooms: A biliteracy lens. *International Journal of Bilingual Education and Bilingualism, 15*(3), 261–278. https://doi.org/10.1080/13670050.2012.658016

James, Carl. (2008). Multiculturalism, diversity, and education in the Canadian context: The search for an inclusive pedagogy. In C. A. Grant & J. L. Lei (Eds.), *Global constructions of multicultural education theories and realities* (pp. 169–199). Lawrence Erlbaum.

Jay, Joelle, & Johnson, Kerri. (2002). Capturing complexity: A typology of reflective practice for teacher education." *Teaching and Teacher Education, 18*(1), 73–85.

Kleyn, Tatyana, & García, Ofelia. (2019). Translanguaging as an act of transformation. In L. C. de Oliveira (Ed.), *The handbook of TESOL in K-12* (pp. 69–82). Wiley.

Kouri, Scott. (2020). Settler education: Acknowledgement, self-location, and settler ethics in teaching and learning. *International Journal of Child, Youth and Family Studies, 11*(3), 56–79. https://doi.org/10.18357/ijcyfs113202019700

Kovach, Margaret. (2021). *Indigenous methodologies: Characteristics, conversations, and contexts.* 2nd ed. University of Toronto Press.

Kubota, Ryuko. (2020). Promoting and problematizing multi/plural approaches in language pedagogy. In S. M. C. Lau & S. Van Viegen (Eds.), *Plurilingual pedagogies: Critical endeavours for equitable language in education* (pp. 303–321). Springer.

Lau, Sunny Man Chu. (2022). Critical ESL education in Canada. In P. G. Price (Ed.), *The Oxford encyclopedia of race and education.* Oxford University Press.

Li, Wei. (2011). Moment analysis and translanguaging space: Discursive construction of identities by multilingual Chinese youth in Britain. *Journal of Pragmatics, 43,* 1222–1235.

Mace, William. (1977). James J. Gibson's strategy for perceiving: Ask not what's inside your head, but what your head's inside of. In R. Shaw & J. Bransford (Eds.), *Perceiving, acting, and knowing: Towards an ecological psychology* (pp. 43–65). Lawrence Erlbaum.

Macedo, Donaldo. (2019). Rupturing the yoke of colonialism in foreign language education: An introduction. In D. Macedo (Ed.), *Decolonizing foreign, second, heritage, and first languages* (pp. 1–49). Routledge.

Marshall, Steve, & Moore, Danielle. (2018). Plurilingualism amid the panoply of lingualisms: Addressing critiques and misconceptions in education. *International Journal of Multilingualism, 15*(1), 19–34. https://doi.org/10.1080/14790718.2016.1253699

Motschenbacher, Heiko. (2016). Inclusion and foreign language education: What linguistics can contribute. *International Journal of Applied Linguistics, 67*(2), 159–189. https://doi.org/10.1075/itl.167.2.03mot

Muñoz-Basols, Javier. (2019). Going beyond the comfort zone: multilingualism, translation and mediation to foster plurilingual competence. *Language, Culture and Curriculum, 32*(3), 299–321. https://doi.org/10.1080/07908318.2019.1661687

Nettle, Daniel. (1999). *Linguistic diversity.* Oxford University Press.

Otsuji, Emi, & Pennycook, Alastair. (2011). Social inclusion and metrolingual practices. *International Journal of Bilingual Education and Bilingualism, 14*(4), 413–426.

Patton, Michael. (2015). *Qualitative research and evaluation methods.* 4th ed. SAGE Publishing.

Pennycook, Alastair. (2022). Critical applied linguistics in the 2020s. *Critical Inquiry in Language Studies, 19*(1), 1–21.

Piccardo, Enrica. (2019). "We are all (potential) plurilinguals": Plurilingualism as an overarching, holistic concept. *Cahiers de l'ILOB/OLBI Working Papers, 10,* 183–204. https://doi.org/10.18192/olbiwp.v10i0.3825

Québec. (1977). *Charte de la langue française.* Publications Québec. http://www.legisquebec.gouv.qc.ca/fr/pdf/cs/C-11.pdf

Québec. (2021). *Projet de loi n° 96.* Québec Official Publisher. http://m.assnat.qc.ca/en/travaux-parlementaires/projets-loi/projet-loi-96-42-1.html

Saldaña, Johnny. (2021). *The coding manual for qualitative researchers.* 4th ed. SAGE Publishing.

Simpson, Leanne Betasamosake. (2014). Land as pedagogy: Nishnaabeg intelligence and rebellious transformation. *Decolonization: Indigeneity, Education & Society, 3*(3), 1–25.

Statistics Canada (2016). *The Aboriginal languages of First Nations people, Métis and Inuit.* https://www12.statcan.gc.ca/census-recensement/2016/as-sa/98-200-x/2016022/98-200-x2016022-eng.cfm

Sterzuk, Andrea. (2020). Building language teacher awareness of colonial histories and imperialistic oppression through the linguistic landscape. In D. Malinowski, H. H.

Maxim, & S. Dubreil (Eds.), *Language teaching in the linguistic landscape* (pp. 145–162). Springer.

Tanchuk, Nicolas, Kruse, Marc, & McDonough, Kevin. (2018). Indigenous course requirements: A liberal-democratic justification. *Philosophical Inquiry in Education*, *25*(2), 134–153.

Todd, Kamala. (director). (2008). *Indigenous plant diva* [film]. National Film Board of Canada. https://www.nfb.ca/film/indigenous_plant_diva/

Tuck, Eve, & Yang, K. Wayne. (2012). Decolonization is not a metaphor. Decolonization: Indigeneity, Education & Society, 1(1), 1–40.

UNESCO. (2017). *A guide for ensuring inclusion and equity in education*. UNESCO. https://inclusiveeducation.ca/wp-content/uploads/sites/3/2013/07/UNESCO-InclusionEducation.pdf

Van Lier, Leo. (2004). *The ecology and semiotics of language learning: A sociocultural perspective*. Springer.

Van Lier, Leo. (2011). Language learning: An ecological-semiotic approach. In E. Hinkel (Ed.), *Handbook of research in second language teaching and learning*, Vol. 2 (pp. 383–394). Routledge.

Whitley, Jess, & Hollweck, Trista. (2020). Inclusion and equity in education: Current policy reform in Nova Scotia, Canada. *Prospects, 49*, 297–312.

Wolfe, Patrick. (2006). Settler colonialism and the elimination of the native. *Journal of Genocide Research*, *8*(4), 387–409.

Wolfram, Walt. (1993). Ethical considerations in language awareness programs. *Issues in Applied Linguistics, 4*, 225–255.

Appendix

Landguaging Exercises (Individual and Group)

Locating the Classroom on the Land

1. **Individual Self-Location**
   a. Reflecting on your general educational experiences (i.e., elementary, high school, CEGEP/college, university):
      - Which land(s) were you educated on?
      - Who are the people indigenous to those lands?
      - Identify the sociocultural knowledges you were taught on these lands. Think about specific book you were assigned, the histories you were taught, the art and movies you've seen, the holidays celebrated, and the languages studied in class.
   b. Did your education include the sociocultural knowledge(s) of:
      - The people indigenous to the lands you were situated on?
      - Your own ancestral/ethnic background(s)?
      - Someone else? Who?
2. **Group Self-Location**
   a. In your ESL curricula, which sociocultural knowledges do you feel most comfortable teaching?
      - Those of the people indigenous to the land you were living on?
      - Those of your own ancestral/ethnic background(s)?
      - Someone else? Who?

Provide examples from ESL teaching activities to illustrate your point. Think about books, songs, movies, TV shows, or holidays discussed.

Locating the Language on the Land

1. **Individual Self-Location**
   a. Reflecting on your general language learning experiences (i.e., elementary, high school, CEGEP/college, university):
      • Which land(s) were you educated on?
      • Who are the people indigenous to those lands?
      • Identify the languages you've learned on these lands.
   b. Reflecting on your specific English-language learning experiences (i.e., elementary, high school, CEGEP/college, university), how many varieties/dialects of English were you exposed to? Think about books you've read, shows/movies you've seen, songs you've heard, and consider the generation/region it was from.
   c. Did your language education include that of:
      • The people indigenous to the lands you were situated on?
      • Your own ancestral/ethnic background(s)?
      • Someone else? Who?
2. **Group Self-Location**
   a. On what lands have you taught English?
   b. In that English curricula, which language(s) did you feel most comfortable including:
      • Those of the Indigenous peoples whose lands you were living on?
      • Those of your own ancestral/ethnic background(s)?
      • Those from your past educational experiences?
      • Someone else? Who?
   c. In your English curricula, did you feel comfortable including:
      • Multiple dialects of English?
      • Other languages?
      Provide examples from ESL/EFL teaching activities to illustrate your point. Think about poems, songs, movies, TV shows, or holidays discussed.
   d. What is the relationship between the dialects/language(s) you teach and know and the land you live on?

Lal Zimman is associate professor of linguistics and affiliated faculty in feminist studies and comparative literature at the University of California, Santa Barbara, where he runs the Trans Research in Linguistics Lab (TRILL). His research, teaching, and advocacy work has contributed to the development of trans linguistics, through which he draws on a range of qualitative and quantitative methods to investigate linguistic phenomena that impact the lives of trans people and communities. Zimman has published on gender difference in the voice and the practices of speech-language pathologists who work with trans people, the lexical strategies trans people use to challenge norms for talking about the gendered body, trans-inclusive language practices, changes in the use of singular "they," and the relationship between trans inclusion and anti-Blackness. He is also general editor for the Oxford University Press Series in Language, Gender, and Sexuality.

Cedar Brown is a PhD student in linguistics at University of California, Santa Barbara, where they have written an MA thesis on language change in an online trans community. Previously they completed their honours thesis at the University of Melbourne on pronoun sharing. They investigate changes regarding language and language practices drawing upon sociocultural linguistics, computational linguistics, sociophonetics, trans linguistics, raciolinguistics, and queer theory. They are coeditor and contributor to a special issue on trans linguistics that is forthcoming at *Gender and Language*.

Abstract: On college campuses working toward trans inclusion, instructors are often encouraged to ask students to share their pronouns on the first day of class. However, critics of this practice have suggested that it pressures students to out themselves or lay claim on an identity they may still be questioning. This chapter discusses the results of a survey of transgender students at a public California university, most of whom reported appreciating the opportunity to share their pronouns in class. However, the comments of students with more negative or ambivalent feelings about this norm allow the possibility of identifying contextual factors that make instructors more or less effective in creating a space in which trans students felt safe sharing their pronouns. Rather than promoting one-size-fits-all approaches to trans inclusion, the authors offer recommendations for more context-sensitive, flexible, and multimodal approaches to pronouns in the classroom that center and normalize trans students' pronouns.

Key Words: gender, pronouns, transgender, nonbinary, inclusive language, classroom practices

15

Beyond Pronouns 101

Linguistic Advocacy for Trans-Inclusive Language in the College Classroom

Lal Zimman (he/him or they/them)
University of California, Santa Barbara

Cedar Brown (they/them or he/him)
University of California, Santa Barbara

Introduction

Within a neoliberal university setting, diversity, equity, and inclusion (DEI) efforts frequently demand that student affairs staff develop and deliver workshops, training modules, and written guides to act as correctives to institutional inequality (e.g., Ahmed, 2012).[1] Many institutions have identified trans-inclusive language, and specifically pronouns, as an important domain for intervention; this focus is supported by a growing body of literature demonstrating that trans people's experiences with misgendering have significant impacts on their health and well-being (e.g., Ross et al., 2022; Sevelius et al., 2020). Trans-inclusive language trainings are typically designed to offer one-size-fits-all, simple solutions, such as those documented by Lal elsewhere (Zimman, 2017). These can ostensibly be implemented by all instructors, from experts in language and gender who are devoted trans allies—or trans themselves—to those trained in fields that tend to resist inclusion and diversity. Because educational institutions' engagements with DEI work are motivated largely by marketing concerns, publicity management, and self-protection against litigation (byrd, 2022; Urciuoli, 2003), they have minimal incentive to engage with sociolinguistic justice in nuanced ways. Within this structure, developing recommendations often falls on transgender students, junior faculty and underresourced staff in campus LGBTQ+ centers. Such essentialist logic leads to a kind of tokenization (see Yoo et al., 2023), in which trans individuals are expected to represent all trans people, distilling our experiences with inclusion and misgendering without being provided with

Lal Zimman and Cedar Brown, *Beyond Pronouns 101* In: *Inclusion in Linguistics*. Edited by: Anne H. Charity Hudley, Christine Mallinson and Mary Bucholtz, Oxford University Press. © Anne H. Charity Hudley, Christine Mallinson, and Mary Bucholtz 2024. DOI: 10.1093/oso/9780197755303 003.0016 the time or resources for deep systematic engagement. They must then navigate the institutional minefields surrounding "academic freedom"—a supposedly apolitical concept that purports to protect the intellectual activities of all faculty, but which is frequently mobilized to protect and perpetuate the influence of racist, transphobic, and otherwise oppressive ideas (miles-hercules, this volume; Pearce, 2021; Popowich, 2020; Sultana, 2018).

This chapter reveals how cookie-cutter recommendations for trans inclusion fail to represent the various complex ways trans, nonbinary, and gender-nonconforming students feel about being asked for their pronouns in class. We discuss a survey we conducted about transgender students' experiences with pronoun rounds, or exchanges in which people introduce themselves by providing their pronouns along with their names. The use of pronoun rounds on the first day of class is one of the most widespread approaches to trans inclusion in the classroom. For example, Tre Wentling's (2015) discussion of misgendering in academic contexts emphasizes, "Educators must create the space for students to introduce themselves with both their name and pronoun" (p. 474). As this sort of advice becomes increasingly common, more careful investigations are needed to explore how educators go about trying to create that space. Recently, linguists have begun to contribute to these conversations in greater depth by offering ethical, methodological, and pedagogical guidance on trans-inclusive language, particularly surrounding singular "they" (e.g., Anderson, 2022; Conrod, 2022; Melendez & Crowley, 2022).

As trans linguists, we see the tools of our discipline as having enormous potential to support advocacy around language and trans affirmation that has in many ways yet to be fulfilled (miles-hercules, this volume; Zimman, 2021). Yet cis linguists must also be cautious so as not to treat their own linguistic expertise as greater or more valuable than the lived linguistic knowledge that trans people carry. Toward this end, the chapter uses a trans linguistic (Zimman, 2020) methodology and analytic lens to highlight difficulties that student respondents to our survey of trans people at our university identified with classroom pronoun rounds and to identify ways college instructors can more effectively prevent misgendering in their classes. We therefore not only problematize the notion that quick and easy fixes can address the systemic problem of misgendering, but also follow critical theorists of trans education (e.g., Catalano, 2015; Martino et al., 2020; Miller, 2019; Siegel, 2019) and sociolinguistic justice in education (e.g., Bucholtz et al., 2014; 2016; Charity Hudley & Flores, 2022; Charity Hudley & Mallinson, 2018) by offering formalized alternatives and elaborations that are more context-sensitive and multimodal in nature.

Most participants in our survey had a positive view of being asked for their pronouns (Zimman et al., 2022), but in this chapter we highlight the complexity of students' feelings about this practice. In their comments, students noted several problematic aspects of the way pronoun rounds are often enacted: the creation of unwanted visibility for trans people; making pronoun requests in ways that reinforce the normativity of cis identities; how instructors and other class members behave during and after pronoun rounds, such as whether people's stated pronouns are actually used; and the way pronoun rounds can limit the fluidity of gender. We then offer ways that instructors in general and linguists in particular can contribute to efforts to address trans inclusion within the classroom (and beyond). In order to avoid the shortcomings of one-size-fits-all recommendations, we identify ways to improve pronoun round practices that take into account the particular contexts in which they occur. At the same time, our discussion can only provide a snapshot of some current norms and practices surrounding the use of trans people's pronouns, and these norms are certain to shift over time. Trans-inclusive language requires an ongoing commitment: As trans activists advance new understandings of trans affirmation and update our language accordingly, so too must cisgender (i.e., nontransgender) allies be receptive to shifts in the repertoire of trans-inclusive language. Pronoun rounds are, on their own, woefully insufficient to address transphobia, within or outside of the classroom. Instead, pronouns remain just one small part of the work that must be done to address the many harms of transphobia, including how it intersects with racism, ableism, heterosexism, and classism. However, trans allies' pronoun-related practices can open the door to build coalitions between trans and cis people with a range of positionalities and relationships to systemic power (Cohen, 1997).

Analysts, Data, and Methods

This section offers context regarding our subjectivities as authors, our data, and the methods used in the analysis to follow.

Who We Are

We write this chapter as social beings with personal, political, and intellectual investments in trans inclusion and affirmation. Because we approach our research as whole human beings, we wish to present some aspects of our positionality that shape our approach to what is written here. Among the characteristics we share is that we are settlers who must acknowledge the ways we have benefitted from the ongoing exploitation of the Indigenous peoples on whose land we have done the research discussed in this chapter, including the Chumash (Santa Barbara, California) and Wurundjeri-Woi Wurrung and Boonwurrung (Melbourne, Australia) peoples.

Lal

I am an associate professor in the linguistics department at the University of California, Santa Barbara (UCSB), a public research-intensive university on Chumash land. I grew up in an affluent part of California within a white and Middle Eastern family that gave me the kind of freedom that allowed me, at age 14, to drop out of high school, come out as trans, and shortly thereafter move to San Francisco, enroll in community college, and begin my transition. By the time I was first exposed to pronoun rounds, which was around the time I finished my PhD in 2012, I had long since reached a sense of equilibrium with my identity as a queer man. Pronoun rounds came too late to impact the ways I was misgendered during my transition, but my relationship with pronouns has nevertheless evolved over time. Although I continue to identify most strongly with he/him pronouns, I find they/them pronouns comfortable and value the way they make my trans identity more visible. Because I began studying linguistics before trans language had become a matter of so much public and academic attention, while still a junior scholar I had both the opportunity and the challenge of charting out an area of study that I have come to call trans linguistics (Zimman, 2020). A central facet of trans linguistics is its grounding in the linguistic needs of trans communities, an emphasis that comes naturally from the fact that it is a field driven by trans scholars. Equally important is what kinds of trans people are doing the driving, and my opportunity to have an early emphasis on this now-blossoming area of study is undoubtedly related to the ways I have benefited—if at times tenuously or complicatedly—from male, white, and class-based privilege throughout my lifetime.

My first published work on trans-inclusive language (Zimman, 2017; 2019b) emerged from workshops I began giving on the subject while teaching at Reed College in Portland, Oregon in 2013–2014, a time and place in which the idea of asking everyone in a classroom about their pronouns was just beginning to take hold. At UCSB, I wanted to expand this connection between research and service to include teaching, so I created a class called "Trans Initiatives in Linguistics." In the class, students collaborate on projects designed to use the tools of linguistics to address the needs of trans, nonbinary, and gender-nonconforming people at the university, especially students but also faculty and staff. It is within this class, for which Cedar has served as Teaching Assistant, that the survey discussed in this chapter was carried out.

Cedar

My involvement in university, arts, and activist spaces across the 2010s coincided with increased awareness of nonnormative pronoun usage and led to me increasingly being in spaces where pronoun sharing occurred. I have had and continue to have a complicated relationship with pronouns, and sharing pronouns has always felt like an uncomfortable negotiation frequently accompanied by anxious spiralling. I began to look at pronoun sharing for my postbachelor honours thesis when I was not yet out as trans. Consequently, coming out and exploring my identity on a personal level has unfolded in conversation with my academic work on pronoun sharing, a practice which often functions as a coming out itself. My honours research involved conducting interviews with community-member experts in Melbourne, Australia (on Wurundjeri-Woi Wurrung and Boonwurrung land) and Washington, DC (on Nacochtank land). I found the practice of interviewing on this subject deeply moving—laden with moments of laughter, moments of connection, and moments where I was brought to tears by what people shared with me. Many of the complexities that I had felt personally around trans-inclusivity practices were reflected, expanded, and extended by the sharings of others. Moving to UCSB for graduate school and working with Lal has allowed me to develop these ideas further through systematically looking at the experiences and practices of people in a single location within a single institution. As I continue with this work, I also continue to reflect on how the stakes of pronouns and pronoun sharing are less pressing for me than for many others who are trans or gender nonnormative. Being a transmasculine nonbinary person who is often unwantedly perceived as a woman is complex and upsetting. However, in contrast to many transfeminine people or otherwise amab (assigned male at birth) nonbinary people, being visibly gender-nonconforming is something that has actually increased my feelings of safety in public spaces, rather than decreased them, as I feel myself getting less unwanted attention than I did when I presented and was perceived as more feminine. While I am still constantly vigilant around transphobia, my whiteness and unmarkedness in other aspects also impacts the way my transness is received by others. Being a grad student at a California university with a trans adviser and many trans and otherwise queer peers has led me to feel a sense of safety in my workplace that I didn't previously experience. That type of safety is not experienced by many people I have spoken to over the course of this research, who may be the only trans person in an organisation or feel that coming out may jeopardise their job or academic standing. I am very aware of the material stakes of sharing pronouns within hostile environments and a goal of my scholarly work is to extend solidarity and support to those currently in that position.

Survey on Pronoun Rounds at UCSB

Our discussion in this chapter draws on the results of the survey project conducted by Lal with the members of the Trans Initiatives in Linguistics class described above, including Cedar as well as Teaching Assistants Brooke English, Aris Keshav, Jordan Tudisco, and students Alice Blank, Jung Ho Hahm, Levi Huntley, Julia Leary, Alex Pigeon, and Forest Stuart. We triangulate our results by drawing on some of the findings from Cedar's previous interview-based research on pronoun rounds (Brown 2020, under review). This component of the research establishes that the patterns we have discovered are not unique to UCSB, but rather reflect broader experiences shared by many trans people who are part of communities where pronoun rounds are practiced.

The UCSB survey was administered in early 2020, although data collection was cut short by the COVID-19 pandemic. The survey questions asked students about their academic experiences, community support, identities, basic needs, and other topics. Language-related questions focused on administrative data (i.e., how the university deals with names and pronoun information), being asked for pronouns in academic settings, and grammatical gender in language classes (e.g., whether students avoided studying languages with binary grammatical gender systems or whether instructors recognized nonbinary options). The survey was designed in Fall 2019 and administered anonymously online via Qualtrics between January and March 2020.[2] Respondents were recruited from a number of sources, including email lists and social media accounts for the UCSB Resource Center for Sexual and Gender Diversity and official and unofficial trans/queer student groups, flyers posted on and off campus, and word of mouth. Participants were not directly compensated, but were given the opportunity to enter a raffle for one of 10 gift cards worth $25 each. All names used in this chapter are pseudonyms.

An important aspect of this study is whose perspectives are represented within its responses. There were approximately 80 respondents who answered at least some sections of the UCSB survey, primarily undergraduate (74%) and graduate students (19%), with slightly different sets of questions depending on university role (grad, undergrad, faculty, or staff). Participants were free to respond to as many or as few questions as they wished, and not all respondents completed the survey, so the number of responses per question varies between 50 and 80; most of the questions discussed here have 54 to 56 student responses. All respondents were transgender, nonbinary, and/or gender-nonconforming. In discussing the results, we use *trans+* as an umbrella term for anyone whose gender identities and/or presentations go beyond what is expected based on their sex assignment at birth, whether or not they identify with the label "trans." Most respondents described themselves as nonbinary (76%), in many cases along with other categories. The next biggest group was trans men (12%), while trans women consisted of just 5% of respondents and 4% described themselves as gender-nonconforming (but not trans or nonbinary). Most respondents identified with they/them pronouns (82%), either exclusively (28%) or in combination with she/her and/or he/him (54%).

Another important aspect of the survey data is whose perspectives are missing from it. Trans women, transfeminine people, and other people who were assigned male at birth are highly underrepresented at just 22%. In addition, despite UCSB being a designated Minority-Serving Institution, trans+ people from ethnoracial groups underrepresented in academia also consisted of only 22% of responses: 18% were Latinx, compared to 27% of all students at UCSB (UCSB Institutional Research, Planning & Assessment 2022); 4% were Native American, compared to 1% of all students; and 2% were Black, compared to 4% of all students. Additionally, 20% identified as Asian/Asian American or Pacific Islander (compared to 28%), 4% as Middle Eastern or North African (not collected by the university), and 2% as "Other" (compared to less than 1% in the university's data). White respondents, meanwhile, were overrepresented at 52% (compared to 38%). One in five respondents chose more than one category, the most common combination of which was Asian/Pacific Islander and white. The overrepresentation of whiteness also shaped our approach to our analysis, which we describe in the next section.

The patterns of representation in our survey may be related to the structural and material impacts of transphobia—poverty, homelessness, poor health, and physical and sexual violence—which are born disproportionately by trans women and trans feminine people of color (e.g., Grant et al. 2012). Though trans people in the United States seek and earn postsecondary degrees at rates higher than the general population (Grant et al. 2012, p. 39), our data suggests that the same intersectional disparities are reflected in trans student populations, at least in the population of students who are sufficiently connected to the resources and networks we used to recruit survey participants—such as UCSB's Resource Center for Sexual and Gender Diversity, trans student groups, and digitally mediated groups networks informally connected to the university—and to have the time and emotional bandwidth to participate in it.

Methods

In our discussion of the survey that follows, we focus on responses to a specific set of questions regarding pronoun rounds. Student participants were asked how they felt about being asked to share their pronouns in class. They had the option to select any combination of the answers: "Positive. Overall, I like being asked in this context (or would like to be)," "Neutral, uncertain, or conflicted," "Negative. Overall, I don't like being asked in this context (or would not like to be)," and "Other." Those who indicated that they felt positively were then given a list of potential reasons to choose from (Table 15.1), while those who indicated negative feelings were given a separate list (Table 15.2). Respondents who indicated uncertainty or ambivalence, or who selected "Other," were given an open-form text box in which to write their answers. Our lists of potential reasons for and against pronoun rounds were developed collectively by members of the Trans Initiatives in Linguistics class. As community-insider researchers (see Clemons, 2024; De Jesus, this volume), we were able to draw on our lived experiences as trans people to imagine numerous potential reasons students might have for their positive or negative feelings. The fact that only a few participants selected "Other" reasons for or against pronoun rounds (see Tables 15.1 and 15.2) suggests that we were successful in our attempt to provide a comprehensive list to choose from.

Because our data overrepresents white trans+ people and transmasculine people, we intentionally highlight the contributions of respondents who are transfeminine and/or people of color. We take as instructive that both of these groups are relatively well-represented among those who expressed less than positive feelings about pronoun rounds.

Trans+ Students' Responses to Pronoun Rounds

The overall picture of the UCSB survey indicates that most of the 54 respondents to questions about pronoun rounds (70%, n = 38) reported positive feelings about being asked for their pronouns in the classroom, while a smaller number expressed a negative view (13%, n = 7). The remainder indicated that they felt uncertain or ambivalent, though some of these selected both "positive" and "uncertain."

Table 15.1 Reasons given for positive orientation to pronoun rounds in responses to UCSB survey

Reason	# of responses (out of 38)
"It creates visibility for trans+ people."	n=31 (82%)
"I want to make sure I get everyone else's pronouns right."	n=31 (82%)
"I prefer to share my pronouns before anyone has to guess which one to use."	n=25 (66%)
"Other students respond more positively to my pronouns when the teacher establishes that pronouns are important."	n=24 (63%)
"I want to show my support for or solidarity with people who use they/them or other nonbinary pronouns."	n=24 (63%)
"People often get my pronouns wrong unless they are told which ones to use."	n=23 (61%)
"I feel like it validates my identity."	n=21 (55%)
"I like sharing my pronouns with everyone."	n=18 (47%)
"I prefer to share my pronouns in a group."	n=12 (32%)
Other	n=2 (1%)

Table 15.1 lists the answer options presented to respondents who reported positive feelings about pronoun rounds and the frequency with which each response was selected.

Most frequently, survey respondents said they liked that sharing pronouns in introductions creates visibility for trans+ people and helps them avoid misgendering others as well as avoiding being misgendered themselves. Quite a few preferred being asked over letting people guess or assume their gender, which they reported frequently led to them being misgendered. The instructor's authority was an important part of pronoun rounds for many respondents as well. Pronoun rounds were seen as both validating trans+ identities and showing solidarity with people who use they/them pronouns. Some respondents also addressed practical considerations, such as the preference to tell everyone their pronouns or to do so in a group. Respondents who selected "Other" gave slight variations on these responses.

It is notable how few respondents reported preferring to share their pronouns in a group context, compared to other reasons for feeling positive about pronoun rounds. This suggests that the desire to avoid misgendering is strong enough that it overrides the discomfort many trans+ people feel about pronoun sharing in group settings, as suggested by the responses in Table 15.2.

Among the seven students in the UCSB survey who indicated a negative view of classroom pronoun rounds, the most common reason was that it draws unwanted attention to them or to trans+ people in general. This is

Table 15.2 Reasons given for negative orientation to pronoun rounds in responses to UCSB survey

Reason	# of responses (out of 7)
"It draws too much attention to me and/or other trans+ people."	n=6 (86%)
"I don't like sharing my pronouns with strangers."	n=3 (43%)
"It feels awkward or instructors don't do it well."	n=3 (43%)
Other	n=3 (43%)
"Other students respond negatively."	n=2 (29%)
"I want to know what pronouns people will use for me if they have to assume."	n=2 (29%)
"I think it's unnecessary to ask people about their pronouns. People who use unexpected pronouns will just let others know."	n=2 (29%)
"I prefer to share my pronouns one-on-one."	n=1 (14%)
"I feel like it invalidates my identity."	n=1 (14%)

essentially the inverse of one of the most common reasons selected by those who like pronoun rounds in classrooms, namely that it creates visibility for trans+ people. The next most commonly selected reasons were not wanting to share pronouns with strangers and feeling that the practice is awkward or poorly executed by instructors. A few students were also concerned about negative responses from other students, preferred to share pronouns in one-on-one contexts, or felt that sharing pronouns invalidated their identities and that they would rather let people make an assumption about their pronouns. Two people felt that students who use "unexpected pronouns" (i.e., pronouns other than those that would likely be normatively assigned to them) should take the initiative to share them instead of everyone being asked.

Based on examination of the open-form comments contributed by participants who selected "Uncertain" or "Other" options in response to questions about classroom pronoun rounds, we identified four major themes regarding the undesirable aspects of pronoun rounds in classes: unwanted visibility, how the instructor executes the communicative event, how the pronouns are taken up by the instructor and other students, and limitations that pronoun rounds impose on the fluidity of gender. Many of these themes are also evident in Cedar's interviews (Brown 2020, forthcoming), and we quote responses from those interviews below to provide broader contextualization for the UCSB survey results.

While a traditional approach to survey data would put more value in the large number of positive responses, we use a negative case analysis approach (Emigh, 1997; Tenzek, 2017), in which negative responses are the primary focus. We excavate our results in this way to highlight the experiences of students who are not being served by current institutionalized practices of pronoun sharing.

Unwanted Visibility

The themes of unwanted visibility and being publicly outed were common in the open responses of participants who selected "Uncertain" or "Other" regarding how they feel about being asked for their pronouns in the classroom (mentioned by 89% of the 19 who left such comments). Respondents described the experience as "uncomfortable," "unnerving," and "othering." Certain contextual factors contributed to these feelings as well, including the size of the class, its subject matter, and whether other trans+ people were visible in the space or whether the students had pre-existing relationships with others in the class. Overall, trans+ students' assessment of the safety of a given classroom significantly impacted whether they felt they could share their pronouns. Jessie, a 31-year-old white nonbinary transfeminine UCSB undergraduate, stated "It feels remarkably unsafe to out myself to a large classroom." Even where safety was not explicitly referenced, participants were clearly attuned to the population of the class. This was the case for Alex, a 21-year-old transfeminine nonbinary Latinx and white undergraduate, who wrote, "it's really unnerving to be the only one in a class that uses different pronouns" than what others expect from them.

The theme of unwanted visibility could also be seen in the conversation that Cedar had with Carmen S, a South Asian genderqueer arts practitioner living in Melbourne, who did not identify with any pronouns at the time of the interview. In talking with Cedar about the experience of starting to use the name Carmen S instead of a pronoun, Carmen S described feeling "a little bit panicked" when asked to provide name and pronouns. Although a pronoun round ostensibly signals openness to whatever form of reference its participants might name, Carmen S reported an internal monologue including the question, "What do I say that won't like suddenly become a ruckus?" (Brown, 2020, p. 51). In this way, Carmen S oriented to the potential disruption of a self-introduction that deviates from the expected and recognizable responses: the pronoun sets she/her, he/him, or even they/them. The fact that Carmen S considered the various options with an eye toward finding one that wouldn't be disruptive further underscores the heightened attention and scrutiny that trans+ people often feel during a pronoun round.

Because contextual factors shaped whether students felt uncomfortably singled out or placed at the center of attention while sharing their pronouns, there is no single way of doing pronoun rounds that will work equally well in every case. In fact, reliance on one-size-fits-all approaches to pronoun rounds may actively undermine students' ability to feel safe in class.

Instructor Execution

The second set of objections to pronoun rounds in the survey responses concerns the way the instructor executes the communicative event. While asking for pronouns is often strategically positioned in DEI trainings as "easy" or "simple" in order to encourage instructors to implement the practice, some ways of asking were recognized as helpful by participants in our study and others problematized. Instructors' power and authority can be harnessed to make space for people to share their pronouns and have them respected. However, it also creates a responsibility for the instructor. In cases where authority figures do not effectively establish a trans-affirming space, it sets a tone of disrespect that is reproduced by other students.

In the UCSB survey, trans+ students identified several types of instructor behavior that worked against the creation of a space where students felt they could safely share their pronouns. One of the most commonly problematized behaviors was asking students about their pronouns on a selective basis, seemingly based on who the instructor perceived to be trans. Marc, a 26-year-old Black trans man who was a UCSB undergraduate, expressed ambivalence about pronoun rounds in classes: "Unless the practice of asking everyone in a space for their pronouns is more normalized and widespread, I'm skeptical of the benefits it can produce." This issue is so common that it is frequently addressed in pronoun trainings, workshops, and resources for university instructors. Such resources often explain that asking only those who "look trans" about their pronouns means missing anyone who does not fit a stereotyped notion of what a trans+ person looks like. If these already marginalized trans+ people want to make their pronouns known, they must then find a way to assert them without instructor support, potentially calling attention to the fact that they were assumed to be cisgender. Despite widespread encouragement to ask everyone in a class to share their pronouns, one quarter of our survey respondents had been singled out by an instructor, sometimes in front of the entire class, to be asked for their pronouns.

Another problematic aspect of instructors' implementations of pronoun rounds that was discussed by participants was the presence or absence of an explanation about why pronouns were being requested. Although some students are well-versed in pronoun rounds, at least some cisgender students in any given class are likely engaging in this communicative practice for the first time, such that its norms might be considered part of the hidden curriculum (Mantenuto et al., this volume; Sanders et al., this volume). They may be unfamiliar with the norms and functions of pronoun rounds, leaving them without a sense of how to participate or what to do with the information their classmates provide.

A final theme in participants' comments about instructor implementation of pronoun rounds was whether pronoun sharing seemed mandatory. This situation was described by several people as creating a forced choice between either outing themselves as trans+ or misgendering themselves and inviting others to do the same. Even trans people who are comfortable sharing their identities may feel that identifying themselves as trans+ in a classroom risks invoking transphobia or unequal treatment. Marc, the Black trans man quoted earlier, also noted that pronoun sharing is "a good concept in theory," but one that could "still force people to misgender themselves/share the wrong pronouns in order to be taken seriously."

At the same time, other students found it more difficult to share their pronouns when the practice was clearly optional. This tension occurred in part because participants noted that cisgender people often fail to share their pronouns even when asked to do so. This tendency can turn into a chain reaction in which cis student after cis student introduces themself without pronouns, whether out of forgetfulness, active resistance, or simply the expectation that their pronouns will be respected whether they specify them or not. When it comes time for a person who wants to share their pronouns to do so, they must essentially single themself out and call attention to their identity through the sudden shift back to mentioning pronouns. As Daniel, a 20-year-old Latinx trans man undergraduate, put it, students in a pronoun round "tend to stop adding in their pronouns for whatever reason and are not reminded to add them," which makes him "uncomfortable to say [his pronouns] after a long string of others not saying them."

Some of these behaviors, such as avoiding only asking individuals who "seem trans" for their pronouns, can be and frequently are targeted in DEI training. However, the deeper engagement required to explain the purpose of pronoun rounds to students is often neglected, even by instructors with familiarity with gender and language or trans inclusion. Additionally, making pronoun sharing optional while still incentivizing those who are comfortable naming their pronouns to do so requires a more complex set of discursive strategies, as we discuss later in this chapter.

How Requests Are Taken Up

The third major objection to pronoun rounds in classrooms had to do with the way instructors and other students responded when pronouns were shared as well as whether they actually used those pronouns. Respondents reported that people reacted to pronoun sharing through marked facial expressions, gaze, or laughter, including laughing when providing their own pronouns. This behavior was also highlighted in conversations from Cedar's previous research. In one such conversation (Brown 2020, p. 57–58), Jon (no pronouns), a white nonbinary transfeminine person involved in community organizing spaces in Washington, DC, talks about cisgender people's disrespect toward pronoun sharing. Jon describes how cis people and deeply closeted trans people (who, despite being affected by transphobic systems and behaviours, can nonetheless act in ways that perpetuate cisnormativity and transphobia which harm other trans people) "sometimes laugh it off." Jon highlights the contrast between a perception of "being funny" with the actuality of "being hostile." This hostility was located in the "mak[ing] real light" of pronoun sharing, where the implied cisnormativity was seen as expressing disaffiliation toward those for whom pronoun rounds are important.

For many survey participants, asking for pronouns was meaningless or even actively harmful if those pronouns were not then used by members of the class. Several participants had low expectations for the likelihood or even the possibility that others would gender them correctly. Gabi (they/them), a 20-year-old Latinx and Native American nonbinary undergraduate, said, "I know some people will not use my pronouns and it's likely the teacher will forget as well." Alex, the 20-year-old Latinx and white transfeminine undergraduate quoted earlier, was even more pessimistic: "Even if I were confident enough to say that I use they/them pronouns, people would forget in the middle of the quarter or just give me looks. So I don't bother and just use he/him pronouns to not stick out." To quote Nour, a 20-something Moroccan genderqueer/gender-nonconforming/nonbinary person in Cedar's previous work, "It's often worse to have people misgender you after you've explicitly shared your pronouns" (Brown 2020, p. 49).

Additionally, our survey participants indicated they would like more agency over how misgendering is handled in class. That is, they hoped for an opportunity to indicate to an instructor or teaching assistant whether corrections should take place in the moment, later on, or not at all; whether it depended on who did the misgendering (a fellow student versus an instructor or teaching assistant); and who should issue corrections, if anyone. Because this information can become complicated if students' preferences depend on contextual factors, it is likely impossible for a pronoun round to convey all the metalinguistic information needed to create an affirming space for trans+ people's pronouns.

Limiting the Complexity and Fluidity of Gender

The final major objection to pronoun rounds on the first day of class is that they limit the complexity and fluidity of gender. Pronoun rounds are typically done only once in any given class, with the assumption that names and pronouns do not change unless someone indicates otherwise. Yet the logic of the pronoun round is based in the recognition of how difficult it can be for an individual to volunteer their pronouns unasked, and their purpose is therefore to normalize communicating about how we refer to one another.

People who are exploring their gender or have a fluid experience of gender may especially appreciate opportunities to answer the question of pronouns in a context-sensitive way. That is, rather than a one-time request in response to which everyone is expected to make a definitive statement about their pronouns, pronoun exchanges are ideally part of ongoing conversations. Especially if students want to get a sense of the class community before sharing pronouns, the first day of class is often not the best time to collect that information. Exemplifying the idea that pronoun conversations should be ongoing was a comment from Sarah, a 28-year-old Middle Eastern/North African trans woman graduate student: "The framing I have heard that I like best is 'What pronouns would you like to use right now in this space?'"

Summary

The survey we have discussed in this chapter indicates that many transgender, nonbinary, and gender-nonconforming students appreciate being asked for their pronouns in the classroom. At the same time, respondents' feelings depended on several contextual factors. Students said they felt more comfortable sharing their pronouns in smaller classes, classes with other visible trans+ students, and classes that address gender-related content. It was critical that all members of a class be asked for their pronouns so that trans+ people were not singled out or made the focus of attention. They also found it easier to share their pronouns when they didn't have pre-existing relationships with other students from contexts in which they were not out as trans. How the instructor led the pronoun rounds was of great importance, and the example set by those in power was recognized as highly influential. Instructors were most effective at creating space for trans+ students to share their pronouns when they included an explanation for why pronouns were being requested and when they set the expectation that members of the class use one another's stated pronouns. Participants also identified benefits of asking for pronouns regularly, rather than just once, and in ways that are more context-specific. One of the paradoxes in the study was that, on one hand, participants stressed that it was difficult to share their pronouns when it seemed mandatory, but that it was also hard to reinsert pronouns when cisgender students opt not to share their own. In an attempt to reconcile these complicating factors, we now turn to our recommendations for college instructors.

Recommendations

Based on our research, we offer below a set of recommendations for more effective implementations of classroom pronoun rounds in ways that recognize trans people's complex feelings about these communicative events. Because we are critical of any broad-brush recommendations surrounding pronouns, we offer the following actionable steps paired with ideas for how to take context into account when implementing them.

1. **Asking everyone** for their pronouns can be a critically important practice for making trans people feel included. However, this does not mean the question should be asked in the same way in every setting. Especially in classes that are large, have few or no visibly trans or gender-nonconforming members, or address content far removed from gender or other social issues, students should be given more options for sharing their pronouns, such as either in class or privately via a student survey or email. In short, **class size, course content, and student population should be taken into account**; when in doubt, it is wise to lean toward giving students greater flexibility about whether and how to share their pronouns. At the same time, a large class full of students unlikely to be well-versed in trans inclusion should not be used as an excuse to avoid talking about pronouns, but an opportunity to begin that work, demonstrate to trans students that you understand the importance of their needs, and create options for trans students to share their pronouns if they so desire. A survey can also give students the option to indicate what they would like to happen if they are misgendered in class, an example of which can be found on the supplementary website associated with these

volumes. If you are unfamiliar with pronouns and trans issues, it can be daunting to approach sharing pronouns in a context-dependent way, without having a fixed, universally applicable template. However, we encourage you to think critically about how the themes we have identified in our chapter may show up in the space you are facilitating or teaching and to be responsive and curious. If you receive negative feedback from students, it is not that you have necessarily done it "wrong," but that you may need to challenge or update the logics and principles you have been applying to pronoun sharing.

2. It is important to **talk about why** you are asking for pronouns, to give examples of how pronouns tend to be shared (e.g., the she/her/hers template), and to set expectations about behavior during and after the pronoun round. It can be helpful to remind students that gender identity is not necessarily visible, and that, in order to respectfully refer to one another, it is important to ask and then listen to the answer. Your course policies surrounding in-class interactions—something all instructors should have—should also include respectful use of pronouns. The goal of such a policy is not to be punitive, but to set an expectation that members will collectively work to acknowledge and respect the humanity of those in the classroom through preventing misgendering. Additionally, it is important to tell students that pronouns can be difficult to share and to clarify that responding to the practice or to classmates' answers with laughter or derision can create a hostile learning environment for their peers and will not be tolerated. Developing and practicing explanations for the rationale and behavior around pronoun sharing in advance can be helpful for those who are new to such discussions. It can also be an ongoing discussion throughout the course, so it is not too late to discuss such things even if you haven't included it in the course policy or the first few weeks of class. On the supplementary website associated with these volumes, we provide examples of explanations for why pronoun rounds are important and how they can be included in course policies. It also includes links to some short videos in which trans people speak about pronouns that you can play for your class as part of establishing expectations.

3. Students should be **encouraged, but not required,** to share their pronouns. But because the absence of a pronoun might be an intentional choice rather than forgetfulness, we recommend referring to students who do not share a pronoun as they/them unless otherwise instructed. If this policy is made clear before a pronoun round, cis students who go by she/her or he/him may be more motivated to remember to specify their

pronouns, whereas students who use they/them are centered, normalized, and given the latitude that cis people typically enjoy: to name their pronouns or not. Importantly, this strategy requires you to become an effective user of they/them pronouns. Familiarize yourself with guides that explain how to use singular "they" such as those provided by the Modern Language Association, University of Chicago English Language Institute, and the Linguistic Society of America (LSA). Tools also exist to help you practice using these pronouns, and links to all of these resources can also be found on the website. We understand that using they/them pronouns for everyone who doesn't share their pronouns in class can be intimidating—and this is something that we, as trans instructors ourselves, don't always do perfectly. However, in order to foster a classroom environment that does not prioritize cis students and does not encourage the arrogant assumption that you know someone's gender better than they do, it is a practice that we can all strive towards. It is crucially important, however, that you don't disproportionately use they/them pronouns for students you perceive as gender-nonconforming and binary pronouns for others but, rather, apply a blanket policy of referring to all students as their stated pronouns or they/them.

4. Asking about pronouns **need not be limited to the beginning of the term or to specific modalities.** Very small classes can start each meeting with brief check-ins from students that include names and pronouns. Some larger classes can set a norm where students are invited to share names and/or pronouns before they raise a question or make a comment. Students can also use or make name/pronoun placards, stickers, or other visual ways to signal how they should be referred to. Classes can also maintain spreadsheets or other databases of information (e.g., on course management software) where students can update information about how people should refer to them. Sofia Melendez and Archie Crowley (2022) discuss a variety of strategies for collecting and sharing pronoun-related information along with more in-depth discussion of each option than we can provide in this space; their work is highly recommended.

5. When mentoring trans students, **there are many ways to support them** as students, scholars, and human beings. Start by ensuring that they are connected with trans people, communities, and resources, both on campus and beyond. Some universities are well-equipped with trans-informed LGBTQ+ centers, while others may have fewer or no formal resources; especially in the latter case, it is important to know safe individuals to whom students can turn and who can help students feel

prepared and supported for whatever they might face. In some cases, there may be more community to be found off campus than on, and distance from isolating campus communities may sometimes be what is needed (see also De Jesus, this volume). Looking beyond campus can also involve connecting students with national resources. Within linguistics, there are the Association for Nonbinary and Trans Language Researchers (ANTLR) and the LSA's Committee on LGBTQ+[Z] in Linguistics (COZIL); these are welcoming spaces for trans linguists regardless of research area. There are also interdisciplinary spaces in which trans scholars who study trans topics can connect, such as the Lavender Languages and Linguistics Conference and Summer Institute and the Center for Applied Transgender Studies. Links for all of these groups can be found on the companion site.

As we work toward these goals, it is critical to be mindful of the ways trans inclusion and representation may enact other forms of marginalization. This can happen when transness is represented by relatively privileged trans people and when efforts to prevent or address misgendering fail to account for the different opportunities students may have had to learn about trans-inclusive language depending on their linguistic, cultural, and educational histories, among other factors. Just as our analytic method focused on trans participants who are also subject to racism and/or transmisogyny, we encourage linguists to focus specifically on the ways trans people of color, trans femmes, disabled trans people, and people whose cultural systems include other models of gender-nonconformity (who may or may not use the word "trans") are served or not by inclusion efforts.

Conclusion

Linguists have a critical role to play in advancing inclusive pronoun practices within our institutions. As we have shown, linguistic research, especially when done by insider researchers, can shed light on how pronouns function in trans people's lives. Linguists are also well-positioned to settle debates about pronouns that often take place around trans inclusion: We can share our knowledge that pronouns have always been political (Bodine, 1975; Silverstein, 2003), that languages differ widely in the kinds of distinctions their pronouns do and do not make (Hellinger & Bußmann, 2001), and that changes in singular "they" have been taking place for quite some time (Anderson, 2022; Conrod, 2020). In many campus communities, this linguistic work is already underway and could benefit from the authority that linguists-as-accomplices can offer (Arnold, 2019; Bucholtz et al., 2016). At the same time, cis linguists should take care not to treat their linguistic expertise as greater than the lived linguistic knowledge that trans people already hold. Furthermore, pronoun-related activism should push linguists to reconsider aspects of our professional training that are incompatible with meaningful advocacy for trans inclusion, such as the way we talk about grammatical prescriptivism and descriptivism. Resistance to prescriptivism has strong political potential when used to question linguistic hierarchies and inequalities, but the same stance can also be abused as a justification for misgendering people (Conrod, 2022; miles-hercules, this volume), and our students deserve clarification on where we truly stand.

Linguists have a unique opportunity—and, as a result, a responsibility—to use our course content to support trans advocacy, but unfortunately this obligation remains largely unmet. The first day of class can involve not just an invitation to share pronouns but time for talking about pronouns and related aspects of language as part of the academic material. This approach is important considering how few students are exposed to open classroom conversations about why pronoun rounds are used. The links to pronoun use in sociocultural linguistics are especially clear, but there are many possibilities for making connections across linguistics. Classes in linguistic structure or typology might consider the ways social and grammatical meaning is encoded in languages; historical linguists could focus on the processes through which pronominal systems can change; and morphosyntacticians can interrogate the very category of pronoun. Courses that investigate the voice, cognition, and other topics through experimental methods can discuss how gender is often naturalized and treated as a simple physiological binary in scientific research and how this limits knowledge production (Zimman, 2018; forthcoming; miles-hercules, this volume). A class on sign language linguistics or other highly embodied forms of language might offer alternative ways for thinking about bodies that transcend socially constructed binaries (Moges, 2020). Introductory linguistics classes could use pronouns as a first foray into discussing prescriptivism, language ideologies, or the creation of testable hypotheses. At the same time, it is important to approach these discussions with care and intentionality. If you feel uncertain about your ability to direct such a discussion, make sure you do the necessary homework by reading linguistic research that takes a trans-inclusive approach to gender in pronouns and other grammatical forms. We recommend offering preparatory reading material for students as well, such as one of the academic or nonacademic pieces linked from the resources on the companion website or short summaries of key content following the lecture notes genre described by Nathan Sanders, Pocholo Umbal, and Lex Konnelly (this volume). Cis linguists should seek input from student affairs staff and—with appropriate compensation for their expertise—trans students and colleagues, and they should always teach such content under the assumption that trans people are present in the room, even if no one openly identifies as such. At well-resourced institutions, professional trans consultants can be hired to do in-depth reviews of classroom practices. The companion website also includes an outline for a lesson on pronouns, grammatical gender, and singular "they" that could be adapted for courses in a variety of subfields.

Finally, these practices should not be limited to engagements with students, but should inform all of our relationships, professional and otherwise. Assumptions around what pronouns people use are just as harmful to trans people in publications as they are in the classroom, and our discipline should develop equitable norms around pronouns in citation such as listing authors' pronouns along with their names (as these two volumes do), confirming the pronouns of the scholars we cite, or avoiding pronouns and using they/them pronouns in cases where an author's pronouns cannot be confirmed. While professional conferences frequently offer pronoun badges or stickers to add to name tags, we have seen trans attendees be misgendered even while wearing colorful tags that boldly read "THEY/THEM" (Zimman, 2019a). Research participants are likewise frequently placed into binary gender categories and referred to with binary pronouns without much thought about what assumptions this practice imposes on the data, let alone the humans represented by it. Even those of us who think carefully about pronouns in academic or activist settings may revert to binary assumptions in other parts of our lives. There is much work to be done.

Trans inclusion and transphobia must be addressed throughout the discipline, and trans linguists need cis linguists' support to do it. However, this goal is not possible without the presence of a critical mass of trans linguists to guide these efforts. The classroom therefore presents an especially potent opportunity to create spaces of affirmation and learning through which trans students' linguistic activism can be nurtured. Professional organizations are frequently slow or reluctant to take strong stances in support of trans people—troublingly, the LSA did not release a statement against misgendering until 2021 (Ananthanarayan et al., 2021)—and universities are often more worried about the institutional repercussions of limiting transphobia than about the impact transphobia has on trans students and employees. It is therefore all the more critical that classrooms become spaces in which trans people are cherished and trans well-being is prioritized. Trans-inclusive and trans-affirming language cannot undo systems of oppression on their own, but they can function as harm reduction strategies that allow new generations of trans linguists to emerge and trans students in all disciplines to thrive.

Notes

1. Our greatest thanks to participants in our research and students in the Trans Initiatives class at UCSB: Alice Blank, Brooke English, Jung Ho Hahm, Levi Huntley, Aris Keshav, Julia Leary, Alex Pigeon, Forest Stuart, and Jordan Tudisco. We also extend gratitude to members of the Trans Research in Linguistics Lab at UCSB for their feedback, especially Jazmine Exford, Dozandri Mendoza, and Jordan Tudisco, who shared with us their experiences doing (trans-)inclusive language trainings while working in student services positions. Finally, we thank attendees at the 2022 Meeting of the Society for Linguistic Anthropology for their comments and questions as well as the editors and reviewers for this volume for their valuable feedback and guidance.
2. The study (exempt protocol 5-19-0894) was approved by UCSB's Institutional Review Board on November 25, 2019.

References

Ahmed, Sara. (2012). *On being included: Racism and diversity in institutional life*. Duke University Press.

Ananthanarayan, Sunny, Bradley, Evan, Conrod, Kirby, Crowley, Archie, Inscoe, J., Konnelly, Lex, & Zimman, Lal. (2021). LSA statement against linguistic misgendering. https://www.linguisticsociety.org/content/lsa-statement-against-linguistic-misgendering

Anderson, Catherine. (2022). Pronouns and social justice in the linguistics classroom. *Journal of Language and Sexuality, 11*(2), 251–263.

Arnold, Lynnette. (2019). Accompanying as accomplices: Pedagogies for community engaged learning in sociocultural linguistics. *Language and Linguistics Compass, 13*, e12329.

Bodine, Ann. (1975). Androcentrism in prescriptive grammar: Singular "they," sex-indefinite "he," and "he or she." *Language in Society, 4*(2), 129–146.

Brown, Cedar. (2020). *They identify themselves: Ideology and identity in pronoun sharing practices* [Honours thesis, University of Melbourne].

Brown, Cedar. (forthcoming). Misgender or out yourself: Vulnerability in pronoun sharing practices. *Gender and Language*.

Bucholtz, Mary, Lopez, Audrey, Mojarro, Alina, Skapoulli, Elena, VanderStouwe, Chris, & Warner-Garcia, Shawn. (2014). Sociolinguistic justice in the schools: Student researchers as linguistic experts. *Language and Linguistics Compass, 8*(4), 144–157.

Bucholtz, Mary, Casillas, Dolores Inés, & Lee, Jin Sook. (2016). Beyond empowerment: Accompaniment and sociolinguistic justice in a youth research program. In Robert Lawson & Dave Sayers (Eds.), *Sociolinguistic Research: Application and Impact* (pp. 25–44). Routledge.

byrd, derria. (2022). How diversity fails: An empirical investigation of organizational status and policy implemented on three public campuses. *Education Sciences, 12*(3), Article 211.

Charity Hudley, Anne H., & Mallinson, Christine. (2018). Introduction: Language and social justice in higher education. *Journal of English Linguistics, 46*(3), 175–185.

Charity Hudley, Anne H., & Flores, Nelson. (2022). Social justice in applied linguistics: Not a conclusion, but a way forward. *Annual Review of Applied Linguistics, 42,* 144–154.

Clemons, Aris Moreno. (2024). Apolitical linguistics doesn't exist, and it shouldn't: Developing a Black feminist praxis toward political transparency. In Anne H. Charity Hudley, Christine Mallinson, & Mary Bucholtz (Eds.), *Decolonizing linguistics.* Oxford University Press.

Cohen, Cathy J. (1997). Punks, bulldaggers, and welfare queens: The radical potential of queer politics? *GLQ: A Journal of Lesbian and Gay Studies, 3*(4), 437–465.

Conrod, Kirby. (2020). Pronouns and gender in language. In Rusty Barrett & Kira Hall (Eds.), *The Oxford handbook of language and sexuality.* Oxford University Press. Online pre-print: https://academic.oup.com/edited-volume/42645/chapter-abstract/358160984.

Conrod, Kirby. (2022). Variation in English gendered pronouns: Analysis and recommendations for ethics in linguistics. *Journal of Language and Sexuality, 11*(2), 141–164.

Catalano, D. Chase J. (2015). "Trans enough?" Pressures trans men negotiate in higher education. *TSQ: Transgender Studies Quarterly, 2*(3), 411–430.

Emigh, Rebecca Jean. (1997). The power of negative thinking: The use of negative case methodology in the development of sociological theory. *Theory and Society, 26*(5), 649–684.

Grant, Jaime M., Mottet, Lisa A., Tanis, Justin, Harrison, Jack, & Keisling, Mara. (2012). *Injustice at every turn: A report of the national transgender discrimination survey.* National Center for Transgender Equality and the National Gay and Lesbian Task Force.

Hellinger, Marlis, & Bußmann, Hadumod. (Eds.). (2001–2003). *Gender across languages: The linguistic representation of women and men* (Vols. 1–3). John Benjamins.

Martino, Wayne, Kassen, Jenny, & Omercajic, Kenan. (2020). Supporting transgender students in schools: Beyond an individualist approach to trans inclusion in the education system. *Educational Review, 7*(4), 753–772.

Melendez, Sofia, & Crowley, Archie. (2022). Pronoun practices in the higher education classroom. *Journal of Language and Sexuality, 11*(2), 264–277. doi:10.1075/jls.20022.cro

Miller, sj. (2019). *About gender identity justice in schools and communities.* Teachers College Press.

Moges, Rezenet. (2020). The signs of Deaf female masculinity: Styles of gendering/queering ASL. In Kira Hall & Rusty Barrett (Eds.), *The Oxford handbook of language and sexuality.* Oxford University Press. Online preprint: https://academic.oup.com/edited-volume/42645/chapter-abstract/402650399

Pearce, Ruth. (2021). Academic freedom and the paradox of tolerance. *Nature Human Behaviour, 5,* 1461.

Popowich, Sam. (2020). The antinomies of academic freedom: Reason, trans rights, and constituent power. *Canadian Journal of Academic Librarianship / Revue Canadienne de bibliothéconomie universitaire, 6,* 1–28.

Ross, Lori E., Kinitz, David J., & Kia, Hannah. (2022). Pronouns are a public health issue. *American Journal of Public Health, 112*(3), 360–362.

Sevelius, Jae M., Chakravarty, Deepalika, Dilworth, Samantha E., Rebchook, Greg, & Neilands, Torsten B. (2020). Gender affirmation through correct pronoun usage: Development and validation of the Transgender Women's Importance of Pronouns (TW-IP) Scale. *International Journal of Environmental Research and Public Health, 17*(24), Article 9525. 10.3390/ijerph17249525

Siegel, Derek P. (2019). Transgender experiences and transphobia in higher education. *Sociology Compass, 13,* e12734.

Silverstein, Michael. (2003). Indexical order and the dialectics of sociolinguistic life. *Language & Communication, 23*(3–4), 193–229.

Sultana, Farhana. (2018). The false equivalence of academic freedom and free speech: Defending academic integrity in the age of white supremacy, colonial nostalgia, and anti-intellectualism. *ACME: An International Journal for Critical Geographies, 17*(2), 228–257.

Tenzek, Kelly E. (2017). Negative case analysis. In Mike Allen (Ed.), *The SAGE encyclopedia of communication research methods*, 4, (1085–1087). SAGE Publishing.

UC Santa Barbara Institutional Research, Planning & Assessment. (2022). 2021–2022 Campus profile: University of California, Santa Barbara. https://bap.ucsb.edu/institutional-research/campus-profiles

Urciuoli, Bonnie. (2003). Excellence, leadership, skills, diversity: marketing liberal arts education. *Language & Communication, 23*(3), 385–408.

Wentling, Tre. (2015). Trans* disruptions: Pedagogical practices and pronoun recognition. *TSQ: Trans Studies Quarterly, 2*(3), 469–476.

Yoo, Joyhanna, Lee, Cheryl, Cheng, Andrew, & Ànand, Anusha. (2023). Asian American racialization and model minority logics in linguistics. *Daedalus, 152*(3), 130–146. https://www.jstor.org/stable/48739986

Zimman, Lal. (2017). Transgender language reform: Some challenges and strategies for promoting trans-affirming, gender-inclusive language. *Journal of Language and Discrimination, 1*(1), 84–105.

Zimman, Lal. (2018). Transgender voices: Insights on identity, embodiment, and the gender of the voice. *Language and Linguistics Compass, 12*(8), e12284.

Zimman, Lal. (2019a). Getting pronoun badges right: Five recommendations for event organizers. *Trans Talk*. https://medium.com/trans-talk/getting-pronoun-badges-right-five-recommendations-for-event-organizers-5458116b2ffc

Zimman, Lal. (2019b). Pronouns and possibilities: Transgender language activism and reform. In Netta Avineri, Laura R. Graham, Eric J. Johnson, Robin Conley Riner, & Jonathan Rosa (Eds.), *Language and Social Justice in Practice* (pp. 176–183). Routledge.

Zimman, Lal. (2020). Transgender language, transgender moment: Toward a trans linguistics. In Kira Hall & Rusty Barrett (Eds.), *The Oxford handbook of language and sexuality*. Oxford University Press. Online preprint: https://academic.oup.com/edited-volume/42645/chapter-abstract/358161844

Zimman, Lal. (2021). Beyond the cis gays' cis gaze. *Gender and Language, 15*(3), 423–429.

Zimman, Lal. (forthcoming). What is a gendered voice? Intersectional perspectives on ethics, empiricism, and epistemologies in the sociophonetics of gender. In Sam Gray, Akshay Aitha, Kutay Serova, & Madeline Snigaroff (Eds.), *Proceedings of Chicago Linguistics Society, 58*.

Zimman, Lal, Brown, Cedar, Leary, Julia, English, Brooke, Tudisco, Jordan, Keshav, Aris, Stuart, Forest, and Blank, Alice. (2022). *Trans+ at UCSB: Report on a 2020 survey*. Trans Research in Linguistics Lab. https://trillucsb.org/resources-and-projects/trans-at-ucsb-reports.

Florian Schwarz is associate professor and undergraduate chair of linguistics at the University of Pennsylvania, where he also serves as the associate director for Education of MindCORE, Penn's hub for the integrative study of the mind. His research focuses on meaning, combining formal tools from semantics and pragmatics with experimental methods from psycholinguistics to study phenomena such as presuppositions, implicatures, and definite descriptions. He is associate editor of the Open Access journal *Glossa Psycholinguistics*, founded in 2021, as well as of *Natural Language Semantics*. Together with Anna Papafragou, he initiated the interdisciplinary conference *Experiments in Linguistic Meaning*. With Jérémy Zehr, he maintains PCIbex, a free and Open Access online experiment platform. In his teaching, he strives to make formal concepts and approaches accessible, and to provide an inclusive and welcoming environment to all students, as reflected in particular in his active learning version of Linguistics 106: Introduction to Formal Linguistics.

Abstract: One part of working toward more diversity in linguistics is to make introductory courses more welcoming and inclusive. The need for this is especially pressing in theoretical and formal linguistics, where the lack of diversity is particularly pronounced. Active learning pedagogy has been shown to be a useful tool toward this goal, especially when paired with focused efforts toward creating an inclusive classroom culture. The author reports on his conversion of Linguistics 106: Introduction to Formal Linguistics to an active learning class format, reporting both the details of implementation and data on class outcomes and evaluations. Overall, the outcomes suggest that the new format enhances student performance and provides a more inclusive class experience. While no formal data on the impact on specific racial backgrounds is available, there is hope that these changes especially benefit students from diverse backgrounds and contribute toward making introductory linguistics teaching more welcoming and inclusive.

Key Words: formal linguistics, syntax, semantics, active learning, flipped classroom, pedagogy

16

Increasing Inclusion Through Structured Active Learning

Curriculum Changes in an Introduction to Formal Linguistics Class

Florian Schwarz (he/him/his)
University of Pennsylvania

Introduction

Various minoritized groups remain underrepresented in linguistics, and working toward changing this takes efforts at many levels. Many institutions have statements of commitments to making the field and its context in academia more inclusive and diverse. The Linguistic Society of America's Committee on Ethnic Diversity in Linguistics was founded on the recognition that "some ethnic and racial minorities . . . are significantly underrepresented in the linguistics workforce, . . . and that it is in the interest of the field of linguistics . . . to be enriched by the participation of all its ethnic groups" (LSA, 1994). Similarly, many universities, such as the University of Pennsylvania (Penn) where I work, have explicit general commitments to inclusion: "We must take responsibility for creating curricula and . . . learning environments that are affirming and inclusive" (Penn Arts & Sciences, 2020). But bringing about concrete changes requires individual action, ideally with support aligning with these commitments from the relevant institutions. This chapter describes an effort in this direction that I have made in my introductory teaching, with various forms of support from Penn.[1]

Working toward greater inclusivity in introductory undergraduate teaching is one important piece of the overall endeavor. If the first encounter with the field fails to provide an inclusive environment, this inevitably undermines long term work toward diversity and inclusion. The issue seems particularly pressing on the formal and technical side of linguistics, where the lack of diversity is perhaps most pronounced, and where the subject matter and the way it is taught are commonly seen as off-putting to students of color

Florian Schwarz, *Increasing Inclusion Through Structured Active Learning* In: *Inclusion in Linguistics*.
Edited by: Anne H. Charity Hudley, Christine Mallinson and Mary Bucholtz, Oxford University Press.
© Anne H. Charity Hudley, Christine Mallinson, and Mary Bucholtz 2024. DOI: 10.1093/oso/9780197755303.003.0017

as well as those with less technical academic background. As a white male trained in traditional theoretical linguistics working at an Ivy League institution, I've come to realize that maintaining the status quo in my teaching is the default, and that working toward any change would require comprehensive efforts. At the same time, I recognize that I face limitations in what I can do based on my own background that is very much aligned with the lack of diversity in the field. But I decided to seriously face the question of how I can make my teaching more inclusive and accessible to a wider range of students. Research on science, technology, engineering, and mathematics (STEM) teaching points to structured active learning pedagogy as an effective tool for increasing inclusion. This chapter describes how I converted my class Linguistics 106: Introduction to Formal Linguistics, which covers concepts from discrete mathematics as tools for syntax and semantics, to what at Penn is called Structured Active In-Class Learning (SAIL).[2] I report data from three instances of the class postconversion from 2019 to 2021 with some comparison to preconversion instances in 2014, 2016, and 2018.

My efforts were supported by Penn's Center for Teaching and Learning (CTL) through a SAIL grant in 2018–2019 and an accompanying year-long SAIL seminar, as well as through continuing training for teaching assistants. CTL also separately offers a seminar for faculty on inclusion in the classroom, which I subsequently participated in. Furthermore, Penn's College of Arts and Sciences supported the class financially by providing funding for undergraduate learning assistants (whose role is described in more detail below) after the first year in the new format.

Active Learning as a Tool for Inclusion

Active learning pedagogy (sometimes also referred to as "flipped" or "inverted" classroom teaching) has been argued to enhance the learning experience of all students while also increasing inclusion. Its general approach is to reduce class time spent on lecturing to allow students more active engagement with course materials during class. There also is an emphasis on student engagement with materials before and after class, as well as a shift to more frequent, low-stakes assessments, with less emphasis on exams. A meta-analysis by Scott Freeman and colleagues (2014) aggregates extensive evidence showing that active learning leads to general performance improvements in STEM classes. More recently, another meta-analysis on the impact of active learning on underrepresented minoritized and low-income students concludes, "Active learning benefits all students but offers disproportionate benefits for individuals from underrepresented groups. Widespread implementation of high-quality active learning can help reduce or eliminate achievement gaps in STEM courses and promote equity in higher education" (Theobald et al., 2020, p. 6476). (Active structured learning can also be highly effective in online and hybrid teaching environments (Gavassa et al., 2019), which aligns with my experiences during the last two offerings of my course during the COVID-19 pandemic.) An analysis of underlying factors contributing to the enhanced benefits of this approach for some student populations finds that homework and the frequent opportunity to practice were especially valued by Black students (Eddy & Hogan, 2014). Furthermore, the authors report that in a traditionally taught version of the class, "Black students were significantly less likely . . . to speak up in class, but this disparity disappeared under moderate structure. We suspect that the increased sense of the classroom as a community may have contributed to this increased participation" (Eddy & Hogan, 2014, p. 465).

Given that a decreased sense of belonging in students from underrepresented groups has been argued to affect decisions against majoring in STEM fields (Rainey et al., 2018), the potential for such positive impacts of active learning pedagogy on inclusion is both promising and important. But as Elli Theobald and colleagues (2020) recognize, structuring a class's curriculum along active learning principles alone "is not a silver bullet for mitigating achievement gaps" (p. 6479). They propose a "heads-and-hearts hypothesis," pairing active learning pedagogy with a culture of inclusion, which emphasizes "treating students with dignity and respect . . . and demonstrating a genuine interest in students' intellectual and personal growth and success." In line with this, I set out to both utilize active learning pedagogy as a tool for inclusion while also paying special attention to providing an inclusive classroom culture in the specific implementation of this approach.

Converting a Formal Linguistics Class to Active Learning

Linguistics 106: Introduction to Formal Linguistics has been offered at Penn since 1997, and was intended as complementing Linguistics 001: Introduction to Linguistics by providing more in-depth coverage of formal tools from discrete mathematics and their use in theoretical linguistics. I took over teaching of this class in 2009, and over time adapted the previous format and content to more directly integrate analysis of linguistic phenomena using these formal tools and added a section on my own area of semantics to complement the previous focus on syntax. The overall emphasis is on general conceptual grounding and gaining facility with formalisms. In its current form as I have developed it over the years, the class covers four main areas. The first module introduces set theory. The next module introduces formal language and automata theory, including regular and more complex languages. The third module explores context-free grammars for modeling parts of English syntax. The final module introduces basic set-theoretic semantics, including basic statement logic. The overall goal is to introduce students to the use of formal tools in linguistic theory and to hone general analytical reasoning skills. These are of use across the many disciplines and directions that the enrolled students, who come from a diverse range of academic backgrounds, wind up pursuing.

The course is introductory with no prerequisites. It satisfies two general education requirements in Penn's College of Arts and Sciences: the formal reasoning and analysis foundational requirement, satisfied by courses that "focus on deductive reasoning and the formal structure of human thought, including its linguistic, logical and mathematical constituents. These courses emphasize mathematical and logical thinking and reasoning about formal structures and their application to the investigation of real-world phenomena." And the sector requirement on natural science across disciplines, which is satisfied by classes with "diverse perspectives generated by applying the principles of the natural sciences to broader applications." The class generally enrolls close to 50 students, including everyone from freshmen to seniors from various academic backgrounds, making for a diverse group with respect to familiarity with formalisms. In terms of racial background, enrollment typically mirrors that of Penn undergraduate students overall, with roughly 8% Black students, 10% Hispanic/Latinx students, and overall 53% female students.[3] Many humanities students see the class as a welcome alternative to the other course options for satisfying the college requirements, which most prominently include calculus. But there also are students from computer science and engineering, who are curious how formalisms familiar to them are utilized in linguistics. While the class is not required for the linguistics major, it is a common entry-level course for students that later join the major.

The nature of the materials, together with the diverse range of academic backgrounds of enrolled students, naturally lends itself to an active learning format. For most students, the formalisms covered in the class are entirely new, and mastering them requires a substantial leap from passively grasping the main gist of a given topic to actively being able to apply the relevant analytical tools in problem-solving. This requires ample opportunity for practice with structured support along the way.

The original class structure was traditional, with two 50-minute lectures per week and one additional meeting of two smaller recitation sections led by a graduate teaching assistant. Some of the elements of the course structure before conversion might already be considered moderately structured in accordance with the active learning literature, in that homework and quizzes counted toward the bulk of the grade, with less weight given to the midterm and final exam: Nine homework assignments counted for 60% of the grade, and short daily quizzes after class for 10%. A midterm and final exam each counted another 15%.

A common complaint from students before the course conversion was lack of opportunity to practice skills before being evaluated for performance. While they appreciated the regular hands-on practice that came with homework, the fact that these assignments provided the first extensive opportunity for practicing skills but also counted toward 60% of the course grade made this less productive and more stressful than ideal for an initial phase of learning. Review and discussion in recitation sections also did not seem to offer enough active engagement with the materials, based on students' reports. And while lectures frequently incorporated questions for the students, contributions mostly came from a small number of students with a strong formal background, typically mostly male and with white or Asian background. Hearing only these students talk in class may have intimidated others, undermining their confidence in their own abilities. While I often stressed to students that the best way to learn was to practice using the formal tools on their own, there wasn't enough opportunity to do so with the original course structure.

Reflecting on these issues over the years and having made various smaller scale changes along the way, I came to realize that a more substantial overhaul was needed to make the class content more relatable and accessible, and to provide a more inclusive and engaging environment for all students. I applied for a SAIL grant from Penn's Center for Teaching and Learning and began the planning of the new format in spring 2018 and participated in CTL's SAIL seminar in the academic year 2018–2019. The new version of the class, with two extended 80-minute meetings per week to incorporate time previously used for recitation sessions, dedicates class time almost exclusively to hands-on problem-solving in small groups, paired with structured work before and after class. The previous lecture content was condensed into one to three short video lectures per class, lasting 15 to 25 minutes in total. Students were encouraged to further engage with the lecture materials using the extensive written lecture notes, which were prepared by me and formed the basis of the video lecture content. It is worth noting that making the core class content available asynchronously has the advantage of supporting different learning styles. For each video, there was a short quiz due before class, to be completed within a fairly limited amount of time (15–20 minutes). A total of 30 quizzes counted for 20% of the grade, with generous partial credit given for any answer attempts, in line with a low-stakes approach that allows students to demonstrate their current level of understanding without undue impact on their grade. The quiz questions drew on the previously used daily quizzes and basic-level questions from homework from the old course format. Other questions from preconversion homework assignments focusing mostly on more complex problems formed 10 revised homework assignments worth 30% of the grade. The midterm and final exams remained essentially unchanged in both format and weight (15% each) from the earlier version of the course.

The in-class group work formed the heart of the new class setup. I set up groups of four or five students in a semirandom fashion, starting from a completely randomly created list and then adjusting to balance out gender, seniority, and backgrounds. When possible, two or more students of color were grouped together to provide the opportunity of them working together. Groups were changed in the middle of the semester following the same approach, but also taking into account performance to date (including the midterm), only combining students in the bottom and middle third, as well as the middle and top third in one group to avoid large performance spans within groups, which can be counterproductive and lead to frustration over time. Students worked at a table with ample access to whiteboard space (during online teaching, Zoom breakout rooms were used). I started each class with a brief review of core concepts, then the groups turned to the day's problem sets. These generally began with basic applications of a given formalism (e.g., solving set-theoretic equations) and then continued to more complex and open-ended problems (e.g., constructing an automaton that models a certain formal language). Problem sets were split into basic problems and challenge problems to provide enough stimulating materials for all students without expecting everyone to finish all problems. Each group member was assigned a rotating role, such as scribe, a reporter who presented group work to class, whiteboard person, or manager, as recommended by Kathryn Johnson (2019, p. 210). A new grade component for group work participation counted for 20% of the grade. Rather than evaluating participation based on amount of work completed or points for correct answers, full credit was given for "making a good faith effort," which was understood as actively participating in groupwork, and the group as a whole working on the in-class problem sets throughout a given class. (Given high overall student commitment to in-class work, usually everyone present earns full participation credit, with very few individual exceptions over the years.)

In addition to the changes in class structure and pedagogical approach, various concrete steps were taken to actively foster a welcoming and inclusive environment in the classroom. One important ingredient was the addition of two undergraduate learning assistants to the instructional team. These are typically recruited from students who previously took the class, with the aim of reflecting the gender and racial diversity of the students taking the class. In addition to ensuring sufficient levels of support for group work, including undergraduate students in the instructional team serves to lower the barrier for students to reach out with questions and problems of understanding, as some may have reservations about approaching more senior members of the instructional team with such issues. Furthermore, both graduate and undergraduate student members of the instructional team participated in the CTL's SAIL TA training, which includes sessions on managing group dynamics, giving feedback and providing guidance for students to work through resolving questions they have along the way.

During class sessions, each of the four of us (graduate TA, two undergraduate TAs, and myself) attended to three of the 12 tables, rotating across class sessions. We answered specific questions or went over particular issues upon request, or just dropped by and listened in to stimulate discussion as needed. In doing so, we strived to encourage questions at all levels, and to ensure that all students in a given group were actively involved in the problem-solving process. Occasional breaks brought back the entire class to go over common issues or let groups report on their work. To set the stage at the beginning of the semester, I presented recommendations for group work that highlighted the diverse academic backgrounds in the class, with varying degrees of ease with formalisms, in the first class. The key guideline was to "help each other learn: If you already know materials well, use this as a challenge to think through teaching them to others. If all is new to you, don't be shy to ask questions" (Schwarz, 2021). In addition, students were asked to be kind and patient with each other and encouraged to call on the instructional team for help. Finally, advice from prior students on how to do well in the class, taken from a feedback survey administered at the end of semester (discussed below), was shared.

Outcomes and Evaluation of New Class Format

The conversion was successful as measured by attendance rates, student performance, and student evaluation responses and feedback. One commonly voiced concern about providing virtually all course content outside of class time is whether students will bother to come to class at all. The participation component of the course grade, cumulatively worth 20%, aimed to counter this potential challenge. While no precise quantitative comparison is possible due to lack of attendance data preconversion, attendance clearly was not an issue after the conversion, and most likely increased substantially compared to previous lecture attendance. Students very rarely missed class, not only because attendance was worth some points, but also because they experienced class time as extremely valuable learning time, as witnessed by the student feedback discussed below. Also worth noting, not only but especially in the context of the many challenges during the COVID-19 pandemic, is that the administration of in-class problem sets via Canvas, the learning management system used at Penn, made it easy for students with excused absences to complete assignments on their own, enabling them both to engage with the relevant materials and to earn participation points. More generally, having these materials available both in class and outside of class provides flexibility for students with different learning styles and for those who don't do well with group work, as they can continue work on these on their own if desired.

Grade outcomes by class format for 286 students (140 in traditional format, 146 in SAIL) are summarized in Table 16.1. Grades are higher in the active learning format.

I had originally hoped to include racial background in my analysis of course performance data. However, access to official data on this is considered sensitive by the administration, and to date I do not have access to the relevant information. I therefore can only report statistical analyses on the general impact of the new course structure on student performance overall. Mixed-effect models with a random slope for year were fit in R using the lme4-package to test for statistical significance of the differences, with p-values from the lmerTest package. As a proxy for the amount of background on and ease with working with formalisms, STEM major was included as a second factor, in addition to class format, to separately capture potential variation in student backgrounds across class instances. Total grades were higher in the SAIL versions ($\beta = .051$, SE $= 0.013$, $p < .05$) and for STEM majors ($\beta = .037$,

Table 16.1 Percentage of total points by grade category and class format in the traditional and new versions of Linguistics 106

Format	Total	Exams	Homework	Quizzes
Traditional	87.3%	87.3%	88.8%	78.5%
SAIL	92.5%	90.8%	92.4%	91.8%

SE = 0.009, p < .001). While there was no significant interaction (p =.35), the increase for SAIL was numerically greater for non-STEM majors: pairwise comparisons using the emmeans package find a significant increase of 6.0 percentage points (SE = 0.016, p <.05) for these, versus a marginally significant 4.3-point increase for STEM majors (SE = 0.016, p = .052). A parallel pattern was found for exam grades, with a 3.3-point increase for SAIL and a 6.2 increase for STEM; again, the SAIL effect was driven by non-STEM students (non-STEM: β = .046, SE = 0.015, p < .05; STEM: β = .020, SE = 0.016, p = .48). For homework, the SAIL effect was marginally significant (β = 0.37, SE = 0.015, p =.064), while the STEM major effect remained robust (β = .032, SE = 0.009, p < .001). The SAIL effect was comparable numerically for both major groups. Quizzes saw the most dramatic increase in the SAIL format (β = .13.3, SE = 0.020, p < .01), likely at least in part due to removing more complex and advanced questions; there also was a STEM effect (β = .033, SE = 0.012, p < .01), and no clear difference in SAIL effect across major types.

In sum, grades improved throughout in the SAIL version, compared to the traditional format. STEM majors had higher grades than non-STEM majors both before and after the conversion, but at least numerically, the gap between them shrank through more pronounced improvements for the latter group. (However, statistically, this did not reach the level of a significant interaction.) This can be seen as a form of greater inclusion in general terms, making mathematical formalisms more uniformly accessible to different students. Due to the lack of access to demographic information on students' racial backgrounds, I cannot directly assess at the moment how the changes impacted students from different backgrounds specifically. But given that the present findings align with prior results showing that active learning improves overall student performance, together with findings from earlier work that students from underrepresented groups disproportionately benefit from this teaching format, there is reasonable hope that the changes I made in my pedagogical approach have real potential to increase inclusion in this formal introductory linguistics class.

Students' course evaluations also indicate that the new format is more effective. Penn's standard course evaluations allow for direct comparison of preconversion and postconversion instances of the course. Mean ratings for relevant questions are summarized in Table 16.2.

Student evaluations are higher for SAIL, and statistical significance was again assessed via mixed-effect models. The increase in overall course quality was significant (β = .55, SE = 0.11, p < .001). Other individual questions with significant increases in ratings were "ability to . . . solve problems" (β = .27, SE = 0.12, p < .05), "challenged . . . to consider new ideas" (β = .32, SE = 0.11,

Table 16.2 Means of responses to prompts on Penn's official course evaluations in the traditional and new versions of Linguistics 106

Rating Prompt (from 0 - Poor/Strongly Disagree to 4 - Excellent/ Strongly agree)	Trad.	SAIL
Overall quality of the course.	2.55	**3.10***
As a result of taking this course, I have a better understanding of factual knowledge, principles and/or theories in this area.	3.34	3.47
This course helped me to improve my ability to analyze, solve problems and/or think critically.	3.05	**3.32***
This course helped me to understand how this field asks and answers questions.	3.17	3.34
This course challenged me to consider new ideas, concepts, or ways of thinking.	3.08	**3.40***
As a result of taking this course, I am more excited by this field of study.	2.63	**2.98***
Please rate the difficulty of the course.	2.23	2.31
Please rate the amount of work required for this course.	2.12	2.40

$p < .01$), and being "excited by this field" ($\beta = .35$, SE = 0.15, $p < .05$). The small numeric increases in difficulty and amount of work required were not significant.

In order to gather additional student input beyond Penn's standard course evaluations, two feedback surveys were administered, in the middle of the semester and at the end of the SAIL version of the class. These aimed at gathering more targeted information on the specific structural elements of the class, and also were intended to inform potential future adjustments to the course structure. On a scale from one (strongly disagree) to seven (strongly agree), students indicated that the in-class work prepared them well for homework assignments (6.14), and that in-class feedback from the instructional team in class helped their understanding (5.99). Similarly, they found working with their group helpful to increase understanding (5.73). This positive experience of the group work arose in the context of groups working cooperatively and providing space for students to ask questions: the statement "I feel comfortable about telling the other members of my group when I don't understand something" was rated 5.91, and students also highly rated agreement with the statement "The members of my group are all actively contributing to the in-class problem set work" (5.95).

The final survey included additional questions to assess the learning effectiveness of different course components. On a scale from one (not effective at all) to five (very effective), doing homework assignments (4.46) and in-class group work on problems (4.44) were rated most effective, followed by asking the instructional team questions during class (4.32) and taking the video quizzes (4.26). With regards to the in-class group work, working through the problems with others was rated most effective (4.39). Explaining material to other students was almost as highly rated (4.36), followed by explanations from others (4.24). Overall, students rated the course structure as "well-suited for enhancing my learning experience" at 4.38.

Key ingredients to the successful use of group work for effective learning would seem to be a high level of comfort with asking questions, a commitment to helping others, and support from the instructional team. Additional individual practice outside of class in form of quizzes and homework was also seen as effective.

While these quantitative data present a compelling case for the success of the active learning conversion, my own impressionistic observations as well as students' comments to more open-ended survey questions provide an even richer picture. During group work, I noticed that the classroom always was filled with an excited buzz of activity and high levels of energy. This stands out particularly during one class a quarter of the way into the semester where I do lecture for an extended period of time: both the students and I have low levels of energy after that, compared to the usual active learning sessions. More generally, while lecturing can often leave one feeling drained and exhausted, I leave the active learning sessions feeling energized and excited by seeing the students' progress. Similarly, the students typically show no signs of wanting to stop working toward the end of class, and it is not uncommon that I have to actively stop the groupwork after the regular class time is over. Another aspect of the new format that I very much enjoy is that I get to know the students a lot more closely, given all the chance of interaction I have with them twice a week. There is simply hardly any chance for that in a traditional lecture class with 50 students. With regards to the students' experience, their own words best serve to illustrate it. Examples of comments on the problem sets include the following:

- "Doing [problem sets] as a group made us focus more on having everyone understand the topics, and the fact that we were not graded . . . also helped take a lot of the stressful aspects of problem sets away."
- "If [problem sets] were graded based on answers, I would most likely would not have spoken up as much in my group in fear of offering a wrong answer that would affect my peers and my grade. I also would have been more focused on finishing . . . rather than trying to understand the material."

Other comments spoke to the effectiveness of the overall setup:

- "The video lectures and subsequent in-class group work was an *amazingly effective* way of learning. As a hardcore humanities major, anything involving quantitative reasoning has always been a challenge for me but this class might be one of the best quantitative classes I've ever taken."
- "I've never felt so consistently engaged and prepared in each class."
- "I can't imagine just going off of in-class lectures and not having the in-class problem set time- it's so crucial to my learning."

One of the most illuminating aspects of student feedback came in response to the question "What advice do you have for future students who wish to do well in this course, both in general and with regards to the structure of the course?" In addition to a constant mantra of "watch the videos and come to class prepared, stay on top of your work," a lot of the comments again spoke to the importance of the in-class group work and contributing to making it productive and inclusive:

- "The group work is crucial in making sure you understand the information adequately. Ask any and all questions you have!!"
- "Definitely reach out to your group mates when you have questions . . . Group work helped reduce a lot of the stress and anxiety from thinking that everyone understands the topics (because most of the time everyone is also as confused as you are)."
- "Admit to your group when you don't understand something! They will more than likely be more than happy explain, and hearing a concept explained by someone who just learned it themselves can be really helpful"
- "Befriend and work with your groupmates, they are your most valuable resource. Learn from them when they know more than you, and teach them if you know you're right."
- "Learn your group members' strengths and work together as a team to solve the problems."
- "Also, take the in-class problems seriously. It's easy to get lazy and shift the burden of work to your group, but that won't help you. You'll just have to make up the efforts come homework or studying time."
- "Watching the video lectures is so important! Don't be the one person in your group who depends on the others to understand the material. Be sure to ask lots of questions when you don't understand something."

- "For a class heavy in formalisms like this one, having a little bit of fun with your group while you do the problems helps you to pick up the concepts."

As these comments vividly illustrate, the students are very much aware of what aspects of this class setup are most central to enhancing learning. In addition to the structured class components that help students stay on track throughout, they see a cooperative and inclusive spirit as entirely crucial for successful group work, much in line with the "heads-and-hearts" hypothesis (Theobald et al., 2020).

In addition to the many ways in which the conversion of the class format has been a success, challenges and problems of course remain. One challenge is that a small number of students (typically only two or three) simply do not like working in groups and thus are rather discontent with the active learning format. While in principle, they could do more of the work on their own, I have not encouraged this due to the value I see in the collaborative approach, but this does leave a tension that is so far unresolved. Furthermore, navigating the make-up of the individual groups can at times be challenging, especially when there are students who struggle to get along and collaborate productively. Another challenging issue is how to best make the in-class problem sets available to students, given that they are computer-based. One option is to only give the student with the scribe-role in the group access to the quiz on Canvas, but this can make it difficult for everyone to access the relevant information. Another option is to give all students access, but this requires students to have a computer available to bring to class, and perhaps more importantly, can inhibit collaborative work and be a source of distraction.

Conclusion and Outlook

The change to an active learning format for Linguistics 106 has led to higher student performance and is overall strongly welcomed by students, based on their evaluations and feedback. While at present, a direct quantitative analysis of racial and gender inclusion is not possible due to lack of access to demographic data, the overall positive outcomes together with the findings from the prior literature suggest that this teaching approach increases inclusion. While there are many limitations, the hope is that this will provide inspiration for more active learning courses and investigation of their effects in linguistics. At Penn, the new Linguistics 106 class format has been welcomed by the department and the School of Arts and Sciences as an addition to the curriculum, as reflected in logistical and financial support, for example, through making available suitable classroom spaces, providing training and feedback for teaching and learning assistants, and covering their stipends. Several other classes are now also using active learning strategies, including our Introduction to Sociolinguistics class and a new introductory course on Data Science for Studying Language and the Mind.

In closing, I offer some reflections on various possible directions for extending the approach taken here. To anyone considering adapting their teaching in similar ways, but with some hesitation about undertaking a major revamping of a course, I'd note that it is perfectly possible to gradually incorporate active teaching elements over time. While the present course underwent a focused overhaul, I implemented many of the changes slowly over time and then fully integrated them into the new format during the transition. Any structured activity that allows students to apply newly learned concepts in a supportive environment, and which fosters a collaborative learning experience where students can get questions of their own clarified by others as well as do some explaining themselves, has the potential to contribute to a more inclusive class environment.

By the same token, no undertaking of this sort is ever completely finished. For example, one promising direction is to combine the change in pedagogical methods with adjustments to the content and phenomena covered with an eye toward greater inclusivity, much in line with various other chapters in this volume. While in the STEM context of prior research on active learning, changing course content does not seem to have played much of a role, likely because of the perceived independence of the subject matter from issues of inclusion, such a step is a natural as an extension of the "heads and hearts hypothesis," especially in the linguistics context. First and foremost, this change could start with revisiting the languages and possibly dialects that example data is drawn from (see also Sanders et al., this volume). The empirical ground covered in Linguistics 106 is relatively narrow, due to its focus on formal tools. Apart from a few illustrative case studies from Luiseño and Warlpiri, as well as some exercises on formal properties of stress systems in non–Indo-European languages, the focus is mostly on Standard English. A systematic exploration of where there is room for a wider range of data from other languages and other dialects of English could further contribute to greater inclusion of students of color and multilingual students.

With regards to extending the active learning approach to other classes in linguistics, there clearly is promise in utilizing similar approaches for the teaching of other subject matter, though it likely will require adjustments of various sorts. But as the field of linguistics is fundamentally concerned with analysis of one sort of another of different levels of linguistic structure—from minimal sound pairs to narrative structure—and the relation of linguistic form to its contexts of use, it seems highly suited for spending substantial parts of class time on students practicing whatever analytical skills are involved in a given course. Since much of linguistic data is, or can be made, easily accessible, our field indeed seems very well positioned to incorporate learning-by-doing into classroom activities.

As a matter of both practical concern and availability of resources, it is worth noting that much of the effort in implementing curricular changes of the sort described here can be seen as an up-front investment with future payoff for the individual instructor. For example, by strategically using exercise implementations in learning management systems, which not only allow for automatic grading but also for extensive custom feedback displayed after work is submitted, the need for laborious manual checking of practice work can be avoided, while still providing detailed feedback for students to review. Taken together with the decreased need for instructor preparation time for individual classes and lecturing, this approach leaves much more time and energy for instructors to work with students individually and in small groups in a more targeted manner, providing help and explanation where it is needed. In my experience, this shift in focus is both seen as more effective by the students and in many ways more rewarding for the instructor. At the same time, it is clear that institutional support for such individual efforts is of great importance, and I personally have been privileged to benefit from the resources and support at Penn, both in terms of financial support and pedagogical resources and training.

If more classes in a given program shift toward active learning, one additional consideration is whether the novelty will wear off for students, and whether their experiences of workload and time management overall may affect the effectiveness of this type of approach. Impressionistically, student feedback suggests that many students genuinely see the format as providing a more successful learning experience, in a way that I would hope would remain stable even if students take multiple classes of this sort in parallel. But only time will tell—at least to the extent that this type of teaching format is more widely adapted. In any case, the overall evidence so far lends substantial promise to extending active learning strategies to other topics and contexts in linguistics. This is of particular importance for introductory offerings in formal and theoretical linguistics, to provide a more welcoming and inclusive entry point to parts of the overall field that are in the most dire need of increasing diversity. Hopefully, along the way, those in the field joining such efforts can also gather more wide-ranging data to more comprehensively assess its success overall and its impact on increasing inclusion in linguistics.

Notes

1. Thanks are in order to a number of people. First and foremost, I could not have undertaken this project without Ryan Budnick, my teaching assistant for both the last preconversion class and the first class in the new format. He enthusiastically agreed to work together in the process and went above and beyond in so many ways. Most importantly, he took on the huge task of taking the lead in creating the in-class problem sets, whose high quality is a key ingredient for the success of this teaching model. I also received invaluable support and guidance from Penn's Center for Teaching and Learning, and particularly benefited from input and advice from Bruce Lenthall, Emily Elliott, and Jamiella Brooks. The other graduate and undergraduate teaching assistants—Alexandros Kalomoiros, Gwendolyn Hildebrand, Nikhil Lakhani, Michael Ehart, Stefan Pophristic, Tess Christensen, and Nikhil Avadhani—have also contributed in many important ways to the success of the class over the different SAIL instances. Finally, thanks to Hannah Gibson, Anne Charity Hudley, Christine Mallinson, and Mary Bucholtz for helpful suggestions and discussions on earlier versions of the chapter.
2. For some examples of related work on active learning efforts in linguistics, which I was unaware of at the time of converting my class, see Jon Bakos (2019), Valentyna Filimonova (2020), David Marlow (2010), and Lauren Squires (2017).
3. Full details are available at Penn Diversity, https://diversity.upenn.edu/diversity-at-penn/facts-and-figures. Official numbers for the class enrollment and the linguistics major are not available at the time of writing.

References

Bakos, Jon. (2019). Corpus-based sociolinguistics activities in an active-learning language classroom. *American Speech*, 94(2), 302–310. doi:10.1215/00031283-7592095

Eddy, Sarah L., & Hogan, Kelly A. (2014). Getting under the hood: How and for whom does increasing course structure work? *CBE—Life Sciences Education*, 13(3),453–468. doi:10.1187/cbe.14-03-0050

Filimonova, Valentyna. (2020). Problem-based learning in introductory linguistics. *Language*, 96(1), e1–e21. doi:10.1353/lan.2020.0012

Freeman, Scott, Eddy, Sarah L., McDonough, Miles, Smith, Michelle K., Okoroafor, Nnadozie, Jordt, Hannah, & Wenderoth, Mary Pat. (2014). Active learning increases student performance in science, engineering, and mathematics. *Proceedings of the National Academy of Sciences*, 111(23), 8410–8415. doi:10.1073/pnas.1319030111

Gavassa, Sat, Benabentos, Rocio, Kravec, Marcy, Collins, Timothy, & Eddy, Sarah. (2019) Closing the achievement gap in a large introductory course by balancing reduced in-person contact with increased course structure. *CBE—Life Sciences Education*, 18(1), ar8. doi:10.1187/cbe.18-08-0153

Johnson, Kathryn M. S. (2019). Implementing inclusive practices in an active learning STEM classroom. *Advances in Physiology Education*, 43(2), 207–210. doi:10.1152/advan.00045.2019

Linguistic Society of America (LSA). (1994). Committee on Ethnic Diversity in Linguistics (CEDL). (n.d.). https://www.linguisticsociety.org/about/who-we-are/committees/ethnic-diversity-linguistics-cedl

Marlow, David W. (2010). Engaging syntax: Using a personal response system to encourage grammatical thought. *American Speech, 85*(2), 225–237. doi:10.1215/00031283-2010-012

Penn Arts & Sciences. (2020). Inclusion and anti-racism initiatives. https://www.sas.upenn.edu/2020-inclusion-and-anti-racism-initiatives

Rainey, Katherine, Dancy, Melissa, Mickelson, Roslyn, Stearns, Elizabeth, & Moller, Stephanie. (2018). Race and gender differences in how sense of belonging influences decisions to major in STEM. *International Journal of STEM Education, 5*(1), 10. doi:10.1186/s40594-018-0115-6 https://pubmed.ncbi.nlm.nih.gov/30631700/

Schwarz, Florian. (2021). LING 106: Introduction to formal linguistics: Lecture 1. Lecture notes, University of Pennsylvania.

Squires, Lauren. (2017). Mini-experiments for teaching across the English linguistics syllabus. *American Speech, 92*(2), 231–252. doi:10.1215/00031283-4202042

Theobald, Elli J., Hill, Mariah J., Tran, Elisa, Agrawal, Sweta, Arroyo, E. Nicole, Behling, Shawn, Chambwe, Nyasha, Cintrón, Dianne Laboy, Cooper, Jacob D., Dunster, Gideon, Grummer, Jared A., Hennessey, Kelly, Hsiao, Jennifer, Iranon, Nicole, Jones, Leonard II, Jordt, Hannah, Keller, Marlowe, Lacey, Melissa E., Littlefield, Caitlin E., . . . Freeman, Scott. (2020) Active learning narrows achievement gaps for underrepresented students in undergraduate science, technology, engineering, and math. *Proceedings of the National Academy of Sciences, 117*(12), 6476–6483. doi:10.1073/pnas.1916903117

Nathan Sanders is associate professor, teaching stream, and undergraduate associate chair in the Department of Linguistics at the University of Toronto, located in the traditional territory of many nations, including the Mississaugas of the Credit, the Anishinaabe, the Wendat, and the Haudenosaunee. He studied mathematics and linguistics at the Massachusetts Institute of Technology and earned his MA and PhD from the University of California, Santa Cruz, with a dissertation on phonology and sound change in Polish. He works on the phonetics and phonology of signed and spoken languages, historical phonology, linguistic typology, and innovative and inclusive teaching in linguistics. He has published articles in *Language, Sign Language & Linguistics, Natural History*, and *Journal for Research and Practice in College Teaching*, he is co-author of the second edition of the online textbook *Essentials of Linguistics* and co-editor of the book *Language Invention in Linguistics Pedagogy*. He lives in downtown Toronto with his extensive boardgame collection.

Lex Konnelly earned their PhD in linguistics and sexual diversity studies at the University of Toronto. Their research is situated in the interrelated areas of sociocultural linguistics, variationist sociolinguistics, and linguistic anthropology, with an emphasis on linguistic innovation in transgender, nonbinary, and gender-diverse communities of practice. Their doctoral research explores the role of language in gender-affirming healthcare access. In addition to their disciplinary and community-based advocacy work, they have published articles in *Gender and Language, Journal of Language and Sexuality, Language in Society*, and *Language & Communication*, among others. They are a white settler originally from the unceded Coast Salish Territory of the Lekwungen and W̱SÁNEĆ nations now known as Victoria, BC, and they now live in Tkaronto, Ontario, with their partner and their two cats.

Pocholo Umbal earned his PhD in linguistics at the University of Toronto, where he is now an assistant professor. His research interests include sociolinguistics and language contact, with a focus on the sociophonetics of spoken languages in diasporic communities. His doctoral research explores variable speech patterns in Toronto Heritage Tagalog. He has also previously investigated variation in Canadian English (multi-)ethnolects and his work has appeared in *American Speech* and *Language in Society*, among other venues. In addition, he works alongside a coalition of Asian-identified linguists to increase representation of Asian (broadly defined) scholars in the field. He was born in Manila, Philippines, and immigrated to Canada at a young age, settling in Vancouver, BC, which is situated on the unceded traditional territories of the xʷməθkʷəy̓əm (Musqueam), Sḵwx̱wú7mesh (Squamish), and səlilwətaɬ (Tsleil-Waututh) Nations. He now lives in Etobicoke, Ontario, with his partner.

Abstract: This chapter discusses a three-year pedagogical initiative at the University of Toronto to bring more equity, diversity, and inclusion into the linguistics classroom and to address linguistic injustice more generally in teaching beyond linguistics courses. In an effort to provide a model for anyone interested in doing similar work in their own departments, the authors focus on implementational details, concrete steps, outcomes, and generalizable action-based advice on how individual pieces of our project can be adapted in different contexts. They provide an overview of the initiative and details of a number of its resulting products, including a variety of materials that they developed and collected into a publicly accessible online repository. The authors also discuss numerous connections and collaborations that helped expand the scope of the initiative, and conclude by offering helpful suggestions and further reflections on why this work is important and why linguists must prioritize it.

Key Words: pedagogy, language-based bias, collaboration, teaching materials, resource sharing

17

An Action-Based Roadmap for Equity, Diversity, and Inclusion in Teaching Linguistics

Nathan Sanders (he/him)
University of Toronto

Lex Konnelly (they/them)
University of Toronto

Pocholo Umbal (he/him)
University of Toronto

Introduction

In this chapter, we describe aspects of a three-year pedagogical initiative at the University of Toronto to bring more equity, diversity, and inclusion (EDI) into the linguistics classroom and to address linguistic injustice more generally in teaching beyond linguistics.[1] This initiative follows a larger trend of rapid momentum in EDI work in Canadian universities, which are increasingly prioritizing EDI policies at a range of different levels, from departmental and university-wide programming to recruitment of diverse talent among faculty, staff, and students (Tamtik & Guenter, 2019), with 77% of Canada's universities explicitly referencing EDI in their strategic planning or long-term planning documents, and 70% either already having or currently developing an EDI action plan (Universities Canada, 2019).

At our own institution, the Faculty of Arts & Science has placed emphasis on EDI as part of the University's fundamental institutional values (University of Toronto Faculty of Arts & Science, 2020). Universities in Canada and elsewhere are coming to recognize that initiatives that address EDI issues are crucial to advancing higher education and are intentionally working to establish campus communities as affirming places to foster intellectual and

Nathan Sanders, Lex Konnelly, and Pocholo Umbal, *An Action-Based Roadmap for Equity, Diversity, and Inclusion in Teaching Linguistics* In: *Inclusion in Linguistics*. Edited by: Anne H. Charity Hudley, Christine Mallinson and Mary Bucholtz, Oxford University Press. © Anne H. Charity Hudley, Christine Mallinson, and Mary Bucholtz 2024.
DOI: 10.1093/oso/9780197755303.003.0018

epistemological innovation. In a best-case scenario, these initiatives may even help to disrupt the extractive, ivory tower relationship between universities and the wider communities in which they are embedded. Of course, universities are still inherently conservative institutions, so there are limits to what can be done from an EDI perspective within the confines of university structures (Shin & Sterzuk, 2019; Stein, 2020).

We present our work on this initiative in an effort to provide a model for anyone interested in doing similar EDI work in their own departments and courses (see Arnold, this volume; Schwarz, this volume; and Thomas, this volume for other models with different approaches and scope). We know from our own experience that it can be overwhelming to know where to start, so our focus in this chapter is on implementational details, concrete steps, and outcomes. Throughout, we offer generalizable action-based advice on how individual pieces of our project can be adapted in different contexts.

We begin with an overview of our initiative, including its history, motivation, structure, and logistics, as well as our own positionality. We then discuss several products that resulted from this initiative, including a variety of materials that we developed and collected into a publicly accessible online repository, as well as numerous connections and collaborations that we built with colleagues in our own department, at other departments within our university, at other institutions, and with the public at large. We conclude with a summary of our primary suggestions and limitations based on our experiences, as well as further reflections on why this work is important and why linguists must prioritize it.

We must briefly note that there is great variation among scholars pursuing EDI-based pedagogy with respect to the terms and acronyms used, so it is important to make choices that reflect your own goals and strategies. Our use of the term "EDI" matches the language in various policies and initiatives at the University of Toronto. This helps situate our project within larger institutional frameworks, which makes it easier to talk about this work with colleagues, to get engagement from various people and units, and to receive grant funding. That said, EDI is not just a strategic terminological choice for our project. It also accurately captures aspects of the scope of our work. We align with the principle of *equity* in endeavouring to mitigate biases in our course materials and, wherever possible, to challenge prevailing assumptions in linguistics, especially when it comes to (re)imagining our pedagogical practices in ways that leverage students' diverse linguistic backgrounds and eliminate the hidden curricula of language-related inequities. *Diversity* is also a central pillar of our content generation: throughout our collaborations with instructors within our own department and elsewhere, we have sought to diversify the kinds of materials that students are exposed to (whether through data sets on underdocumented languages or the Diverse Names Database, each of which we devote greater discussion to below). Finally, we recognize the importance of *inclusion* for ensuring that our linguistics classrooms are spaces where our students' diverse backgrounds are respected and valued, so that students see themselves reflected in course content. In recognizing themselves in linguistics, we hope that students can in turn recognize linguistics as a place for them to thrive and to make meaningful contributions in their own right.

Though this has been the language that works for us, others may use a different order of the acronym elements depending on their institution-specific conventions (for example, DEI seems to be more common in the United States), or they may adopt new terms entirely depending on what is most authentic to their mission. For example, the expanded acronym JEDI has become popular due to the inclusion of *J* for *justice* to highlight active dismantling of unjust structures (while also evoking the heroic Jedi of the *Star Wars* franchise, though this association is not without its problems; see Hammond et al., 2021), while many Canadian institutions sometimes use an extra *D* and/or *I* (as in EDID at the University of Alberta and EDII at the University of Waterloo) for *decolonization* and *Indigeneity*, to place focus on efforts needed to specifically address Canada's colonial history and its devastating effects on Indigenous peoples. We encourage our readers to reflect on what terminology best encompasses their own visions for creating change in their departments and what may be most effective or advantageous for securing funding or other forms of administrative support.

Project Overview

Various forms of systemic harm and injustice, many of which often manifest in relation to language, permeate society, especially in education (see, e.g., Blundon, 2016; Bucholtz, 2016; Charity Hudley & Mallinson, 2011; Cochran, 2019; Fletcher, 1983; Flores & Rosa, 2015; Kohli & Solórzano, 2012; Lippi-Green, 2012; Russell et al., 2018; Zhang & Noels, 2021). Like many academic fields, linguistics is not immune to these forms of injustice, and linguists have increasingly issued calls to action for linguists to address these issues, not just in society at large, but in our own field (for example Charity Hudley, 2020; Conrod, 2019; Mallinson, 2024; Leonard, 2018; Rickford & King, 2016).

Of particular concern for both linguists and the field of linguistics more generally is that these issues are often not discussed in core content in linguistics courses (Spring et al., 2000; Hercula, 2020). Undergraduate students form the next generation of linguists, and they therefore need to know early on how linguistic injustice persists in society and what linguists can do to combat it. It is also necessary for students from racialized and other minoritized groups to feel included and validated as they study linguistics: when students see themselves represented in course material, they may be more likely to see the discipline as a place for them, which may in turn contribute to increased representation of underrepresented groups in linguistics (cf. Charity Hudley et al. 2020; Rickford, 1997). We therefore see introductory courses as optimal sites of intervention to revise existing curricula, in order to engage students in these conversations (see Arnold, this volume; Calhoun et al. 2021). Further, as Sarah Hercula (2020, p. 13) argues, introductory linguistics courses also have many students who will not go on to become linguists, but who nevertheless "have the potential to impact language-related policy and practice in fields outside linguistics and academia, such as engineering and business." In short, whether or not our students continue on to become linguists like us, it is our responsibility to impart to them the significance of linguistic injustice, so that they may take this knowledge forward beyond linguistics and the academy, in whatever way they so choose.

Addressing injustice in linguistics more generally is a collective effort, and there is increasing demand within the field for conversations on these issues, such as in the teaching sections of flagship journals such as *Language* and *American Speech*, where pedagogical linguistic scholarship can be published and circulated more widely. Linguists therefore have a responsibility to the field in sharing their work and experiences, so that other educators can realize that this work can and should be done. Informed by this backdrop and by long-standing discussions in our linguistics department at the University of Toronto, we put together a proposal for a three-year initiative to help bring an increased focus on EDI to the linguistics classroom. In Sanders et al. 2020, we provide an initial introduction to this project, titled "Innovations in Linguistic Equity, Diversity, and Inclusion in the Linguistics Curriculum and Beyond." In this chapter, we summarize key aspects of our proposal and elaborate further on more recent developments in the two years since that initial report.

In the summer of 2019, working with Naomi Nagy and Keren Rice, Nathan applied for a grant through the Learning & Education Advancement Fund (LEAF) at the University of Toronto, totaling almost CAD$45,000, spread out over three years. There may be similar institutional grants at your own institution, depending on the funding situation and your status (for example, tenure-track faculty will generally have greater access to funding opportunities than contingent faculty or students). You may need to search around and be creative in finding the right grant to apply for. Our original grant proposal included relevant background and bibliography on linguistic injustice, a detailed plan of action for all three years showing expansion of the project from department-internal to other institutions and fields, and description of specific deliverables and plans for sustainability. Here, we highlight three key aspects of our proposal: budget, strategic writing, and consultation.

First, appropriate compensation for student labour is crucial, especially given the spirit of the project itself, so the majority of the grant was earmarked to pay for the labour of two Lead EDI Teaching Assistants (Lex and Pocholo), working a combined 245 hours per year during the academic year.

Second, write for your audience and your future self. For most institutional grants, the background justification requires careful attention, since the committee adjudicating grant proposals will likely not contain any linguists. Thus, technical terminology from within linguistics needs to be avoided and replaced with phrasing that would be more transparent to nonlinguists. In addition, find aspects of your proposal that can be highlighted as connecting to larger issues of broad concern to the institution, such as interdisciplinarity, Indigeneity, social justice, and public outreach. Extracting quotes from the institution's mission statement is a good way to make it clear that the proposal is grounded in institutional values, which will increase its chances of being approved.

In addition, giving as many specifics in the proposal as possible helps on two fronts. It gives the funding entity a better idea of what they are funding and more security in knowing that the project will actually be successfully carried out. Moreover, it gives the team a plan to follow. With this outline in place, we were able to start working on the first day knowing what we needed to do, so that less time was needed for initial organization and planning. Putting that work in early in the proposal stage left more time during the project itself for working on the project's goals directly. Of course, no plan is infallible, and we shifted as necessary, but having some basic structure in place greatly facilitated our ability to do the work we wanted to do.

Finally, getting advance support from the department and administration is also crucial. Before submitting the proposal, we workshopped it with faculty and graduate students in the department, the department chair, and members of the relevant decanal office. Rather than submitting the proposal in a vacuum, we worked months in advance to get broad advice and input from multiple perspectives, which helped better shape the proposal into something that would be useful to as many people as possible, and again, would give it greater likelihood to be approved.

Positionality

Our commitment to promoting EDI in linguistics is fueled in large part by our own lived experiences. Because language is so deeply and unavoidably personal (Thomas, this volume), each member of our team is informed by their own unique relationship to language. Nathan is a white, cisgender, queer, hearing American Canadian linguist who has worked on signed languages. He grew up in the rural southern United States speaking a highly stigmatized variety of English, and as a result of significant dialect discrimination in his early adulthood, he shifted to a more mainstream variety and lost fluent access to his original dialect. This experience fueled a feeling of loss of connection to his family and has long informed his views on language ideologies and discrimination. Lex, a white, queer, transmasculine, nonbinary Canadian linguist, is especially attuned to the relationship between language and gender, both the ways in which language creates and reinforces oppression for transgender communities, as well as the immense linguistic innovation and advocacy that gender-diverse people are constantly engaged in. Pocholo, a queer, Filipino Canadian linguist, is acutely aware of how nonnormative or nonmainstream language varieties can be barriers to both economic and academic success among racialized communities. Thus, our personal experiences with our own marginalized identities help ground this work. That said, we are mindful about our own limitations, and how these are reflected in what we have been able to accomplish. For example, while our own research before and during this project has focused on foregrounding issues related to gender, sexuality, and immigrant and deaf communities, we have been cautious in approaching issues related to other minoritized communities outside our own experiences and research. Recognizing our limitations is the first step to forging meaningful partnerships with other educators and students, whose lived experiences and expertise complement ours.

The Linguistics Equity, Diversity, and Inclusion Repository

Many fields have robust literatures and pedagogical resources concerning EDI issues in teaching and learning. The fields of education and curriculum and instruction studies more broadly have been highly productive in cultivating a rich canon of anti-oppressive scholarship meant to inform pedagogies across disciplines (such as Bettez, 2011; Hobbel, 2010; hooks, 1994), reverberating throughout other fields such as mathematics (Bond & Chirnoff,

2015; Brantlinger, 2013; Wagner & Stintson 2013; Yusun & Gagné 2021), social work (Nicotera, 2019), sociology (Alexander, 2005; Rudy & Konefal, 2007), and health and physical education (Gerdin et al., 2021), among others. Closer to linguistics, the field of language education has also grappled with these issues. One particular area that has gained attention and is currently being challenged is the rampant heteronormativity in pedagogical materials and classroom practices (Gray, 2013; Paiz, 2019). For example, most language education textbooks inadvertently foreground heterosexism by containing examples with female and male characters with stereotypical gender roles and heterosexual relationships (see also LSA, 2022). In the classroom, questions about gender identity and expression are often not discussed (Neto, 2018). These practices reinforce the hegemony of heterosexual relationships and effectively erase lesbian, gay, bisexual, transgender, queer, intersex, and Two-Spirit (LGBTQI2S+) identities and experiences, which in turn often have serious ramifications, especially for queer and/or questioning students (Vandrick, 1997). In response, researchers have made calls to action to queer the field of language teaching (Nelson, 2007; Neto, 2018; Paiz, 2019).

In linguistics, EDI issues often already organically arise in some subfields, such as sociolinguistics and language revitalization and reclamation, where the relationship between language and society plays a crucial role in research. However, many course instructors in other subfields are also equally keen to incorporate EDI principles into their classrooms, but they may not see how these topics fit into their subfields, or they may feel that they do not have the time or expertise to do this work properly (cf. Bowern & Dockum, 2024; Gibson et al., 2024). To address these concerns, we used this project as an opportunity to consult with these kinds of interested instructors to find ways that EDI could be incorporated into their courses and to develop relevant course materials tailored to their goals and their courses' learning outcomes.

Of course, many instructors around the world are already implementing many of the principles outlined here, but within the field of linguistics specifically, these materials are often not published (and thus, not widely accessible), or their existence is not widely known (with a few notable exceptions, such as the initiative described in Charity Hudley, 2020). This problem is common in linguistics pedagogy more broadly, because the scholarship of teaching and learning in the discipline is not yet as robust as in many other fields (Hercula, 2020, p. 15). For example, even though there are teaching sections of some linguistics journals, there are currently no standalone journals dedicated to the scholarship of teaching and learning in linguistics as there are in other fields (e.g., *Teaching Sociology*, *Teaching Anthropology*, *Physics Education*, among others). As a result, pedagogical materials in linguistics, especially those that specifically integrate a social justice component, are less widely available and may be more challenging to come by. To address this issue, we built the Linguistics Equity, Diversity, and Inclusion Repository (LEDIR) (https://ledir.ling.utoronto.ca, citable as Sanders et al., 2021–2022), which contains the materials we created for this project, including lecture notes, data sets, the Diverse Names Database, and the *Handbook for Inclusive Linguistics Teaching*. We describe each of these resources in more detail in the following sections.

Lecture Notes

We created lecture notes (short readings for students) to bring EDI content as course material into a standard phonetics course, where these issues are not traditionally treated as material to be learned. This course is a requirement for our major and was taught by Nathan in the first year of the project, making it an ideal course to work on. The lecture notes we designed are short readings, no more than two pages each, that can be used to supplement any phonetics course with explicit discussion of EDI issues relevant to phonetics. The text and references of these lecture notes are available on LEDIR and in Sanders et al. (2020).

We designed these lecture notes following a few guiding principles. First, the content should be directly relevant to phonetics and fully integrated into the course, so that the material would matter to the students and not appear to be tacked on or optional, which would undermine the effectiveness of the pedagogical effort. Second, the lecture notes should be small enough to not detract from the main course content. Finally, the content should cover a range of different topics. We ended up with three new sets of lecture notes: (1) two pages (written primarily by Lex) on gender and the vocal tract, challenging gendered assumptions about vocal tract length, especially the 17.5 cm length traditionally used in linguistics as a default (male) vocal tract length (as in Behrman, 2018; Gobl & Ní Chasaide, 2010; Howard & Angus, 2017), and bringing up issues of body and gender diversity, including trans identities and the phonetic effects of hormone replacement therapy; (2) one page (written primarily by Pocholo) on the effect of social biases on speech perception, highlighting the role of race in the perception of intelligibility; and (3) half a page (written primarily by Nathan) on the status of signed languages in phonetics and linguistics more broadly, focusing on the problematic ways that signed languages, deafness, and deaf people are often minimized or ignored in linguistics, with spoken languages and hearing people treated as implicit defaults.

Similar lecture notes in this vein can be created for a variety of courses. A basic strategy we recommend is to pick a general topic within EDI (such as gender diversity, racism, or signed languages) and find a unit of the course material where that topic could be inserted in a small way as an extension of the existing content. This approach means that the instructor does not have to do extensive revision of the planned material, minimizing their workload and not disrupting their original course plan. Even just a few of these small changes to the course content can have a large impact on student experience. For example, in anonymous course evaluations for Nathan's phonetics course where these lecture notes were used, students lauded the inclusion of these topics and the expanded view of phonetics presented in the course.

Not only do lecture notes provide students with content that may be more directly applicable to their life outside the linguistics classroom, but for those students with marginalized identities and backgrounds, this increased representation can make them feel more included in the larger conversation about language and linguistics in ways they traditionally have not been. It also helps students with more socially privileged identities better understand how these issues are relevant in ways they may not have thought of before. An important next step is developing a means to assess whether students have recognized the importance of these issues, and to receive other types of feedback. Questions that elicit relevant feedback can be integrated into course evaluation surveys that instructors invite student responses at the end of the semester.

Diverse Data Sets

We also worked with instructors in several courses to expand representation of minoritized languages in their course material and problem sets, with an eye toward intentional, purpose-driven diversity of data. In creating your own data sets, we recommend taking into account the sociocultural context of your institution. Because we are at a Canadian university, we focused on underrepresented languages that also reflect the linguistic diversity of Canada, in particular, Indigenous languages and heritage languages of immigrant communities. Again, this approach is a way to better represent the backgrounds of the students in the classroom and help them feel more included as part of the field (cf. Calhoun et al., 2021). Further, in introducing minoritized languages, it is important to go beyond the usual background information (language family, number of users, etc.). For example, when presenting data for Stoney Nakoda for a phonology course, we also include resources pointing to documentation and revitalization efforts underway, such as the Stoney Mobile Dictionary (https://www.stoneyeducation.ca/stoney-dictionary-app), created by community members and used in Stoney language classes in secondary schools at the Alexis Nakota Sioux Nation in Alberta (Bell, 2019). This kind of extra information helps show students that languages are not just data to be analyzed, but that they are used by real human beings in real communities with real concerns. This information can provide an opportunity to reflect on broader social and cultural issues, such as the role of Canada's colonial history in the severe decline of Indigenous languages.

The Diverse Names Database

Our third resource emerged from our concern that, while constructed linguistic example sentences are a core vehicle for linguists in teaching a wide range of phenomena to our students, it is well-established that these examples, particularly in syntax textbooks and journals, systematically underrepresent women and perpetuate harmful gender stereotypes. For example, feminine-gendered arguments are often presented as nonsubjects, more likely to be unnamed, and more often referred to in kinship terms in relation to masculine-gendered referents (Bergvall, 1996; Macaulay & Brice, 1994, 1997; Pabst et al., 2018, published as Cépeda et al. 2021; Kotek et al. 2020; 2021; Richy & Burnett, 2019). In the classroom, linguists may not realize that they are relying on their own biases in creating examples, particularly when coming up with examples spontaneously in the midst of class discussion. As an intervention on the inequity of names chosen in example sentences for linguistic course content, we developed the Diverse Names Database (DND; Sanders et al., 2020; Sanders, 2021b; Konnelly et al., 2021; Konnelly et al., forthcoming b), a database of names from 78 languages, categorized three ways by gender (all-gender, feminine-leaning, and masculine-leaning), confirmed with native speakers and/or academic experts on these languages. An excerpt from the DND appears in Table 17.1.

Our goal was to create an easily accessible spreadsheet with names for three gender groups for each of the 26 letters of the English alphabet. Although

Table 17.1 Excerpt from the Diverse Names Database

all-gender		*feminine-leaning*		*masculine-leaning*	
Amal	Arabic	Anahera	Māori	Aimo	Finnish
Bounmy	Lao	Boróka	Hungarian	Baber	Urdu
Cahyo	Javanese	Chana	Hebrew	Carlu	Corsican
⋮	⋮	⋮	⋮	⋮	⋮
Xquenda	Zapotec	Xulia	Galician	Xuan	Asturian
Yunuen	Purépecha	Yolotl	Nahuatl	Yama	Pashto
Zhyrgal	Kirghiz	Zuriñe	Basque	Zaharia	Romanian

using the English alphabet as a base structure reinforces the hegemony of English, English is the language of instruction at our institution, and the English alphabet makes the DND more suited to typical situations in linguistics instruction, where it is common to abbreviate names to a single letter (as in predicate logic, where sentences like *Amal is happy* may be represented as $H(a)$). Because of this dependence on the English alphabet, a subset of the DND or an entirely different version would be warranted in situations where the language of instruction is not English. An underlying design principle was fundamental simplicity: we wanted to create a tool that could be consulted quickly and easily. To find names for the DND, we largely employed a scavenger methodology, trawling as many sources as possible (grammars, journal articles, baby name databases, professional and personal contacts, etc.), prioritizing understudied languages and a broad range of language families. We also included phonetic transcriptions from native speaker consultants wherever possible. The resulting database represents over 30 language families from over 110 countries. This resource has been one of the more successful products of our project, with at least a dozen linguists reporting to us that they have used names from it.

Though it can be greatly useful, the DND also comes with potential drawbacks that must be carefully weighed. While it presents opportunities for greater inclusiveness and affirmation with respect to both gender and cultural representation, applications of the DND may raise additional issues that linguists should be mindful of, and names from the DND should not be unthinkingly inserted into examples. For example, English is often the default language of instruction in North American universities, as well as within many other academic contexts around the world. In an Anglophone classroom, using names that do not conform to English phonotactics can thus be an important tool for unsettling the social power of English. However, the inclusion of names that are not easily assimilated to English pronunciations may risk exoticization or may elicit microaggressive commentary or mispronunciations from students that can be distressing for their minoritized peers to overhear. There is a careful balance to be struck, and instructors need to be prepared to respond when the balance tips one way or the other: either fitting names to English phonotactics and reinforcing English as a hierarchical standard, or not fitting English phonotactics but inadvertently othering communities whose names are treated as marked by Anglophones. Similar principles apply where English is not a dominant language or the language of instruction. There is not a single right answer, and incorporating greater cultural representations will necessarily involve being prepared to deal with issues as they arise, and importantly, advocating for why it matters to get people's names correct.

Put simply, the DND must be integrated with intention and with regard for classroom dynamics and a commitment to anti-racist teaching more generally. Our hope is that the DND will be a supportive resource for both instructors and students in constructing more diverse, inclusive, and affirming examples in assignments and other course materials. This tool is one possible step forward in increasing gender and cultural diversity and representation in linguistics example sentences and thus providing a more equitable and inclusive experience for linguistics students and the field. Moving forward, we plan to keep the DND updated and respond to feedback from its use to thoughtfully expand it for different contexts and purposes.

The Handbook for Inclusive Linguistics Teaching

The final LEDIR resource we discuss here is the *Handbook for Inclusive Linguistics Teaching*, which is designed to help fill a gap in linguistics training. As in many fields, linguists often do not receive extensive, if any, discipline-specific pedagogical training as part of their graduate education; they are typically expected to just pick it up as needed from observing what has worked or not worked in their own education. As new instructors, they may feel uncertain about teaching in general, and even experienced linguistics instructors may not have a strong grasp of inclusive teaching practices or the principles underlying them. Again, although there has been a shift in recent years, particularly in the creation and expansion of teaching-focused faculty positions and venues for publication of linguistics pedagogy research, our field still has a long way to go in prioritizing how we teach linguistics.

The handbook, which is geared towards both instructors and teaching assistants in linguistics and related fields, contains practical recommendations that can be easily integrated into many aspects of a course. These recommendations come from our years of experience as instructors and teaching assistants in many linguistics courses at the University of Toronto, where the usual course setup consists of large lectures (upwards of 250 students, led by the instructor) with smaller associated tutorial sessions (around 35 students, led by graduate student teaching assistants). As a living document, development of the handbook is ongoing, especially with increasing connections to the robust literature on pedagogy in order to better create stronger links between scholarship on teaching and learning as well as our own teaching practices.

The full handbook is available on LEDIR. We offer a brief summary here. A major goal of the handbook is to help foster an inclusive space for all students in the classroom. Inclusivity involves acknowledging, recognizing, and working towards combating structural violence and injustice, so that all people feel welcomed and respected. Further, inclusivity normalizes differences; that is, it recognizes that differences are "natural, acceptable, and ordinary" (Baglieri & Knopf, 2004, p. 525). Inclusive teaching for us, then, is conceptualized as a set of pedagogical practices aimed at creating a learning environment where all students are treated equitably and are provided with genuinely equal access to opportunities and resources. There are multiple ways to work towards building a more inclusive classroom.

First, course syllabi should contain explicit language about valuing diversity and inclusion. Research has found that "when teachers model positive language and attitudes toward difference, students also are affirmed in the development of their peer relationship" (Baglieri & Knopf, 2004, p. 527). We therefore believe that it is imperative that we begin our classes by being explicit about our commitment to diversity and inclusion. In particular, we should remind students that all languages and language varieties are valid (Martinez et al., 2017). This reminder includes affirming that nonstandardized as well as standardized varieties of the language of instruction are equally valid resources that students can use to facilitate their learning in class discussions and in writing.

Second, as linguists, we also have a discipline-specific opportunity to empower students as language experts by letting them know that their linguistic backgrounds and experiences are valued and can be an advantage in their learning of linguistics concepts. This message can be part of a larger effort towards diversification of linguistic examples. For example, data volunteered by students is more humanized than a decontextualized data set. Thus, when teaching syntactic concepts like question formation, instructors could ask students to translate a question like *What did Yama eat?* into languages and varieties that they know and examine how the process of question formation in the language of instruction patterns similarly or differently from their examples. Drawing from students' own languages allows them to make stronger connections between the more abstract concepts they are learning and how those concepts manifest in real language use. In this way, we echo Lisa Delpit (2006, p. 225) in viewing teachers as "cultural brokers who have the opportunity to connect the familiar to the unknown."

It is also important for instructors to practice self-awareness by reflecting about our own positionalities in order to better understand those of our students and ultimately connect with them (Dewsbury & Brame, 2019). By acknowledging certain assumptions that we bring to the classroom, we are able to be more critical of what and how we teach our students. This perspective can also help us to remember to use inclusive language to avoid common linguistic microaggressions (Bucholtz, 2016), such as mispronouncing students' names (Kohli & Solórzano, 2012) or using the wrong pronouns or a previous name for transgender or nonbinary students (Cochran, 2019).

In summary, the handbook provides instructors with multiple ways to think about adopting curriculum design, assessment, and teaching practices that make students of all background and lived experiences feel that they are supported, respected, and valued. The handbook in combination with the other resources on LEDIR described above provide many tools that can help address a variety of EDI issues in linguistics classrooms.

Workshops, Outreach, and Collaboration

It is important for a project like the one we have described here to foster connections, to build and share expertise, to receive feedback for improvement, and to distribute the work so that others may benefit. In this section, we provide an overview of the types of relationships we established over the course of our LEDIR initiative, and how these relationships have both supported and informed the goals and values of our efforts thus far.

Over the course of the project, we held multiple workshops with different subsets of our teaching community in the department. One workshop was led by Lex and Pocholo with a team of teaching assistants from a large introduction to linguistics lecture course in a discussion of classroom practices that foster inclusion and representation. The content of this workshop ultimately evolved into the handbook described above. In this workshop, we highlighted common situations where language-related biases can easily come in (for example, names, example sentences, and relying on native speakers in discussions).

In addition, in collaboration with the Writing-Integrated Teaching program in the Faculty of Arts & Science at the University of Toronto, we designed and jointly led a workshop on making linguistics writing more affirming, geared towards supporting instructors and teaching assistants on how to guide their students to write about communities in affirming ways, especially when they are not members of those communities themselves. In this workshop, we considered the kind of language typically or historically used to describe marginalized identities and people (specifically, trans and nonbinary, immigrant, deaf, and Indigenous), with a focus on harmful terms, descriptors, discourses, and ideologies that readings, instructors, and students often use. We then discussed numerous ways to mitigate these biases, including suggestions of specific alternative and more affirming language which does not undermine the linguistic knowledge and scientific rigour being created and shared. The workshop was positively received by both faculty and graduate students in attendance (both informally and in a follow-up survey), and their constructive comments will help shape and improve the future iterations of the workshop. These kinds of small-scale workshops are a great way to plant transformative seeds in a department, especially for inexperienced instructors and teaching assistants.

A fundamental part of this work is engaging with departments and communities outside of our own immediate institutional space. Getting inclusive teaching strategies in linguistics out there, known, and recognized is crucial to having it adopted elsewhere. We quickly realized that there was an immense appetite for conversations on EDI in pedagogy, both within linguistics and outside of our discipline. Of course, it is important to take advantage of the many opportunities we as linguists have to publicize our work to our colleagues in the discipline and solicit their feedback. We presented portions of this project at two annual meetings of the Canadian Linguistic Association (Konnelly et al., 2021; Sanders et al., 2020), in a webinar on racial justice in linguistics teaching hosted by the Linguistic Society of America (Namboodiripad & Sanders, 2020), and at an invited talk for a workshop on inclusive teaching at the Semantics and Linguistic Theory conference (Sanders, 2021b).

But the work that we are engaging in also has value outside of our own discipline, and to this end, going beyond our field is likewise important. In Fall 2020, we were invited to present our work at an interdisciplinary teaching and learning symposium in the Faculty of Arts & Science at the University of Toronto. We gave a short presentation similar in scope and purpose to this chapter, to show our colleagues from other departments how to undertake similar initiatives and to highlight the various funding and general support pathways that enabled us to do this work. It also gave us the opportunity to talk about the importance of linguistic injustice to a wider audience, doing double duty as both a how-to guide on EDI-based pedagogy and an educational talk to nonlinguists on the relationship between language and social justice.

As a result of this talk, a faculty member in the Department of English requested that a member of our team come visit her second-year undergraduate course on the history of English and facilitate a discussion on any aspect of our project that would expand her students' understanding of the relevant EDI issues. The presenter, Lex, discussed prescriptivism, language attitudes, and linguistic injustice, a conversation that students were eager to engage with. As a discipline that focuses on the study of language, English is in many ways a natural fit for such a discussion. We recommend that colleagues who are interested in building connections outside of their home department consider looking to these academically related communities first, since we found that making our work accessible to those who already had some baseline familiarity with the close analysis of language was an ideal stepping-stone to moving to more distant fields.

Due to word of mouth about our project, Pocholo was also invited to present on our project at an inclusive pedagogy panel discussion at the University of Toronto Mississauga. The panel discussion centred around representation of LGBTQI2S+ issues in many different departments, including linguistics, situations that show clear gaps in inclusion in curriculum and pedagogy, and initiatives that instructors and teaching assistants have developed to centre LGBTQI2S+ perspectives. As one of our project goals is to make our materials portable to other interested departments and fields of study, Pocholo took this opportunity to invite educators to think about ways in which they can integrate discussion of social justice issues within their courses. For example, he highlighted the ways in which the linguistic concepts we teach are often imbued with assumptions that perpetuate heteronormativity (such as binary gender constructions when studying language variation) and how harmful these assumptions can be for our LGBTQI2S+ students. He therefore urged instructors to be mindful about underlying assumptions and assumed defaults in their courses: Where do these constructs come from? Who established them? Who benefits from them? One of the key messages of this presentation was that these considerations are applicable regardless of the academic field, and so we must create classroom environments where students have opportunities to reflect about these issues in an effort to create more affirming spaces for all.

Our project also drew the attention of ezCPD.ca, a professional development organization for legal professionals, which invited Nathan to give a webinar on linguistic injustice in legal settings (Sanders, 2021a). This kind of public outreach is crucial for projects like this, to highlight real-world applications for nonspecialists outside the academy, and it demonstrates how a project nominally focused on pedagogy can have broader impact outside academia.

Importantly, in all of these cases, the work essentially promoted itself. People heard about the project through word of mouth and internet searches, and they wanted to know more. Presentations led to more presentations, and connections led to more connections. Starting outreach as soon as possible, even in just one venue, can pay off down the road in more opportunities to distribute the work. A key factor is that all of our materials are publicly available on LEDIR. This was a decision we made early on in the project: anyone who wants access to our project materials should have access. Having these resources locked away in secret, distributed only to a select few, goes against the very principles of inclusion and equity that our work is based upon. We encourage other linguists to also make their materials publicly accessible wherever possible, so that we can collectively normalize an open-sourced, accessible, and critical pedagogical approach in the discipline (but for the complexities of Open Access, see Villarreal & Collister, 2024).

This work has also led to in-depth collaborations with instructors in other departments and at other institutions. A few examples include a presentation and forthcoming publication with a colleague in the Department of Mathematics at the University of Toronto on the effects of linguistic biases on the assessment of writing in math (Konnelly et al., 2022, forthcoming a); ongoing research with a colleague at another university in Canada on the effects of marginalized identities in online learning in linguistics courses throughout the country; and collaboration with a colleague at a university in the United States to expand the DND into a mobile app for ease of use while teaching. Each of these collaborations were completely unforeseen in the original conception of the initiative, a fact that highlights the importance of leaving space for flexibility in a large multifaceted project with broad appeal. Many people are interested in EDI issues, which touch on so many different aspects of our lives, so we expect that there will be plenty of opportunities to make further connections and expand this work.

Challenges and Limitations

We offer here a few cautionary notes about some of the issues we encountered while doing this work. The biggest challenge we faced was that the intended scope of the project was much more ambitious than what was practical with the time and resources we had available. There are many facets to both EDI and pedagogy, and it is impossible to address them all. During our first year of the project, we learned that we needed to spend more time reflecting on what our top priorities were, so that we could refocus our efforts in a narrower range. This meant that we could not accomplish everything we originally wanted, but it allowed us to better allocate our time to a more manageable set of tasks, so that work did actually get done. Doing this earlier would have been even better, so we recommend sitting down at the beginning of a project like this and being very selective in identifying which outcomes are must-haves and which can take lower priority. It is also important to understand the inherent limitations of certain topics. For example, we were initially very interested in reducing the reliance on English in a semantics course, but this turned out to be much more difficult than we anticipated. Part of the problem is that none of us are semanticists, but this is also a larger problem for the field of semantics itself (cf. Sanders, 2021b; see also Larson, 2022 for one path for addressing this problem). Relatedly, we were limited by our particular lived experiences. We had early frank discussions about our positionality, so that we could better determine which topics we needed to seek out more appropriate perspectives for. Of course, in any work in which a marginalized community is discussed, it is important to include and centre the work and experiences of members of that community, but we knew it was even more important to do so for those communities we were not a part of. We want to emphasize here how important it is to do this work early, so that the entire team knows when outside expertise is needed and has a plan for who to contact for that expertise. It is not enough to recognize the lack of relevant lived experience in the project; you must identify who you can have productive discussions with and which resources are available. Then, rather than scrambling at the last minute for rushed advice, you can instead take the time to forge more meaningful and longer-lasting collaborations.

Conclusion

Throughout this project, we have been guided by Anne Charity Hudley and Christine Mallinson's (2018, p. 514) questions about "what linguistics is, who it is for, and who it benefits." Adopting more inclusive teaching practices and materials in linguistics involves more than showcasing linguistics as a scientific field that is deeply embedded in the social world; it requires actively participating in the process of making that a reality. Our hope is that the proliferation of initiatives like this one and others described in this volume will drive a shift towards increased engagement and retention of students who have been historically underrepresented in the field. We also hope that these initiatives will give all students who come out of our courses a deeper understanding of how language perpetuates power imbalance and inequality in society.

Our intention for this chapter is not only to highlight how pedagogical interventions like this project can be adopted by others, but also why it is necessary for linguists to prioritize work toward social justice in our discipline. We hope our model will inspire other linguists to answer our call to action to confront linguistic injustice in their teaching, but we recognize that there are many other ways to address these issues, and a broad range of tactics are necessary. Our model contains only some of the many different tools that can be used to help change the underlying structures of our teaching as part of a larger process of deconstructing how linguistics is taught. We linguists must view this deconstruction as part of our scholarly and pedagogical practice, because if we do not actively work to challenge linguistic discrimination, we are helping to perpetuate it. We encourage our readers to leverage the tools that work for them and to respond to the many different manifestations of linguistic injustice in linguistics classrooms and elsewhere with innovative solutions that make sense in their unique context. We do not have all the answers, and no one group or individual can do this kind of work perfectly. Social justice is a communal effort, and we must all contribute and support each other.

Note

1. We thank Naomi Nagy, Keren Rice, and the members of the Language Variation and Change Research Group in the Department of Linguistics at the University of Toronto for early advice and support, especially in developing the proposal. We also thank Sali Tagliamonte, Alana Boland, and especially Thuy Huynh for helping finalize the proposal and budget. We thank Anne Charity Hudley for initial inspiration and continued wisdom throughout the life of the initiative. We thank audiences at the 2020 and 2021 annual meetings of the Canadian Linguistic Association, the Linguistic Society of America's Racial Justice, Equity, Diversity, and Inclusion in the Linguistics Curriculum webinar series, the 31st Semantics and Linguistic Theory conference, the 13th Toronto Undergraduate Linguistics Conference, the University of Toronto Faculty of Arts & Science Teaching and Learning Community of Practice, ezCPD.ca, the University of Toronto Mississauga 2022 Workshop on Linguistic Equity and Justice, and the 6th Northeastern Conference on Research in Undergraduate Mathematics Education for their feedback on various aspects of this work. We thank Henry Ivry, Jessie Richards, and Will Heikoop for discussions in helping plan for the future of the project. Finally, we thank Lauren Gawne and our editors for valuable feedback on earlier drafts of this chapter and Catherine Anderson, Susana Béjar, Marisa Brook, Ann Gagné, Peter Jurgec, Colin McCarter, Maura O'Leary, Avery Ozburn, Virgilio Partida-Peñalva, Carol Percy, Jason Siefken, Lisa Sullivan, Ai Taniguchi, Guillaume Thomas, and Erin Vearncombe for various discussions and collaborations that have enriched this project.

References

Alexander, Susan M. (2005). Social justice and the teaching of sociology. *Sociological Focus, 38*(3), 171–179. https://www.jstor.org/stable/20832266

Baglieri, Susan, & Knopf, Janice H. (2004). Normalizing difference in inclusive teaching. *Journal of Learning Disabilities, 37*(6), 525–529. https://doi.org/10.1177/00222194040370060701

Behrman, Alison. (2018). *Speech and voice science*, 3rd ed. Plural Publishing.

Bell, Roberta. (2019, December 5). Stoney language app connects elders, youth at Alexis Nakota Sioux Nation. CBC News. https://www.cbc.ca/originalvoices/language/nakoda/

Bergvall, Victoria L. (1996). Humpty Dumpty does syntax: Through the looking-glass, and what Alice found there. *Natural Language & Linguistic Theory, 14*(2), 433–443. https://www.jstor.org/stable/4047856

Bettez, Silvia Cristina. (2011). Building critical communities amid the uncertainty of social justice pedagogy in the graduate classroom. *The Review of Education, Pedagogy, and Cultural Studies, 33*(1), 76–106. https://doi.org/10.1080/10714413.2011.550191

Blundon, Patricia Hart. (2016). Nonstandard dialect and educational achievement: Potential implications for First Nations students. *Canadian Journal of Speech-Language Pathology and Audiology, 40*(3), 218–231. https://cjslpa.ca/files/2016_CJSLPA_Vol_40/No_03/CJSLPA_2016_Vol_40_No_3_Blundon_218-231.pdf

Bond, Gareth, & Chernoff, Egan J. (2015). Mathematics and social justice: A symbiotic pedagogy. *Journal of Urban Mathematics Education, 8*(1), 24–30. https://doi.org/10.21423/jume-v8i1a256

Bowern, Claire, & Dockum, Rikker. (2024). Decolonizing historical linguistics in the classroom and beyond. In Anne H. Charity Hudley, Christine Mallinson, & Mary Bucholtz (Eds.), *Decolonizing linguistics*. Oxford University Press.

Brantlinger, Andrew. (2013). Between politics and equations: Teaching critical mathematics in a remedial secondary classroom. *American Educational Research Journal, 50*(5), 1050–1080. https://doi.org/10.3102/0002831213487195

Bucholtz, Mary. (2016). On being called out of one's name: Indexical bleaching as a technique of deracialization. In H. Samy Alim, John R. Rickford, & Arnetha F. Ball (Eds.), *Raciolinguistics: How language shapes our ideas about race* (pp. 273–289). Oxford University Press.

Calhoun, Kendra, Charity Hudley, Anne H., Bucholtz, Mary, Exford, Jazmine, & Johnson, Brittney. 2021. Attracting Black students to linguistics through a Black-centered introduction to linguistics course. *Language, 97*(1), e12–e38. http://doi.org/10.1353/lan.2021.0007

Cépeda, Paola, Kotek, Hadas, Pabst, Katharina, & Syrett, Krysten. (2021). Gender bias in linguistics textbooks: Has anything changed since Macaulay & Brice 1997? *Language, 97*(4), 678–702. https://doi:10.1353/lan.2021.0061

Charity Hudley, Anne H. (2020). Fostering a culture of racial inclusion in linguistics: For the children of the 9th ward circa 2005. Plenary address at the 94th Annual Meeting of the Linguistic Society of America. https://www.youtube.com/watch?v=PSyvCJHLJvw

Charity Hudley, Anne H., & Mallinson, Christine. 2011. *Understanding English language variation in U.S. schools*. Teachers College Press.

Charity Hudley, Anne H., & Mallinson, Christine. 2018. Dismantling "The Master's Tools": Moving students' rights to their own language from theory to practice. *American Speech, 93*(3–4), 513–537. https://doi.org/10.1215/00031283-7271305

Charity Hudley, Anne H., Mallinson, Christine, & Bucholtz, Mary. (2020). Toward racial justice in linguistics: Interdisciplinary insights into theorizing race in the discipline and diversifying the profession. *Language, 96*(4), e200–e235. http://doi.org/10.1353/lan.2020.0074

Cochran, Katharine. (2019). Trans in higher ed: Understanding the experiences of transgender and nonbinary college students [Doctoral dissertation, University of Wisconsin-Milwaukee].

Conrod, Kirby. (2019). Doing gender and linguistics. Keynote lecture given at They, Hirself, Em, and You: Nonbinary Pronouns in Research and Practice conference. Queen's University, June 11-13.

Delpit, Lisa. (2006). Lessons from teachers. *Journal of Teacher Education, 57*(3), 220–231. https://doi.org/10.1177/0022487105285966

Dewsbury, Bryan, & Brame, Cynthia J. (2019). Inclusive teaching. *CBE–Life Sciences Education, 18*(2), 1–5. https://doi.org/10.1187/cbe.18-11-0226

Fletcher, John D. (1983). What problems do American Indians have with English? *Journal of American Indian Education, 23*(1), 1–14. https://eric.ed.gov/?id=ED247051

Flores, Nelson, & Rosa, Jonathan. (2015). Undoing appropriateness: Raciolinguistic ideologies and language diversity in education. *Harvard Educational Review, 85*(2), 149–171. https://doi.org/10.17763/0017-8055.85.2.149

Gerdin, Göran, Smith, Wayne, Philpot, Rod, Schenker, Katarina, Moen, Kjersti Mordal, Linnér, Susanne, Westlie, Knut, & Larsson, Lena. (2021). *Social justice pedagogies in health and physical education.* Routledge.

Gibson, Hannah, Jerro, Kyle, Namboodiripad, Savithry, & Riedel, Kristina. (2024). Towards a decolonial syntax: Research, teaching, publishing. In Anne H Charity Hudley, Christine Mallinson, & Mary Bucholtz (Eds.), *Decolonizing linguistics.* Oxford University Press.

Gobl, Christer, & Chasaide, Ailbhe Ní. (2010). Voice source variation and its communicative functions. In William J. Hardcastle, John Laver, & Fiona E. Gibbon (Eds.), *The handbook of phonetic sciences,* 2nd ed. (pp. 378–423). Wiley-Blackwell.

Gray, John. (2013). LGBT invisibility and heteronormativity in ELT materials. In John Gray (Ed.), *Critical perspectives on language teaching materials* (pp. 40–63). Palgrave Macmillan.

Hammond, J. W., Brownell, Sara E., Kedharnath, Nita A., Cheng, Susan J., & Byrd, W. Carson. (2021, September 23). Why the term "JEDI" is problematic for describing programs that promote justice, equity, diversity and inclusion. *Scientific American Inequality.* https://www.scientificamerican.com/article/why-the-term-jedi-is-problematic-for-describing-programs-that-promote-justice-equity-diversity-and-inclusion/

Hercula, Sarah E. (2020). *Fostering linguistic equality: The SISE approach to the introductory linguistics course.* Palgrave Macmillan.

Hobbel, Nikkola. (2010). *Social justice pedagogy across the curriculum: The practice of freedom.* Routledge.

hooks, bell. (1994). *Teaching to transgress: Education as the practice of freedom.* Routledge.

Howard, David M., & Angus, Jamie A. S. (2017). *Acoustics and psychoacoustics,* 5th ed. Routledge.

Kohli, Rita, & Solórzano, Daniel G. (2012). Teachers, please learn our names! Racial microaggressions and the K–12 classroom. *Race Ethnicity and Education, 15*(4), 441–462. https://doi.org/10.1080/13613324.2012.674026

Konnelly, Lex, Sanders, Nathan, Siefken, Jason, & Umbal, Pocholo. (2022). Are writing questions in math fair? Talk presented at the 6th Northeastern Conference on Research in Undergraduate Mathematics Education. Virtual: October 15.

Konnelly, Lex, Umbal, Pocholo, & Sanders, Nathan. (2021). The diverse names database: A tool for creating more equitable, diverse, and inclusive linguistic example sentences. Poster presentation in the Special Session on Pedagogy at the Congrès annuel de l'Association canadienne de linguistique 2021/Annual meeting of the Canadian Linguistic Association. Virtual. June 4-7.

Konnelly, Lex, Sanders, Nathan, Siefken, Jason, & Umbal, Pocholo. (forthcoming a). Are writing questions in math fair? *Journal of the Scholarship of Teaching and Learning.*

Konnelly, Lex, Umbal, Pocholo, & Sanders, Nathan. (forthcoming b). On the use of names and example sentences in the linguistics classroom. *Canadian Journal of Linguistics.*

Kotek, Hadas, Babinski, Sarah, Dockum, Rikker, & Geissler, Christopher. (2020). Gender representation in linguistic example sentences. *Proceedings of the Linguistic Society of America, 5*(1), 514–528. https://doi.org/10.3765/plsa.v5i1.4723

Kotek, Hadas, Babinski, Sarah, Dockum, Rikker, & Geissler, Christopher. (2021). Gender bias and stereotypes in linguistic example sentences. *Language, 97*(4), 653–677. http://doi.org/10.1353/lan.2021.0060

Larson, Richard K. (2022). *Semantics as science.* MIT Press.

Leonard, Wesley Y. (2018). Reflections on (de)colonialism in language documentation. In Bradley McDonnell, Andrea L. BerezKroeker, & Gary Holton (Eds.), *Reflections on Language Documentation 20 Years After Himmelmann 1998* (pp. 55–65). University of Hawai'i Press.

Lippi-Green, Rosina. (2012). *English with an accent: Language, ideology and discrimination in the United States,* 2nd ed. Routledge.

Linguistic Society of America (LSA). (2022). Gender bias and stereotypes in linguistics research and teaching. Webinar. https://www.youtube.com/watch?v=LFGeB1r3u9s

Macaulay, Monica, & Brice, Colleen. (1994). Gentlemen prefer blondes: A study of gender bias in example sentences. In Mary Bucholtz, A.C. Liang, Laurel A. Sutton, & Caitlin Hines (Eds.), *Cultural Performances: Proceedings of the Third Berkeley Women and Language Conference* (pp. 449–461). Berkeley Women and Language Group.

Macaulay, Monica, & Brice, Colleen. (1997). Don't touch my projectile: Gender bias and stereotyping in syntactic examples. *Language, 73*(4), 798–825. https://doi.org/10.2307/417327

Mallinson, Christine. (2024). Linguistic variation and linguistic inclusion in education. *Annual Review of Linguistics,* 10. https://doi.org/10.1146/annurev-linguistics-031120-121546.

Martinez, Danny C., Zitlali Morales, P., and Aldana, Ursula S. (2017). Leveraging students' communicative repertoires as a tool for equitable learning. *Review of Research in Education, 41*(1), 477–499. https://doi.org/10.3102/0091732X17691741

Namboodiripad, Savithry, & Sanders, Nathan. (2020). Centering linguistic diversity and justice in course design. Racial Justice, Equity, Diversity, and Inclusion in the Linguistics Curriculum webinar series, Linguistic Society of America. https://www.linguisticsociety.org/resource/webinar-centering-linguistic-diversity-and-justice-course-design

Nelson, Cynthia D. (2007). Queer thinking about language teaching: An overview of published work. In Helene Decke-Cornill and Laurenz Volkmann (Eds.), *Gender Studies in Foreign Language Teaching* (pp. 63–76). Guter Narr.

Neto, João Nemi. (2018). Queer pedagogy: Approaches to inclusive teaching. *Policy Futures in Education, 15*(5), 589–604. https://doi.org/10.1177/1478210317751273

Nicotera, Anthony. (2019). Social justice and social work, a fierce urgency: Recommendations for social work social justice pedagogy. *Journal of Social Work Education, 55*(3), 460–475. https://doi.org/10.1080/10437797.2019.1600443

Pabst, Katharina, Cépeda, Paola, Kotek, Hadas, Syrett, Krysten, Donelson, Katharine, & McCarvel, Miranda. (2018). Gender bias in linguistics textbooks: Has anything changed since Macaulay & Brice (1997)? Paper presented at the 92nd annual meeting of the Linguistic Society of America. Salt Lake City, UT: January 4-7.

Paiz, Joshua M. (2019). Queering practice: LGBTQ+ diversity and inclusion in English language teaching. *Journal of Language, Identity & Education, 18*(4), 266–275. https://doi.org/10.1080/15348458.2019.1629933

Richy, Célia, & Burnett, Heather. (2019). Jean does the dishes while Marie fixes the car: A qualitative and quantitative study of social gender in French syntax articles. *Journal of French Language Studies, 30*(1), 1–26. https://doi.org/10.1017/S0959269519000280

Rickford, John R. (1997). Unequal partnership: Sociolinguistics and the African American speech community. *Language in Society, 26*(2), 161–197. https://www.jstor.org/stable/4168760

Rickford, John R., & King, Sharese. (2016). Language and linguistics on trial: Hearing Rachel Jeantel (and other vernacular speakers) in the courtroom and beyond. *Language, 92*(4), 948–988. http://doi.org/10.1353/lan.2016.0078

Rudy, Alan P., & Konefal, Jason. (2007). Nature, sociology, and social justice: Environmental sociology, pedagogy, and the curriculum. *American Behavioral Scientist, 51*(4), 495–515. https://doi.org/10.1177/0002764207307739

Russell, Stephen T., Pollitt, Amanda M., Li, Gu, and Grossman, Arnold H. (2018). Chosen name use is linked to reduced depressive symptoms, suicidal ideation, and suicidal behavior among transgender youth. *Journal of Adolescent Health, 63*(4), 503–505. https://doi.org/10.1016/j.jadohealth.2018.02.003

Sanders, Nathan. (2021a). Language-based biases in legal contexts. ezCPD.ca webinar. http://sanders.phonologist.org/Papers/sanders-lg-biases-legal.pdf

Sanders, Nathan. (2021b). Teaching semantics from a JEDI perspective: Some considerations. Invited presentation in the Workshop on Inclusive Teaching in Semantics at the 31st Semantics and Linguistic Theory conference. Brown University: May 7-9. https://www.youtube.com/watch?v=6jzTtXxqUkU

Sanders, Nathan, Umbal, Pocholo, & Konnelly, Lex. (2020). Methods for increasing equity, diversity, and inclusion in linguistics pedagogy. *Actes du congrès annuel de l'Association canadienne de linguistique 2020 | Proceedings of the 2020 Annual Conference of the Canadian Linguistic Association.* https://cla-acl.artsci.utoronto.ca/actes-2020-proceedings/

Sanders, Nathan, Umbal, Pocholo, & Konnelly, Lex. (2021–2022). The Linguistics Equity, Diversity, and Inclusion Repository. https://ledir.ling.utoronto.ca/

Shin, Hyunjung, & Sterzuk, Andrea. (2019). Discourses, practices, and realities of multilingualism in higher education. *TESL Canada Journal, 36*(1), 147–159. https://doi.org/10.18806/tesl.v36i1.1307

Spring, Cari L., Moses, Rae, Flynn, Michael, Steele, Susan, Joseph, Brian D., and Webb, Charlotte. (2000). The successful introductory course: Bridging the gap for the nonmajor. *Language, 76*(1), 110–122. https://doi.org/10.1353/lan.2000.0124

Stein, Sharon. (2020). "Truth before reconciliation": The difficulties of transforming higher education in settler colonial contexts. *Higher Education Research & Development, 39*(1), 156–170. https://doi.org/10.1080/07294360.2019.1666255

Tamtik, Merli, & Guenter, Melissa. (2019). Policy analysis of equity, diversity and inclusion strategies in Canadian universities: How far have we come? *Canadian Journal of Higher Education, 49*(3), 41–56. https://doi.org/10.47678/cjhe.v49i3.188529

Universities Canada. (2019). *Equity, diversity and inclusion at Canadian universities: Report on the 2019 survey.* https://www.univcan.ca/media-room/publications/equity-diversity-and-inclusion-at-canadian-universities-report-on-the-2019-survey/

University of Toronto Faculty of Arts & Science. (2020). Academic plan 2020–2025: Leveraging our strengths. https://www.artsci.utoronto.ca/about/strategic-overview/academic-plan-2020-2025/academic-plan-pdf

Vandrick, Stephanie. (1997). The role of hidden identities in the postsecondary ESL classroom. *TESOL Quarterly, 31*(1), 153–157. https://doi.org/10.2307/3587980

Villarreal, Dan, & Collister, Lauren. (2024). Open Methods: Decolonizing (or not) research methods in linguistics. In Anne H. Charity Hudley, Christine Mallinson, & Mary Bucholtz (Eds.), *Decolonizing linguistics.* Oxford University Press.

Wagner, Anita A., & Stinson, David W. 2013. *Teaching mathematics for social justice: Conversations with educators.* National Council of Teachers of Mathematics.

Yusun, Timothy, & Gagné, Ann. (2021). Towards a supportive math pedagogy: Power dynamics and academic integrity considerations. *Canadian Perspectives on Academic Integrity, 4*(1), 70–90. https://doi.org/10.11575/cpai.v4i1.71341

Zhang, Ying Shan Doris, & Noels, Kimberly. (2021). The frequency and importance of accurate heritage name pronunciation for post-secondary international students in Canada. *Journal of International Students, 11*(3), 608–627. https://doi.org/10.32674/jis.v11i3.2232

PART 4

FOSTERING COMMUNITY PARTNERSHIPS AND PUBLIC ENGAGEMENT

Lauren Gawne is senior lecturer in linguistics at La Trobe University (Melbourne, Australia), and co-produces Lingthusiasm with Gretchen McCulloch. She was a writer and consultant for Crash Course Linguistics.

Gretchen McCulloch is an author who writes about linguistics for public audiences, including her 2019 book *Because Internet*, and co-produces Lingthusiasm with Lauren Gawne. She was a writer and consultant for Crash Course Linguistics.

Nicole Sweeney is an executive producer at Complexly and was the producer for Crash Course Linguistics.

Rachel Alatalo is a managing editor at Complexly and was the script editor for Crash Course Linguistics.

Hannah Bodenhausen is a producer at Complexly and was the video editor for Crash Course Linguistics.

Ceri Riley previously worked at Complexly and was the content manager for Crash Course Linguistics.

Jessi Grieser is associate professor of linguistics at the University of Michigan. She was the fact checker for Crash Course Linguistics.

Abstract: This case study vignette provides an insight into the choices made in the writing of Crash Course Linguistics. This series of 16 ten-minute videos cover core introductory level topics for English speakers who consume online content. This chapter discusses how the topics were selected and arranged into a series order. The authors also discuss the ways in which inclusion was actively built into the series workflow and content, including in the team that worked on the content, the language examples selected, and topics covered. Throughout, the authors discuss the challenges and benefits of working in a collaborative team that includes a media production company and linguists with a commitment to public engagement and communication linguistics to new audiences. Sharing these observations about putting Crash Course Linguistics together is part of the authors' commitment to using public communication to advance the standard of public engagement with the field, and the field's approach to inclusive practice.

Key Words: lingcomm, video, YouTube, audience, collaboration

18
Creating Inclusive Linguistics Communication

Crash Course Linguistics

Lauren Gawne (she/they)
La Trobe University, Lingthusiasm

Gretchen McCulloch (she/her)
Lingthusiasm

Nicole Sweeney (she/her)
Complexly

Rachel Alatalo (they/them)
Complexly

Hannah Bodenhausen (she/her)
Complexly

Ceri Riley (she/her)
Complexly

Jessi Grieser (she/her)
University of Michigan

Introduction

Popular media and social media are places where people first discover the discipline of linguistics.[1] In order to ensure that the broadest possible population feels that linguistics is relevant to their experiences, linguistics communication (lingcomm) should be undertaken with inclusivity as a central aim. Public-facing linguistics content that sets a high standard for inclusivity also helps set

Lauren Gawne, Gretchen McCulloch, Nicole Sweeney, Rachel Alatalo, Hannah Bodenhausen, Ceri Riley, and Jessi Grieser,
Creating Inclusive Linguistics Communication In: *Inclusion in Linguistics*. Edited by: Anne H Charity Hudley, Christine Mallinson and Mary Bucholtz, Oxford University Press. © Anne H. Charity Hudley, Christine Mallinson, and Mary Bucholtz 2024.
DOI: 10.1093/oso/9780197755303.003.0019

higher expectations, and provides more useful resources, inside the discipline as well. This case study outlines a specific lingcomm project where inclusion was an intentional goal: script writing and production for the Crash Course Linguistics online educational series.[2] In sharing this experience we hope to demonstrate the critical considerations that go into producing high-quality lingcomm, and provide a model for lingcomm that takes an inclusive approach.

Lingcomm is its own area of expertise with a skill set that draws on both knowledge of linguistics and skill at communicating this knowledge to audiences outside of the academy. This skill set is rarely overtly taught or encouraged within linguistic academia, in spite of the valuable contribution it can make to the reputation and reach of the discipline. Striving for inclusive lingcomm broadens the number of people who have a positive conceptualization of linguistics and its relevance to their lives, providing more pathways into discovery and learning, and the range of backgrounds and experiences these people bring to their engagement with the discipline. This pathway could be formal education, or individuals (un)learning about linguistic injustice in their own lives. For us, a primary concern of inclusive lingcomm is that audiences see themselves in the media they consume while being educated and entertained. Additionally, for teachers and professors, these materials provide an easily accessible way to broaden inclusion in their introductory classes. Regardless of whether lingcomm resources are used for formal study or personal education, everybody has their lived experience of and with language, and part of our critical approach to lingcomm is ensuring that as many people feel included in linguistics as possible. Inclusion of a wide range of linguistic experiences, including nonstandard Englishes, signed as well as spoken modality and a global norm of multilingualism, was central to the conceptualization and execution of this project, as discussed in the following section.

Our work is situated at the intersection of discussions around more inclusive practices in the field of linguistics (Charity Hudley et al., 2020) and in the field of science communication (Canfield et al., 2020). Within science communication we draw on evidence-based practice in how to communicate technical concepts to nonspecialist audiences. Key approaches that have influenced our approach to lingcomm include the evidence that explaining concepts before introducing technical jargon increases likelihood of comprehension (McDonnell at al., 2016) and the approach to misinformation in the Debunking Handbook (Lewandowsky et al., 2020) where audiences need an updated mental model to replace incorrect information.

We start with an introduction to Crash Course and the Linguistics series before looking at some of the specific choices we made in writing the series.

Throughout, we discuss the perspectives the different team members brought to the project, and the challenges and benefits of collaborations between academic linguists and existing media organizations to create thoughtful lingcomm projects. We conclude with a discussion of the importance of critical approaches to lingcomm to inclusion in linguistics. Our aim is to guide you, the reader, in the ways these collaborations might occur, point you toward some best practices in inclusion in scicomm, and demonstrate the ways inclusive scicomm might also inform inclusive practice in and outside of academe.

Crash Course Linguistics: The Series

Crash Course provides free, online educational videos with high production quality, predominantly distributed through YouTube. These videos cover a wide range of topics, from Literature, Psychology, and World History to Astronomy, Statistics, and Organic Chemistry. The content is a fast-paced introduction to high school and college level content, providing a more compelling introduction for self-directed learners than the traditional textbook model, while also being rigorous enough to serve as a classroom resource. In 2020 Complexly, a for-profit company, produced Crash Course Linguistics (Nielsen, 2020) in collaboration with Public Broadcasting System (PBS), a private nonprofit corporation in the US that co-funded production and also distributes the show on its own online educational network. As an established media company, Complexly provided funding for paying the host, writers, editors, animators (through their close collaborator, Thought Café), and other roles. However, this funding was limited from the beginning to a 16-episode series (160 minutes) and any decision to expand it or create a second season is at the discretion of Complexly, which along with PBS hold the media rights to this intellectual property.

Complexly has a long-held commitment to making educational materials inclusive and accessible. Founders Hank and John Green, both white cis men from the US, have been hosting video series since 2012, but as the company grew, Crash Course began to recruit presenters of various genders, races and ethnicities. Complexly approached the writing team based on their lingcomm and research experience. The three writing team members had experience running their own lingcomm projects (including the Lingthusiasm podcast from McCulloch and Gawne), and a commitment in existing projects to communicating about a diverse range of linguistic experiences. This existing work provided evidence to Complexly of the linguistics writing team's own goals.

All participants were paid for their contribution, either as salaried members of the Complexly team, or as contractors on a per-script basis.

For the linguists on the team, Complexly's reputation and prior work helped us feel confident in their commitment to an inclusive approach. The primary challenge for inclusive lingcomm with Complexly was thus less about selling the team on the need for inclusion in the first place, and more establishing exactly what inclusion consisted of for linguistics and how we could implement that vision together. We recognize that working with existing companies is not without risk for linguists and that not all media companies may share these same priorities. For Complexly, the writing team's prior work on public-facing lingcomm helped demonstrate a capacity to deliver subject content in an engaging and ethical way. The initial planning conversations were vital for ensuring everyone was on the same page regarding the aims of the project, and inclusion was central to those early discussions.

As noted above, this chapter is a collaboration of the writing team for the series and members of the Complexly production team. From the writing team, Gawne is a white linguist from Australia, McCulloch is a white linguist from Canada, and Grieser is a Black linguist from the US. Sweeney, Alatalo, Bodenhausen, and Riley were members of Complexly's production team for the series. The first three are white people from the US. Riley is multiracial (Malaysian Chinese American), Alatalo is nonbinary, and the rest of the team is made up of cis women. Acknowledgment that the team is predominantly white, predominantly cis female, and all users of normative varieties of English helped us to see the limits of our lived experiences.

Planning the series included operating within time constraints; Complexly had an upper limit of 16 episodes of about 10 minutes each for the series. There was also a two-minute preview that introduced the field of linguistics and outlined the topics covered in the series. The structure drastically limited the number of topics and examples we could cover in an episode. Table 18.1 is an overview of the series.

Each Crash Course series is presented by a single host, recruited and cast by Complexly. Crash Course Linguistics was presented by Taylor Behnke, host of the YouTube channel It's Radish Time, which includes personal diary-style videos and discussions of social justice. This commitment to social justice in Behnke's own work formed part of our enthusiasm for working with her. Her experience studying linguistics as an undergraduate made it easier for her to read terminology and International Phonetic Alphabet transcription. Behnke's linguistic repertoire as a multiracial Black American woman also informed the selection of topics in the sociolinguistics video through a series of planning discussions between her and the writers; for example, in

Table 18.1 List of episodes in the Crash Course Linguistics series

Episode	Topic
00	Crash Course Linguistics Preview
01	What is Linguistics? (broad introduction)
02	Morphology
03	Syntax 1 - Morphosyntax
04	Syntax 2 - Trees
05	Semantics
06	Pragmatics
07	Sociolinguistics
08	Phonetics 1 - Consonants
09	Phonetics 2 - Vowels
10	Phonology
11	Psycholinguistics
12	Language acquisition
13	Language change and historical linguistics
14	World languages
15	Computational linguistics
16	Writing systems

one segment, Behnke codeswitches into African American English to illustrate features of this variety and critique linguistic appropriation. Recruiting Behnke as the "face" of linguistics for the Crash Course audience was part of our active attempt to reduce raciolinguistic gatekeeping (Rosa & Flores, 2017) in early engagement with linguistics by having a young biracial woman as the professional face of linguistics, discussing the scientific study of language in a way that positively draws on features from racialized varieties as part of introducing core linguistic concepts (Arnold, this volume, discusses this challenge in the classroom). Centering features from racialized varieties while introducing core linguistics concepts and having a multiracial person as the authoritative host should not be treated as groundbreaking choices, but they were considerations we actively made in development of the series.

A Focus on Inclusion in Crash Course Linguistics

Awareness of our audience—people across the globe who use English, with internet access and an interest in language and linguistics, or a general sense of curiosity—and of the role of the series as a model for lingcomm more generally, informed our commitment to inclusion was a foundational goal in Crash Course Linguistics. Inclusion in lingcomm means not only presenting a range of languages and varieties in ways which do not privilege hegemonic languages, varieties, or language users, but also making linguistic knowledge itself accessible. In sharing these specific examples we hope to demonstrate that building intentionally inclusive lingcomm content, while requiring forethought and careful planning, ultimately strengthens the end product and invites broader participation in the field. We overtly flag ways you can use these observations in making your own lingcomm projects more inclusive.

In any lingcomm project with an external commercial organization, due diligence needs to be done ahead of time to ensure that the entire team shares your aim of inclusivity, and that the definition of inclusion is agreed upon. The different backgrounds of our team members helped expand our combined definition of inclusion; Complexly and Thought Café had a long tradition of ensuring inclusive representation with regard to race and gender, while the linguists on the team also wanted to ensure that a diversity of languages, modalities, and linguistic varieties were represented in the examples used to illustrate linguistics concepts. While we drew on the different perspectives of the team members, we also discussed the limitations of the team and sought external script checks when discussing signed languages and minoritized varieties, particularly examples in Indigenous languages. Expanding the linguistic repertoire for a project can be a challenge with any organization, whether commercial or not-for-profit (e.g., a university publisher), particularly when editorial decisions are made outside of the direct production team's control.

In this case, Crash Course already had a strong commitment to inclusivity. For example, the writers' guidelines for all Crash Course series make such requests as: avoid too much jargon, use conversational language, don't be US-centric or Eurocentric. The Complexly production team also has a strong established practice of ensuring inclusion, such as using animated characters and stock images that allow all audience members to see people that look like them in the videos, and they continued this practice in the Crash Course Linguistics series. Before starting the project the writing team drafted the episode syllabus and a range of principles that we would aspire to meet, including our commitment to including signed as well as spoken modalities and the need to center perspectives that focus on descriptivism and linguistic justice. The production team worked together to make sure we met those goals in each episode, with Complexly editors using the list of principles to flag when, for example, an episode did not include mention of signed examples.

Thanks to this intensive collaborative editing process we managed to meet these goals. The writing team were involved not only in script-writing (McCulloch & Gawne) but also in video fact-checking (Grieser). The animation team was receptive to feedback, such as not including nation-state boundaries on maps when they were not relevant to the languages being shown. The Crash Course team also ensured that we were held to our own principles as we turned in scripts, and the rigorous editing process ensured the scripts were as clear and compelling as possible. This is support that would not have been available without a larger commercial production. Choosing to accept collaboration offers from thoughtful partners like Complexly is an important part of creating inclusive lingcomm to reach the widest possible audience. Subsequent to the production of Crash Course Linguistics, Complexly have asked the writing team for content checks on other series, indicating an expansion of awareness regarding linguistic inclusiveness as a result of this project. Public engagement work for linguistics can be enhanced beyond the lifespan of a project when collaboration is mutually enriching in this way.

Aspiring to create compelling lingcomm for a wide international audience provides an opportunity to re-envision and selectively choose the best pedagogical approaches. One strategy we used was to consult with the Linguistic Society of America's Committee on Advanced Placement (AP) Linguistics, which had recently conducted a survey of college level introductory linguistics courses on offer in North America as part of their work toward a high-school level AP curriculum. We drew upon the survey findings to ensure we covered a relevant range of topics for high school and college viewers. It also led us to reconsider the order in which episodes were presented. Rather than the prevalent curriculum reported to the AP Linguistics committee, which moves from the smallest linguistic units to the largest (i.e., from phonetics to morphology to syntax and so on), we took an approach used in a minority of introductory programs that starts with words and morphemes and then moves to syntax, semantics, pragmatics, and then loops back to phonetics/phonology via sociolinguistics. We chose this order as phonetics is especially dense with terminology, making it intimidating to casual beginners. Words are a more straightforward starting place for linguistics newcomers than phonetics, as people feel they have an intuition of what is a word (even if it's not quite how linguists approach words). By beginning with words and their structure, we could tap immediately into questions viewers were likely to already have. This content structure was already used by one of our authors (Gawne) in her introductory college linguistics class, and subsequently used by another contributor (Grieser) in her own introductory course with great success.

In another inclusive strategy, the languages discussed in each episode were carefully considered so that there was a balance of geographic diversity and language families, as well as a balance of languages likely to be familiar and new to much of the audience. The languages used throughout the series in part reflect the research interests and linguistic repertoires of the authors. We drew on the language experience of the team, the majority of whom know multiple languages, including Spanish, Mandarin, Nepali, Latin, and French, but these are all majority languages with a skew toward Europe. Having a team from Canada, Australia, and the US with different training and research interests helped us broaden the range of languages included, illustrating the benefit of building inclusive teams to increase the potential for inclusive output. The introduction of every video included an opening animation that had written facts about language presented not only in English, but also in French, Russian, Chinese, Arabic, German, Korean, Vietnamese, and Klingon, reflecting the linguistic diversity and interests of the Thought Café animation team. The lack of expertise in minoritized or Indigenous languages in the production team led to the limitation of languages in this section to global/national languages. Throughout the series we mentioned over 100 languages and families. We also discussed different varieties of some languages; for English we made mention of African American English, Appalachian English, Australian English, Standardized American English, and British English, as well as Middle English and Old English. In the signed modality we included examples from both British Sign Language (BSL) and Auslan (the signed language of Australia) and discussed how they are related languages in the same family with South African Sign Language (SASL) and New Zealand Sign Language (NZSL).

We found it easier to include more languages for some topics than others. Historical linguistics (episode 13) and sociolinguistics (episode 7) lend themselves to discussing a diversity of languages because foundational concepts are best illustrated through a plurality of examples from a range of languages (see also Bowern & Dockum, 2024; Sanders et al., this volume). The 10-minute episode constraint meant that for other topics the focus was on introducing technical processes, terminology or different theoretical approaches. For example, in the episode on semantics (episode 5) we decided to introduce predicate calculus in English without simultaneously performing it on another language, as there is already a lot to unpack working on a standard English model. The list of languages used as illustrative examples and those that are additionally mentioned can be found online (Grieser et al., 2021).

Another vital component of our commitment to linguistic diversity was ensuring that signed languages were included throughout (for additional examples of active inclusion, see Hou & Ali, this volume, and Sanders et al., this volume) to counter the often unintentional but very real audism of approaches to linguistics that only include spoken languages. This strategy included overtly referencing specific signed languages, as well as moving away from oralist descriptions of linguistic phenomena; for example, discussing both sounds and handshapes in our episodes on phonetics and phonology. We consulted with a number of deaf and hearing signed language linguists on these examples, including Gabrielle Hodge, Lynn Hou, and Adam Schembri. Including signed languages across the videos was a minimum benchmark for us, but with more videos we would have liked to have more extended discussion of signed examples of linguistic phenomena. This content is not covered in many introductory textbooks, but for public communication work to introduce people to the field it is important not simply to reproduce existing pedagogy but to engage with the primary linguistic research literature to find new examples or contact scholars where necessary (a strategy also discussed in Bancu, Peltier, et al., 2024). A larger-scale project benefits from a network of team members and consultants from different linguistic backgrounds and minoritized identities to ensure a range of languages and social groups are actively involved in shaping lingcomm content. In this project that network was built informally via the professional networks of the linguist writing team, but a more formalized advisory committee would have made this work easier, and better recognized the contribution of these experts.

As well as diversity at the general level of named languages, we also sought to ensure a realistic and inclusive representation of language at the social level. We worked with host Taylor Behnke to write the narrative for this episode around her linguistic experience as a queer biracial American woman. As Jamie Thomas (this volume) notes, "language is unavoidably personal," and so we added small touches of Behnke's personal experience to other episodes, such as including her own anecdote about her first words in the episode on language acquisition (episode 12). Behnke's experience of language and its role in identity was made most explicit in episode 7. This episode normalizes linguistic variation and specifically demonstrates the grammaticality of African American English (showcasing research in Jackson & Green, 2005) while referencing work from John Baugh (1983) and Kelly Wright (2019) to demonstrate the real effect of linguistic discrimination in people's lives, particularly with regard to African American English in the context of the US. We decided to focus on the social context of African American English to help people use linguistics to confront their own ideologies, as even audiences outside of the US have some engagement with this variety. In this way we have taken the same approach as Jenny Lederer (this volume) to place linguistic authority in the hands of language users. This is one of the more overt examples of how, throughout the series, we approached lingcomm in a way that heeded the call from Anne Charity Hudley et al. (2020) to dismantle raciolinguistic ideologies in how we discussed language and its use.

Inclusion in lingcomm fundamentally means bringing nonlinguists along for the ride. One of the major choices we made was to encourage audience identification with linguistic experiences rather than ideological debates within the discipline. For example, in discussing child language acquisition (episode 12) we decided to focus on affirming parents raising bilingual and multilingual children, rather than academic debates about the innateness of children's capacity for language. Similarly, in discussing historical linguistics (episode 13), we expanded our approach beyond the oft-discussed Proto-Indo-European to include other proto-languages (including Proto-Algonquian, Proto-Austronesian and Proto-Bantu); we also discussed language contact with a focus on pidgins and creoles (Bowern & Dockum, 2024, discuss in more detail the ways that historical linguistics can grapple with its colonialist roots). Issues we addressed that further connected linguistics to topics of social importance include the damaging effect of residential schools on First Nations communities and languages (Truth and Reconciliation Commission of Canada, 2015); bias in language tech (Bender et al., 2021), where we used existing research to frame our discussion (Suresh & Guttag, 2019); and gender identity, including singular *they* and neopronouns drawing on the work of Kirby Conrod (2019). This focus on topics that connect to lived experiences and real-world issues is also a theme of Plackowski's (this volume) approach to classroom teaching.

Another consideration when making lingcomm inclusive is to ensure that audiences aren't alienated by an avalanche of terminology. The aim of lingcomm is not to create content that people are required to memorize, but to give them the broader conceptual point. Sometimes this can mean using terminology without focusing on it too heavily. For example, in introducing the International Phonetic Alphabet (episodes 8 and 9) our focus was on explaining the larger organizing principle behind the IPA chart, so that the audience has a better chance of recalling this when they encounter it in the future. Rather than focus on teaching the names of specific places of articulation, for example, we capitalized on the ability to animate a midsagittal section to show how the IPA chart corresponds to those places of articulation. Sometimes, serving the audience and making linguistics accessible means prioritizing some content while not including other commonly taught elements: In our introduction to morphology we omitted a discussion of inflectional and derivational morphology in favor of using the time to introduce cross-linguistic variation in the amount of morphology (with our examples including Chinese, German, English, ASL (American Sign Language), and Murrinhpatha). In the episode on vowels we deprioritized the discussion of tense/lax distinctions, including it in the same section as length and tone features, which are more common cross-linguistically.

Limitations and Future Considerations

Even a project with a large team and access to funding and resources still has its limitations. We have discussed above how our awareness of the limitations of the linguistic experiences of the production team led us to seek input and feedback from a wider range of experts, in a partial effort to move beyond those limited experiences Here we discuss some of the broader limitations posed by creating a commercially produced product for a particular internet-using audience.

One major limitation in terms of audience inclusivity is that Crash Course Linguistics is delivered entirely in English. Subtitles are only available in English as well. Crash Course used to attract community-created captions in other languages, but YouTube removed the option to create such captions in 2020. This means that, for now, Crash Course Linguistics is only accessible to those who speak or read English.

The series was also designed for an online-savvy audience, with passing reference to internet tropes and memes in some videos. Inclusivity does not mean making projects that are generic enough to be consumable by a generic audience, but to continue to work toward different approaches for different audiences. Public engagement with linguistics needs to happen in a broader range of languages and contexts to continue to move toward inclusivity.

A final limitation of this series, and most lingcomm, is the lack of tracking engagement and impact for lingcomm work. We know engagement has been strong, since YouTube keeps play counts public. Each video has been watched 100,000 times or more (there's half a million views on the first video as of writing this in mid-2022). As for impact, we have received some feedback from viewers that the series was their introduction to the field and they subsequently moved on to engage with other lingcomm projects such as Lingthusiasm. We have also had some colleagues tell us they are using the videos in their introductory classes. If you make use of any public resources, including the many excellent lingcomm projects in this volume, we encourage you to contact the creators to let them know how you've been using their work to help them build evidence of the value of their lingcomm work.

Conclusion: Lingcomm Is Important for Inclusion in Linguistics

Public-facing educational resources are often people's first encounter with linguistics. With Crash Course Linguistics, we wanted those resources to show that linguistics is a lens that can help learners address their own priorities, including racial justice, anti-colonialism, and anti-audism. For learners who may initially have been attracted to linguistics by one topic in particular, we hope to have also expanded their horizons to develop a fuller picture. Thoughtful lingcomm moves beyond uncritically re-explaining the received wisdom of the field with more humor and less jargon, and toward re-examining the validity of the core assumptions of the field and reconceptualizing how and if they should be presented. This also helps raise standards within the discipline when it comes to inclusion, by normalizing approaches to key topics that center the linguistic experiences of a wider range of people, particularly those whose varieties of language are minortized, racialized, or otherwise made absent from the curriculum.

For those who are creating lingcomm projects, we set forth a few guiding principles to help make your work more inclusive. First, know who your audience is. Knowing who you're creating for helps you shape your choices so that you can make space for those who are not used to seeing their own experiences in linguistics and make choices that are directly relevant to their experiences. Second, assemble a team with a variety of perspectives. For this project, having a team that included even some linguistic and social variation, as well as a collaborative combination of linguists and nonlinguists was a valuable way to ensure that the content was clearly communicated. Third, ensure that everyone agrees on the scope of the project, which includes overt discussion of the inclusivity aims. In our case, this principle allowed us all to be able to refer to expectations, which was particularly important for making sure we met the goals the Complexly team set for itself as well as the goals the writing team set. Fourth, push yourself to do more than recapitulate existing examples and find new ways to approach topics. Generating new key examples involved drawing on a network of informal consultants and fact-checkers. Inclusive lingcomm also requires that we encourage more people to engage the public in linguistics, so that there are more perspectives shared with new audiences.

As more and more people across the globe make web-based, public resources like Crash Course their first encounter with academic topics, we have an obligation to those viewers as well as to our academic disciplines to make those encounters as inclusive of the diversity of those learners' experiences as possible. Such efforts, we hope, are reflexive—changing who is publicly represented as belonging in linguistics, and in so doing, making space and an invitation for more people to belong.

Notes

1. See for example the list compiled by McCulloch of general-audience oriented linguistics content at his All Things Linguistic blog, https://allthingslinguistic.com/post/176495707 872/a-long-list-of-linguistics-youtube-channels-and, which spans genres and is created by both lay and academically trained linguists. This list continues to grow, and recently has been augmented by the arrival of the TikTok platform, where many lay and academic linguists produce short videos explaining discrete concepts (for examples, search for the tag #lingtok).
2. This chapter is a collaboration between team members from Complexly and from the linguist writing team. The majority written by the two linguists with academic employment and therefore more often represents their perspective. Unfortunately, there is still too little incentive for academic linguists to participate in sustained public engagement, and too little incentive for public media creators to engage with academic literature.

References

Bancu, Ariana, Peltier, Joy P. G., Bisnath, Felicia, Burgess, Danielle, Eakins, Sophia, Gonzales, Wilkinson, Saltzman, Moira, Sedarous, Yourdanis, Stevers, Alicia, & Baptista, Marlyse. (2024). Revitalizing attitudes toward Creole languages. In Anne H. Charity Hudley, Christine Mallinson, & Mary Bucholtz (Eds.), *Decolonizing linguistics*. Oxford University Press.

Baugh, John. (1983). *Black street speech: Its history, structure and survival*. University of Texas Press.

Bender, Emily. M., Gebru, Timnit., McMillan-Major, Angelina, & Shmitchell, Shmargaret. (2021). On the dangers of stochastic parrots: Can language models be too big? In *Proceedings of the 2021 ACM Conference on Fairness, Accountability, and Transparency*, 610–623.

Bowern, Claire, & Dockum, Rikker. (2024). Decolonizing historical linguistics in the classroom and beyond. In Anne H. Charity Hudley, Christine Mallinson, & Mary Bucholtz (Eds.), *Decolonizing linguistics*. Oxford University Press.

Canfield, Katherine N., Menezes, Sunshine, Matsuda, Shayle B., Moore, Amelia, Mosley Austin, Alycia N., Dewsbury, Bryan M., Feliú-Mójer, Mónica I., McDufie, Katharine W. B., Moore, Kendall, Reich, Christine A., Smith, Holly M. & Taylor, Cynthia. (2020). Science communication demands a critical approach that centers inclusion, equity, and intersectionality. *Frontiers in Communication, 5*, 2. http://doi.org/10.3389/fcomm.2020.00002/full

Charity Hudley, Anne H., Mallinson, Christine, & Bucholtz, Mary. 2020. Toward racial justice in linguistics: Interdisciplinary insights into theorizing race in the discipline and diversifying the profession. *Language, 96*(4), e200–e235. http://doi.org/10.1353/lan.2020.0074

Conrod, Kirby. (2019). Pronouns raising and emerging [Doctoral dissertation, University of Washington].

Grieser, Jessi, McCulloch, Gretchen, & Gawne, Lauren. (2021). Languages mentioned in Crash Course Linguistics. *FigShare*. http://doi.org/10.26181/61031a232e96e

Jackson, Janice E., & Green, Lisa. (2005). Tense and aspectual be in child African American English. In Henk J. Verkuyl, Henriette de Swart, & Angeliek van Hout (Eds.), *Perspectives on Aspect* (pp. 233–250). Springer.

Lewandowsky, Stephan, Cook, John, Ecker, Ullrich, Albarracin, Dolores, Amazeen, Michelle A., Kendou, Panayiota, Lombardi, Doug, Newman, Eryn J., Pennycook, Gordon, Porter, Ethan, & Rand, David G. (2020). *The debunking handbook 2020*. Centre for Climate Change Communication.

McDonnell, Lisa, Barker, Megan K., & Wieman, Carl. (2016). Concepts first, jargon second improves student articulation of understanding. *Biochemistry and Molecular Biology Education, 44*(1), 12–19. https://doi.org/10.1002/bmb.20922

Nielsen, M. (director). (2020). *Crash Course Linguistics*. YouTube video series. Complexly/PBS Digital Studios.

Rosa, Jonathan., & Flores, Nelson. (2017). Unsettling race and language: Toward a raciolinguistic perspective. *Language in society, 46*(5), 621–647. https://doi.org/10.1017/S0047404517000562

Suresh, Harini, & Guttag, John V. (2019). A framework for understanding unintended consequences of machine learning. *arXiv* preprint arXiv:1901.10002.

Truth and Reconciliation Commission of Canada. (2015). Honouring the truth, reconciling for the future: Summary of the final report of the Truth and Reconciliation Commission of Canada. http://www.trc.ca/websites/trcinstitution/File/2015/Findings/Exec_Summary_2015_05_31_web_o.pdf

Wright, Kelly E. (2019). Experiments on linguistic profiling of three American dialects [Doctoral dissertation, University of Michigan].

Jennifer Sclafani is assistant professor of applied linguistics at the University of Massachusetts Boston. Her research and teaching focus on language and social justice, intercultural communication, political discourse analysis, gender and the media, and language and identity in contexts of migration and globalization. Her analysis of the language of Donald Trump has been published as a book, *Talking Donald Trump: A Sociolinguistic Study of Style, Metadiscourse, and Political Identity*, and her analyses of US presidential politics have been featured in news outlets including the *Washington Post*, *Scientific American*, *CNN Politics*, *BBC Radio 4*, *PBS News Hour*, *CBC Radio*, and *The Guardian*, among others. She also researches issues of heritage language maintenance and identity among return migrants to Greece and teachers' discourse related to their work with multilingual learners.

Iuliia Fakhrutdinova is a PhD candidate and research and teaching assistant in the Department of Applied Linguistics at the University of Massachusetts Boston. She is also a Foreign Fulbright awardee, Muskie Internship Program alumna, and Stanford US–Russia Forum fellow. She obtained her MA in Teaching English to Speakers of Other Languages (TESOL) from Saint Michael's College, Vermont. Her research interests include refugee background education, immigrant education, literacy, culture, identity, multilingualism, transnationalism, translanguaging, narratives, critical pedagogy, and critical discourse analysis. Her dissertation explores the negotiated identities of refugee-background women during resettlement. Iuliia volunteered as a teacher of refugee-background adult emergent readers for two years in the Vermont Refugee Resettlement Program, and currently she is a volunteer teacher in refugee and immigrant resettlement agencies in the Boston area and Afghan Women Solidarity from all over the world.

Panayota Gounari is professor of applied linguistics at the University of Massachusetts Boston. Using her background in critical applied linguistics and critical pedagogy, she investigates social issues through the lens of critical discourse studies (CDS) and their implications for pedagogy, always aiming to produce socially committed research. Her current research focuses on far-right populist discourses and authoritarianism, the discourse of the critical race theory debate, and the discourses of collective memory and historical revisionism. She has also written on critical pedagogy and educational and linguistic policy reforms. Her most recent book, *From Twitter to Capitol Hill: Far-Right Authoritarian Populist Discourses, Social Media, and Critical Pedagogy*, explores far-right authoritarian populist discourses in social media in the context of Trump's presidency and the January 6 insurrection, in an attempt to illuminate how online extremism works and the ways discourses shape social events.

Vannessa Quintana Sarria is a PhD candidate and research assistant in the Department of Applied Linguistics at the University of Massachusetts Boston. She obtained a BA in foreign languages with a concentration in English and French from Valle University in Cali, Colombia, and an MA in foreign languages with a concentration in Spanish from North Carolina State University. Her scholarship explores the experiences of multilingual English language teachers, language teacher identities, and language teacher education. Currently, she is advancing her dissertation data collection in a Massachusetts high school with six teachers who work with emergent bilinguals in an SEI program. She also works as a research assistant with the Centering Relationships, Equity, and Access for Teachers of English Learners (CREATE) project with the purpose of increasing educator and district capacity to serve ELs in eight high-needs urban school districts in Greater Boston.

Abstract: This chapter presents the Justice Language Action Project, an educational outreach project that provides professional development in critical discourse analysis and language awareness to K-12 teachers and assists them in incorporating these perspectives into social justice-themed curricular units for their classrooms. The project was designed to address the needs of teachers in urban districts with high numbers of English learners and other minoritized students. These teachers were working to respond to the unprecedented challenges of the 2020–2021 school year— specifically, the longstanding educational inequities exacerbated by the pandemic and the traumatic events that sparked the Black Lives Matter movement across the nation. First, the authors describe the four-day workshop that they led in August 2021. Next, they describe the units that teachers created and their experiences, successes, and challenges in implementation. The chapter offers this model to other linguists seeking to engage in community partnerships to foster equity and inclusion in K-12 classrooms.

Key Words: critical language awareness, critical pedagogy, K-12 education, praxis, professional development

19

The Justice Language Action Project

Critical Linguistics for Inclusion and Equity in K-12 Classrooms

Jennifer Sclafani (she/her)
University of Massachusetts Boston

Panayota Gounari (she/her)
University of Massachusetts Boston

Iuliia Fakhrutdinova (she/her)
University of Massachusetts Boston

Vannessa Quintana Sarria (she/her)
University of Massachusetts Boston

Introduction: The Justice Language Action Project

The COVID-19 pandemic presented extreme challenges and crucial awakenings for educators and students worldwide, as schooling shifted to remote and hybrid formats (Barnett et al., 2021; Daniels, 2020; Onyema et al., 2020). In the United States, the challenges of the pandemic have heightened issues of equity and access to resources for minoritized students and have highlighted longstanding challenges facing urban communities and school systems. While many schools responded by amplifying social-emotional supports to address students' immediate needs, these traumatic events have continued to take a toll on K-12 students, especially those most vulnerable, including English learners and minoritized students in underfunded districts.

During the tumultuous summer of 2020, when schools were shifting to remote teaching, and social unrest following the murder of George Floyd was sweeping the country (Li & Lalani, 2020; Parker et al., 2020), the first author, Jennifer, was teaching an online graduate course at the University of Massachusetts Boston (UMass Boston) on literacy and culture to a group of in-service teachers, who were simultaneously preparing for the upcoming

Jennifer Sclafani, Panayota Gounari, Iuliia Fakhrutdinova, and Vannessa Quintana Sarria, *The Justice Language Action Project*
In: *Inclusion in Linguistics*. Edited by: Anne H. Charity Hudley, Christine Mallinson and Mary Bucholtz, Oxford University Press.
© Anne H. Charity Hudley, Christine Mallinson, and Mary Bucholtz 2024. DOI: 10.1093/oso/9780197755303.003.0020

school year and learning new apps to engage students remotely. They were also worrying whether many of their students, especially English learners, would even have the digital and material resources to attend class from home. In class discussions, these teachers expressed concern over how they would integrate critical discussions about race and social justice in response to the Black Lives Matter protests and civil unrest that students were witnessing first-hand in their communities. As a final project for the course, in lieu of a traditional research paper, teachers were invited to create or refine a curricular unit they currently taught that integrated the course topics of critical, digital, and multimodal literacies to support them in their preparation for the unprecedented 2020–2021 pandemic school year. The resulting projects from the summer course represented a variety of creative, critical, and integrative lessons, ranging from a 10th grade Spanish unit on the social history of the repressive Chilean military dictatorship to an English as a Second Language (ESL) unit interrogating xenophobia through a multimodal exploration of Gene Luen Yang's (2006) graphic novel *American Born Chinese*. Unfortunately, with the quick transition to the academic year, there was little time for teachers to exchange and reflect on their projects with each other or receive and integrate peer and instructor feedback.

In an attempt to address these needs, Jennifer conceptualized the Justice Language Action Project (JLAP) as a professional and curricular development project with three goals: (1) to equip K-12 educators with a critical awareness of the power of language and discourse; (2) to provide them with a platform and community of peers with whom they could reflect on how the COVID-19 pandemic and the US movement for racial justice affected their personal lives and professional activities; and (3) to assist them in developing pedagogical materials that work to foster positive social change in their classrooms and communities. She proposed the idea to her colleague Panayota, whose teaching specializations include critical discourse studies and critical pedagogy, and with the help of PhD candidates and paid research assistants Iuliia and Vannessa, the four of us developed the first JLAP professional development workshop in spring 2021 and delivered it in August 2021.

The goal of JLAP is to introduce critical language awareness to elementary, middle, and high school classrooms in the Boston area through partnerships with teachers who have taken coursework in the UMass Boston graduate program in applied linguistics as part of their preparation for the Massachusetts ESL licensure. Through this partnership, teachers receive focused training in critical discourse analysis and learn about classroom applications. The multiday workshop provides them with space for reflection, conversation, and feedback as they develop social justice-themed curricular units for their classrooms. The units culminate in the creation of collaborative student-generated digital projects in which students interrogate, research, and reform the social, environmental, and educational policies affecting their lives.

JLAP has five stages:

1. Professional development workshop on critical discourse analysis and language awareness
2. Development of CDLA-grounded instructional units
3. Implementation of instructional units and creation of collaborative projects
4. Follow-up interviews and focus groups with participants on collaborative projects
5. Publication and community sharing of collaborative projects

In this chapter, we describe the various stages of this project as a model of inclusion and as an example of an effective community partnership in linguistics that enhances public understandings of language and promotes the social justice mission of public K-12 education. We begin by describing our positionalities and the theoretical frameworks that have inspired and guided the design of this project. Next, we describe the implementation of the four-day workshop and provide examples of materials and units created by participants. We then reflect on the classroom impact of this project by discussing participants' written reflections and findings from our follow-up interviews. Finally, we address some shortcomings of the pilot workshop, discuss future directions of JLAP, and share ideas and resources that we believe would benefit other linguists engaging in social justice-oriented educational partnerships.

Positionalities

Iuliia is an educator who aims to transform our classrooms into spaces where we critically discuss social issues (e.g., racism, gender inequality, refugee crisis, climate change, bullying) through critical language awareness, critical discourse analysis, and critical pedagogy. As a cisgender Asian woman, ethnically Tatar Korean, daughter, international doctoral student, researcher, and educator, she grew up in a working-class immigrant family that migrated from Uzbekistan to Russia when she was 11, and later came to study in the United States. These experiences influenced her perspective on politics, culture, language, race, ethnicity, religion, gender, sexual orientation, migration, and education. Her early experiences in teacher-centered classrooms where teachers were afraid to talk about politics raised many questions for her; she is a strong believer that our schools are the ideal places to express our identities and politics, and have uncomfortable conversations.

Jennifer is a third-generation Bostonian, daughter of a public school teacher, and a product of the Massachusetts public school system. Growing up in a linguistically diverse neighborhood, she witnessed the challenges of her multilingual peers at school, observed the obstacles that teachers like her father with limited resources and institutional support faced when working with English learners, and experienced the dominant subtractive ideologies of multilingualism that colored the educational experiences of all students and their peer relationships. She is concerned by the ideological rifts between generations of immigrants that have emerged as the demographics of Boston have evolved in recent decades and is committed to working with educators to implement culturally and linguistically sustaining pedagogies in their classrooms to ensure safety and develop critical consciousness among their students.

Panayota is a critical educator, a political being, and a lifelong learner. As a scholar who works at the intersection of applied linguistics and critical pedagogy, she produces socially committed scholarship. She is passionate about researching, analyzing, and questioning language in use, as it is embodied in discourses, in social contexts, and in the realities it shapes. She is committed to researching, critiquing, supporting, and ultimately improving and transforming public education at all levels. She is practicing a pedagogy for critical consciousness, political awareness, and collective action, and she is implementing pedagogical practices that foster inquiry, epistemological curiosity, intellectual freedom, creativity, and dialogue. She is the granddaughter of Greek refugees from Asia Minor, and the daughter of working-class, left educators. She is Greek, multilingual, and multicultural.

Vannessa is a racialized multilingual English teacher who is committed to working with teachers like herself to counteract problematic narratives of nativism, monolingualism, and white supremacy in English language education. Her work with immigrant students, teachers, and school staff in Boston schools has emphasized the importance of secondary English teachers in adolescent immigrant life. Teachers are sometimes the only reliable role models in students' lives and are responsible for shepherding students through life-changing decisions like college, career, friends, immigration, and employment. However, dominant ideological orientations play into educators' teaching principles, and Vannessa views JLAP as a way to support their critical liberation from these ideologies. She is committed to working with language educators from different places of origin, races, and linguistic backgrounds as they develop practices that support teaching English in equitable and empowering ways.

Theoretical Framework

This project is informed by critical approaches to discourse analysis that underscore the power of ideology to maintain systems of oppression and also pay close attention to how the complex participation frameworks of mass-mediated social interaction shape language meaning (Kress & Van Leeuwen, 2020; Rogers, 2011; Wodak & Meyer, 2015). The workshop is grounded in critical pedagogy (Apple, 2013; Freire, 1970/2005; Giroux, 1983; hooks, 1994; Gounari, 2019) and its implementation in language teaching (Canagarajah, 2006; Crookes, 2012; Kubota & Austin, 2007; Pennycook, 2001), critical language awareness (Fairclough, 2014), raciolinguistics (Alim et al., 2016), and linguistically responsive approaches to pedagogy (Bucholtz et al., 2018; Charity Hudley & Mallinson, 2010; 2013; Paris & Alim, 2014). The final collaborative project is inspired by the concept of identity texts (Cummins & Early, 2010), and specifically, more recent iterations of this concept that incorporate critical and muliliteracy perspectives (e.g., Mirra et al., 2018).

These frameworks, which ground our own teaching and research in applied linguistics, facilitate teachers' ability to lift up their students through linguistically sustaining pedagogical practices that recognize and build on their identities, backgrounds, intelligences, skills, and interests. In this sense, the workshop is an extension of what JLAP participants learned in their graduate coursework and encourages them to put to use some of the pedagogical strategies (e.g., translanguaging in Garcia et al. (2017)) that they have encountered in their course readings. Through JLAP, we specifically wanted to push participants to make meaningful text-to-world connections and develop new strategies that guide their students not only to express their own identities from a linguistic framework but also to work for social change in their own communities.

Professional Development Workshop Design

We recruited JLAP participants among current and recent UMass Boston graduate students who were current or pre-service teachers or teacher educators in Boston public schools in a variety of settings, including dual language programs, classrooms with high numbers of mainstreamed English learners, and ESL programs. Due to pandemic restrictions, we ran our first workshop in an intensive four-day synchronous remote format via Zoom in August 2021 and were able to include students from our online MA program located in other geographical locations as well. Participants were paid a stipend for their participation in the workshop through university funds. The pilot workshop, which we report on here, served seven participants—four from Boston, one from Vermont, one from Washington, DC, and one from Michigan—and was co-taught by the four of us. Five of the participants were in-service or pre-service teachers, one was a teacher educator, and one was contemplating a career switch from consulting at the time of the workshop but was hesitant about pursuing a career in teaching.

The workshop took place for four hours a day over four consecutive days and was structured as follows:

Day 1: Introductions, workshop objectives, critical media literacy icebreakers
Day 2: Training and data workshops in critical discourse analysis and critical language awareness (CDLA)
Day 3: Reading and discussion of case studies of classroom applications of CDLA, brainstorming for instructional unit creation
Day 4: Individual work on instructional units, peer and instructor sharing and feedback sessions

During the first day of the workshop, instructors and participants engaged in a unit titled "Exploring Our Positionalities" (e.g., De Costa & Norton, 2017; Gounari, 2020; Martin & Van Guten, 2002; Varghese et al., 2005), in which instructors and participants discussed their identities, schooling experiences, teaching experiences, and how these inform their beliefs and teaching practices. Participants were also encouraged to record their written reflections in an online journal that they shared with the instructors throughout the workshop. Next, in a unit titled "Media Through Our Own Eyes," participants reflected on where and how they access the news and how their media choices, sources, and intake both reflect and affect their identities and positionalities. Participants also compared and contrasted their own media consumption practices with those of their students, family members, friends, and colleagues, and discussed how these practices function as lenses, filters, and mirrors that shape the way they view the world and their own positions and agency with regard to social change.

The second day was run as an intensive introduction to CDLA, with a focused discussion on how linguistic forms work to construct, uphold, and transform power relations and systems of oppression in society. Participants gained analytic practice by examining various media outlets' representation of social issues related to immigration and racism in the United States (e.g., Fox, 2021; Keene, 2021; Villavicencio, 2020), considering the linguistic representation of social actors and argumentation schemes employed. They also discussed the transformative power of language and analyzed the ways in which language can be harnessed to effect change through an analysis of speeches by US Congresswomen Ilhan Omar (2019) and Alexandria Ocasio-Cortez (2020), and poet Amanda Gorman (2021), and the stances, identities, and ideologies evoked therein. Throughout these discussions, participants were encouraged to make connections between the data analysis workshops and their own teaching contexts, reflect on what they learned, and consider potential applications in their online journals.

On the third day, participants examined classroom applications of CDLA documented in the applied linguistics and education literature. Units included four case studies: (1) literacy lessons and cultural stereotypes in a third grade dual language classroom (Esquivel, 2019); (2) the use of discourse norms of African American English to socialize students into literature study in a high school ELA classroom (Lee, 2004); (3) the study of US geography from Indigenous American perspectives (Bishop, 2022); and (4) a critical examination of commercial educational materials marketed for studying climate change in the science curriculum (Colston & Thomas, 2019). As instructors, we also introduced additional pedagogical resources from our own teaching and from platforms we researched in preparation for the workshop, such as the journal *Rethinking Schools* (https://rethinkingschools.org/) and the website Zinn Education Project (https://www.zinnedproject.org/). Throughout these units, participants brainstormed how they might adapt the materials or pedagogical approaches in the case studies for their own content areas, grade levels, and student populations.

Curricular Unit Design: An Example

During the final day of the workshop, participants designed social justice-themed instructional units for their classrooms, incorporating elements of critical language awareness that they had discussed and seen exemplified in the case studies on Day Three. Curricular units ranged from a fourth-grade environmental science unit on erosion to a high school English language arts unit integrating Shakespeare and persuasive writing. One participant chose not to create a K-12 curricular unit and instead designed a professional diversity training workshop on linguistic and cultural diversity for her coworkers. Below, we share one example of a thematic unit that a pre-service teacher, Maria Mo, designed for a middle school classroom. Maria's cross-disciplinary unit connects journalism and media studies with creative writing and aims to linguistically equip students to critique hegemonic ideologies reproduced in the news through the production of counternarratives (Solórzano & Yosso, 2002). This unit aptly illustrates how participants can put focused CDLA training to work by developing lessons that encourage their students to similarly reflect on their social worlds and work to create social change. Furthermore, the unit may be adapted to different grade levels as well as for English learners, making it an invaluable tool not only for Maria's own future classroom, but for other teachers to adapt and implement in their own classrooms. (With her permission, we use Maria's real name in order to give her appropriate credit for the unit she created. All other names of participants are pseudonyms.)

Maria's unit integrates blackout poetry and CDLA in the study of media texts to chisel, interrupt, and transgress dominant narratives in the news. The unit begins by showing the TED talk by Nigerian writer Chimamanda Ngozi Ndichie (2009) on "the danger of a single story," in which the author promotes access to literature representing a multitude of cultural perspectives so that children may see their own realities represented in the books they read. Next, the unit introduces the idea of reclaiming power over the text through the production of counternarratives. In Maria's own words in her curricular unit plan, "By blacking out large portions of the text, dominant narratives become a kind of background noise, a negative space to bring into light and highlight the alternative stories."

The class then participates in a guided reading of a politically charged article on a current topic in the news, such as the immigration situation at the United States-Mexico border. The teacher leads students as they color code unfamiliar words, main ideas, and quotations. Depending on the level of the class, students may also locate passive verbs, deleted agents, nominalizations, and other linguistic features of interest to CDLA that reveal underlying attitudes or political ideologies. Next, the teacher leads students in a critical discussion of the content of the article. Some guiding questions that Maria developed include:

- What do you know to be true or untrue of this article?
- What are the truths that you want to highlight?

- What do you want the text to say instead? What are the words that can convey that?
- If taken out of context, what words/phrases/sentences resonate with you?
- What are some negative words that can acquire a positive meaning if taken out of context?

The second phase of the unit transitions from what the text *does* say to what it *can* say. Students receive a second copy of the article and are instructed to black out parts of the text while keeping some words and phrases that resonate with them. In small groups, they experiment with blacking out different words, phrases, and sentences to create a poem out of the remaining words. They receive feedback from peers and discuss the new meanings they have created through the process. Maria provided us with a sample blackout poem that she created (see Figure 19.1).

Once the students gain familiarity with creating blackout poetry from the news, they are asked to choose their own article and create a blackout poem with it. Multilingual students are also encouraged to use their translanguaging skills, replacing some English words with words in their home languages. A further possibility is to play with the visual layout of the article. As Maria describes in her unit plan, "students can add an artistic twist by blacking out words, not so that an emerging poem makes sense, but that the final product is an image that reflects a theme, idea, or reaction from the article (e.g., blackening out a Fox News article so that the resulting article, a story on children crossing the border, looks like a cage)."

The students then share their blackout poetry with the class. This can be done through any one or more of these venues: a poetry reading, a

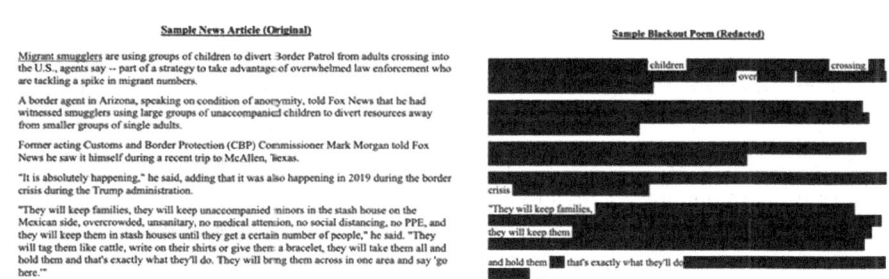

Figure 19.1 Blackout poem example

Alt-text: Left: A 5-paragraph news article about migrant smugglers using children to divert Border Patrol agents at US-Mexico border. Right: same article with most text redacted. Remaining text reads, "children crossing over crisis They will keep families, they will keep them and hold them that's exactly what they'll do."

self-published class book, a collage on a poster or bulletin board, or a gallery walk activity. Students also share their work with the broader community by sharing photos of their poems via social media. For assessment purposes, students may be asked to write a reflection on the writing process and explain their choices to highlight and hide certain elements of the news article through the blackout poetry activity.

Classroom Impact

In addition to reviewing the journals that participants kept during the workshop, we assessed the impact of JLAP in several ways. We have conducted follow-up interviews with participants to learn about JLAP's impact on their teaching practices and overall classroom experiences. Multiple participants expressed that even if they had not yet fully implemented their unit, the training they received and the ideas they shared with their peers during the workshop altered how they approach teaching, and heightened their awareness of the linguistic choices made in the texts they teach as well as their own language and positionality.

For example, Daisy, an experienced ESL teacher, reported that although she needed to make substantial changes before her unit could be effectively implemented with her own students after participating in the workshop, she had become more aware of her own positionality as the only white teacher in a predominantly Black school district and had gained a more reflexive stance in her interactions with both her ESL students and the non-ESL students and teachers at her school. In her online journal, she wrote:

> If I look at my position as a teacher (part of my identity) in relation to the other students in that building and their needs and their culture, I recognize that my viewpoint was limited and actually oppositional . . . I suddenly became aware of my relation to the student body and [another] teacher (who demands critical thinking and has high standards for his students) in a way I had not before . . . It also sparks a desire to bring language justice to all students. And when I do that, then 'activist' will become part of my identity too.

In our interview with Daisy five months after the workshop ended, she informed us that instead of pursuing her original idea of creating a critical media literacy unit on the topic of COVID-19 vaccination misinformation, she planned to create a professional development workshop for teachers on critical sociolinguistic awareness. When asked whether sociolinguistic variation was currently addressed in one of her classes, which she co-teaches with a Black teacher and a biracial (Black and white) teacher, she referred to this topic as "the elephant in the room":

> We never mention the d fferences at all, it's not mentioned, it's not noted, it's not pointed out, if someone speaks different or something like that. But I know that some kids just will not talk to me. They don't want to, they don't want to talk to me. They don't relate to me, they just see me, and cut off. I see it. I sense it. And some kids I can get through to because they know that I'm for real and that I'm really there to help them.

In our discussion, Daisy acknowledged the limits of her own ability to approach these topics in the classroom as a perceived outsider and as one of the few white teachers in her school, and highlighted the sensitivity surrounding talk about race and language in this context. However, she remains committed to finding ways to integrate critical language awareness into both teachers' professional development and the school's ESL and content area curricula. In response to issues like the one Daisy raised here, we plan to expand our discussion of positionality in future JLAP workshops to extend beyond participants' identities and encourage them to critically reflect on their relationships with their students in more depth.

Another teacher, Camila, who had been promoted to the role of director of a large public Massachusetts ESL program during the summer that the JLAP workshop was held, used the workshop to brainstorm ways in which she could improve ESL teachers' professional development in her district. During our follow-up interview, she highlighted her own identity as a former English learner in the same district that she now directs. With this intimate understanding of the barriers that her current students face, she discussed the topic of testing as a site of reform she hopes to tackle:

> I think working with teachers, this whole conversation about grading and how do you approach grading with students, what is fair, what's right, and I think all of those things are part of social justice, right? Because grad ng is very subjective, so we're looking at students failing. We had about 700 students failing, 70% of them were English learners or students of color, then why? Right? Because grading is so subjective! Are teachers aware of their biases or the things that they put in place in their classrooms that a-e barriers for these students to succeed?

Although testing was not a featured topic in the workshop, Camila was able to make the connection between our discussions of positionality and the use of CDLA in order to identify a potential social justice issue in her district. She is currently planning ways to address this concern in her role as director.

To take a final example of participant feedback, Nancy, a teacher educator, reported to us that she was able to directly borrow lessons from the workshop on CDLA to use in her own classes, but she also discussed some of the structural barriers preventing her from fully moving from theory to practice with certain teacher populations she works with: "There were teachers from New Hampshire, and they're like 'Yep, so you know, like I'm not allowed to say my opinion about anything, and you know especially with the political.'" Here Nancy refers to the New Hampshire state ban on teaching critical race theory in schools that was signed into law in June 2021 (at the time of writing, the law is being challenged in a federal lawsuit). In our discussion, Nancy reported that at one point she was "called out for being a CRT teacher" by a student, but that despite their disagreements, Nancy was "fair" with the student, who came to appreciate their differences in the end. Based on what we learned from Nancy's account, it appears that even in contexts where the local political landscape may run counter to teachers' efforts to implement antiracist pedagogies, with careful implementation they can open the dialogue and engage students in alternative perspectives.

In addition to helping us evaluate the impact of JLAP on the participants' classrooms, the journals and interviews also enabled us to determine which aspects of the workshop resonated most with the participants, how they had internalized the ideas in the months following the intensive summer workshop, and what barriers they might encounter in connecting theory to practice. At the same time, they helped us identify shortcomings and areas for improvement, as we discuss in the next section.

Challenges and Directions for Improvement

As we reflect on some shortcomings of the pilot JLAP workshop and its greater impact on the communities we aim to serve, we would like to share some lessons we learned along the way to stimulate further conversations about linguistic outreach and the development of partnerships between linguists and educators.

First, it became clear to us during the first unit of the workshop that we did not allow enough time or flexibility when we communicated to our participants our expectations that they would develop full curricular units during the short time frame of the workshop. Our participants displayed hesitation about their ability to meet these expectations, and we consequently adjusted how we communicated the goals of the workshop over the following days. For example, a few participants felt too constrained by their current curricula and were more comfortable designing a simple one-day lesson plan that could be later elaborated into an instructional unit. Other participants were not currently teaching and had difficulty designing a unit for a hypothetical classroom.

One surprise to us was that Maria, whose blackout poetry lesson we described above, was one of the participants who was hesitant about creating a unit because she was not currently teaching. Yet in the end she was able to effectively design her unit so that it could be easily tailored to students in a variety of grades and in different types of classrooms with high populations of English learners (e.g., dual language, sheltered English immersion). When Maria shared her unit with the other participants, several expressed their desire to adapt her idea to their own classrooms. We also shared excerpts from Maria's unit at the Linguistic Society of America annual conference (Sclafani et al., 2022), where we heard from an audience member who is planning to adapt it for her college-level Spanish class. We realized that although our original concept of community sharing focused on the communities of our participants' students, the peer network we established through the workshop has created valuable opportunities for educators to share their ideas with each other. As we further develop JLAP, we plan to create a publicly available digital repository for participants to share their units with the wider community of socially engaged educators and report back their implementation experiences.

In addition, we realized that the workshop has the potential to reach beyond the K-12 educator population that we had originally envisioned it serving. Two participants in our workshop who did not work in the K-12 setting elected to create instructional units for other populations. The teacher educator adapted the CDLA and critical media literacy lessons for her own student teachers, and the participant considering a career change designed a diversity training seminar for colleagues in her current work with law enforcement professionals. These two examples widened our own perspective regarding the utility of the workshop, and we plan to expand our recruitment to include educators who work with undergraduates and in community college contexts in future iterations of the workshop.

Conclusion

The Justice Language Action Project was designed to fulfill an immediate need in our own context: our graduate students' lack of time and space to truly connect theory and practice in their work as educators during a turbulent period of their own professional, academic, and personal lives. Through this CDLA-grounded professional development, it is our hope that their students, and especially their English learners who were impacted most by the traumatic events of the COVID-19 pandemic and its effects on education, benefit from the enhanced reflexivity and pedagogical ideas that participants created and shared during this workshop.

We are currently working to revise and expand JLAP to cater to teachers working in specific content areas (e.g., foreign languages, STEM) and we are developing an open online resource for teachers involved in the project to share their curricular units and materials with colleagues. We believe it is of utmost importance that linguists continue to work beyond disciplinary boundaries and develop community partnerships that use critically informed understandings of language to work for social change. We view this project as a seed for the further development of partnerships among linguists and educators to work together to advance models of inclusion for linguistically, socioeconomically, and culturally diverse student populations.

References

Alim, H. Samy, Rickford, John, & Ball, Arnetha F. (Eds.). (2016). *Raciolinguistics: How language shapes our ideas about race*. Oxford University Press.

Apple, Michael W. (2013). *Can education change society?* Routledge.

Barnett, W. Steven, Grafwallner, Rolf, & Weisenfeld, Georgenne G. (2021). Corona pandemic in the United States shapes new normal for young children and their families. *European Early Childhood Education Research Journal, 29*(1), 109–124.

Bishop, Michelle. (2022). Indigenous education sovereignty: Another way of "doing" education. *Critical Studies in Education, 63*(1), 1–16.

Bucholtz, Mary, Casillas, Doloros Inés, & Lee, Jin Sook. (Eds.). (2018). *Feeling it: Language, race, and affect in Latinx youth learning*. Routledge.

Canagarajah, A. Suresh. (2006). TESOL at forty: What are the issues? *TESOL Quarterly, 40*(1), 9–34.

Charity Hudley, Anne, & Mallinson, Christine. (2010). *Understanding English language variation in U.S. schools*. Teachers College Press.

Charity Hudley, Anne, & Mallinson, Christine. (2013). *We do language: English variation in the secondary English classroom*. Teachers College Press.

Colston, Nicole, & Thomas, Julie. (2019). Climate change skeptics teach climate literacy? A critical discourse analysis of children's books. *Journal of Science Communication, 18*(4), 1–22.

Crookes, Graham. (2012). Critical pedagogy in language teaching. In Carol A. Chapelle (Ed.), *The encyclopedia of applied linguistics* (355–359). Blackwell.

Cummins, Jim, & Early, Margaret. (2010). *Identity texts: The collaborative creation of power in multilingual schools*. Trentham Books Ltd.

Daniel, Sir John. (2020). Education and the COVID-19 pandemic. *Prospects, 49*(1), 91–96.

De Costa, Peter I., & Norton, Bonny. (2017). Introduction: Identity, transdisciplinarity, and the good language teacher. *The Modern Language Journal, 101*(S1), 3–14.

Esquivel, Johanna. (2019). Critical discourse analysis in the bilingual classroom: Uncovering stereotypes in children's picture books. *NABE Journal of Research and Practice, 9*(3–4), 198–209.

Fairclough, Norman. (2014). *Critical language awareness.* Taylor & Francis.

Fox, Ben. (2021, April 19). US under Biden will no longer call migrants 'illegal aliens'." AP News. https://apnews.com/article/donald-trump-coronavirus-pandemic-immigration-7c8c0bad5dedb750c2aa7c1e9d8aa3cb

Freire, Paulo. (1970/2005.) *Pedagogy of the oppressed.* Continuum.

Garcia, O., Johnson, S. I., & Seltzer, K. (Eds.). (2017). *The translanguaging classroom. Leveraging student bilingualism for learning.* Caslon.

Giroux, Henry. (1983). *Theory and resistance in education: A pedagogy for the opposition.* Bergin & Garvey.

Gorman, Amanda. (2021). Inauguration poem, "The hill we climb." [speech transcript]. *Town and Country.* https://www.townandcountrymag.com/society/politics/a35279603/amanda-gorman-inauguration-poem-the-hill-we-climb-transcript/

Gounari, Panayota. (2019). Education in the Trump era: Educators' mobilizations as critical public pedagogy. *International Journal of Critical Media Literacy, 1*(2), 228–245.

Gounari, Panayota. (2020). Introduction to the special issue on critical pedagogies. *L2 Journal, 12*(2). doi:10.5070/L212249913.

hooks, bell. (1994). *Teaching to transgress: Education as the practice of freedom.* Routledge.

Keene, Houston. (2021, June 28). Ilhan Omar says every illegal immigrant in US should have "pathway to citizenship." *Fox News.* https://www.foxnews.com/politics/ilhan-omar-illegal-immigrants-pathway-citizenship

Kress, Gunther, & Van Leeuwen, Theo. (2020). *Reading images: The grammar of visual design.* Routledge.

Kubota, Ryuko, & Austin, Theresa. (2007). Critical approaches to world language education in the United States: An introduction. *Critical Inquiry in Language Studies, 4*(2–3), 73–83.

Li, Cathy, & Lalani, Farah. (2020, April 29). The COVID-19 pandemic has changed education forever. This is how. *World Economic Forum.* https://www.weforum.org/agenda/2020/04/coronavirus-education-global-covid19-online-digital-learning/

Lee, Carmen D. (2004). African American vernacular English as resource in cultural modeling classrooms. In John S. Brown and Christian Heath (Eds.), *Bakhtinian Perspectives on Language, Literacy, and Learning* (pp. 129–147). Cambridge University Press.

Martin, Renée J., & Van Gunten, Dawn M. (2002). Reflected identities: Applying positionality and multicultural social reconstructionism in teacher education. *Journal of Teacher Education, 53*(1), 44–54.

Mirra, Nicole, Morrell, Ernest, & Filipiak, Danielle. (2018). From digital consumption to digital invention: Toward a new critical theory and practice of multiliteracies. *Theory Into Practice, 57*(1), 12–19.

Ndichie, Chimamanda Ngozi. (2009). The danger of a single story [video]. TED Conferences. https://www.ted.com/talks/chimamanda_ngozi_adichie_the_danger_of_a_single_story

Ocasio-Cortez, Alexandria. (2020). Verbal assault against women "not new. And that is the problem." [speech transcript, July 23, 2020]. *Rev.* https://www.rev.com/blog/transcripts/rep-alexandria-ocasio-cortez-floor-speech-about-yoho-remarks-july-23"https://www.rev.com/blog/transcripts/rep-alexandria-ocasio-cortez-floor-speech-about-yoho-remarks-july-23

Omar, Ilhan. (2019). Trump's attacks on me target women, people of color & immigrants everywhere. [Speech transcript, May 1, 2019]. *Democracy Now.* https://www.democracynow.org/2019/5/1/im_a_survivor_of_war_i

Onyema, Edeh Michael, Nwafor, Chika, Obafemi, Faith, Sen, Shuvro, Atonye, Fyneface Grace, Sharma, Aabha, & Alsayed, Alhuseen Omar. (2020). Impact of coronavirus pandemic on education. *Journal of Education and Practice, 11*(13), 108–121.

Paris, Django, & Alim, H. Samy. (2014). What are we seeking to sustain through culturally sustaining pedagogy? A loving critique forward. *Harvard Educational Review, 84*(1), 85–100.

Parker, Kim, Horowitz, Juliana Menasce, & Anderson, Monica. (2020). Amid protests, majorities across racial and ethnic groups express support for the Black Lives Matter movement. Pew Research Center's Social & Demographic Trends Project. https://policycommons.net/artifacts/616390/amid-protests-majorities-across-racial-and-ethnic-groups-express-support-for-the-black-lives-matter-movement/1597028/

Pennycook, Alastair. (2001). *Critical applied linguistics: A critical introduction.* Lawrence Erlbaum.

Rogers, Rebecca (Ed.). (2011). *An introduction to critical discourse analysis in education.* Routledge.

Sclafani, Jennifer, Gounari, Panayota, Fakhrutdinova, Iuliia, & Quintana Sarria, Vannessa. (2022). Applying critical language awareness: A professional development model for educators. Paper presented at the Linguistics Society of America Annual Meeting, Washington, DC, January 6–9.

Solórzano, Daniel G., & Yosso, Tara J. (2002). Critical race methodology: Counter-storytelling as an analytical framework for education research. *Qualitative Inquiry, 8*(1), 23–44.

Varghese, Manka, Morgan, Brian, Johnston, Bill, & Johnson, Kimberly A. (2005). Theorizing language teacher identity: Three perspectives and beyond. *Journal of Language, Identity, and Education, 4*(1), 21–44.

Villavicencio, Karla Cornejo. (2020, April 10). I can't be your hero, baby. *This American Life.* Podcast, Chicago Public Media. https://www.thisamericanlife.org/700/embiggening"https://www.thisamericanlife.org/700/embiggening

Wodak, Ruth, & Meyer, Michael (Eds.). (2015). *Methods of critical discourse studies,* 3rd ed. SAGE Publishing.

Yang, Gene Luen. (2006). *American born Chinese.* First Second Books.

Marie Bissell is a PhD student in the Department of Linguistics at Ohio State University. She previously received her MA in English (linguistics) from North Carolina State University. Her research focuses on sociophonetic aspects of sound change, especially with respect to vowels, in the domains of both perception and production. More broadly, she is interested in applying quantitative methods to questions about dialectology and language change.

José Álvarez-Retamales is a PhD student in the Department of Linguistics at New York University. They previously received their MA in English (sociolinguistics) from North Carolina State University. Their research focuses on discursive constructions of Blackness and how it correlates with sociophonetic variables. Their work seeks to answer raciolinguistic queries in the Caribbean and the Latinx diaspora in the US.

Matthew Champagne is an MS student in the Department of Educational Policy Studies and Evaluation at the University of Kentucky. He previously received his MA in English (linguistics) from North Carolina State University. His research focuses on psychometric methodology and improving assessment and evaluation of Standardized English Learner (SEL) students as well as educational finance forecasting.

Jessica Hatcher currently works in conversational AI consulting. She earned her MA in English linguistics and BA in English education from North Carolina State University. Her research interests lie mostly across the intersections of sociolinguistics and education, especially the application of sociolinguistics within K-12 educational settings.

Shalina Omar is a data scientist at Guidehouse, a consulting firm based in Washington, DC. She received her MA in English (linguistics) from North Carolina State University and her MS in Analytics from the Institute for Advanced Analytics at the same university. Her sociolinguistic research and interests have included linguistic subordination, invisible bias, cross-dialectal and cross-linguistic influence and communication, and linguistic performance of identity.

Walt Wolfram is William C. Friday Distinguished University Professor at North Carolina State University, where he also directs the North Carolina Language and Life Project. He has pioneered research on social and ethnic dialects since the 1960s and published more than 20 books and over 300 articles. He is currently focused on the application of sociolinguistic information for the public.

Abstract: This chapter aims to provide a practical template for groups and organizations who are new to conducting linguistic diversity outreach programs, which are essential educational tools for disseminating linguistic knowledge and scholarship to members of the general public. This work is grounded in the notion that linguists have an obligation to give back to the communities whose linguistic data are studied and analyzed in the academy. In this chapter, the authors illustrate two case studies of linguistic diversity outreach programs that have been implemented by the Linguistics Diversity Ambassadors (LDA), a graduate student-led organization at North Carolina State University.

Key Words: linguistic outreach, community engagement, sociolinguistics, student organizations, case studies

20

Linguistic Literacy and Advocacy in Action

Case Studies in Community Engagement from the Language Diversity Ambassadors at North Carolina State University

Marie Bissell (she/her)
Ohio State University

José Álvarez-Retamales (they/them)
New York University

Matthew Champagne (he/they)
independent scholar

Jessica Hatcher (she/her)
independent scholar

Shalina Omar (she/her)
independent scholar

Walt Wolfram (he/him)
North Carolina State University

Introduction

Public access to and knowledge about scholarship in linguistics helps individuals understand the real-life impacts of linguistic stereotyping and discrimination. However, the responsibility for clear communication that scholars in the academy hold is often overlooked. Members of the public are not readily able to access articles buried in academic journals, so it is up to linguists to disseminate our findings in a way that makes them understandable by and pertinent to community members (see also Gawne et al., this volume). This

Marie Bissell, José Álvarez-Retamales, Matthew Champagne, Jessica Hatcher, Shalina Omar, and Walt Wolfram, *Linguistic Literacy and Advocacy in Action* In: *Inclusion in Linguistics.* Edited by: Anne H. Charity Hudley, Christine Mallinson and Mary Bucholtz, Oxford University Press. © Anne H. Charity Hudley, Christine Mallinsor , and Mary Bucholtz 2024.
DOI: 10.1093/oso/9780197755303.003.0021

chapter is first and foremost constructed to provide actionable ideas and practical knowledge for the expansion of linguistic outreach programs.

Language Diversity Ambassadors (LDA) is a student organization of graduate students in linguistics and sociology at North Carolina State University who conduct linguistics outreach programs at the university itself, in the surrounding Raleigh community, and throughout the state of North Carolina. The organization has worked to make linguistics accessible and relevant to the lived experiences of community members by developing linguistics outreach programs. In particular, the organization has focused on giving people educational tools and knowledge to advocate for their linguistic practices and perspectives (Wolfram et al., 2004; Wolfram, 2013). Our primary programming focus is to explicitly and critically examine power hierarchies and how they are produced and reproduced by language (Godley & Minnici, 2008 Godley & Reaser, 2018). By working to increase community-wide awareness about linguistic stereotyping and discrimination, we seek to counter bias at the ideological level while working hard to disseminate the results of linguistic scholarship so that others may change the ways they think and act with regards to language diversity (Charity, 2008). We invite nonlinguist audiences to explore, engage with, and appreciate the validity of the social, historical, and lived experiences of the speakers who use a variety of dialects. Through the LDA, we have implemented several programs in compliance with NC State's institutional review board policies to move closer to these goals; in this chapter, we present a few case studies to facilitate others in their endeavors to build and maintain linguistic outreach programs at their own institutions and communities.

The first case study covers the Language Diversity Enrichment Program (LDEP), a week-long, daily summer camp designed to introduce high school students, who are frequently multidialectal and attending public schools in the Raleigh area, to linguistic diversity as well as provide them the opportunity to reflect on their own lived experiences in relation to their linguistic practices. The goals of this program are to get young people to think about language and linguistics in their own lives and to make linguistics more accessible to a wider audience outside of the academy. We present this case study as an example of a week-long engagement with multiple days of planned curriculum and opportunities for student reflection and follow-up. We aspire for this chapter to provide an adaptable template for those hoping to implement similar programs in their own communities.

The second case study details a recurring program, College Mentors for Kids (CMK), where representatives from the LDA teach and facilitate activities with groups of students from local public elementary schools in kindergarten through fifth grade as part of a pre-existing after-school program. These students came from a variety of racial and socioeconomic backgrounds. The CMK programs were designed to get elementary-aged students to begin thinking critically—and to get excited—about their own linguistic experiences, as well as to scaffold early outreach experience for the LDA facilitators. In many cases, a K-12 student's first formal introduction to the ideas of linguistic diversity and appreciation can only happen through short-term engagements, so we provide this case study as a model for one-time workshop-style activities that can be optimized for all ages.

This chapter has two main aims. First, we present two outreach efforts planned and implemented by the LDA at North Carolina State University, along with their limitations and challenges. Second, we provide clear overviews of how we facilitated these programs, so that others may reflect upon and incorporate these ideas about linguistic variation and subordination into their own linguistic outreach and advocacy endeavors.

Background: Language Diversity Ambassadors

One focus of our outreach efforts is educating local communities at North Carolina State University and the surrounding city of Raleigh about the role that language variation plays in oppressive power dynamics, such as those broadly described by Pierre Bourdieu (1991). These efforts echo Paulo Freire's notion of critical pedagogies (1994; 2000), or the idea that educating is, in and of itself, a political act that is grounded in sociohistorical and cultural contexts and can be used to foster and further social justice efforts. We operationalize a particular kind of critical pedagogy, critical language pedagogies. Amanda Godley and Jeffrey Reaser (2018) described critical language pedagogies as educational practices which work to advocate for individuals who participate in marginalized linguistic communities. This set of practices centers language ideologies and their relationship to broader power structures, and educational materials focus on having students critically examine these concepts. By foregrounding these ideas in our outreach curricula, we aim to provide spaces where students can learn more about—and celebrate—their own linguistic practices.

Crucially, our efforts aim to change language ideologies that link linguistic variation to power imbalances; however, these practices are not without their difficulties. Educators who subscribe to the idea of, and utilize, asset-based approaches generally believe that a student's linguistic and communicative background is an inherent benefit to learning the standardized variety of

English typically taught in language arts curriculum (MacSwan, 2020). While most socially focused linguists and language educators are probably keyed in to this idea already, some asset-based approaches at times can detract from some social realities. For example, as outlined in Django Paris (2012), an effective linguistic asset-based approach is one that works to embrace, explore and sustain the cultural practices and contexts in which a language or dialect is used. Further, Django Paris and H. Samy Alim (2014) proposed that language pedagogies that engage with the sociocultural and historical aspects of language use must recognize and teach language's dynamic and unique relationship to social and political power and racial and ethnic identity construction and maintain a self-critical component as to foster and promote continued, progressive, inclusive educational efforts. Additionally, Jonathan Rosa and Nelson Flores (2017) emphasized that educational practices which prima facie appear to be inclusive in nature, such as the recognition and inclusion of nonhegemonic English features in speech and language screeners for children, still position non-Anglo varieties of English as variant and Other in nature. In sum, even the inclusion of asset-based approaches can still fail to meet the needs of students. As language diversity ambassadors, we continually work to recognize the precarious territory in which our efforts may exist.

While our efforts can be traced back to these theoretical roots, such work would not be possible without the foundation that previous linguistics-based educational outreach efforts have provided, especially by previous efforts of the organization now known as the North Carolina Language and Life Project (NCLLP). The idea that linguists should give back in some way to communities and language users from whom language data is collected was popularized by William Labov's (1982) principles of error correction, in which he proposed that linguists have an ethical obligation to push back against harmful, popularly held linguistic prejudices. We also adopt Labov's principle of debt incurred, which proposes that linguists who obtain data from a community are obligated to share these findings with that community. Generally, Labov argued that linguists should not be "neutral investigators" of language, but instead that linguists should take an active role in community engagement, whether by demystifying linguistic misinformation or by advocating for communities to learn more about their language practices.

Walt Wolfram (1998) broadened the scope of these principles by proposing the principle of linguistic gratuity. This principle states that linguists who engage in community-based research should work both to critically examine the community-researcher relationship and to cultivate a mutually beneficial and collaborative relationship, wherein a community may also receive symbolic, economic, or cultural capital for their time, energy, and data. Such efforts can include the creation of sociolinguistic-based course curricula; the publication of documentaries where community members can discuss the history, cultural practices, and lived experiences of community members; the creation of language exhibits to be displayed in prominent community hubs; and perhaps most importantly, the cultivation of the personal relationships between researchers and community members (Wolfram et al., 2008). It is imperative that researchers recognize that language is an integral component of culture that is not severable from the people and communities that use it (see also Plumb et al., 2024; Riestenberg et al., 2024).

While the NCLLP has established itself within the North Carolina State University Linguistics Program as a semi-independent not-for-profit organization, many of the targeted outreach events and programs have been, and continue to be, graduate student-led. One such effort includes the Educating the Educated program on the university's campus (Dunstan et al., 2015). This program included crafting and presenting targeted, interactive workshops for undergraduate students aimed at addressing various linguistic-based misconceptions and misinformation, as well as surveying workshop participants to note what parts of the workshop were most beneficial or impactful, which areas could be improved upon, and most importantly, what students took away from these programs. Stephany Dunstan and colleagues (2015) also suggest the use of a campus infusion model that highlights pathways across university campuses where linguistic diversity work can have the highest impact, including student and academic affairs offices, diversity and inclusion offices, and human resources departments. These programs were implemented as workshops or trainings for a variety of key groups, including new staff hires in these offices and new first year students at NC State. Ongoing outreach efforts, featuring informational booths at the university's welcome week and a dedicated linguistic diversity week each year, were implemented by the Linguistic Diversity Ambassadors (LDA).

The LDA organization was founded and is led by graduate students and supervised by faculty. Described in detail in Dunstan and colleagues (2018), the LDA provides its members with professional development, outreach, and advocacy opportunities outside of the coursework and research typically associated with graduate school. With respect to professional development, students can collectively and synergistically brainstorm potential workshops for the campus community, craft cross-platform advertising and social media marketing campaigns for various events, and build and increase interinstitution and intrainstitution participation by reaching out to various departments and venues on and off the NC State campus. Due to the nature of its inception and continued leadership, the focus and mission of the LDA has been, and continues to be, peer-to-peer linguistics education. In particular, LDA members are "encouraged to bring their own ideas to the table for creatively presenting [linguistic] information to their peers, and additionally to seek opportunities for partnerships on campus based on their interests and skillsets" (Dunstan et al., 2018, p. 218). In addition to participating heavily in this program, the LDA has also spearheaded many other on-campus and off-campus initiatives. It has led many events such as informational booths at the university's welcome event and the North Carolina State Fair, language diversity teaching in a public school on Ocracoke Island in the Outer Banks for 30 years, and on-campus workshops covering topics ranging from queer linguistics to code-switching, and screening documentaries (Dunstan et al., 2018; Wolfram & Dunstan, 2021). Members of the LDA, including the authors, have historically come from a wide variety of racial, ethnic, socioeconomic, sexual orientation, regional and linguistic backgrounds. We are of the opinion that these variable experiences strengthen our ability to communicate with wider audiences.

The institutional structure that supports these efforts is key to enabling graduate students to occupy important roles within the LDA. By empowering graduate students to seek out, develop, and facilitate linguistic outreach programs, not only does the LDA create a space to disseminate findings from linguistic research and share individual linguistic experiences, but this organization also provides an example of how outreach and advocacy efforts can arise when a group of students wanting to make positive changes in their community organize their collective efforts and are supported in therein by like-minded faculty. The programs we discuss below were entirely graduate student-led from conception to implementation. Giving graduate students the opportunity to directly interact with individuals and communities foregrounds the LDA's mission in the training of future language scientists, such that graduate students are immersed in local language communities from the very beginning of their time at NC State (cf. Franz et al., 2022).

The LDA works to educate individuals about their own linguistic practices to help fight linguistic prejudice (Lippi-Green, 2012) and biases at an ideological level. The importance of education-based linguistic empowerment for community members cannot be overstated, especially in the context of efforts to bring the voices of marginalized individuals into conversation with scholarship in the academy. Service to one's community is fundamental to being a responsible social scientist, especially in the context of education about social inequalities and their manifestations in people's everyday lives. By advocating for people in their linguistic practices (Wolfram, 2013; Wolfram & Waldorf, 2019, we interrogate and engage in collective dialogues about power discrepancies and how they are constructed and reinforced by linguistic practices. Developing self-awareness of one's own linguistic biases, ideologies, and practices allows for critical examination of what role the individual plays in combating systemic issues like linguistic subordination and discrimination.

Language Diversity Education Program for High Schoolers

The first case study we present is the Language Diversity Education Program (LDEP), an educational summer camp for high schoolers run by the LDA since 2017. The program was suspended in 2019 and restarted in 2021. This week-long, half-day camp is designed to bring linguistics to public education beyond single-event engagements (e.g., one-time class lectures by LDA members at local high schools) and make linguistics more accessible to high school students (see also Plackowski, this volume). LDEP is free and open to any interested high schooler: we have been able to reach students from other states visiting North Carolina for the summer, students from more rural areas of North Carolina, and students from both public and private schools in the local Raleigh area. Transportation is not provided, but some schools arrange transportation for their own students who attend in larger groups. It's worth noting that some schools have a requirement for students to complete a summer program. This requirement drove many students toward our program as it was more financially accessible than other programs in the state.

In a fundamental sense, LDEP aims to implement the Students' Right to Their Own Language resolution (NCTE & CCCC, 1974/2014). This statement is central to LDA's mission, given that one major focus of the outreach program is communicating that linguistic diversity should be celebrated instead of stigmatized, especially in educational spaces. Additionally, in this program we seek to instruct students about linguistic diversity in North Carolina as a whole, connecting students to the state's history, cultures, people, and regions. Having students think critically about language and variation was essential to the goals of this curriculum, such that students could seek to evaluate and reevaluate their own language attitudes. Finally, we hope that the curriculum will spur future interest in language and linguistics among young people. This program is aligned with broader goals proposed by the Linguistics in the School Curriculum Committee of the Linguistic Society of America, including encouraging young people to think critically about language variation.

The LDEP curriculum is planned with the following structure: (1) introducing topics for preliminary discussion; (2) prompting students to share and incorporate their lived experiences; and (3) encouraging discussion and interactive activities. Although the topics change from year to year based on graduate students' areas of interest and expertise, the specific educational tools we've used so far have been mostly consistent. These tools are intended to maximize student engagement by gauging students' ideas and thought processes.

One tool that has been especially fruitful is linguistic surveys, which provide insights into students' thoughts and opinions prior to beginning an activity and then again after completing an activity. By assessing students' pre-existing perspectives, we are better able to meet students where they are with respect to their experiences. The post-activity surveys allow us to determine the students' biggest takeaways from the lesson. Students also complete exit tickets each day, which are used to identify the biggest takeaways from that day's class, which in turn allow us to adjust future days' curriculum to reiterate key concepts, to incorporate more information about topics that students had shown interest in, and to reflect on our teaching tools to better serve students' learning styles. Finally, we invite students to journal to reflect on what they had learned or topics they were thinking about. Journaling activities are mostly unstructured to permit students to freely record their thoughts and questions. At the end of the program, students are given the option to either keep their journal or share it with the facilitators, and most students chose to share their journal with the facilitators.

All students are taught basic linguistic concepts, with a focus on descriptivism versus prescriptivism and linguistic discrimination. We always cover several language varieties, including African American Language, American Sign Language, Spanglish in North Carolina, and regional North Carolina dialects (Appalachian, Outer Banks, etc.). Students are first introduced to relevant vocabulary, including *linguist*, *accent*, and *dialect*. Central to these introductory endeavors was learning about students' experiences with each topic, including their perceptions of their own accent, their knowledge of code-switching, and linguistic profiling (Baugh, 2000; Baugh, 2016). We also use professionally produced videos to introduce students to linguists working on diverse topics, especially through the North Carolina Language and Life Project (NCLLP).

Students also participate in interactive exercises that range widely by year. One activity involves the students completing draw-a-map activities for learning about perceptual dialectology, especially in the context of North Carolina. Through this activity, students are able to learn about language ideologies by critically comparing their perceptions to others'. One year, students took part in an ultrasound activity in which they were able to view their own articulations of speech sounds in real-time and learn about the physiology of language. Various group activities, skits, and discussions are also interspersed to facilitate the exchange of ideas and feedback among peers.

The logistics of putting together this experience for high schoolers are arranged by the LDA graduate students with the help of faculty. Advertising has consisted of connecting with high school guidance counselors, hanging flyers in public libraries, and using word of mouth among graduate student and faculty contacts. Social media advertising has also been used in the past, along with promotional materials on the NC State's Linguistics Program website.

One important aspect of LDEP is the range of experiences the graduate student facilitators bring to the program. Some facilitators have no teaching experience, while others have previously worked in public schools or taught at the university level as a teaching assistant. Individual facilitators design their own lessons in collaboration with the other graduate students and faculty, and emphasis is placed on recognizing LDEP students' existing experiences as forms of linguistic expertise. Treating students as fellow scientists from the beginning of the program allows learning to go both ways, with both facilitators and students sharing their experiences and gaining new insights into language and its complexities. This framing of the program helps participants more seriously reflect on the program's content and goals.

In both journal entries and exit surveys, participants have reported they have learned about the role that language ideologies play in their evaluations of linguistic variation, especially in the context of how they think about dialects that have been historically stigmatized. Through their ongoing journals, participants often shared that the curriculum had changed the way they thought about their own dialect usage in educational settings. Participants have also reported feeling like their own linguistic experiences were both valued and validated by the facilitators. We present this case study as an example template for how we designed and executed a curriculum over the course of a week. Multiday programs are a wonderful way to incorporate different topics, cater to the interests of your audience, and take advantage of feedback and follow-up. We hope the LDEP program will inspire and guide readers who want to create a program tailored to their own communities.

The College Mentors for Kids Program

Our second case study is the College Mentors for Kids (CMK) program, which is an example of a shorter or workshop-style community outreach event. One-time or short-term workshops have different audiences and purposes than longer-style programs like the summer camp detailed above. In this program, organized by other students at NC State, college students from outside of LDA are paired with elementary school student partners. The pairs meet for weekly activities that focus on introducing the children to higher education and careers, culture and diversity, and community service. The LDA group partnered with the CMK group for several sessions to facilitate activities for their culture and diversity focus area. We describe these sessions below.

The audience for the College Mentors for Kids program is elementary students in downtown Raleigh. Between 40 and 50 total students engage in these outreach programs split between two age groups: kindergarten to second grade and third to fifth grade. While the teaching objectives are similar for the two age groups, the activities are adjusted to be age-relevant for each group, and each session lasts for two hours. Most of the activities the LDA have completed with the students have been inspired by linguistic outreach programs at other universities, such as Ohio State's Buckeye Language Lab at the Center of Science and Industry Museum in Columbus (Wagner et al., 2015). Facilitators collaborate on designing the activities for each two-hour session.

The goals for these sessions are threefold: to get students to think critically about language, to get them excited about language, and to get them to engage with their own linguistic practices and experiences. Especially with respect to the third goal, we focus on having the students place themselves and their language use in the broader realm of linguistic diversity. Like the linguistics summer camp for high schoolers, we aim to facilitate two-way learning, such that both the facilitators and the children leave the sessions thinking more critically about language. These workshops are the first or one of the first outreach facilitation experiences for some LDA members, introducing them to community-based approaches to linguistic diversity. Additionally, the LDA facilitators are expected to educate themselves about engaging with the local community and its linguistic practices, to connect to the language communities to which the kids belonged. Facilitators prepare for the program by reading several key articles about linguistic outreach from the NCLLP and discussing best practices with Walt Wolfram, the program's faculty director (Charity, 2008; Wolfram et al., 2008; Wolfram, 2013 Dunstan et al., 2018; Hazen, 2018).

This case study presents a template both for a two-hour workshop and for adjusting linguistic diversity curricula for different age groups. Learning about language and linguistic diversity and empowering others in their own language is important for all ages, so it is essential that the lessons and activities are appropriately adjusted to be engaging for their intended audiences. A few of the LDA members had backgrounds in teaching and education, and they were able to adjust activities appropriately for different audiences. The CMK program additionally serves as the first outreach experience for many LDA facilitators. To connect with the community and empower others to think critically about language ideologies at every age level, those who wish to do such outreach need a place to practice learning-by-doing from the facilitator standpoint. A shorter workshop-style event with both new and experienced facilitators acts as scaffolding for longer and more complex outreach events.

Both age groups individually engage with two broad activities before moving on to age-specific activities targeted for each age group. The first broad activity category for both age groups is lexical variation. This activity consists of projecting pictures of everyday items on a screen and soliciting students' words for them (e.g., *soft drink/soda/pop/coke, tennis shoes/sneakers/ gym shoes, trunk/boot*). We also prompt students to think about whether they use different words in different social contexts, like at home, with friends, or at school. Facilitators also show maps from the *New York Times* dialect quiz pertaining to these lexical differences (Katz & Andrews, 2013) to show how vocabulary for the same things can differ geographically. We treat this activity as a gateway to the acknowledgment and acceptance of language variation as a natural phenomenon, as well as an opportunity for the students to connect with their own everyday experiences. Facilitators also use these discussions to transition from talking about strictly lexical variation to other aspects of dialects, such as phonological variation.

The second broad activity category is an exploration of American Sign Language (ASL). Children, all of whom so far have been hearing and unfamiliar with ASL, are taught the ASL alphabet, how to sign their own names with fingerspelling, and how to sing "Happy Birthday" in ASL. These activities introduce students to different language modalities in a way that is fun and hands-on. Because Deaf and Hard of Hearing communities are frequently marginalized, these short activities are helpful for providing students the opportunity to engage with linguistic communities that they are less familiar with.

For the younger group, facilitators lead a wug-creation activity. The children are shown a picture of a wug following Jean Berko's (1958) model, then asked to create the plural form of "wug." Facilitators point out that the children know how to create the plural without knowing the word. Then, students are invited to create their own wugs (or other funny creatures) out of paper and art supplies and name the creature themselves (Farris-Trimble & Reid, 2018). Finally, children share their newly named creatures and their appropriate plurals with the group. We chose this activity for the younger children to keep them physically engaged in an activity and entertained while still learning. Students can also take their creations home, potentially spurring conversations with caregivers about the activity they had completed. This activity functions to validate the linguistic knowledge of students before completing other activities about linguistic diversity.

For the older group, facilitators lead several activities relating to linguistic subordination and discrimination. The first activity invites students to recognize and critically evaluate language ideologies in video clips from movies and television. The children view clips of stereotyped characters (e.g., Scar's evil/smart British accent in *The Lion King*, Foghorn Leghorn's dumb/silly Southern accent from *Looney Tunes*) and then are asked to describe traits associated with different accents. Connecting with students using media they are already familiar with fosters more critical engagement, and this design also allows students to understand the assumptions and associations that people make about specific language varieties. Finally, we seek to challenge children's stereotypes about what someone's accent says about their personal traits, helping them connect the ideas from the activities to their current language spaces.

The second activity geared toward the older children serves as a continuation of the conversation about linguistic discrimination and directly addresses discrimination through linguistic profiling (Baugh, 2000; Baugh, 2016). Facilitators play a video of a Department of Housing and Urban Development fair housing Public Service Announcement, which is widely used in discussions of linguistic profiling (The Language & Life Project, 2008). In the video, a white man calls a landlord to ask about an apartment for rent. The man uses different racially and ethnically marked accents and gets rejected over and over until he uses a more recognizably white accent and is told the apartment is still available for rent. The students first listen to the video without visuals so that they couldn't see it was one talker using different accents and are asked what they believe is the topic of the Public Service Announcement. This prompts students to think about what they were hearing and why the landlord's response to the final voice is different, preparing them for a conversation about linguistic profiling and discrimination. Facilitators then play the same video but now with both the audio and its accompanying visuals. The students can often identify the message of discrimination but have expressed surprise at seeing all the voices coming from one person, which highlights the kinds of information we can pick up and assume from hearing an accent.

In addition to introducing children to the concept of linguistic profiling in general, we also seek to present linguistics as a way to engage with social inequalities. We emphasize the idea that seemingly harmless assumptions or associations about language can perpetuate social inequalities. Through this activity, the facilitators drive home the importance of acceptance of and appreciation for linguistic diversity, encouraging children to recognize and combat linguistic discrimination in their everyday lives.

Conclusion

The programs that we have discussed in this chapter specifically built upon existing efforts and models of linguistic outreach that have been implemented by the North Carolina Language and Life Project, such as its annual week-long curriculum taught by faculty and graduate students at Ocracoke School in the Outer Banks of North Carolina (Wolfram, Reaser, & Vaughn, 2008). The materials we have developed for the LDEP and CMK programs are available on the supplemental website associated with these volumes, as one of our aims is to facilitate the growth of language science outreach programs at other universities and educational institutions.

In doing this work, we stand on the shoulders of many dedicated linguists, activists, and outreach professionals. However, we are not the only student group that focuses on language and social justice-based efforts. For example, several efforts at the College of William & Mary and the University of California, Santa Barbara, have also worked to promote the inclusion of historically marginalized groups in linguistics and to implement student-centered mentorship programs in linguistics in addition to various linguistic outreach events (Franz et al., 2022). Phillip Carter (2018) also noted how mass media outlets can be a powerful tool for linguistic outreach via a case study of a Hispanic-serving Institution. It is our sincere hope that the two case studies that we outline in this chapter will be helpful to those who wish to engage with their own communities about language variation, change, and ideology, and perhaps most importantly, who desire to create a world where it is a bit easier to do linguistic work that matters.

References

Baugh, John. (2000). Racial identification by speech. *American Speech*, 75(4), 362–364.

Baugh, John. (2016). Linguistic profiling and discrimination. In Nelson Flores, Ofelia García, & Massimiliano Spotti (Eds.), *The Oxford handbook of language and society* (pp. 349–368). Oxford University Press.

Berko, Jean. (1958). The child's learning of English morphology. *Word, 14*(2–3): 150–177. doi:10.1080/00437956.1958.11659661

Bourdieu, Pierre. (1991). *Language and symbolic power*. Harvard University Press.

Carter, Phillip. (2018). Hispanic serving institutions and mass media engagement: Implications for sociolinguistic justice. *Journal of English Linguistics, 46*(3), 246–262.

Charity, Anne H. (2008). Linguists as agents for social change. *Language and Linguistics Compass, 2*(5), 923–939.

Dunstan, Stephany B., Wolfram, Walt, Jaeger, Andrey J., & Crandall, Rebecca E. (2015). Educating the educated: Language diversity in the university backyard. *American Speech, 90*(2), 266–280.

Dunstan, Stephany B., Eads, Amanda, Jaeger, Andrey J., & Wolfram, Walt. (2018). The importance of graduate student engagement in a campus language diversity initiative. *Journal of English Linguistics, 46*(3), 215–228.

Farris-Tremble, Ashley, & Reid, Danica. (2018). Little linguists: Teaching elementary schoolers to be language scientists [conference presentation]. LSA 2018, Salt Lake City, UT, United States.

Franz, Hannah, Charity Hudley, Anne, Scarborough King, Rachael S., Calhoun, Kendra, miles-hercules, deandre, Muwwakkil, Jamaal, Edwards, Jeremy, Duffie, Cecily A., Knox, Danielle, Lawton, Bishop, & Merrit, John Henry. (2022). The role of the graduate student in inclusive undergraduate research experiences. *Pedagogy: Critical Approaches in Teaching Literature, Language, Composition, and Culture, 22*(1), 121–141.

Freire, Paulo. (1994). *Pedagogy of hope: Reliving pedagogy of the oppressed*. Bloomsbury.

Freire, Paulo. (2000). *Pedagogy of the oppressed, 30th anniversary ed*. Continuum.

Godley, Amanda J., & Minnici, Angela. (2008). Critical language pedagogy in an urban high school English class. *Urban Education, 43*(3), 319–346.

Godley, Amanda J., & Reaser, Jeffrey. (2018). *Critical language pedagogy: Interrogating language, dialects, and power in teacher education*. Peter Lang.

Hazen, Kirk. (2018). Sociolinguistic outreach for the new South. In Jeffrey Reaser, Eric Wilbanks, Kara Wojcik, & Walt Wolfram (Eds.), *Language variety in the new South: Contemporary perspectives on change and variation* (321–343). University of North Carolina Press.

Katz, Josh, & Andrews, Wilson. (2013, December 19). How y'all, youse, and you guys talk. *New York Times*. https://www.nytimes.com/interactive/2014/upshot/dialect-quiz-map.html.

Labov, William. (1982). Objectivity and commitment in linguistic science: The case of the Black English trial in Ann Arbor. *Language in Society, 11*(2), 165–201.

Lippi-Green, Rosina. (2012). *English with an accent: Language, ideology, and discrimination in the United States*. Routledge.

MacSwan, Jeff. (2020). Academic English as standard language ideology: A renewed research agenda for asset-based language education. *Language Teaching Research 24*(1), 28–36.

National Council of Teachers of English and the Conference on College Composition and Communication. (1974/2014). Students' right to their own language (with bibliography). https://cccc.ncte.org/cccc/resources/positions.

Paris, Django. (2012). Culturally sustaining pedagogy: A needed change in stance, terminology, and practice. *Educational Researcher, 41*(3), 93–97.

Paris, Django & Alim, H. Samy. (2014). What are we seeking to sustain through culturally sustaining pedagogy? A loving critique forward. *Harvard Educational Review, 84*(1), 85–100.

Plumb, May Helena, Dubcovsky, Alejandra, Guzmán, Moisés García, Lillehaugen, Brook Danielle, & Lopez, Felipe H. (2024). Growing a bigger linguistics through a Zapotec agenda: The Ticha Project. In Anne H. Charity Hudley, Christine Mallinson, & Mary Bucholtz (Eds.), *Decolonizing linguistics*. Oxford University Press.

Riestenberg, Katherine J., Freemond, Ally, Lillehaugen, Brook Danielle, & Washington, Jonathan N. (2024). Prioritizing community partners' goals in projects to support Indigenous language revitalization. In Anne H. Charity Hudley, Christine Mallinson, & Mary Bucholtz (Eds.), *Decolonizing linguistics*. Oxford University Press.

Rosa, Jonathan, & Flores, Nelson. (2017). Unsettling race and language: Toward a raciolinguisitc perspective. *Language in Society, 46*(5), 621–647.

The Language & Life Project. (2008, September 10). Fair Housing PSA [video file]. https://www.youtube.com/watch?v=zup2qlFuCDc.

Wagner, Laura, Speer, Shari R., Moore, Leslie C., McCullough, Elizabeth A., Ito, Kiwako, Clopper, Cynthia G., & Campbell-Kibler, Kathryn. (2015). Linguistics in a science museum: Integrating research, teaching, and outreach at the language sciences research lab. *Language and Linguistics Compass, 9*(10), 420–431.

Wolfram, Walt. (1998). Scrutinizing linguistic gratuity: Issues from the field. *Journal of Sociolinguistics, 2*(2), 271–279.

Wolfram, Walt. (2013). Community commitment and responsibility. In J. K. Chambers & N. Schilling (Eds.), *The Handbook of Language Variation and Change* (pp. 557–576). Oxford: John Wiley and Sons.

Wolfram, Walt, Rowe, Ryan, & Grimes, Drew. (2004). Sociolinguistic involvement in community perspective: Opportunity and obligation. *LAVIS II, University of Alabama.*

Wolfram, Walt, Reaser, Jeffrey, & Vaughn, Charlotte. (2008). Operationalizing linguistic gratuity: From principle to practice. *Language and Linguistics Compass, 2*(6), 1109–1134.

Wolfram, Walt, & Waldorf, KellyNoel. (2019). Talking Black in America: The role of the documentary in public education. *English Today, 35*(1), 3–13.

Wolfram, Walt, & Dunstan, Stephany. (2021). Linguistic inequality and sociolinguistic justice in campus life: The need for programmatic intervention. In Gaillynn Clements & Marnie Joe Petray (Eds.), *Linguistic discrimination in US higher education* (156–173). Routledge.

Abstract: This conclusion to *Inclusion in Linguistics* provides a set of action plans to make linguistics a genuinely and intersectionally inclusive discipline and profession not merely in philosophy but, crucially, in practice. The resulting roadmap highlights specific recommendations made by the authors of the foregoing chapters, with particular attention to how to foster inclusion intersectionally, structurally, and educationally in all aspects of linguistics research, teaching, community partnerships, public engagement, and institutional and professional service. Central to these goals is the need to dismantle the barriers that make linguistics exclusionary and instead to embrace practices that center, support, and sustain minoritized scholars and students as well as sociopolitically marginalized communities. An inclusive linguistics will not look like the current version of the discipline, and it will not be confined to the ivory tower. Building a truly just, equitable, and inclusive linguistics will require ongoing and collective efforts.

Key Words: accessibility, community partnerships, educational partnerships, inclusion, public linguistics, social justice, structural change

Conclusion

Inclusion in Linguistics

Christine Mallinson (she/her)
University of Maryland, Baltimore County

Jon Henner† (he/him,☞/✋)
University of North Carolina, Greensboro

Anne H. Charity Hudley (she/her)
Stanford University

Mary Bucholtz (she/her, they/them)
University of California, Santa Barbara

Introduction

In the introduction to this volume, we discussed statements and action plans for justice, equity, diversity, access, and inclusion that have been put forward by linguistics departments and universities in recent years. Changes must come in culture and climate, and they must have structural and material impact. The chapters in *Inclusion in Linguistics* have presented models for how to do this work in linguistics research, teaching, community partnerships, public engagement, and institutional and professional service in ways that center justice, equity, and inclusion at their core—and in so doing, they have offered pathways for what an inclusive linguistics can look like. We now extend the conversation in this conclusion by building on the themes and insights shared in the chapters in this volume to create roadmaps for how to achieve greater inclusion in linguistics and in academia by implementing direct actions for implementable and measurable change. (Parallel recommendations and roadmaps are also presented in the conclusion of our companion volume,

---

Jon Henner died on August 14, 2023. His contributions to this chapter were complete except for the final copyediting and proofreading which was done by the editors.

Christine Mallinson, Jon Henner, Anne H. Charity Hudley, and Mary Bucholtz, *Conclusion* In: *Inclusion in Linguistics*. Edited by: Anne H. Charity Hudley, Christine Mallinson and Mary Bucholtz, Oxford University Press.
© Anne H. Charity Hudley, Christine Mallinson, and Mary Bucholtz 2024. DOI: 10.1093/oso/9780197755303.003.0022

Decolonizing Linguistics. The supplementary website associated with these volumes also include numerous materials designed to provide practical guidance and actionable ideas to other scholars looking to replicate and extend such initiatives.)

In a prior publication, Anne Charity Hudley and Christine Mallinson (2018) established the need for linguists to "operationalize a call to action in a way that moves us from sentiment to practice" (p. 524), focusing on the areas of student, faculty, campus, and community inclusion. That article presented guiding questions to inform how scholars can conceptualize and take action on diversity, equity, and inclusion, which drew upon previous work by faculty in the College of William and Mary Linguistics Program (2017) and upon a comprehensive plan for diversity and inclusion established by the Virginia Commonwealth University Department of English (2011). In this conclusion, we have adopted a similar guiding framework whereby we conceptualize and summarize how contributors to this volume are advancing student, faculty, campus, and community inclusion in their work, and how these insights inform next steps for change.

We also connect this framework to our guiding principles surrounding how we conceptualize inclusion. Often when people discuss inclusion, they focus on the integration of marginalized groups into an institution without structurally changing it: That is, they aim for superficial changes that do not alter how the institution operates. The most extreme example of this problem is the tendency for discussions of inclusion to assume that all members of marginalized groups can physically integrate into the institution as a material structure with material practices. This is self-evidently not the case for disabled people, who are expected to navigate physical spaces and activities that were not designed for them. In other words, inclusion that does not encompass physical access for disabled people is not inclusion at all. The physical environment must be manipulated to make it just for people whose bodies and minds are considered non-normative by the dominant culture. In this era of post-COVID-19 politics, when conferences have reduced the number of online accessible talks and masks are no longer required, the idea that inclusion must also centrally incorporate disabled people is even more critical. Similarly, linguists cannot claim to support linguistic variation while holding that the language produced by disabled people is unacceptable variation (cf. Hill, 2022). At the most fundamental level, inclusion requires accessibility. In this volume, several contributors discuss steps to address the woefully insufficient level of disability inclusion in linguistics and work toward a more comprehensive vision for inclusion that recognizes that theory and rhetoric without direct action for change are not enough.

As this example illustrates, we must strive for intersectional inclusion by rejecting the marginalization of scholars who are traditionally underrepresented in our discipline and profession. In our conceptualization, the category of underrepresented scholars not only includes scholars of color, women scholars, LGBTQ+ scholars, scholars from economically marginalized backgrounds, and others from historically and systemically marginalized groups (cf. Koester, 2022; Leslie et al., 2015; O'Grady, 2021); it also includes deaf scholars, disabled scholars, and scholars who work outside of traditionally elite colleges and universities, such as scholars at community colleges, Historically Black Colleges and Universities (HBCUs), Tribal Colleges and Universities (TCUs), and institutions of higher education across the Global South. Many of these scholars are assumed to be less capable, less talented, and less brilliant than their peers with greater structural privilege (Gutiérrez y Muhs et al., 2012; Leslie et al., 2015); for some, their very presence as faculty members on college and university campuses is viewed as a threat. Their intellectual interests are often marginalized as well. These scholars are often more interested in exploring applied research, research on education and pedagogy, community-centered collaborations, public-facing work, and intersections between and across fields, and they may not meet arbitrary and exclusionary criteria about what does or doesn't "count" as linguistics, which leads to bias within our discipline (cf. Charity Hudley & Flores, 2022).

Action Plans for Intersectional Inclusion

Addressing these challenges requires not only rejecting exclusionary disciplinary boundaries but also actively engaging in dialogue with underrepresented scholars and those who work in collaboration with sociopolitically subordinated communities and welcoming their insights into the discipline's theoretical and methodological paradigms. The chapters in Part 1 of this volume provide many recommendations for how to implement intersectional inclusion models in linguistics across disability, sexuality, geography, and gender identity, as well as race.

In Chapter 1, "How to Train Your Abled Linguist: A Crip Linguistics Perspective on Pragmatic Research," Jon Henner discusses the problems that arise when linguists examine autistic language through an ableist theoretical lens. Henner points out that linguists need to broaden what they consider to be appropriate language as well as appropriate linguistics. He suggests that linguists read more widely, particularly in disability justice and studies, instead of making assumptions about language based on flawed studies of disabled populations. In Chapter 2, "Critically Examining Inclusion and Parity for Deaf Global South Researchers of Colour in the Field of Sign Language Linguistics," Lynn Hou and Kristian Ali recommend that PhD-granting linguistics programs revise their admissions requirements to minimize bias against deaf students, while investing in cluster recruiting for deaf students as well as community capacity building to connect students and local deaf signing communities and to promote opportunities for collaboration on community-based research projects. They also recommend that conference, workshop, and summer school organizers promote greater attendance by Global South deaf researchers of color, including through increased financial support as well as community-building and research collaboration opportunities. Finally, the authors call for more open and explicit dialogue about disparities and inequities facing deaf linguists, particularly Global South deaf researchers of color, including increased attention to the ethical responsibilities necessary for equitable and inclusive research with deaf and signing communities.

Chapters 3 and 4 both offer suggestions for scholar allies and accomplices. In Chapter 3, "We Need to Be Telling Our Own Stories: Creating a Home for Filipinx Americans in Linguistics," Julien De Jesus recommends that scholars who work with and mentor Filipinx Americans begin by educating themselves on Filipino history and culture. Filipinx mentees and colleagues are not obligated to be educators nor advocates for their own experiences and ways of viewing the world. De Jesus also recommends getting involved with Filipinx scholarship, inviting Filipinx scholars to present their work locally, and fostering Filipinx network opportunities as ways that non-Filipinx scholars can better support their students and colleagues. Similarly, in Chapter 4, "(Trans)forming Expertise: Transness, Equity, and the Ethical Imperative of Linguistics," deandre miles-hercules concludes their discussion of the need for inclusion of trans and nonbinary linguists in the field by providing a list of rules for how to be an accomplice, which include holding cis colleagues accountable for micro/macroaggressions, supporting scholars targeted by hate groups for speaking out against inequity, and refusing to remain silent about misconduct within the discipline. The final rule is to teach graduate students to follow these same rules, in order to make linguistics a space that is more inclusive of trans and nonbinary lives and perspectives.

In Chapter 5, "Toward a Big Tent Linguistics: Inclusion and the Myth of the Lone Genius," Rikker Dockum and Caitlin M. Green provide advice for readers in different stages of their linguistics career. For undergraduates, they recommend following podcasts and social media featuring linguists from a range of diverse social backgrounds providing information about linguistics that may not be covered in classes; they also suggest that undergraduates advocate for more inclusive linguistics coursework. For graduate students, they recommend reaching out to professional networks or clusters that focus on inclusive linguistics research. For scholars post-PhD, they suggest both revising syllabi to include more inclusive research and volunteering to review articles in order to help change what types of papers get published. For tenure-track professors, the authors recommend examining course design policies and reviewing ethics guidelines for journal editing. For tenured and full professors, they recommend strategies for amplifying the work of junior colleagues. Finally, they advise that public linguists use their platform ethically and that linguists beyond the academy bring linguistic inclusion to their professional spheres.

Action Plans for Structural Inclusion

In creating an inclusive linguistics, we must broaden pathways for who can access higher education generally as well as linguistics specifically. As Charity Hudley and Mallinson (2018) state, "we must think about the comprehensive support of underrepresented students as a central focus of the social justice mission of linguistics" (p. 526). In the US, linguistics is most often taught at universities that are active in the Linguistic Society of America (2021), which sets many of the policy and funding priorities for linguistics as a discipline. Further, as Jason Haugen, Amy V. Magaris, and Sarah Calvo (forthcoming) find, 25% of all faculty in North American linguistics PhD programs graduated from just three departments, and 50% from just 10 departments. These factors lead to a concentration of resources and prestige in ways that limit inclusion. Moreover, students from the communities whose language patterns are extensively studied by linguists—especially African American students and Native and Indigenous students—are often not those who end up in linguistics classrooms (see Calhoun et al., 2021). Such inequities can also be found among faculty ranks, where tenure-track faculty are often economically and socially privileged, particularly in elite spaces (O'Grady, 2021). Throughout academia, faculty of color remain highly underrepresented (Flaherty, 2022), including in linguistics (Charity Hudley et al., 2020; Rickford 2014; for a visualization, see Chang, 2022).

This challenge reveals the need for an intersectionally informed approach to racial inclusion in linguistics departments as well as the attendant need to expand linguistics at Minority Serving Institutions, HBCUs, TCUs, and community colleges. We must ensure that there are pathways for students from groups that are overstudied by linguists yet underrepresented in college and university spaces to gain access to linguistics content and courses. This issue is particularly critical at HBCUs, which tend not to offer linguistics as an undergraduate major and typically fold linguistics content into areas such as communication sciences and rhetoric. Pathways for inclusion may therefore necessitate that linguistics departments and programs establish partnerships with these other degree programs, especially those that tend to serve larger numbers of students from minoritized groups than linguistics typically does, including partnerships across institutions (cf. Charity Hudley et al., 2019).

Addressing these challenges requires ensuring that faculty, departments, and universities affirm students' linguistic and academic identities without tokenization; include their linguistic insights as intellectual contributions to academic research in ways that draw upon who they are and what they want to study without further marginalization; and guide them in learning how to negotiate multiple linguistic terrains in ways that promote their retention, persistence, belonging, and success in higher education. This goal also requires that student inclusion be viewed not as separate from but rather as intertwined with faculty and community inclusion. In order for students to ascertain their department's and institution's commitments to anti-racism, social justice, and inclusion and equity work, they also need to look at who is hired, whose scholarship is published, whose teaching areas are supported, who receives tenure and who is pushed out, who is given leadership roles, who is valued for their community-facing work, how communities are involved in academic endeavors, and so on (cf. Flaherty, 2021).

The chapters in Part 2 of this volume provide many recommendations for how to work toward inclusion across various underexamined disciplinary contexts in support of underrepresented scholars and students. In Chapter 6, "Increasing Access and Equity for First-Generation Scholars in Linguistics," Iara Mantenuto, Tamaya Levy, Stephanie Reyes, and Zhongyin Zhang recommend strategies to more comprehensively support first-generation scholars in linguistics, including the need for outreach efforts, more institutional support and professional support including mentorship, and greater awareness about this diverse and intersectional group, their needs, and the challenges they may face in the discipline and in academia. In Chapter 7, "For the Culture: Pathways in Linguistics for Black and HBCU Scholars," Candice Y. Thornton similarly identifies many barriers that affect Black students and students who attend HBCUs from engaging in linguistics. To address these barriers for greater inclusion, Thornton recommends pathways such as increased financial support for students, coordinated efforts for more Black-centered coursework about language that appeals to students across disciplines, and sustained, comprehensive mentoring and student research opportunities.

In Chapter 8, "Towards Greater Inclusion in Practice and Among Practitioners: The Case for an Experience-Based Linguistics in India," Reenu Punnoose and Muhammed Haneefa draw from the neighboring discipline of sociology to assert the need for linguistics to become more reflexive about its practice, its practitioners, and the relationship between the two; the authors also interrogate the role of colonialism and caste inequality that have led to the current exclusionary intellectual traditions and professional practices of linguistics in India. They call for reframing Indian linguistics around experience and empiricism in ways that do not relegate it as secondary to theory and that instead view theory and experience as imperative for each other's existence and for the production of knowledge. They also urge educators to reimagine the curriculum by increasing opportunities for students to take linguistics courses that are community-facing and interdisciplinary and that allow students to collaborate outside of academia, such as through internships and educational partnerships with local schools. Finally, they call on Global North linguists, especially those who have benefited from studying languages of India and the Global South, to actively and more fully include scholars and students from India and the Global South in the field, such as by increasing the numbers of underrepresented students in their programs, by offering virtual participation options at conferences, and by diversifying editorial boards, professional organizations, and funding agencies.

In Chapter 9, "Power Shift: Toward Inclusive Natural Language Processing," Emily M. Bender and Alvin Grissom II discuss how current big data/machine learning approaches to language technology privilege the knowledge of dominant communities and concentrate power in ways that need to be critically examined so that the risks of language technology can be mitigated. To do so, they recommend supporting language technology work that is led and governed by marginalized communities, especially when that technology has implications for Indigenous languages and stigmatized language varieties. They also encourage linguists to get involved in efforts to demand transparency as new approaches to language technology are created and deployed. This task requires linguists to be proactive in making and claiming space for ourselves to be in the room where decisions about language technology design and deployment are being made—and even to prepare ahead of time for the eventuality of becoming a whistleblower in situations where we recognize the potential for negative impacts of new proposed technologies to arise.

Action Plans for Educational Inclusion

Another way that linguists must advance inclusion is by broadening pathways for how and where linguistics is taught and in what form. To do so requires creating an inclusive curriculum that ensures belonging and promotes success at every stage, which begins in the years before students enter college and continues through college, into graduate school, and in the profession. Courses about language, whether housed in linguistics programs or in related majors, must be situated in the curriculum in such a way as to make them accessible to and inclusive of students from minoritized and marginalized backgrounds, which means ensuring that there are articulated pathways for these students to enter college or university, to pursue a course of study in linguistics, and to have the institutional support necessary to succeed.

Addressing these challenges requires that linguistics coursework include information on underrepresented languages and varieties as well as readings and research by scholars of color (Cite Black Women Collective, 2017) and by scholars from the communities who use those languages and varieties, as asserted in many of the chapters in this volume and its accompanying volume, *Decolonizing Linguistics.* Courses must also foster inclusive learning environments (University of Arizona Department of Linguistics Committee on Equity, Respect, and Inclusion, 2017), employ inclusive assessment tools and avoid those that are inequitable (Clayton, 2016; Posselt, 2016), and use high-impact teaching practices, including involving minoritized undergraduate and graduate students in research activities (AAC&U, n.d.). These and other evidence-based techniques have been found to promote the success of underrepresented students, which leads to the greater diversification of linguistics and higher education and ultimately the professoriate. The chapters in Part 3 of this volume provide many recommendations for methods of inclusion in teaching linguistics.

In Chapter 10, "Disrupting English Class: Linguistics and Social Justice for *All* High School Students," Amy L. Plackowski reminds us that linguists need to produce course content, particularly free and accessible resources, that is relevant to the needs of teachers, of great interest to students, and sufficiently scaffolded to allow for independent and ready use in classrooms. Plackowski also recommends that linguists partner with local educators to make linguistics more widely available in schools. One strategy for doing so is to collaborate with professional teacher organizations; another is to get involved with the Linguistic Society of America's Linguistics in the School Curriculum Committee (LiSC), which Plackowski chairs and which helps facilitate networking between university linguists and school educators.

In Chapter 11, "Bilingual Education in Cabo Verdean: Toward Visibility and Dignity," Abel Djassi Amado, Marlyse Baptista, Lourenço Pina Garcia, Ambrizeth Helena Lima, and Dawna Marie Thomas call attention to the clear need for and relevance of partnerships between academic linguists and local school systems. They illustrate how the Cabo Verdean Center for Applied Research (CVCAR), an organization of scholars of Cabo Verdean descent representing the community, worked closely with Boston Public Schools to develop and implement the Cabo Verdean Heritage Language and Culture Curriculum at a local high school. This highly effective effort was not isolated but rather was situated in the context of advocacy for the cultural and linguistic interests of the Cabo Verdean community of Boston as well as for bilingual education more generally.

In Chapter 12, "Community College Linguistics for Educational Justice: Content and Assessment Strategies That Support Antiracist and Inclusive Teaching," Jamie A. Thomas reminds us that universities and small liberal arts colleges are not the only places where linguistics is taught. Community colleges often offer linguistics courses, and the kinds of students who attend these classes come from varied backgrounds and may be at different life stages. A field that wants to diversify should therefore target students at community colleges. As Thomas shows, linguistics needs to consider the reality of students' lives and to broaden the ranks of linguistics to include the insights of groups other than those who are white, abled, monolingual, and from other backgrounds that historically and systemically have been overrepresented in the academy.

In Chapter 13, "Texts, Tweets, Twitch, TikTok: Computer-Mediated Communication as an Inclusive Gateway to Linguistics," Jenny Lederer points out that the data and examples used in many introductory textbooks are not congruent with how undergraduates use and understand language. She suggests that students be taught to collect their own data from social media to create materials that are more relevant to students, particularly BIPOC (Black, Indigenous, and People of Color) students, who typically do not see their own linguistic practices reflected in linguistics textbooks.

In Chapter 14, "Pedagogies of Inclusion Must Start from Within: Landguaging Teacher Reflection and Plurilingualism in the L2 Classroom," Rhonda Chung and John Wayne N. dela Cruz explain that classrooms cannot operate outside the languaging—and "landguaging"— environments that their students live in, because plurilingual students bring their communities and languages into the classroom with them, including the lands that their languages are rooted in. They assert that instructors of Teaching English as a Second Language (TESL) who do not confront the allochthonous nature of their monolingual teaching practices ignore the plural reality of their students and reproduce colonization not only within their own classroom but in the spaces where ESL instructors are trained. As they suggest, in order to create inclusive, anti-colonial language pedagogies, TESL programs must create translanguaging learning spaces with their multidialectal/plurilingual students that are sensitive to the land where language teaching and learning unfolds.

Building an inclusive classroom space often means rethinking established practices. In Chapter 15, "Beyond Pronouns 101: Linguistic Advocacy for Trans-Inclusive Language in the College Classroom," Lal Zimman and Cedar Brown provide guidance to instructors on how to handle classroom discussions about students' personal pronouns. Contrary to the conventional recommendation that all students should be asked to provide their pronouns publicly on the first day of class, based on their research the authors suggest using gender-neutral pronouns for all students until specific pronouns are offered. Zimman and Brown also emphasize that students should not be put into situations where they may feel forced to share their pronouns or singled out by an instructor.

In Chapter 16, "Increasing Inclusion Through Structured Active Learning: Curriculum Changes in an Introduction to Formal Linguistics Class," Florian Schwarz encourages teachers of formal linguistics to utilize an active learning or "flipped classroom" format in which all content is delivered outside of class, a pedagogical approach that has been shown to be especially effective in creating more inclusive and equitable STEM instruction for students of color. Schwarz reassures instructors who may be skeptical that students will even attend class in such a format, let alone learn the material, by sharing students' feedback on the course throughout the quarter as well as measures of attendance and performance that demonstrate the benefits of active learning in linguistics.

In Chapter 17, "An Action-Based Roadmap for Equity, Diversity, and Inclusion in Teaching Linguistics," Nathan Sanders, Lex Konnelly, and Pocholo Umbal advance inclusive teaching practices in linguistics at a larger scale by sharing their work to create the publicly available Linguistics Equity, Diversity, and Inclusion Repository (LEDIR). This pedagogical intervention includes databases, syllabi, lecture notes, and other materials developed at the University of Toronto, and the chapter provides concrete details, steps, and outcomes that are designed for other scholars to follow as they adapt these resources for use in other instructional and institutional settings.

Action Plans for Community-Centered and Public Linguistics

Finally, for full inclusion, we must ensure that both the general public and especially minoritized communities benefit from our academic endeavors. To do so requires critically examining how we as scholars, our colleagues, our departments, and our universities support efforts to support marginalized groups on campus or in the local community—such as community-based learning endeavors, public engagement projects, and so on. The question we must ask at every point is: Who is the work benefiting and how? We need an inclusive view of linguistic scholarship that includes interdisciplinary and transdisciplinary work as well as collaborations and community-centered partnerships with real-world outcomes that expand the scope and relevance of linguistics. We also need to more fully harness the media and other forms of public outreach as a mechanism for fostering linguistic inclusion, dismantling damaging language ideologies, and ensuring that language-related issues are made relevant to community and public concerns. The chapters in Part 4 of this volume provide many recommendations for inclusive collaborations, community partnerships, and public engagement.

In Chapter 18, "Creating Inclusive Linguistics Communication: Crash Course Linguistics," Lauren Gawne, Gretchen McCulloch, Nicole Sweeney, Rachel Alatalo, Hannah Bodenhausen, Ceri Riley, and Jessi Grieser provide recommendations for inclusive linguistic communication based on their experience developing an online educational series on linguistics, such as ensuring that inclusion plans are discussed overtly and throughout the design of public engagement initiatives and taking care that a broad range of languages, contexts, perspectives, and experiences are covered.

In Chapter 19, "The Justice Language Action Project: Critical Linguistics for Inclusion and Equity in K-12 Classrooms," Jennifer Sclafani, Panayota Gounari, Iuliia Fakhrutdinova, and Vannessa Quintana Sarria present their Justice Language Action project as a model for other scholars seeking to design educationally inclusive transdisciplinary projects. Their own project maximizes its impact by including graduate students as facilitators, focusing on teachers as their target audience, and promoting critical language awareness among students.

Finally, in Chapter 20, "Linguistic Literacy and Advocacy in Action: Case Studies in Community Engagement from the Language Diversity Ambassadors at North Carolina State University," Marie Bissell, José Álvarez-Retamales, Matthew Champagne, Jessica Hatcher, Shalina Omar, and Walt Wolfram

444 Inclusion in Linguistics

provide additional concrete models for linguistic outreach programs. The programs they describe, a summer camp for elementary students and an after-school mentoring program for high school students, are led by graduate students. Programs like these foster student self-empowerment on at least two levels, both by shifting the balance of power from faculty to graduate students and by providing young people from diverse linguistic backgrounds with the tools they need to advocate for themselves for their linguistic rights.

Conclusion

The chapters in this volume have offered theoretical as well as practical discussions about pathways for challenging exclusion and fostering greater equity and social justice within and through the discipline of linguistics. We encourage further extension of these efforts and we urge readers to continue these conversations and draw on the inspiration of these chapters to take needed action in ways that benefit faculty, students, campuses, and communities in your local context.

The next steps in this process require us to continue to resist intellectual forms of erasure. The chapters in this volume directly reject the discourse of disciplinary policing perpetuated in many linguistics circles—which includes the gatekeeping ideologies that certain areas of study "aren't linguistics," that doing research that is inclusive of culture and community is less worthy or valuable, that such work diminishes the scholarly impact of the discipline, or that it may negatively affect a scholar's reputation and opportunities for professional advancement. Such ideologies rely upon assimilatory replication models of academia that are grounded in and designed to maintain white-supremacist, colonial, normatively embodied, abled, and cis male-hegemonic ideals of prestige and thereby prevent urgently needed social change. Such models also ignore the scholarly and intellectual contributions of generations of scholars from historically and currently marginalized and colonized groups. Chapters from this volume have effectively challenged these models by demonstrating the critical significance, deep relevance, and broad impact of efforts for genuine inclusion in linguistics and academia.

We must also continue to extend these efforts to advance inclusion in tandem with decolonization throughout the global community, particularly in the Global South and across the African Diaspora. Although conceptualizations of race differ across the world, inequities based on race, color, class, education, and the like are interrelated in ways that reach beyond geographic and national boundaries (see, e.g., Alim, Rickford, & Ball,

2016; DeGraff, 2005; Mufwene, 2001; Ndhlovu 2021). There is no racial justice without linguistic justice—and no linguistic justice without racial justice (Charity Hudley, 2018). The same is true for justice on the basis of gender identity, disability, and all other current axes of oppression. We must continue to interrogate and dismantle privilege and structural power within linguistics and resist the within-discipline exclusionary practices and rhetoric that position some scholars, subdisciplines, institutions, research areas, and so on as worthier than others and thereby make reparative and inclusive work more challenging. As chapters in this volume have made clear, the need and the opportunities for inclusion work in linguistics and academia are wide-ranging and far-reaching.

Through the open and transparent conversations and the frameworks, strategies, and practices for inclusion that are presented throughout this volume, linguists can create and pursue—indeed, linguists are already creating and pursuing—bold yet realistic pathways for greater inclusion in the discipline. The collective intellectual contributions, actions, and courage of linguists who are working for justice and inclusion across subfields of linguistics and around the world inspire us as we collectively continue this work.

References

AAC&U. (n.d.). High-impact practices.https://www.aacu.org/trending-topics/high-impact

Alim, H. Samy, Rickford, John R., & Ball, Arnetha F. (Eds.) (2016). *Raciolinguistics: How language shapes our ideas about race.* Oxford University Press.

Calhoun, Kendra, Charity Hudley, Anne, Bucholtz, Mary, Exford, Jazmine, & Johnson, Brittney. (2021). Attracting Black students to linguistcs through a Black-centered introduction to linguistics course. *Language, 97*(1), e12–e38. https://doi.org/10.1353/lan.2021.0007

Chang, Charles B. [@CharlesBChang]. (2022, January 29). I'll bite during today's lunch break. Faculty in highly-ranked #Linguistics departments in #Wordle grids (using @CalvinKLai's methodology [Tweet]. Twitter. https://twitter.com/CharlesBChang/status/1487495915619315712

Charity Hudley, Anne H. (2018). Engaging and supporting underrepresented undergraduate students in linguistic research and across the university. *Journal of English Linguistics, 46*(3), 199–214. https://doi.org/10.1177/0075424218783445

Charity Hudley, Anne H., Zimman, Lal, Conner, Tracy, Calhoun, Kendra, Muwwakkil, Jamaal, miles-hercules, deandre, & Keshav, Maya. (2019). A roadmap for inclusion in sociocultural linguistics [presentation]. New Ways of Analyzing Variation 48, University of Oregon.

Charity Hudley, Anne H., & Flores, Nelson. (2022). Social justice in applied linguistics: Not a conclusion, but a way forward. *Annual Review of Applied Linguistics, 42,* 144–154. https://doi.org/10.1017/S0267190522000083

Charity Hudley, Anne H., & Mallinson, Christine. (2018). Dismantling "the master's tools": Moving students' rights to their own language from theory to practice. *American Speech, 93*(3–4), 513–537. https://doi-org.stanford.idm.oclc.org/10.1215/00031283-7271305

Charity Hudley, Anne H., Mallinson, Christine, & Bucholtz, Mary. (2020). Toward racial justice in linguistics: Interdisciplinary insights into theorizing race in the discipline and diversifying the profession. *Language, 96*(4), e200–e235. https://doi.org/10.1353/lan.2020.0074

Cite Black Women Collective. (2017). https://www.citeblackwomencollective.org/

Clayton, Victoria. (2016, March 1). The problem with the GRE. *The Atlantic*. https://www.thea tlantic.com/education/archive/2016/03/the-problem-with-the-gre/471633/

College of William and Mary Linguistics Program. (2017). Diversity and inclusion plan. Unpublished document.

DeGraff, Michel. (2005). Linguists' most dangerous myth: The fallacy of Creole exceptionalism. *Language in Society, 34*, 533–591. https://doi.org/10.1017/S0047404505050207

Flaherty, Colleen. (2021, January 6). Illusion of inclusion. *Inside Higher Ed*. https://www.ins idehighered.com/news/2021/01/06/faculty-members-color-see-illusion-inclusion

Flaherty, Colleen. (2022, December 2). Faculties so white. *Inside Higher Ed*. https://www.ins idehighered.com/news/2022/12/02/report-finds-faculty-diversity-isnt-meeting-student-needs?utm_campaign=ihesocial&utm_content=highered_https://www.insi&utm_med ium=social&utm_source=twitter

Gutiérrez y Muhs, Gabriella, Nieman, Yolanda Flores, Gonzalez, Carmen G., & Harris, Angela P. (Eds.). (2012). *Presumed incompetent*. University Press of Colorado.

Haugen, Jason, Margaris, Amy V., & Calvo, Sarah. (forthcoming). A snapshot of academic job placements in linguistics in the US and Canada. *Canadian Journal of Linguistics*.

Hill, Joseph. (2022, October 14). *Same but different: What sociolinguistic lessons can we find in the study of sign language?* [plenary address]. New Ways of Analyzing Variation 50, Stanford, California.

Koester, Rylie. (2022, January 28). Geoscience researchers call for updated metaphor to help make field more inclusive and equitable. *Phys Org*. https://phys.org/news/ 2022-01-geoscience-metaphor-field-inclusive-equitable.html?fbclid=IwAR1jZ_jEp-VhDpiXIA6ktollSg7azDBXeEbfxlbdOY4YVXOjOlI5iY2yako

Leslie, Sarah-Jane, Cimpian, Andrei, Meyer, Meredith, & Freeland, Edward. (2015). Expectations of brilliance underlie gender distributions across academic disciplines. *Science, 347*(6219), 262–265. https://www.science.org/doi/10.1126/science.1261375

Linguistic Society of America. (2021). *The state of linguistics in higher education*, 8th ed. [annual report]. https://www.linguisticsociety.org/sites/default/files/Annual%20Report%202 020%20Jan2021%20-%20final_0.pdf

Mufwene, Salikoko S. (2001). *The ecology of language evolution*. Cambridge University Press.

Ndhlovu, F. (2021). Decolonising sociolinguistics research: methodological turn-around next? *International Journal of the Sociology of Language, 2021*(267–268), 193–201. https://doi.org/ 10.1515/ijsl-2020-0063

O'Grady, Cathleen. (2021, April 1). Academia is often a family business. That's a barrier for increasing diversity. *Science*.https://www.science.org/content/article/academia-often-fam ily-business-s-barrier-increasing-diversity?utm_campaign=NewsfromScience&utm_sou rce=Social&utm_medium=Twitter

Posselt, Julie R. (2016). *Inside graduate admissions: Merit, diversity, and faculty gatekeeping*. Harvard University Press.

Rickford, John R. (2014, January 5). *Increasing the representation of under-represented ethnic minorities in linguistics* [presentation]. Linguistic Society of America, Minneapolis, Minnesota.

University of Arizona Department of Linguistics Committee on Equity, Respect, and Inclusion. (2017). Sample language for inclusion in syllabi. https://linguistics.arizona.edu/sample-language-inclusion-syllabi

Virginia Commonwealth University Department of English. (2011). VCU Department of English diversity plan. Unpublished document.

Printed in the USA/Agawam, MA
February 8, 2024

860826.010